CRIMINOLOGY

ninth edition

by the late
EDWIN H. SUTHERLAND

and DONALD R. CRESSEY
University of California, Santa Barbara

ninth edition

by the late
EDWIN H. SUTHERLAND

and
DONALD R. CRESSEY
University of California
Santa Barbara

J. B. LIPPINCOTT COMPANY
PHILADELPHIA/NEW YORK/TORONTO

Criminology

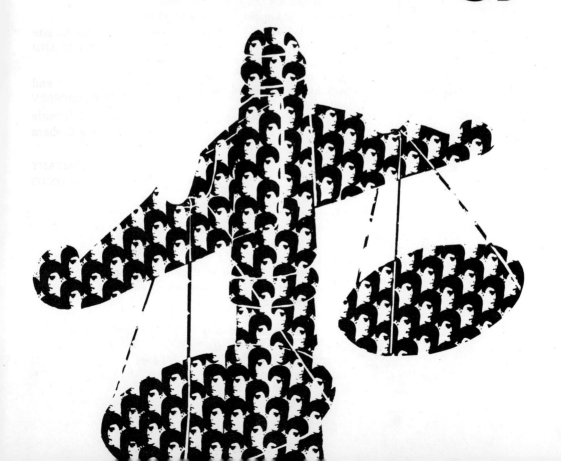

10 9 8 7 6 5 4 3 2 1

Library of Congress Catalog Card Number: 74-8508
ISBN-0-397-47295-1
Printed in the United States of America

This is a revised edition of Edwin H. Sutherland
and Donald R. Cressey's *Criminology*, copyright,
1970, by J. B. Lippincott Company. Original
copyright, 1924, by J. B. Lippincott Company,
under the title *Criminology*, of which Edwin H.
Sutherland was sole author. Rewritten and
reset under the title *Principles of Criminology*,
with Sutherland as sole author, in 1934, 1939,
and 1947.
Rewritten and reset, with Edwin H. Sutherland
and Donald R. Cressey as co-authors, in 1955,
1960, 1966, and 1970.

Library of Congress Cataloging in Publication Data
Sutherland, Edwin Hardin, 1883-1950.
    Criminology.
    A revision of the authors' Principles of criminology,
first published in 1924 under title: Criminology, by
E. H. Sutherland.
    Includes bibliographies.
    1. Crime and criminals. I. Cressey, Donald Ray,
1919-   joint author. II. Title.
HV6025.S83 1974   364   74-8508
ISBN 0-397-47295-1

Like the fifth, sixth, seventh, and eighth editions, which I prepared, this ninth edition of *Criminology* is an extension of the work done by Professor Edwin H. Sutherland in the earlier editions. Since this textbook first appeared, in 1924, it has always been more than a mere set of lesson plans or lectures for students. In his preface to the fourth (1947) edition, Professor Sutherland said: "Much factual information regarding crime has been accumulated over several generations. In spite of this, criminology lacks full scientific standing. The defects of criminology consist principally of the failure to integrate this factual information into consistent and valid general propositions." Like the earlier editions, the ninth attempts to correct some of these defects.

Criminology has always been designed to place emphasis upon the organization and systematization of knowledge, and this edition adheres to that tradition. In fact, it was the task of writing earlier editions of this book that led Professor Sutherland to formulate his differential association theory, a principle which a number of social scientists have found useful for putting order into a wide range of data on delinquency and crime causation. When preparing the fifth edition, I found this principle to be useful, also, for organizing the research materials on the effectiveness of various systems and techniques for rehabilitating criminals—probation, parole, group therapy, vocational training, and so forth—and this system of organization has continued into the ninth edition.

Part 1 examines facts of crime and delinquency and relates them to the differential association, differential social organization, and other theories. The factual data examined include variations of crime and delinquency rates with age, sex, race, poverty, educational status, urbanization, and other variables, as well as the incidence among criminals and delinquents of various biological, psychological, and social traits, characteristics, and processes. The differential association theory and alternative theories of crime causation are evaluated in the light of their comparative capacity to "make sense" of the facts.

In part 2 factual materials pertaining to control of crime are related to sociological and psychological theories of punishment and treatment, as well as to the differential association and differential social organization theories. Imprisonment, probation, parole, corporal punishment, group therapy, and psychoanalysis, for example, are identified as societal reactions to crime; variations in these societal reactions are observed; and theories to account for the variations are presented. The contemporary conflict between punishment and treatment of criminals is documented, and the consequences of this conflict for the "politics of crime" and for practices and organization of police, courts, probation departments, parole departments, and prisons are examined. The implications of the differential association and differential social organization theories for criminal justice administration and for reform and rehabilitation both of criminals and of criminal law are explored.

The eighth edition differed from earlier editions in three principal respects. *First,* it was directed more to the student than to the professor. Many of the foreign language footnotes and multiple citations of scholarly documenting the same point were deleted, as was complete coverage of some of the more esoteric topics such as the origin of the concept "infamy." However, because I believe that important points should be repeated as an aid to student learning, I continued the practice of "saying it thrice." *Second,* there had been a tendency in earlier editions to give continued coverage to criminological fads that appeared over the years. At one time everyone seemed concerned about comic books and delinquency, at another time about the importance of community coordinating councils in delinquency prevention, or the use of authority in social work, or about scandals in the bail system, or whatever. Discussions such as these thrive for a few years, then disappear; the eighth edition referred to them, but not in the detail of earlier editions. Lastly, the eighth edition concentrated on those studies that "made a difference"—in the sense that they changed the direction of research.

The first seven editions of this book—which covered a span of a half century—attempted to systematize most of the criminological studies produced in the English-speaking world, and some of those produced in other parts of the world. But research reports on delinquency, crime, the sociology of the criminal law, and the administration of justice have been produced at an accelerated rate in recent years. When I prepared the seventh edition, I found it impossible to cite, let alone discuss, all the recent research findings. The ninth edition, similarly, concentrates on selected studies and topics.

Substantial portions of some chapters have been rewritten, and changes have been introduced in all chapters. Statistics have been brought up to date wherever possible, and stress has been placed on discussion of the processes by which these statistics are manufactured by various official agencies. The arrangement of materials within chapters is essentially that of the eighth edition.

Once again I have decided that the formal statement of the theory of differential association should not be modified. The theory has been found defective, and suggestions for its modification have been made. These suggestions have been incorporated in the text. However, if considered as a "principle" rather than as a "theory," differential association continues to make good sense of most of the phenomena in the delinquency and crime area. It was a harbinger of the "conflict orientation" that is now becoming popular in sociological circles once again. Moreover, the formal statement, as written by Sutherland, continues to be tested, analyzed, discussed, and extended. It would be inappropriate to modify the theory in such a way that research work now in progress would be undermined. Moreover, the "great debates" about the present statement of the theory probably are of more value to undergraduates than would be a revised formal statement that would take some of the criticisms into account. Finally, the theory in its present form has become rather basic to the thinking of American researchers, who are beginning to refer to "the theory of differential association," or just "differential association," without citing Sutherland or anyone else, apparently on the assumption that readers are familiar with the theory and its origins. I continue to believe that it would not be wise to revise the statement in such a way that these references became meaningless.

Santa Barbara, California
January, 1974   DONALD R. CRESSEY

Contents

Part 1 THE STUDY OF DELINQUENCY AND CRIME

Criminology is the body of knowledge regarding delinquency and crime as social phenomena. It includes within its scope the processes of making laws, of breaking laws, and of reacting toward the breaking of laws. These processes are three aspects of a somewhat unified sequence of interactions. Certain acts which are regarded as undesirable are defined by the political society as crimes. In spite of this definition some people persist in the behavior and thus commit crimes; the political society reacts by punishment, treatment, or prevention. This sequence of interactions is the subject matter of criminology.

Criminology consists of three principal divisions, as follows: (a) the sociology of law, which is an attempt at systematic analysis of the conditions under which criminal laws develop and also an explanation of variations in the policies and procedures used in administration of criminal justice; (b) criminal etiology, which is an attempt at scientific analysis of the causes of crime; and (c) penology, which is concerned with control of crime. The term penology is unsatisfactory because this division includes many methods of social control which are not penal in character.

The objective of criminology is the development of a body of general and verified principles and of other types of knowledge regarding this process of law, crime, and reaction to crime. This knowledge will contribute to the development of other sciences, and through these other social sciences it will contribute to an understanding of social behavior. In addition, criminology is concerned with the immediate application of knowledge to programs of social order and crime control. This concern with practical programs is justified, in part, as experimentation which may be valuable because of its immediate results but at any rate will be valuable in the long run because of the increased knowledge which results from it. If practical programs wait until theoretical knowledge is complete, they will wait for eternity, for theoretical knowledge is increased most significantly by practical programs. John Dewey described the relationship between knowledge and control thus:

. . . it is a complete error to suppose that efforts at social control depend upon the prior existence of a social science. The reverse is the case. The building up of social science, that is, of a body of knowledge in which facts are ascertained in their significant relations, is dependent upon putting social planning into effect. . . . Physical science did not develop because inquirers piled up a mass of facts about observed phenomena. It came into being when men intentionally experimented, on the basis of ideas and hypotheses, with observed phenomena to modify them and disclose new observations. This process is self-corrective and self-developing. Imperfect and even wrong hypotheses, when acted upon, brought to light significant phenomena which made improved ideas and improved experimentations possible. The change from a passive and accumulative attitude into an active and productive one is the secret revealed by the progress of physical inquiry.[1]

While experimentation may increase theoretical knowledge and thereby contribute to ultimate improvements in policies, it is unnecessarily wasteful unless it is directed by the best organized and critical thought available. Moreover, experimentation with humans, unlike natural science experiments, poses grave ethical problems, even when directed by the best organized critical thought. The average citizen is confronted by a confusing and conflicting complex of popular beliefs and programs in regard to crime. Some of these are traditions from eighteenth-century philosophy; some are promulgations of special-interest groups; and some are mere emotional reactions. Organized and critical thinking in this field is therefore peculiarly difficult and also peculiarly necessary. ●

Conventional definition of crime and the criminal law

Criminal behavior is behavior in violation of the criminal law. No matter what the degree of immorality, reprehensibility, or indecency of an act, it is not a crime unless it is prohibited by the criminal law. The criminal law, in turn, is defined conventionally as a body of specific rules regarding human conduct which have been promulgated by political authority, which apply uniformly to all members of the classes to which the rules refer, and which are enforced by punishment administered by the state. The characteristics which distinguish this body of rules regarding human conduct from other rules are, therefore, *politicality, specificity, uniformity,* and *penal sanction.* However, these are characteristics of an ideal, completely rational system of criminal law; in practice the differences between the criminal law and other bodies of rules for human conduct are not clear-cut. Also, the ideal characteristics of the criminal law are only rarely features of the criminal law in action. ●

Characteristics of the criminal law

The vast majority of the rules which define certain behavior as crime are found in constitutions, treaties, common law, enactments by the legislatures of the state and its subdivisions, and in judicial and administrative regulations. However, the criminal law is not merely a collection of written proscriptions. The agencies of enforcement are the police and the courts, and these agencies, rather than the legislature, determine what the law is. According to one school of thought, police and courts merely "apply" the law in an evenhanded manner to all persons who come before them. However, both the techniques used by justice administrators in interpreting and applying the statutes and the

[1] John Dewey, "Social Science and Social Control," *New Republic,* 67:276-277 July 29, 1931.

body of ideals held by them are a part of the law in action, as truly as are the written statutes.

The court decision in one controversy becomes a part of the body of rules used in making decisions in other controversies. Consequently, law students must read court decisions in order to learn law. Further evidence supporting this view that the courts as well as the legislatures make law is found whenever the nation is confronted with the problem of selecting a justice of the Supreme Court. At such times it is explicitly recognized that the nature of the law itself, not merely its administration, is determined to a considerable extent by the proportion of liberals and conservatives on the supreme bench. Thus, behind the behavior of courts is public opinion. Also, between the courts and the legislature are intermediate agencies such as the police. Many statutes are never enforced; some are enforced only on rare occasions; others are enforced with a striking disregard for uniformity. Enforcement and administrative agencies are affected by shifts in public opinion, budget allocations, and in power. As a consequence, the law often changes while the statutes remain constant.

Politicality is regarded almost universally as a necessary element in criminal law. The rules of the trade union, the church, or the family are not regarded as criminal law, nor are violations of these rules regarded as crimes. Only violations of rules made by the state are crimes. This distinction between the state and other groups is not only arbitrary but also is difficult to maintain when attention is turned to societies where patriarchal power, private self-help, popular justice, and other forerunners of legislative justice are found. This may be illustrated by the gypsies, who have no territorial organization and no written law, but who do have customs, taboos, and a semijudicial council which makes definite decisions regarding the propriety of behavior of members of the group and often imposes penalties. These councils have no political authority in the territory in which they happen to be operating, but they perform the same function within the gypsy group that courts perform in the political order. Similarly, early Chinese immigrants in Chicago established an unofficial court which had no political authority, but which, in practice, exercised the functions of an authorized court in controversies among the Chinese people. The American "Cosa Nostra" has a legislative and judicial system for administering the functional equivalent of the criminal law among its members.[2] Thus, the element of politicality is arbitrary and is not sharply defined. The earlier systems of law, together with the present relation between public opinion and legal precepts, raise the question, When should

---

[2] See Jean-Paul Clebert, *The Gypsies*, trans. Charles Duff (London: Vista Books, 1963), pp. 123-33; and Donald R. Cressey, *Theft of the Nation: The Structure and Operations of Organized Crime in America* (New York: Harper and Row, 1969), pp. 162-220.

the rules of a group be regarded as the law and violations of these rules as crimes?[3]

Specificity is included as an element in the definition of criminal law because of the contrast in this respect between criminal law and civil law. The civil law may be general. An old German civil code, for instance, provided that whoever intentionally injured another in a manner contrary to the common standards of right conduct was bound to indemnify him. The criminal law, on the other hand, generally gives a strict definition of a specific act, and when there is doubt as to whether a definition describes the behavior of a defendant, the judge is obligated to decide in favor of the defendant. In one famous case, for example, the behavior of a person who had taken an airplane was held to be exempt from the consequences of violating a statute regarding the taking of "self-propelled vehicles," on the ground that at the time the law was enacted "vehicles" did not include airplanes.[4] Some laws, to be sure, are quite general, as the laws in regard to nuisances, conspiracy, vagrancy, disorderly conduct, use of the mails to defraud, and official misfeasance. The criminal law, however, contains no general provision that any act which, when done with culpable intent, injures the public can be prosecuted as a punishable offense.[5] Consequently it frequently happens that one act is prohibited by law while another act, which is very similar in nature and effects, is not prohibited and is not illegal.[6]

Uniformity or regularity is included in the conventional definition of criminal law because law attempts to provide evenhanded justice without respect to persons. This means that no exceptions are made to criminal liability because of a person's social status; an act described as a crime is crime, no matter who perpetrates it. Also, uniformity means that the law-enforcement process shall be administered without regard for the status of the persons who have committed crimes or are accused of committing crimes. This ideal is rarely followed in practice, principally because it results in injustices. Rigid rule is softened by police discretion and judicial discretion. Rigid rule treats all persons in the class to which the law refers exactly alike, while police and judicial discretion

---

[3] See E. Adamson Hoebel, *The Law of Primitive Man: A Study in Comparative Legal Dynamics* (Cambridge: Harvard University Press, 1954).

[4] *McBoyle v. United States,* 283 U.S. 25 (1931).

[5] A German law of June 28, 1935, seems to be an exception to this generalization. It provided: "Whoever commits an action which the law declares to be punishable or which is deserving of punishment according to the fundamental idea of a penal law and the sound perception of the people, shall be punished. If no determinate penal law is directly applicable to the action, it shall be punished according to the law, the basic idea of which fits it best." Lawrence Preuss, "Punishment by Analogy in Nationalist Socialist Penal Law," *Journal of Criminal Law and Criminology,* 26:847, March-April, 1936. See also Frederick Hoefer, "The Nazi Penal System," *Journal of Criminal Law and Criminology,* 35:385-393, March-April, 1945, and 36:30-38, May-June, 1945.

[6] See Jack P. Gibbs, "Crime and the Sociology of Law," *Sociology and Social Research,* 51:23-38, October, 1966.

take cognizance of the circumstances of the offense and the characteristics of the offender, a process which has come to be called "individualization."[7] Much of what happens to persons accused of delinquency or crime is determined in a process of negotiation. Equity, also, developed as a method of doing justice in particular situations where iron regularity would not do justice. As precedents in equity have accumulated, the decisions tend to become uniform, and thus similar to law. In line with the present tendency toward judicial discretion, authority has been conferred by legislative assemblies upon many administrative bodies to make regulations applicable to particular situations such as length of prison term and parole.

Penal sanction, as one of the elements in the orthodox definition of law, refers to the notion that violators will be punished or, at least, threatened with punishment by the state. Punishment under the law differs from that imposed by a mob in that it is to be applied dispassionately by representatives of the state in such a manner that it may win the approval of the cool judgment of impartial observers. A law which does not provide a penalty that will cause suffering is regarded as quite impotent and, in fact, no criminal law at all. However, the punishment provided may be very slight; in the courts of honor a verdict was reached, a party was declared guilty, and the disgrace of the declaration of guilt was the only punishment. In view of the difficulty of identifying the criminal law of nonliterate societies, where the institution of "the state" is not obvious, the suggestion has been made that the penal sanction is the only essential element in the definition of criminal law, and that wherever proscriptions are enforced by a penal sanction, there criminal law exists. This is in contrast to the tort law, where the court orders the defendant to reimburse the plaintiff, but does not punish him for damaging the plaintiff.

The punitive aspect of criminal law clearly is on the wane. In the juvenile court and to a smaller extent in the criminal courts, the tendency is to discover and use methods which are effective in forestalling crime, whether they are punitive or not. By using juvenile court procedures, we have attempted to avoid applying the "stigma of crime" to the acts of children. In theory, the juvenile court does not determine the guilt or innocence of a criminal; it merely acts in behalf of a child who is in need of help. The court's objective is treatment, not the meting out of penalties. However, except for children who are called delinquent because they have been neglected, or are "predelinquent," juvenile delinquencies are acts which would be crimes if committed by an adult. Consequently, juvenile delinquencies continue to be acts which are punishable by law, even if the punishment is kept in the background.[8] Similarly, the states and the federal government

---

[7] See Donald R. Cressey, "Control of Crime and Consent of the Governed, An Introduction," chap. in Gresham M. Sykes and Thomas E. Drabek, eds., *Law and the Lawless* (New York: Random House, 1969), pp. 271-287.

[8] See the discussion in chap. 20, pp. 440-461.

for a generation or two have been enacting laws for the regulation of manufacturing, commerce, agriculture, and other occupations. The persons affected by such laws are ordinarily respectable and powerful, and the legislatures have adapted the procedures to the status of these persons. Violations of these laws are crimes, but they are not always tried in the criminal courts. Instead, they are handled in civil and equity courts or in administrative commissions; the conventional penalties of fine and imprisonment are kept in the background to be used only as a last resort, and coercion in the first instance consists of injunctions and cease-and-desist orders. Thus these persons of social importance avoid the "stigma of crime," just as, to a lesser degree, juvenile delinquents do. The acts remain as crimes, however, for they are punishable by law.[9]

The conventional view is that a crime is an offense against the state, while, in contrast, a tort in violation of civil law is an offense against an individual. A particular act may be considered as an offense against an individual and also against the state, and is either a tort or a crime or both according to the way it is handled. A person who has committed an act of assault, for example, may be ordered by the civil court to pay the victim a sum of $500 for the damages to his interests, and he may also be ordered by the criminal court to pay a fine of $500 to the state. The payment of the first $500 is not punishment, but payment of the second $500 is punishment.

This distinction between individual damage and social harm is extremely difficult to make in the legal systems of nonliterate societies, where court procedures are relatively informal. Even in modern society, the distinction is dubious, for it rests upon the assumption that "individual" and "group" or "state" are mutually exclusive. For practical purposes, the individual is treated as if he were autonomous, but in fact an act which harms an individual also harms the group in which he has membership. Also, in modern society the indefiniteness of the distinction between torts and crimes is apparent when the victim of an act which is both a tort and a crime uses the criminal law as a method of forcing restitution which could not be secured with equal facility in the civil courts. Prosecutors frequently complain about the use of the criminal law as a collecting agency, especially because the victim who is reimbursed by the offender prior to trial then refuses to act as a witness. ●

**The sociology
of criminal law**

For many centuries, philosophers of jurisprudence have attempted by deductive reasoning to determine the principles underlying the development and use of criminal law. Divine will, the will of the sovereign, nature, reason, history, public opinion, and other prin-

---

[9] Edwin H. Sutherland, "Is 'White Collar Crime' Crime?" *American Sociological Review,* 10:132-139, April, 1945; idem, *White Collar Crime* (New York: Dryden Press, 1949), pp. 29-55.

ciples have been presented.[10] Sociologists have, since about 1960, taken up this search for principles, but in the name of the sociology of law. Generally speaking, sociologists have recently revived an interest in the sociology of law that flourished in the 1920s, although it was not called by that name. Many of the recent specialists in the sociology of law have taken a clue from Roscoe Pound, the principal figure in "sociological jurisprudence," a school of legal philosophy.[11] This is reasonable, because fifty years ago Pound took many of his clues from sociologists like E. A. Ross, Albion W. Small, and, especially, Lester F. Ward. Pound stated that a final answer to the question, "What is law?" is impossible because law is a living, changing thing, which may at one time be based on sovereign will and at another time on juristic science, which may at one time be uniform and at another time give much room for judicial discretion, which may at one time be very specific in its proscriptions and at another time much more general.[12]

Pound's statement is a call for the study of "law in action," and sociologists are beginning to respond. Pound maintained that the law regulates social interests and arbitrates conflicting interests, claims, and demands. Sociologists are beginning to see that the emergence of criminal laws, like the administration of justice, reflects the wishes of interest groups. In pluralistic societies, the criminal law does not merely balance various social interests; it *is* a balance of social interests. As Quinney has said, "First . . . society is characterized by diversity, conflict, coercion, and change, rather than by consensus and stability. Second, law is a *result* of the operation of interests, rather than an instrument which functions outside of particular interests. Though law may operate to control interests, it is in the first place *created* by interests. Third, law incorporates the interests of specific persons and groups in society. Seldom is law the product of the whole society."[13]

Four principal theories regarding the origin of the criminal law as an agency of social control, and of specific criminal laws, can be discerned. Three of the theories invoke a "consensus model," whereby a group or society expresses its will or spirit in the form of criminal law, while the fourth uses a "conflict model" consistent with the observation that politically organized society is based on an interest structure.

---

[10] See John W. Burgess, *The Sanctity of Law* (Boston: Ginn, 1927); Roscoe Pound, *Interpretations of Legal History* (New York: Macmillan, 1923); idem, *Law and Morals* (Chapel Hill, N.C.: University of North Carolina Press, 1926); Morris R. Cohen, *Reason and Law* (Glencoe, Ill.: Free Press, 1950).

[11] See Gilbert Geis, "Sociology, Criminology, and Criminal Law," *Social Problems*, 7:40-47, Summer, 1959.

[12] Pound, *Interpretations of Legal History*, chap. 3.

[13] Richard Quinney, "Introduction: Toward a Sociology of Criminal Law," in Richard Quinney, ed., *Crime and Justice in Society* (Boston: Little, Brown, 1969), p. 25.

The classical theory regarded the criminal law as originating in torts, or wrongs to individuals. According to this theory, all wrongs produced efforts at self-redress in the injured parties and were therefore treated as injuries to particular individuals. Later, by a series of transitions, the group took charge of the transaction, and the wrongs came to be regarded as injuries to the group or to the state. These transitions included a requirement that the avenger announce his intention of seeking revenge; a requirement that the avenger secure the consent of the group before taking vengeance; the regulation of the amount of injury that could be done to the wrongdoer by the injured party; the limitation of time and place in which vengeance could be secured; public investigation of the merits of the case in connection with the requirements mentioned previously or independently of these; and participation of some members of the group in the efforts of the injured party to secure self-redress.

There can be no doubt that some crimes did originate in torts and became crimes through one or more of the steps described. The theory is inadequate, however. It assumes the priority of the individual to the group, and this is not justified, for it is certain that in early societies some wrongs were regarded as wrongs against the group. Such wrongs were regarded as dangerous to the group directly, as in treason and in violations of the hunting rules, or indirectly, as in sacrilege and witchcraft, which might bring down the wrath of the gods upon the group.[14] Furthermore, for those crimes which originated from torts, the process is not adequately described. It is at this point, in part, that some of the other theories are concentrated.

A second theory is that the criminal law originated in the rational processes of a unified society. When wrongs occurred, the society took action and made a regulation to prevent a repetition of such wrongs. The criminal law, then, is simply a reflection of "the will of the people" or of "public opinion."[15] It is obvious that some criminal laws are made in a rational manner, but the theory is inadequate as a general description of how the criminal law has developed. An alternative interpretation is that the enactment of a statute is an expression of emotion. Something occurs which upsets a group, and it rushes to the legislature to secure a prohibition of such acts. One of the founders of American sociology, Professor Robert Park, said in one of his lectures, "We are always passing laws in America. We might as well get up and dance. The laws are largely to relieve emotion, and the legislatures are quite aware of that fact."

---

[14] S. R. Steinmetz, *Ethnologische Studien zur ersten Entwicklung der Strafe* (Leiden: Harrassowitz, 1894), 2:327-348; H. Oppenheimer, *The Rationale of Punishment* (London: University of London Press, 1913), pp. 66-91; and Hoebel, *Law of Primitive Man.*

[15] See N. Friedman, *Law in a Changing Society* (Berkeley: University of California Press, 1959).

A third theory is that the criminal law originated in and is a crystallization of the mores. Customs developed with little or no rational analysis, but after persisting for a time, they achieved an ethical foundation. Infraction of such customs produced antagonistic reactions of the group, which were expressed in the form of criminal law with penal sanctions. While primitive law and modern common law might reflect some consensus of this kind, there clearly is little general "public opinion" at the base of modern statutes which deal with airplanes, labor unions, factories, automobiles, television, and taxes.[16]

A fourth theory is that criminal law originated in conflict of interests of different groups. When an interest group secures the enactment of a law, it secures the assistance of the state in a conflict with a rival interest group; the opposition of the rival group thus becomes criminal. According to this theory, wrongful acts are characteristic of all classes in present-day society; the upper classes are subtle in their wrongdoing, the underprivileged classes are direct. The upper classes are politically important, and they prohibit the wrongful acts of the underprivileged classes, but the laws are defined and implemented in such manner that many of the wrongful acts of the upper classes do not come within their scope. In this theory, the criminal law originates in the conflict of groups and in the inconsistency of the mores.

Chambliss has used this theory in an excellent analysis of the emergence of vagrancy laws in England and the United States.[17] He demonstrates that these laws emerged in order to provide an abundance of cheap labor to landowners during a period when serfdom was breaking down. When landowners were no longer dependent upon cheap labor, and when industrialists and businessmen supplanted landowners as a powerful interest group, the vagrancy laws remained dormant. But after the turn of the sixteenth century, emphasis was placed on "rogues" and others suspected of being engaged in criminal activities, rather than on the "idle" and "those refusing to work." This shift reflected the increased importance of commerce in England. A new interest group, of great importance to the society, emerged; the vagrancy laws were altered so as to afford protection to this group.

From this perspective, and in light of the discussion in the preceding section, crime can be seen to involve four elements: a value which is appreciated by a group or a part of a group which is politically powerful; isolation of or normative conflict in another part of this group so that its members do not appreciate the value or appreciate it less highly and consequently tend to endanger it; political declaration that behavior endangering the

---

[16] See Richard C. Fuller, "Morals and the Criminal Law," *Journal of Criminal Law and Criminology*, 32:624-630, March-April, 1942; and Clarence Ray Jeffery, "Crime, Law and Social Structure," *Journal of Criminal Law, Criminology, and Police Science*, 47:423-435, November-December, 1956.

[17] William J. Chambliss, "A Sociological Analysis of the Law of Vagrancy," *Social Problems*, 12:67-77, Summer, 1964.

value is henceforth to be a crime; and pugnacious resort to coercion decently applied by those who appreciate the value to those who disregard the value. When a crime is committed, all these relationships are involved. Crime *is* this set of relationships when viewed from the point of view of a social system rather than of the individual. The theory of differential association, to be discussed in chapter 4 and later sections, can logically be derived from the notion that crime consists of this set of relationships.

No positive conclusion can be reached about the comparative efficiency of the various theories concerning the origin of criminal law. Certainly some criminal laws—such as those prohibiting sacrilege, witchcraft, and, possibly, murder—are expressions of consensus. But, just as certainly, criminal laws prohibiting vagrancy, cattle rustling, automobile theft, and discrimination against Negroes and women are expressions of special interests. Research on social aspects of criminal law is greatly needed. While the medical profession is constantly engaged in research work as to the origin of diseases and the effects of treatment, the legal profession has until recently engaged in practically no research work of an analogous kind. Even now, professors of law concentrate their research work on study of what the law *is*. Four of the small number of exceptions to this approach are the analysis by Jerome Hall of the development of the law of theft in modern society, the analysis by a group of Norwegian scholars of the changes in the laws relevant to domestic servants, the analysis by William Chambliss of vagrancy laws, and the more general analysis by Leon Radzinowicz of the development of criminal law in England.[18] ●

The differentiae of crime

The rules of criminal law contain only definitions of specific crimes, such as burglary, robbery, and rape, but legal scholars have been able to abstract certain general principles from such definitions. These general principles are said to apply to all crimes and are the criteria ideally used in determination of whether any particular behavior is or is not criminal. They are consistent with the ideal characteristics of the whole body of the criminal law—politicality, specificity, uniformity, and penal sanction—and, in fact, they may be viewed as translations of the ideal characteristics of the criminal law into statements of the ideal characteristics of all crimes. The concern is shifted from determination of the characteristics of a body of rules to

---

[18] Jerome Hall, *Theft, Law, and Society,* 2d ed. (Indianapolis: Bobbs-Merrill, 1952); Vilhelm Aubert, Torstein Eckhoff, and Knut Sveri, *En Lov i Sökelyset: Sosialpsykologisk undersökelse ave den Norske Hushjelplov* [A law in the searchlight: social psychological research on the Norwegian law pertaining to domestic servants] (Oslo: Akademisk Forlag, 1952); Leon Radzinowicz, *A History of English Criminal Law and Its Administration from 1750,* vols. 1-4 (New York: Macmillan, 1948-1968).

determination of the general characteristics of the many specific acts described in those rules. Thus, for example, penal sanction is a general characteristic of the criminal law, and liability to legally prescribed punishment is a characteristic of all acts or omissions properly called crime. Obviously, a set of criteria used for deciding whether or not any specific act is a crime must be more precise than statements of the general characteristics of a body of rules.

One extensive and thorough analysis of crimes has resulted in a description of seven interrelated and overlapping differentiae of crime.[19] Ideally, behavior would not be called crime unless all seven differentiae were present. The following brief description of the differentiae is greatly simplified.

First, before behavior can be called crime there must be certain external consequences or "harm." A crime has a harmful impact on social interests; a "mental" or emotional state is not enough. Even if one decides to commit a crime but changes his mind before he does anything about it, he has committed no crime. The intention is not taken for the deed.

Second, the harm must be legally forbidden, must have been proscribed in penal law. Antisocial behavior is not crime unless it is prohibited by law. As indicated previously, the law must have specifically prohibited the harm which occurs. Penal law does not have a retroactive effect; there is a long-standing tradition against the enactment of ex post facto legislation.

Third, there must be "conduct"; that is, there must be an intentional or reckless action or inaction which brings the harmful consequences about. One who is physically forced to pull the trigger of a gun does not commit murder, even if someone dies from the bullet.

Fourth, "criminal intent," or *mens rea,* must be present. Hall suggests that legal scholars have often confused intentionality (deliberate functioning to reach a goal) and motivation (the reasons or grounds for the end-seeking).[20] *Mens rea* is identified with the former, not with the latter. The "motives" for a crime might be "good," but the intention itself might be an intention to effect a harm forbidden by the criminal law, a criminal intent. Thus if a man decides to kill his starving children because he feels that they will pass on to a better world, his motive is good, but his intention is wrong. Persons who are "insane" at the time they perpetrate legally forbidden harms do not commit crimes, for the necessary *mens rea* is not present.[21]

Fifth, there must be a fusion or concurrence of *mens rea* and conduct. This means, for example, that a policeman who goes into a house to make an arrest and who then commits a crime

---

[19] Jerome Hall, *General Principles of Criminal Law,* 2d ed. (Indianapolis: Bobbs-Merrill, 1960). See especially pp. 14-26.
[20] Ibid., pp. 84-93.
[21] See the discussion in chap. 8, pp. 156-157.

while still in the house after making the arrest cannot be considered a trespasser from the beginning. The criminal intent and the conduct do not fuse or concur.

Sixth, there must be a "causal" relation between the legally forbidden harm and the voluntary misconduct. The "conduct" of one who fails to file an income tax return is his failure to take pen and ink, fill out the form, etc.; the "harm" is the absence of a return in the collector's office. In this case, the "causal" relation between the two obviously is present. But if, for example, one man shot another (conduct) and the victim suffocated while in a hospital recovering from the wound, the relationship between conduct and harm (death) is not so clear-cut.

Seventh, there must be legally prescribed punishment. Not only must the harm be proscribed by law but, as indicated above, the proscription must carry a threat of punishment to violators. The voluntary conduct must be punishable by law.

These differentiae of crime are all concerned with the nature of the behavior which can properly be called crime, but in making decisions about most cases each criterion need not be considered separately and individually. If the *mens rea,* conduct, the legally proscribed harm are obviously present, for example, the "causal" relation between harm and misconduct almost certainly will be present. In sum, the differentiae represent the kinds of subject matter with which both criminal lawyers and criminal-law theorists must deal.

There are, of course, many exceptions to the generalization that these are the elements of all crimes. Criminal-law theory is not a body of precise principles, and consequently there are deviations from that which is logical and ideal. For purposes of illustration, we may cite two major exceptions to the above differentiae.

First, criminal intent, in the ordinary meaning of the concept, need not be present for some crimes. In some cases—the so-called strict-liability cases—the offender's intent is not considered. Instead, the person is held responsible for the results of his conduct, regardless of his intention. The handling of "statutory rape" is a case in point—no matter how elaborate the calculations, inquiries, or research which a male utilizes in reaching the conclusion that his female companion is above the age of consent, if he has sexual relations with her and it is subsequently shown that she was below the age of consent, he has committed statutory rape. Certain "public welfare" offenses, such as traffic offenses and the selling of adulterated food, are handled under the same rule. Similarly, under the "felony-murder — misdemeanor-manslaughter doctrine" defendants are held criminally liable for much more serious offenses than they intended to commit. If one sets fire to a building and a fireman dies trying to extinguish the flames, the offender is liable for murder; if the offense had been a misdemeanor rather than arson, he would have been liable for manslaughter.

Hall has severely criticized this doctrine and the general conception of strict liability in the criminal law. He contends that it is "bad law," stating that "there is no avoiding the conclusion that strict liability cannot be brought within the scope of penal law."[22] A behavioristic school in jurisprudence, however, insists that the intent can be determined only by the circumstances of the act, and that a translation of these circumstances into mental terms confuses rather than clarifies the procedure. It contends that the doctrine of *mens rea* should be greatly modified or even abandoned. In criminology, the inclusion in the concept "crime" of behavior which was not intended by the actor makes general theoretical explanation of all crime extremely difficult. No current theoretical explanation of criminal behavior can account for the strict-liability offenses.

Second, "motive" and "intention" are confused in many court decisions. In the crime of libel, for instance, motive is explicitly considered. In many states, one cannot publish truthful, albeit damaging, statements about another unless his motive is good. Criminal conspiracy also frequently involves consideration and evaluation of a defendant's motives as well as his intention. In most instances, however, motivation ideally is taken into account only in the *administration* of the criminal law, i.e., in making a decision as to the severity of the punishment which should be accorded a criminal. •

The relativity of crime

Crime is relative from the legal point of view and also from the social point of view. The criminal law has had a constantly changing content. Many early crimes were primarily religious offenses, and these remained important until recent times; now few religious offenses are included in penal codes.[23] It was a crime in Iceland in the Viking age for a person to write verses about another, even if the sentiment was complimentary, if the verses exceeded four stanzas in length. A Prussian law of 1784 prohibited mothers and nurses from taking children under two years of age into their beds. The English villein in the fourteenth century was not allowed to send his son to school, and no one lower than a freeholder was permitted by law to keep a dog. The following have at different times been crimes: printing a book, professing the medical doctrine of circulation of the blood, driving with reins, sale of coin to foreigners, having gold in the house, buying goods on the way to market or in the market for the purpose of selling them at a higher price, writing a check for less than one dollar. On the other hand, many of our present laws were not known to earlier

---

[22] Hall, *General Principles of Criminal Law,* p. 336. See also Jerome Hall, "Analytic Philosophy and Jurisprudence," *Ethics,* 77:14-28, October, 1966; and Colin Howard, *Strict Responsibility* (London: Sweet and Maxwell, 1963).

[23] Kai T. Erikson, *Wayward Puritans: A Study in the Sociology of Deviance* (New York: John Wiley, 1966).

generations—quarantine laws, traffic laws, sanitation laws, factory laws.

Laws differ, also, from one jurisdiction to another at a particular time. The laws of some states require automobile owners to paste certificates of ownership or inspection certificates on the windshield, while adjoining states prohibit the pasting of anything on the windshield. Georgia has a $1,000 fine or six months' incarceration as the maximum penalty for adultery, while in Louisiana adultery is not a crime at all.[24]

In a particular jurisdiction at a particular time there are wide variations in the interpretation and implementation of the law. These variations are related to the specific characteristics of the crimes, to the status of the offenders, and to the status of the enforcers. Sudnow has shown that what is "burglary" or "robbery" or almost any other crime is highly negotiable.[25] Further, gross forms of fraud, such as those committed by confidence men, are easily detected by the regular police, but expert investigators must deal with the subtler forms of fraud which flourish in many areas of business and of the professions. When such experts are provided by politicians interested in making subtle fraud "real crime," what has been mere chicanery is interpreted and dealt with as crime. In this sense, also, crime is relative to the status of the criminals and the situations in which they violate law. ●

Classification of crimes

Since crime is not a homogeneous type of behavior, efforts have been made to classify crimes. They are frequently classified in respect to atrocity as felonies and misdemeanors. The more serious are called felonies and are usually punishable by death or by confinement in a state prison; the less serious are called misdemeanors and are usually punishable by confinement in a local prison or by fines. As a classification of crimes this is not very useful, as was pointed out long ago by Sir James Stephen, and it is difficult to make a clear-cut distinction between the classes. Though one may agree that assaults, as a class, are more serious offenses than permitting weeds to grow on a vacant lot in violation of a municipal ordinance, the effects of permitting the weeds to grow, in a particular case, may be more serious because of the hay fever produced by the pollen and the resulting incapacitation of many people. The fact that many things which are classed as felonies in one state are classed as misdemeanors in nearby states shows how difficult it is to make a real distinction between them. Even within a single state the distinction is often vague.

---

[24] Robert C. Bensing, "A Comparative Study of American Sex Statutes," *Journal of Criminal Law, Criminology, and Police Science,* 42:57-72, May-June, 1951.

[25] David Sudnow, "Normal Crimes: Sociological Features of the Penal Code in a Public Defender Office," *Social Problems,* 12:255-276, Winter, 1965.

The greatest objection to the classification of crimes as felonies and misdemeanors is that it is used also as a classification of criminals. The individual who commits a felony is a felon; the individual who commits a misdemeanor is a misdemeanant. It is assumed that misdemeanants are less dangerous and more susceptible to rehabilitative measures than felons. But it is quite fallacious to judge either dangerousness or the probability of reformation from one act, for an individual may commit a misdemeanor one week, a felony the second week, and a misdemeanor the third. The acts do not represent changes in his character or changes in his dangerousness.

Moreover, the definition of a crime as misdemeanor or felony is influenced by various considerations other than atrocity or dangerousness. Since 1852, when a felony was first defined in Massachusetts as a crime punishable by confinement in the state prison, at least four changes have been made in the laws of that state determining the conditions under which a sentence is served in state prison rather than in a jail or house of correction. These changes, which also changed crimes from felonies to misdemeanors or the reverse, were not made because of alterations in views regarding the atrocity of crimes but for purely administrative reasons, generally to relieve the congestion of the state prison. In the administration of justice, thousands of persons charged with committing felonies successfully arrange to have the charge reduced to a misdemeanor, and the distinction between the two classes of offense is lost. Consequently there seems to be good reason to abandon this classification.

Bonger, the Dutch criminologist, classified crimes by the motives of the offenders as economic crimes, sexual crimes, political crimes, and miscellaneous crimes (with vengeance as the principal motive).[26] But no crime can be reduced to one motive. A desire for excitement or vengeance may be very important in such crimes as burglary, which Bonger classified as economic crime. The classification is clearly inadequate.

Crimes are frequently classified for statistical purposes as crimes against the person, crimes against property, and crimes against public decency, public order, and public justice. Most recorded crimes are crimes against public order or public morality, such as disorderly conduct and drunkenness; next in frequency come the crimes of dishonesty without violence. Of the persons arrested by the police in 1971, 34 percent were arrested for drunkenness or disorderly conduct or vagrancy. The crimes which are regarded as most serious are relatively few, according to this criterion. Homicide constituted 0.2 percent, rape 0.2 percent, burglary 5 percent, and robbery 2 percent, a

---

26 W. A. Bonger, *Criminality and Economic Conditions* (Boston: Little, Brown, 1916), pp. 536-537.

total for these serious offenses of 7.4 percent of all arrests.[27] It is probable that if all cases of fraud could be recorded, fraud would rank close to drunkenness and disorderly conduct in frequency.

In a classification of crimes for theoretical purposes, each class should be a sociological entity, differentiated from the other classes by variations in causal processes. Professional crime, for instance, would be a class, or more likely a combination of classes, differentiated from other crimes by the regularity of this behavior, the development of techniques, and the association among offenders and consequent development of a group culture. Within this class might be included some cases of murder, arson, burglary, robbery, and theft, but not all of the cases in any of those legal categories.[28] Similarly, specific criteria for describing cases as "criminal violation of financial trust" have been developed, with the result that some, but not all, cases of embezzlement, confidence game, forgery, larceny by bailee, and other crimes are included.[29] The new classification avoided the error of extending a legal concept beyond its legal meaning, e.g., calling all the behavior "embezzlement," and at the same time it provided a rigorous definition of the behavior being studied. Jerome Hall has made an excellent analysis of theft from this point of view.[30] It is not worthwhile at present to attempt a complete classification of crimes from this viewpoint. Such a classification should be based on research work rather than on a priori speculation.[31] ●

The criminal   Who is a criminal? An answer consistent with the previous discussion is: a person who commits a crime. However, in the democratic legal tradition even one who admits to having committed a crime is not designated a criminal until his criminality has been proven by means of the accepted court procedures.

---

[27] Federal Bureau of Investigation, U.S. Department of Justice, *Uniform Crime Reports for the United States, 1971* (Washington: Government Printing Office, 1972), p. 126.

[28] See chap. 13, below; see also Don C. Gibbons and Donald L. Garrity, "Some Suggestions for the Development of Etiological and Treatment Theory in Criminology," *Social Forces,* 38:51-58, October, 1959; and Jack P. Gibbs, "Needed: Analytical Typologies in Criminology," *Southwestern Social Science Quarterly,* 12:321-329, March, 1960; and Marshall B. Clinard and Richard Quinney, *Criminal Behavior Systems,* 2d ed. (New York: Holt, Rinehart and Winston, 1973).

[29] Donald R. Cressey, *Other People's Money: A Study in the Social Psychology of Embezzlement* (Glencoe, Ill.: Free Press, 1953), pp. 19-22; idem, "Criminological Research and the Definition of Crimes," *American Journal of Sociology,* 56:546-551, May, 1951.

[30] Hall, *Theft, Law, and Society.*

[31] Cf. Jerome Hall, "Some Basic Questions Regarding Legal Classification for. Professional and Scientific Purposes," *Journal of Legal Education,* vol. 5 (1953), no. 3, pp. 329-343; and Sudnow, "Normal Crimes."

Consequently, a prison warden would not be justified in receiving as a prisoner a person who had not been officially convicted and sentenced, and public officials could not rightfully deny civil rights to persons who had not been convicted of some crime. Similarly, criminologists cannot rightfully designate as "criminals" persons who have behaved in an antisocial manner but who have not violated a criminal law.[32] However, for scientific purposes it is not necessary that every decision be made in court; the criminologist must only know that a certain class of acts is defined as crime and that a particular person has committed an act of this class. Just as there is justification for writing of "crimes known to the police" and "unsolved crimes," there is justification for writing of "unapprehended criminals" and "criminals at large."[33]

This answer, that a criminal is one who commits a crime, however, raises other questions, for even the criminal law does not specify the length of time a person remains a criminal after he has committed a crime. Is one a criminal only during the time he is committing the crime, until he has "paid the penalty," or during the remainder of his life? Is a boy a delinquent if no one labels him a delinquent? These questions are perhaps unimportant and are difficult to answer only because we use the words *criminal* and *delinquent* to stigmatize persons who violate the law. In public thought the word *criminal* is generally applied only to those who are ostracized by official society. It is in this sense that Tarde stated that criminals are "social excrement."[34]

Some criminologists are inclined to restrict the term *criminal* to those persons who conform to a social type which is defined by those persons and by society generally as criminal. The term then refers to the violator of law who has a body of skills, attitudes, and social relationships which signify maturity in criminal culture. This usage is analogous to the practice of reserving the terms *plumber, electrician,* or *preacher* for those who engage regularly and expertly in certain occupations. If the term is restricted in this manner, it is not applied to many occasional violators of law, even those who commit murder. The *criminal* then becomes *the real criminal.* Most of the inmates of state prisons would not be *criminals* by this criterion. The use of the word *criminal* in this manner does not direct attention to most of the pertinent problems of criminology. ●

---

[32] Cf. Paul W. Tappan, "Who is the Criminal?" *American Sociological Review,* 12:96-102, February, 1947; Frank E. Hartung, "White-collar Offenses in the Wholesale Meat Industry in Detroit," *American Journal of Sociology,* 56:25-34, July, 1950; and Robert G. Caldwell, "A Reexamination of the Concept of White Collar Crime," *Federal Probation,* 22:30-36, March, 1958.

[33] See Donald R. Cressey, "Foreword" to Edwin H. Sutherland, *White Collar Crime,* new ed. (New York: Holt, Rinehart and Winston, 1961), pp. 4-8.

[34] Gabriel Tarde, *Penal Philosophy,* trans. Rapelje Howell, Modern Criminal Science Series (Boston: Little, Brown, 1912), p. 222.

Possibility of a science of criminology

Criminology is not a science, but criminologists hope it will become a science. The argument has been made, however, that criminology cannot possibly become a science. According to this argument, general propositions of universal validity are the essence of science; such propositions can be made only regarding stable and homogeneous units; crime is not a stable and homogeneous unit but varies from one time or place to another; therefore universal propositions cannot be made regarding crime, and scientific studies of criminal behavior are impossible.

The emphasis on universal propositions might be regarded by some students as exaggerated, but all will agree on the value of such universal propositions when they can be obtained and the desirability of organizing a study so that such propositions may be reached. Furthermore, this criticism neglects the possibility of selecting areas and types of crimes in which definitions are essentially uniform, or at least of taking into account variations in definitions. As indicated above, it is possible to some extent for the criminologist, by selection of criminal cases, to redefine crime for his own purposes. But, in general, the difficulties arising from the legal definition of crime should be recognized.

Sellin implicitly acknowleged the criticism described above and suggested that criminologists study all violations of conduct norms, whether crime or not. He argued that a solid basis for a science of criminology cannot be found unless the arbitrary definitions of the legislatures are replaced by definitions drawn up by scientists and for scientific purposes.[35] Even if this is done, it is not possible to escape the evaluations of behavior which are made by groups and the labeling decisions that are made as a result. Courage, for instance, cannot be defined as a fixed aspect of behavior, for behavior which is called courageous in one situation is called cowardly in another, and the difference in the names applied to the behavior makes the behavior different. Juvenile delinquency and some forms of crime have the same attribute. Physiologically, acts can be defined apart from group evaluations; sociologically they cannot be. In this respect crime is like all other social phenomena, and the possibility of a science of criminal behavior is similar to the possibility of a science of any other behavior. Social science has no stable unit, as it deals with phenomena involving group evaluations.

A universal explanation of crime must necessarily be extremely broad and may not be especially enlightening or valuable for purposes of control. In medicine, a great leap forward was made principally by defining and explaining particular diseases. Similarly, in criminology the significant explanations probably will relate not to crime as a whole, but to particular

---

[35] Thorsten Sellin, *Culture Conflict and Crime* (New York: Social Science Research Council, 1938). See also Denis Szabo, *Déviance et Criminalité* (Paris: Armand Colin, 1970), p. 17.

types or classes of crimes, each class being defined in terms of universal elements. Obviously, legal definitions should not confine the work of the criminologist; he should be completely free to push across the barriers of legal definitions whenever he sees noncriminal behavior which resembles criminal behavior.

Some students, admitting the criticisms outlined above, have abandoned the effort to make criminology a science and place their emphasis on study of social control. A study of lawmaking, lawbreaking, and reactions to lawbreaking from the point of view of the efficiency of the law as a method of control is a useful objective in a criminology of this nature.[36] ●

The problem of crime

The seriousness of the social problem of crime hardly needs to be described. The general public is, by definition, always the victim of crime. The general public suffers losses from crime either directly (as in treason or theft and destruction of public property) or indirectly (in the form of the expense of maintaining the police and the courts and in the form of uneasiness or even terror because of the prevalence of crime). In this sense every individual in the state is a victim of crime. In addition, some individuals are victims of crime in a more specific sense. The victims of crime may lose anything that has value. Personal safety, money, and property are perhaps basic values, because they contribute to the satisfaction of many wishes. About ten thousand persons a year are victims of homicides, of which perhaps one-third are felonious homicides not due to negligence.

The financial losses from fraudulent business transactions are probably many times as great as the financial losses from burglary, robbery, and ordinary larceny. Each working day trusted employees make off with over $8 million of their employers' cash or merchandise, a total annual loss of over $2 billion. In comparison, it was estimated that in 1965 crimes against the person resulted in a loss of approximately $815 million. This figure takes into account the value of property taken, loss of earnings, medical and hospital expenses, and related costs. Losses from property crimes amount to about $3,932,000 annually. The most publicized and feared crimes, the FBI Index crimes, are estimated to cost about $600 million. The cost of illegal goods and services, such as prostitution, drugs, and gambling, is estimated to be $8,075,000,000.[37] One chain of stores has about five hundred burglaries and robberies a year, with a total loss of about $100,000 a year. The same chain had one embezzlement which caused a loss of more than $600,000. A

---

[36] See Marc Ancel, *Social Defence: A Modern Approach to Criminal Problems* (London: Routledge and Kegan Paul, 1965).

[37] President's Commission on Law Enforcement and Administration of Justice, *Task Force Report: Crime and Its Impact—An Assessment* (Washington: Government Printing Office, 1967), pp. 45-53.

management consulting firm recently found dishonesty in 50 percent of the assignments it undertook in one year, when there was no prior hint of dishonesty. The firm makes surveys of employee morale, performance in connection with plant layout, efficiency, and other matters which are essentially engineering in nature. In more than 50 percent of *these cases* they found dishonesty. The same firm unearthed more than $60 million worth of dishonesty in one year with more than 60 percent attributable to supervisory and executive personnel.[38] Such business losses are ordinarily passed on to the consumer in the form of higher prices.

Loss of status in the community is frequently a result of crime. The victim of rape, especially, suffers this loss, and the loss is immensely magnified by the continued publicity given to it in the newspapers. Also, loss of status may be suffered by persons not ordinarily considered to be the victims, as the relatives of the prostitute or of the murderer or embezzler. The victim is sometimes immediately aware of the loss he suffers, but the realization is frequently delayed. The child who is employed in violation of the child-labor law, for instance, may not have an immediate realization of the loss he suffers by this crime and, in fact, may never realize the relation of his childhood labor to his subsequent career.

In crimes of personal violence, the victims and the offenders are generally of the same social group and have residences not far apart. Negroes murder Negroes, Italians murder Italians, and Chinese murder Chinese. These crimes of personal violence are generally committed against persons with whom the offenders have personal dealings.[39] Crimes against property, however, are generally committed against strangers. They may be either direct and personal attacks, as in robbery or burglary, or may be much more general and public, as in fraudulent stock and bond sales or fraudulent advertisements. In modern society these general and impersonal crimes have become much more serious in their effects than have the direct and personal attacks. Although the impersonal crimes generally represent no antagonism toward the victims, they do represent a ruthless and reckless pursuit of interests at variance with the interests of the victim.

It is urged by some persons that crime makes certain contributions to society which offset this loss to some extent. One suggested contribution is that it promotes the solidarity of the group,

---

[38] Norman Jaspan with Hillel Black, *The Thief in the White Collar* (Philadelphia: J. B. Lippincott, 1960), p. 10.

[39] Harold Garfinkel, "Research Note on Inter- and Intra-Racial Homicides," *Social Forces*, 27:369-381, May, 1949; President's Commission, *Task Force Report: Crime and Its Impact*, p. 82; Marvin E. Wolfgang and Franco Ferracuti, *The Subculture of Violence: Towards an Integrated Theory in Criminology* (London: Tavistock, 1967).

just as does war.[40] While it is true that the group is welded together by certain spectacular crimes of murder or rape, it is probable that many other crimes promote dissension, suspicions, and divisions in society. Moreover, the solidarity which is aroused in this manner is generally rather futile, for it is an emotional expression which drives criminals into organized groups. In this respect crime, like war, may have some effect in producing group solidarity, but the values can be produced more effectively in other ways.

Again, it is urged that we must have crime in order to prevent morality from going to an extreme. If, under an existing régime, all criminals were eliminated, the standards would be set a little higher. If those at the bottom who violated the new standards were eliminated, the standards would be set still higher. Thus the group would become more and more strict in its morality until the situation became impossible. This argument, also, is not entirely convincing. At least, many primitive groups retained essentially the same standards with practically no violations for long periods of time.[41] ●

AUBERT, VILHELM. "Researches in the Sociology of Law." *American Behavioral Scientist,* 7:16-20, December, 1963.

BECKER, HOWARD S. *Outsiders: Studies in the Sociology of Deviance.* New York: Free Press, 1963.

BLUMBERG, ABRAHAM S. *Criminal Justice.* Chicago: Quadrangle Books, 1967.

CHAMBLISS, WILLIAM J., & ROBERT B. SEIDMAN. *Law, Order, and Power.* Reading, Mass.: Addison-Wesley, 1971.

CICOUREL, AARON V. *The Social Organization of Juvenile Justice.* New York: John Wiley, 1968.

CLINARD, MARSHALL B., & RICHARD QUINNEY. *Criminal Behavior Systems: A Typology.* 2nd ed. New York: Holt, Rinehart and Winston, 1973.

COSER, LEWIS A. *The Functions of Social Conflict.* Glencoe, Ill.: Free Press, 1956.

EVAN, WILLIAM M., ed. *Law and Society.* New York: Free Press, 1962.

FRIEDMAN, LAWRENCE M., & STEWART MacAULAY. *Law and the Behavioral Sciences.* Indianapolis: Bobbs-Merrill, 1969.

GIBBS, JACK P. "Crime and the Sociology of Law." *Sociology and Social Research,* 51:23-38, October, 1966.

GURVITCH, GEORGES. *Sociology of Law.* New York: Philosophical Library, 1941.

Suggested readings

---

[40] George Herbert Mead, "The Psychology of Punitive Justice," *American Journal of Sociology,* 23:577-602, March, 1918; A. C. Hall, *Crime in Its Relation to Social Progress* (New York: Columbia University Press, 1902), pp. 1-10. See also Robert A. Dentler and Kai T. Erikson, "The Functions of Deviance in Groups," *Social Problems,* 7:98-107, Fall 1959; and Lewis A. Coser, "Some Functions of Deviant Behavior and Normative Flexibility," *American Journal of Sociology,* 68:172-181, September, 1962.

[41] William J. Chambliss and Robert B. Seidman, *Law, Order, and Power* (Reading, Mass.: Addison-Wesley, 1971), pp. 19-25.

HALL, JEROME. *General Principles of Criminal Law.* 2d ed. Indianapolis: Bobbs-Merrill, 1960.

HALL, JEROME. *Theft, Law, and Society.* 2d ed. Indianapolis: Bobbs-Merrill, 1952.

HANN, ROBERT G. "Crime and the Cost of Crime: An Economic Approach." *Journal of Research in Crime and Delinquency,* 9:12-30, January, 1972.

HILLS, STUART L. *Crime, Power, and Morality.* Scranton, Pa.: Chandler, 1971.

HOBSBAWM, E. J. *Primitive Rebels.* New York: W. W. Norton, 1959.

MARTIN, J. P., & J. BRADLEY. "Design of a Study of the Cost of Crime." *British Journal of Criminology,* 4:591-603, October, 1964.

MICHAEL, J., & M. J. ADLER. *Crime, Law, and Social Science.* New York: Harcourt, Brace, 1933.

POUND, ROSCOE. *Criminal Justice in America.* New York: Holt, 1930.

QUINNEY, RICHARD. *The Social Reality of Crime.* Boston: Little, Brown, 1970.

QUINNEY, RICHARD. "Crime Control in Capitalist Society: A Critical Philosophy of Legal Order." *Issues in Criminology,* 8:75-99, Spring, 1973.

RADZINOWICZ, LEON. *A History of English Criminal Law and Its Administration from 1750,* vols. 1-4. New York: Macmillan, 1948-1968.

REISS, ALBERT J., JR. "Law and Sociology: Some Issues for the 70's." *University of Richmond Law Review,* 5:31-46, 1970.

SCHAFER, STEPHEN. *Theories in Criminology.* New York: Random House, 1969.

SCHUR, EDWIN M. *Law and Society.* New York: Random House, 1969.

SCHWARTZ, RICHARD D., & JEROME H. SKOLNICK. *Society and the Legal Order: Cases and Materials in the Sociology of Law.* New York: Basic Books, 1970.

SKOLNICK, JEROME H. "The Sociology of Law in America: Overview and Trends." In *Law and Society,* a supplement to *Social Problems,* Summer, 1965, pp. 1-39.

SUTHERLAND, EDWIN H. *White Collar Crime.* New York: Dryden Press, 1949.

TIMASHEFF, N. S. *An Introduction to the Sociology of Law.* Cambridge: Harvard University Committee on Research in the Social Sciences, 1939.

TREVES, RENATO, & J. F. GLASTRA van LOON. *Norms and Actions: National Reports on Sociology of Law.* The Hague: Martinus Nijhoff, 1968.

TURK, AUSTIN. *Criminality and Legal Order.* Chicago: Rand McNally, 1969.

WOLFGANG, MARVIN E., ed. *Crime and Culture.* New York: John Wiley, 1968.

Indexes of delinquency and crime

The statistics about crime and delinquency are probably the most unreliable and most difficult of all social statistics. It is impossible to determine with accuracy the amount of crime in any given jurisdiction at any particular time. Some behavior is labeled "delinquency" or "crime" by one observer but not by another. Obviously a large proportion of all law violations goes undetected. Other crimes are detected but not reported, and still others are reported but not officially recorded. Consequently any record of crimes, such as crimes known to the police, arrests, convictions, or commitments to prison, can at most be considered an "index" of the crimes committed. But these "indexes" of crime do not maintain a constant ratio with the true rate, whatever it may be. We measure the extent of crime with elastic rulers whose units of measurement are not defined.

Ordinarily, a statistical index, such as a "cost of living index," is a compilation of fluctuations in a sample of items taken from the whole; the relationship to the whole is known, and the index serves as a convenient shortcut to a sufficient approximation of variation in the whole. But in crime statistics the rate as indicated by any set of figures cannot be a sample, for the whole cannot be specified. Both the true rate and the relationship between the true rate and any "index" of this rate are capricious "dark figures" which vary with changes in police policies, court policies, and public opinion.[1] The variations in this "dark figure" in crime statistics make it almost foolhardy to attempt a comparison of crime rates of various cities, and it is hazardous even to compare national rates or the rates of a given city or state in a given year with the rates of the same jurisdiction in a different year. International comparisons are even more difficult. ●

Crimes known to the police

The crimes which are reported to the police and recorded by the police are designated "crimes known to the police." These statistics are an inadequate index of the true crime rate. Yet the decision to use this rate is probably the best way out of a bad situation, for as Professor Sellin has repeatedly pointed out, "The value of criminal statistics as a basis for measurement of crimi-

---

[1] Donald R. Cressey, "The State of Criminal Statistics," *National Probation and Parole Association Journal*, 3:230-241, July, 1957; Albert D. Biderman and Albert J. Reiss, Jr., "On Exploring the Dark Figure of Crime," *Annals of the American Academy of Political and Social Science*, 374:1-15, November, 1967; and Roger Hood and Richard Sparks, *Key Issues in Criminology* (London: World University Library, 1970), chaps. 1 and 2.

nality in geographic areas decreases as the procedures take us farther away from the offense itself."[2] That is, these police records are a more reliable index than arrest statistics; arrest statistics are more reliable than court statistics; and court statistics are more reliable than prison statistics.

Even within a single police department, many crimes are "lost" between recording and arrest, the exact number varying with the honesty and efficiency of the police department and with the policy regarding handling cases informally, without actual arrest. In 1971, the police of 4,500 cities who reported crimes to the Federal Bureau of Investigation "cleared by arrest" 84 percent of the murders, 55 percent of the rapes, 66 percent of the aggravated assaults, 27 percent of the robberies, 19 percent of the burglaries, 19 percent of the larcenies, and 16 percent of the automobile thefts known to them.[3] Similar rates are reported for European countries, but statistical comparisons are hazardous because "clearance" is defined in so many different ways.[4] No matter how defined, high clearance rates do not necessarily reflect diligent detective work on the part of policemen. But because they often are viewed as indexes of police efficiency, they tend to be highly inflated. Police commonly use a technique called "slate cleaning" to improve their clearance rate. A burglar, for example, might confess to a hundred burglaries, thus "clearing" them, in return for a promise that he will be granted a light sentence upon conviction of the burglary for which he was arrested. Probably not more than five percent of all crimes committed in the United States are cleared by means of field detective methods.

Similarly, many crimes are "lost" between arrest and prosecution. Just as some types of crime are cleared by arrest more frequently than others, some types of crime are more frequently prosecuted than others. In 2,990 cities in the United States in 1971, persons were held for prosecution in 96 percent of the murder cases, 45 percent of the rape cases, 46 percent of the aggravated assault cases, 27 percent of the robbery cases, 14 percent of the burglary cases, 17 percent of the larceny cases, and 14 percent of the automobile theft cases known to the police.

In addition, many crimes are "lost" between prosecution and conviction; this process, too, is selective—some types of crime are "lost" more frequently than others. In 2,900 cities in 1971,

---

[2] Thorsten Sellin, "The Significance of Records of Crime," *Law Quarterly Review*, 67:489-504, October, 1951.

[3] Federal Bureau of Investigation, U.S. Department of Justice, *Uniform Crime Reports for the United States, 1971* (Washington: Government Printing Office, 1972), p. 104.

[4] See Manuel Lopez-Rey, *Crime: An Analytical Appraisal* (London: Routledge and Kegan Paul, 1970), pp. 60-62. See also Donald J. Black, "Production of Crime Rates," *American Sociological Review*, 35:733-747, August, 1970.

39 percent of the persons charged with murder were found guilty, as compared to 27 percent of those charged with rape, 35 percent of those charged with aggravated assault, 20 percent of those charged with robbery, 23 percent of those charged with burglary, 50 percent of those charged with larceny, and 17 percent of those charged with automobile theft. It is obvious that prison statistics are not in constant ratio to the crimes committed, for there are wide variations in the use of fines, probation, and other alternatives to imprisonment. These variations indicate that if crimes known to the police are a good index of crimes committed, then arrests, prosecutions, convictions, and commitments to prison are not—at least for purposes of comparing types of crime.

However, even the number of crimes known to the police is not an adequate index of crime. There are five examples of evidence for this assertion.

First, the number of crimes known to the police is certainly much smaller than the number actually committed. National surveys done for President Johnson's Crime Commission revealed that the incidence of crime in the United States is several times the incidence reported in *Uniform Crime Reports*. Persons interviewed in 1965-1966 about the extent to which they had been victims of crimes revealed that "crimes known to the police" for 1965 include at most only about half the crimes of violence and less than half of the property crimes committed. The rate of forcible rapes reported by the persons interviewed was about 3½ times, the rates for burglary about three times, and the rates for aggravated assault and robbery about double the rates reported to the FBI's statistical division.[5] In one year, the detectives of a Chicago department store arrested two-thirds as many adult women for shoplifting as were formally charged with petty larceny of all forms (including shoplifting) by the police in the entire city of Chicago.[6] Store detectives turn only about 25 percent of apprehended shoplifters over to the police.[7]

Victims may consider the crime insignificant and not worth reporting; they may hope to avoid embarrassing the offender, who might possibly be a relative, school friend, or fellow employee; they may wish to avoid the publicity which might result if the crime were reported; they might have agreed to the crime, as in gambling offenses and some sexual offenses; they may wish to

---

[5] President's Commission on Law Enforcement and Administration of Justice, *The Challenge of Crime in a Free Society* (Washington: Government Printing Office, 1967), p. 20.

[6] Loren E. Edwards, *Shoplifting and Shrinkage Protection for Stores* (Springfield, Ill.: Charles C Thomas, 1958), p. 130. See also Mary Owen Cameron, *The Booster and the Snitch* (New York: Free Press, 1964).

[7] Roger K. Griffin, "Shoplifting: A Statistical Study," *Security World*, November, 1970, pp. 21-25.

avoid the inconvenience of calling the police, appearing as a witness, etc.; they may be intimidated by the offender; they may be antagonistic to the police or opposed to the punitive policies of the legal system; or they may feel that the police are so inefficient that they will be unable to catch the offender even if the offense is reported.[8] The police themselves overlook many offenses, often because "enforcing the law" would be unfair to the suspect, because the law is vague, or because booking the offender would be too much work.

Second, the number of crimes known to the police is a reasonably accurate index of crime only if the police are honest, efficient, and consistent in making their reports. Police have an obligation to protect the reputation of their cities, and when this cannot be done efficiently under existing administrative machinery, it is sometimes accomplished statistically. Politicians up for reelection are likely to be accused of neglect of duty if the crime rate has gone up during their administration, and they are likely to be praised if the crime rate has declined. Consequently, political administrations often try to show statistically that during their term in office the crime rate declined. In 1966 the New York City Police Commissioner found that only 22 percent of the department's auto theft and rape cases, 45 percent of the aggravated assaults, and 54 percent of the larcenies were properly recorded—as against 92 percent of the robbery cases and 96 percent of the burglaries. With these corrections, the rate for serious crimes would rise immediately from 1,608 per 100,000 population to 2,203, an increase of about 37 percent.[9] In Madison, Wisconsin, juvenile delinquency rates increased tremendously in one year, principally because the proportion of juveniles contacted by the police who were referred to the court increased from 15 to 47 percent.[10] Individual policemen select out for recording and further processing only a proportion of the crimes, delinquencies, and suspected crimes and delinquencies they observe. No one knows what the proportion is in each case. It is known, however, that policemen with professional training process more delinquents than those without professional training.[11] Variations in crime rates among cities or among other jurisdictions must be interpreted with extreme caution, for the differences may be due merely to differential recording practices in the various police departments and by individual policemen.

---

[8] F. H. McClintock, "The Dark Figure," *Collected Studies in Criminological Research,* vol. V, 1970, pp. 9-34.

[9] Marvin E. Wolfgang, *Crimes of Violence,* a document submitted to the President's Commission on Law Enforcement and Administration of Justice, 1967, p. 33.

[10] Lyle W. Shannon, "Types and Patterns of Delinquency Referral in a Middle-Sized City," *British Journal of Criminology,* 4:24-36, July, 1963.

[11] James Q. Wilson, "The Police and the Delinquent in Two Cities," in Stanton Wheeler, ed., *Controlling Delinquents* (New York: John Wiley, 1967).

Third, the value of crimes known to the police as an index of crime is sharply limited by the fact that the ratio of crimes committed to crimes reported and recorded varies according to offense. As Sellin has said:

> . . . we cannot use the *total* recorded criminality. We must extract from that total the data for only those offences in which the recorded sample is large enough to permit the assumption that a reasonably constant relationship exists between the recorded and the total criminality of these types. We may make that assumption *when the offence seriously injures a strongly embraced social value, is of a public nature in the sense that it is likely to come to the attention of someone beside the victim, and induces the victim or those who are close to him to co-operate with the authorities in bringing the offender to justice.*[12]

Fourth, variations in the criminal law may affect the volume of crimes known to the police, reducing the value of the index for comparative purposes. Behavior which is crime in one place or time may not be crime in another place or time; the difference reduces the value of the index for long-range comparative purposes. Further, categorization of an offense in one of the classifications used for recording may be unsystematized and irregular, so that variation in a particular offense is created when none exists in fact.[13] Whether a suspect is charged with petty theft, burglary, or grand larceny sometimes depends on the whim of the policeman as he records the offense. Most contemporary "kidnaping," for example, is actually the taking possession of a victim in the course of a robbery. Philadelphia magistrates pay little attention to the charges against the bums who come before them; in one year, as a consequence, there were 1,430 commitments of vagrants to the house of correction, but only 1,241 arrests for vagrancy.[14] Similarly, comparisons of the crime rates of various countries are seriously limited by wide variations in the national legal systems. For example, "robo" in the Argentine penal code includes what the United States codes call "robbery," but it also includes some kinds of behavior which the typical United States code would call burglary or breaking and entering.[15] International comparisons should be of decided value in securing an understanding of criminality because these statistics show the wider variations which may not be apparent within a particular country. In Scandinavia, considerable interest has developed in a program for the international codification of criminal laws and for the development of international statistics

---

[12] Sellin, "Significance of Records of Crime," pp. 496-497.

[13] Cf. Samuel A. Stouffer, "Indices of Psychological Illness," in Paul F. Lazarsfeld and Morris Rosenberg, eds., *The Language of Social Research* (Glencoe, Ill.: Free Press, 1955), pp. 63-65.

[14] Caleb Foote, "Vagrancy-Type Law and Its Administration," *University of Pennsylvania Law Review*, 104:603-650, March, 1956, at p. 612.

[15] Lois B. DeFleur, "A Cross-Cultural Comparison of Offenders and Offenses: Cordoba, Argentina, and the United States," *Social Problems*, 14:483-492, Spring, 1967.

of crime and criminals. The essential problem is to develop units that can be used for international comparisons.

Fifth, the number of crimes known to the police must, for purposes of comparison, be stated in proportion to the population or to some other base, and the determination of this base is often difficult. United States census figures on the general population collected in the first year of a decade often must be used throughout the decade as the base for computing crime rates. Since the increasing United States population is not taken into account, the number of crimes per 100,000 population appears to increase each year throughout the decade. If 1970 population figures are used to compute the crime rates for both 1970 and 1979, for example, the latter year shows a higher rate, not because of an increase in crime, but because the population increase between 1970 and 1979 is not included in the base for the 1979 rate. Also, the population figures must be corrected for variations in age, sex, racial composition, and urban-rural composition, and much of this information is available only in the years in which decennial enumerations of the population are made.[16] Moreover, in many cases it is necessary to have other information. For instance, the number of automobile thefts in a community must be stated in proportion to the number of automobiles in the community. More generally, crimes of theft should be stated in proportion to the amount of property available to be stolen, not merely in proportion to population. Moreover, Engelmann and Throckmorton have argued convincingly that a more accurate view of all crime rates is obtained if the number of crimes is stated in proportion to the frequency of interaction among people, rather than merely in proportion to the number of people.[17] The difficulty of securing an adequate base for computing a rate is evident. ●

Sources of statistics on crime in the United States

Police, court, and prison statistics may be published by the agency which manufactures them, or they may be reported to a central state or federal agency which organizes, combines, and publishes the statistics from many agencies. Only rarely do the local or central agencies do more than catalog the incidence of various crimes. Computation of rates, analyses of interrelationships between various statistical facts, and the making of inferences about the statistics are left to outside research workers. The various agencies, in other words, merely take censuses of various dimensions of the criminal population, just as the Department of Commerce takes censuses of the total United States population. Some

---

[16] See Ronald Chilton and Adele Spielberger, "Is Delinquency Increasing? Age Structure and the Crime Rate," *Social Forces,* 49:487-493, March, 1971.

[17] Hugo O. Engelmann and Kirby Throckmorton, "Interaction Frequency and Crime Rates," *Wisconsin Sociologist,* 5:33-36, Spring, 1967. See also Sarah L. Boggs, "Urban Crime Patterns," *American Sociological Review,* 30:899-908, December, 1965.

of the agencies explicitly state the limitations of the statistics which they publish, but most of them do not.

Since 1930, the United States Department of Justice has published a periodical bulletin on crime statistics, *Uniform Crime Reports.* The number of known crimes reported to the FBI by the police of about 3,000 cities and towns is used as an index of "major" crimes (murder, rape, aggravated assault, burglary, robbery, larceny, and automobile theft), and the "arrests" (fingerprint records sent to the FBI) are used as an index of other crimes. The bulletin was first published monthly, became a quarterly in 1932, was converted into a semiannual publication during World War II, and became an annual publication in 1959. Local police departments are supplied with a manual on reporting, but participation by police departments is on a voluntary basis. Consequently not all communities are covered, and the large metropolitan centers are overrepresented. In 1971 the total population represented in one set of statistics on arrests numbered 181 million, while the total population of the United States was over 206 million.[18]

Although the *Uniform Crime Reports* have many limitations, and the FBI will not vouch for their accuracy, they comprise the best available statistics on crime in the United States. Table I shows the estimated number of serious crimes reported as known to the police in 1971, and Table II shows the number of police department arrests recorded in 1971 by the FBI on the basis of the fingerprint cards sent to it. In the latter table it should be

Federal reports

TABLE I

Estimated number of major crimes in the United States, 1971[19]

Crime index classification	Estimated crime, 1971		Percent change over 1970	
	Number	Rate per 100,000 inhabitants	Number	Rate
Total	5,995,200	2,906.7	+ 7.4	+5.8
Murder	17,360	8.5	+11.1	+9.0
Forcible rape	41,890	20.3	+11.3	+9.7
Robbery	385,190	187.1	+10.8	+9.2
Aggravated assault	364,600	176.8	+10.1	+8.5
Burglary	2,368,400	1,148.3	+ 8.8	+7.2
Larceny, $50 and over	1,875,200	909.2	+ 7.2	+5.6
Auto theft	941,600	456.5	+ 2.1	+ .6

[18] Federal Bureau of Investigation, *Uniform Crime Reports, 1971,* p. 100. For a history of this bulletin and a critique of the statistics reported in it, see Marvin E. Wolfgang, "Uniform Crime Reports: A Critical Appraisal," *University of Pennsylvania Law Review,* 111:708-738, April, 1963.

[19] Federal Bureau of Investigation, *Uniform Crime Reports, 1971,* p. 6. The estimated crime totals for the United States appearing in this table are not comparable to such totals published in *Uniform Crime Reports* in the years prior to 1959. "Negligent manslaughter" has been omitted. "Larceny" no longer includes petty offenses, and "rape" no longer includes "statutory rape."

Total arrests, distribution by sex, 1971[20]

Offense charged	Number			Percent		
	Total	Male	Female	Total	Male	Female
Total	**6,966,822**	**5,923,052**	**1,043,770**	**100.0**	**100.0**	**100.0**
Criminal homicide	17,317	14,604	2,713	.2	.2	.2
Forcible rape	16,582	16,582	—	.2	.3	—
Robbery	101,728	95,293	6,435	1.5	1.6	.6
Aggravated assault	140,350	121,729	18,621	2.0	2.1	1.8
Burglary—breaking or entering	315,376	299,870	15,506	4.5	5.1	1.5
Larceny—theft	674,997	485,087	189,910	9.7	8.2	18.2
Auto theft	130,954	123,160	7,794	1.9	2.1	.7
Other assaults	307,107	265,226	41,881	4.4	4.5	4.0
Arson	11,154	10,034	1,120	.2	.2	.1
Forgery and counterfeiting	45,340	34,223	11,117	.7	.6	1.1
Fraud	95,610	68,233	27,377	1.4	1.2	2.6
Embezzlement	7,114	5,342	1,772	.1	.1	.2
Stolen property— buying, receiving, possessing	75,516	68,495	7,021	1.1	1.2	.7
Vandalism	121,850	112,279	9,571	1.7	1.9	.9
Weapons—carrying, possessing, etc.	114,569	106,475	8,094	1.6	1.8	.8
Prostitution and commercialized vice	52,916	11,807	41,109	.8	.2	3.9
Sex offenses (except forcible rape and prostitution)	50,695	44,626	6,069	.7	.8	.6
Narcotic drug laws	400,606	336,476	64,130	5.8	5.7	6.1
Gambling	86,698	79,582	7,116	1.2	1.3	.7
Offenses against family and children	56,456	51,594	4,862	.8	.9	.5
Driving under the influence	489,545	456,043	33,502	7.0	7.7	3.2
Liquor laws	231,192	199,966	31,226	3.3	3.4	3.0
Drunkenness	1,491,782	1,383,913	107,869	21.4	23.4	10.3
Disorderly conduct	621,057	522,815	98,242	8.9	8.8	9.4
Vagrancy	80,180	62,631	17,549	1.2	1.1	1.7
All other offenses (except traffic)	869,270	727,618	141,654	12.5	12.3	13.6
Suspicion	54,374	46,421	7,953	.8	.8	.8
Curfew and loitering law violations	101,943	80,297	21,646	1.5	1.4	2.1
Runaways	204,544	92,631	111,913	2.9	1.6	10.7

noted that only 20.1 percent of the arrests were for the seven "major" crimes and that there is a great discrepancy between the estimated number of major crimes committed and the number of arrests for those crimes.

The Department of Justice also publishes statistics on commitments to state and federal penal institutions in the United States.

---

[20] Ibid., p. 124.

This series, *National Prisoner Statistics,* was originally published until 1950 by the Bureau of the Census, with the title *Prisoners in State and Federal Prisons and Reformatories.* In 1950 it was transferred to the Federal Bureau of Prisons, and in 1971 to the Law Enforcement Assistance Administration. Included are data on the number of commitments to the various institutions, the number of prisoners present at the end of each year, and the number of prisoners discharged under each of the various systems of release. The annual report of the Federal Bureau of Prisons, *Federal Prisons* (formerly named *Federal Offender*), gives statistical data on persons convicted of violations of federal laws. Table III presents

Prisoners in institutions and received from court, 1939-1970,
Rates per 100,000 of the estimated civilian population[21]

	Present at end of year			Received from court		
Year	All institutions	Federal institutions	State institutions	All institutions	Federal institutions	State institutions
1939	137.1	15.0	122.0	—	—	—
1940	132.0	14.6	117.3	55.5	11.5	44.1
1941	126.0	14.1	112.0	52.3	11.7	40.6
1942	116.4	12.9	103.5	45.5	10.6	34.9
1943	108.0	12.7	95.3	39.4	9.6	29.8
1944	104.2	14.3	89.9	39.5	11.0	28.4
1945	100.5	14.0	86.5	40.0	10.7	29.4
1946	99.7	12.5	87.2	43.7	10.6	33.0
1947	105.2	11.9	93.3	45.0	9.0	36.0
1948	106.6	11.2	95.4	43.6	8.5	35.1
1949	110.0	11.3	98.6	46.3	8.8	37.5
1950	110.3	11.4	98.9	46.1	9.5	36.7
1951	108.9	11.4	97.4	44.1	9.3	34.9
1952	108.8	11.6	97.1	45.8	9.9	35.9
1953	110.2	12.3	97.9	47.1	10.4	36.7
1954	113.8	12.4	101.3	50.3	10.4	40.0
1955	113.4	12.3	101.1	47.9	9.3	38.5
1956	113.5	12.1	101.4	46.7	8.1	38.6
1957	114.9	12.0	102.9	47.4	7.8	39.5
1958	118.8	12.5	106.3	51.2	8.0	43.3
1959	117.7	12.8	104.9	49.5	7.9	41.6
1960	118.6	12.9	105.7	49.3	7.6	41.7
1961	120.8	13.0	107.8	51.3	7.4	43.9
1962	118.3	12.9	105.3	48.1	7.3	40.8
1963	115.7	12.3	103.4	46.8	6.9	39.9
1964	112.6	11.4	101.2	46.0	6.6	39.4
1965	109.5	10.9	98.6	45.4	6.6	38.8
1966	102.7	9.9	92.8	40.0	5.9	34.1
1967	99.1	10.0	89.2	39.6	5.8	33.8
1968	94.3	9.9	84.3	36.3	5.6	30.7
1969	97.6	9.7	87.8	37.6	5.8	31.8
1970	96.7	9.8	86.8	39.1	5.9	33.1

[21] Federal Bureau of Prisons, "Prisoners in State and Federal Institutions for Adult Felons, 1968-1970", *National Prisoner Statistics,* no. 47, April, 1972, table 1, p. 2, and table 2, p. 3.

National Prisoner Statistics data on the recent trends in rates of commitments to both state and federal institutions.

Local coroners keep records of known homicides, and the National Office of Vital Statistics (or a similar agency) has since 1900 published in *Vital Statistics of the United States* an annual homicide rate based on these records. Until about 1930, only the coroners' statistics from the New England states were summarized but now the entire population of the United States is covered. These statistics were issued by the Bureau of the Census until 1946; now that bureau merely reprints—in *Statistical Abstracts of the United States*—the data published by the U.S. Public Health Service. Table IV shows that the number of deaths by homicide per one-hundred thousand adults increased in the middle 1960s and has remained rather constant since that time. These statistics on homicide do not, however, necessarily show that murders and manslaughter, as ordinarily understood, have increased. Homicide includes justifiable and noncriminal violence, such as killing in self-defense, killing a prisoner who is trying to escape, and similar acts. It also includes deaths caused by negligence, now common in automobile accident cases. Because *Vital Statistics* does not report the portion of all homicides which are justifiable or due to negligence, the publication tells us little about trends in murder, as popularly understood. It should be noted further that coroners' reports pertain to medical causes of death, and not to arrests or prosecutions of persons accused of murder.

TABLE IV

Number and rate of homicides, United States: 1930 to 1970[22]

Years[a]	Number	Rate[b]
1930	10,473	12.4
1935	10,587	11.7
1940	8,329	8.6
1945	7,412	7.2
1950	7,942	7.3
1955	7,418	6.5
1960	8,464	7.0
1965	10,712	8.3
1966	11,589	—
1967	13,425	10.0
1968	14,686	10.8
1969	14,480	10.4
1970 est.	15,610	11.0

[a] Prior to 1960, excludes Alaska and Hawaii. Excludes Armed Forces abroad.
[b] Per 100,000 resident population 16 years old and over; enumerated as of April 1 for 1930, 1940, 1950, 1960, and 1970; estimated as of July 1 for all other years.

The homicide rate per 100,000 population fluctuates markedly from country to country. The United States consistently shows a rate higher than most European countries and lower than most South American countries, as illustrated in Table V.

---

[22] U.S. Bureau of the Census, *Statistical Abstract of the United States, 1972,* 93rd edition (Washington, 1972), table 229, p. 146.

TABLE V

Homicide rates for selected countries (per 100,000 population)[23]

Country	Rate	Year reported
Mexico	45.6	1969
South Africa	36.2	1966
Colombia	21.5	1967
France	16.7	1969
United States	9.5	1968
England/Wales	3.5	1969
Ireland	3.4	1969
Canada	2.5	1969
Japan	2.3	1968
Federal Republic of Germany	1.3	1967

Wide differences in homicide rates are found within the United States. In 1971, Atlanta had the highest rate of any American city with more than a million population, having nearly twice as high a rate as New York or Cleveland, and more than five times the rate of Pittsburgh and Boston.

Statistics on juvenile delinquency are also published by the federal government, through the Children's Bureau of the Social Security Administration. Until 1939, the reports were issued as bulletins called *Children in the Courts;* from 1939 to 1945 they appeared occasionally as supplements to the Children's Bureau publication, *The Child;* since 1945 they have been published irregularly in mimeographed form and in a special Children's Bureau Statistical Series. Until 1955, only about 400 courts, out of approximately 3,000 courts that deal with children's cases, made reports to the bureau. In 1955, the bureau revised its statistical reporting plan to include a national sample representative of all juvenile courts. The earlier Children's Bureau statistics have been criticized on the ground that a very small proportion of the population is represented, that the standards for reporting are not uniform, that definitions of delinquency vary from jurisdiction to jurisdiction, that the ages of children over whom the courts have jurisdiction vary, and that there are variations in the proportions of juvenile delinquents who are referred to the courts.[24] Table VI shows the recent trends in juvenile delinquency, as measured by the representative national sample for 1957-1969.

Generally, the states are less efficient than the federal government in making crime statistics available. In most states, one or more state departments obtain reports from a particular type of county

State reports

---

[23] *Demographic Yearbook,* 22nd issue, United Nations Publications, 1971, pp. 694-708.

[24] See James F. Short, Jr., and F. Ivan Nye, "Extent of Unrecorded Juvenile Delinquency: Tentative Conclusions," *Journal of Criminal Law, Criminology, and Police Science,* 49:296-302, November-December, 1958.

TABLE VI Trend in delinquency cases disposed of by juvenile courts,
United States, 1957-1970[25]

Year	Delinquency cases[a,b]	Child population (10-17 years of age)	Rate[c]
1957	440,000	22,173,000	19.8
1958	470,000	23,443,000	20.0
1959	483,000	24,607,000	19.6
1960	510,000	25,364,000	20.1
1961	503,000	26,029,000	19.3
1962	555,000	26,962,000	20.6
1963	601,000	28,031,000	21.4
1964	686,000	29,189,000	23.5
1965	697,000	29,479,000	23.6
1966	745,000	30,008,000	24.8
1967	811,000	30,750,000	26.4
1968	900,000	31,374,000	28.7
1969	988,500	31,971,000	30.9
1970	1,052,000	32,531,000	32.3

[a] "Excluded from this report, for the first time, are the ordinary traffic cases handled by juvenile courts, except where traffic cases, usually the more serious ones, are adjudicated as 'juvenile delinquency' cases and are reported as such. Variations in types of courts having jurisdiction in traffic cases of juveniles and frequent changes in laws affecting this jurisdiction, together with changes in administrative practices and inadequate reporting of such cases, make it very difficult to determine meaningful national estimates on the extent and trends in juvenile traffic offenses."

[b] Data for 1957-1969 estimated from the national sample of juvenile courts. Data for 1970 estimated from all courts reporting whose jurisdictions included almost three-fourths of the population of the U.S.

[c] Based on the number of delinquency cases per 1,000 U.S. child population, 10-17 years of age.

or municipal official, but no attempt is made to use a uniform system of reporting in order to make the resulting summaries comparable. The attorney general may receive information from district attorneys; the department of correction may receive information from sheriffs; the department of public welfare from juvenile courts and welfare agencies dealing with delinquency, etc. In a few states, the only criminal statistics are those published by individual institutions or agencies. Only thirteen states— including California, Hawaii, Louisiana, Massachusetts, Michigan, Minnesota, New York, Pennsylvania, Rhode Island, South Dakota, and Texas—have central statistical bureaus which collect and pub-

[25] U.S. Department of Health, Education, and Welfare, *Juvenile Court Statistics, 1970* (Washington: National Center for Social Statistics, 1972), p. 11. See fig. I, p. 242, below.

lish statistical information drawn from reports made by a variety of local, county, or state agencies. For some states, crimes known to the police, arrests, and convictions are summarized, but in most states the statistics are restricted to the number of persons admitted to probation, prison, and parole. The data in Table VII are from the Bureau of Statistics, California Department of Justice; this bureau acts as a statistical agency for the Department of Corrections.

Statistics on specific crimes are published regularly by some federal and state agencies, and certain private organizations maintain running accounts of the offenses committed against them. The Federal Deposit Insurance Corporation, the Treasury Department, and the Department of Justice, for example, all publish annual indexes of the number of violations of certain federal laws. Similarly, the American Bankers Association keeps records of offenses against banks; fidelity bonding companies keep records of crimes against bonded business firms, and large corporations record their annual losses to various kinds of crime. Ordinarily, the statistics reported by a single agency or private organization are not comparable with the statistics compiled and published for the entire nation or for an entire state.

Other reports

TABLE VII

Male prisoners newly received from court,
California, 1967 and 1968[26]

Offense	1967		1968		Percent change in rate— 1968 over 1967
	Number	Rate per 100,000 population[a]	Number	Rate per 100,000 population[a]	
Total	**4,782**	**24.94**	**4,667**	**23.59**	**− 5.4**
Homicide	293	1.50	327	1.65	10.0
Robbery	929	4.76	906	4.58	− 3.8
Assault	317	1.62	336	1.70	4.9
Burglary	838	4.29	772	3.90	− 9.1
Theft, except auto	404	2.07	387	1.96	− 5.3
Auto theft	237	1.21	218	1.10	− 9.1
Forgery and checks	541	2.77	463	2.34	−15.5
Sex offenses	318	1.63	305	1.54	− 5.5
Narcotics	667	3.41	631	3.19	− 6.5
Other offenses	328	1.68	322	1.63	− 3.0

[a] Estimates of State population from State Department of Finance, Financial and Population Research Section publication.

[26] *California Prisoners, 1968* (Sacramento: Department of Corrections, 1969), p. 17.

Government agencies and private foundations also have promoted and conducted a number of crime surveys, one general aim of which has been the discovery of the proportions of crimes not reported in the usual statistics of crime. Among the more famous surveys are the Cleveland survey, the Missouri survey, the Illinois survey, the study by the Wickersham commission, the Oregon survey, the Attorney General's survey, and the recent survey made by the President's Commission.[27]

Occasionally, a comprehensive firsthand investigation by an independent research worker produces new statistical indexes. Short and Nye have demonstrated that statistics compiled from reports of delinquencies by offenders are acceptable and desirable in scientific analyses.[28] ●

The pervasiveness of crime in the United States

Crime is much more general and pervasive than the ordinary statistics indicate, and an entirely incorrect impression regarding criminality is formed if conclusions are limited to these statistics. Opposition to law has been a tradition in the United States. Popular rebellions against laws constitute an almost continuous series from the early colonial period to the present. Violations of many of the early laws were quite as general as were violations of the national prohibition law in the 1920s and violations of current laws prohibiting gambling, homosexual conduct, and possession of marijuana. The manufacture of nails and of other commodities in violation of English law, the sale of firearms and of liquor to Indians, smuggling and other violations of laws regulating commerce, Shays's Rebellion in 1787, the Whiskey Rebellion in 1794, trading with the enemy during the War of 1812, riots against the Catholics, the Irish, and the Mormons, Dorr's Rebellion in 1841-1842, trading in slaves, harboring fugitive slaves, Negro disfranchisement, violation of antitrust laws, violation of banking laws, violation of prohibition laws, and violation of draft laws during the Vietnam War are some of these popular rebellions.[29] The earlier violations of this type cannot be measured statistically, and it is not possible to determine from the descrip-

---

[27] Roscoe Pound and Felix Frankfurter, eds., *Criminal Justice in Cleveland* (Cleveland: The Cleveland Foundation, 1922); Missouri Association for Criminal Justice, Survey Committee, *The Missouri Crime Survey* (New York: Macmillan, 1926); Illinois Association for Criminal Justice, *The Illinois Crime Survey* (Chicago: Author, 1929); National Commission on Law Observance and Enforcement, *Reports* (Washington: Government Printing Office, 1931); Wayne L. Morse and Ronald H. Beattie, *Survey of the Administration of Justice in Oregon* (Eugene, Ore.: University of Oregon Press, 1932); *Attorney General's Survey of Release Procedures,* 5 vols. (Washington: Government Printing Office, 1939-40); President's Commission on Law Enforcement and Administration of Justice, *The Challenge of Crime in a Free Society* (Washington: Government Printing Office, 1967), pp. 21-22.

[28] James F. Short, Jr., and F. Ivan Nye, "Reported Behavior as a Criterion of Deviant Behavior," *Social Problems,* 5:207-213, Winter, 1957-58.

[29] See Kai T. Erikson, *Wayward Puritans: A Study in the Sociology of Deviance* (New York: John Wiley, 1966).

tions whether the number of persons involved in popular rebellions has increased or decreased.

The criminal tradition is also reflected in the fact that certain occasions are defined as holidays from morality. Halloween, New Year's Eve, election nights, spring celebrations, campus demonstrations, and important football victories are occasions of this nature. Crimes are committed on these occasions by persons who ordinarily would not commit them, and may take the form of destruction of property and of assaults. Individual crimes are committed primarily in a spirit of exuberance, and they coincide with institutionalized collective behavior involving many persons. There is much evidence that the delinquency of boys in the deteriorated areas is an extension of this attitude through the entire year.

Labor strikes were once very much like these moral holidays. More recently student strikes have resembled them. There is a gathering of persons with a common interest, an attitude during the early period of the strike which is much like that of a picnic, and an exuberance which is like that of the spring celebration. Assaults and destruction of property occur on these occasions, just as on other holidays from morality. The violation of law, however, is much more purposive in the strike than in these other outbursts. Factory workers, skilled tradesmen, farmers, and students, without much differentiation, violate the laws on such occasions. These holidays from morality are so generally recognized that penalties for lawlessness seldom result.

The fact that almost all persons have at some time deliberately committed crimes, often of a serious nature, is further evidence of our criminal tradition. In an older study, 1,020 men and 678 women were asked to check which of forty-nine offenses they had committed.[30] In the distribution of the questionnaire an effort was made to obtain a balanced religious and racial cross-section of the population, but the group of subjects contained an excess of persons from upper social classes. Ninety-one percent of the subjects admitted that they had committed one or more offenses, excluding juvenile delinquencies, for which they could have received a jail or prison sentence. Men had an average of eighteen and women an average of eleven adult offenses. Thirteen percent of the men admitted to grand larceny, 26 percent to auto theft, 17 percent to burglary, and 11 percent to robbery. The corresponding figures for women were 11, 8, 11, and 1. Sixty-four percent of the men and 27 percent of the women admitted to committing at least one felony.

Such percentages can be accepted only with many reservations. However, the study certainly reveals that the number of crimes committed is far greater than the number reported in crime statistics, as do studies conducted in Norway, Sweden, and Finland.

---

[30] James S. Wallerstein and Clement J. Wyle, "Our Law-Abiding Law-Breakers," *Probation*, 25:107-112, March-April, 1947.

The Finnish study showed that only 5 percent of self-reported larcenies and 1 percent of self-reported violations of alcohol laws were detected by police.[31] In a study of juvenile delinquencies Short found that a group of sixty-five college boys reported that they had committed an average of 9.9 offenses against property, 12.3 behavior-problem offenses, 9.6 offenses against persons, 16.5 sex offenses, 20.8 "casual offenses," and 12.6 miscellaneous offenses. A group of ninety-four training-school boys reported that they had committed an average of 13.4 offenses against property and 19.1 behavior-problem offenses; their average number of other offenses was about the same as that of the college boys. In comparison with the training-school boys, the college men had only very rarely been arrested for their offenses.[32] One explanation for this differential lies in the fact that many of the complaints to juvenile authorities are made by parents against their own children—parents of college students do not file complaints as frequently as do parents of noncollege students. Further, policemen and other officials use discretion in making arrests, often to the advantage of the suspect that does not fit the stereotype of the "bad actor."[33]

White-collar crimes—crimes committed by persons of respectability and high social status in the course of their occupations—also are extremely widespread, but an index of their frequency is not found in police reports. Prosecution for this kind of crime frequently is avoided because of the political or financial importance of the parties concerned, because of the apparent triviality of the crimes, or because of the difficulty of securing evidence sufficient for prosecution, particularly in the cases of crimes by corporations.[34] Even more important, methods other than prosecution in the criminal courts are frequently used to protect society against white-collar crime—action may be taken in the civil courts or in hearings before boards and commissions. Consequently, a precise statement regarding the extent of white-collar crime is impossible. Differences in administrative procedures, however, do not justify the designation of this behavior as some-

[31] Nils Christie, Johs. Andenaes, and Sigurd Skirbekk, "A Study of Self-Reported Crime," *Scandinavian Studies in Criminology*, 1 (1965): 86-116; Inkeri Anttila and R. Jaakkola, "Unrecorded Criminality in Finland," *Kriminologinen Tutkimuslaitos*, 2 (1966): 5-22.

[32] James F. Short, Jr., "A Report on the Incidence of Criminal Behavior, Arrests, and Convictions in Selected Groups," *Research Studies of the State College of Washington*, 22:110-118, June, 1954. See also Short and Nye, "Reported Behavior as a Criterion of Deviant Behavior," and Maynard L. Erickson and Lamar T. Empey, "Court Records, Undetected Delinquency and Decision-making," *Journal of Criminal Law, Criminology, and Police Science*, 54:456-469, December, 1963.

[33] Aaron V. Cicourel, *The Social Organization of Juvenile Justice* (New York: John Wiley, 1968); Irving Piliavin and Scott Briar, "Police Encounters with Juveniles," *American Journal of Sociology*, 70:206-214, September, 1964.

[34] See Edwin H. Sutherland, "White Collar Criminality," *American Sociological Review*, 5:1-12, February, 1940.

thing other than crime.[35] In general, underlying these failures to prosecute is the lack of a developed social feeling and ethical code in the groups concerned and, to some extent, in the general public. The danger from robbery or assault is clearly realized, for they involve direct sensory processes and are based on social relations which have existed for many centuries. Theft by fraudulent advertisements and prospectuses is a recent development and affects persons who may be thousands of miles away from the thief. Codes of behavior have not been developed in regard to this behavior. These white-collar criminals, however, are by far the most dangerous to society of any type of criminal from the point of view of effects on private property and social institutions.

An analysis has been made of the number of instances in which seventy of the largest United States mining, manufacturing, and mercantile corporations violated, over a period of about forty years, the laws outlawing the following practices: restraint of trade; misrepresentation in advertising; infringements of patents, trademarks, and copyrights; "unfair labor practices" as defined by the National Labor Relations Act and other laws; rebates; financial fraud and violation of trust; violations of war regulations; and some miscellaneous activities.[36] The records reveal that every one of the seventy corporations had violated one or more of the laws, with an average of about thirteen adverse decisions per corporation and a range of from one to fifty adverse decisions per corporation. The corporations had a total of 307 adverse decisions on charges of restraint of trade, 222 adverse decisions on charges of infringements, 158 adverse decisions under the National Labor Relations Act, 97 adverse decisions under the laws regulating advertising, and 196 adverse decisions on charges of violating other laws. Thus, generally, the official records reveal that these corporations violated the trade regulations with great frequency. The "habitual criminal" laws of some states impose severe penalties on criminals convicted the third or fourth time. If this criterion were used here, about 90 percent of the large corporations studied would be considered habitual white-collar criminals. Moreover, this enumeration of official decisions is far from complete, and it is concerned with violations of only a few laws. Even a complete enumeration of all adverse decisions against all corporations would represent only a crude index of the total amount of crime perpetrated by those corporations.

Financial corporations and institutions also have a high incidence of hidden criminality. The comptroller of the currency re-

---

[35] See Vilhelm Aubert, "White-Collar Crime and Social Structure," *American Journal of Sociology*, 58:263-271, November, 1952; John C. Spencer, "White-Collar Crime," chap. in Tadeusz Grygier, Howard Jones, and John C. Spencer, eds., *Criminology in Transition* (London: Tavistock, 1965), pp. 233-266; André Normandeau, "Les Deviations en Affaire et de Crime en Col Blanc," *Revue International de Criminologie et de Police Technique*, 4:247-248, 1965; and Hans Joachim Schneider, "Wirtschaftkriminalität in Kriminologischer und Strafrechtlicher Sicht," *Juristenzeitung*, 15:461-467, August, 1972.

[36] Edwin H. Sutherland, *White Collar Crime* (New York: Dryden Press, 1949).

ported that approximately three-fourths of the national banks examined in a particular quarter were found to be violating the national banking laws. Dishonesty was found in 50.4 percent of the national bank failures during the period 1865-1899, and in 61.4 percent during the period 1900-1919.[37] Some years ago, lie detector tests of the employees of certain Chicago banks showed that 20 percent of them had taken money or property from the bank, and in almost all cases these tests were supported by subsequent confessions.[38]

Fraud, also, is frequently a white-collar crime. The statistics on crime in European countries show a general trend toward a decrease in crimes of violence and an increase in crimes involving fraud. It is probable that the trend is even more pronounced in America, but neither the trend nor the present extent of fraud can be determined by available statistics. It is probable, also, that fraud is the most prevalent crime in America. Misleading balance sheets which public accountants have been able to invent and develop; wash sales by which the value of a security is fraudulently determined; concessions in rent by real estate dealers for the purpose of fraudulently increasing the sales price of property; excessive and misleading claims made by the manufacturers, vendors, and advertisers of patent medicines, toothpaste, cosmetics, and many other articles; transfer of deteriorated securities from the banker's own possession to the trust funds under his direction; and a considerable part of present-day salesmanship and of advertising—all these examples illustrate this kind of criminality. These things represent either active fraud with the intent to deceive the prospective purchaser or else misrepresentation by silence.

Expert techniques of concealment have developed in many occupations for the purpose of preventing the purchaser from learning the defects of the commodity. Not many farmers would sell hogs with the knowledge that the hogs were infected with cholera and would die within a few days, and those farmers who did this would be regarded as dishonest, even if the misrepresentation consisted merely in silence regarding the danger. On the other hand, not many brokers or bankers would hesitate to sell securities which, by advance information, they had learned would soon be worthless, and the few who did refrain from immediate sale would be regarded as foolish. The physical disease of the hogs is more readily appreciated than the financial disease of the securities, and the effects are likely to be more definitely

---

[37] These statistics were included in the annual reports of the comptroller of the currency and of the Department of the Treasury until 1923, when they were discontinued.

[38] Fred E. Inbau, "Scientific Evidence in Criminal Cases," *Journal of Criminal Law and Criminology*, 24:1140-1158, March-April, 1934.

recognized. Defects in commodities are frequently concealed and labels often misrepresent. Shirting of inferior quality may be filled with clay in order that the defects may be concealed until the sale is consummated. This is essentially the same principle that was used by the old horsetrader in concealing the blemishes in his horses. Manufacturers offer merchants a wide variety of "list prices" for the same item, so that the merchants can advertise that they sell at a very small percentage of "list price." These cases of misrepresentation and fraud have not been subject to prosecution in most cases, for the courts have operated on the principle *caveat emptor,* which has meant that the purchaser must protect himself against ordinary dishonesty and could appeal to the courts for protection only against extraordinary dishonesty. President Roosevelt in 1933 insisted that the principle be reversed and *caveat vendor* be substituted, especially with regard to securities.

An immense amount of fraud is involved in insurance, both on the part of the insured and the insurers. Murders are committed, houses burned, automobiles destroyed, and sickness or injury feigned in order that insurance may be collected. Fraud in personal injury cases is unusually extensive, and was once an important source of income for unscrupulous lawyers, known as "ambulance chasers," who generally worked on contingent fees. Fraud in these cases seldom results in prosecution, although murder and arson may be occasion for prosecution of those crimes as such. The insurance company is seldom free to prosecute for fraud, for it seldom has clean hands. The insurance company adopts the usual policy that "business is business" and that sentiment must be eliminated; it makes a settlement at the lowest possible figure rather than at the figure which the nature of the loss justifies. For this purpose, claim agents, lawyers, and physicians for the insurance company frequently practice misrepresentation. Physicians for the company, for instance, frequently minimize the extent of injuries, in the expectation that the physician on the other side will magnify them. Also, in many cases the claim agent collects an additional sum for settlement and divides this with the attorney for the injured party.

Fraud is also present in the legal profession. Popular feeling inclines to the belief that a lawyer cannot be successful if completely honest and that almost any law firm will take any case within its field of specialization no matter how extreme the dishonesty required for representing the interests of the client. Though absence of official statistics makes it impossible to determine the truth or falsity of this popular opinion, it probably exaggerates the extent of dishonesty in the profession. While fraud is still common, flagrant practices seem to have decreased in the past generation, due to increased "professionalization" of legal occupations. Bar associations have been organized to promote codes of ethics and to prosecute unethical and openly-criminal practices. Nevertheless, the "spirit of combat" in legal trials continues to make it necessary for some lawyers to practice fraud and misrepresentation by misstatement and concealment of whole truth if they are to win cases. Such practices generally are not grounds for disbarment proceedings by bar associations but, again, they illustrate our criminalistic traditions.

Fraudulent reports of property and income for tax purposes are general. The person who reported his personal property honestly would generally be regarded as a freak, for the only method by which a person can avoid paying more than his share of the taxes is by accepting the common level of dishonesty. Most citizens would probably prefer to make honest reports, if they were assured that others would do the same. Dishonesty in reporting incomes has become more dangerous, but the general methods of concealing a part of the income or making fraudulent claims for exemptions are extremely widespread.

Many churches and denominational colleges have misapplied funds, under the direction of boards of trustees composed of clergy, lawyers, and businessmen. Gifts for endowments have been used for current expenses; gifts for missions have been used for pastors' salaries; and in other ways funds have been misapplied.

The extraordinary development of fraud in modern life has been an aspect of the drive for profits, which in itself has been regarded as one of the primary virtues, and which, for that reason, has appeared to remove somewhat the taint from illegal practices. Persons practicing fraud have ordinarily felt no pangs of conscience, for the effects of fraudulent behavior have not become apparent in individual victims known to the defrauders, but have been impersonal and diffuse. If the effects were discernible in particular persons known to the defrauders, and if the practices were not purified by attachment to the virtuous search for profits, many business and commercial practices would be clearly recognized as crimes.

Although bribery is not always white-collar crime, it is another extremely prevalent crime for which arrests are seldom made. Bribery of public officials is a crime both for the bribe-taker and the bribe-giver. Influencing of private persons by giving them gifts, money, or services is not crime, but it is closely akin to bribery in effects and attitudes. Both public and private "influence peddling" may be in the form of a direct exchange of money, but it is much more frequently a concealed and indirect method of putting a person under obligation to return a service.

In many cities and states an immense amount of white-collar bribery of public officials occurs in connection with the purchase of supplies, the making of contracts, the enforcement of regulations, and the enactment of legislation. It is involved when fuel oil is purchased, when school books are purchased, when roads or buildings are constructed, when land is bought for public purposes, when franchises are granted to railroads, bus companies, steamship companies, and other public utility companies, and on hundreds of other occasions. Agents of book-publishing companies have testified regarding their methods of bribing school boards, and many public investigations have shown the wide prevalence of bribery of public officials. In some cities, any purchase of commodities which is strictly honest is an oversight. Much of the wealth of some public officials was secured from these bribes, and it came from the most important of the financial and commercial concerns as well as from the agencies of the so-called underworld.

Enforcement of regulations regarding insurance, banking, factories, housing, building construction, streets, garbage, public utilities, weights and measures, and most other important functions is often a matter of bargaining between the agents of the state and the agencies subject to the law. The process, once started, grows and involves firms which were previously honest. The honest firm is forced to bribe the inspector in order to protect itself against arbitrary and persecutory enforcement of laws, but the inspector's expectation of securing bribes has grown out of bribes given previously by other concerns. Campaign contributions may protect a firm against demands for petty graft and may be effective in protecting agencies and interests against laws which may decrease profits.

Corruption is extremely prevalent, also, in private business. Buyers for department stores, hotels, factories, railways, and almost all other concerns which make purchases on a large scale accept and sometimes demand gifts or money payments. In doing so, they violate the trust their employer has placed in them, although not necessarily in a criminal way. The cost of the gifts is added to the price of the merchandise being sold, so that the employer and, eventually, the consumer actually are forced to subsidize the employee. Agents of general credit bureaus and of credit bureaus of special trade associations have reported that they are frequently approached by businessmen who offer bribes if information which tends to lower their credit rating is concealed or if their credit rating is raised. Persons who have had experience in both business and politics claim that the honesty standards among politicians are higher than they are among businessmen.

Aiding and abetting criminals is itself a crime. Although, for obvious reasons, this crime is seldom reported to the police, the number of persons who, in the course of their business, aid and abet criminals is very great. Cigar stores and nightclubs are sometimes the arsenals of gunmen, though the proprietors may not themselves engage in crimes of violence. Some lawyers are regularly retained to advise professional criminals and to protect the professional criminals in case of arrest, and are an essential part of any criminal organization. Certainly some part of the perjury by witnesses in trials grows out of the suggestions and instructions of lawyers. Reputable business concerns frequently purchase the proceeds of thefts with a clear realization of the source of the commodities. The manufacturers and distributors of guns, especially machine guns, of silencers, and of material for bombs are important assistants of gangsters. All large cities and most of the smaller ones have persons who make a business of "fixing" cases for professional thieves. The police, bailiffs, clerks, prosecutors, and judges frequently cooperate with these "fixers," either for direct money payments or under orders from political leaders who control appointments and elections.

The police constantly break the laws. The laws of arrest are rigidly limited, but the police exercise their authority with little reference to these limitations and in violation of law. If illegal arrests are regarded as kidnapings, then the number of kidnapings by the police is thousands of times as great as the number of kidnapings by burglars and robbers. The courts, similarly, are not immune from criminal contagion, and this is true especially of the lower courts.

Thus crime is found in most occupations and is very prevalent. The people of the business world are probably more criminalistic in this sense than are the people of the slums. The crimes of the slums are direct physical actions—a blow, a physical grasping and carrying away of the property of others. The victim identifies the criminal definitely or indefinitely as a particular individual or group of individuals. The crimes of the business world, on the other hand, are indirect, devious, anonymous, and impersonal. A vague resentment against the entire system may be felt, but when particular individuals cannot be identified, the antagonism is futile. The perpetrators thus do not feel the resentment of their victims, and the criminal practices continue, spread, and go unreported.

It should not be concluded, however, that correcting the deficiencies of crime statistics is merely a matter of making better counts. Sociologists in recent years have devised methods of data collection which make it unnecessary to rely upon arrest statistics and other compilations in order to study delinquency and crime. Studies using techniques such as participant observation, interviews, questionnaires, surveys of unreported crimes and victimization, and plain logical argument have given a broader perspective on "the crime problem." But the very conception of some behaviors as "criminal" or "delinquent" depends upon conditions outside the behavior itself, making it all but impossible to count accurately, by any technique, the incidence of "crime" or "delinquency." Study of the variables related to the settings and circumstances in which statistics are collected has recently been given high priority in criminological circles.[39] Once sociologists

---

[39] Stanton Wheeler and Leonard S. Cottrell, Jr., *Juvenile Delinquency: Its Prevention and Control* (New York: Russell Sage Foundation, 1966), pp. 22-27; Howard S. Becker, *Outsiders: Studies in the Sociology of Deviance* (New York: Free Press, 1963), pp. 8-14; and John I. Kitsuse, "Societal Reaction to Deviant Behavior: Problems of Theory and Method," *Social Problems*, 9:247-256, Winter, 1962.

simply analyzed the available statistical "facts" about crime, among other things. Now they are beginning to show that the datum for study is the process by which the statistical information is manufactured, assembled, and published.[40] Some observers of this change have called it a shift toward a "sociology of law." Quinney has, more accurately, called it a shift to the study of "the politics of crime."[41] ●

AKMAN, DOGAN D., & ANDRE NORMANDEAU. "Towards the Measurement of Criminality in Canada." *Acta Criminologica,* 1:135-254, January, 1968.

Suggested readings

CRESSEY, DONALD R. "The State of Criminal Statistics." *National Probation and Parole Association Journal,* 3:230-241, July, 1957.

DOLESCHAL, EUGENE. *Criminal Statistics.* Washington: U.S. Government Printing Office, 1972.

EATON, JOSEPH W., & KENNETH POLK. *Measuring Delinquency.* Pittsburgh: University of Pittsburgh Press, 1961.

EDELHERTZ, HERBERT. *The Nature, Impact and Prosecution of White-Collar Crime.* Washington: U.S. Government Printing Office, 1970.

ERICKSON, MAYNARD L., & LAMAR T. EMPEY. "Court Records, Undetected Delinquency and Decision-making." *Journal of Criminal Law, Criminology, and Police Science,* 54:456-469, December, 1963.

GEHLKE, C. E. "Development of Criminal Statistics in the Past Century." *Proceedings of the American Prison Association,* 1931, pp. 176-190.

GEIS, GILBERT, ed. *White-Collar Criminal.* New York: Atherton Press, 1968.

HARTUNG, FRANK E. "White Collar Crime: Its Significance for Theory and Practice." *Federal Probation,* 17:31-36, June, 1953.

KAMISAR, YALE. "How to Use, Abuse—and Fight Back with—Crime Statistics." *Oklahoma Law Review,* 25:239-258, May, 1972.

LEJINS, PETER P. "Uniform Crime Reports." *Michigan Law Review,* 64:1011-1030, December, 1966.

McCLINTOCK, F. H., & N. HOWARD AVISON. *Crime in England and Wales.* London: Heinemann, 1968.

PRICE, J. E. "A Test of the Accuracy of the Crime Statistics." *Social Problems,* 14:214-222, Winter, 1966.

QUINNEY, EARL R. "The Study of White Collar Crime: Toward a Reorientation in Theory and Research." *Journal of Criminal Law, Criminology, and Police Science,* 55:208-214, June, 1964.

---

[40] Cicourel, *Social Organization of Juvenile Justice;* John I. Kitsuse and Aaron V. Cicourel, "A Note on the Uses of Official Statistics," *Social Problems,* 11:131-139, Fall, 1963.

[41] Richard Quinney, "Crime in Political Perspective," *American Behavioral Scientist,* 8:19-22, December, 1964.

ROBINSON, LOUIS N. "History of Criminal Statistics (1908-1933)." *Journal of Criminal Law and Criminology,* 24:125-139, May-June, 1933.

SCHMID, CALVIN F., & STANTON E. SCHMID. *Crime in the State of Washington.* Olympia, Wash.: Law and Justice Planning Office, 1972.

SELLIN, THORSTEN, & MARVIN E. WOLFGANG. *The Measurement of Delinquency.* New York: John Wiley, 1964.

SHANNON, LYLE W. "Types and Patterns of Delinquency Referral in a Middle-Sized City." *British Journal of Criminology,* 14:24-36, July, 1963.

SMIGEL, ERWIN O., & H. LAURENCE ROSS, eds. *Crimes Against Bureaucracy.* New York: Van Nostrand, 1970.

SUTHERLAND, EDWIN H. *White Collar Crime.* New York: Dryden Press, 1949.

WALKER, NIGEL. *Crimes, Courts and Figures: An Introduction to Criminal Statistics.* London: Penguin, 1971.

WHEELER, STANTON. "Criminal Statistics: A Reformulation of the Problem." *Journal of Criminal Law, Criminology, and Police Science,* 58:317-324, September, 1967.

WOLFGANG, MARVIN E. "Uniform Crime Reports: A Critical Appraisal." *University of Pennsylvania Law Review,* 111:708-738, April, 1963.

Perspectives and methods   3

Systematic study of criminal behavior is of rather recent origin. During the medieval and early modern periods many unorganized and ephemeral explanations of crimes were stated and accepted. Probably the principal explanation during this time was that crime was due to innate depravity and the instigation of the devil. The English indictment used as late as the nineteenth century not only accused the defendant of violating the law, but also of "being prompted and instigated by the devil and not having the fear of God before his eyes." And the Supreme Court of North Carolina, as late as 1862, declared: "To know the right and still the wrong pursue proceeds from a perverse will brought about by the seductions of the evil one."[1]

During the period when this explanation was used most frequently the conception of natural causation was not developed

---

[1] Quoted in Harold Shepherd, "The Psychopathic Laboratory," *Journal of Criminal Law and Criminology,* 13:486, January-February, 1923.

even with reference to such things as disease, and, of course, was not developed with reference to criminality. Little interest was manifested in motives, intentions, circumstances, or other immediate conditions of the offender and his offense. Punishments were arbitrary and unequal. The general principle in crime control was that of heaping tortures on the damned in accordance with divine example. •

Schools of criminology have developed during the last two centuries. A "school of criminology" is a system of thought, together with the supporters of that system of thought. The system of thought consists of a theory of crime causation integrated with policies of control implied in the theory. Obviously, many popular "explanations" of crime are not included in this definition. But every control policy and control technique is based, implicitly or explicitly, on a theory or set of assumptions about the cause or causes of crime. The relationship between control policies and etiological theories will be elaborated in part II (beginning on page 294, below).

Outline of schools of criminology

The principal schools of criminology are listed in table VIII. These schools can be distinguished from each other only in the writings of the more extreme adherents, who were customarily the early writers in each school. Each of the schools, with the possible exception of the last, has been discredited as a complete explanation of criminal behavior, and has then merged with the other explanations. Furthermore, the outline below cannot do justice to the many variations in each school of thought or to the interrelations among the schools. The dates of origin are approximations. Each of these schools will be de-

TABLE VIII

Schools of criminology

School	Date of origin	Content of explanation	Methods
Classical-neoclassical	1765	Hedonism	Armchair
Cartographic	1830	Ecology, culture, composition of population	Maps, statistics
Socialist	1850	Economic determinism	Statistics
Typological 1. Lombrosian	1875	Morphological type, born criminal	Clinical, statistics
2. Mental testers	1905	"Feeblemindedness"	Clinical, tests, statistics
3. Psychiatric	1905	Psychopathy	Clinical, statistics
Sociological and social psychological	1915	Groups and social processes	Clinical, statistics, fieldwork

scribed briefly, and in later chapters the more pertinent research pertaining to each school will be discussed. ●

The classical school   The classical school of criminology and of criminal law developed in Italy and England during the last half of the eighteenth century and spread to other European countries and to America. It was based on hedonistic psychology. According to this psychology, man governs his behavior by considerations of pleasures and pains; the pleasures anticipated from a particular act may be balanced against the pains anticipated from the same act, or the algebraic sum of pleasures and pains from one act may be balanced against the algebraic sum of pleasures and pains from another act. The actor was assumed to have a free will and to make his choice with reference to the hedonistic calculation alone. This was regarded as the final and complete explanation of the causes of crime, and no need for further investigation of causation could be imagined.

Beccaria in 1764 made the principal application of this doctrine to penology.[2] His objective was to make punishment less arbitrary and severe than it had been. He contended that all persons who violated a specific law should receive identical punishments regardless of age, sanity, position, or circumstance. This was justified on the ground that the rights of individuals could be preserved only by treating all individuals alike, and also on the ground that the punishment must be definitely determined in advance in order that it might be taken into account in the calculation of pains and pleasures that would result from violation of the law. According to this school the penalty should be just severe enough so that the pains would exceed the pleasures derived from violation of the law.

This extreme idea of equality was soon modified at two points: children and "lunatics" were exempted from punishment on the ground that they were unable to calculate pleasures and pains intelligently, and the penalties were fixed within narrow limits rather than absolutely, so that a small amount of judicial discretion was possible. With these modifications, the classical doctrine became the backbone of the body of the criminal law and has persisted in popular thought and judicial decisions to the present day. The modified classical doctrine is the essence of the neoclassical school of criminology.

The psychology underlying the work and policies of the classical-neoclassical school, and of much contemporary criminal law, is now generally questioned. It is individualistic, intellectualistic,

---

[2] Cesare Beccaria, *An Essay on Crimes and Punishments* (London: Almon, 1767); see also Marcello T. Maestro, *Voltaire and Beccaria as Reformers of the Criminal Law* (New York: Columbia University Press, 1942). Bentham applied the hedonistic psychology to legislation: Jeremy Bentham, *An Introduction to the Principles of Morals and Legislation* (London: Pickering, 1823).

and voluntaristic. It assumes freedom of the will in a manner which gives little or no possibility of further investigation of the causes of crime or of efforts to prevent crime. All the schools which developed in the nineteenth and twentieth centuries accepted the hypothesis of natural causation, and for that reason they are sometimes called positivistic. ●

The cartographic or geographic school used methods similar to those used in more recent years by ecologists and epidemiologists. The leaders of this school were concerned primarily with the distribution of crimes in certain areas, both geographical and social. They were interested in crime as a necessary expression of social conditions. Quetelet and A. M. Guerry were the leaders of this approach in France, and they had a large number of followers in that country and in England and Germany. The school flourished from about 1830 to 1880. Not only did the adherents of this method analyze the distribution of general crime rates, but they made special studies of juvenile delinquency and of professional crime which are comparable with those of the present century.[3] The basic notion was, and is, that crime is caused by the conflicts of values arising when legal norms' fail to take into consideration the behavioral norms that are specific to the lower socioeconomic classes, various age groups, religious groups, and interest groups living in certain geographic areas. Early proponents of the school also saw crime rooted in "poverty, misery and depravity,"[4] but they tended to hold each individual criminal responsible for falling to his lowly state. Later proponents merged with the socialist school. ●

The cartographic school

The socialist school of criminology, based on writings of Marx and Engels, began about 1850 and emphasized economic determinism. The basic idea is that poverty results from private ownership of the means of production and from exploitation of the working classes; this poverty, in turn, causes people to turn to crime. The research approach is empirical. Many statistical studies—most of them done by non-Marxists—show that variations in crime rates are associated with variations in economic conditions. The earlier studies used statistical methods, measures of crime, and measures of economic conditions that were quite naive by present-day standards.

The socialist school

[3] Alfred Lindesmith and Yale Levin, "The Lombrosian Myth in Criminology," *American Journal of Sociology,* 42:653-671, March, 1937; Yale Levin and Alfred Lindesmith, "English Ecology and Criminology of the Past Century," *Journal of Criminal Law and Criminology,* 27:801-816, March-April, 1937.

[4] Henry Mayhew, *London Labour and the London Poor: Cyclopedia of the Conditions and Earnings of Those That Will Not Work* (London: Charles Griffin, 1861), 1:6.

The Soviet Union and other communist nations continue to base control policies and interpretations of crime statistics on the basic principles of this school. Fifty years of economic and political change has not eliminated crime in the Soviet Union, as it was expected to do. Some Soviet young people whose fathers and mothers were born after the 1917 revolution, and to whom words like *bourgeoisie* and *landlord* are abstract notions, commit crimes and delinquencies, just as do some young people in capitalist countries. Although the Soviet Union publishes no questional crime statistics as other nations do, it is experiencing a crime problem. This is suggested by the fact that in July, 1966, the Soviet government adopted special measures to "step up the fight against crime."[5] But persistence of crime and delinquency is not taken as evidence that the theory is defective. Instead, crime and delinquency are attributed to two sources: persistence of old traditions, ideologies, and prejudices which have carried over from capitalism and other socioeconomic structures; and imperfect implementation of the Marxian theory. "Besides the objective causes, there are subjective causes which help to perpetuate crimes, among them economic mismanagement at various levels, poor instruction in moral behavior by either the family or the school and poor organization of the leisure time of young people. It follows, then, that crime in the Soviet Union is not a form of social protest. It is the product of deficiencies of the past."[6] ●

Typological schools

Three schools of criminology which have been called "typological" or "bio-typological" have developed. They are similar in their general logic and methodology; all of them are based on a postulate that criminals differ from noncriminals in certain traits of personality, which promote unusual tendencies to commit crimes in situations in which others do not commit crimes; these tendencies to commit crimes may be inherited or may be the necessary expression of unique personal traits. The three typological schools differ from each other as to the specific traits which differentiate criminals from noncriminals.

The Lombrosians

Lombroso was the leader of a school which was known as the "Italian school." The first statement of his theory was in the form of a pamphlet, published in 1876; it grew to a three-volume

---

[5] Nikolai A. Shchyolokov, "Crime and Social Health," *Soviet Life*, September, 1968, pp. 16-17. See also P. Hollander, "A Converging Social Problem: Juvenile Delinquency in the Soviet Union and the United States," *British Journal of Criminology*, 9:148-166, 1969; Walter D. Connor, "Deviant Behavior in Capitalist Society—the Soviet Image," *Journal of Criminal Law, Criminology, and Police Science*, 61:554-564, December, 1970.

[6] Ibid., p. 17.

book in subsequent editions.[7] In its earlier and more clear-cut form this theory consisted of the following propositions: (*a*) Criminals are, by birth, a distinct type. (*b*) This type can be recognized by stigmata or anomalies, such as asymmetrical cranium, long lower jaw, flattened nose, scanty beard, and low sensitivity to pain.[8] The criminal type is clearly represented in a person with more than five such stigmata, incompletely represented by three to five, and not necessarily indicated by less than three. (*c*) These physical anomalies do not in themselves cause crime; rather they identify the personality which is predisposed to criminal behavior, and this personality is either a reversion to the savage type—an atavism—or else a product of degeneration. (*d*) Because of their personal natures, such persons cannot refrain from crime unless the circumstances of life are unusually favorable. (*e*) Some of Lombroso's followers concluded that the several classes of criminals, such as thieves, murderers, and sex offenders, are differentiated from each other by physical stigmata.

The Lombrosian school was directed at first against the classical school, and it concentrated on the question of determinism versus free will. Later it was directed against Tarde's theory of imitation[9] and concentrated on the question of biological versus social determinism. As a result of these controversies, Lombroso gradually modified his conclusions, especially as to the "born criminal," and reduced the proportion of criminals who were "born criminals" from approximately 100 percent to about 40 percent. Garofalo, Ferri, and other followers of Lombroso made other modifications, so that the school lost its clear-cut characteristics.

The conception that criminals constitute a distinct physical type was disproved to the satisfaction of most scholars when Goring, an English physician, made a comparison of several thousand criminals and several thousand noncriminals and found no significant difference between them.[10] Lombroso and his followers had never made a careful comparison of criminals and noncriminals and had little knowledge of the "savage" whom the criminals were supposed to resemble. The morphological emphasis has continued in modified form in South America. It was in vogue in the United States until about 1915, and it continues, currently, in attempts to locate the cause of some criminality in chromosome imbalances.[11]

---

[7] Cesare Lombroso, *L'uomo delinquente* (Torino, Italy: Bocca, 1896-97). See Marvin E. Wolfgang, "Pioneers in Criminology: Cesare Lombroso (1835-1909)," *Journal of Criminal Law, Criminology, and Police Science*, 52:361-391, November-December, 1961.

[8] The belief that criminals have unique physical characteristics appeared long before Lombroso. See C. Bernaldo de Quiros, *Modern Theories of Criminality*, trans. Alfonso de Salvio (Boston: Little, Brown, 1911), pp. 4-5.

[9] Gabriel Tarde, *Penal Philosophy* (Boston: Little, Brown, 1912).

[10] Charles Goring, *The English Convict* (London: His Majesty's Stationery Office, 1913). See pp. 99-100.

The mental testers

When the Lombrosian school fell into disrepute, its logic and methodology were retained, with "feeblemindedness" substituted for physical type as the characteristic which differentiated criminals from noncriminals. This school was represented most clearly by Goddard's theory that "feeblemindedness," inherited as a Mendelian unit, causes crime for the reason that the mentally retarded person is unable to appreciate the consequences of his behavior or appreciate the meaning of law.[12] Goddard's tests showed that almost all criminals were "feebleminded," and he asserted, also, that almost all "feebleminded" persons were criminals. As mental tests became standardized and were applied to a larger number of criminal and noncriminal persons, the importance attributed to mental retardation in the causation of crime decreased greatly, and this school of thought tended to disappear.

The psychiatric school

The psychiatric school is a continuation of the Lombrosian school without the latter's emphasis on morphological traits. In the earlier years it emphasized, as did Lombroso, psychoses, epilepsy, and "moral insanity," but it has attributed increasing importance to emotional disturbances and other minor psychopathies as the school of mental testers fell into disrepute. Also, in the later history of this school, it has held that these emotional disturbances are acquired in social interaction rather than by biological inheritance. Many variations are found within this school, but the major influence has been the Freudian theory, especially in its earlier form, which placed great emphasis on frustration and "the unconscious." The central thesis of the psychiatric school at present is that a certain organization of the personality, developed entirely apart from criminal culture, will result in criminal behavior regardless of social situations. For example, Aichhorn claimed that a delinquent personality is formed in the first few years of a child's life. If the child is not socialized in a manner such that he learns to control his instincts for pleasure, he will come into conflict with society. His ego will be faulty because he was unable to adjust to the problem of leaving the pleasures of childhood for the reality of adult life.[13] Criminal patterns are said to be omnipresent for selection by a person with this organization of the personality, and if they were not present would be invented. The most extreme writers

---

[11] M. F. Ashley Montagu, "Chromosomes and Crime," *Psychology Today*, 2:42-49, October, 1968; and Donald J. West, ed., *Criminological Implications of Chromosome Abnormalities* (Cambridge: Institute of Criminology, 1969).

[13] August Aichhorn, *Wayward Youth* (New York: Viking Press, 1936). See the more general discussion in David Feldman, "Psychoanalysis and Crime," chap. in Bernard Rosenberg, Israel Gerver, and F. William Howton, eds., *Mass Society in Crisis* (New York: Macmillan, 1964), pp. 50-58.

hold that all or almost all criminals develop by processes similar to this; the less extreme writers attempt to isolate a smaller fraction of the criminals for explanation in this manner. The less extreme writers tend to merge with the sociologists. ●

Of the schools of criminology, this one is the most varied and diverse. Analysis of the causes of crime in a sociological manner actually began with the cartographic and socialist schools. Also, many nineteenth-century European scholars belonging to neither of these schools interpreted crime as a function of social environment. Among these were Von Liszt (Germany), Prins (Belgium), Van Hamel (Holland), and Fointsky (Russia). Tarde, a French social psychologist and a contemporary of Lombroso, refuted the prevailing biological notions and developed a theory emphasizing the importance of "imitation" in crime causation. His basic notion was that one behaves according to the customs of his society; if a man steals or murders, he is merely imitating someone else.

The sociological and social psychological school

The greatest development of the sociological school has taken place in the United States. Late in the nineteenth century, criminology was accepted as a field of study by the growing university departments of sociology, and in the United States since that time systematic studies of crime and criminals have been made primarily by sociologists. A survey made in 1901 indicated that criminology and penology were among the first courses offered under the general title "sociology" in United States colleges and universities,[14] and the *American Journal of Sociology* included articles and book reviews on criminology when it was first published in 1895. However, American sociologists, like most European scholars, were deeply impressed by many of the Lombrosian arguments,[15] and it was not until about 1915, after the publication of Goring's work, that a strong environmentalist position was cultivated. It was probably this trend which prompted a sociologist to write in 1914:

> The longer the study of crime has continued in this country, the greater has grown the number of causes of crime which may be described as social. This is the aspect in the development of American criminology which has given to that study in this country the title of "The American School."[16]

---

[14] Frank L. Tolman, "The Study of Sociology in Institutions of Learning in the United States," *American Journal of Sociology*, 7:797-838, May, 1902; 8:85-121, July, 1902; 8:251-272, September, 1902; 8:531-558, January, 1903.

[15] See, for example, Carroll D. Wright, *Outline of Practical Sociology* (New York: Longmans Green, 1899); Maurice F. Parmelee, *The Principles of Anthropology and Sociology in Their Relations to Criminal Procedure* (New York: Macmillan, 1908); Phillip Parsons, *Responsibility for Crime* (New York: Columbia University Press, 1909).

[16] John L. Gillin, "Social Factors Affecting the Volume of Crime," in *Physical Basis of Crime: A Symposium* (Easton, Pa.: American Academy of Medicine, 1914), pp. 53-67.

The central thesis of the sociological school is that criminal behavior results from the same processes as other social behavior. Analyses of these processes as they pertain to criminality have taken two principal forms. First, sociologists have attempted to relate variations in crime rates to variations in social organization, including the variations in larger institutional systems. The following are some of the social conditions which have been discussed in relation to variations in the crime rates of societies and subsocieties: the processes of mobility, culture conflict, normative conflict, competition, and stratification; political, religious, and economic ideologies; population density and composition; and the distribution of wealth, income, and employment. This kind of analysis fell into disfavor in the years between about 1940 and 1955, principally because criminologists have become extremely cautious about basing generalizations on the available crime statistics. Because variations in crime rates may represent mere differences in statistical procedures, rather than real variations in the frequency of crime, sociological analysis of the variations is extremely hazardous. Sociologists are now concentrating much time and attention on the processes by which various agencies manufacture sets of crime and delinquency statistics. Nevertheless, the trend in criminology since about 1955 has been toward analysis of the relationships between aspects of the social structure and variations in crime rates, especially variations by social class.

Second, sociologists have attempted to define the processes by which a person becomes a criminal. These analyses are related to general theories of social learning and have utilized such concepts as imitation, attitude-value, compensation, frustration-aggression, and differential association. The principal orientation at present is generally taken from the social psychological theories of John Dewey, George Mead, Charles Cooley, and W. I. Thomas, and the development of criminal behavior is considered as involving the same learning processes as does the development of the behavior of a banker, waitress, or doctor. The content of learning, not the process itself, is considered the significant element which determines whether one becomes a criminal or a noncriminal. ●

Epidemiology and individual conduct

The basic controversy in criminology in the United States at present is that between the psychiatric school and the sociological school. Members of the sociological school recognize that psychogenic traits must be taken into account in the explanation of criminal behavior, and members of the psychiatric school have recognized the importance of social and cultural conditions. But there is disagreement over the extent to which "personality" and "culture" should be emphasized in criminological theories, largely because there is no consensus as to the specific manner in which personality and culture interact to produce specific forms of noncriminal behavior. Some writers in both schools have made classifications of criminals, with the conception that one class is due to personality and another to culture.[17] Lindesmith and Dunham suggested that criminals constitute a continuum, with personality and culture as two variables; personality as a cause is zero at one extreme and 100 percent at the other, with culture ranging between the same extremes in reverse order. Thus, at one extreme would be the individualized type, represented by the psychotic, whose "crime" is an expression of individual values and not supported by a culture; at the other extreme is the "social criminal," represented by the professional thief, whose objectives are approved by the general society, and whose methods are approved only within his smaller subculture.[18]

This conception of the relation between personality and culture seems to form a basis for merging the psychiatric and sociological approaches to an explanation of criminal behavior, but it is unduly simplified. The problem of how, or whether, basic personality traits and culture combine in the less extreme cases remains as a point of controversy. Perhaps a new school of criminology will soon develop. Ideally, the theory forming the basis of this school will have two distinct but consistent aspects. First, there will be a statement that explains the statistical distribution of criminal behavior in time and space (epidemiology), from which predictive statements about unknown statistical distributions can be derived. Second, there will be a statement that identifies, at least by implication, the process by which persons come to exhibit criminal behavior, from which can be derived predictive statements about the behavior of individuals. Concentration on either the epidemiological segment or the individual conduct segment of a theoretical problem is sometimes necessary, but it is erroneous and inefficient to ignore the second segment or to turn it over to another academic discipline. This means that as time goes on, the psychiatric school, which now concentrates on individual criminality, will attempt to explain crime rates with a consistent set of theory, and that those sociologists who concentrate only on explaining the distribution of crime will develop a consistent set of theory of explanation of individual criminal conduct. ●

In contrast with the preceding schools of criminology, which attempt to formulate theoretical explanations of criminal behavior, many scholars have insisted that crime is a product of a

The multiple-factor approach

---

[17] See Guy Houchon, "Contribution à la Methode Differentielle en Criminologie," *Revue Internationale de Criminologie et de Police Technique,* 18:19-32, March, 1964.

[18] A. R. Lindesmith and H. W. Dunham, "Some Principles of Criminal Typology," *Social Forces,* 19:307-314, March, 1941. See also Richard O. Nahrendorf, "Typologies of Crime and Delinquency: Classification or Methodology?" *Sociologia Internationalis,* 5 (1967): 15-33.

large number and great variety of factors, and that these factors cannot now, and perhaps cannot ever, be organized into general propositions which have no exceptions; that is, they insist that no scientific theory of criminal behavior is possible. The multiple-factor approach, which is not a theory, is used primarily in discussions of individual cases of crime, but one form of this approach is also used in analyses of variations in crime rates.

Persons who study individual cases by means of this approach are convinced that one crime is caused by one combination of circumstances or "factors," while another crime is caused by another combination of circumstances or "factors." This eclecticism is often considered more rigorously "empirical" than explanations stated in terms of an integrated theory. William Healy's emphasis upon "multiple causation" in the cases of individual delinquents, at a time when many persons were seeking arguments for discounting the biological and physical explanations of crime, played an important role in the rise of this assumption.[19] Healy was determined that no theoretical orientation or preconception would influence his findings and that he would simply observe any "causal factor" present. The inevitable consequence of such crass empiricism was the discovery, in a now-famous study, of no less than 170 distinct conditions, every one of which was considered as conducive to delinquency.[20] The following is an example of multiple-factor thinking about individual cases:

> Elaborate investigations of delinquents give us conclusive evidence that there is no single predisposing factor leading inevitably to delinquent behavior. On the other hand, the delinquent child is generally a child handicapped not by one or two, but usually by seven or eight counts. We are safe in concluding that almost any child can overcome one or two handicaps, such as the death of one parent or poverty and poor health. However, if the child has a drunken unemployed father and an immoral mother, is mentally deficient, is taken out of school at an early age and put to work in a factory, and lives in a crowded home in a bad neighborhood, nearly every factor in his environment may seem to militate against him.[21]

Although this statement seems to be based on an assumption that each "factor" is of equal importance, adherents of the multiple-factor notion ordinarily argue that either the presence of one or two "important" factors or seven or eight "minor" factors will cause delinquency.

When variations in crime rates are the object of consideration, conditions found to be statistically associated with high crime

[19] William Healy, The Individual Delinquent (Boston: Little, Brown, 1915).

[20] Cyril Burt, The Young Delinquent, 4th ed. (London: University of London Press, 1944), p. 600.

[21] Mabel A. Elliott and Francis E. Merrill, Social Disorganization (New York: Harper, 1941), p. 111. A similar statement appears in Martin H. Neumeyer, Juvenile Delinquency and Modern Society, 2d ed. (New York: Van Nostrand, 1955), pp. 80-81. The quoted statement is modified in recent editions of Social Disorganization.

rates are taken as the units of study. Thus, in the United States, males have a higher crime rate than females, Negroes than whites, young adults than middle-aged, and city residents than rural residents. The advocates of the multiple-factor approach to the study of crime rates make little or no attempt to discover the crime-producing processes that are common to males, Negroes, young adults, and city residents. However, they do not impute causal power to the "factors" either; this is in contrast to the persons who use the multiple-factor approach in studying individual cases. Ogburn used this procedure in comparison of crime rates of American cities,[22] and Reckless advocated its use under the name "actuarial method":

> The actuarial approach assumes that individuals have a greater or lesser liability to be caught and reported as violators [of the criminal law] by virtue of the position they occupy in society as determined by their age, sex, race, nativity, occupational level, and type of residence. The behavior which is studied is only that which is reported in contrast to that which is not recorded. The liability is strictly that of becoming the sort of violator who is reported.[23]

The adherents of the multiple-factor "theory" sometimes take pride in their position, pointing to the narrow, particularistic explanations of other schools and to their own broadmindedness in including all types of factors.[24] However, the position seems to be based upon a confusion of single-factor explanations and single theories of criminality. Sometimes the adherents of the multiple-factor notion agree on the desirability of a generalized and integrated theory and on the possibility of developing such a theory in the long run, but they point to the breakdown of all such explanations and insist that the most economical procedure for the present generation is to accumulate factual knowledge rather than add to the futile attempts at new generalizations. Often the contribution of multiple-factor studies to criminal-law administration, rather than to the development of a body of scientific principles, is emphasized.

Albert Cohen has made one of the best critiques of the multiple-factor approach in criminology, and some of the comments above are from his work.[25] There are three major points in the critique, which is directed at the approach as it is used in the study of individual cases. He points out, first, that there has been a

---

22 William F. Ogburn, "Factors in the Variation of Crimes Among Cities," *Journal of the American Statistical Association*, 30:12-34, March, 1935.

23 Walter C. Reckless, *The Etiology of Delinquent and Criminal Behavior* (New York: Social Science Research Council, 1943), p. 74. See also Gunnar Dahlberg, "Risken att Dommas for Svaare Brott" [The risk of being sentenced for serious crime], *Nordisk Tidskrift for Kriminalvidenskap*, 31 (1943): 145-201.

24 See Sheldon Glueck, "Theory and Fact in Criminology," *British Journal of Delinquency*, 7:92-109, October, 1956.

25 Albert K. Cohen, "Juvenile Delinquency and the Social Structure" (Ph.D. dissertation, Harvard University, 1951), pp. 5-13. See also his *Delinquent Boys: The Culture of the Gang* (Glencoe, Ill.: Free Press, 1955).

confusion of explanations by means of a *single factor* and explanation by a *single theory* or system of theory applicable to all cases. A single theory does not explain crime in terms of a single factor, and it is often concerned with a number of *variables*. A variable is a characteristic or aspect—such as "velocity" or "income"—with respect to which something may vary. We make statements of fact in terms of the *values* of these variables, e.g., "The crime rate is high among persons with incomes of less than $2,000 per year." The pertinent variable here is "income," and its value is "$2,000." But neither a statement of one fact ("single factor") nor a series of such statements ("multiple factors") about crime is a theoretical explanation of crime. A theoretical explanation, a single *theory*, organizes and relates the variables; it is an abstract statement of how the known variations in the values of one variable are related to known variations in the values of other variables. A test of the theory is how well it accounts for all of the variations in the values of the variables.

Second, "factors" are not only confused with "causes," but each factor also is assumed to contain *within itself* a capacity to produce crime, a fixed amount of crime-producing power. Thus, one factor is not always considered powerful enough to produce crime in individual cases—several factors must conspire to do so. As Cyril Burt said, "It takes many coats of pitch to paint a thing thoroughly black." Sometimes the basis for imputing causal power to a factor in an individual case is statistical association between high crime rates and that factor. Thus, if a study of various areas of a city has revealed that high crime rates and "poor housing" are usually found together, an investigator studying a juvenile delinquent who lives in a poor house may assign causal power to the condition of the house. Or if the delinquency rate among "only children" is high, causal power may be assigned to the fact that a particular child is an "only child." Statisticians have pointed out that this practice is fallacious, and it is not an intrinsic part of the "actuarial approach."[26] Sometimes, also, the basis for imputing causal power to a factor cannot be determined at all, for it is based upon rather subjective, intuitive judgments of the investigators. Furthermore, each factor is assumed to be independent of all other factors and to operate independently of the actor's definition of the situation. However, the factor "only child," for example, has been shown to have no intrinsic qualities which produce delinquency or nondelinquency; instead, the meaning of being an only child varies with differences in local customs,

---

[26] William S. Robinson, "Ecological Correlations and the Behavior of Individuals," *American Sociological Review*, 15:351-357, June, 1950; Leo A. Goodman, "Some Alternatives to Ecological Correlation," *American Journal of Sociology*, 64:610-625, May, 1959.

national or ethnic mores, and various other social conditions.[27]

Third, Cohen points out, the "evil-causes-evil fallacy" usually characterizes multiple-factor studies, although it is neither a necessary part of the approach nor peculiar to it. This fallacy is that "evil" results (crime) must have "evil" precedents (broken home, psychopathic personality, etc.). Thus, when we "explain" crime or almost any other "social problem," we tend merely to catalog a series of sordid and ugly circumstances which any "decent citizen" would deplore, and attribute causal power to those circumstances. In criminology, this fallacious procedure might stem from a desire to eradicate crime without changing other existing conditions which we cherish and esteem; that is, criminologists tend to identify with the existing social order and seek "causes" of crime in "factors" which might be eliminated without changing social conditions which they hold dear, or which may be safely deplored without hurting anyone's feelings. •

Methods of studying crime

The explanations of crime have been derived from two general types of methodology. The first is the commonsense methodology by which people become acquainted with a community, a business, politics, or religion. This methodology is used by the historian and by all social scientists. It consists of the collection and arrangement of all data that are believed to be significant. It is not the methodology of science outlined in the textbooks on logic. It is impressionistic and deals with general tendencies rather than with specific interpretations. Because of this it is possible to take into account a great variety of conditions which are eliminated in the more specific studies. One of the most important of these omissions in criminology is the immense amount of fraud in modern social life which cannot be presented statistically and which seldom results in arrest or imprisonment, but which, nevertheless, is either vaguely or clearly in violation of law and is similar to the other crimes in its social effects and in the attitudes with which it is perpetrated.

The second general methodology is the systematic study of persons who are arrested or convicted of crimes or of the statistics of such arrests and convictions. This methodology is more precise and "scientific" than the first; it deals with specific variables and, usually, specific types of criminal behavior.[28] The more popular techniques or "methods" included within the scope of this methodology are discussed below. In later chapters, many examples of research studies utilizing the various methods will be given.

---

[27] William W. Wattenberg, "Delinquency and Only Children: A Study of a 'Category,' " *Journal of Abnormal and Social Psychology*, 44:356-366, July, 1949.

[28] Guy Houchon, "Modèles de Recherche et Equipment en Criminologie," *Annales de la Faculté de Droit de Liège*, 1965, pp. 241-304.

Statistics
of crimes

One common criminological method is the determination of the correlation between arrests or convictions and certain specific physical or social variables. Bonger used this method and presented a mass of materials purporting to show a close correlation between crime rates and economic conditions.[29] Others have used the same method in an effort to determine the statistical significance of seasons, of unemployment, of congestion of population. Thus, the correlations may be between crime rates and certain conditions over a period of time, or they may be between crime rates and certain conditions in space. One of the difficulties of this method has been the lack of reliable crime statistics, and lack of concern for the processes by which statistics are produced. Another difficulty is that it at most merely identifies general relationships. It may determine, for instance, that more crimes are committed against the person in hot weather than in cold weather, but it does not tell whether this is due to the direct effect of temperature upon temper, or to a greater frequency of contacts between people in hot weather than in cold weather, or to a greater frequency of intoxication in hot weather, or to something else. Consequently this method is of value in collecting facts but does not necessarily lead to theoretical statements about the facts.

Statistics of
traits and
conditions
of criminals

A second statistical method is comparison of the frequency with which one or more traits or conditions appears among criminals with the frequency with which it occurs among noncriminals. Thus, personality tests have been used to determine the relative frequency of emotional disturbances among criminals and noncriminals. An enumeration is also made of the criminals who come from homes broken by death, divorce, and desertion of one or both parents in comparison with the number of law-abiding persons who come from such homes. Similarly, race, sex, age, nativity, alcoholism of self or of parents, education, and other conditions are studied. In the course of such studies many traits and conditions are compared, but in general each one is abstracted from the others. Often, as indicated above, each trait showing a relatively high incidence among criminals is considered one of many "factors" in crime. No pretense is made of studying any criminal as a unit, and no effort is made to determine the cause of the criminality of a particular person by this method.

Valuable information, preliminary to the formulation of a theory, may be secured in this way; the ideal study of this kind would reveal that certain traits or conditions were present among all criminals, or all criminals of a certain type, and that these traits or conditions were absent among all noncriminals. But there are several difficulties and inadequacies in this method:

---

[29] W. A. Bonger, *Criminality and Economic Conditions* (Boston: Little, Brown, 1916), pp. 1-246.

(a) There is practically no information accessible in regard to criminals, as such. The only information generally available concerns prisoners. Prisoners are a selected group of criminals, and an enumeration of traits or conditions of prisoners would, presumably, yield results different from an enumeration of the same traits or conditions of all criminals. This is a difficulty that confronts any method of studying criminals, but it is more distinctly a limitation of this method than of some of the others because this method depends on mass information. Apparently, the best that can be done at present is to recognize the apparent biases in the statistics and make allowances for them, or attempt to secure other statistics regarding the classes of criminals not adequately represented in prisons.

(b) The data regarding prisoners are doubtful in many respects. Such evident conditions as race, sex, and age can be determined with a fair degree of accuracy, but it is impossible to secure other data, such as income, home conditions, or employment history, without intensive investigations in the communities in which the prisoners lived prior to confinement. Beyond these rather formal items, reliable information can be secured from prisoners only with great difficulty. Even when prisoners are cooperative, unreliability enters because of errors of memory, perception, and interpretation.

(c) When this method is used, it is necessary to make comparisons with the general population and also with specialized occupational, racial, sex, age, and other groups from which criminals come. It is often necessary to assume, therefore, that the sample of the general population contains only noncriminals, that it does not contain persons who have violated the criminal law without detection or apprehension. This assumption is unwarranted. Standards for the entire population and especially for particular groups are also lacking. It has been customary for those who use this method to enumerate their cases and then, without knowing how prevalent the same traits are in the general population, assert that the enumerated traits are important "causes of" or "factors in" crime. For instance, it is frequently reported that a specified part of the criminal population is found, on examination, to be psychopathic, and that this trait is therefore extremely important in the causation of crime. But no one knows how large a percentage of the general population would also be found, by the same standards, to be psychopathic.[30] It was once frequently asserted that "feeblemindedness" was much more common among criminals than among noncriminals, but the general administration of army tests during World War I revealed that the proportion of the population estimated to be "feebleminded" had been far too small.

---

[30] See Michael Hakeem, "A Critique of the Psychiatric Approach to Crime and Correction," *Law and Contemporary Problems*, 23:650-682, Autumn, 1958.

(d) It is possible to secure measurements of only a few traits or conditions, and therefore this method cannot by itself locate the cause or causes of crime. It does not explain the mechanisms by which criminality is produced. We may find, for instance, that the male is ten times as criminalistic, judged by commitments to prison, as the female. But males are also ten times as likely to be killed by lightning. Is this a sex difference, or a result of differences in occupations, or the general mode of life, or something else? If we find that there is a close correlation between the criminality of juveniles and the alcoholism of their parents, we want to know whether this connection is due to a constitutional defect that is responsible both for the alcoholism of the parent and the delinquency of the child, or whether the child is delinquent because the parent spends money for alcohol that ought to be used to obtain necessities for the child, or because the discipline of the home is irregular or brutal, or because the child becomes emotionally disturbed, or because alcoholism of parents creates a condition whereby the child comes into contact with an excess of delinquent behavior patterns. As Thomas stated about fifty years ago, "Taken in themselves, statistics are nothing more than symptoms of unknown causal processes."[31]

(e) Sometimes the traits and conditions which are compared are so loosely defined that their frequency distribution in the two populations can only be asserted, not demonstrated. The incidence of "constitutional inferiority," "bad home environment," and "psychological tensions," for example, cannot be determined with accuracy simply because the concepts are so vague that investigators cannot agree on their presence or absence in individual cases.

(f) The statistical enumeration of traits and conditions tells us that certain of these are important and perhaps measures the importance in mathematical terms. It may tell us how much more frequently delinquency occurs in children from homes broken by divorce, desertion, or death than in children from homes not so broken. But we need to know more than that: why some children from broken homes do not become delinquent. We need to know not only why mentally retarded persons become criminals more frequently than normal persons (if they do), but also why some mentally retarded persons do not become delinquent and why some normal persons do become delinquent. That is, we should have information that will enable us to state that a person with such and such a nature or such and such attitudes in such and such a situation will always become delinquent. Perhaps it will never be possible to construct precise laws of this kind, but it is certain that the statistics of traits of criminals will not be sufficient in themselves.[32] The differential

---

[31] W. I. Thomas, The Unadjusted Girl (Boston: Little, Brown, 1923), p. 244.
[32] See Marvin E. Wolfgang and Harvey A. Smith, "Mathematical Models in Criminology," International Social Science Journal, 18 (1966): 200-223.

association theory, presented in chapter 4, represents an attempt to organize, integrate, and give meaning to statistical information about crimes and criminals, among other things.

In the individual case study method, the criminal, rather than the trait or condition, is regarded as the unit. The traits and conditions of one criminal are all studied together. It is not necessary to abstain from statistics in this method, and it differs from the method just described largely in that the individual, rather than any abstracted trait or condition, is the unit of study. The same traits may be studied by each method. If the importance of the home environment to crime is determined by a comparison of the grades or indices of the homes of criminals and of noncriminals, it is not the individual case method. If the importance of the home environment is determined by a consideration of the home in relation to the rest of the life situation of a criminal, it is the individual case method. The differences in the methods are further emphasized by recalling that the purpose of the comparison of the home indices of criminals and noncriminals is to determine the relative frequency of home conditions of specified kinds among the two groups. The purpose of the individual case study is to determine how and why certain types of homes produce delinquency—how they produce delinquency, rather than how frequently delinquency is found in them.

The study of individual cases can be made on a multiple-factor level, or it can be used to discover meaningful hypotheses to be tested by other methods or by analyses of other cases. The first use of the method, the enumeration of multiple factors, has already been discussed. The assertion that a certain combination of factors caused the delinquency in an individual case often rests on an implicit, "hidden" theory which the person making the study has in mind. It is important, in scientific work, that these implicit theories be made explicit. In his pioneer study of delinquents, Healy listed factors located by means of reviewing the child's family and "developmental" histories, by examining his environment (including home and neighborhood), by taking physical and psychological measurements, and by making medical and psychiatric examinations.[33] The list of specific items under these heads covers nine pages in his book. But Healy emphasized the importance of studying psychological factors, e.g., mental dissatisfaction, irritative mental reactions to environmental conditions, obsessional imagery, adolescent mental instabilities and impulsions, emotional disturbances, worries and repressions, antisocial grudges, mental peculiarities or aberrations, and mental defects.[34] This would indicate that the "causal factors" considered as "significant" to the delinquency

Individual case study

---

[33] Healy, *The Individual Delinquent*, pp. 53-63.
[34] Ibid., pp. 28, 32.

of each case actually were those which supported a hidden, implicit psychiatric hypothesis about delinquency. In later books, Healy explicitly stated this hypothesis and reported on specific efforts to test it by the method of examining the traits of delinquents and nondelinquents.[35] An alternative interpretation is that the earlier case studies were conducted on an exploratory basis, and that the psychiatric theory was suggested by them. While this hypothesis is doubtful in this particular instance, exploratory examination of case histories, including life histories and autobiographies of criminals and delinquents, can provide significant hypotheses about the etiology of criminal behavior.

The individual case study method is subject to two general criticisms: (a) Explanations of the specific delinquencies are too much subject to the individual whim or prejudice of the investigator. Consequently, there is danger of making much of conditions which are really insignificant and neglecting conditions that are very significant. This means that one sees in the materials of an individual case those things which fit into his own pre-existing scheme for explaining delinquency, even if that scheme is not stated. The check on this explanation is the judgment of other investigators who examine the same case and carefully state their causal hypotheses. (b) Most of the persons making case studies are employed by agencies dealing with delinquents, and their studies must result in advice regarding procedure. Consequently, there is a probability that the studies will be directly oriented toward temporary modification of delinquency rather than toward understanding delinquency causation. The items which can be readily modified may be selected as causes, or considerations of practicability in dealing with the offender may determine both the kind of statistics produced and the explanation which is given. There is a tendency to be concerned with any physical or other defect that may need to be corrected, even if it is not considered relevant to the causation of the individual's criminality.

Limited case study   In an attempt to explain drug addiction, Lindesmith used a method which is aimed at the production of universal generalizations rather than a multiple-factor "theory." This system also has been used in a study of embezzlement.[36] The method involves case studies, directed by explicit hypotheses, of rigorously defined categories of behavior. The procedure has essentially the following steps: First, a rough definition of the behavior to be explained is formulated. Second, a hypothetical explanation of

---

[35] William Healy and Augusta F. Bronner, *New Light on Delinquency and Its Treatment* (New Haven: Yale University Press, 1936).

[36] Alfred R. Lindesmith, *Opiate Addiction* (Bloomington, Ind.: Principia Press, 1947), and *Addiction and Opiates* (Chicago: Aldine, 1968); Donald R. Cressey, *Other People's Money: A Study in the Social Psychology of Embezzlement* (Glencoe, Ill.: Free Press, 1953). See also Howard S. Becker, *Outsiders: Studies in the Sociology of Deviance* (New York: Free Press, 1963).

the behavior is formulated. Third, one case is studied in the light of the hypothesis with the object of determining whether the hypothesis fits the facts in that case. Fourth, if the hypothesis does not fit the facts, either the hypothesis is reformulated or the behavior to be explained is redefined, so that the case is excluded. This definition must be more precise than the first one, and it may not be formulated *solely* to exclude a negative case. The negative case is viewed as a sign that something is wrong with the hypothesis, and redefinition takes place so that the cases of behavior being explained will be homogeneous. Fifth, practical certainty may be attained after a small number of cases have been examined in this way, but the location by the investigator, or anyone else, of a negative case disproves the explanation and requires a reformulation. Sixth, this procedure of examining cases, redefining the behavior, and reformulating the hypothesis is continued until a universal relationship is established, each negative case calling for a redefinition or a reformulation. The negative case—that is, the one which does not fit the hypothesis —is the important point in the procedure, for it calls for redefinition or reformulation. Seventh, for purposes of proof, cases outside the area circumscribed by the definition are examined to make certain that the final hypothesis does not apply to them. This step is in keeping with the observation that scientific generalizations consist of descriptions of conditions which are always present when the phenomenon being explained is present but which are never present when the phenomenon is absent.

This method is not statistical in the ordinary sense, nor is it the case study method in the ordinary sense. It combines the individual case study method and the method of statistical examination of traits of criminals, for it examines individual cases of criminality in the light of a hypothesis and then, for purposes of proof, attempts to determine whether or not that hypothesis also pertains to cases of noncriminality. At the same time, however, it differs from either of these methods: it does not attempt to secure a general picture of the person, but only such facts as bear upon the hypothesis, and it attempts to go beyond statistical tendencies to a theoretical explanation. The method has been criticized on the ground that it merely produces precise definitions of various types of behavior, rather than causal explanations of that behavior.[37]

Another method of studying crime is by association with criminals "in the open." Those who have had intimate contacts with criminals "in the open" know that criminals are not "natural" in police stations, courts, and prisons, and that they must be studied in their everyday life outside of institutions if they are to be understood. By this is meant that the investigator must

Study of the criminal "in the open"

---

[37] Ralph H. Turner, "The Quest for Universals in Sociological Research," *American Sociological Review*, 18:604-611, December, 1953.

associate with them as one of them, seeing their lives and conditions as the criminals themselves see them. In this way, he can make observations on attitudes, traits, and processes which can hardly be made in any other way. Also, his observations are of unapprehended criminals, not the criminals selected by the processes of arrest and imprisonment.

There is no doubt of the desirability of securing information in this way, but it is clearly limited by considerations of practicability. Few individuals can acquire the technique to pass as criminals, or even to be trusted by criminals. One individual cannot build upon the work of another to a very great extent, for precise, controlled techniques of observation can scarcely be employed. Moreover, when confidence men study confidence men by this method, it is impossible to determine whether the published conclusions are social science or part of a confidence game. It is extremely difficult to secure information regarding the origin of most of the attitudes of the criminals, for few of them can recall the subtle details of their life histories. Moreover, it cannot be assumed that criminals know much about crime causation, even if they volunteer information regarding the processes by which they became criminals. Nevertheless, the more information we can secure in this way, the less likely we are to be led astray by the other methods.[38]

Experimental method It is possible to test hypotheses regarding the causes of delinquency by changing the behavior of individuals or of groups, under controlled conditions. This is somewhat like the experimental method in the physical and biological sciences, although the control is necessarily much less complete in social situations. The Chicago Area Projects were undertaken primarily to test the hypothesis that community disorganization causes high crime rates.[39] Hypotheses regarding the processes by which persons become criminals can also be tested by application to criminals of therapeutic methods based upon the hypotheses. The Cambridge-Somerville Youth Study was an experiment of this kind.[40] However, the results of such experiments must be interpreted with extreme caution: evidence that a person's behavior changes in the expected direction when therapy based upon a theory is applied to him cannot, by itself, be taken as evidence that the theory correctly describes the process by which the behavior was originally acquired. His change might have been produced by things rather extraneous to the therapy, or the therapy might have been based on several theories, rather than on a single theory. The careful observation and elimination of such extraneous things is the essence of a *controlled* experiment. ●

---

[38] Cf. Ned Polsky, *Hustlers, Beats, and Others* (Chicago: Aldine, 1967).
[39] See the discussion below, pp. 625-626.
[40] See the discussion below, pp. 630-631.

All the methods which have been described have a proper place in the program for developing an understanding of criminal behavior. Much futile argument has been devoted to controversies between methods and especially to the controversy between the statistical and the nonstatistical methods. The value of any method is determined by its relation to the problem which is stated, and the statement of a problem is justified by the position of that problem in the total body of knowledge. At a particular stage in the development of knowledge some problems are more important than others, and consequently some methods are more useful than others.

The "exploratory method" is needed continuously. This is a congeries of methods, including statistical descriptions and comparisons in the form of averages, percentages, and correlations, field observations, and armchair speculations. This exploratory method is justified in new areas of study because it may pave the way for later definitive studies, based on general theory. Both in the total field of criminal behavior and in smaller areas within this field, the exploratory method is the only method available for developing hypotheses and theories. Several generalizations have been made by different schools of thought regarding criminal behavior as a whole. None of these generalizations is completely satisfactory, and revision of them calls for new hypotheses to be tested. Similarly, if a particular area of criminal behavior, such as kleptomania or automobile theft, is selected for study, the researcher must become acquainted with the available statistical data and use other exploratory methods before he is prepared to formulate definite hypotheses regarding it.

The principal argument presented in this chapter is that the multiple-factor approach, defined as mere enumeration of a series of factors related in some manner or other to criminal behavior, is not adequate. The pride which some criminologists take in this multiple-factor approach is entirely misplaced. This "theory" should be recognized as an admission of defeat, for it means that criminological studies must always be "exploratory." The criminologist can carry his conclusions beyond multiple factors and reduce the series of factors to simplicity by the method of logical abstraction.

For purposes of understanding criminal behavior, definitive generalizations are needed regarding criminal behavior as a whole, with specifications of the general theory applied to particular criminal behaviors. The relation between the general theory and the particular criminal behaviors is analogous to the relation between a germ theory of disease and the particular germs which cause particular diseases.

Work along both of these lines is desirable. Continued efforts should be made to state valid generalizations regarding criminal behavior as a whole, and continued efforts should be made to explain particular criminal behaviors. Research work of the

Conclusion

former type should guide the efforts of those who are attempting to explain particular criminal behaviors, and conclusions from the studies of particular areas of criminal behaviors should lead to revisions of the generalizations regarding criminal behavior as a whole. Just as the germ theory of disease does not explain all diseases, so it is possible that no one theory of criminal behavior will explain all criminal behavior. In that case, it will be desirable to define the areas to which any theory applies, so that the several theories are coordinate and, when taken together, explain all criminal behavior.[41] ●

Suggested readings

BECKER, HOWARD S. *Outsiders: Studies in the Sociology of Deviance.* New York: Free Press, 1963.

BURGESS, E. W. "The Study of the Delinquent as a Person." *American Journal of Sociology,* 28:657-680, May, 1923.

CANTOR, NATHANIEL. "The Search for Causes of Crime." *Journal of Criminal Law and Criminology,* 22:854-863, March-April, 1932.

CICOUREL, AARON V. *Method and Measurement in Sociology.* New York: Free Press, 1965.

CLINARD, MARSHALL B. "Contributions of Sociology to Understanding Deviant Behaviour." *British Journal of Delinquency,* 13:110-129, October, 1962.

COHEN, ALBERT K. "Sociological Research in Juvenile Delinquency." *American Journal of Ortho-Psychiatry,* 27:781-788, October, 1957.

CRESSEY, DONALD R. *Other People's Money: A Study in the Social Psychology of Embezzlement.* Glencoe, Ill.: Free Press, 1953.

DOLESCHAL, EUGENE. *Crime and Delinquency Research in Selected European Countries.* Washington: U.S. Government Printing Office, 1971.

DOUGLAS, JACK D., ed. *Crime and Justice in American Society.* Indianapolis: Bobbs-Merrill, 1970.

FERDINAND, THEODORE N. *Typologies of Delinquency: A Critical Analysis.* New York: Random House, 1966.

GRUPP, STANLEY E. *The Positive School of Criminology: Three Lectures by Enrico Ferri.* Pittsburgh: University of Pittsburgh Press, 1968.

---

[41] Cf. Marshall B. Clinard and Andrew L. Wade, "Toward the Delineation of Vandalism as a Sub-Type in Juvenile Delinquency," *Journal of Criminal Law, Criminology, and Police Science,* 48:493-499, January-February, 1958; Don C. Gibbons and Donald L. Garrity, "Some Suggestions for the Development of Etiological and Treatment Theory in Criminology," *Social Forces,* 38:51-58, October, 1959; Marshall B. Clinard and Richard Quinney, *Criminal Behavior Systems: A Typology,* 2nd ed. (New York: Holt, Rinehart and Winston, 1973), pp. 1-18; Edwin D. Driver, "A Critique of Typologies in Criminology," *Sociological Quarterly,* Summer, 1968, pp. 356-373; and Nahrendorf, "Typologies of Crime and Delinquency."

HARTUNG, FRANK E. "A Critique of the Sociological Approach to Crime and Correction." *Law and Contemporary Problems,* 23:703-734, Autumn, 1958.

HIRSCHI, TRAVIS, & HANAN C. SELVIN. *Delinquency Research: An Appraisal of Analytic Methods.* New York: Free Press, 1967.

JEFFERY, CLARENCE RAY. "Pioneers in Criminology: The Historical Development of Criminology." *Journal of Criminal Law, Criminology, and Police Science,* 50:3-19, May-June, 1959.

LINDESMITH, ALFRED R. *Addiction and Opiates.* Chicago: Aldine, 1968.

MANNHEIM, HERMANN. *Comparative Criminology.* Boston: Houghton Mifflin, 1965.

MANNHEIM, HERMANN, ed. *Pioneers in Criminology.* Chicago: Quadrangle Books, 1960.

MARTIN, JOHN M., JOSEPH P. FITZPATRICK, & ROBERT E. GOULD. *The Analysis of Delinquent Behavior: A Structural Approach.* New York: Random House, 1970.

QUINNEY, RICHARD. *The Social Reality of Crime.* Boston: Little, Brown, 1970.

RADZINOWICZ, LEON. *Ideology and Crime.* London: Heinemann, 1966.

RECKLESS, WALTER C. "American Criminology." *Criminology: An Interdisciplinary Journal,* 8:4-20, May, 1970.

SLAWSKI, CARL J. "Crime Causation: Toward a Field Synthesis." *Criminology: An Interdisciplinary Journal,* 3:375-396, February, 1971.

WHEELER, STANTON. "The Social Sources of Criminology." *Sociological Inquiry,* 32:139-159, Spring, 1962.

WILKINS, LESLIE T. *Social Deviance: Social Policy, Action and Research.* Englewood Cliffs, N.J.: Prentice-Hall, 1965.

WILSON, THOMAS P. "Conceptions of Interaction and Forms of Sociological Explanation." *American Sociological Review,* 35: 697-710, August, 1970.

WOLFGANG, MARVIN E. "Criminology and the Criminologist." *Journal of Criminal Law, Criminology, and Police Science,* 54:155-162, June, 1963.

4 A sociological theory of criminal behavior

The preceding discussion has suggested that a scientific explanation consists of a description of the conditions which are always present when a phenomenon occurs and which are never present when the phenomenon does not occur. Although a multitude of conditions may be associated in greater or lesser degree with the phenomenon in question, this information is relatively useless for understanding or for control if the data are left as a hodge-podge of unorganized factors. Scientists strive to organize their knowledge in interrelated general propositions, to which no exceptions can be found. ●

The problem for criminolog-ical theory

If criminology is to be scientific, the heterogeneous collection of "multiple factors" known to be associated with crime and crim-inality should be organized and integrated by means of explana-tory theory which has the same characteristics as the scientific theory in other fields of study. That is, the conditions which are said to cause crime should always be present when crime is present, and they should always be absent when crime is absent. Such a theory or body of theory would stimulate, simplify, and give direction to criminological research, and it would provide a framework for understanding the significance of much of the knowledge acquired about crime and criminality in the past. Furthermore, it would be useful in control of crime, provided it could be "applied" in much the same way that the engineer "applies" the scientific theories of the physicist.

There are two complementary procedures which may be used to put order into criminological knowledge, to develop a causal theory of criminal behavior. The first is logical abstraction. Negroes, urban-dwellers, and young adults all have compara-tively high crime rates. What do they have in common that results in these high crime rates? Research studies have shown that criminal behavior is associated, in greater or lesser degree, with the social and personal pathologies, such as poverty, bad housing, slum-residence, lack of recreational facilities, inade-quate and demoralized families, mental retardation, emotional instability, and other traits and conditions. What do these con-ditions have in common which apparently produces excessive criminality? Research studies have also demonstrated that many persons with those pathological traits and conditions do not commit crimes and that persons in the upper socioeconomic class frequently violate the law, although they are not in poverty, do not lack recreational facilities, and are not mentally retarded or emotionally unstable. Obviously, it is not the conditions or traits themselves which cause crime, for the conditions are some-times present when criminality does not occur, and they also are sometimes absent when criminality does occur. A causal explan-ation of criminal behavior can be reached by abstracting, logi-cally, the mechanisms and processes which are common to the rich and the poor, the blacks and the whites, the urban- and the rural-dwellers, the young adults and the old adults, and the emotionally stable and the emotionally unstable who commit crimes.

In arriving at these abstract mechanisms and processes, crim-inal behavior must be precisely defined and carefully distinguished from noncriminal behavior. The problem in criminology is to explain the criminality of behavior, not behavior, as such. The abstract mechanisms and processes common to the classes of criminals indicated above should not also be common to noncriminals. Criminal behavior is human behavior, has much in common with noncriminal behavior, and must be explained within the same general framework used to explain other human behavior. However, an explanation of criminal behavior should be a specific part of a general theory of behavior. Its specific task should be to differentiate criminal from noncriminal behavior. Many things which are necessary for behavior are not for that reason important to the criminality of behavior. Respiration, for instance, is necessary for any behavior, but the respiratory process cannot be used in an explanation of criminal behavior, for it does not differentiate criminal behavior from noncriminal behavior.

The second procedure for putting order into criminological knowledge is differentiation of levels of analysis. This means that the problem is limited to a particular part of the whole situation, largely in terms of chronology. The causal analysis must be held at a particular level. For example, when physicists stated the law of falling bodies, they were not concerned with the reasons why a body began to fall except as this might affect the initial momentum. It made no difference to the physicist whether a body began to fall because it was dropped from the hand of an experimental physicist or rolled off the edge of a bridge because of vibration caused by a passing vehicle. Also, a round object would have rolled off the bridge more readily than a square object, but this fact was not significant for the law of falling bodies. Such facts were considered as existing on a different level of explanation and were irrelevant to the problem with which the physicists were concerned.

Much of the confusion regarding criminal behavior is due to a failure to define and hold constant the level of explanation. By analogy, many criminologists would attribute some degree of causal power to the "roundness" of the object in the above illustration. However, consideration of time sequences among the conditions associated with crime and criminality may lead to simplicity of statement. In the heterogeneous collection of factors associated with criminal behavior, one factor often occurs prior to another factor (in much the way that "roundness" occurs prior to "vibration," and "vibration" occurs prior to "rolling off a bridge"), but a theoretical statement about criminal behavior can be made without referring to those early factors. By holding the analysis at one level, the early factors are combined with or differentiated from later factors or conditions, thus reducing the number of variables which must be considered in a theory.

A motion picture several years ago showed two boys engaged in a minor theft; they ran when they were discovered; one boy had longer legs, escaped, and became a priest; the other had shorter legs, was caught, committed to a reformatory, and became a gangster. In this comparison, the boy who became a criminal was differentiated from the one who did not become a criminal by the length of his legs. But "length of legs" need not be considered in a criminological theory, for there is no significant relationship between criminality and length of legs; certainly many persons with short legs are law-abiding, and some persons with long legs are criminals. The length of the legs does not determine criminality and has no necessary relation to criminality. In the illustration, the differential in the length of the boys' legs may be observed to be significant to subsequent criminality or noncriminality only to the degree that it determined the subsequent experiences and associations of the two boys. It is in these experiences and associations, then, that the mechanisms and processes which are important to criminality or noncriminality are to be found. A "one-level" theoretical explanation of crime would be concerned solely with these mechanisms and processes, not with the earlier factor, "length of legs." ●

Two types of explanations of criminal behavior

Scientific explanations of criminal behavior may be stated either in terms of the processes which are operating at the moment of the occurrence of crime or in terms of the processes operating in the earlier history of the criminal. In the first case, the explanation may be called "mechanistic," "situational," or "dynamic"; in the second, "historical" or "genetic." Both types of explanation are desirable. The mechanistic type of explanation has been favored by physical and biological scientists, and it probably could be the more efficient type of explanation of criminal behavior. However, criminological explanations of the mechanistic type have thus far been notably unsuccessful, perhaps largely because they have been formulated in connection with the attempt to isolate personal and social pathologies among criminals. Work from this point of view has, at least, resulted in the conclusion that the immediate determinants of criminal behavior lie in the person-situation complex.

The objective situation is important to criminality largely to the extent that it provides an opportunity for a criminal act. A thief may steal from a fruit stand when the owner is not in sight but refrain when the owner is in sight; a bank burglar may attack a bank which is poorly protected but refrain from attacking a bank protected by watchmen and burglar alarms. A corporation which manufacturers automobiles seldom violates the pure food and drug laws, but a meat-packing corporation might violate these laws with great frequency. But in another sense, a psychological or sociological sense, the situation is not exclusive of the person, for the situation which is important is the situation as defined by the person who is involved. That is, some persons define a situation in which a fruit-stand owner is out of sight as a "crime-committing" situation, while others do not so define it. Furthermore, the events in the person-situation complex at the time a crime occurs cannot be separated from the prior life experiences of the criminal. This means that the situation is defined by the person in terms of the inclinations and abilities which he has acquired. For example, while a person could define a situation in such a manner that criminal behavior would be the inevitable result, his past experiences would, for the most part, determine the way in which he defined the situation. An explanation of criminal behavior made in terms of these past experiences is an historical or genetic explanation.

The following paragraphs state such a genetic theory of criminal behavior on the assumption that a criminal act occurs when a situation appropriate for it, as defined by the person, is present. The theory should be regarded as tentative, and it should be tested by the factual information presented in the later chapters and by all other factual information and theories which are applicable. ●

The following statements refer to the process by which a particular person comes to engage in criminal behavior.

Genetic explanation of criminal behavior

1. *Criminal behavior is learned.* Negatively, this means that criminal behavior is not inherited, as such; also, the person who is not already trained in crime does not invent criminal behavior, just as a person does not make mechanical inventions unless he has had training in mechanics.

2. *Criminal behavior is learned in interaction with other persons in a process of communication.* This communication is verbal in many respects but includes also "the communication of gestures."

3. *The principal part of the learning of criminal behavior occurs within intimate personal groups.* Negatively, this means that the impersonal agencies of communication, such as movies and newspapers, play a relatively unimportant part in the genesis of criminal behavior.

4. *When criminal behavior is learned, the learning includes (a) techniques of committing the crime, which are sometimes very complicated, sometimes very simple; (b) the specific direction of motives, drives, rationalizations, and attitudes.*

5. *The specific direction of motives and drives is learned from definitions of the legal codes as favorable or unfavorable.* In some societies an individual is surrounded by persons who invariably define the legal codes as rules to be observed, while in others he is surrounded by persons whose definitions are favorable to the violation of the legal codes. In our American society these definitions are almost always mixed, with the consequence that we have culture conflict in relation to the legal codes.

6. *A person becomes delinquent because of an excess of definitions favorable to violation of law over definitions unfavorable to violation of law.* This is the principle of differential association.

It refers to both criminal and anticriminal associations and has to do with counteracting forces. When persons become criminal, they do so because of contacts with criminal patterns and also because of isolation from anticriminal patterns. Any person inevitably assimilates the surrounding culture unless other patterns are in conflict; a southerner does not pronounce r because other southerners do not pronounce r. Negatively, this proposition of differential association means that associations which are neutral so far as crime is concerned have little or no effect on the genesis of criminal behavior. Much of the experience of a person is neutral in this sense, e.g., learning to brush one's teeth. This behavior has no negative or positive effect on criminal behavior except as it may be related to associations which are concerned with the legal codes. This neutral behavior is important especially as an occupier of the time of a child so that he is not in contact with criminal behavior during the time he is so engaged in the neutral behavior.

7. *Differential associations may vary in frequency, duration, priority, and intensity.* This means that associations with criminal behavior and also associations with anticriminal behavior vary in those respects. "Frequency" and "duration" as modalities of associations are obvious and need no explanation. "Priority" is assumed to be important in the sense that lawful behavior developed in early childhood may persist throughout life, and also that delinquent behavior developed in early childhood may persist throughout life. This tendency, however, has not been adequately demonstrated, and priority seems to be important principally through its selective influence. "Intensity" is not precisely defined, but it has to do with such things as the prestige of the source of a criminal or anticriminal pattern and with emotional reactions related to the associations. In a precise description of the criminal behavior of a person, these modalities would be rated in quantitative form and a mathematical ratio be reached. A formula in this sense has not been developed, and the development of such a formula would be extremely difficult.

8. *The process of learning criminal behavior by association with criminal and anticriminal patterns involves all of the mechanisms that are involved in any other learning.* Negatively, this means that the learning of criminal behavior is not restricted to the process of imitation. A person who is seduced, for instance, learns criminal behavior by association, but this process would not ordinarily be described as imitation.

9. *While criminal behavior is an expression of general needs and values, it is not explained by those general needs and values, since noncriminal behavior is an expression of the same needs and values.* Thieves generally steal in order to secure money, but likewise honest laborers work in order to secure money. The attempts by many scholars to explain criminal behavior by general drives and values, such as the happiness principle, striv-

ing for social status, the money motive, or frustration, have been, and must continue to be, futile, since they explain lawful behavior as completely as they explain criminal behavior. They are similar to respiration, which is necessary for any behavior, but which does not differentiate criminal from noncriminal behavior.

It is not necessary, at this level of explanation, to explain why a person has the associations he has; this certainly involves a complex of many things. In an area where the delinquency rate is high, a boy who is sociable, gregarious, active, and athletic is very likely to come in contact with the other boys in the neighborhood, learn delinquent behavior patterns from them, and become a criminal; in the same neighborhood the psychopathic boy who is isolated, introverted, and inert may remain at home, not become acquainted with the other boys in the neighborhood, and not become delinquent. In another situation, the sociable, athletic, aggressive boy may become a member of a scout troop and not become involved in delinquent behavior. The person's associations are determined in a general context of social organization. A child is ordinarily reared in a family; the place of residence of the family is determined largely by family income; and the delinquency rate is in many respects related to the rental value of the houses. Many other aspects of social organization affect the kinds of associations a person has.

The preceding explanation of criminal behavior purports to explain the criminal and noncriminal behavior of individual persons. As indicated earlier, it is possible to state sociological theories of criminal behavior which explain the criminality of a community, nation, or other group. The problem, when thus stated, is to account for variations in crime rates and involves a comparison of the crime rates of various groups or the crime rates of a particular group at different times. The explanation of a crime rate must be consistent with the explanation of the criminal behavior of the person, since the crime rate is a summary statement of the number of persons in the group who commit crimes and the frequency with which they commit crimes. One of the best explanations of crime rates from this point of view is that a high crime rate is due to social disorganization. The term *social disorganization* is not entirely satisfactory, and it seems preferable to substitute for it the term *differential social organization*. The postulate on which this theory is based, regardless of the name, is that crime is rooted in the social organization and is an expression of that social organization. A group may be organized for criminal behavior or organized against criminal behavior. Most communities are organized for both criminal and anticriminal behavior, and, in that sense the crime rate is an expression of the differential group organization. Differential group organization as an explanation of variations in crime rates is consistent with the differential association theory of the processes by which persons become criminals. ●

Differential association and individual criminality

Professor Sutherland introduced the theory of differential association in the 1939 edition of *Criminology*. He modified the theory in the 1947 edition, but this version was not changed in the 1955, 1960, 1966, or 1970 editions. Neither has it been changed in the current edition. The theory is presently in a period of great popularity, judging by the number of journal articles reporting on how it is being tested, analyzed, and extended. It would be inappropriate to modify the statement in such a way that research work now in progress would be undermined. Accordingly we shall merely elaborate on the basic statement by describing some of the principal interpretive errors apparently made by readers and some of the principal criticisms advanced by criminologists and others.[1]

Some literary errors

The basic statement of the theory of differential association is not clear. In two pages, nine propositions are presented, with little elaboration, purporting to explain both the epidemiology of crime and delinquency and the presence of criminality and delinquency in individual cases. It therefore is not surprising that Sutherland's words do not always convey the meaning he seemed to intend. Most significantly, as we shall see later, the statement gives the impression that there is little concern for explaining variations in crime and delinquency rates. This is a serious error in communication. In reference to the delinquent and criminal behavior of individuals, however, the difficulty in communication seems to arise as much from failure to study the words presented as from the words themselves. Five principal errors, and a number of minor ones, have arisen because readers do not always understand what Sutherland seemed to be trying to say.

First, it is common to believe, or perhaps to assume momentarily, if only for purposes of research and discussion, that the theory is concerned only with contacts or associations with criminal and delinquent behavior patterns. Vold, for example, says, "One of the persistent problems that always has bedeviled the theory of differential association is the obvious fact that not everyone in contact with criminality adopts or follows the criminal pattern."[2] At first glance, at least, such statements seem to overlook or ignore the words "differential" and "excess" in the theory, which states that a person becomes delinquent because of an *excess* of definitions favorable to violation of law over definitions unfavorable to violation of law. "This is the

---

[1] The remainder of this chapter is taken, with modifications, from Donald R. Cressey, "Epidemiology and Individual Conduct: A Case from Criminology," *Pacific Sociological Review*, 3:47-58, Fall, 1960. Students interested in documentation of the points made here should refer to this article, which is reprinted in Donald R. Cressey and David A. Ward, eds., *Crime, Delinquency, and Social Process* (New York: Harper and Row, 1969), pp. 557-577.

[2] George B. Vold, *Theoretical Criminology* (New York: Oxford University Press, 1958), p. 194.

principle of differential association. It refers to both criminal and anticriminal associations and has to do with counteracting forces." DeFleur and Quinney recently rearranged and analyzed the nine assertions of the differential association theory in the logical language of set theory.[3] This work both discovered and demonstrated that "the principle" or "the theory" is in all nine assertions, not in the sixth assertion (about the excess of definitions) alone. But it also showed clearly that the sixth assertion does not say that persons become criminals because of associations with criminal behavior patterns; it says that they become criminals because of exposure to an *overabundance* of such associations, in comparison with associations with anticriminal behavior patterns. After restating the theory of differential association in the language of set theory, DeFleur and Quinney translated their finished product back into English as follows:

> Overt criminal behavior has as its necessary and sufficient conditions a set of criminal motivations, attitudes, and techniques, the learning of which takes place when there is exposure to criminal norms in excess of exposure to corresponding anticriminal norms during symbolic interaction in primary groups.[4]

Clearly, then, it is erroneous to state or imply that the theory is invalid because a category of persons—such as policemen, prison workers, or criminologists—have had extensive association with criminal behavior patterns but yet are not criminals.

Second, it is commonly believed that the theory says persons become criminals because of an excess of associations with *criminals*. Because of the manner in which the theory is stated, and because of the popularity of the "bad companions" theory of criminality in our society, this error is easy to make. The theory of differential association is concerned with ratios of associations with *patterns of behavior,* no matter what the character of the person presenting them. Phrases such as "definitions of legal codes as favorable or unfavorable," "definitions favorable to violation of law over definitions unfavorable to violation of law," and "association with criminal and anticriminal patterns" are used throughout the formal statement. Thus, if a mother teaches her son that "Honesty is the best policy," but also teaches him, perhaps inadvertently, that "It is all right to steal a loaf of bread when you are starving," she is presenting him with an anticriminal behavior pattern and a criminal behavior pattern, even if she herself is honest, noncriminal, and even anticriminal. One can learn criminal behavior patterns from persons who are not criminals, and one can learn anticriminal behavior patterns from hoods, professional crooks, habitual offenders, and gangsters.

Third, in periods of time ranging from five to twelve years after

---

[3] Melvin L. DeFleur and Richard Quinney, "A Reformulation of Sutherland's Differential Association Theory and a Strategy for Empirical Verification," *Journal of Research in Crime and Delinquency,* 3:1-22, January, 1966.

[4] Ibid., p. 7.

the first publication of the above statement (1947), at least five authors have erroneously believed that the theory consists of the version published in 1939.[5] This error is not important to the substance of the current statement of the theory, but discussing it does tell something about the nature of the theory. The 1939 statement was qualified so that it pertained only to "systematic" criminal behavior, rather than to the more general category "criminal behavior."[6] The word "systematic" was then deleted, and Sutherland explained that it was his belief that all but "the very trivial criminal acts" were "systematic," but he deleted the word because some research workers were unable to identify "systematic criminals," and other workers considered only an insignificant proportion of prisoners to be "systematic criminals."[7] The theory now refers to all criminal behavior. Limitation to "systematic" criminality was made for what seemed to be practical rather than logical reasons, and it was abandoned when it did not seem to have practical utility.

Fourth, it is commonplace to say that the theory is defective because it does not explain why persons have the associations they have. Although such expressions are valuable statements of what is needed in criminological research, they are erroneous when applied to differential association. Determining why persons have the associations they have is a highly relevant research problem, and we shall later see that when the differential association theory is viewed as a principle that attempts to account for variations in crime rates it does deal in a general way with differential opportunities for association with an excess of criminal behavior patterns. Nevertheless, the fact that the "individual conduct" part of the theory does not pretend to account for a person's associations cannot be considered a defect in it.

Fifth, other authors have erroneously taken "theory" to be synonymous with "bias" or "prejudice," and have condemned the statement on this ground. For example, in connection with criticizing Sutherland for deleting "systematic" from the earlier

---

[5] Robert G. Caldwell, *Criminology* (New York: Ronald Press, 1956), pp. 182-184; Ruth S. Cavan, *Criminology*, 2d ed. (New York: Crowell, 1955), p. 701; Mabel A. Elliott, *Crime in Modern Society* (New York: Harper and Bros., 1952), p. 274; Richard R. Korn and Lloyd W. McCorkle, *Criminology and Penology* (New York: Holt, 1959), pp. 297-298; Vold, *Theoretical Criminology*, pp. 197-198.

[6] See Edwin H. Sutherland, *Principles of Criminology*, 3d ed. (Philadelphia: J. B. Lippincott, 1939), pp. 5-9. This statement proposed generally that systematic criminality is learned in a process of differential association but then went on to use "consistency" as one of the modes of affecting the impact of the various patterns presented in the process of association. Thus, "consistency" of the behavior patterns presented was used as a general explanation of criminality, but "consistency" also was used to describe the process by which differential association takes place. Like the word "systematic," "consistency" was deleted from the next version of the theory.

[7] Edwin H. Sutherland, "Development of the Theory," in Albert K. Cohen, Alfred R. Lindesmith, and Karl F. Schuessler, eds., *The Sutherland Papers* (Bloomington, Ind.: Indiana University Press, 1956), p. 21.

version of his theory, Caldwell wrote that by 1947 "we had not acquired enough additional facts to enable [Sutherland] to explain all criminal behavior."[8] This statement does not clearly recognize that facts themselves do not explain anything, and that theory tries to account for the relationships between known facts, among other things. Confusion about the role of theory also is apparent in Clinard's statement that the theory is "arbitrary," Glueck's statement that "social processes are dogmatically shaped to fit into the prejudices of the preexisting theory of 'differential association,' " and Jeffery's statement that "the theory does not differentiate between criminal and noncriminal behavior, since both types of behavior can be learned."[9]

Additional errors stemming from the form of the formal statement, from lack of careful reading of the statement, or from assumptions necessary to conducting research, have been made, but not with the frequency of the five listed above. Among these are (a) confusion of the concept "definition of the situation" with the word "situation," (b) confusion of the notion that persons associate with criminal and anticriminal behavior patterns with the notion that it is groups that associate on a differential basis, (c) belief that the theory is concerned principally with learning the *techniques* for committing crimes, (d) belief that the theory refers to learning of behavior patterns that are neither criminal nor anticriminal in nature, (e) belief that "differential association," when used in reference to professional thieves, means maintaining "a certain necessary aloofness from ordinary people,"[10] (f) failure to recognize that the shorthand phrase "differential association" is equivalent to "differential association with criminal and anticriminal behavior patterns," with the consequent assumption that the theory attempts to explain all behavior, not just criminal behavior, and (g) belief that the theory is concerned only with a raw ratio of associations between the two kinds of behavior patterns and does not contain the statement, explicitly made, that "differential association may vary in frequency, duration, priority, and intensity."[11]

---

[8] Caldwell, *Criminology*, p. 182.

[9] Marshall B. Clinard, *Sociology of Deviant Behavior* (New York: Rinehart, 1957), p. 204; Sheldon Glueck, "Theory and Fact in Criminology," *British Journal of Delinquency*, 7:92-109, October, 1956; Clarence Ray Jeffery, "An Integrated Theory of Crime and Criminal Behavior," *Journal of Criminal Law, Criminology, and Police Science*, 49:533-552, March-April, 1959.

[10] Walter C. Reckless, *The Crime Problem*, 2d ed. (New York: Appleton-Century-Crofts, 1955), p. 169. This kind of error may stem from Sutherland himself, for in his work on the professional thief he used the term "differential association" to characterize the members of the behavior system, rather than to describe the process presented in the first statement of his theory, two years later. See Edwin H. Sutherland, *The Professional Thief* (Chicago: University of Chicago Press, 1937), pp. 206-207.

[11] If these "modalities," as Sutherland called them, are ignored, then the theory would equate the impact of a behavior pattern presented once in a television drama with the impact of a pattern presented numerous times to a child who deeply loved and respected the donor. It does not so equate the patterns.

Some popular criticisms

Identification of some of the defects that various critics have found in the theory also should make the theory clearer. Five principal types of criticism have been advanced in the literature. It would be incorrect to assume that a criticism advanced by many readers is more valid or important than one advanced by a single reader, but commenting on every criticism would take us too far afield. We can only mention, without elaboration, some of the criticisms advanced by only one or two authors. It has been stated or implied that the theory of differential association (a) is defective because it omits consideration of free will, (b) is based on a psychology assuming rational deliberation, (c) ignores the role of the victim, (d) does not explain the origin of crime, (e) does not define terms such as "systematic" and "excess," (f) does not take "biological factors" into account, (g) is of little or no value to "practical men," (h) is not comprehensive enough because it is not interdisciplinary, (i) is not allied closely enough with more general sociological theory and research, (j) is too comprehensive because it applies to noncriminals, and (k) assumes that all persons have equal access to criminal and anticriminal behavior patterns. Some of these comments represent pairs of opposites, one criticism contradicting another, and others seem to be based on one or more of the errors described above. Still others are closely allied with the five principal types of criticism, and we shall return to them.

One popular form of "criticism" of differential association is not, strictly speaking, criticism at all. A number of scholars have speculated that some kinds of criminal behavior are exceptional to the theory. Thus, it has been said that the theory does not apply to rural offenders, to landlords who violated OPA regulations, to criminal violators of financial trust, to "naïve check forgers," to white-collar criminals, to perpetrators of "individual" and "personal" crimes, to irrational and impulsive criminals, to "adventitious" and/or "accidental" criminals, to "occasional," "incidental," and "situational" offenders, to murderers, nonprofessional shoplifters and noncareer type of criminals, to persons who commit crimes of passion, and to men whose crimes were perpetrated under emotional stress.[12] It is important to note that

---

[12] Marshall B. Clinard, "The Process of Urbanization and Criminal Behavior," *American Journal of Sociology,* 48:202-213, September, 1942; idem, "Rural Criminal Offenders," *American Journal of Sociology,* 50:38-45, July, 1944; idem, "Criminological Theories of Violations of Wartime Regulations," *American Sociological Review,* 11:258-270, June, 1946; Donald R. Cressey, "Application and Verification of the Differential Association Theory," *Journal of Criminal Law, Criminology, and Police Science,* 43:43-52, May-June, 1952; Edwin M. Lemert, "Isolation and Closure Theory of Naïve Check Forgery," *Journal of Criminal Law, Criminology, and Police Science,* 44:293-307, September-October, 1953; Korn and McCorkle, *Criminology and Penology,* pp. 299-300; Elliott, *Crime in Modern Society,* pp. 347-348, 402; Vold, *Theoretical Criminology,* pp. 197-198; Jeffery, "Integrated Theory of Crime and Criminal Behavior"; Daniel Glaser, "Criminality Theories and Behavioral Images," *American Journal of Sociology,* 61:441, March, 1956.

only the first five comments—those referring to rural offenders, landlords, trust violators, check forgers, and some white-collar criminals—are based on research. At least two authors have simply stated that the theory is subject to criticism because there are exceptions to it; the kind of behavior thought to be exceptional is not specified.[13]

The fact that most of the comments are not based on research means that the "criticisms" actually are proposals for research. Should a person conduct research on a particular type of offender and find that the theory does not hold, a revision is called for, provided the research actually tested the theory, or part of it. As indicated, this procedure has been used in five instances, and these instances need to be given careful attention. But in most cases, there is no evidence that the kind of behavior said to be exceptional is exceptional. For example, we do not know that "accidental" or "incidental" or "occasional" criminals have not gone through the process specified in the theory. Perhaps it is sometimes assumed that some types of criminal behavior are "obviously exceptional." However, one theoretical analysis indicated that a type of behavior that appears to be obviously exceptional—"compulsive criminality"—is not necessarily exceptional at all.[14]

A second principal kind of criticism attacks the theory because it does not adequately take into account the "personality traits," "personality factors," or "psychological variables" in criminal behavior. This is real criticism, for it suggests that the statement neglects an important determinant of criminality. Occasionally, the criticism is linked with the apparent assumption that some kinds of criminality are "obviously" exceptional. However, at least a dozen authors have proposed that the statement is defective because it omits or overlooks the general role of personality traits in determining criminality.

In an early period Sutherland stated that his theory probably would have to be revised to take account of personality traits.[15] Later he pointed out what he believed to be the fundamental weakness in his critics' argument: *Personality traits* and *personality* are words that merely specify a condition, like mental retardation, without showing the relationship between that condition and criminality. He posed three questions for advocates of *personality traits* as supplements to differential association: (1) What are the personality traits that should be regarded as significant? (2) Are there personal traits, to be used as supplements to differential association, which are not already included

---

[13] Harry Elmer Barnes and Negley K. Teeters, *New Horizons in Criminology*, 3d ed. (Englewood Cliffs, N.J.: Prentice-Hall, 1959), p. 159; Donald R. Taft, *Criminology* (New York: Macmillan, 1956), p. 340.

[14] Donald R. Cressey, "The Differential Association Theory and Compulsive Crimes," *Journal of Criminal Law, Criminology, and Police Science*, 45:49-64, May-June, 1954.

[15] Sutherland, "Development of the Theory" (1942), pp. 25-27.

in the concept of differential association? (3) Can differential association, which is essentially a *process* of learning, be combined with personal traits, which are essentially the *product* of learning?[16]

Sutherland did not attempt to answer these questions, but the context of his discussion indicates his belief that differential association does explain why some persons with a trait like "aggressiveness" commit crimes, while other persons possessing the same trait do not. It also reveals his conviction that terms like *personality traits, personality,* and *psychogenic trait components* are (when used, with no further elaboration, to explain why a person becomes a criminal) synonyms for *unknown conditions*.[17]

Closely allied with the "personality trait" criticism is the assertion that the theory does not adequately take into account the "response" patterns, "acceptance" patterns, and "receptivity" patterns of various individuals. The essential notion here is that differential association emphasizes the social process of transmission but minimizes the individual process of reception. Stated in another way, the idea is that the theory deals only with external variables and does not take into account the meaning to the recipient of the various patterns of behavior presented to him in situations which are objectively quite similar but nevertheless variable, according to the recipient's perception of them. One variety of this type of criticism takes the form of asserting that criminals and noncriminals are sometimes reared in the "same environment"—criminal behavior patterns are presented to two persons, but only one of them becomes a criminal.

Sutherland was acutely aware of the social psychological problem posed by such concepts as "differential response patterns." Significantly, his proposed solution to the problem was his statement of the theory of differential association.[18] One of the principal objectives of the theory is to account for differences in individual responses to opportunities for crime and in individual responses to criminal behavior patterns presented. To illustrate, one person who walks by an unguarded and open cash register, or who is informed of the presence of such a condition in a nearby store, may perceive the situation as a "crime-committing" one, while another person in the identical circumstances may perceive the situation as one in which the owner should be warned against carelessness. The difference in these two perceptions, the theory holds, is due to differences in the prior associations with the two types of definition of situation, so that

---

[16] Edwin H. Sutherland, *White Collar Crime* (New York: Dryden Press, 1949), p. 272.

[17] See the discussion in chap. 7, below.

[18] See Edwin H. Sutherland, "Susceptibility and Differential Association," in Cohen, Lindesmith, and Schuessler, eds., *Sutherland Papers*, pp. 42-43. See also Solomon Kobrin, "The Conflict of Values in Delinquency Areas," *American Sociological Review*, 16:653-661, October, 1951.

the alternatives in behavior are accounted for in terms of differential association. The differential in "response pattern," or the difference in "receptivity" to the criminal behavior pattern presented, then, is accounted for by differential association itself.[19] Elsewhere, we have pointed out that one of the greatest defects in the theory is its implication that receptivity to any behavior pattern presented is determined by the patterns presented earlier, that receptivity to those early presentations was determined by even earlier presentations, and so on back to birth.[20] But this is an assertion that the theory is difficult to test, not an assertion that it does not take into account the "differential response patterns" of individuals.

If "receptivity" is viewed in a different way, however, the critics appear to be on firm ground.[21] The theory does not identify what constitutes a definition "favorable to" or "unfavorable to" the violation of law. The same objective definition might be "favorable" or "unfavorable," depending on the relationship between the donor and the recipient. Consequently, the theory indicates that differential associations may vary in "intensity," which is not precisely defined but "has to do with such things as the prestige of the source of a criminal or anticriminal pattern and with emotional reactions related to the associations." This statement tells us that some associations are to be given added *weight*, but it does not tell us how, or whether, early associations affect the *meaning* of later associations. If earlier associations determine whether a person will later identify specific behavior patterns as "favorable" or "unfavorable" to law violation, then these earlier associations determine the very meaning of the later ones, and do not merely give added weight to them. In other words, whether a person is prestigeful or not prestigeful to another may be determined by experiences that have nothing to do with criminality and anticriminality. Nevertheless, these experiences affect the meaning (whether "favorable" or "unfavorable") of patterns later presented to the person and, thus, they affect his "receptivity" to the behavior patterns.[22]

A fourth kind of criticism is more damaging than the first three, for it insists that the ratio of learned behavior patterns used to explain criminality cannot be determined with accuracy in specific cases. Short, for example, has pointed out the extreme difficulty of operationalizing terms such as "favorable to" and "unfavorable to"; nevertheless, he has devised various measures of differential

---

[19] Cf. Elihu Katz, Martin L. Levin, and Herbert Hamilton, "Traditions of Research on the Diffusion of Innovation," *American Sociological Review*, 28:237-252, April, 1963.

[20] Cressey, "Application and Verification of the Differential Association Theory."

[21] I am indebted to Albert K. Cohen for assistance with this paragraph and with other points.

[22] This actually is the important point Vold was making in the quotation cited at footnote 2, above.

association and has used them in a series of significant studies.[23] Glaser has argued that "the phrase 'excess of definitions' itself lacks clear denotation in human experience,"[24] and Glueck has asked, "Has anybody actually counted the number of definitions favorable to violation of law and definitions unfavorable to violation of law, and demonstrated that in the pre-delinquency experience of the vast majority of delinquents and criminals, the former exceeds the latter?"[25] In a study of trust violators, Cressey found that embezzlers could not identify specific persons or agencies from whom they learned behavior patterns favorable to trust violation. The general conclusion was, "It is doubtful that it can be shown empirically that the differential association theory applies or does not apply to crimes of financial trust violation or even to other kinds of criminal behavior."[26] It should be noted that these damaging criticisms of the theory of differential association as a precise statement of the mechanism by which persons become criminals do not affect the value of the theory as a general principle which organizes and makes good sense of the data on crime rates. As we shall see below, a theory accounting for the distribution of crime, delinquency, or any other phenomenon can be valid even if a presumably coordinate theory specifying the process by which deviancy occurs in individual cases is incorrect, let alone untestable.

The fifth kind of criticism states in more general terms than the first four that the theory of differential association oversimplifies the process by which criminal behavior is learned. Such criticism ranges from simple assertions that the learning process is more complex than the theory states or implies, to the idea that the theory does not adequately take into account some specific type of learning process, such as differential identification. Between these two extremes are assertions that the theory is inadequate because it does not allow for a process in which criminality seems to be "independently invented" by the actor.

But it is one thing to criticize the theory for failure to specify the learning process accurately and another to specify which aspects of the learning process should be included and in what way.[27] Clinard, Glaser, and Matthews, among others, have introduced the process of identification.[28] Weinberg, Sykes and Matza,

---

[23] James F. Short, Jr., "Differential Association and Delinquency," *Social Problems*, 4:233-239, January, 1957.

[24] Glaser, "Criminality Theories and Behavioral Images."

[25] Glueck, "Theory and Fact in Criminology," p. 96.

[26] Cressey, "Application and Verification of the Differential Association Theory," p. 52.

[27] Despite the fact that Sutherland described a learning process, it should be noted that he protected himself by saying, "The process of learning criminal and anticriminal patterns involves all the mechanisms that are involved in any other learning."

[28] Clinard, "The Process of Urbanization and Criminal Behavior"; idem, "Rural Criminal Offenders"; idem, "Criminological Theories of Violations of War-

and Cressey, among others, have stressed other aspects of more general social psychological theory.[29] Even these attempts are, like the differential association statement itself, more in the nature of general indications of the kind of framework or orientation one should use in formulating a theory of criminality than they are statements of theory. Burgess and Akers have recently given the most promising lead in this area by specifying that the conditions and mechanisms through which delinquent and criminal behavior are learned are those indicated in the theory of human learning variously referred to as "reinforcement theory," "operant behavior theory," and operant conditioning theory.[30] ●

Students should carefully note that the theory of differential association is concerned with making sense of the gross facts about crime, rather than concentrating exclusively on individual criminality.[31] Examination of Sutherland's writings clearly indi-

Differential association and crime rates

time Regulations"; Glaser, "Criminality Theories and Behavioral Images"; idem, "Differential Association and Criminological Prediction," *Social Problems*, 8:6-14, Summer, 1960; idem, "The Differential Association Theory of Crime," in Arnold Rose, ed., *Human Behavior and Social Process* (Boston: Houghton Mifflin, 1962), pp. 425-443; Victor Matthews, "Differential Identification: An Empirical Note," *Social Problems*, 15:376-383, Winter, 1968.

[29] S. Kirson Weinberg, "Theories of Criminality and Problems of Prediction," *Journal of Criminal Law, Criminology, and Police Science*, 45:412-429, November-December, 1954; idem, "Personality and Method in the Differential Association Theory," *Journal of Research in Crime and Delinquency*, 3:165-172, July, 1966; Gresham Sykes and David Matza, "Techniques of Neutralization: A Theory of Delinquency," *American Sociological Review*, 22:664-670, December, 1957; Cressey, "Application and Verification of the Differential Association Theory"; idem, "The Differential Association Theory and Compulsive Crimes"; idem, "Social Psychological Foundations for Using Criminals in the Rehabilitation of Criminals," *Journal of Research in Crime and Delinquency*, 2:49-59, July, 1965; idem, "The Language of Set Theory and Differential Association," *Journal of Research in Crime and Delinquency*, 3:22-26, January, 1966.

[30] Robert L. Burgess and Ronald L. Akers, "A Differential Association — Reinforcement Theory of Criminal Behavior," *Social Problems*, 14:128-147, Fall, 1968. See also Ronald L. Akers, Robert L. Burgess, and Weldon T. Johnson, "Opiate Use, Addiction, and Relapse," *Social Problems*, 15:459-469, Spring, 1968.

[31] One of Sutherland's own students, colleagues, and editors has said, "Much that travels under the name of sociology of deviant behavior or of social disorganization is psychology — some of it very good psychology, but psychology. For example, Sutherland's theory of differential association, which is widely regarded as preeminently sociological, is not the less psychological because it makes much of the cultural milieu. It is psychological because it addresses itself to the question: How do people become the kind of individuals who commit criminal acts? A sociological question would be: What is it about the structure of social systems that determines the kinds of criminal acts that occur in these systems and the way in which such acts are distributed within these systems?" Albert K. Cohen, "The Study of Social Disorganization and Deviant Behavior," chap. 21 in Robert K. Merton, Leonard Broom, and Leonard S. Cottrell, Jr., eds., *Sociology Today* (New York: Basic Books, 1959), p. 462.

cates that when he formulated the theory he was greatly, if not primarily, concerned with organizing and integrating the factual information about crime rates. In his account of how the theory of differential association developed, he made the following three relevant points:

> More significant for the development of the theory were certain questions which I raised in class discussions. One of these questions was, Negroes, young-adult males, and city dwellers all have relatively high crime rates: What do these three groups have in common that places them in this position? Another question was, even if feeble-minded persons have a high crime rate, why do they commit crimes? It is not feeble-mindedness as such, for some feeble-minded persons do not commit crimes. Later I raised another question which became even more important in my search for generalizations. Crime rates have a high correlation with poverty if considered by areas of a city but a low correlation if considered chronologically in relation to the business cycle; this obviously means that poverty as such is not an important cause of crime. How are the varying associations between crime and poverty explained?[32]

> It was my conception that a general theory should take account of all the factual information regarding crime causation. It does this either by organizing the multiple factors in relation to each other or by abstracting them from certain common elements. It does not, or should not, neglect or eliminate any factors that are included in the multiple-factor theory.[33]

> The hypothesis of differential association seemed to me to be consistent with the principal gross findings in criminology. It explained why the Mollaccan children became progressively delinquent with length of residence in the deteriorated area of Los Angeles, why the city crime rate is higher than the rural crime rate, why males are more delinquent than females, why the crime rate remains consistently higher in deteriorated areas of cities, why the juvenile delinquency rate in a foreign nativity group is high while the group lives in a deteriorated area and drops when the group moves out of the area, why second-generation Italians do not have the high murder rate their fathers had, why Japanese children in a deteriorated area of Seattle had a low delinquency rate even though in poverty, why crimes do not increase greatly in a period of depression. All of the general statistical facts seem to fit this hypothesis.[34]

The formal statement of the theory indicates, for example, that a high crime rate in urban areas can be considered the end product of criminalistic traditions in those areas. Similarly, the fact that the rate for all crimes is not higher in some urban areas than it is in some rural areas can be attributed to differences in conditions which affect the probabilities of exposure to criminal behavior patterns.[35] The important general point is that in a multi-group type of social organization, alternative and inconsistent

---

[32] Sutherland, "Development of the Theory," p. 15.
[33] Ibid., p. 18.
[34] Ibid., pp. 19-20.
[35] Cf. Henry D. McKay, "Differential Association and Crime Prevention: Problems of Utilization," *Social Problems,* 8:25-37, Summer, 1960.

standards of conduct are possessed by various groups, so that an individual who is a member of one group has a high probability of learning to use legal means for achieving success, or learning to deny the importance of success, while an individual in another group learns to accept the importance of success and to achieve it by illegal means. Stated in another way, there are alternative educational processes in operation, varying with groups, so that a person may be educated in either conventional or criminal means of achieving success. As indicated above, this situation may be called "differential social organization" or "differential group organization." "Differential group organization" should explain the crime rate, while differential association should explain the criminal behavior of a person. The two explanations must be consistent with each other.

It should be noted that, in the three quotations above, Sutherland referred to the differential association statement as both a "theory" and a "hypothesis," and did not indicate any special concern for distinguishing between differential association as it applies to the epidemiology of crime and differential association as it applies to individual conduct. In order to avoid controversy about the essential characteristics of theories and hypotheses, it seems preferable to call differential association, as it is used in reference to crime rates, a "principle." Many "theories" in sociology are in fact principles that order facts about rates—now called epidemiology—in some way. Durkheim, for example, invented what may be termed a "principle of group integration" to account for, organize logically, and integrate systematically the data on variations in suicide rates. He did not invent a theory of suicide, derive hypotheses from it, and then collect data to determine whether the hypotheses were correct or incorrect. He tried to "make sense" of known facts about rates, and the principle he suggested remains the most valuable idea available to persons who would understand the differences in the rates of suicide between Protestants and Jews, urban-dwellers and rural-dwellers, etc.

The differential association statement, similarly, is a "principle of normative conflict" which proposes that high crime rates occur in societies and groups characterized by conditions that lead to the development of extensive criminalistic subcultures. The principle makes sense of variations in crime rates by observing that modern societies are organized for crime as well as against it, and then observing further that crime rates are unequally distributed because of differences in the degree to which various categories of persons participate in this normative conflict. Sutherland invented the principle of normative conflict to account for the distribution of high and low crime rates; he then tried to specify the mechanism by which this principle works to produce individual cases of criminality. The mechanism proposed is differential association:

The second concept, differential association, is a statement of [normative] conflict from the point of view of the person who commits the crime. The two kinds of culture impinge on him or he has association with the two kinds of cultures and this is differential association.[36] ●

The value of differential association

.As an organizing principle, normative conflict makes understandable most of the variations in crime rates discovered by various researchers and observers, and it also focuses attention on crucial research areas.[37] The principle of normative conflict does not make good sense out of all the statistical variations, but it seems to make better sense out of more of them than do any of the alternative theories.

On the other hand, it also seems safe to conclude that differential association is not a precise statement of the process by which one becomes a criminal. The idea that criminality is a consequence of an excess of intimate associations with criminal behavior patterns is valuable because, for example, it negates assertions that deviation from norms is simply a product of being emotionally insecure or living in a broken home, and then indicates in a general way why only some emotionally insecure persons and only some persons from broken homes commit crimes. Also, it directs attention to the idea that an efficient explanation of individual conduct is consistent with explanations of epidemiology. Yet the statement of the differential association process is not precise enough to stimulate rigorous empirical test, and it therefore has not been proved or disproved. This defect is shared with broader social psychological theory. Although critics agree, as we have indicated, that the differential association statement oversimplifies the process by which normative conflict "gets into" persons and produces criminality, an acceptable substitute that is consistent with the principle of normative conflict has not appeared.

It is important to observe, however, that the "individual conduct" part of the theoretical statement does order data on individual criminality in a general way and, consequently, might be considered a principle itself. Thus, "differential association" may be viewed as a restatement of the principle of normative conflict, so that this one principle is used to account for the distribution of criminal and noncriminal behavior in both the life of the individual *and* in the statistics on collectivities. In this case, both individual behavior data and epidemiological rate data may be employed as indices of the variables in the principle, thus provid-

---

[36] Sutherland, "Development of the Theory," pp. 20-21.

[37] Cf. Llewellyn Gross, "Theory Construction in Sociology: A Methodological Inquiry," chap. 17 in Llewellyn Gross, ed., *Symposium on Sociological Theory* (Evanston, Ill.: Row, Peterson, 1959), pp. 548-555. See also Donald R. Cressey, "The State of Criminal Statistics," *National Probation and Parole Association Journal*, 3:230-241, July, 1957; and DeFleur and Quinney, "Reformulation of Sutherland's Differential Association Theory."

ing two types of hypotheses for testing it.[38] Glaser has shown that differential association makes sense of both the predictive efficiency of some parole prediction items and the lack of predictive efficiency of other items.[39] In effect, he tested the principle by determining whether parole prediction procedures which could have proven it false actually failed to prove it false. First, he shows that a majority of the most accurate predictors in criminology prediction research are deducible from differential association theory, while the least accurate predictors are not deducible at all. Second, he shows that this degree of accuracy does not characterize alternative theories. Finally, he notes that two successful predictors of parole violation—type of offense and noncriminal employment opportunities—are not necessarily deducible from the theory, and he suggests a modification that would take this fact into account. ●

AKERS, RONALD L. *Deviant Behavior: A Social Learning Approach.* Belmont, Calif.: Wadsworth, 1973.

BANDURA, ALBERT. *Principles of Behavior Modification.* New York: Holt, Rinehart and Winston, 1969.

BORDUA, DAVID J. "Some Comments on Theories of Group Delinquency." *Sociological Inquiry,* 32:245-260, Spring, 1962.

CLARK, ROBERT E. *Reference Group Theory and Delinquency.* New York: Behavioral Publications, 1972.

COHEN, ALBERT K. *Deviance and Control.* Englewood Cliffs, N.J.: Prentice-Hall, 1966.

COHEN, ALBERT K., ALFRED R. LINDESMITH, & KARL F. SCHUESSLER, eds. *The Sutherland Papers.* Bloomington, Ind.: Indiana University Press, 1956.

CRESSEY, DONALD R. "Epidemiology and Individual Conduct: A Case From Criminology." *Pacific Sociological Review,* 3:47-58, Fall, 1960.

DeFLEUR, MELVIN L., & RICHARD QUINNEY. "A Reformulation of Sutherland's Differential Association Theory and a Strategy for Empirical Verification." *Journal of Research in Crime and Delinquency,* 3:1-22, January, 1966.

EMPEY, LAMAR T. "Delinquency Theory and Recent Research." *Journal of Research in Crime and Delinquency,* 4:28-42, January, 1967.

---

[38] I am indebted to Daniel Glaser for calling this point to my attention.

[39] Glaser, "Differential Association and Criminological Prediction." See also idem, "A Reconsideration of Some Parole Prediction Factors," *American Sociological Review,* 19:335-341, June, 1954; and idem, "The Efficiency of Alternative Approaches to Parole Prediction," *American Sociological Review,* 20:283-287, June, 1955; and Daniel Glaser and Richard R. Hangren, "Predicting the Adjustment of Federal Probationers," *National Probation and Parole Association Journal,* 4:258-267, July, 1958; and David M. Downes, *The Delinquent Solution: A Study in Subcultural Theory* (London: Routledge and Kegan Paul, 1966), pp. 97-98.

GLASER, DANIEL. "Differential Association and Criminological Prediction." *Social Problems,* 8:6-14, Summer, 1960.

GLASER, DANIEL. "The Differential Association Theory of Crime." Chapter in *Human Behavior and Social Processes,* edited by Arnold Rose, pp. 425-443. Boston: Houghton Mifflin, 1962.

HALL, PETER M. "Identification with the Delinquent Subculture and Level of Self-Evaluation." *Sociometry,* 29:146-158, June, 1966.

HARTUNG, FRANK E. *Crime, Law, and Society.* Detroit: Wayne State University Press, 1965.

JEFFERY, CLARENCE RAY. "Criminal Behavior and Learning Theory." *Journal of Criminal Law, Criminology, and Police Science,* 56:294-300, September, 1965.

LISKA, ALLEN E. "Interpreting the Causal Structure of Differential Association Theory." *Social Problems,* 16:485-492, Spring, 1969.

LOFLAND, JOHN. *Deviance and Identity.* Englewood Cliffs, N. J.: Prentice-Hall, 1969.

MATTHEWS, VICTOR M. "Differential Identification: An Empirical Note." *Social Problems,* 15:376-383, Winter, 1968.

MATZA, DAVID. *Becoming Deviant.* Englewood Cliffs, N. J.: Prentice-Hall, 1969.

McKAY, HENRY D. "Differential Association and Crime Prevention: Problems of Utilization." *Social Problems,* 8:25-37, Summer, 1960.

MILESKI, MAUREEN, & DONALD J. BLACK. "The Social Organization of Homosexuality." *Urban Life and Culture,* 1:187-202, July, 1972.

NAESS, SIRI. "Comparing Theories of Criminogenesis." *Journal of Research in Crime and Delinquency,* 1:171-180, July, 1964.

PASCHKE, WALTER R. "The Addiction Cycle: A Learning Theory–Peer Group Model." *Correctional Psychiatry and Journal of Social Therapy,* 16:74-81, 1970.

REISS, ALBERT J., JR., & LEWIS RHODES. "An Empirical Test of Differential Association Theory." *Journal of Research in Crime and Delinquency,* 1:5-18, January, 1964.

SCHEFF, THOMAS J. "Social Support for Stereotypes of Mental Disorder." *Mental Hygiene,* 47:461-469, July, 1963.

SEVERY, LAWRENCE J. "Exposure to Deviance Committed by Valued Peer Group and Family Members." *Journal of Research in Crime and Delinquency,* 10:35-46, January, 1973.

SEWELL, WILLIAM H. "Some Recent Developments in Socialization Theory and Research." *Annals of the American Academy of Political and Social Science,* 349:163-181, September, 1963.

SHERWOOD, JOHN J. "Self Identity and Referent Others." *Sociometry,* 28:66-81, March, 1965.

SHORT, JAMES F., JR. "Differential Association as a Hypothesis: Problems of Empirical Testing." *Social Problems*, 8:14-25, Summer, 1960.

STRATTON, JOHN R. "Differential Identification and Attitudes Toward the Law." *Social Forces*, 46:256-262, December, 1967.

TRASSLER, GORDON. *The Explanation of Criminality*. London: Routledge and Kegan Paul, 1962.

VOLD, GEORGE B. *Theoretical Criminology*. New York: Oxford University Press, 1958.

VOSS, HARWIN L. "Differential Association and Reported Delinquent Behavior: A Replication." *Social Problems*, 12:78-85, Summer, 1964.

WEINBERG, S. KIRSON. "Personality and Method in the Differential Association Theory." *Journal of Research in Crime and Delinquency*, 3:165-172, July, 1966.

5 Crime, delinquency, and social structure

The purpose of this chapter is to present the general historical background of present-day crime and delinquency in terms of the social processes by which they developed. This is, for the most part, in the nature of hypothesis rather than demonstrated fact. Further, the assumption is made that the actual incidence of crime is much greater than is indicated by the various statistics. ●

Differential social organization

In nonliterate and peasant societies the influences surrounding a person were relatively steady, uniform, harmonious, and consistent. Until the early part of this century, China exemplified this situation perfectly except in a few of the coastal cities. The individual was surrounded by all of his relatives, and this larger family determined his career and his ambitions. His principal satisfactions were found in cooperation with that group, which was considered as extending beyond his own life into the distant future. Within this group he had perfect individual security, for the group cared for him in case of sickness, accident, old age, insanity, or any other emergency. Such charity involved no stigma or disgrace whatsoever. This large family, moreover, was supported by the surrounding community, which also was harmonious in its traditional culture.

In such a situation the behavior of the individual was almost completely predictable, for he had few alternative patterns to follow. The social organization provided few opportunities for "individualism" in behavior. The local group had little contact with outsiders, since the community was a self-supporting and self-contained society, and this isolation also was conducive to consistency in the behavior patterns presented to persons in the socialization process. Within this group, few crimes were committed; the occasional offenses were committed chiefly by nonresidents upon members of the group, or by members of the group upon nonmembers. This social isolation is illustrated by certain Labrador Indians, who have been characterized as follows:

> They are primary in pattern since, through the intimate association of individuals forming them, the social fusion of kin results in producing a community whole within which there is a tendency toward harmony and the most thoroughgoing cooperation. Strife is scarcely present, violence strenuously avoided; competition even courteously disdained. These, they think, lead to ridicule. In their place are met subjection of self, generosity in respect to property, service, and opinion, the qualities which we often speak of as being found in "good sports" and which seem to develop as social habits. And these are the qualities that to them represent honor and a welcome place in the thoughts of their associates.[1]

At present no such consistency and uniformity is evident in Western civilization, although certain isolated rural settlements are the closest approach to it. In contemporary urban society, a child is confronted with various ways of behaving even within his own home, for no parent can act consistently in modern life; the parent himself is the recipient of many alternative roles and behavior patterns.[2] Similarly, groups outside the home have standards of conduct which often are extremely different from those within the home. A great deal of behavior is in the nature of role-playing, and when roles are conflicting or ambiguous, the behavior is inconsistent. Sellin has described the normative conflicts within contemporary communities thus:

> Every person is identified with a number of social groups, each meeting some biologically conditioned or socially created need. Each of these groups is normative in the sense that within it there grow up norms of conduct applicable to situations created by that group's specific activities. As a member of a given group, a person is not only supposed to

---

[1] Frank G. Speck, "Ethical Attributes of Labrador Indians," *American Anthropologist,* 35:559-594, October-December, 1933. See also Robert Redfield, "Primitive Law," *University of Cincinnati Law Review,* 33:1-22, Winter, 1964; R. K. Denton, *The Semai: A Non-Violent People of Malaya* (New York: Holt, Rinehart, and Winston, 1968); and Michael Banton, "Authority in the Simpler Societies," *Police Journal,* 43:261-267, 1970.

[2] See Aubrey Wendling and Delbert S. Elliott, "Class and Race Differentials in Parental Aspirations and Expectations," *Pacific Sociological Review,* 11:123-133, Fall, 1968.

conform to the rules which it shares with other groups, but also to those which are peculiarly its own. A person who as a member of a family group—in turn the transmitting agency for the norms which governed the groups from which the parents come—possesses all its norms pertaining to conduct in routine life situations, may also as a member of a play group, a work group, a political group, a religious group, etc., acquire norms which regulate specialized life situations and which sustain, weaken, or even contradict the norms earlier incorporated in his personality. The more complex a culture becomes, the more likely it is that the number of normative groups which affect a person will be large, and the greater is the chance that the norms of these groups will fail to agree, no matter how much they may overlap as a result of common acceptance of certain norms. A conflict of norms is said to exist when more or less divergent rules of conduct govern the specific life situation in which a person may find himself. The conduct norm of one group of which he is a part may permit one response to this situation, the norm of another group may permit perhaps the very opposite response.[3]

This condition of normative conflict is ordinarily considered social "disorganization" or "unorganization" because the social pressures for conformity on the part of the person are not uniform and harmonious. In this condition, the society does not possess consensus with respect to societal goals or else does not possess consensus regarding means of achieving agreed-upon societal goals. Consequently, the individual is confronted with alternative goals or means, or he exists under conditions in which the norms of many members of the society are unknown to other members.[4] He finds that behavior which is "right" or "correct" in one group is "wrong" or "improper" from the point of view of other groups in which he has membership; or, in the condition of *anomie*, he literally does not know how to behave, for he does not know what is expected of him. The presence of this heterogeneous set of conflicting norms is considered social disorganization largely on the ground that an earlier form of social organization has disappeared or is disappearing. Actually, the social conditions in which the influences on the person are relatively inharmonious and inconsistent are themselves a kind of social organization. Such social organization is characteristic of all except the earliest societies and the most isolated contemporary societies, although there are wide variations in the degree of heterogeneity and in the pervasiveness of the normative inconsistencies.

So far as delinquency and crime are concerned, a heterogeneity of norms in a society means that both a delinquent or criminal subculture and an antidelinquent or anticriminal subculture have developed. Society has become organized in such

---

[3] Thorsten Sellin, *Culture Conflict and Crime* (New York: Social Science Research Council, 1938), pp. 29-30. See also John Dewey, *Human Nature and Conduct* (New York: Henry Holt, 1930), p. 130.

[4] See Judith Blake and Kingsley Davis, "Norms, Values and Sanctions," chap. 13 in Robert E. L. Faris, ed., *Handbook of Modern Sociology* (Chicago: Rand McNally, 1964), pp. 456-484.

a way that a premium has been placed both on refraining from crime and on perpetrating crime. A person may now be a member of a group organized against crime while, at the same time, he is a member of a group organized for criminal behavior. For example, a person who accumulates large sums of money through white-collar crimes may be an ardent advocate of community recreational facilities which, he believes, will prevent juvenile delinquency. Under such conditions of differential group organization one would expect the crime rates to be relatively high, for there are "rules for crime" as well as "rules against crime." The person participates in delinquent subcultures as well as in nondelinquent and antidelinquent subcultures. A sociological problem of first-rate importance is discovery of the conditions under which "rules for crime" and "rules for delinquency" have developed. The task here is not to identify the processes by which criminal behavior patterns are adopted by an individual or a group; it is to identify the processes which brought the behavior patterns into existence in the first place. •

Development of normative conflict

One recent impetus to development of delinquent and criminal subcultures was the colonization of America, which threw the Old World out of economic balance. This was followed by the final breakup of the feudal system, in which the ownership of the land had been limited, and in which the fixed social classes had mutual duties to each other. Experimental science developed, resulting in the rise of modern technology. With the development of machinery, the production of wealth passed from the control of the consumer to the control of the capitalist; the laborer followed his work from the home to the factory; and thus the city developed around the factory and the marketplace. The traditional restrictions on economic activity were irksome as world commerce began to develop, and rebellion against these restrictions resulted in a system of relatively free competition, with an accompanying individualistic ideology according to which social welfare is best attained if every person works only for his own selfish interests. Thus, the new system placed great emphasis upon individual enterprise, and it became shameful for an individual to withdraw from economic competition. Each person was expected to pursue his private ends in the most efficient manner possible, and the expected result was increased economic wealth for all.

The democratic revolutions, with accompanying ideologies of natural and inalienable rights, cannot be clearly separated from this economic revolution. The participants in the relatively new economic system resisted any measures which would inhibit free competition, and the slogan "the least government the best" was given homage. Each participant rebelled against restrictions on his own behavior and therefore attempted to keep government weak. However, as competition developed, it became apparent that competitive advantages could be secured through governmental manipulation. Individuals and industries secured tariffs, franchises, patents, and other special privileges. Both by emphasis on a "hands-off" policy and by emphasis on special privileges, government was made less effective as a controller of behavior.

The attitudes and ideology which developed with the industrial and democratic revolutions were opposed to the authoritarian principle in government and in other institutions. Economic and political individualism was useful at the time of revolt against the fixed statuses and restrictions of the feudal system and against the absolutism of the political system. But individualism is not a positive principle of social organization, and when the revolutions were ended, the usefulness of the negative principle was ended. Since that time, the ideology of individualism has encouraged each citizen to disregard social welfare in the interest of his selfish satisfactions. Under such conditions of normative conflict, the significance of laws becomes relative: some are obeyed and others are not, depending on whether one "believes in" them.[5] Public welfare need not be considered, for it will be best realized if each person works for his own selfish interests.[6] The gangster and the grafter believe that social welfare need not be an object of consideration, and that they may get what they can by whatever methods they can. The gangster is a man who acquires by personal merit and a gun that which is denied him by the complex orderings of a stratified society. As Veblen said:

> The ideal pecuniary man is like the ideal delinquent in his unscrupulous conversion of goods and persons to his own ends, and in a callous disregard of the feelings and wishes of others and of the remoter effects of his actions, but he is unlike him in possessing a keener sense of status and in working more farsightedly to a remoter end.[7]

Similarly, with the industrial and democratic revolutions the ambition for luxurious standards of life became effective for all social classes, since the values which previously restricted these standards to the nobility had been altered. Emile Durkheim, the noted French sociologist, made the following observation about stable societies:

> The economic ideal assigned each class of citizens is itself confined to certain limits, within which the desires have free range. But it is not infinite. This relative limitation and the moderation it involves make men contented with their lot while stimulating them moderately to improve it; and this average contentment causes the feeling of calm, active happiness, the pleasure in existing and living which character-

---

[5] Marshall B. Clinard, *The Black Market: A Study of White Collar Crime* (New York: Rinehart, 1952), pp. 331, 334.

[6] Cf. Edward A. Duddy, "The Moral Implications of Business as a Profession," *Journal of Business,* 15:70-71, April, 1945.

[7] Thorstein Veblen, *Theory of the Leisure Class* (New York: Macmillan, 1912), p. 237. See also David Matza and Gresham M. Sykes, "Juvenile Delinquency and Subterranean Values," *American Sociological Review,* 26:712-719, October, 1961.

izes health for societies as well as for individuals. Each person is then at least, generally speaking, in harmony with his condition, and desires only what he may legitimately hope for as the normal reward of his activity. Besides, this does not condemn man to a sort of immobility. He may seek to give beauty to his life; but his attempts in this direction may fail without causing him to despair.[8]

But rapid technological advancements and discovery of vast unexploited markets raised the level of aspirations by presenting what appeared to be unlimited possibilities for accumulation of wealth.[9] After the disappearance of the nobility, businessmen constituted the elite, and wealth became respected above all other attainments; necessarily, poverty became a disgrace. Wealth was therefore identified with worth, and worth was made known to the public by conspicuous consumption. The desire for symbols of luxury, ease, and success, developed by competitive consumption and by competitive salesmanship, spread to all classes, and the simple life was no longer satisfying. Now, "it is everlastingly repeated that it is man's nature to be eternally dissatisfied, constantly to advance, without relief or rest, toward an indefinite goal. The longing for infinity is daily represented as a mark of moral distinction. . . . The doctrine of the most ruthless and swift progress has become an article of faith."[10]

Planned acquisition through hard work and careful saving became a virtue, and failure to acquire became evidence of poor character. The doctrine of equality meant that each man was to compete against "all comers," even if his social and economic status put him at great disadvantage in doing so. As Durkheim said:

> Overweening ambition always exceeds the results obtained, great as they may be, since there is no warning to pause here. Nothing gives satisfaction and all this agitation is uninterruptedly maintained without appeasement. Above all, since this race of an unattainable goal can give no other pleasure but that of the race itself, if it is one, once it is interrupted the participants are left empty-handed. At the same time the struggle grows more violent and painful, both from being less controlled and because competition is greater. All classes contend among themselves because no established classification any longer exists. Effort grows, just when it becomes less productive.[11]

In sum, this analysis maintains that in the attempt to locate and train the most talented persons to occupy technical roles, industrial societies maintain that goals of personal, material success are available to all, regardless of social origins. By maintaining that great rewards are available to all, and by maintaining that achievement of the rewards is a sign of moral worth,[12]

---

[8] Emile Durkheim, *Suicide: A Study in Sociology,* trans. John A. Spaulding and George Simpson (Glencoe, Ill.: Free Press, 1951), p. 250. This book was first published in Paris in 1897.

[9] Cf. S. Kirson Weinberg, "Urbanization and Male Delinquency in Ghana," *Journal of Research in Crime and Delinquency,"* 2:85-94, July, 1965.

[10] Durkheim, *Suicide,* p. 257.

[11] Ibid., p. 253.

[12] See Max Weber, *The Protestant Ethic and the Spirit of Capitalism,* trans. Talcott Parsons (London: Allen and Unwin, 1930).

an optimum number of persons can be motivated to compete for the rewards. But the social structure of industrialized societies is not necessarily consistent with this set of values, this culture. The social structure is the patterned sets of relationships among people and, as Merton has pointed out, in industrial society this structure effectively blocks access to success goals for some parts of the population.[13]

One result is invention of a set of values which makes it "all right," even if illegal, to achieve success by routes other than the standard ones provided in the social structure. A set of values of this kind is "deviant," or "delinquent," or "criminal," in the sense that it inspires persons to achieve success by means which are not sanctioned by the legal institutions of society. Normative conflict is present, and both individuals and groups now have the opportunity to learn both the illegitimate means and the legitimate means for achieving personal success. In this kind of social arrangement, the generally approved "rules of the game" may be known to those who evade them, but the emotional supports which accompany conformity to these rules are offset by the stress on the success goal and by the "rules for violating rules" which develop in these circumstances. As Merton has said, "It is only when a system of cultural values extols, virtually above all else, certain *common* success-goals for the population at large while the social structure rigorously restricts or completely closes access to approved modes of reaching these goals *for a considerable part of the same population*, that deviant behavior ensues on a large scale."[14]

Cloward and Ohlin have summarized the general observations on the origins of delinquent and criminal subcultures and, thus, the observations on the origins of normative conflict, in the following terms:

Interaction among those sharing the same problem [discrepancies between aspiration and opportunity] may provide encouragement for the withdrawal of sentiments in support of the established system of norms. Once freed of allegiance to the existing set of rules, such persons may devise . . . delinquent means of achieving success. A collective delinquent solution to an adjustment problem is more likely to evolve by this process in a society in which the legitimacy of social rules can be questioned apart from their moral validity. . . . What seems expedient, rational, and efficient often becomes separable from what is traditional, sacred, and moral as a basis for the imputation of legitimacy. Under such conditions it is difficult for persons at different social positions to agree about the forms of conduct that are both expedient and morally right. Once this separation takes place, the

---

[13] Robert K. Merton, *Social Theory and Social Structure*, rev. and enl. ed. (Glencoe, Ill.: Free Press, 1957), chaps. 4 and 5.

[14] Ibid., p. 146. It should be noted that in this statement Professor Merton slips into a theory of deviant behavior, rather than limiting himself to a theory of the origin of deviant subcultures. "Deviant behavior on a large scale" can arise only *after* invention of deviant subcultures. This point will be discussed in chapter 9.

supporting structure of the existing system of norms becomes highly vulnerable.[15]

Many types of delinquent, criminal, and deviant subcultures exist in contemporary society, with the result that normative conflict is present on a large scale. Accordingly, no juvenile gang, neighborhood group, ethnic group, or social class needs to invent a criminal subculture in order to take on a high rate of criminality. Although new sets of values which make delinquency and criminality "all right" even if illegal are invented from time to time, most apparent inventions are merely variations on old themes, invented long ago. As Bordua has observed, "Each generation does not meet and solve anew the problems of class structure barriers to opportunity but begins with the solution of its forbears. This is why reform efforts can be so slow to succeed."[16]

However, it appears that various types of delinquent subcultures have arisen, and thrive, at different locations in the social structure.[17] The evidence is fragmentary, impressionistic, and uncoordinated, but it seems to indicate that some types of delinquent and criminal subcultures have arisen in large metropolitan centers and particularly in those areas of cities that are characterized by poverty, while other types have arisen among middle-class persons or, as indicated by values conducive to the commission of white-collar crimes, among upper-class persons. Because the sets of delinquent and criminal values are located in different parts of the social structure, they are not equally available for adoption by all segments of the society. Working-class persons living in areas inhabited by certain racial and ethnic groups in large American cities have available to them for adoption a different kind of criminal subculture than do upper-class persons.[18] High delinquency and crime rates of various kinds become, from this perspective, "location data" which direct the attention of researchers to the study of the origin and continuation of various kinds of delinquent and criminal subcultures in various parts of the society.[19]

In one of the best studies using "location data" as a stimulus to exploration of the origin of a type of delinquent subculture, Cohen examined "non-utilitarian" delinquency.[20] Statistical data indicated that a destructive kind of "hell-raising" vandalism was more prevalent among working-class boys than among middle-

---

[15] Richard A. Cloward and Lloyd E. Ohlin, *Delinquency and Opportunity: A Theory of Delinquent Gangs* (Glencoe, Ill.: Free Press, 1960), pp. 108-109.

[16] David J. Bordua, "Delinquent Subcultures: Sociological Interpretations of Gang Delinquency," *Annals of the American Academy of Political and Social Science*, 338:119-136, November, 1961.

[17] Cloward and Ohlin, *Delinquency and Opportunity*, pp. 26-27.

[18] See Irving Spergel, *Racketville, Slumtown, Haulburg: An Exploratory Study of Delinquent Subcultures* (Chicago: University of Chicago Press, 1964).

[19] Cloward and Ohlin, *Delinquency and Opportunity*, pp. 33-34.

[20] Albert K. Cohen, *Delinquent Boys: The Culture of the Gang* (Glencoe, Ill.: Free Press, 1955), esp. pp. 121-137.

class boys. Traditionally, criminologists have assumed that such data indicated the existence of a delinquent subculture and, thus, a high incidence of normative conflict among working-class boys, and then they have gone on to try to explain how the delinquent subculture is taken over by individual boys. Cohen, on the other hand, followed the leads provided by Durkheim and Merton and asked why such a subculture is there to be taken over. The theory he developed in response to this question maintains that the nonutilitarian delinquent subculture has arisen in response to a conflict between the aspirations inspired by middle-class values and the ability and opportunity that working-class boys have for fulfilling these aspirations. Middle-class values have been incorporated into the law and into other general codes of legitimate and moral conduct, codes which prescribe proper conduct for everyone.

At the same time, however, society is organized in such a way that all working-class persons cannot achieve the goals implied in these values—goals such as personal "success" and achievement of the kind requiring rational, honest labor, careful long-range planning, and deferral of gratifications. For example, while all boys might be inspired with the notion that "anyone" who works honestly and soberly can graduate from college, and with the idea that it is a "good thing" to graduate from college, the fact is that some boys entering this competition will be defeated, for they are not adequately equipped for the competition. In response to this conflict between values and social structure, rules have been developed for achieving personal success by turning the middle-class rules "upside down." Once this subculture had been invented, boys could achieve a symbol of status, for example, either by doing well in school or by vandalizing the school at night. Or, more generally, they could achieve a symbol of status either by getting a good education, working hard, and saving their money until they were able to join the country club, or by doing none of these things and, instead, ripping up the country club's golf greens late at night.

It should be noted that Cohen's theory does not attempt to account for the delinquency or nondelinquency of any particular boy. It is a theory that explains why certain values are more readily available for learning by some boys than by others. Since the rules for nonutilitarian delinquency are carried, by and large, by working-class persons, they are more readily available for learning by working-class persons than by middle-class persons. Further, since the rules for delinquency arise in connection with differences between culturally defined aspirations regarding "success," on the one hand, and opportunities for achieving this success, on the other, they are more readily available for learning by boys than by girls.

Walter B. Miller's work on working-class delinquency indicates more concern for diffusion of delinquency values within the working class than for the origin of these rules for delinquency among working-class people. Unlike Cohen, he has not developed a specific theory which attempts to account for the development of certain of the rules for delinquency. Instead, he develops the notion that working-class values include a delinquent subculture.[21] Accordingly, he finds the origin of the delinquent subculture in the values of the working class, but he does not report in detail on the structural conditions leading to the invention of these values. Essentially, Miller sees working-class values emerging from the shaking-down process of immigration, internal migration, and vertical mobility.[22] Normative conflict has developed on a class basis, and, accordingly, rules for delinquency are present for learning by lower-class boys.

For example, Miller observes an intense concern for "toughness" and "masculinity" in lower-class culture, a concern which is expressed in a set of rules demanding that boys "act tough" in certain circumstances. Since "acting tough" and "being tough" often are defined as delinquency by the agencies of law enforcement, the stress on toughness amounts to a delinquent subculture. Miller emphasizes the importance of the structure of the family relationships in the working class to development of this delinquent subculture in that class:

A significant proportion of lower-class males are reared in a predominantly female household and lack a consistently present male figure with whom to identify and from whom to learn essential components of a "male" role. Since women serve as a primary object of identification during the pre-adolescent years, the almost obsessive lower-class concern with "masculinity" probably resembles a type of compulsive reaction-formation.[23]

According to Miller's theory, delinquent subcultures develop, then, because of problems of adjustment confronting lower-class males and because of conflicts between (a) values which, on a class basis, stress achievement and (b) social structure which, on a class basis, restricts that achievement. His thesis has been reduced by Cloward and Ohlin to three main propositions: (1) The lower class is characterized by distinctive values. (2) These values vary markedly from the middle-class values which undergird the legal code. (3) The result is that conformity with certain lower-class values may automatically result in violation of the law.[24] As Miller says, "Engaging in certain cultural practices which comprise essential elements of the total life pattern of lower-class culture automatically violates certain legal norms."[25]

[21] Walter B. Miller, "Lower Class Culture as a Generating Milieu of Gang Delinquency," *Journal of Social Issues*, vol. 14 (1958), no. 3, pp. 5-19.

[22] See Bordua, "Delinquent Subcultures," and Walter B. Miller, "Implications of Urban Lower Class Culture for Social Work," *Social Service Review*, 33:219-236, September, 1959.

[23] Miller, "Lower Class Culture as a Generating Milieu of Gang Delinquency," p. 9.

[24] Cloward and Ohlin, *Delinquency and Opportunity*, p. 65.

[25] W. C. Kvaraceus and W. B. Miller, *Delinquent Behavior: Culture and the Individual* (Washington: National Education Association, 1959), pp. 68-69.

This observation is consistent with one made earlier by two astute observers of American social life:

Activities [such as] gregarious theft and gang warfare by the boys and gregarious sex by the girls appear to be channels for the playful, sociable and conformist impulses of the lower-class youth. If, in many urban areas, we find a lower-class boy or girl who is not delinquent in this sense, we can be fairly sure that he or she is either headed up the class ladder or is psychologically deviant or both, being unwilling or unable to join in the group activities sanctioned by his peers.[26]

Cloward and Ohlin have attempted to account for the invention of delinquent subcultures in terms which closely resemble those used by Cohen. Their concern, like that of Miller, is more for the question of why delinquent subcultures persist and diffuse once they are invented, than for the question of how they get invented in the first place. Nevertheless, they follow the writings of Durkheim and Merton to the conclusion that at least three different types of delinquent subcultures have been invented as a response to a clash between values which promote unlimited aspirations and a social structure which restricts accomplishment of the aspirations. They then go on to observe that among some segments of the population even the possibilities of legitimately achieving *limited* success goals are also restricted, and they find three delinquent subcultures being invented in these areas of poor opportunity.

Two of these subcultures provide illegal avenues to success goals; these are the "criminal subculture," which contains rules for the pursuit of material gain by means such as theft, extortion, and fraud, and the "conflict subculture," which contains rules for the achievement of status through manipulation of force or the threat of force. The other subculture, the "retreatist subculture," contains rules favoring the consumption of drugs. The basic notion here is that the subcultures are invented when aspirations are frustrated and when the frustration is diagnosed as due to the conditions of the social order rather than to personal attributes of the interacting but frustrated population.[27]

If a delinquent subculture, once invented, is to persist, there must be devices for passing the norms, values, and "rules for delinquency" on to newcomers, whether these newcomers are children of the participants or immigrants from another area where the subculture did not exist. For example, the "criminal subculture" described by Cloward and Ohlin is rather stable, and one source of this stability is the network of bonds that

---

[26] Reuel Denney and David Riesman, "Leisure in Urbanized America," in Paul K. Hatt, ed., *Reader in Urban Sociology* (Glencoe, Ill.: Free Press, 1951), p. 471. See also David M. Downes, *The Delinquent Solution: A Study in Subcultural Theory* (London: Routledge and Kegan Paul, 1966).

[27] Cloward and Ohlin, *Delinquency and Opportunity*, pp. 111-124. See also Wendling and Elliott, "Class and Race Differentials."

exists between age levels.[28] Children are linked with adolescent delinquents and share their normative conflict; adolescent delinquents, in turn, are linked with young adult offenders, who, in turn, are linked with adult criminals.[29] The delinquent subculture is carried by a broad, age-linked population. On the other hand, the "conflict subculture" is less stable, probably because devices for socializing newcomers into it have not developed to the same degree. While any newcomer must learn the values of the conflict subculture, the subculture is carried by adolescents, not by children and adults. Accordingly, those persons who have been socialized do not move onward through a set of age-graded patterns; they tend to be guided by other values when they reach young adulthood, rather than moving on to an "adult" form of violence. The population carrying the values of the conflict subculture is small and diffuse.

Discovery of the processes leading to the invention of delinquent and criminal subcultures whose existence establishes normative conflict in a society does not explain either the behavior of individual delinquents and criminals or the distribution of crime and delinquency rates. Even in societies disproportionately stressing success goals to the degree that delinquent subcultures are invented, most persons do not use illegitimate means for achieving the approved ends.[30] Rather, in a multigroup type of social organization, conflicting standards of conduct are possessed by various groups. Normative conflict is not distributed evenly throughout the society. An individual who is a member of one group will use one means for achieving the success goal, while an individual having membership in another group will use another means. McKay has pointed out that alternative educational processes are in operation and that a child may be educated in either "conventional" or criminal means of achieving success.[31] Cloward has shown that even unsanctioned means of attaining success are not available to everyone; some persons may be "double failures," in the sense that neither legitimate nor illegitimate means for achieving success are available to them:

---

[28] Ibid., p. 44. Cloward and Ohlin do not make a careful distinction between gang activities and the delinquent subcultures on which gang activities are based, with the result that it is difficult to determine when they are concerned with the invention of a delinquent subculture and when they are concerned with the distribution of the values of this subculture to individuals. See the discussion of gangs in chap. 9, pp. 187-197, below. For an excellent study of the way the behavioral rules making up a deviant subculture get invented, see John K. Irwin, "Surfers: A Study of the Growth of a Deviant Subculture" (Master's thesis, Department of Sociology, University of California, Berkeley, 1965).

[29] See Gerald Robin, "Gang Member Delinquency," *Journal of Criminal Law, Criminology, and Police Science*, 55:59-65, March, 1964.

[30] Cf. Blake and Davis, "Norms, Values and Sanctions."

[31] Henry D. McKay, "The Neighborhood and Child Conduct," *Annals of the American Academy of Political and Social Science*, 261:32-42, January, 1949. See also South Side Community Committee, *Bright Shadows in Bronzetown* (Chicago: Author, 1949), pp. 26-28.

"Note, for example, variations in the degree to which members of various classes are fully exposed to and thus acquire the values, education, and skills which facilitate upward mobility. It should not be startling, therefore, to find similar variations in the availability of illegitimate means."[32] ●

The industrial and democratic revolutions were accompanied by increased mobility as well as by a conflict between increased aspirations and conditions of the social structure. The new condition of mobility was compatible with the individualistic ideology, and it was at the same time incompatible with political absolutism.[33] In the first place, the large family and the homogeneous neighborhood, which had been the principal agencies of social control, disintegrated, primarily as a result of mobility. They were replaced by the small family, consisting of parents and children, detached from other relatives, and by a neighborhood in which the mores were not homogeneous. Many family functions were transferred to other social institutions, resulting in a weak family unit in which the members had relatively few activities or interests in common. Similarly, the neighborhood ceased to function as an effective socializing agency in which the pressures for conformity were intimate, personal, and consistent.

Second, with increased mobility the problem of control was greatly intensified, for the boundaries of frequent and effective interaction were extended from the local community to nations and then to most of the earth in the form of commerce, travel, newspapers, and other means of communication. When interaction was confined to the local community, spontaneous and sentimental influences controlled behavior, for the effect of the behavior of a person was immediately apparent to himself and to others. When interaction extended beyond the area of intimate association, the effects of the behavior were not immediately discernible either to the members of any local community or to the participants in the broader area of interaction. Because of increased mobility, a condition of anonymity was created, and the agencies by which control had been secured in almost all earlier societies were greatly weakened. It is probable that the family and neighborhood would have been relatively impotent to control their members in activities with outsiders, even if they had been retained in their original strength, for these agencies cannot be effective in the control of behavior occurring far away from their location. A certain national loyalty, somewhat com-

Mobility

---

[32] Richard A. Cloward, "Illegitimate Means, Anomie, and Deviant Behavior," *American Sociological Review*, 24:164-176, April, 1959. See also Albert K. Cohen and James F. Short, Jr., "Research in Delinquent Subcultures," *Journal of Social Issues*, vol. 14 (1958), no. 3, pp. 20-37.

[33] Seymour M. Lipset and Reinhard Bendix, *Social Mobility in Industrial Society* (Berkeley: University of California Press, 1959).

parable to the loyalties in the earlier primary groups, flourished in connection with the doctrine of the divinity of royalty, but apparently the common people did not take this doctrine as seriously as did royalty, and when the belief in the doctrine disintegrated, no effective substitute was found.

We may conclude that mobility of persons and of commodities widens the area within which control becomes necessary and at the same time weakens the local agencies of control in the communities into which the migrants move. However, this conclusion is not based on sufficient evidence to justify a definitive statement regarding the significance of mobility to criminality. It is possible that rapid changes in technology may create conditions under which the criminal laws, written for social conditions as they existed before the technological changes, must almost necessarily be violated if the new technologies are to be retained.[34] Certain students of law, on the other hand, have insisted that the prevalence of crime is due to the fact that the law has been extended much more rapidly than the general mores, and that when the law is not thus supported by general mores it is relatively important and is violated frequently. In either case, the most relevant variable is the normative conflict which has arisen to provide alternative patterns of conduct, some of which are clearly violations of the criminal law.[35]

A few studies of the relationship between horizontal mobility and the crime rate have been made, most of them in the 1930s, but they have been directed toward analysis of the direct effects of mobility in a contemporary situation. They fail to measure the full significance of mobility, for the effects of this process on criminality are principally indirect and are diffused over a period of time and over a wide area.[36] The data are presented, however, as illustrations of the first efforts to study this process. McKenzie found a correlation of 0.39 between juvenile delinquency and mobility by wards in Columbus, and Sullenger found a correlation of 0.34 in a similar study in Omaha.[37] Carpenter concluded that a criminal group studied in Buffalo was much more migratory than a control group in the same city.[38] A more recent study, of a sample of 787 Dutch children, showed that children who had never moved had the lowest delinquency rates, that those who had moved 1-3 times had intermediate rates, and

[34] W. F. Ogburn, *Social Change*, 2d ed. (New York: Viking Press, 1952), pt. 4.

[35] See Weinberg, "Urbanization and Male Delinquency in Ghana."

[36] O. Kinberg, "On So-Called Vagrancy," *Journal of Criminal Law and Criminology*, 24:552-583, September-October, 1933.

[37] R. D. McKenzie, "The Neighborhood," *American Journal of Sociology*, 28: 166, September, 1921; T. E. Sullenger, *Social Determinants in Juvenile Delinquency* (New York: John Wiley, 1936), p. 179. See also his, "The Social Significance of Mobility: An Omaha Study," *American Journal of Sociology*, 55:559-564, May, 1950.

[38] Niles Carpenter and William M. Haenszel, "Migratoriness and Criminality in Buffalo," *Social Forces*, 9:254-255, December, 1930.

that children who had moved four or more times had the highest delinquency rates.[39] Reiss showed that 39 percent of a group of delinquent probationers in Chicago had resided at their present address for less than three years, and the Gluecks found that 33.6 percent of their delinquents, as compared with only 14.8 percent of the nondelinquents, were at their present address for less than one year.[40]

These statistics give some understanding of the reason why the word *traveler* in medieval England was used in popular discourse to designate the thief. Such statistics, however, are entirely inadequate as demonstrations of the significance of horizontal mobility, for the important point is that mobility has affected all persons in modern society and not merely those who are nonresidents at the time of a crime. ●

Like "social disorganization," the concept "culture conflict" has been used to refer to social conditions characterized by a lack of consistency and harmony in the influences which direct the individual. The concept has not been clearly formulated, however, for it sometimes is used as a synonym for "normative conflict" and sometimes is restricted to only the normative conflict arising from migration of conduct norms from one area to another.[41] Here, we shall use the term in the latter sense, to refer to a special kind of normative conflict. As we have seen, normative conflict can develop *within* a culture, without the introduction of norms from other cultural areas. It also can arise when the norms of one cultural area come into conflict with those of another. Most of the American research on the relationships between "culture conflict" and crime has been concerned with normative conflict arising in the latter process, the interpenetration of cultural codes. This emphasis no doubt reflects an interest in America's "immigrant problem."

Culture conflict

Conflicts between the norms of behavior of divergent cultural codes may arise in at least three ways.[42] First, the codes may clash on the border of contiguous culture areas. Speck observed, for example, that:

> Where the bands popularly known as the Montagnais have come more and more into contact with Whites, their reputation has fallen lower among the traders who have known them through commercial relationships within that period. The accusation is made that they have become less honest in connection with their debts, less trust-

[39] W. Buikhuisen and H. Timmerman, "Verhuizing en Criminaliteit" [Moving and Crime], *Nederlands Tijdschrift voor Criminologie*, 12:34-39, March, 1970.

[40] Albert J. Reiss, Jr., "The Accuracy, Efficiency, and Validity of a Prediction Instrument," *American Journal of Sociology*, 56:552-561, May, 1951. Sheldon and Eleanor T. Glueck, *Unraveling Juvenile Delinquency* (New York: Commonwealth Fund, 1950), p. 80.

[41] See Donald R. Cressey, "Culture Conflict, Differential Association, and Normative Conflict," chap. 4 in Marvin E. Wolfgang, ed., *Crime and Culture: Essays in Honor of Thorsten Sellin* (New York: John Wiley, 1968), pp. 43-54.

[42] Sellin, *Culture Conflict and Crime*, pp. 63-67.

worthy with property, less truthful, and more inclined to alcoholism and sexual freedom as contacts with the frontier towns have become easier for them.[43]

With increased mobility and the development of communication processes, the "border" between such divergent cultures has become extremely broad, for knowledge concerning divergent conduct norms no longer arises solely out of direct personal contacts. The old social relations and standards of behavior which had been adequate for control while Palestine was relatively isolated from the rest of the world have proved inadequate in more recent years, when the cultures of other groups have been introduced into Israel through impersonal means. Remarkable changes in criminality have occurred.[44] Similar effects have also been observed in South Africa:

> An important factor in producing criminal behavior is culture conflict. This discontinuity is seen in the movement of hundreds of thousands of Bantus from the "Veld," the native reserves, and even other parts of Africa to the cities where a new set of physical and personal associations surrounds the individual. There is a breakdown in primary controls that follows detribalization with the introduction of cash economy, accelerated mobility, personal anonymity, and new leisure time pursuits. . . . One aspect of nonconforming behavior has been gang life among the (African) juvenile offenders.[45]

In the United States, Evelyn Crook found that 86 percent of the delinquent girls who were studied resided on racial or language "frontiers," where two or more racial groups came in contact, and only 14 percent resided in the interior of a racial or language group. In Israel, 42 percent of the prostitutes in a research sample were found to be immigrants from North Africa; North Africans comprised 50 percent of the foreign born in the sample, but only 13 percent in the total population.[46]

Second, in "colonization" the laws and norms of one cultural group may be extended to cover the territory of another, with the result that traditional ways of behaving suddenly become illegal. For example, when Soviet law was extended to Siberian tribes, women who obeyed the Soviet law and laid aside their veils were killed by their relatives for violating the norms of the tribes. Wearing a veil was illegal from the point of view of Soviet law, and not wearing a veil was illegal from the point of view of tribal law. Similarly, before French law was introduced in Algeria, the killing of an adulterous woman was the right and

---

[43] Speck, "Ethical Attributes of Labrador Indians," p. 561.

[44] See Shlomo Shoham, "Culture Conflict as a Frame of Reference for Research in Criminology and Social Deviation," chap. 5 in Wolfgang, Crime and Culture, pp. 55-82.

[45] R. Williamson, "Crime in South Africa: Some Aspects of Causes and Treatment," Journal of Criminal Law, Criminology, and Police Science, 48:185-192, July-August, 1957.

[46] Evelyn B. Crook, "Cultural Marginality in Sexual Delinquency," American Journal of Sociology, 39:493-500, January, 1934; Shoham, op. cit., p. 79.

duty of the woman's father or brother; but under the French law such killing became a crime, punishable by death.

Third, when participants in one culture migrate to another culture, they may take with them ways of behaving which clash with the norms of the receiving culture. This process is the reverse of the one just discussed, and it occurs when the migrant group is politically weaker than the group whose territory is invaded. If the Algerians in the above illustration had moved to France, they would have introduced divergent norms in that nation.

After a period of dominance by English customs and laws, many conflicting norms were introduced in the United States by this process. Generally, the immigrant population, having reached maturity in the Old World environment, remains relatively isolated and has a relatively low crime rate when the immigrants settle in America, but some studies show that the sons of immigrants have a much higher crime rate than their parents or the native-born of native parentage, apparently because the second generation, like the Siberian women, finds it difficult to identify the proper ways of behaving. Also, some studies, though not all, have concluded that the native-born children with one parent native-born and the other foreign-born have a higher rate than native-born children with both parents foreign-born or both parents native-born, and this also seems to be due to the greater divergence of norms in those cases. •

Tendencies toward integration

The individualistic system in business and poltics has been modified in the last generation or two in its material aspects. Free competition was ruining individuals, and they were driven into collective activities. Huge corporations, huge banks, chain stores, chain theaters, chain newspapers, and broadcasting companies have developed. Trade associations, trade unions, chambers of commerce, and many other associations have also been formed. To an increasing extent, the behavior and opportunities of individuals are determined and defined by these collectivities and associations. Thus, the general development has been from feudalism and absolutism to individualism, and from individualism to private and public collectivism. But the transition from individualism has been confined principally to material effects. Corporations and associations have no more interest in general social welfare than did the competing individuals who preceded them. The ideology of individualism still remains in a world of corporate activity. This may be seen in the frequency with which the directors and officers of corporations are traitors to their stockholders, in the competition between associations for financial advantages, and in many other ways.

Four tendencies toward social integration, aside from the corporate activities described above, may be discovered in the modern world. First, a wider uniformity of behavior and a greater degree of identification of self with others are secured by newspapers, radio, theaters, television, and public education. This interest, however, is restricted in scope or is concerned with ephemeral incidents. Its importance may be indicated in relation to bribery of athletes. In 1919, when a notorious gambler and gangster bribed some of the baseball players in the world series to throw the game, a tremendous pressure for punishment of the players and the briber was exerted. Bribery of a member of the president's cabinet provoked less popular antagonism than the bribery of these baseball players. An almost identical reaction to bribery of college basketball players occurred thirty years later. The players were dismissed, and in some states laws were enacted which made the penalty for giving bribes in athletic contests more severe than the penalty for robbery with a gun. On this point, the public, or that part of it which counted in athletics, presented a united front. It is possible that baseball or some other sport could become the nucleus around which public morality may be unified, as has been claimed of cricket in England; but in general the public interests, like the communication media which largely create them, are fluctuating, unstable, and concerned with unimportant things.

A second tendency toward uniformity of thought and attitudes is seen in the recent artificial efforts to develop nationalism in Europe, as in the Nazi regime in Germany, Fascism in Italy, Sovietism in Russia, and dictatorships in other countries. These movements, like the New Deal in the United States, were gropings toward social organization to replace the individualism which had broken down or was breaking down economically, legally, and politically.

Third, the rise of suburban living in the United States, a leveling-off of the birth rate, and the near-elimination of immigration should permit the development of a cultural homogeneity that has not been possible since the early nineteenth century. The passing of the population-expansion phase of our history, together with industrial decentralization, may lead to a cessation of city growth, may permit the development of neighborhoods and residential suburbs of a primary-group type, and may reduce the speculative aspect of economic life.

A fourth tendency toward homogeneity may be found in the development of scientific activities and intellectual honesty. The number of scientific people in modern society is not large, but the results of science have permeated all society to a greater or lesser extent. The attitude of scientific inquiry is an important variable to be considered in analysis of changes in some of the old institutions. A characteristic of the changes in social organization described earlier was their incompatibility with intellectual honesty.[47] ●

---

[47] Noam Chomsky, "The Responsibility of Intellectuals," *The New York Review of Books*, February 23, 1967; and Kai T. Erikson, "Sociology: That Awkward Age," *Social Problems*, 19:431-436, Spring, 1972.

ARNOLD, THURMAN. *The Folklore of Capitalism.* New Haven: Yale University Press, 1937.

BARRON, MILTON L. "Juvenile Delinquency and American Values." *American Sociological Review,* 16:208-214, April, 1951.

BELL, DANIEL. "Crime as an American Way of Life." *Antioch Review,* 13:131-154, June, 1953.

BLAKE, JUDITH, & KINGSLEY DAVIS. "Norms, Values, and Sanctions." Chapter 13 in *Handbook of Modern Sociology,* edited by Robert E. L. Faris, pp. 456-484. Chicago: Rand McNally, 1964.

BORDUA, DAVID J. "Delinquent Subcultures: Sociological Interpretations of Gang Delinquency." *Annals of the American Academy of Political and Social Science,* 338:119-136, November, 1961.

CLINARD, MARSHALL B. *The Black Market: A Study of White Collar Crime.* New York: Rinehart, 1952.

CLOWARD, RICHARD A. "Illegitimate Means, Anomie, and Deviant Behavior." *American Sociological Review,* 24:164-176, April, 1959.

CLOWARD, RICHARD A., & LLOYD E. OHLIN. *Delinquency and Opportunity: A Theory of Delinquent Gangs.* Glencoe, Ill.: Free Press, 1960.

COHEN, ALBERT K. *Delinquent Boys: The Culture of the Gang.* Glencoe, Ill.: Free Press, 1955.

DE FLEUR, LOIS B. *Delinquency in Argentina: A Study of Cordoba's Youth.* Pullman, Wash.: Washington State University Press, 1970.

DEWEY, JOHN. "Individualism, Old and New." *New Republic,* 61:239-241, 294-296; 62:13-16, 184-188, January-April, 1930.

DURKHEIM, EMILE. *Suicide: A Study in Sociology.* Translated by John A. Spaulding and George Simpson. Glencoe, Ill.: Free Press, 1951.

HALL, A. C. *Crime in Its Relation to Social Progress.* New York: Columbia University Press, 1902.

KATZ, ELIHU, MARTIN L. LEVIN, & HERBERT HAMILTON. "Traditions of Research on the Diffusion of Innovation." *American Sociological Review,* 28:237-252, April, 1963.

MATZA, DAVID, & GRESHAM M. SYKES. "Juvenile Delinquency and Subterranean Values." *American Sociological Review,* 26:712-719, October, 1961.

MILLER, WALTER B. "Subculture, Social Reform and the 'Culture of Poverty'." *Human Organization,* 30:111-125, Summer, 1971.

RHODES, H. T. F. *The Criminals We Deserve.* London: Methuen, 1937.

SELLIN, THORSTEN. *Culture Conflict and Crime.* New York: Social Science Research Council, 1938.

SHORT, JAMES F., JR., & FRED L. STRODTBECK. *Group Process and Gang Delinquency.* Chicago: University of Chicago Press, 1965.

Suggested readings

SPERGEL, IRVING. *Racketville, Slumtown, Haulburg: An Explor-atory Study of Delinquent Subcultures.* Chicago: University of Chicago Press, 1964.

SZABO, DENIS (en collaboration avec Marc LeBlanc, Lise Deslau-riers et Denis Gagné). "Interprétations Psycho-Culturelles de L'Inadaptation Juvénile dans la Société de Masse Contempo-raine." *Acta Criminologica,* 1:9-134, January, 1968.

VEBLEN, THORSTEIN. *Theory of the Leisure Class.* New York: Macmillan, 1912.

WEBER, MAX. *The Protestant Ethic and the Spirit of Capitalism.* Translated by Talcott Parsons. London: Allen and Unwin, 1930.

WEINBERG, S. KIRSON. "Urbanization and Male Delinquency in Ghana." *Journal of Research in Crime and Delinquency,* 2:85-94, July, 1965.

WIRTH, LOUIS. "Culture Conflicts and Delinquency." *Social Forces,* 9:484-492, June, 1931.

WIRTH, LOUIS. "Urbanism as a Way of Life." *American Journal of Sociology,* 44:1-24, July, 1938.

WOLFGANG, MARVIN E., ed. *Crime and Culture: Essays in Honor of Thorsten Sellin.* New York: John Wiley, 1968.

WOOD, ARTHUR L. "Political Radicalism in Changing Sinhalese Villages." *Human Organization,* 23:99-107, Summer, 1964.

Physical and physiological conditions

6

Although crime and criminality are by definition social phenom-ena, men have for centuries entertained the notion that they are the products of nonsocial causes. This notion has been expressed in many essays and research studies on the relationship between crime rates and certain physical conditions of the earth, and on the relationship between criminality and certain aspects of the biological makeup of the criminal. The data have been largely confined to arrest and incarceration rates and to criminals who are arrested and prosecuted; the white-collar criminal and the unap-prehended criminal are not represented. This chapter shows how some, but not all, physical and physiological conditions affect social status, self-identification, and social interaction, thus affect-ing ratios of association with criminal behavior patterns and anti-criminal behavior patterns. ●

Physical environment

For many generations, scholars have attempted to find relation-ships between crime and physical conditions, which would enable them to "demonstrate" physical determinants of criminal behavior. They have reported that crimes against property are more frequent in winter months and that crimes against the person are more frequent in summer months; and, analogous to this, that crimes against property increase, and crime against the person decrease, with the distance from the equator.[1] It has been claimed also that crime rates vary with changes in barometric pressure and with direction of the wind.[2] Other scholars have reported that crimes are frequent in mountainous areas and infrequent in plains areas, or are frequent near the coast and infrequent in the interior.

These reports and claims may be appraised in two propositions. First, the association between crime rates and these physical conditions at best is slight; in some cases not even a slight association has been demonstrated.[3] Second, these physical conditions provide the habitat for human life and consequently may facilitate or impede contacts among human beings and perhaps in that sense be related to opportunities for criminal behavior.[4] For example, the greater frequency of crimes against the person in summer months is presumably due to the greater frequency of contacts among human beings in those months. Some years ago, Schmid reported that in Seattle homicides reach the maximum in the winter and explained that this was due to the influx of migratory laborers in the late autumn.[5] It has not been demonstrated that changes in physical conditions change either the attitudes and values which are conducive to criminal behavior or the attitudes and values conducive to noncriminal behavior. ●

Heredity

In the early part of the present century the discussion of causes of crime was concentrated on the controversy between heredity and environment, and this controversy continues, with decreasing attention, in the present generation. Five methods have been used in the effort to reach conclusions on the question of whether criminality is hereditary: comparison of criminals with the

---

[1] The research studies on this point are reviewed in G. Aschaffenburg, *Crime and Its Repression* (Boston: Little, Brown, 1913), pp. 16-30; Gerhard J. Falk, "The Influence of the Seasons on the Crime Rate," *Journal of Criminal Law, Criminology, and Police Science*, 43:199-213, July-August, 1952; and Sidney J. Kaplan, "The Geography of Crime," in Joseph S. Roucek, ed., *Sociology of Crime* (New York: Philosophical Library, 1961), pp. 160-192.

[2] G. A. Mills, "Suicide and Homicide in Their Relation to Weather Changes," *American Journal of Psychiatry*, 91:669-677, November, 1934; Manfred Curry, "The Relationship of Weather Conditions, Facial Characteristics, and Crime," *Journal of Criminal Law and Criminology*, 39:253-261, July-August, 1948.

[3] Ernest LaRoche and Louis Tillery, "Weather and Crime in Tallahassee during 1954," *Journal of Criminal Law, Criminology, and Police Science*, 47:218-219, July-August, 1956; Alex D. Pokorny and Fred Davis, "Homicide and Weather," *American Journal of Psychiatry*, 120:806-808, February, 1964.

[4] Henry Allen Bullock, "Urban Homicide in Theory and Fact," *Journal of Criminal Law, Criminology, and Police Science*, 45:565-575, January-February, 1955.

[5] C. F. Schmid, "A Study of Homicides in Seattle," *Social Forces*, 4:745-756, June, 1926.

"savage," family trees, Mendelian ratios in family trees, statistical associations between crimes of parents and of offspring, and comparison of identical and fraternal twins.

Lombroso and his followers used comparisons of criminals and "savages" as their method of studying inheritance of criminality.[6] They held that the typical criminal was a born criminal and attributed this to atavism, or throwback to lower animal and savage life. Their principal evidence that criminality was atavistic was the resemblance of the criminal subjects to the savage, but the characteristics of the savage were assumed, not determined by reliable methods. The result was that Lombroso had no significant proof or explanation of the inheritance of criminality.

Family trees have been used extensively by certain scholars in the effort to prove that criminality is inherited. Perhaps the most famous example is the study of the Jukes family by Dugdale and Estabrook, who reported that of about 1,200 members of this family, 140 were criminals, 7 were convicted of murder, 60 of theft, and 50 of prostitution.[7] Dugdale's methods were so questionable that his conclusions have been roundly denounced.[8] Nevertheless, in the early part of the current century the descendants of Jonathan Edwards, a famous preacher during the colonial period, often were compared with the Jukes family. None of Edwards' descendants were said to be criminals, while many were presidents of the United States, governors of states, members of the Supreme Court and of other high courts, and famous writers, preachers, teachers. The specific difficulty about this comparison is that some of Jonathan Edwards' ancestors did have criminal records. His maternal grandmother was divorced on the ground of adultery, his grandaunt murdered her son; his granduncle murdered his own sister. If criminality be inherited, Jonathan Edwards and many of his descendants should have been criminals. The more general argument against a conclusion from the study of family trees is that it shows only that a trait appears in successive generations; this does not prove that the trait is inherited. The use of the fork in eating has been a trait of many families for several generations, but this does not prove that a tendency to use a fork is inherited. Dahlström showed that in a family of criminals whose records for four generations were known, six children removed from the family before the age of seven became respectable members of society, and two removed after the age of seven became criminals.[9]

Over sixty years ago, Goring attempted to prove by elaborate correlations that the criminalistic tendency is inherited, and that

---

[6] See above, pp. 52-55.

[7] Richard Dugdale, The Jukes: A Study in Crime, Pauperism, and Heredity (New York: Putnam, 1877); A. H. Estabrook, The Jukes in 1915 (Washington: Carnegie Institution, 1916).

[8] Samuel H. Adams, "The Juke Myth," Saturday Review, 38:13, 48-49, April 2, 1955.

[9] Sigürd Dahlström, "Is the Young Criminal a Continuation of the Neglected Child?" Journal of Delinquency, 12:97-121, June, 1928.

environmental conditions are of slight importance to criminality. He found that criminality, measured by imprisonment, of fathers and sons was correlated by a coefficient of +.60, which is very nearly the same as the coefficient for stature, span, length of forearm, eye color, and other physical traits; brothers had a coefficient of correlation for criminality of +.45, which also is approximately the same as for physical traits.[10] Goring reasoned that if the influence of environmental factors on his two correlations were very low, heredity would, by elimination, be the explanation. He divided environmental factors into "contagion" and "force of circumstances," such as poverty and ignorance, and his argument regarding them is as follows: (a) The resemblance of fathers and sons regarding criminality is not due to "contagion." First, the coefficient of correlation is no higher in crimes of stealing, in which fathers are examples for their sons, than in sex crimes, which fathers ordinarily attempt to conceal from their sons, and in which therefore they are not examples. Second, children taken away from the influence of parents at an early age, by imprisonment, become confirmed criminals to a greater extent than those taken at a later age. (b) This resemblance is not due to the "force of circumstances" because, after the influence of defective intelligence is eliminated by the use of partial correlations, the correlation between criminality and "force of circumstances" is negligible.

The defects in Goring's arguments undermined his conclusion that criminality is inherited. The following are the principal defects: (a) He did not measure the influence of "environment." He considered only eight environmental factors, which are a relatively small part of the total environment. (b) He assumed that mental ability is hereditary. (c) His comparison of stealing and sex offenses is based on an assumption that parental contagion is restricted entirely to techniques of crimes, and he did not consider the possibility that transmission of more general values is more important. (d) The removal of a child from the home to prison at an early age does not remove the child from a criminalistic to a noncriminalistic environment, as Goring assumed. (e) He restricted his study to male criminals, although he mentions the fact that the ratio of brothers to sisters in respect to imprisonment is 102 to 6. If criminality is inherited to the same extent that color of the eyes is inherited, it must affect females to the same extent as males unless it is sex-linked. Since, according to Goring, the criminal diathesis consists entirely of physical and mental inferiority, sex linkage is not plausible.

The fifth method of measuring the relation of heredity to criminality is the comparison of identical twins, which are the product of a single egg, with fraternal twins, which are the product of two eggs fertilized by two sperms. Heredity is assumed to be identical in the former and different in the latter. Lange made a study of

---

[10] Charles Goring, *The English Convict* (London: His Majesty's Stationery Office, 1913), p. 369.

thirty pairs of adult male twins; thirteen of the pairs were identical twins, and seventeen fraternal twins. One member of each pair was a criminal, and whenever the twin was also criminal, the pair was termed "concordant." The problem was to determine whether concordance would be more frequent among the group of identical twins than among the group of fraternal twins. He found that 77 percent of the pairs of identical twins and only 12 percent of the pairs of fraternal twins were concordant, that is, both criminal. The similarity of identical twins with reference to criminality was thus 6.4 times as great as the similarity of fraternal twins.[11] This great similarity was assumed to be a measure of the inheritance of criminality, but it is subject to skepticism on two points. First, the number of cases of each type is very small, and a shift of one or two cases from one category to the other would produce a significant difference in the conclusions. Second, the classification of a particular pair of twins as identical or fraternal must be doubtful in many cases, since evidence as to the birth process is seldom available.

Lange's work was hailed as proof of the inheritance of criminality. However, three later studies of twins in European countries by methods similar to those of Lange show for all the cases in the three studies that the frequency of similarity in criminal behavior among identical twins was only 1.4 times as great as the frequency among fraternal twins.[12] One of the most extensive studies of the criminality of twins was later made by Rosanoff and others on adult criminality, juvenile delinquency, and child behavior problems. This study showed, for all types of cases combined, approximately three times as much concordance among identical twins as fraternal twins.[13] The procedures in this study, however, are so inaccurate that the conclusions are worthless. This may be illustrated with reference to the juvenile delinquents in the study. A juvenile delinquent was rigorously defined as a child under eighteen years of age brought before the juvenile court on a delinquency petition and either placed on probation or committed to a correctional institution. According to the brief descriptions given in the Rosanoff report, all delinquents of the fraternal type conform to this definition, while nine of the twenty-nine male juvenile delinquents of the identical-twin type fail to conform to the definition, and consequently should not be included as concordant cases. If correction be made for those cases which do not conform to the definition, concordance appears among identical twins only 1.1 times as frequently as it appears among fraternal twins.

[11] Johannes Lange, Verbrechen als Schicksal (Leipzig: Thieme, 1919); trans. by Charlotte Haldane, with the title Crime and Destiny (New York: Boni, 1930).

[12] A. M. Legras, Psychose en Criminaliteit bei Tweelingen (Utrecht: Kemink, 1932); F. Stumpfl, Die Ursprünge des Verbrechens (Leipzig: Thieme, 1936); Heinrich Kranz, Lebensschicksale Krimineller Zwillinge (Berlin: Springer, 1936).

[13] A. J. Rosanoff, Leva M. Handy, and Isabel A. Rosanoff, "Etiology of Child Behavior Difficulties, Juvenile Delinquency, and Adult Criminality," Psychiatric Monographs, no. 1 (Sacramento: California Department of Institutions, 1941).

This difference is not sufficiently great to create a presumption of inheritance.

The most extensive study of twins is now being completed by Christiansen in Denmark. All six thousand pairs of twins born in Denmark between 1880 and 1910 are being studied. A preliminary report indicates that the name of at least one member of nine hundred pairs of these twins had by 1968 been entered in Denmark's Central Police Register.[14] Concordance was found in 36 percent of 67 pairs of one-egg male twins and in 12 percent of 114 pairs of two-egg male twins, in 21 percent of 14 pairs of one-egg female twins and in 4 percent of 23 pairs of two-egg twins, and in 4 percent of 226 pairs of two-egg male-female twins. Concordance, whether of one-egg or two-egg twins, was higher for serious crimes than for minor offenses, for females than for males, and for twins reared in rural districts as compared with twins reared in urban areas.

Even if a difference between the two types of twins in reference to concordance in criminality be accepted, the conclusion that criminality is inherited does not necessarily follow. The difference between the two types of twins may be explained in whole or in part by the fact that the environments of identical twins are more nearly alike, psychologically, than the environments of fraternal twins. Because of the difficulty of distinguishing one identical twin from the other, the reactions of other persons toward identical twins will be more nearly alike than the reactions of others toward fraternal twins.[15] These reactions of others are the most important part of the "environment." In general, therefore, the study of twins has failed as completely as other procedures to demonstrate the inheritance of criminality.

Some recent research has indicated that sex chromosome imbalances are disproportionately represented among patients in mental hospitals, and this finding has led to a flurry of studies of criminals. The general hypothesis is that an extra Y chromosome, or more, in males causes the individual to be uncontrollably aggressive. However, it has not been shown that chromatin abnormality produces criminality, or even aggressiveness. A recent review of research concluded: "XYY males in an institutional setting are *less* violent or aggressive when compared to matched chromosomally normal fellow inmates; and their criminal histories involve crimes against property rather than person."[16]

---

14 Karl O. Christiansen, "Threshold of Tolerance in Various Population Groups Illustrated By Results From Danish Criminological Twin Study," in A. V. S. Reuck and Ruth Porter, eds., *Ciba Foundation Symposium on the Mentally Abnormal Offender* (London: J. and A. Churchill, 1968), pp. 107-116.

15 Ernest R. Mowrer, "Some Factors in the Affectional Adjustment of Twins," *American Sociological Review*, 16:468-471, August, 1954; H. H. Newman, *Multiple Human Births: Twins, Triplets, Quadruplets, and Quintuplets* (New York: Doubleday, 1940), p. 160.

16 Richard S. Fox, "The XYY Offender: A Modern Myth?", *Journal of Criminal Law, Criminology, and Police Science*, 62:59-73, March, 1971. See also Theodore R. Sarbin and Jeffrey E. Miller, "Demonism Revisited: The XYY Chromosomal Anomaly," *Issues in Criminology*, 5:195-207, Summer, 1970.

Two positive propositions and one negative proposition can be stated as conclusions regarding the relation of heredity to crime. *First,* criminals, like all human beings, have some inherited traits which make it possible for them to behave like human beings. This proposition, however, does not aid in explaining why some human beings commit crimes and others do not. *Second,* some inherited characteristics may be significantly related to criminal behavior by virtue of the fact that members of a society have learned to react to them in a certain way. For example, the color of the skin of the Negro is reacted to in a certain way in the United States, and the crime rate is high among Negroes. But this proposition is not relevant to explaining criminality on the basis of heredity, for traits which are not inherited may be reacted to in a significant way and may likewise be associated with criminal behavior. The *third* proposition is that, except in the two senses previously stated, heredity has not been demonstrated to have any connection whatever with criminal behavior. If persons with certain inherited traits are more likely to commit crimes than persons with other inherited traits, these traits have not been identified, and their connection with criminal behavior has not been demonstrated.[17] It is obviously impossible for criminality to be inherited as such, for crime is defined by acts of legislatures, and these vary independently of the biological inheritance of the violators of the laws. ●

Anatomical conditions

Lombroso insisted that criminals differed from noncriminals with reference to certain physical traits which he called "stigmata of degeneracy." He found these physical deviations in all parts of the anatomy, but placed particular emphasis on deviations in the shape of the cranium. Goring made careful measurements of several thousand prisoners in comparison with the general population and reached the conclusion that prisoners differed anatomically from the general population only in being slightly shorter in stature and slightly lighter in weight. Goring's work is generally accepted as having demolished the early Lombrosian view that criminals are characterized by certain stigmata and constitute an inferior biological type. However, in the late 1930s Hooton, an American anthropologist, attempted to revive the Lombrosian theory. He made elaborate measurements of thousands of prisoners and of a few nonprisoners. He found some differences between the two classes and concluded that "the primary cause of crime is biological inferiority."[18]

---

[17] Cf. M. F. Ashley Montagu, "The Biologist Looks at Crime," *Annals of the American Academy of Political and Social Science,* 217:46-57, September, 1941; L. S. Penrose, "Genetics and the Criminal," *British Journal of Delinquency,* vol. 6 (1955), no. 1, pp. 15-25.

[18] E. A. Hooton, *Crime and the Man* (Cambridge, Mass.: Harvard University Press, 1939), p. 130. See also idem, *The American Criminal: An Anthropological Study* (Cambridge, Mass.: Harvard University Press, 1939).

Three principal criticisms of Hooton's procedures and conclusions have been made. *First*, his control groups were so small and so selected that they were worthless as a sample of the noncriminal population, and, consequently, he had no means of showing that criminals differ from noncriminals. Other studies have generally reached the conclusion that criminals are not significantly different in physical traits from noncriminals.[19] *Second*, he found few significant differences between criminals and noncriminals and used a surprisingly large number of measurements which were practically identical. *Third*, he had no criterion of biological inferiority. He apparently assumed that persons who were imprisoned were inferior; by this logic males should be appraised as biologically inferior to females, since a larger proportion of males are imprisoned. A sociologist and a biologist pointed out that Hooton's criminals differed from the anthropoid apes in more respects than did the control groups; if similarity to anthropoid apes be accepted as a criterion of inferiority, the noncriminals are the inferior group, and the criminals the superior group.[20]

The general body build, or somatotype, also has received considerable attention as a possible explanation of criminal behavior.[21] Kretschmer developed a classification of somatotypes in relation to psychoses and general personality. Attempts have been made to use Kretschmer's classification in the study of criminals, but thus far no relationship has been found between his body types and criminal behavior.

Sheldon also attempted to differentiate criminals from noncriminals on the basis of body type.[22] He found three somatotypes—the endomorphic, which is round and soft; the mesomorphic, which is round and hard; and the ectomorphic, which is thin and fragile—and claimed that three temperamental types and three psychiatric types are closely related with these somatotypes. After making a study of two hundred young adults in a Boston welfare agency, whom he described as "more or less delinquent," he concluded that delinquents are different from nondelinquents in their somatotypes and in their related temperamental and psychiatric types. Also he assumed that these differences are in the direction of inferiority and that the inferiority is inherited. His data, in fact, do not justify the conclusion that the delinquents are different

---

[19] These studies have been reviewed and summarized in W. Norwood East, "Physical Factors in Criminal Behavior," *Journal of Clinical Psychopathy*, 8:7-36, July, 1946.

[20] Robert K. Merton and M. F. Ashley Montagu, "Crime and the Anthropologist," *American Anthropologist*, 42:384-408, August, 1940.

[21] An excellent summary and appraisal of the general morphological theories of criminal behavior has been made by William A. Lessa, "An Appraisal of Constitutional Types," *Memoirs of the American Anthropological Society*, no. 62. (*American Anthropologist*, vol. 45, no. 4, pt. 2, 1943); and "Somatomancy — Precursor of the Science of Human Constitution," *Scientific Monthly*, 75:355-365, December, 1952.

[22] William H. Sheldon, *Varieties of Delinquent Youth: An Introduction to Constitutional Psychiatry* (New York: Harpers, 1949).

from the nondelinquents in general, the conclusion that the difference, if it exists, indicates inferiority, or the conclusion that the inferiority, if it exists, is inherited.[23]

The Gluecks used the logic of Kretschmer and Sheldon in a study of juvenile delinquents.[24] Like Sheldon, they have adopted a system characterized by a noted physical anthropologist as a "new Phrenology in which the bumps of the buttocks take the place of the bumps on the skull."[25] ●

Physical and physiological defects

Physical defects such as blindness, deafness, and lameness are sometimes regarded as important in relation to delinquency and criminality. These physical defects may be due to heredity, to antenatal conditions, to difficulties in the birth process, and to postnatal conditions. Regardless of their origin, their frequency in the criminal population in comparison with the noncriminal population is not known. Optometrists have reported wide differences between delinquents and other schoolchildren in respect to defective vision, and offer the explanation that children with defective vision are more likely to become delinquent because of the physical irritation caused by defective vision and because of the difficulty in reading, which drives them into truancy and gang activities. A Norwegian study found that of all males born in Oslo in 1933, 5 percent had become registered lawbreakers by January 1, 1958. A comparison of the offenders' and nonoffenders' conditions of health revealed only slight differences. For example, 12 percent of the offenders and 9 percent of the nonoffenders had been given medical discharges from military service, and there were insignificant differences in regard to other medical decisions. The differences were all in the same direction, however: The offenders were placed in somewhat lower "grades" of physical fitness. A British study of institutionalized boys found that double the expected proportion had been rejected from military service on physical grounds.[26]

Though physical defects have not been shown to be present in criminal populations to a significantly higher degree than in noncriminal populations, they are significant in some individual cases. However, this significance depends upon the reactions of other

---

[23] Edwin H. Sutherland, "Critique of Sheldon's *Varieties of Delinquent Youth,*" *American Sociological Review,* 16:10-14, February, 1951.

[24] Sheldon and Eleanor T. Glueck, *Physique and Delinquency* (New York: Harper, 1956). See also Sanford J. Fox, "Delinquency and Biology," *University of Miami Law Review,* 16:65-91, Fall, 1961.

[25] S. L. Washburn, "Review of W. H. Sheldon, *Varieties of Delinquent Youth,*" *American Anthropologist,* 53:561-563, December, 1951.

[26] Nils Christie, *Unge Norske Lovovertredere* [Young Norwegian Lawbreakers] (Oslo: Universitetsforlaget, 1960), pp. 211-219, 306-307; T. C. N. Gibbens, *Psychiatric Studies of Borstal Lads* (Oxford: Oxford University Press, 1963).

persons toward the defects.[27] The child with enlarged tonsils who consistently holds his mouth open, the child with crossed eyes, and the child who stutters or lisps may or may not meet ridicule and suffer loss of social status which leads him to identification with delinquents. Both the person with a physical defect and other persons are likely to find the defect irritating, and for the person with the defect the sequence may be of irritation, retardation and dissatisfaction with school or work, truancy, association with delinquents, and a general view of one's self as an outcast.

Undernourishment, disease, and poor health are sometimes reported to be found among criminals in excessive proportions. For example, it has recently been claimed that delinquency, crime, and suicide are all caused by a diet containing too much sugar.[28] While there is no reason to minimize the importance of good diet and health, it is apparent that the connection between crime and physical ailments is not close or necessary.

Other physiological abnormalities which are less evident have also been regarded as important by some writers. During the decade of the twenties popular and semipopular writers placed much emphasis on the endocrine glands as determiners of personality and of criminal behavior. Endocrinologists in general have been much more cautious than these popular writers, and they generally state that no conclusion has been reached regarding the relation between the endocrine glands and criminal behavior.[29] ●

Age ratios in crime

Despite all their limitations, statistics on crime give information important to our understanding of crime and to hypotheses and theories about it. Similarities and differences in crime rates for certain categories of persons are so consistent that a gross relationship between the category and crime can reasonably be concluded to exist. In these cases, it is practical to assume that if the part of an observed relationship which is due merely to the methods of collecting and recording statistics were eliminated, a real relationship would still remain. After specifying this assumption, we can go ahead and use the statistics.

Even if they are gross, relationships which consistently appear and which cannot be readily "explained away" by citing the differential reactions of the persons and agencies manufacturing delinquency and crime statistics must be taken into account in any theory of crime and criminality. There are at least six types

---

[27] Erving Goffman, *Stigma: Notes on the Management of Spoiled Identity* (Englewood Cliffs, N. J.: Prentice-Hall, 1963); Fred Davis, "Deviance Disavowal: The Management of Strained Interaction by the Visibly Handicapped," *Social Problems*, 9:120-132, Fall, 1961.

[28] J. I. Rodale, *Natural Health, Sugar and the Criminal Mind* (New York: Pyramid, 1968).

[29] See, for example, R. G. Hoskins, *Endocrinology* (New York: W. W. Norton, 1941), p. 348; and Edward Podolsky, "The Chemical Brew of Criminal Behavior," *Journal of Criminal Law, Criminology, and Police Science*, 45:675-678, March-April, 1955.

of such consistent relationships that are of great theoretical significance to students of crime and criminality. Age and sex will be discussed here, race and nativity in chapter 7, size of community in chapter 9, and social class in chapter 11.

Many varieties of statistics, in many jurisdictions, in many different years, collected by many types of agencies, uniformly report such a high incidence of crime among young persons, that it may reasonably be assumed that there is a statistically significant difference between the rate of crime among young adults and the rate among other age groups. Statistics are likely to exaggerate the crime rate of young adults: old people may have prestige enough to avoid fingerprinting and arrest, and young children might not be arrested as readily as either young adults or old adults, leaving young adults to bear the responsibility for more than their share of all the crimes committed. But there does seem to be a difference, even if it is not as great as the statistics indicate when they are taken at face value. In this sense, there are two general relationships between age and criminality.

A. The age of maximum general criminality is during or shortly before adolescence. Recent English statistics show that the age category of maximum convictions for indictable crimes is 14-17. While American statistics place this age slightly higher, these statistics are based on fingerprints submitted by local police departments to the Federal Bureau of Investigation, and American police departments seldom take fingerprints of young people. Similarly, in Scandinavian countries, 13-15 is the age of maximum criminality.[30] Table IX shows the American arrest rates for various age groups in 1971.

B. The age of maximum criminality is not the same under all conditions. The extent to which the crime rate among young persons exceeds the crime rate among other age groups varies by offense, sex, place, and time.

1. The age of maximum criminality varies with the type of crime. For example, males aged 15-19 have higher arrest rates for auto theft and burglary than does any other group of males. Table X presents some recent data on the percentages of all arrests which were arrests of young persons. The table shows, for instance, that homicides and assaults are committed by persons who are much older, on the average, than are the persons committing automobile theft and burglary. Persons under the age of 25 constituted 44 percent of all homicide arrests, 76 percent of the arrests for robbery, 80 percent of the arrests for burglary, 73 percent of the arrests for larceny, and 84 percent of the arrests for motor vehicle theft. In a study of homicides committed in Philadelphia between 1948 and 1952, Wolfgang found that the age group 20-24 predominated, with a homicide rate of 12.6 per

---

[30] F. H. McClintock and N. Howard Avison, *Crime in England and Wales* (London: Heinemann, 1968), p. 165; Knut Sveri, *Kriminalitet og Alder* [Criminality and Age] (Stockholm: Almquist and Wiksell, 1960), pp. 80, 161.

TABLE IX

Arrest rates for different age groups—1971
(rates per 100,000 population)[a]

Age groups	Arrest rates for all offenses (excluding traffic)	Arrest rates for willful homicide, forcible rape, robbery, aggravated assault	Arrest rates for larceny, burglary, motor vehicle theft
11 to 14	3,455.7	107.1	1,312.5
15 to 17	9,410.4	354.7	2,636.9
18 to 20	8,549.6	417.4	1,697.5
21 to 24	6,723.5	364.3	954.2
25 to 29	4,974.7	266.8	557.5
30 to 34	4,305.8	197.7	370.7
35 to 39	4,078.0	149.7	265.9
40 to 44	3,790.8	105.8	194.5
45 to 49	3,229.2	71.7	138.0
50 and over	1,457.9	24.5	59.7
Overall rate	3,365.0	131.9	541.6

[a] Population estimates from U.S. Bureau of the Census, *Population—Estimates and Projections* (Washington: Government Printing Office, November, 1971), p. 13.
Source: Federal Bureau of Investigation, U.S. Department of Justice, *Uniform Crime Reports for the United States, 1971* (Washington: Government Printing Office, 1972), pp. 122-123.

TABLE X

Percent of arrests accounted for by different age groups—1971
(percent of total)

Offense charged	Persons 11-17	Persons 18-24	Persons 25 and over
Population[a]	13.9	12.4	52.3
Willful homicide	10.2	33.9	55.5
Forcible rape	20.5	43.5	36.0
Robbery	31.5	44.6	23.1
Aggravated assault	17.0	30.0	52.5
Burglary	47.8	32.4	16.7
Larceny (includes larceny under $50)	47.1	25.5	22.0
Motor vehicle theft	52.6	31.3	15.7
Willful homicide, rape, robbery, aggravated assault	22.2	36.4	40.8
Larceny, burglary, motor vehicle theft	48.0	29.3	19.6

[a] U.S. Bureau of the Census, *Statistical Abstract of the United States, 1972*, 93d ed. (Washington, 1972).
Source: Federal Bureau of Investigation, *Uniform Crime Reports, 1971*, pp. 122-123.

100,000; the median age of the offenders was 31.9.[31] A similar study of homicide in Chicago in 1965 showed the modal age of the offenders to be 20-24.[32]

---

[31] Marvin E. Wolfgang, "A Sociological Analysis of Criminal Homicide," *Federal Probation*, 25:48-55, March, 1961.
[32] Harwin L. Voss and John R. Hepburn, "Patterns in Criminal Homicide in Chicago," *Journal of Criminal Law, Criminology, and Police Science*, 59:499-508, December, 1968.

The type of crimes committed by the adult felons in the California prisons shows a marked variation by age. Among the male felons received in 1969, the highest median age at admission was for the offense group "lewd act with child," 39.6 years. Other high median ages were 36.1 for other sex offenses (excluding rape), and 31.9 years for forgery and checks. The lowest median ages were for robbery (23.9 years) and theft (24.7 years). Among female felons, the highest median age was for the women convicted of homicide, 32.3 years. Women admitted for theft were the second oldest group (31.2 years), and those admitted for burglary were the youngest (28.7 years).[33]

2. The age of maximum criminality varies by sex. Generally speaking, females commit crimes at later ages than do males. In 1971, for example, 50.6 percent of the American males arrested for larceny were under 18 years of age, but 45.5 percent of the females arrested for the same offense were under 18. Yet sex offenses, narcotic drug offenses, crimes against family and children, driving while intoxicated, and homicide and forgery appear earlier in the lives of women than in the lives of men. In 1971, 10.1 percent of the females and 8.1 percent of the males arrested for forgery were under age 18.[34]

3. The age of first delinquency varies from place to place. In areas of high rates of delinquency, the children who become delinquent do so at an earlier age than do the children living in areas with low rates of delinquency.

4. The type of crime most frequently committed by persons of various ages varies from place to place. In some areas of Chicago, delinquent boys between 12 and 13 years old commit burglaries, while in other areas delinquent boys of those ages commit petty larcenies or engage in gang violence. In rural areas, offenders of any specified age are likely to be convicted of crimes different from those committed by offenders of the same age who live in urban areas.

5. For all crimes, and for each specific crime, the rate decreases steadily from the age of maximum criminality to the end of life. This conclusion is derived from the general statistics of many nations, although Pollak has found some conflicting statistics in a study of criminals in Pennsylvania.[35] In the United States, burglary and automobile theft decrease rather regularly after ages 15-19, as does the crime rate generally; homicide decreases rather regularly after ages 20-29, where it is concentrated. Some crimes decrease more dramatically with increasing age than do others;

---

[33] *California Prisoners, 1969* (Sacramento: Department of Corrections, 1972), pp. 36, 38-39.

[34] Federal Bureau of Investigation, *Uniform Crime Reports, 1971* (Washington: Government Printing Office, 1972), p. 120.

[35] Otto Pollak, "Criminality of Old Age," *Public Charities Association [of Pennsylvania] Herald*, 22:4, November, 1945. See also idem, "The Criminality of Old Age," *Journal of Criminal Psychology*, 3:213-235, October, 1941.

for example, the evidence is fairly conclusive that larceny decreases in old age more than do sex offenses.[36]

6. The crime rates among different age groups vary from time to time. Juvenile delinquency rates seem to have increased enormously during the last twenty years in proportion to the crime rates at older ages.

7. Both the probability that a crime will be repeated and the length of time between first and second offenses vary with the age at which the first offense is committed. Generally speaking, the younger a person is when he commits his first offense, the higher the probability that he will commit a second offense and the shorter the interval between first offense and second offense.[37] A recent Danish study found that, in a group of 569 adult male offenders, 70 percent of those whose first offense was committed at age 20 or below had committed at least one additional offense.[38]

8. Juvenile delinquency is probably related in some manner to adult criminal behavior, but it is not correct to say that the juvenile delinquent of today is the adult criminal of tomorrow, as has frequently been stated. The error is due to the fact that practically all juveniles commit delinquencies, but not all of them develop into adult criminals. Moreover, many persons acquire their first formal record of crime after passing the juvenile age. Frum found that the criminal histories of 46 percent of the 319 recidivists in the Indiana Reformatory and State Prison officially started prior to age 18.[39] There is evidence, also, that after about age 25 the percentage of criminals who are first offenders increases with increasing age.

In sum, the available statistics on crime tell us that young persons have higher crime rates than older persons, but that there are variations in the ratio of young persons to old persons in the criminal population. Thus, crime rates vary with age, but in any age group the rates vary with specific social conditions. Age appears to have an important effect, directly or indirectly, on the frequency and type of crime committed.

One of the theories presented as an explanation of the age ratios in crime is that they are due directly to biological traits such as physical strength and vigor: crimes are committed frequently by persons who are strong and active and infrequently

---

[36] David O. Moberg, "Old Age and Crime," *Journal of Criminal Law, Criminology, and Police Science,* 43:764-776, March-April, 1953; Martin Roth, "Cerebral Disease and Mental Disorders of Old Age as Causes of Antisocial Behavior," in A.V.S. Reuck and Ruth Porter, eds., *The Mentally Abnormal Offender* (London: J. and A. Churchill, 1968), pp. 36-37.

[37] Thorsten Sellin, "Recidivism and Maturation," *National Probation and Parole Association Journal,* 4:241-250, July, 1958; Hermann Mannheim and Leslie T. Wilkins, *Prediction Methods in Relation to Borstal Training* (London: Her Majesty's Stationery Office, 1955), p. 64.

[38] Preben Wolf, "A Contribution to the Topology of Crime in Denmark," *Scandinavian Studies in Criminology,* 1 (1965): 201-226.

[39] Harold S. Frum, "Adult Criminal Offense Trends Following Juvenile Delinquency," *Journal of Criminal Law, Criminology, and Police Science,* 49:29-49. May-June, 1958.

by persons who are weak and passive. Another biological theory is that inheritance is the direct cause—persons strongly predisposed by heredity to commit crime do so at a very young age, while those with a weaker tendency delay longer.

These biological theories obviously provide no explanation of many of the variations in the age ratios in crime; indeed, it may be said that they do not explain even one of the facts outlined above when that fact is considered in its ramifications. On the other hand, all of these facts are consistent with the general theory that crime and criminality are products of social experiences and social interaction. It must be agreed, however, that the sociological theories of crime causation have not been sufficiently demonstrated as to any of these facts. •

Sex ratios in crime

Sex status is of greater statistical significance in differentiating criminals from noncriminals than any other trait. If an investigator were asked to use a single trait to predict which persons in a town of 10,000 population would become criminals, he would make the fewest mistakes if he simply chose sex status and predicted criminality for the males and noncriminality for the females. He would be wrong in many cases, for most of the males would not become criminals, and a few of the females would become criminals. But he would be wrong in more cases if he used any other single trait, such as age, race, family background, or a personality characteristic. As is the case with age, there are two general relationships to be observed between crime and sex status.

A. The crime rate for men is greatly in excess of the rate for women—in all nations, all communities within a nation, all age groups, all periods of history for which organized statistics are available, and for all types of crime except those peculiar to women, such as infanticide and abortion.[40] In the United States at present, the rate of arrest of males is about eight times the rate of arrest for females; about fifteen times as many males as females are committed to correctional institutions of all kinds; and about twenty times as many males as females are committed to prisons and reformatories housing serious offenders. Approximately 80 percent of the delinquency cases in juvenile courts are boys. These statistics are supported by studies of self-reported delinquency, but the ratios of males to females in such studies is lower than that indicated by official sources.[41] In 1961, the sex ratio of Canadians convicted of indictable offenses was 1,100; but for sex offenses the ratio was 12,900, for motor-vehicle offenses 5,000, for homicide 1,100, for commercialized vice 250, and for family

---

[40] See Hans Göppinger, *Kriminologie* (Munich: C. H. Beck, 1971), pp. 336-338.
[41] Michael J. Hindelang, "Age, Sex, and the Versatility of Delinquent Involvements," *Social Problems*, 18:522-535, Spring, 1971.

offenses 140.[42] In random samples (3,032 men and 606 women) of Danish citizens who were between the ages of twenty and seventy in 1953, 19 percent of the men and 2 percent of the women were listed in the official registers of criminals in Denmark.[43] Even if correction could be made for the statistical bias in favor of females, the male crime rate probably would still greatly exceed that of females.[44]

B. The extent to which the crime rate among males exceeds the crime rate among females is not the same under all conditions. There are variations in the sex ratio in crime, just as there are variations in the age ratio in crime:

1. The extent to which the rate for males exceeds the rate for females varies from one nation to another. Male criminals are 342 times as numerous as females in Belgium and 2,744 times as numerous in Algiers and Tunis in proportion to the populations of the several groups. In Ceylon, 98 percent of the delinquents placed on probation in 1946-1956 were male.[45] The sex ratio among 807,000 Japanese criminals investigated by the police in 1967 was 1,600; of 3,143 criminals investigated for robbery, only 36 were females.[46] Nine studies in various nations and districts of Africa since 1955 show sex ratios ranging from 20,400 to 900.[47] The female crime rate shows some tendency to approach closest to the male in countries in which females have the greatest freedom and equality with males, such as western Europe, Australia, and the United States, and to vary most from the male rate in countries in which females are closely supervised, such as Algiers.[48] If countries existed in which females were politically and socially dominant, the female rate, according to this trend, should exceed the male rate.

---

[42] P. J. Griffen, "Rates of Crime and Delinquency," chap. 4 in W. T. McGrath, ed., *Crime and its Treatment in Canada* (Toronto: Macmillan, 1965), pp. 59-90.

[43] Wolf, "Contribution to the Topology of Crime in Denmark."

[44] Cf. Otto Pollak, *The Criminality of Women* (Philadelphia: University of Pennsylvania Press, 1950), pp. 44-56, 154; and Bertha J. Payak, "Understanding the Female Offender," *Federal Probation*, 27:7-12, December, 1963.

[45] Ceylon Department of Census and Statistics, *Juvenile Probationers in Ceylon* (Ceylon: Government Press, 1957), p. 10.

[46] Japanese Ministry of Justice, *Statistical Data on Criminality in Japan* (Tokyo, 1970), p. 8. The sex ratio always is expressed as the number of males per 100 females. A ratio over 100 thus means that males exceed females, while a ratio less than 100 means that females exceed males.

[47] G. Houchon, "Les Mécanismes Criminogènes dans une Société Urbaine Africaine," *Revue Internationale Criminologie et de Police Technique,* 21 (1967): 271-292.

[48] E. Hacker, *Kriminalstatistische und Kriminalaetiologische Berichte* (Miskolc, Hungary: Ludwig, 1941); Commonwealth Immigration Advisory Council, *Third Report of the Committee Established to Investigate Conduct of Migrants* (Canberra, Australia: Commonwealth Government Printer, 1957), p. 14; Sveri, *Kriminalitet og Alder*, p. 50.

2. The extent to which the rate for males exceeds the rate for females varies with the social positions of the sexes in different groups within a nation. An analysis of statistics in prewar Poland indicated sex ratios that ranged from 176 to 1,163 in forty-two groups in categories according to age, province of residence, rural-urban residence, religion, and civil status.[49] In the United States, the sex ratio is less extreme among blacks than it is among whites, and it is probable that black males and females more closely resemble each other in social standing than do white males and females. In 1957, the sex ratio among Negroes committed to New York State prisons was 1,075, but the ratio among whites was over 3,000, and the sex ratio among the Negroes admitted to Florida prisons in 1970 was 2,043, as compared to 2,456 for whites.[50]

3. The extent to which the rate for males exceeds the rate for females varies with the size of community of residence. In American cities the crime rate of females is closer to the crime rate of males than is the case in rural areas and small towns. The ratio of male arrests to female arrests for crimes against the person in Massachusetts in 1970 was 17 to 1 in "towns," most of which have less than twelve thousand population, and 11 to 1 in cities above twelve thousand; for offenses against property the ratio was 8 to 1 in towns and 6 to 1 in cities.[51]

4. The extent to which the crime rate among males exceeds the crime rate among females varies with age. In the United States, the sex ratio among persons committed to penal institutions tends to increase with increasing age. At ages 15-17 the sex ratio is about 1,300, while at 60-64 it is about 2,500. The English statistics of convictions for indictable crimes in 1958 show a sex ratio of 772 for all ages; however, for the ages under 17 the ratio is 1,266; for the years 17-21 it is 850; and for the ages 21 and over it is 589.[52] In earlier years, these data were compiled for all age groups, and they indicated that after age 10 the two sexes became progressively more alike with advancing age until the age of 40, with little change thereafter. For Norway in 1959, the male rate per thousand population of the same age was only three times the female rate at age 60 and over, eight times the female rate at ages 40-59, and twelve times the female rate at ages 25-39. The greatest differences were at ages 9, 12, and 24, where the male

[49] L. Radzinowicz, "Variability in the Sex Ratio of Criminality," *Sociological Review*, 29:76-102, January, 1937.

[50] New York State Commission of Correction, *Thirty-First Annual Report, 1957* (New York: Sing Sing Prison Press, 1958), p. 405; Florida Division of Corrections, *Seventh Biennial Report* (Tallahassee: Author, 1971), p. 70.

[51] *Statistical Reports of the Commissioner of Correction, 1963* (Boston: Massachusetts Public Document No. 115, 1971), p. 65. Communities of less than twelve thousand are "towns," but a community with more than twelve thousand becomes a city only if it chooses to give up the "town" designation.

[52] Great Britain Central Statistical Office, *Annual Abstract of Statistics*, vol. 95 (London: Her Majesty's Stationery Office, 1958), p. 71.

rate exceeded the female rate by 30 times, 36 times, and 30 times, respectively.[53]

5. The extent to which the crime rate among males exceeds the crime rate among females varies with area of residence within a city. Generally, the higher the crime rate of an area, the lower the sex ratio in crime. However, it has been shown that some areas with high delinquency rates also have unusually high sex ratios among their delinquents.[54]

6. The extent to which the crime rate among males exceeds the crime rate among females varies with time. There is some evidence that the sex ratio is decreasing. In 1938, females were 5 percent of the persons under age 18 whose arrests were reported to the FBI; in 1947 females were 10 percent; in 1957 they were 12.7 percent; in 1964 they were 16 percent; and in 1967 they were 18 percent. Between 1960 and 1965 the male arrest rate for serious crimes increased 18 percent, but the female rate increased 62 percent.[55] In England and Wales, the sex ratio of the persons cautioned by the police for all serious ("indictable") crimes in 1957 was 600; by 1967 it had decreased to 400. In 1957, 81 out of each 100,000 males and 13 out of each 100,000 females were cautioned; by 1967 the male rate had increased 1.5 times, and the female rate had increased 2.5 times.[56] In war years, when women take over the occupations of men and in other ways approach social equality with men, the female crime rate increases.

7. Among young criminals, the extent to which the crime rate for males exceeds the crime rate for females varies with the degree of integration in the family. Among delinquents from broken homes, the sex ratio is lower than it is among delinquents from unbroken, "integrated" homes.[57] Further, there is some evidence from specialized studies that the sex ratio in delinquency is lower in females in which male children outnumber the females than in families in which the number of each sex is more nearly equal.[58]

As indicated, no other trait has as great statistical importance as does sex in differentiating criminals from noncriminals. But no one feels that he has an explanation of criminality when he

Conclusion

---

[53] Sveri, *Kriminalitet og Alder*, p. 84.

[54] E. Manheim, *Youth in Trouble* (Kansas City, Mo.: Department of Welfare, 1945), pp. 64-65.

[55] President's Commission on Law Enforcement and Administration of Justice, *Task Force Report: Crime and Its Impact — An Assessment* (Washington: Government Printing Office, 1967), p. 78.

[56] Manuel Lopez-Rey, *Crime: An Analytic Appraisal* (London: Routledge and Kegan Paul, 1970), pp. 197-198.

[57] Jackson Toby, "The Differential Impact of Family Disorganization," *American Sociological Review*, 22:505-512, October, 1957.

[58] Raymond F. Sletto, "Sibling Position and Juvenile Delinquency," *American Journal of Sociology*, 39:657-669, March, 1934.

learns that the criminal is male. Some scholars have claimed that the higher rate of delinquency of the male sex is due to the biological characteristics of the male. This conclusion has no more justification than the conclusion that a death rate of males by lightning six times as high as of females is due to the biological differences between the sexes.

The variations in the sex ratio in crime are so great that it can be concluded that maleness is not significant in the causation of crime in itself but only as it indicates social position, supervision, and other social relations. Moreover, since boys and girls live in the same homes, in equal poverty, and with equally ignorant parents, and live in the same neighborhoods, which are equally lacking in facilities for organized recreation, these conditions of the social environment cannot be considered as causes of delinquency. The significant difference is in the social positions of the girls and women as compared with the boys and men, and the difference in social positions either determines the frequency and intensity of the delinquency and antidelinquency patterns which impinge upon them or determines the frequency of opportunities for crimes which are available to them.[59]

Probably the most important difference is that the girls are supervised more carefully and behave in accordance with anti-criminal behavior patterns taught to them with greater care and consistency than in the case of boys. From infancy, girls are taught that they must be nice, while boys are taught that they must be rough and tough; a boy who approaches the behavior of girls is regarded as a "sissy." This difference in care and supervision presumably rested originally on the fact that the female sex is the one which becomes pregnant. The importance of avoiding the personal and familial consequences of illicit pregnancy led to special protection of the girl, not only in respect to sex behavior but also in respect to social codes in general.[60] Grosser has shown that stealing has a different functional significance for boys and girls; it can be integrated with and can express features of the masculine adolescent role, but it cannot do so for the basic features of the feminine role.[61] ●

---

[59] Cf. Pollak, Criminality of Women, pp. 137-148.

[60] Talcott Parsons has presented the thesis that girls are less delinquent than boys partially because the girls receive an apprenticeship training from their mothers for the careers into which they are to enter, while boys remain, during the same age, isolated from the occupational activities of their fathers, which leads to frustration of the boys and consequent delinquency. If this thesis were valid, the delinquency rates of the two sexes should be more nearly alike in rural districts, where both boys and girls receive this apprenticeship training, than in urban districts, where the girls alone receive it. But Toby has shown that the delinquency rates are more nearly the same for the two sexes in the urban districts, where the training in this respect differs more widely. See Talcott Parsons, Essays in Sociological Theory (Glencoe, Ill.: Free Press, 1949), pp. 219, 257-259; Toby, "Differential Impact of Family Disorganization."

[61] George H. Grosser, Juvenile Delinquency and Contemporary American Sex Roles (Ph.D. dissertation, Harvard University, 1952).

The general conclusion from this survey of the facts regarding physical and physiological conditions is that these conditions have not, in any case, been demonstrated to be a direct force in the production of crime or delinquency. On the contrary, it is apparent that these conditions are significant in crime causation only to the extent that they affect social interaction. ●

Suggested readings

ALBERT, ETHEL M. "The Roles of Women: A Question of Values." Chapter in *Man and Civilization: The Potential of Women,* edited by Seymour M. Farber and Roger H. L. Wilson, pp. 105-115, New York: McGraw-Hill, 1963.

BERTRAND, MARIE-ANDREE. "Self-Image and Delinquency: A Contribution to the Study of Female Criminality and Woman's Image." *Acta Criminologica,* 2:71-138, January, 1969.

DAVIS, FRED. "Deviance Disavowal: The Management of Strained Interaction by the Visibly Handicapped." *Social Problems,* 9:120-132, Fall, 1961.

FINK, ARTHUR E. *Causes of Crime: Biological Theories in the United States, 1800-1915.* Philadelphia: University of Pennsylvania Press, 1938.

FRIEDENBERG, EDGAR Z. *The Vanishing Adolescent.* New York: Dell, 1962.

HABER, LAWRENCE D., & RICHARD T. SMITH. "Disability and Deviance: Normative Adaptations of Role Behavior." *American Sociological Review,* 36:87-97, February, 1971.

HINDELANG, MICHAEL J. "Age, Sex, and the Versatility of Delinquent Involvements." *Social Problems,* 18:522-535, Spring, 1971.

LOPEZ-REY, MANUEL. *Crime: An Analytic Appraisal.* New York: Praeger, 1970.

MORRIS, RUTH. "Female Delinquency and Relational Problems." *Social Forces,* 43:82-99, December, 1964.

STOTT, D. H. "Evidence for a Congenital Factor in Maladjustment and Delinquency." *American Journal of Psychiatry,* 118: 781-794, 1962.

TOBY, JACKSON. "The Differential Impact of Family Disorganization." *American Sociological Review,* 22:505-512, October, 1957.

TURNER, RALPH H. "Deviance Avowal as Neutralization of Commitment." *Social Problems,* 19:308-321, Winter, 1972.

WOLFGANG, MARVIN E. "Pioneers in Criminology: Cesare Lombroso (1835-1909)." *Journal of Criminal Law, Criminology, and Police Science,* 52:361-369, November-December, 1961.

WOLFGANG, MARVIN E., & FRANCO FERRACUTI. *The Subculture of Violence.* London: Social Science Paperbacks, 1967.

Race and nativity 7

We previously examined the age and sex ratios in crime, described certain variations in the ratios, and made a preliminary attempt to explain the ratios and the variations. In this chapter we shall consider the variations in two more ratios, the race ratio and the nativity ratio. Any general theory of criminal behavior should explain all the ratios and, also, the variations in the ratios. A theory which makes sense of the sex ratio and its variations, for example, should also explain the age ratio, the race ratio, and the nativity ratio. ●

Race ratios and crime

Crimes are sometimes regarded as a direct product of racial traits, and racial traits are regarded as biologically determined. For example, some persons believe that Negroes are a primitive race and are innately inclined toward crime. This belief is composed of two constituent notions: that Negroes cannot control their emotions and consequently have a high rate of crime against the person, and that they have no moral sense regarding property rights and consequently have a high rate of crime against property.[1] A survey of the facts regarding the crimes of various races in the United States would indicate whether such biological notions are valid, but it is difficult to obtain the facts. The statistics on the crimes of various racial groups are by no means facts.

In the first place, the classification of persons as "white," "Negro," or something else is arbitrary. Fifty years ago Herskovits drew a sample of 5,000 "Negroes" from all parts of the United States, but his anthropological study of them suggested that at most 22 percent were of unmixed ancestry.[2] It is reasonable to assume that this proportion has decreased in the last half-century. There is no avoiding the fact that at least 80 percent of the offenders contributing to the "black" crime rate are part "white."

In the second place, arrest rates and other official statistics are reported for selected areas and cities, but the population of the several races in those areas cannot be determined. Even racial classifications based on social definitions or regional legislation do not indicate how persons are classified for census purposes.

---

[1] See the discussion by Gunnar Myrdal, An American Dilemma, rev. ed. (New York: Harpers, 1962), p. 655.

[2] Melville J. Herskovits, The Anthropometry of the American Negro (New York: Columbia University Press, 1930), p. 177. See also Marvin E. Wolfgang and Bernard Cohen, Crime and Race: Conceptions and Misconceptions (New York: Institute of Human Relations Press, American Jewish Committee, 1970).

In many estimates of Negro crime, the arrest rate of Negroes in a city, state, or area is determined by comparing the number of arrests with the total population of Negroes in the United States.

A third error in the statistics arises because the procedures used in the administration of criminal justice are biased against minority groups, especially blacks. Later chapters—especially those dealing with the police and courts—will identify some of these biases. The transgressions of lower-class persons, and especially the transgressions of Negroes, are much more visible than the transgressions of white middle-class persons.[3] Numerous studies have shown that African-Americans are more likely to be arrested, indicted, convicted, and committed to an institution than are whites who commit the same offenses, and many other studies have shown that blacks have a poorer chance than whites to receive probation, a suspended sentence, parole, commutation of a death sentence, or pardon.[4] Thus, almost any "index" of the crime rate is likely to exaggerate the rate for Negroes, as compared with the rate among whites. Myrdal concluded that one could merely "suspect" that Negroes commit more crimes than whites.

However, it is also true that many crimes committed by Negroes—especially those committed against other Negroes—receive no official attention from the police or courts, and this practice of overlooking some crimes offsets to some unknown degree the bias in other arresting, reporting, and recording practices. An extensive study of the administration of justice indicated that many guilty persons are acquitted because the conduct complained about is considered "normal" to the subculture of the defendant.[5] For example, in commenting on differential treatment of certain sex cases, a judge remarked: "In statutory rape or carnal knowledge cases the man might be just above the legal age and the girl just below. Usually in such cases, particularly among the Negroes, there is mutual consent and in the Negro

---

[3] See William J. Chambliss, ed., *Crime and the Legal Process* (New York: McGraw-Hill, 1969), pp. 85-89; and Leroy C. Gould, "Who Defines Delinquency: A Comparison of Self-Reported and Officially Reported Indices of Delinquency for Three Racial Groups," *Social Problems*, 16:325-336, Winter, 1969.

[4] See, for example, Thorsten Sellin, "Race Prejudice in the Administration of Justice," *American Journal of Sociology*, 41:212-217, September, 1935; Sidney Axelrad, "Negro and White Institutionalized Delinquents," *American Journal of Sociology*, 57:569-574, May. 1952; Marvin E. Wolfgang, Arlene Kelly, and Hans C. Nolde, "Comparison of the Executed and the Commuted Among Admissions to Death Row," *Journal of Criminal Law, Criminology, and Police Science*, 53:301-311, September, 1962; Nathan Goldman, *The Differential Selection of Juvenile Offenders for Court Appearance* (New York: National Council on Crime and Delinquency, 1963); Irving Piliavin and Scott Briar, "Police Encounters with Juveniles," *American Journal of Sociology*, 60:206-214, September, 1964; and Robert M. Terry, "The Screening of Juvenile Offenders," *Journal of Criminal Law, Criminology, and Police Science*, 58:173-181, June, 1967.

[5] Donald J. Newman, *Conviction: The Determination of Guilt or Innocence Without Trial* (Boston: Little, Brown, 1966), pp. 155-159.

group this type of behavior is not particularly frowned upon and is felt to be normal. You have to take this factor into consideration." In urban Negro communities the problems of divergent mores, real or assumed, are most apparent at the police level. While discrimination against blacks is manifested in arresting them more readily than whites for many types of crime, it also is manifested in police activity resulting in underarresting Negroes for conduct which would likely result in arrest in other precincts. Underarrest, in turn, affects conviction rates. Newman concluded:

Assaults involving Negro perpetrators and Negro victims commonly do not result in arrest, unless extremely serious, on the general philosophy that such conduct is normal in this subculture. The police have an informal policy of discouraging Negro assault victims from filing complaints, and it was reported that officers newly assigned to primarily Negro districts quickly adopt this practice regardless of the attitudes and policies they brought with them from white districts. . . . The policy of underarresting Negroes for such crimes as assault has a deceptive influence on conviction and sentencing statistics. For example, if only assault conviction records were used as the basis for comparing court treatment of the two races, it might appear as if there were a court bias against Negro defendants. Most Negroes charged with assault are convicted while a higher percentage of whites similarly charged are dismissed or acquitted; furthermore, the Negro defendant is more likely to receive a longer or more severe sentence. The difference, of course, is primarily due to differential arrest practices.[6]

The practice of underarresting blacks is sometimes based on the notion that strict enforcement against the more visible crimes of lower-class persons is a form of discrimination. But it sometimes is based on the prejudiced assumption that poor persons, and especially Negroes, are degenerates who cannot be expected to live up to the standards of morality codified in the law. One judge interviewed by Newman dismissed an assault charge against the male partner in a white "hillbilly" common-law relationship, then explained: "These people couldn't care less about marriage, divorce or other relationships. They are ignorant and their moral standards are not like ours. They come from the backwoods in the South where even incest is the accepted thing." Another judge, obviously subscribing to the notion that blacks are an inferior people with natural proclivities to crime, discouraged rigorous enforcement against gambling among Negroes on the ground that this "would merely drive them onto the streets, with a consequent rise in rapes, burglaries, and other serious crimes."

Some crimes of other minority groups also are overlooked, often for different reasons, and with entirely different consequences to the crime statistics. For example, Chambliss and Nagasawa recently reported that in the Seattle area delinquencies of Japanese-Americans were underreported principally because

---

[6] Ibid., p. 157.

teachers, counselors, police, and other officials believe that Japanese-Americans are well behaved. Moreover, part of the Japanese
culture is to show respect for one's elders, and for others in
positions of authority, so when a policeman encounters a Japanese-American it is hard for him to believe that a youth so polite,
neat, and middle-class in demeanor could be involved in any
very serious delinquency. By way of contrast, "Coolness, indifference, and a tough exterior are prized possessions of Negro youth.
When youths who operate in this world are confronted with an
accuser, their response is likely to do more to convince him of
their guilt and their problem than to allay his qualms about the
seriousness of their suspected or known delinquent behavior."[7]

That these suggested differences are by no means universal was
revealed by a study in which Japanese-American delinquents and
their parents were compared with Japanese-American nondelinquents and their parents. The delinquents and their families were
much less "Japanese" than the nondelinquents, especially in
terms of more use of lower-class argot, sloppy dress, hair style,
and general physical appearance. The social participation patterns of the delinquents were typically with non-Japanese lower-
class persons.[8]

At least four excellent localized studies have shown that racial
membership of both the offender and the victim is of great
importance in determining the official reaction to crimes committed by Negroes.[9] Moses said that for the persons in his
study, made in the 1940s, there was "no reason to suspect that
Negroes were more readily convicted than whites."[10] However,
in a more recent study Bullock found that juries tend to give
Negro prisoners convicted of murder shorter sentences than
whites, while Negroes convicted of burglary received longer
sentences than whites. Murder by Negroes tends to be an intra-
racial crime, while burglary by Negroes is mainly interracial.[11]

---

[7] William J. Chambliss and Richard H. Nagasawa, "On the Validity of Official
Statistics — A Comparative Study of White, Black, and Japanese High-School
Boys," *Journal of Research in Crime and Delinquency*, 6:71-77, January, 1969.

[8] Harry H. L. Kitano, "Japanese-American Crime and Delinquency," *Journal of
Psychology*, 66:253-263, July, 1967.

[9] Guy B. Johnson, "The Negro and Crime," *Annals of the American Academy
of Political and Social Science*, 217:93-104, September, 1941; James D. Turner,
"Differential Punishment in a Bi-Racial Community" (Master's thesis, Indiana
University, 1948); idem, "Dynamics of Criminal Law Administration in a
Bi-Racial Community of the Deep South" (Ph.D. dissertation, Indiana Uni-
versity, 1956); Henry Allen Bullock, "Significance of the Racial Factor in the
Length of Prison Sentences," *Journal of Criminal Law, Criminology, and
Police Science*, 52:411-417, November-December, 1961.

[10] Earl R. Moses, "Differentials in Crime Rates Between Negroes and Whites,"
American Sociological Review, 12:411-420, August, 1947. See also William H.
Kephart, *Racial Factors and Urban Law-Enforcement* (Philadelphia: Univer-
sity of Pennsylvania Press, 1957), pp. 174-175.

[11] Bullock, "Significance of the Racial Factor in the Length of Prison
Sentences."

TABLE XI

City arrests by race, 1971 [4,088 agencies: 1971 estimated population 104,783,000][12]

Offense charged	White	Negro	Indian	Chinese	Japanese	All others (includes race unknown)
			Percent distribution			
Total	**66.9**	**29.7**	**2.2**	**0.1**	**0.1**	**1.0**
Criminal homicide:						
(a) Murder and non-negligent manslaughter	30.0	67.7	.5	—	—	1.8
(b) Manslaughter by negligence	71.1	26.2	.2	.1	.3	2.1
Forcible rape	40.9	57.3	.8	—	—	.9
Robbery	28.3	69.6	.7	—	.1	1.3
Aggravated assault	45.7	52.1	1.0	.1	—	1.1
Burglary—breaking and entering	59.3	38.7	.7	.1	.1	1.2
Larceny—theft	65.3	32.6	.8	.1	.1	1.1
Auto theft	58.7	38.6	.9	.1	.1	1.5
Subtotal for above offenses	**58.4**	**39.4**	**.8**	**.1**	**.1**	**1.2**
Other assaults	56.3	41.8	.8	—	—	1.1
Arson	67.7	30.6	.6	.2	.1	.9
Forgery and counterfeiting	63.0	36.1	.5	—	—	.3
Fraud	67.5	31.6	.4	—	—	.5
Embezzlement	71.8	27.2	.2	—	—	.7
Stolen property: buying, receiving, possessing	58.4	40.1	.5	.1	—	.9
Vandalism	75.7	22.7	.5	—	—	1.0
Weapons: carrying, possessing, etc.	43.4	54.5	.7	.1	—	1.3
Prostitution and commercialized vice	34.6	64.2	.4	.1	—	.7
Sex offenses (except forcible rape and prostitution)	73.2	24.4	.7	.1	.1	1.6
Narcotic drug laws	73.6	25.0	.4	.1	.1	.9
Gambling	24.2	71.6	.1	.3	.6	3.2
Offenses against family and children	61.1	37.7	.5	—	—	.7
Driving under the influence	78.0	19.1	1.8	—	.1	1.0
Liquor laws	85.7	12.0	1.8	—	—	.5
Drunkenness	72.4	20.8	6.2	—	—	.6
Disorderly conduct	61.7	35.3	1.2	—	—	1.8
Vagrancy	70.5	26.8	1.7	—	—	1.0
All other offenses (except traffic)	68.1	29.9	1.0	—	.1	1.0
Suspicion	69.0	29.8	.7	.1	—	.4
Curfew and loitering law violations	75.9	21.7	1.1	.1	.2	1.1
Runaways	84.1	13.5	.9	.1	.1	1.4

Table XI shows the distribution of arrests reported to the FBI in 1971 by police agencies in cities with populations over 2,500.[12] About 10 percent of the persons in these cities are classified as Negro. While differential reporting and arresting practices probably affect in a significant way the proportions of arrests for crimes such as assault, burglary, possession of weapons, prostitution, and disorderly conduct, they probably are less closely related to crimes like murder and robbery.

Despite the limitations of the official statistics on the crimes committed by members of the various races, it seems reasonable to assume that in the United States the general crime rate among Negroes is considerably higher than the rate among whites. If we make this assumption, then we can observe that there are two general relationships between crime and race, just as there are two general relationships between crime and age, and between crime and sex. We shall focus on a comparison of the rates of Negroes and of whites.

A. The general crime rate of Negroes exceeds the rate among whites. The official statistics of arrest per 100,000 population of the same race fifteen years of age and over for the entire United States suggest that blacks have arrest rates about three to four times those of the white population. In 1965, the arrest rate per 100,000 for serious offenses ("index crimes" plus larceny under fifty dollars), was 1,696 for Negroes and 419 for whites, for a ratio of four to one.[13] The rate of commitment of Negroes to state and federal prisons is about six times the white rate. The arrest rates of Indians and Chinese are also about three times the rate of whites, but the Japanese have a rate slightly lower than that of whites. The commitment rates of Indians and Chinese are also similar to the rate of Negroes; the rate for Filipinos is a little more than twice as high as the rate for whites, but the commitment rate for Japanese is only about half that of whites.

B. The extent to which the crime rate among Negroes exceeds the crime rate of whites varies with social conditions. In some conditions the rate for blacks is not as far in excess of the rate for whites as it is in other conditions, and in still other conditions the rate for blacks is lower than the rate for whites.

1. The extent to which the rate for Negroes exceeds the rate for whites varies with regions of the United States. The excess is highest in the western states and lowest in the southern states, with northern states occupying an intermediate position.[14] In

---

[12] Federal Bureau of Investigation, U.S. Department of Justice, *Uniform Crime Reports for the United States, 1971* (Washington: Government Printing Office, 1972), p. 136.

[13] President's Commission on Law Enforcement and Administration of Justice, *Task Force Report: Crime and Its Impact — An Assessment* (Washington: Government Printing Office, 1967), p. 78.

[14] The high ratio in the West may be due in part to the fact that blacks in that area tend to be unduly concentrated in the young adult group and in cities, both of which have high crime rates.

Philadelphia in 1954, Negroes made up 20 percent of the population but accounted for 50 percent of the arrests[15]; in Michigan and Ohio at about the same time Negroes were 7 percent of the population and about 40 percent of the prison population.[16] The differences in rates are not distributed in the same way for all offenses; for homicide, for example, the difference is greatest in the South and least in New England. Similarly, Hayner has shown that the crime rate of one Indian tribe is quite different from that of another, and the variations are related to their contacts with white civilization and to their economic resources.[17]

2. The extent to which the crime rate of Negroes exceeds the crime rate of whites varies with sex status. Forslund found the following variations in the arrest and conviction rates per 100,000 of the same status in Stamford, Connecticut in 1959-1961:[18]

	White Males	White Females	Negro Males	Negro Females
Arrest Rate	1,829	175	10,696	1,666
Conviction Rate	1,746	114	14,177	1,607

Thus, the conviction rate for Negro males was about eight times that for white males, but the rate for Negro females was about 14 times the rate for white females. Similarly, in Wolfgang's study of all criminal homicides occurring in Philadelphia between January 1, 1948, and December 31, 1952, the rate per 100,000 by race and sex of offenders showed the following rank order: Negro males—41.7, Negro females—9.3, white males—3.4, and white females—.4.[19] A study of criminal homicide in Chicago in 1965 showed higher rates, but in the same rank order: nonwhite males—54.8, nonwhite females—11.6, white males—6.6, and white females—.7.[20]

3. The extent to which the crime rate of Negroes exceeds the crime rate of whites varies with the offense. When based on

[15] William H. Kephart, "The Negro Offender," American Journal of Sociology, 60:46-50, July, 1954.

[16] Vernon Fox and Joann Volakakis, "The Negro Offender in a Northern Industrial Area," Journal of Criminal Law, Criminology, and Police Science, 46:641-647, January-February, 1956; Ohio Legislative Service Commission, Capital Punishment, Staff Research Report No. 46 (Columbus: Author, 1961), p. 62.

[17] Norman S. Hayner, "Variability in the Criminal Behavior of American Indians," American Journal of Sociology, 47:602-613, January, 1942. See also Hans von Hentig, "Delinquency of the American Indian," Journal of Criminal Law and Criminology, 36: 75-84, July-August, 1945.

[18] Morris A. Forslund, "A Comparison of Negro and White Crime Rates, "Journal of Criminal Law, Criminology, and Police Science, 61:214-217, June, 1970.

[19] Marvin E. Wolfgang, "A Sociological Analysis of Criminal Homicide," Federal Probation, 25:48-55, March, 1961.

[20] Harwin L. Voss and John R. Hepburn, "Patterns in Criminal Homicide in Chicago," Journal of Criminal Law, Criminology, and Police Science, 59:499-508, December, 1968.

imprisonment rates, the excess is greatest for assault and homicide and lowest for rape. Table XI shows the proportions of Negroes, whites, and others arrested for various crimes in 1968.[21] The proportions of Negroes among the persons arrested for murder and nonnegligent manslaughter, for robbery, and for gambling were high. It should be noted, however, that even within an offense category, there are variations in the race ratio. For example, while Negroes were 68 percent of those arrested for murder and nonnegligent manslaughter in 1971, they were only 36 percent of those arrested for forgery and 19 percent of those arrested for driving under the influence. It also is known that the excess of crime among Negroes is higher for second offenses than it is for first offenses.

One study indicated that in Virginia the rates for forgery and for drunken driving actually are lower among Negroes than among whites, but this does not take into account the fact that literacy and automobile ownership are probably less frequent among Negroes.[22] McKeown correlated arrest rates for specified crimes in 1930 and in 1939 in fifty-five cities of 100,000-250,000 population and thirty-six cities over 250,000 with the percentage of Negro population in those cities. For murder and nonnegligent manslaughter the coefficients of correlation range from +.67 to +.87 in the two years and the two classes of cities; these high correlations justify a conclusion that cities which have a large percentage of Negro population have high rates of murder and nonnegligent manslaughter. The coefficients for other types of crimes vary widely from one year to the other or from one class of cities to the other, and justify no conclusion regarding the relation between Negro population and crime rates of cities. Moreover, it has been shown that in southern cities, which have large percentages of Negroes, the white populations have very high rates of murder and manslaughter; consequently, the relatively high murder and manslaughter rates in the cities which have large proportions of Negroes cannot be attributed to a racial factor.[23]

4. The extent to which the crime rate of Negroes exceeds that of whites varies with the area of residence within a city. Studies of Houston and Baltimore showed that the Negro delinquency rate was lowest in those areas having the greatest proportion of Negroes in their populations, and highest in those areas with relatively low proportions of Negroes to whites.[24] Although these data do not necessarily indicate that the excess of crime is greatest in

---

[21] Federal Bureau of Investigation, *Uniform Crime Reports, 1971*, p. 136.

[22] Workers' Writers Program, *The Negro in Virginia* (New York: Hastings House, 1940), p. 341.

[23] James Edward McKeown, "Poverty, Race and Crime," *Journal of Criminal Law and Criminology*, 39:480-484, November-December, 1948.

[24] *The Houston Delinquent in His Community Setting* (Houston: Bureau of Research, Council of Social Agencies, 1945), pp. 22-45; Bernard Lander, *Towards an Understanding of Juvenile Delinquency* (New York: Columbia University Press, 1954), p. 82.

areas where whites and Negroes are not segregated, this is probably the case. However, the juvenile delinquency rate of Negroes decreases regularly from the center of the city to the outer zones of the city, as shown by studies in Chicago and other cities. The change in delinquency rates as the residential areas change is substantially the same for black and white children.

5. The extent to which the crime rate of Negroes exceeds the crime rate of whites varies with time. There is no long-range evidence on this point, but it seems probable that the amount of excess has been increasing during the last fifty years. Recent statistics suggest that the amount of excess is increasing for some offenses but decreasing for others. During the period 1960-1965, the Negro arrest rate for robbery increased 24 percent while the white rate increased 3 percent. But for crimes of violence (murder, rape, aggravated assault) the Negro rate increased only 5 percent, while the white rate increased 27 percent. The rates per 100,000 of the same race for burglary, larceny, and automobile theft arrests increased along parallel lines—33 percent for Negroes and 24 percent for whites.[25]

An earlier study indicated that in three decades the Negro juvenile delinquency rate in Chicago increased seven times, while the Negro population increased only three times.[26] The comparable data on the rate and population increases for whites are not available. Negro children have a relatively low delinquency rate when they first settle in a deteriorated area, but their delinquency rate increases with length of residence until a peak is reached; this generally has taken about five years.[27]

6. The extent to which the crime rate of blacks exceeds that of whites varies with educational status. Older studies indicated little crime among graduates of Negro colleges, but it is likely that educated Negroes have been increasingly convicted of crime in recent years, while small semirural Negro communities with high degrees of illiteracy have remained relatively free of crime.[28] Nevertheless, the crime rate of highly educated Negroes is much lower than the rate of poorly educated whites.

In short, such statistics as are available indicate that Negroes have higher crime rates than whites, but that the ratio of crime rates among blacks to crime rates among whites varies with specific social situations. These variations cannot be explained by biological differences among the races. They can be explained only by social interaction. The specific theory of social interaction which explains these racial ratios in crime has not been determined.

---

[25] President's Commission, *Task Force Report: Crime and Its Impact*, p. 78.

[26] Earl R. Moses, "Community Factors in Negro Delinquency," *Journal of Negro Education*, 5:220-227, April, 1936.

[27] Ibid. See also Moses, "Differentials in Crime Rates."

[28] E. Franklin Frazier, "Theoretical Structure of Sociology and Social Research," *British Journal of Sociology*, 4:293-311, December, 1953.

One notion is that the minority group status, as such, somehow produces a high crime rate. The low crime rate of the Japanese is a sufficient refutation of that idea, for this minority group has a lower crime rate than the majority group.

A second notion is that the high crime rate of minority groups is due to frustrations produced by discriminations. Again, the Japanese meet discrimination and are presumably frustrated, but they do not have a high crime rate. Furthermore, while frustration is a vague term which cannot be measured or even defined, the feeling of frustration is probably more pronounced in the upper socioeconomic class of Negroes, whose crime rate is low, than in the lower class of Negroes, whose crime rate is high. A variation of the frustration theory is limited to the high rate of assaults and homicides by Negroes. This theory is that Negroes build up a great feeling of anger because of the discriminations against them, that they do not dare express their anger against the powerful white population, and that they release this anger in attacks on their fellow Negroes. This theory, which is a theory of displacement of emotion, was formulated by Dollard[29] and apparently accepted as valid by Myrdal.

A third theory is that it is the economic status of the minority group, which is a product of discrimination, that explains the high crime rate of the minority group. This theory will be discussed in some detail in chapter 11. The basic idea is that the differential between the Negro's economic status and his recently aroused hope that he will at last be permitted to participate in the "American dream" has produced a potential for direct action in the form of crime. Blue has shown in a statistical study of delinquency of Negro and white children by census tracts in Detroit that when economic status is held constant the partial correlation between race and juvenile delinquency is +.52, while when race is held constant the correlation between economic status and juvenile delinquency is −.59.[30] This indicates that economic status is slightly more closely related to juvenile delinquency than is race. Statistically speaking, Negroes are poor— in 1963, about 10 percent of the families in the United States were nonwhite, but 25 percent of the poverty families (those with incomes of $3,000 or less) were nonwhite. Forty-three percent of all nonwhite families were classified as "poor," as compared with 16 percent of the white families.[31] However, Japanese-Americans resemble other minority groups in their low economic

[29] John Dollard, *Caste and Class in a Southern Town* (New Haven: Yale University Press, 1937).

[30] John T. Blue, "The Relationship of Juvenile Delinquency, Race, and Economic Status," *Journal of Negro Education*, 17:469-477, Fall, 1948. See also Kenneth Polk, "Juvenile Delinquency and Social Areas," *Social Problems*, 5:214-217, Winter, 1957-58.

[31] H. Miller, "Changes in the Number and Composition of the Poor," in M. Gordon, ed., *Poverty in America* (San Francisco: Chandler, 1965), pp. 86-87; and St. Clair Drake, "The Social and Economic Status of the Negro in the United States," *Daedalus*, 94:771-810, Fall, 1965.

position but differ from them in crime rates. Finally, economic determinism is not a satisfactory general explanation of criminal behavior.[32]

According to the differential association theory, the race ratios in crime result from differential associations with criminal and anticriminal patterns. In the United States, race may be related to associations in either or both of two ways. First, the inheritance of certain characteristics may determine the social and economic level at which members of a race must live, and thus possibly throw them into situations where certain criminal patterns impinge upon them with great frequency and intensity. Negroes do not commit white-collar crimes as frequently as do whites, because they are not as frequently in white-collar jobs; they commit crimes which are typical of that part of the society with which they come in contact. Second, confinement of a race to a given locale may mean that the members of the race can hardly escape the traditions which are characteristic of the locale.[33] The traditions may be essentially anticriminal, but in contemporary inner-city ghettos the traditions are in direct conflict with the morality reflected in the criminal law. ●

Nativity ratios and crime

While assimilation of vast numbers of immigrants is no longer a serious social problem in the United States, analysis of data on the nativity of criminals remains a problem of great theoretical significance. During the years when immigration was at its height, many persons argued that immigration was the chief cause of crime. The mechanisms by which immigration produces crime were not specified, but the following were suggested: (a) Immigrants come from inferior "racial stock," or there is a larger proportion of inferior individuals in the "racial stock" of immigrants than among native whites. (b) Immigrants are not trained in the codes and ideals of America and are, therefore, not adjusted. (c) Immigrants are frequently poverty-stricken, and this condition of poverty and the resulting frustration create personal maladjustments of various kinds. (d) Immigrants are highly mobile and, hence, isolated from the inhibiting and restraining influences of primary groups. Each of these notions is based upon the assumption that there is an excessive rate of criminality among the immigrants. Many research studies have been conducted on the crime rates of immigrants, and these studies have yielded a set of statistical data about the nativity ratio in crime

---

[32] See p. 219, below.

[33] See Marvin E. Wolfgang, *Patterns in Criminal Homicide* (Philadelphia: University of Pennsylvania Press, 1958), pp. 65-70, 180-181; Mozell Hill, "The Metropolis and Juvenile Delinquency Among Negroes," *Journal of Negro Education*, 28 (1959): 277-285; Claude Brown, *Manchild in the Promised Land* (New York: Macmillan, 1965); and Victor Eisner, *The Delinquency Label: The Epidemiology of Juvenile Delinquency* (New York: Random House, 1969), pp. 87-107.

and about the variations in this ratio. Consideration of these data should throw light on the validity of the various notions. As is the case with age, sex, and race, there are two general relationships between crime and nativity.

A. Computed on the basis of population numbers only, the native-white rates of arrest and imprisonment in the United States are approximately two times as high as the rates for foreign-born whites. Similarly, the crime rate for native Australians is about twice the rate for immigrants arriving after World War II,[34] and in 1966 the crime rate of the native population of Düsseldorf, Germany, was about twice the rate of foreign-born workers.[35] The conviction rate of native-born Canadian males aged 15-49 was 87/10,000 in 1951-1954, but the rate for foreign-born males was 43. The rates for specific foreign-born groups ranged from 63 for the United States to 42 for Germany, 37 for Asia, and 17 for Italy.[36] When correction is made for the fact that the age and sex distributions of the populations are not the same, the rates of the two groups become more nearly equal, but still show less crime among immigrants than among native whites. For example, 52.5 percent of the immigrants in Australia and only 29 percent of the native Australians are in the "crime-committing ages" (fifteen to thirty-five), so the correction for age gives the immigrants an even lower comparative crime rate. A recent study of the crime rates of Italian immigrants in Zurich, Switzerland, also showed that the crime rate of an immigrant group—in this case, Italians—was lower than that of the native-born despite an unfavorable age ratio.[37] In the earlier studies it was often concluded that immigrants contributed more than their quota of crime, but the present findings rebut this conclusion.[38]

B. The extent to which the crime rate of native whites exceeds the rate among immigrants is not the same under differing social conditions:

1. The extent to which the crime rate among native whites exceeds the crime rate of the foreign-born varies with offenses. Certain types of crime are characteristic of one immigrant group, while other types of crime are characteristic of a different immigrant group. Some groups have high rates for drunkenness and

[34] Commonwealth Immigration Advisory Council, *Third Report of the Committee Established to Investigate Conduct of Migrants* (Canberra, Australia: Commonwealth Government Printer, 1957), p. 4.

[35] Franco Ferracuti, "European Migration and Crime," chap. 12 in Marvin E. Wolfgang, ed., *Crime and Culture: Essays in Honor of Thorsten Sellin* (New York: John Wiley, 1968), pp. 189-219.

[36] P. J. Griffen, "Rates of Crime and Delinquency," chap. 4 in W. T. McGrath, ed., *Crime and Its Treatment in Canada* (Toronto: Macmillan, 1965), p. 83.

[37] Ferracuti, "European Migration and Crime," p. 205.

[38] For examples of the earlier studies, see U.S. Immigration Commission, "Immigration and Crime," *Report*, vol. 36 (Washington: Government Printing Office, 1910); Joseph M. Gilman, "Statistics and the Immigrant Problem," *American Journal of Sociology*, 30:29-48, July, 1924; Edwin H. Sutherland, "Is There Undue Crime Among Immigrants?" *Proceedings of the National Conference of Social Work*, 1927, pp. 572-579.

other misdemeanors, and low rates for felonies, while other groups have high rates for felonies and low rates for misdemeanors.

A high rate of commitment to jails and workhouses, as in the case of the Irish and Finnish immigrants, is usually an expression of the drinking habits and extent of intoxication in those groups. Of German immigrants committed to federal and state prisons in 1932-1936, 4.5 percent were committed for homicide, 3.6 percent for assault, and 14.3 percent for burglary, while of Italian immigrants the percentages were 10.7, 9.4, and 7.1; that is, the Italians had twice the proportion of homicides and assaults, and half the proportion of burglaries. Sixty-five percent of the Yugoslavs convicted of crimes in Stockholm in 1965 had committed crimes against persons, and only 12 percent were drunk at the time of the crime; Greeks, on the other hand, had only 24 percent convictions of crimes against the person, and almost all of them were committed while the offender was intoxicated.[39]

Thus certain crimes or groups of crimes are characteristic of certain national groups. These same types of crimes are, usually, characteristic of the home countries, also. The Italian and Turkish immigrants residing in Germany in 1965 had an extraordinarily high rate of conviction for murder and assault; Italy and Turkey also have high murder and assault rates.[40] Italians in America have a low rate of arrest for drunkenness, and drunkenness is comparatively rare in Italy. The traditions of the home country are transplanted to America and determine the relative positions of the immigrant groups with reference to the types of crimes.[41]

2. The extent to which the crime rate of native whites exceeds the rate among foreign-born persons varies from one immigrant group to another. In 1955, eastern European immigrants in Australia had crime rates about three times as high as southern European immigrants and almost twice as high as northern European immigrants.[42] Of the foreign-born groups in Switzerland in 1965, the Austrians had the highest crime rate, followed by Germans, Italians, Arabs, Turks, and French.[43] Similarly, in the United States in the years when immigration was at its height, persons of Irish nativity had crime rates three to five times as high as German immigrants. The crime rate among Japanese immigrants was exceptionally low.[44] The rate among the children

---

[39] Ferracuti, "European Migration and Crime," pp. 210-211.

[40] Ibid., pp. 211-212.

[41] Cf. Earnest Albert Hooton, Crime and the Man (Cambridge, Mass.: Harvard University Press, 1939), pp. 204-252.

[42] Commonwealth Immigration Advisory Council, Third Report, p. 18. This publication does not specify the nations involved. For a summary of research on the crime rates of various immigrant groups in America, see Arthur Lewis Wood, "Minority Group Criminality and Cultural Integration," Journal of Criminal Law and Criminology, 37:498-510, March-April, 1947.

[43] Ferracuti, "European Migration and Crime," p. 208.

[44] Norman S. Hayner, "Delinquency Areas in the Puget Sound Region," American Journal of Sociology, 39:314-328, November, 1933.

of these immigrants was also exceptionally low, but the grand-children are now beginning to take on the crime rates of the areas where they reside.[45] A study of our adult Puerto Rican citizens in Brooklyn showed, similarly, that the crime rates are dispropor-tionately low.[46] Another study shows that Puerto Rican children are not overrepresented in New York City's juvenile courts.[47]

3. The extent to which the crime rate of native whites exceeds the rate among the foreign-born varies from one native white group to another. The native white sons of immigrants tend to have crime rates higher than those of their fathers but lower than other native whites. Even this variation changes with specific circumstances. Sometimes the rates for the children of immi-grants are higher than those for native whites of native paren-tage. Among the 8,615 juvenile delinquents referred to the Los Angeles County Probation Department in 1956, 34 percent were identified as Mexican-Americans, which probably means that they were the children of immigrants from Mexico. The rate for the Mexican-Americans was three times the rate for "Anglos" (whites who are not of Mexican or Oriental descent) and slightly higher than the rate for Negroes.[48] Forty years ago, Ogburn found that crimes known to the police have a negative correla-tion with the number of children of immigrants in three groups of cities, and that the negative association persists when other factors are held constant; the coefficients of correlation in the three groups of cities range between −0.34 and −0.54.[49]

The Bureau of the Census, in its *Report on Federal and State Prisons* for 1933, presented a table regarding nativity of prisoners in twenty-six states in which reports regarding nativity were complete enough for comparison. In seventeen of these states the children of immigrants had a rate of commitment lower than that for native whites of native parentage, while in the other nine states their rate of commitment was higher. In one of the last studies of the crimes of the foreign-born in the United States, Taft made an anlysis of this table, with corrections for variations in age distribution, and concluded that the states in which the second generation had lower rates were those in which the older

---

[45] Gerald H. Ikeda, "Japanese Americans Fight Delinquency," *California Youth Authority Quarterly,* 12:3-6, Summer, 1959; Harry H. L. Kitano, "Japanese-American Crime and Delinquency."

[46] Julius Alter, "Crimes of Puerto Ricans in Brooklyn" (Master's thesis, Depart-ment of Sociology, Brooklyn College, 1958).

[47] Clarence O. Senior, *Strangers — Then Neighbors* (New York: Anti-Defama-tion League of B'nai B'rith, 1961), p. 31. See also New York City Board of Education, *The Puerto Rican Study, 1953-1957* (New York: Author, 1958), p. 120.

[48] Joseph W. Eaton and Kenneth Polk, *Measuring Juvenile Delinquency* (Pitts-burgh: University of Pittsburgh Press, 1961), pp. 20, 28.

[49] William F. Ogburn, "Factors in the Variation of Crime among Cities," *Jour-nal of the American Statistical Association,* 30:21-24, March, 1935. See also McKeown, "Poverty, Race and Crime," and Hans von Hentig, "The First Generation and a Half: Notes on the Delinquency of Native Whites of Mixed Parentage," *American Sociological Review,* 10:792-798, December, 1945.

immigration was predominant, and the states in which they had higher rates were those in which the newer immigration was predominant.[50]   Taft's study showed, also, that the children of immigrants had higher rates of commitment than their parents in all except one of the twenty-six states, and that offspring of mixed parentage had lower rates of commitment than offspring of foreign parentage in seventeen states and higher rates in nine states.

4. The amount of the excess of crime among the native-born varies with age. Among immigrants who arrive in the United States when they are in early childhood, the crime rate is higher than among immigrants arriving in middle age.[51] Young immigrants take on the relatively high crime rate of native whites to a greater extent than do middle-aged immigrants. Further, the sons of immigrants tend to change from the types of crime characteristic of their parents to those characteristic of the native-born. This is illustrated in table XII, a comparison of the Irish

TABLE XII

Rate of conviction of specified groups

| Offense | Irish | | Native white of native parentage |
	Immigrants	Second generation	
Homicide	2.3	1.0	0.5
Rape	0.0	0.3	0.7
Gambling	1.2	2.7	3.6

immigrants of the first and second generations and the native whites of native parentage with reference to a few crimes of which they were convicted in the New York Court of General Sessions in 1908-1909.[52] The same tendency appears, also, in a comparison of the first and second generations of Italian immigrants with reference to crimes of personal violence in Massachusetts, as shown in table XIII.[53] This seems to show that the tendency to commit crimes of personal violence, which is seen so clearly in the Italian immigrants, is a matter of tradition—a tradition which is not passed on to the second generation.

[50] D. R. Taft, "Nationality and Crime," *American Sociological Review*, 1:724-736, October, 1936.

[51] Van Vechten, "Criminality of the Foreign-Born."

[52] U.S. Immigration Commission, "Immigration and Crime," p. 14; see also pp. 14-16 and 67-86.

[53] Computed from reports of the Massachusetts Department of Correction, 1914-1922; population was secured from the Massachusetts State Census of 1915; the census of 1920 does not give the necessary information; Italians of all ages were included, and native-born, both white and nonwhite, of all ages, were used in computation of the native white rate. A similar analysis for the state of New Jersey was made by Stofflet. E. H. Stofflet, "A Study of National and Cultural Differences in Criminal Tendency," *Archives of Psychology*, no. 185, 1935.

TABLE XIII

Frequency of commitments to state prison and state reformatory of Massachusetts for murder, manslaughter, and assault, in specified groups, 1914-1922, per 100,000 in each group in 1915

Nativity and parentage	Number committed for specified offenses
Born in Italy	192
Native-born, one or both parents born in Italy	24
Native-born, of native parentage	24
Native-born, one or both parents born in any foreign country	22

5. The extent to which the crime rate of native whites exceeds that of immigrants varies with the length of time the immigrants have been in the host country. Both immigrants and their sons tend to take on the crime rate of the specific part of the community in which they locate. The delinquency rates of the second generation are comparatively low when the immigrant group first settles in a community, and they increase as contacts with the surrounding culture multiply. The rate remains low in those foreign colonies which are comparatively isolated from the surrounding culture. However, the rate is lowest in the heart of the colony and increases on the borderlines where the group comes into contact with other groups. Moreover, the rates are comparatively low in the immigrant groups which have moved away from the areas of deterioration into better residential areas. Even the immigrant group itself tends to approach the crime rate of the host country.[54] A study of crime rates in France in the nineteenth century indicated that migrants moving from one province to another changed their crime rates in the direction of the rate of the host province, whether the rate in the host province was higher or lower than the rate in the province from which they migrated.[55] In the first five years of residence in an area of high delinquency in Los Angeles, 5 percent of the children in an immigrant group appeared before the juvenile court; after five more years, 46 percent appeared; and after another ten years, 83 percent of the children came before the court.[56] The delinquency rate increased with length of stay in the area, presumably

---

[54] Evelyn Buchan Crook, "Cultural Marginality in Sexual Delinquency," *American Journal of Sociology*, 39:493-500, January, 1934; Hayner, "Delinquency Areas"; Andrew W. Lind, "The Ghetto and the Slum," *Social Forces*, 9:206-215, December, 1930; idem, "Some Ecological Patterns of Community Disorganization in Honolulu," *American Journal of Sociology*, 36:206-220, September, 1930; Helen G. McGill, "The Oriental Delinquent in the Vancouver Juvenile Court," *Sociology and Social Research*, 22:428-438, May, 1938.

[55] Henri Joly, *La France Criminelle* (Paris: Cerf, 1889), pp. 45-46.

[56] Pauline V. Young, "Urbanization as a Factor in Juvenile Delinquency," *Publications of the American Sociological Society*, 24 (1930): 162-166.

because the immigrant group was assimilating that part of American culture which it experienced, including the delinquency rates. In a personal communication, Dr. Young recently pointed out that in the 1940's the group dispersed to the suburbs, and that by 1970 the image of them as delinquents had completely vanished among law enforcement agencies.

Taken together, the above variations in the nativity ratio force a rejection of each of the four theories described above; each theory is contradicted by at least one of the variations. Also, the fact that there is generally no undue amount of crime among the foreign-born undermines the assumption on which each of the theories is based.

The variations can be explained in terms of differential associations with criminal and anticriminal behavior patterns. Since immigrants often live in poverty, are mobile, and are affected by many other conditions which are described as "criminogenic," it has been argued that their apparently low general crime rate must be due to statistical errors.[57] There is no necessary conflict here, however. Most immigrants have developed respect for law in their home countries, and these habits, ideals, and codes persist after they reach America, so that they are not as criminalistic as native Americans. They are, nevertheless, affected by the behavior patterns of the people living in the areas where they settle, and these patterns are likely to involve norms conducive to delinquency and crime.[58] The comparatively low crime rate of recent southern European migrants in Australia has been attributed to the fact that most such migrants enter Australia under the sponsorship of a member of their own family already in that country; the migrants who had spent many years in displaced-persons camps in Europe made up the group responsible for the greatest number of crimes committed by aliens.[59]

Thus, the important variables in the differential crime rates of the several nationality groups are the strength and consistency of the traditions which they assimilated in their home countries and the strength and consistency of the traditions with which they come in contact in the new country.[60] These traditions also explain the differences in the types of crime characteristics of the various immigrant groups and the variations in the types of crime and crime rates of the second-generation immigrants as compared with their parents. An expert on demography and migration has formulated the principle as follows: "The characteristics of

---

[57] Donald R. Taft, "Does Immigration Increase Crime?" *Social Forces,* 12:69-77, October, 1933.

[58] See Elena Padilla, *Up From Puerto Rico* (New York: Columbia University Press, 1958), p. 229; Richard A. Cloward and Lloyd E. Ohlin, *Delinquency and Opportunity* (Glencoe, Ill.: Free Press, 1960), pp. 194-211; and Daniel Bell, "Crime as an American Way of Life," *Antioch Review,* 13:131-154, June, 1953.

[59] Commonwealth Immigration Advisory Council, *Third Report,* pp. 5, 18.

[60] Cf. Wood, "Minority Group Criminality."

migrants tend to be intermediate between the characteristics of the population at origin and the population at destination."[61] ●

In this chapter and in chapter 6 we have considered some of the facts about the relationship of crime and delinquency to age, sex, race, and nativity. Although these are only some of the social conditions with which crime rates vary, the list is sufficiently long to enable us to draw the important conclusion that crime is social behavior that is closely associated with other kinds of social behavior. In chapters 9 and 11 we will consider additional sets of facts, those pertaining to relationships between crime and size of community and between crime and social class. Here we need only observe that one set of facts indicates that the crime rate is higher for young adults than for persons in later life, higher for men than for women, higher for Negroes than for whites, and higher for native-born than for foreign-born. Such differences may be described as ratios—the age ratio in crime, the sex ratio in crime, etc. A second set of facts shows that these ratios are not constant. They vary in definite ways, depending on social conditions.

Summary and conclusions

These ratios, and variations in ratios, make up some of the facts that a general explanation of crime must fit. They may be called definitive facts, for they define or limit the explanations of crime that can be considered valid. For example, an explanation that attributes crime to poverty helps make good sense out of the overrepresentation of Negroes in the general criminal population, but the theory falls flat when it is recalled that women, who are equal in poverty with men, have very low crime rates; when it is recalled that immigrants, who are probably at least as poor as their sons, sometimes have crime rates lower than their sons; when it is recalled that even poor Negroes do not have high crime rates in their old age, and so on. Similarly, an explanation of crime in terms of a hereditary characteristic, or of a psychological trait such as aggression must show that the characteristic is much more frequent among men than among women, among Negro women than white women, among young persons as compared to old persons, among native whites as compared to immigrants; and it must show that the trait occurs very infrequently among some immigrant groups, among Negroes who live in segregated areas, among southern European immigrants in Australia, etc.

None of the general explanations of crime makes good sense of all the ratios and variations in ratios. Some of them explain one set of facts, and others explain another set of facts, but none of them explains all the facts. However, the theory of differential association and concordant sociological theories that have as their general point the observation that crime and crim-

---

[61] A. S. Lee, "A Theory of Migration," *Demography,* 3 (1966): 47-57.

inality are products of social experience and social interaction make better sense out of more of the facts than do other general theories. ●

Suggested readings

AXELRAD, SIDNEY. "Negro and White Institutionalized Delinquents." *American Journal of Sociology,* 57:569-574, May, 1952.

BONGER, W. A. *Race and Crime.* Translated by Margaret M. Horduk. New York: Columbia University Press, 1943.

BULLOCK, HENRY ALLEN. "Significance of the Racial Factor in the Length of Prison Sentences." *Journal of Criminal Law, Criminology, and Police Science,* 52:411-417, November-December, 1961.

EATON, JOSEPH W., & KENNETH POLK. *Measuring Juvenile Delinquency.* Pittsburgh: University of Pittsburgh Press, 1961.

FALK, GERHARD J. "Status Differences and the Frustration Aggression Hypothesis." *International Journal of Social Psychiatry,* 5:214-222, Winter, 1959.

FINESTONE, HAROLD. "Cats, Kicks, and Color." *Social Problems,* 5:3-13, July, 1957.

FORSLUND, MORRIS A. "A Comparison of Negro and White Crime Rates." *Journal of Criminal Law, Criminology, and Police Science,* 61:214-217, June, 1970.

GEIS, GILBERT. "Statistics Concerning Race and Crime." *Crime and Delinquency,* April, 1965, pp. 142-150.

GOLDBERG, N. "Jews in the Police Records of Los Angeles, 1933-1937." *Yivo Annual of Jewish Social Science,* 5 (1950): 266-291.

GOULD, LEROY C. "Who Defines Delinquency: A Comparison of Self-Reported and Officially Reported Indices of Delinquency for Three Racial Groups." *Social Problems,* 16:325-336, Winter, 1969.

KEPHART, WILLIAM H. "The Negro Offender." *American Journal of Sociology,* 60:46-50, July, 1954.

KITANO, HARRY H. L. "Differential Child-Rearing Attitudes Between First and Second Generation Japanese in the United States." *Journal of Social Psychology,* 53 (1961): 13-19.

KITANO, HARRY H. L. "Japanese-American Crime and Delinquency." *Journal of Psychology,* 66:253-263, July, 1967.

PETERSON, CLAIRE L., & THOMAS J. SCHEFF. "Theory, Method and Findings in the Study of Acculturation: A Review." *International Review of Community Development,* 13 (1965): 155-176.

RUDWICK, ELLIOTT M. "Race Labeling and the Press." *Journal of Negro Education,* 31 (1962): 177-181.

SILVERMAN, ROBERT A. "Criminality Among Jews: An Overview." *Issues in Criminology,* 6:1-39, Summer, 1971.

STOFFLET, E. H. "The European Immigrant and His Children." *Annals of the American Academy of Political and Social Science,* 217:84-92, September, 1941.

TERRY, ROBERT M. "The Screening of Juvenile Offenders." *Journal of Criminal Law, Criminology, and Police Science,* 58:173-181, June, 1967.

VON HENTIG, HANS. "The First Generation and a Half: Notes on the Delinquency of Native Whites of Mixed Parentage." *American Sociological Review*, 10:792-798, December, 1945.

WOLFGANG, MARVIN E., & BERNARD COHEN. *Crime and Race: Conceptions and Misconceptions*. New York: Institute of Human Relations Press, American Jewish Committee, 1970.

WOLFGANG, MARVIN E., ARLENE KELLY, & HANS C. NOLDE. "Comparison of the Executed and the Commuted Among Admissions to Death Row." *Journal of Criminal Law, Criminology, and Police Science*, 53:301-311, September, 1962.

WOOD, ARTHUR LEWIS. "Minority-Group Criminality and Cultural Integration." *Journal of Criminal Law and Criminology*, 37:498-510, March-April, 1947.

8 Personality

A widely held belief is that criminal behavior is due to some characteristic or trait of the personality and that this trait is in the nature of a pathological condition which exists prior to the criminal behavior and is the cause of it. The Lombrosian notion that criminals constitute a distinct physical type has continued as a neo-Lombrosian notion that maintains the same logic but substitutes psychopathological type for physical type. Some scholars have found the explanation of crime in mental defectiveness, others in schizophrenia, others in psychopathic personality, and others in a composite group of emotional disturbances. However, psychiatrists differ as to the importance of these pathological traits; some assert that practically all criminals are psychopathic; others assert that 10 percent or even less are psychopathic.

Mental disorders have been classified in many ways. One of the simpler classifications includes three groups, namely, mental defect or mental retardation, psychosis or insanity, and neuropathic conditions, which include epilepsy, postencephalitic personality, psychopathic personality, and the psychoneuroses. ●

Mental defect

Mental retardation was once used almost as a specific explanation of crime. The explanation was explicitly stated in propositions that all or almost all criminals are "feebleminded." It also was stated implicitly in the proposition that "feebleminded" persons commit crimes, in the absence of special inhibiting conditions, because they do not have sufficient intelligence to appreciate the reasons for laws and the consequences of violations of law; in the proposition that "feeblemindedness" and, thus, the tendency to commit crimes is inherited as a unit character in accordance with Mendel's law of heredity; and in the proposition that a policy of sterilization or segregation of the "feebleminded" is the only effective method of preventing crime and of dealing with criminals.

This statement of propositions does not include the many exceptions made by various authors, and perhaps is unfair even to Harry H. Goddard, who was in the early period the most extreme adherent of the idea that mental defect causes crime. Over fifty years ago Goddard stated:

> Every investigation of the mentality of criminals, misdemeanants, delinquents, and other antisocial groups has proven beyond the possibility of contradiction that nearly all persons in these classes, and in some cases all, are of low mentality. . . . It is no longer to be denied that the greatest single cause of delinquency and crime is lowgrade mentality, much of it within the limits of feeble-mindedness.[1]

During the period when this kind of theory was most popular, an attempt was made to determine what conclusions could be drawn from all the studies of the intelligence of delinquents and criminals.[2] The following conclusions were derived from an analysis of approximately 350 reports of this nature, which included tests of approximately 175,000 criminals and delinquents. *First*, the proportion of delinquents diagnosed "feebleminded" decreased from more than 50 percent in the average study made in the period 1910-1914 to 20 percent in the period 1925-1928. *Second*, wide variations are found in the results of tests given over a period of two decades, variations which are more likely to reflect differences in the methods of the testers than differences in the intelligence of the persons tested. *Third*, when allowance is made for the selection involved in arrest, conviction, and imprisonment, the distribution of intelligence scores of delinquents is very similar to the distribution of intelligence scores of the general population. Zeleny, after equating the procedures of different testers, concluded that the ratio of delinquents and general population in respect to mental deficiency was about 1.2 to 1.[3] *Fourth*, the studies of groups of mentally retarded persons

---

[1] H. H. Goddard, *Human Efficiency and Levels of Intelligence* (Princeton: Princeton University Press, 1920), pp. 73-74. See also idem, *Juvenile Delinquency* (New York: Dodd, Mead, 1921), p. 22.

[2] Edwin H. Sutherland, "Mental Deficiency and Crime," chap. 15 in Kimball Young, ed., *Social Attitudes* (New York: Henry Holt, 1931), pp. 357-375.

[3] L. D. Zeleny, "Feeble-mindedness and Criminal Conduct," *American Journal of Sociology*, 38:564-578, January, 1933. See also Simon H. Tulchin, *Intelligence and Crime* (Chicago: University of Chicago Press, 1939); Edward A. Ferentz, "Mental Deficiency and Crime," *Journal of Criminal Law, Criminology, and Police Science*, 45:299-307, September-October, 1954; and Mary Woodward, *Low Intelligence and Delinquency* (London: Institute for the Study and Treatment of Delinquency, 1963).

in the community do not show an excess of delinquency among them, as compared with the normal population. *Fifth,* mentally retarded prisoners have about the same disciplinary records in prisons as other prisoners. *Sixth,* mentally retarded offenders are successful on parole about as frequently as other parolees. *Seventh,* mentally retarded offenders become recidivists with about the same frequency as other offenders. *Eighth,* persons convicted of sex crimes are more likely to be mentally retarded than persons convicted of other crimes. In general, this analysis showed that the relationship between crime and mental retardation is comparatively slight. Certainly intelligence is not as closely correlated with crime as are age and sex. This does not, however, mean that it may not be a very important condition in individual cases.

An extensive survey of the literature on the general relation between morality and intellect concluded that the relation is positive but low, with correlations usually between 0.10 and 0.30. The only significant point of difference from the analysis described above is on the fourth point, for the survey reported that the mentally retarded population in the community has an unusually large number of delinquencies.[4] Further evidence on this point was later supplied by Kennedy, who compared 256 morons and a matched control group of 129 nonmorons and concluded that morons had a higher rate of arrest and also of recidivism than had nonmorons.[5] The difficulty with this study, however, is that the parents and other family members of the morons also had a higher arrest rate than the family members of the nonmorons. Thus the control group was not matched with the moron group in certain essential respects, and the higher arrest rate of the morons may be due to their family associations rather than to their IQs.

The proposition that "feeblemindedness" is inherited as a unit characteristic has now been generally abandoned. Intelligence, as measured by tests, has proved to be modifiable, as is shown both by retesting of individuals and by comparisons of foster children reared in different environments.[6] Recent psychological thought regarding the relationship between mental deficiency and crime tends to parallel that of Coleman, who makes the following statement:

Popular opinion, based on outdated psychological findings, has it that the great majority of inmates of penal institutions are mentally defective and that mentally defective individuals are especially prone to criminal behavior. Indeed, one of the major reasons why institutionalization was first recommended for the mental defective was to

---

[4] Clara F. Chassell, *The Relation Between Morality and Intellect* (New York: Columbia University Press, 1935), p. 133.

[5] Ruby Jo Reeves Kennedy, *The Social Adjustment of Morons in a Connecticut City* (Hartford: Commission to Survey the Human Resources of Connecticut, 1948). See also Austin E. Grigg, "Criminal Behavior of Mentally Retarded Adults," *American Journal of Mental Deficiency,* 52:370-374, April, 1948.

[6] See Kenneth Eells, *Intelligence and Cultural Differences: A Study of Cultural Learning and Problem Solving* (Chicago: University of Chicago Press, 1951).

protect society from his supposed "criminal propensities." More recent psychological evidence has conclusively demonstrated, however, that inferior mentality is neither the specific cause nor the outstanding factor in crime and delinquency. Although a higher percentage of delinquent children come from the ranks of the mentally defective, particularly from those of borderline intelligence, it is not the mental deficiency per se but the inability of the child to make adequate school or social adjustments that usually results in his delinquency.[7] ●

Psychoses   Although mental disease has been studied for many generations, much disagreement still prevails regarding definitions, classifications, causes, methods of diagnosis, therapy, extent in the general population, and frequency in the criminal population. It is probably improper to speak of adjustment problems as "disease" or even "illness."[8] However, if the disease analogy is used, then the phenomenon is not one disease but a large number of diseases, differing from each other as much as bronchitis differs from tuberculosis. Paresis is a fairly well-established disease with clear symptoms and demonstrable organic origin, but schizophrenia is extremely indefinite in regard to both symptoms and origin.

Increasing emphasis is being placed on the role of social relations in the etiology of many of the psychoses. In a pioneering work along this line, Faris and Dunham studied the residences of psychotic patients received in the public and private hospitals of Illinois and showed a definite relationship between social organization and the incidence of psychoses. Generally, they found that the previous places of residence clustered around the center of the city and decreased in frequency toward the city limits. Moreover, they found that all psychoses did not follow the same pattern of distribution, that one type of social organization tended to produce schizophrenia, another type to produce manic-depressive disorders.[9] More recent studies show both a close relationship between social class position and various kinds of mental disturbance[10] and a close relationship between posthospital performance and social class—the higher the class, the better the

---

[7] James C. Coleman, *Abnormal Psychology and Modern Life* (Glenview, Ill.: Scott, Foresman, 1950), pp. 476-477. See also Franco Ferracuti, "Il Contributo Die Tests Psicologici Alle Teorie Criminologiche Ed Alla Diagnosi Dei Criminali Mentalmente Anormali," *Quaderni Di Criminologia Clinica,* 2:495-506, December, 1960.

[8] Thomas S. Szasz, *The Myth of Mental Illness: Foundations of a Theory of Personal Conduct* (New York: Hoeber-Harper, 1961). See also idem, *The Manufacture of Madness* (New York: Harper and Row, 1970); and Herbert Fingarette, *The Meaning of Criminal Insanity* (Berkeley and Los Angeles: University of California, 1972).

[9] R. E. L. Faris and H. W. Dunham, *Mental Disorders in Urban Areas: An Ecological Study of Schizophrenia and Other Psychoses* (Chicago: University of Chicago Press, 1939).

[10] August B. Hollingshead and Frederick C. Redlich, *Social Class and Mental Illness* (New York: John Wiley, 1958).

performance.[11] One investigator has emphasized that delusional ideas and abnormal reaction patterns are transferred from one person to another, and that this phenomenon is found among persons in close and prolonged personal contact, even when there is no blood relationship.[12]

The major characteristic which psychotics have in common is complete breakdown or severe impairment of the means of communication; they lose contact with "reality." They sometimes are completely isolated from the values of their social groups and, in fact, do not maintain membership in social groups. In other cases the isolation is less extreme. Accordingly, many psychotics do not manage their lives in a way considered satisfactory by most persons, and they sometimes get into trouble with the law. The psychoses may produce social harms in various ways. A hallucinatory voice may repeat a command to kill, and the voice may finally be obeyed. An innocent person may be attacked as a means of revenge for or defense against an imagined misdeed. However, only some of the persons classed as psychotic are dangerous, and certainly not all psychotic persons are hospitalized.

Psychiatric examinations of criminals on admission to state prisons generally show not more than 5 percent to be psychotic, and in many institutions less than 1 percent. This variation is affected both by the preconceptions of the examiners and by variations in the manner of handling defendants who plead that they are "insane," not "criminal." In one clinic, no delinquent was diagnosed as "normal," on the strange ground that "normality is a vague concept because everybody simply projects his own ideal of perfection into it."[13] Offenders admitted to houses of correction and to jails have a slightly higher rate of psychoses than those admitted to prisons. Even so, the rate is seldom higher than 5 percent of the admissions and in many studies is reported to be about 2 percent. The offenders in these institutions often have alcoholic psychoses, from which they may quickly recover. Moreover, when the harms committed are not serious, the court is not as likely to declare a defendant "insane" and commit him to a hospital rather than to a penal institution. The fact that a criminal is psychotic does not mean that his crime was due to his psychosis. Silverman reported that the social backgrounds of 500 psychotic inmates of the Federal Medical Center were remarkably similar to those of nonpsychotic federal prisoners.[14] However,

[11] Simon Dinitz, Mark Lefton, Shirley Angrist, and Benjamin Pasamanick, "Psychiatric and Social Attributes as Predictors of Case Outcome in Mental Hospitalization," *Social Problems*, 8:322-328, Spring, 1961.

[12] Alexander Gralnick, "Folie a Deux — The Psychosis of Association: A Review of 103 Cases and the Entire English Literature, with Case Presentations," *Psychiatric Quarterly*, 16:230-263, September, 1942.

[13] Pierre Rube, "Psychiatric Clinic for Adolescent Delinquents," *Quarterly Journal of Child Behavior*, 4:24-56, January, 1952.

[14] Daniel Silverman, "The Psychotic Criminals: A Study of 500 Cases," *Journal of Clinical Psychopathology*, 8:301-327, October, 1946. See also Daniel Silverman, "Psychoses in Criminals: A Study of 500 Psychotic Prisoners," *Journal of Criminal Psychopathology*, 4:703-730, April, 1943.

he did find that psychotic prisoners were considerably different from psychotic persons outside prisons. This suggests that the social backgrounds which produced criminal behavior in the non-psychotic prisoners also produced criminal behavior in the psychotic prisoners.

Many psychotic persons do not commit crimes or legal harms of any kind. This has been demonstrated in two organized research studies. Dunham, in a study of 870 male schizophrenic patients aged 15-29 in Illinois hospitals, found that only 24 percent had records of juvenile delinquency or adult crime, and a large proportion of these records were for minor offenses; approximately 20 percent of these records were in connection with the current commitment to the hospitals; the paranoid had a significantly higher rate of crime than the catatonic.[15] A similar study of 1,262 patients in the Eloise State Hospital in Michigan showed that 21.1 percent had records of definite crimes, and an additional 4.4 percent had records of threatened or attempted crimes; of these, 39 percent had the recorded behavior before the recognized onset of mental disease, 61 percent after the onset.[16] The law-abiding behavior of most psychotics is explained partly by the types of psychoses and partly by the fact that their characters and inclinations were law-abiding prior to the onset of the psychosis and somehow persisted after the mental disturbance occurred.

Research on the exact role of psychoses in crime is complicated by the fact that a person who is "insane" at the time he commits a legally-forbidden harm does not commit a crime. A person charged with a crime may defend himself in court by showing that he was insane at the time the act occurred, just as another person may plead that his act occurred in self-defense. This means, for example, that one who is insane at the time he kills another has committed no crime; he is committed to a hospital for treatment, rather than to a prison for punishment. Hence, if the legal concept "insanity" were synonymous with the psychiatric term "psychosis," there would be no problem regarding the role of the psychoses in criminality, for persons would be *either* psychotic *or* criminal. In the current medico-legal situation, however, "insanity" differs from what many psychiatrists have in mind when they speak of "psychoses." Consequently, a court may find a defendant to be criminal (i.e., "not insane" and guilty), while a psychiatrist may diagnose the same defendant as schizophrenic or, generally, psychotic.

Generally, "insanity" is used to describe legally harmful behavior perpetrated under circumstances in which the actor (a) did not know the nature or quality of his act or (b) did not know right

[15] H. Warren Dunham. "The Schizophrene and Criminal Behavior," *American Sociological Review*, 4:352-361, June, 1939. See also J. Kloek, "Schizophrenia and Delinquency," in A. V. S. Reuck and Ruth Porter, eds., *The Mentally Abnormal Offender* (Boston: Little, Brown, 1968), pp. 19-28.

[16] Milton H. Erickson, "Criminality in a Group of Male Psychiatric Patients," *Mental Hygiene*, 22:459-476, July, 1938.

from wrong. These rules for determining insanity were formulated in England in 1843 and are known as the "M'Naghten rules." Most psychiatrists hold that they do not incorporate the many advances in their profession since that time. The most frequent argument against them is that in some kinds of behavior the actor does know right from wrong but *nevertheless* exhibits the harmful behavior because it is prompted "from within" by a force which he is powerless to resist.[17] This argument has had some effect on criminal law theory, for at present the courts of about fourteen states hold that punishment for perpetration of a legal harm can be avoided by showing that, while the defendant knew right from wrong, his behavior was prompted by an "irresistible impulse."[18] In 1954 the Court of Appeals in the District of Columbia rejected the M'Naghten rules for determining insanity, holding simply that a defendant is not criminally responsible if his act was the product of "mental disease or mental defect."[19] The M'Naghten rules have also been modified in about six other states. In most states the vagueness of both the criminal law concepts and psychiatric concepts allows some criminals to be declared "insane," and thereby to escape punishment; and it allows some psychotics to be punished for crime rather than treated for mental disease.

During the last generation, development of the electroencephalograph technique, a recording of a so-called "brain wave," has enabled researchers to compare delinquents and criminals with psychotics without actually declaring the delinquents to be psychotic or insane. A recent study of Israeli juvenile delinquents found them to have a high incidence of EEG abnormalities, and this finding was supported by results of Rorschach tests.[20] However, a comprehensive review of thirty years of research on this subject concluded: "Despite numerous electroencephalographic (EEG) studies indicating varying but high rates of abnormality in adult criminals, there is no proof that brain damage or abnormality as reflected in the EEG is a necessary precondition for the development of antisocial reactions."[21] ●

---

[17] See Manfred S. Guttmacher and Henry Weihofen, *Psychiatry and the Law* (New York: W. W. Norton, 1952), pp. 401-423; and Donald R. Cressey, "The Differential Association Theory and Compulsive Crimes," *Journal of Criminal Law, Criminology, and Police Science*, 45:29-40, May-June, 1954.

[18] E. R. Keedy, "Irresistible Impulse as a Defense in Criminal Law," *University of Pennsylvania Law Review*, 100:956-993, May, 1952.

[19] *Durham v. United States*, 214 F. 2d 862-876.

[20] Marcel Assael, Reuven Kohen-Raz, and Suzy Alpern, "Developmental Analysis of EEG Abnormalities in Juvenile Delinquents," *Diseases of the Nervous System*, 28:49-54, January, 1967.

[21] E. Robins, "Antisocial and Dyssocial Personality Disorders," in A. M. Freedman and H. I. Kaplan, eds., *Comprehensive Textbook of Psychiatry* (Baltimore: Williams and Wilkins, 1967), pp. 955-956.

**Post-
encephalitic
personality**

Encephalitis is relatively new as a classified disease. This disease produces lesions in the central nervous system and after-effects in the form of behavior problems, especially if the patient is a child. The primary effect is lethargy, retardation, and irritability. Quarrels, thefts, truancy, and other disorders of behavior are reported frequently. There is, however, little evidence regarding the proportion of cases of this disease in which behavior disorders appear and continue beyond the period of the primary sickness. It has been believed by some psychiatrists that subsequent behavior disorders are almost universal, and they have suggested that many other delinquents may have become disorganized as a result of the disease, though the disease was not recognized as such. If this be true, it is possible that many other children may have had the disease, not recognized as such, and have had no *sequelae* in the form of behavior problems.

This disease is regarded as very significant because it is taken as evidence that injuries to the neural system produce delinquency. As a matter of fact, however, the explanation is not simple. There is the direct physiological theory that the lesions in the central nervous system produce irritability and reduce efficiency and inhibitions, and consequently the child acts impulsively. These effects persist beyond the acute stage of the disease because of habit formation. A second theory is that the inferior performance resulting from the lesions in the central nervous system lowers the status of the child, and the criticisms of parents and teachers when the child does not do as well as previously drive the child desperate. When the child is placed in a group of other postencephalitic children, from whom less is expected, the feeling of inferiority is overcome and the behavior improves.[22] Another theory is that those encephalitic patients who manifest subsequent behavior difficulties are members of families or groups which manifest behavior problems such as psychosis, drunkenness, and criminality. In fact, explanation of the behavior disorders following this disease is not certain, though the injury to the nervous system is evidently of great significance. Also, it is probable that the person's behavior is affected by emotional changes and the reactions of others to these changes, rather than by intellectual deterioration.[23] •

---

[22] For a description of an interesting experiment in the reeducation of post-encephalitic children, see Earl D. Bond and Kenneth E. Appel, The Treatment of Behavior Disorders Following Encephalitis (New York: Commonwealth Fund, 1931). Earl D. Bond and L. H. Smith, "Post-encephalitic Behavior Disorders," American Journal of Psychiatry, 92:17-31, July, 1935.

[23] M. Molitch, "Chronic Post-Encephalitic Behavior Problems," American Journal of Psychiatry, 91:843-861, January, 1935. For a similar conclusion regarding epilepsy, see Leslie E. Keating, "Epilepsy and Behaviour Disorder in Schoolchildren," Journal of Mental Science, 107:161-180, January, 1961.

The terms *psychopath, psychopathic personality,* and *constitutional psychopathic inferior* are used with little or no differentiation to refer to persons who are regarded as emotionally abnormal but who do not manifest the break with reality that characterizes psychotics. Some psychiatrists have classified psychopathic personalities in three groups—the egocentric, the inadequate, and the vagabond—and many descriptive terms have been applied to each category. Others classify them into schizoid types, paranoid types, cyclothymic types, sexual deviants, alcoholics, and drug addicts. The method of diagnosing psychopathic personality is not at all standardized or objective; consequently, a person may be psychopathic or not, depending upon the preconceptions of the person making the examination. Because it is difficult to define or identify a psychopath, the label *psychopathic personality* can be applied to almost anyone. Investigators who are convinced that all, or almost all, criminals must have "bad" personalities can attribute the criminality of persons showing no ordinary psychoses or neuroses to psychopathic personality. Indeed, "delinquency of one kind or another constitutes the most frequently utilized symptomatic basis for diagnosis of psychopathic personality."[24] The concept is often designated a "wastebasket category" into which not-otherwise-explicable criminal behavior is tossed. Preu made the following statement regarding the concept:

Psychopathic personality

> The term "psychopathic personality," as commonly understood, is useless in psychiatric research. It is a diagnosis of convenience arrived at by a process of exclusion. It does not refer to a specific behavioral entity. It serves as a scrapbasket to which is relegated a group of otherwise unclassified personality disorders and problems.[25]

The vagueness of the term, as used in criminology, is indicated by the fact that under the administration of one psychiatrist 98 percent of the inmates admitted to the state prison of Illinois were diagnosed as psychopathic personalities, while in similar institutions with different psychiatrists not more than 5 percent were so diagnosed. Vagueness in diagnosis also has been indicated by Sheldon, who, speaking of 200 boys in a social agency in Boston, declared that it was not uncommon to find that as many as a dozen different psychiatric diagnoses and interpretations had been made on a youngster. Moreover, diagnoses of some boys were contradictory, and others had been given *"all the possible diagnoses."*[26] Numerous persons have attempted to define the

---

[24] P. W. Preu, "The Concept of Psychopathic Personality," in J. McV. Hunt, ed., *Personality and the Behavior Disorders* (New York: Ronald Press, 1944), vol. 2, pp. 922-937.

[25] Ibid. See also Leonard P. Ullman and Leonard Krasner, *A Psychological Approach to Abnormal Behavior* (Englewood Cliffs, N. J.: Prentice-Hall, 1969).

[26] William H. Sheldon, *Varieties of Delinquent Youth: An Introduction to Constitutional Psychiatry* (New York: Harper, 1949), p. 42. See also Nathan W. Ackerman, "Psychiatric Disorders in Children — Diagnosis and Etiology in Our Time," in Paul H. Hoch and Joseph Zubin, eds., *Current Problems in Psychiatric Diagnosis* (New York: Grune and Stratton, 1953), pp. 205-231.

concept *psychopathic personality* with some degree of rigor and to account for the formation of psychopathic personalities.[27]

The most careful investigations of psychopathic personalities among criminals were made by Cason thirty years ago. In reviewing the literature, he found 202 terms which have been used more or less synonymously with the term *psychopath*.[28] He then counted fifty-five "traits or characteristics" which are generally held to be present among psychopaths, and thirty behaviors which are frequently characterized as "forms of psychopathic behavior." A study of the inmates held at the Psychopathic Unit of the Federal Medical Center revealed that some inmates exhibited many of the thirty different forms of psychopathic behavior, and some had few of the behaviors. He selected two groups—the twenty-three inmates having the largest number of the psychopathic behaviors and the twenty-nine inmates having the smallest number—and determined the frequency with which each of the fifty-five traits or characteristics appeared in each group. He found that forty-seven of the fifty-five traits had no statistical significance in differentiating the most psychopathic from the least psychopathic, and, of the eight remaining traits, six were just barely significant. With the exception of the two traits—intolerance and making threats—the traits which are generally regarded as characterizing the psychopaths were not as useful in differentiating the most psychopathic from the least psychopathic as were the facts that a person was born in the eastern states, had engaged in farming, or had violated the Dyer Act against automobile thefts.[29] These studies seem to justify a conclusion that the concept *psychopathic personality* is as useless in the interpretation of criminal behavior as was the older concept *moral imbecile* which has been completely discarded by scholars in this field.

In another study, Cason and Pescor compared 500 prisoners in the Federal Medical Center who had been diagnosed as psychopaths with all federal prisoners and with the civilian population of the United States. Among other things, they found that the psychopathic prisoners were very much concentrated in the age group 20-29, in comparison both with all federal prisoners and with the civilian population.[30] This is highly significant, for it indicates that people cease to be psychopathic after they pass the

[27] See, for example, Karl A. Menninger, "Recognizing and Renaming 'Psychopathic Personalities,'" *Bulletin of the Menninger Clinic*, 5:150-156, December, 1941; and M. D. Gynther, "Crime and Psychopathology," *Journal of Abnormal and Social Psychology*, 64 (1962): 378-380.

[28] Hulsey Cason, "The Psychopath and the Psychopathic," *Journal of Criminal Psychopathology*, 4:522-527, January, 1943.

[29] Hulsey Cason, "The Symptoms of the Psychopath," *Public Health Reports*, 61:1833-1868, December 20, 1946.

[30] Hulsey Cason and M. J. Pescor, "A Statistical Study of 500 Psychopathic Prisoners," *Public Health Reports*, 61:557-574, April 19, 1946; see also Hulsey Cason and M. J. Pescor, "A Comparative Study of Recidivists and Non-recidivists among Psychopathic Federal Offenders," *Journal of Criminal Law and Criminology*, 37:236-238, September-October, 1946.

age of thirty, or that psychopathic persons stop committing federal crimes after the age of thirty, or that psychiatrists do not characterize older persons as psychopaths as readily as they do younger persons. No theory of psychopathy adequately accounts for the first two interpretations. Ullman and Krasner's theory, utilizing both role-playing concepts and modern learning theory, probably offers the most promising research leads in this connection.[31]

During the years immediately following World War II, several states became panic-stricken because of a small number of serious sexual attacks, and their legislatures hurriedly enacted "sexual psychopath" laws, which spread through certain sections of the United States. Because no one has been able to identify a sexual psychopath any more than any other psychopath, the laws have been absurd in principle and futile in operation.[32] ●

Emotional instability and other traits of personality have been studied independently of the concept of psychopathic personality, and delinquent behavior is frequently attributed to one or more of these traits. One of the principal research procedures consists of administering a personality test to a group of delinquents and then comparing their scores with the scores of a control group composed of nondelinquents. Dozens of tests, rating scales, and other devices for measuring personality traits have been used. Studies have been made of instincts, emotions, moods, temperaments, moral judgments, ethical discriminations, as well as of such specific tendencies as aggressiveness, caution, conformity, conscientiousness, deception, self-assurance, social resistance, suggestibility, and many others. Years ago, Thomas said that if these tests had really measured the things they were intended to measure, our knowledge of and control over human nature would be nearly complete, but that, as a matter of fact, the units are not adequately defined, the tests do not measure the things they purport to measure, and the results have not been validated by reference to other data.[33]

Other personality deviations

Some psychiatrists who have attempted to avoid the vagueness of the psychopathic personality concept have merely substituted personality deviations of various kinds. For example, of the 2,537 individuals coming before the Psychiatric Clinic of the New York City Court of General Sessions in one year, 19.4 percent were diagnosed as psychopathic, but 76.1 percent were found to have personality deviations such as aggressiveness, emotional instabil-

---

[31] Ullman and Krasner, *A Psychological Approach to Abnormal Behavior.*

[32] See Edwin H. Sutherland, "The Sexual Psychopath Laws," *Journal of Criminal Law and Criminology,* 40:534-554, January-February, 1950; idem, "The Diffusion of Sexual Psychopath Laws," *American Journal of Sociology,* 56:142-148, September, 1950.

[33] W. I. Thomas and Dorothy S. Thomas, *The Child in America* (New York: Knopf, 1936), p. 263.

ity, and shiftlessness.[34] However, no personality tests were utilized, and the technique for locating such deviations is not precisely described. Moreover, there is no assurance that the deviations found among the criminals would not also be found among the general population.

Schuessler and Cressey in 1950 summarized the results of all studies in which the personality test scores of delinquents and criminals were compared with the scores of control groups. In the 113 studies of this kind, the whole range of traits was included and also the whole range of tests, including the Rorschach and other projective tests. One conclusion of their analysis was that not a single trait was shown in this series of studies to be more characteristic of delinquents than of nondelinquents. The general observation was that "the doubtful validity of many of the obtained differences, as well as the lack of consistency in the combined results, makes it impossible to conclude from these data that criminality and personality elements are associated."[35]

A follow-up survey which examined studies of this kind made between 1950 and 1965 suggests that the results obtained by personality testing are more positive than in the years surveyed by Schuessler and Cressey. Of the ninety-four studies, twenty-nine of which used the Minnesota Multiphasic Personality Inventory, seventy-six (81 percent) found a difference between criminals and noncriminals. Of the studies using tests other than the MMPI, differences were found in 75 percent of the applications. However, after examining the studies closely, the investigators concluded: "Although the results are an improvement over those reported in the Schuessler-Cressey study, the same types of problems and criticisms generally prevailed. . . . The findings are far from conclusive."[36]

The frustration-aggression hypothesis is frequently combined with the deviant-personality-trait conception of delinquency and crime, whether the personality traits are labeled psychopathy or not. It is assumed that unusual frustration results in emotional disturbance which produces aggression, and that delinquency is the consequence. The belief that aggression is a necessary consequence of frustration is certainly incorrect.[37] Most persons are frustrated, but only a few of them are aggressive. The belief that aggression

---

[34] Walter Bromberg, "American Achievements in Criminology," *Journal of Criminal Law, Criminology, and Police Science*, 44:166-176, July-August, 1953.

[35] Karl F. Schuessler and Donald R. Cressey, "Personality Characteristics of Criminals," *American Journal of Sociology*, 55:476-484, March, 1950. Essentially the same conclusion was reached by Lawson G. Lowrey, "Delinquent and Criminal Personalities," in J. McV. Hunt, *Personality and the Behavior Disorders*, pp. 794-821.

[36] Gordon P. Waldo and Simon Dinitz, "Personality Attributes of the Criminal: An Analysis of Research Studies, 1950-65," *Journal of Research in Crime and Delinquency*, 4:185-201, July, 1967.

[37] E. Faris, "Some Results of Frustration," *Sociology and Social Research*, 31:87-92, November, 1946.

has some necessary connection with delinquency and crime is equally incorrect. Most persons who seem to be aggressive are not criminals, and most criminals do not seem to be aggressive. If one were to select the tenth of the population which is most aggressive, assuming that aggression could be measured, it is not at all certain that this aggressive population would contain an unusual proportion of criminals.

The best general study of personal traits in relation to delinquency was made by Healy and Bronner.[38] This was an analysis of 105 delinquents treated over a three-year period in three clinics, in comparison with 105 nondelinquent siblings who lived in the same homes and neighborhoods and were matched with the delinquents, so far as possible, by age and sex. This study resulted in the finding that 91 percent of the delinquents and only 13 percent of their nondelinquent siblings had deep emotional disturbances. This difference is striking and has been regarded as final proof that delinquency is due largely to emotional disturbance. However, this interpretation is open to question for the following reasons:

First, the difference between the delinquents and their nondelinquent siblings is probably exaggerated. The staff in these clinics was composed almost entirely of psychiatrists and psychiatric social workers, and members of these professions have been trained to interpret delinquency in terms of emotional disturbance. Also, the staff became much better acquainted with the delinquents than with the nondelinquents, since they carried on three-year treatment programs for delinquents, and on that account would have been more likely to discover emotional disturbances among the delinquents. The inadequacy of the investigations of the nondelinquents is revealed by the report that only 21 percent of them were "even mildly delinquent."[39] Among university students in classes in criminology, about 98 percent report that they were at least "mildly delinquent" in childhood.

Second, emotional disturbances among delinquents, even if not exaggerated, are not demonstrated to be the cause of the delinquency; delinquent behavior may cause emotional disturbance. No organized effort was made in this study to determine whether the emotional disturbance preceded the delinquent behavior.

Third, the process by which emotional disturbance produces delinquent behavior is not adequately investigated. The basic argument is a deceptively simple one: a child is emotionally disturbed, so he commits a delinquent act. Emotional disturbance, however, does not in itself explain delinquent behavior, as is shown by the 13 percent of the nondelinquents who were said to be emotionally disturbed, and by the fact that there is no correlation between the frequency of emotional instability among school-

---

[38] William Healy and Augusta F. Bronner, *New Light on Delinquency and Its Treatment* (New Haven: Yale University Press, 1936).

[39] Ibid., p. 54.

children and delinquency rates of school districts.[40] The alternative hypothesis is that emotional disturbance produces delinquency when it isolates a person from the law-abiding groups or decreases the prestige of these groups, or when it throws an individual into association with delinquent groups. Under the same conditions of association, delinquent behavior results in those who are not emotionally disturbed. ●

Alcoholism

Estimates of the number of alcoholics in the United States range from 4,500,000 to 6,800,000.[41] Alcoholism is significant in criminology in two respects. First, it may be a crime in itself or may be directly related to violations of certain laws, such as those prohibiting public intoxication and drunken driving. Police arrest statistics submitted to the FBI for 1971 indicated that out of a total of 6,912,448 arrests, 1,491,782 were for drunkenness; another 701,237 arrests were for disorderly conduct and vagrancy, offenses which often involve drunkenness. Second, it may indirectly contribute to the violations of other laws, such as those prohibiting murder, rape, assault and battery, vagrancy, and nonsupport of families.[42] A questionnaire study of 2,325 male felons committed to California's Department of Corrections indicated that 98 percent had used alcoholic beverages, while the usage in the United States population of males twenty-one years of age and older was estimated at 70 percent. Twenty-nine percent of the alcoholic beverage users claimed they were intoxicated at the time they committed the offense for which they were sent to prison. The proportion of those who had been intoxicated varied with the type of crime committed, from a high of 50 percent for automobile theft to a low of 10 percent for narcotics offenses.[43] Alcoholism may also contribute to parental negligence and, in that way, to delinquency—about a third of all delinquents come from homes where there is parental alcoholism or excessive drinking.

Two major problems for a theory of criminal behavior are posed by the alcoholic criminal. The first of these is whether a person who is under the influence of alcohol will violate laws which he would not violate if he were not under that influence; if he does violate the law under such circumstances, he may not be acting under the influence of differential association. No clear-cut

---

[40] G. E. Swanson, "The Disturbance of Children in Urban Areas," *American Sociological Review,* 14:676-678, October, 1949.

[41] Richard H. Blum, "Mind-Altering Drugs and Dangerous Behavior: Alcohol," appendix B in President's Commission on Law Enforcement and Administration of Justice, *Task Force Report: Drunkenness* (Washington: Government Printing Office, 1967), pp. 29-49.

[42] Marvin E. Wolfgang and Rolf B. Strohm, "The Relationship Between Alcohol and Criminal Homicide," *Quarterly Journal of Studies on Alcohol,* vol. 17 (1956), no. 3, pp. 411-425.

[43] State of California, Department of Public Health, Division of Alcoholic Rehabilitation, *Criminal Offenders and Drinking Involvement,* Publication No. 3, 1960, pp. 7, 14.

research work has been done on this problem, and no definite answer can be given. However, considerable information which points in the direction of a negative answer is available. It is known that when people in certain areas become intoxicated, they are almost certain to start fights and violate criminal laws; this is particularly true of the lower socioeconomic class. On the other hand, intoxication in other parts of American society may result only in singing, exchange of dirty stories, or crying. These differences appear to operate in larger groups and do not merely differentiate one person from another.[44] Furthermore, it may be said that even if a person, without change in his associations, acts differently when under the influence of alcohol than at other times, this may conceivably be because he has learned from associations with others certain ways of acting when intoxicated. He may have learned that when he is becoming intoxicated he should act joyful, and consequently he begins to sing, or he may have learned that he should act tough, and consequently he picks a fight. And he may have learned that intoxication is a good excuse for behavior which would be regarded as inexcusable otherwise. The best review and analysis of studies linking alcohol and crime noted that the problem of causal inference is an extraordinarily difficult one:

On the basis of available information it is plausible to assume that alcohol does play an important and damaging role in the lives of offenders, particularly chronic inebriates, and in the production of crime. Yet one cannot be sure on the basis of the work done to date that the alcohol use of offenders exceeds that of nonoffenders with similar social and personal characteristics (if any such match is possible). One cannot be sure that the alcohol use of offenders is any greater at the moments of their offense than during their ordinary noncriminal moments. One cannot be sure that the alcohol-using offenders would not have committed some offense had they not been drinking. One is not sure that the alcohol use of offenders differs from that of the other persons possibly present in the same or like situations which inspired or provoked the criminality of one and not the other. Finally, and this is an important point in view of the fact that all studies have been done on apprehended offenders, one does not know that the relationship now shown between alcohol use and crime is not in fact a relationship between being caught and being a drinker rather than in being a criminal and being a drinker.[45]

The second problem is whether alcoholism is a form of psychopathy. Many psychiatrists in making classifications of psychopathies interpret alcoholism as a form of vagabondage, or an abnormal method of escaping from reality. Scores of papers have been written from the point of view of this interpretation, and it may be regarded as a generally accepted belief. As a matter of fact, it has never been demonstrated, and the concept of escape is so vague that it cannot readily be tested.

---

[44] Craig MacAndrew and Robert B. Edgerton, *Drunken Comportment: A Social Explanation* (Chicago: Aldine, 1969); see also Sherri Cavan, *Liquor License: An Ethnography of Bar Behavior* (Chicago: Aldine, 1966).

[45] Blum, "Mind-Altering Drugs," p. 43.

Moreover, it is commonly asserted that persons who become alcoholic do so because of certain personality traits. An analysis has been made, however, of all the available studies in which alcoholics have been given personality tests in comparison with nonalcoholics or with the general population, and one conclusion from this analysis is that the alcoholics have not been demonstrated to have any trait or traits which differentiate them from nonalcoholics. Particularly, the Rorschach tests, which have been used more frequently than any other tests in studies of alcoholics, fail completely to arrive at any consistent result. Another conclusion which may be drawn from the studies is that there is no such thing as a pre-alcoholic personality, that is, a type of person who is more likely than others to become an alcoholic.[46]

Alcoholism has been defined as a disease by many health organizations, including the American Medical Association and the World Health Organization. But further evidence that alcoholism is not primarily an expression of personal pathology is found in the fact that the Alcoholics Anonymous organization, which had over 400,000 members in 1968, has had some success in treating alcoholics. Although it can be argued that only the alcoholics without personal pathologies join the organization, those who do interact with ex-alcoholics gain assistance in overcoming their craving for alcohol. Alcoholics Anonymous has demonstrated that it is not necessary to attempt to find and treat some underlying defect in the alcoholic's personality. Another method of dealing with alcoholism is a drug called antibuse. A person who drinks after taking this drug becomes quite ill. In deciding malpractice suits against doctors who prescribed the drug, courts have held that the physician should not have given such a substance to a person no longer in control of his drinking. Accordingly, few doctors now prescribe it. Some psychiatrists insisted that antibuse had to be accompanied by psychiatric treatment in order to be successful, but there is some evidence that the drug was as successful when no attention was paid to personality as when accompanied by psychiatric treatment. ●

Narcotic drugs   Drug addiction, like alcoholic intoxication, is often regarded as a symptom of psychopathy; drug addiction is presented in some reports as one of the classes of psychopathies, coordinate with paresis and schizophrenia. The discussion of narcotic addiction is included in this chapter on psychopathic traits and criminal behavior as a matter of convenience rather than of logic, for narcotic addiction is certainly not one of the psychopathies. Lindesmith has shown conclusively that no distinction can be made between psychopathic and normal persons in the genesis of drug addiction. Any person may begin to use narcotic drugs casually, either from motives of curiosity and observance of folk-

---

[46] Edwin H. Sutherland, H. G. Schroeder, and C. L. Tordella, "Personality Traits and the Alcoholic: A Critique of Existing Studies," *Quarterly Journal of Studies on Alcohol,* 11:547-561, December, 1950.

ways in variant cultures or in complete ignorance of the fact that he is using narcotic drugs, which happened especially in earlier generations in connection with medical prescriptions and patent medicines for digestive ailments. Any person, regardless of the traits of his personality, who thus uses narcotic drugs casually until he suffers distress when the drugs are withdrawn, and who becomes aware of the relation between his distress and the withdrawal of the drugs is a drug addict. Psychopathic and normal persons behave in uniform ways in this respect.[47]

Unlike drunkenness, drug addiction itself is not a crime. It never has been a crime under federal law, and a California law making it one was recently declared unconstitutional by the United States Supreme Court.[48] What is against the law is purchase, possession, and sale of narcotics and, in some states, nonmedical use of narcotics and narcotics paraphernalia. Like the skid-row drunk, the addict thus lives in an almost perpetual state of law violation. A large percentage of state and federal prisoners have committed drug-related crimes. In some county jails, as many as 80 percent of the inmates are confined for drug-related offenses.

Narcotic drugs are often said to be factors in the genesis of other criminal behavior. Eleven percent of the persons arrested in 1965 by the New York City police for felonies against property were admitted drug (mostly heroin) users. The proportion of drug users among those arrested for petty larceny was about the same but the figure for involvement of admitted drug users in arrests for felonies against the person was only 2 percent.[49] A more recent study showed a much greater association between criminality and addiction—*all* of the male addicts certified to the New York Narcotic Addiction Control Commission for treatment in summer and fall, 1970, reported commission of criminal offenses, and 79 percent had arrest records.[50] Those arrests that did not involve drug-law violations were principally for petty thefts and vagrancy. Recent studies have also suggested that in America, where the activities necessary to addiction are defined as crime, and where felons are overrepresented in the addict population, crime rates are increased considerably by drug addiction. This is not true in nations that handle drug addicts in such a way that they are not forced into intimate association with criminal behavior patterns.[51]

A precise definition of the process by which narcotic drugs are related to criminal behavior has not been made. The popular belief that these drugs make their users reckless and violent is certainly not correct. The opiates, in fact, have the opposite effect.

---

[47] A. R. Lindesmith, *Addiction and Opiates* (Chicago: Aldine, 1968).

[48] *Robinson v. California*, 370 U.S. 660 (1962).

[49] President's Commission on Law Enforcement and Administration of Justice, *Task Force Report: Narcotics and Drug Abuse* (Washington: Government Printing Office, 1967), p. 10.

[50] James A. Inciardi and Carl D. Chambers, "Unreported Criminal Involvement of Narcotic Addicts," *Journal of Drug Issues*, 2:57-64, Spring, 1972.

[51] Alfred R. Lindesmith, *The Addict and the Law* (Bloomington, Ind.: Indiana University Press, 1965), pp. 124-128.

Cocaine, which should be distinguished from the opiates, is an excitant, and it is said that criminals sometimes take this drug prior to their crimes to stimulate a sense of bravery and recklessness. Even though this be true, the criminal behavior is established before the drug is used. In recent years, cocaine usage has increased in the United States.

A second process which has been suggested is that narcotic addiction produces physical and mental deterioration and therefore reduces the addict's income; at the same time the drug habit demands a continuous supply of expensive drugs, with food and other necessities sacrificed in order to secure the drugs. The non-drug offenses in which the heroin addict becomes involved are generally of the fund-raising variety. The average daily cost to the admitted heroin users arrested in New York City in 1965 was about fourteen dollars. Between three dollars and five dollars in merchandise must be stolen to realize one dollar in cash, so support of a drug habit by stealing cost between forty and seventy dollars worth of merchandise a day. This is an average —some addicts' habits cost much more.[52] Because the need is great, and because satisfaction of the need is expensive, the thefts are often said to be due to economic necessity. This simple explanation is inadequate. All persons have needs; some persons satisfy their needs by legal methods, and some by illegal methods, and neither the fact nor the size of the need seems to differentiate the illegal methods from the legal methods.

A third hypothesis is that the person who becomes a drug addict loses his economic efficiency and his previous associates; he is driven into association with criminals in order to secure a supply of narcotic drugs and thereby associates with criminalistic values which enable him to engage in petty larceny and other illegal methods by which he can acquire a supply of drugs. If he were driven into association with criminals for any other reason, he would have the same tendencies to commit crimes. ●

**Psycho-
analysis
and crime**

A large proportion of the persons working with delinquents and criminals implicitly or explicitly use some form of psychoanalytic theory in their explanations of criminality. There really are many psychoanalytic theories; not one, but all emphasize unconscious emotional difficulties of some kind in the causation of crime.[53] The conventional Freudian theory contends that the mind is composed of three portions or parts: id, ego, and superego. The id consists of "original tendencies," or "impulses" which are possessed at birth. The id impulses are not adapted to social life and must be repressed or expressed in socially acceptable ways if

---

[52] President's Commission, *Task Force Report: Narcotics and Drug Abuse*, p. 10.

[53] For an excellent summary of psychoanalytic explanations of delinquent acts and of delinquent types of personality, see Nigel Walker, *Crime and Punishment in Britain* (Edinburgh: University of Edinburgh Press, 1965), pp. 69-72.

one is to maintain himself in social life. Basically, this is a frustration of drives common to all men. The superego is the embodiment of the moral codes of society, and the id impulses are directed in view of the superego by the ego. The id usually is tamed, but often the impulses remain in the unconscious; the ego represses or forces them into the unconscious because they are painfully in conflict with social conventions. They get into consciousness only in symbolic form, as in dreams or in overt behavior which does not mean what, on its face, it seems to mean. The criminal is a person who has failed to tame the impulses sufficiently, or who has failed to transform them into socially acceptable ways of behaving. Criminal behavior, therefore, may be the direct expression of original urges; it may be symbolic expression of repressed desires; or it may be the result of an ego which has become maladjusted because of the conflicting forces exerted on it by the id and the superego.[54]

The Oedipus complex concept, for example, is based on the premise that incest is a basic desire of human beings—every male loves his mother and is jealous of his father because of the father's sex relations with the mother. In this situation, the id could take over, and the father would be murdered and the mother raped. Or the id urges may be repressed or inhibited because of the strong social taboos against their expression. Or they may be partially repressed, in which case the person may murder his father in some symbolic way, or he may commit an act which is symbolic of the act of sexual intercourse with his mother. Either kind of symbolic act may be a crime—he may "murder" his father by forging checks on his bank account, or he may "rape" his mother by burglarizing a dwelling house. But crime may arise in another way also. Whenever the id dominates the superego, as in instances where it asserts itself through unconscious wishes and desires for intercourse with the mother, the ego feels guilty, for the superego is always operating. To get rid of the guilt feelings, the ego may seek punishment, and, since punishment follows crime, a crime may be committed. The existence of clues to detection and apprehension, such as a fingerprint left at the scene of a crime, is interpreted as evidence of this phenomenon.[55]

The major difficulty with such theory is the fact that the variables cannot be studied scientifically. There is no way to prove or disprove the theory, for the elements of it cannot be observed

---

[54] For detailed discussion of psychoanalytic theory in criminology and for examples of research based upon it, see David Abrahamsen, *The Psychology of Crime* (New York: Columbia University Press, 1960), Kate Friedlander, *The Psychoanalytic Approach to Juvenile Delinquency* (New York: International Universities Press, 1947); Franz Alexander and Hugo Staub, *The Criminal, the Judge, and the Public: A Psychological Analysis*, rev. ed. (Glencoe, Ill.: Free Press, 1956); August Aichhorn, *Wayward Youth* (New York: Viking Press, 1925); Robert Lindner, *Rebel Without Cause* (New York: Grune and Stratton, 1944).

[55] See S. Glover, *The Roots of Crime* (London: Imago, 1960), p. 302.

or measured. From the point of view of a nonbeliever the symbolism often is fantastic, and the psychoanalysts have no way of demonstrating the relation between the symbols and the things they are supposed to represent. Moreover, one who argues that psychoanalytic theory is scientifically invalid in many respects is sometimes psychoanalyzed by the defenders of the theory, on the assumption that he himself must necessarily be expressing some deeply hidden, secret, emotional conflict rather than a worthwhile criticism.[56] ●

Conclusions

The neo-Lombrosian notion that crime is an expression of psychopathy is no more justified than was the Lombrosian notion that criminals constitute a distinct physical type. Some studies have found a large proportion of criminals to be abnormal, but it is possible that these findings arise from poor standardization in methods of diagnosis of abnormality. The preconception of this school of thought was shown in extreme form in a report by psychiatrists on the medical aspects of crime to the effect that a diagnosis of mental disease "is permissible even when the criminal has shown no evidence of mental disease other than his criminal behavior."[57] According to this recommendation, the abnormality which is to be used as the explanation of criminal behavior may be inferred from the criminal behavior which it explains; abnormality and criminal behavior would necessarily be associated according to that circular method of reasoning. Perhaps this is why one psychiatrist has been able to say, "In all my experience I have not been able to find one single offender who did not show some mental pathology. . . . The 'normal' offender is a myth."[58]

Research studies conducted by scholars representing different schools of thought have found no trait of personality to be very closely associated with criminal or delinquent behavior. No consistent, statistically significant differences between personality traits of delinquents and personality traits of nondelinquents have been found. The explanation of criminal behavior, apparently, must be found in social interaction, in which both the behavior of a person and the overt or prospective behavior of other persons play their parts.

---

[56] Cf. Ernest Jones, *The Life and Work of Sigmund Freud,* vol. 2, *The Years of Maturity, 1901-1919* (New York: Basic Books, 1955), p. 127.

[57] Quoted in M. Ploscowe, "Some Causative Factors in Criminality," National Commission on Law Observance and Enforcement, *Report No. 13, Report on Causes of Crime,* vol. 1 (Washington: Government Printing Office, 1931), p. 57.

[58] David Abrahamsen, *Who Are the Guilty? A Study of Education and Crime* (New York: Rinehart, 1952), p. 125. See also Benjamin Karpman, "Criminal Psychodynamics: A Platform," *Archives of Criminal Psychodynamics,* 1:3-100, Winter, 1955.

Suggested readings

ALEXANDER, FRANZ, & HUGO STAUB. *The Criminal, the Judge, and the Public: A Psychological Analysis.* Rev. ed. Glencoe, Ill.: Free Press, 1956.

ALEXANDER, FRANZ G., & SHELDON T. SELESNICK. *The History of Psychiatry.* New York: Harper and Row, 1966.

CHRISTIE, NILS. "Law and Medicine: The Case Against Role Blurring." *Law and Society Review,* 5:357-366, February, 1971.

CRESSEY, DONALD R. "The Differential Association Theory and Compulsive Crimes." *Journal of Criminal Law, Criminology, and Police Science,* 45:29-40, May–June, 1954.

FINGARETTE, HERBERT. *The Meaning of Criminal Insanity.* Berkeley: University of California Press, 1972.

GENDIN, SIDNEY. "Insanity and Criminal Responsibility." *American Philosophical Quarterly,* 10:99-110, April, 1973.

GLASER, FREDERICK B., & JOHN C. BALL. "The British Narcotic 'Register' in 1970." *Journal of the American Medical Association,* 216:1177-1182, May, 1971.

GOODE, ERICH. *The Drug Phenomenon: Social Aspects of Drug Taking.* Indianapolis: Bobbs-Merrill, 1973.

HAKEEM, MICHAEL. "A Critique of the Psychiatric Approach to Crime and Correction." *Law and Contemporary Problems,* 23:650-682, Autumn, 1958.

HAKEEM, MICHAEL. "A Critique of the Psychiatric Approach to the Prevention of Juvenile Delinquency." *Social Problems,* 5:194-206, Winter, 1957.

HALLECK, SEYMOUR L. *Psychiatry and the Dilemma of Crime.* New York: Harper and Row, 1967.

HARE, R. D. *Psychopathy: Theory and Research.* New York: John Wiley, 1970.

LINDESMITH, ALFRED R. *Addiction and Opiates.* Chicago: Aldine, 1968.

LINDESMITH, ALFRED R. *The Addict and the Law.* Bloomington, Ind.: Indiana University Press, 1965.

MENNINGER, KARL. *The Crime of Punishment.* New York: Viking Press, 1968.

O'DONNELL, JOHN A., & JOHN C. BALL, eds. *Narcotic Addiction.* New York: Harper and Row, 1966.

PITTMAN, DAVID J., ed. *Alcoholism.* New York: Harper and Row, 1967.

PLAUT, THOMAS F. A. *Alcohol Problems: A Report to the Nation by the Cooperative Commission on the Study of Alcoholism.* New York: Oxford University Press, 1967.

ROSEN, GEORGE. *Madness in Society.* New York: Harper Torchbooks, 1969.

SCHEFF, THOMAS J., ed. *Mental Illness and Social Processes.* New York: Harper and Row, 1967.

TRICE, HARRISON, & PAUL MICHAEL ROMAN. "Delabeling, Relabeling and Alcoholics Anonymous." *Social Problems,* 17:538-546, Spring, 1970.

ULLMAN, LEONARD P., & LEONARD KRASNER. *A Psychological Approach to Abnormal Behavior.* Englewood Cliffs, N. J.: Prentice-Hall, 1969.

VOLKMAN, RITA, & DONALD R. CRESSEY. "Differential Association and the Rehabilitation of Drug Addicts." *American Journal of Sociology,* 69:129-142, September, 1963.

WALKER, NIGEL, & SARAH McCABE. *Crime and Insanity in England: New Solutions and New Problems.* Edinburgh: University Press, 1973.

WEPPNER, ROBERT S., & MICHAEL H. AGAR. "Immediate Precursors to Heroin Addiction." *Journal of Health and Social Behavior,* 12:11-18, March, 1971.

YABLONSKY, LEWIS. *Synanon: The Tunnel Back.* Baltimore: Penguin Books, 1967.

YOSHIMASU, SHUFU, & SADATAKA KOGI. "Etudes Criminologiques et Psychiatriques au Japon." *Acta Criminologica,* 22:145-163, January, 1969.

Culture areas

9

In the different culture areas of the earth, crime rates have ranged between zero and one hundred percent. Some isolated nonliterate tribes are completely free from violations of their own laws, while other groups have almost universal violations of laws. These standards of behavior, whether lawful or unlawful, are transmitted as traditions over many generations. Most cultural areas, of course, have crime rates between these two extremes, but wide variations exist. Like the variations in the age, sex, race, and nativity ratios in crime, the variations in crime rates from area to area pose challenging problems for a general theory of criminal behavior. ●

Regional distributions

Crime rates not only vary from one nation to another, but also generally among the several sections of each nation. Near the end of the nineteenth century, Ferri reported that the rate of convictions for homicides per million population varied widely in different provinces in each of the principal European countries. In Italy, twenty-seven provinces had rates of less than fifty, while thirteen provinces had rates of more than two hundred. Convictions of homicide in Sardinia were more than fourteen times as frequent in proportion to population as in Lombardy.[1] At about the same time, Aschaffenburg found the offenses against the person were much higher in East Prussia, Bavaria, and the Palatinate than in the other German provinces. He found also that convictions for larceny were much higher in the provinces adjoining the Russian frontier than elsewhere in Germany, while resistance to or attack on officers were most frequent in seaports and in manufacturing districts.[2] The rate of indictable crimes known to the police in England is highest in the counties containing and adjacent to London, next in the counties containing the principal seaports, next in the manufacturing counties in the central part of England, and lowest in the agricultural and mining counties. This same distribution was found in 1893, except that the southwestern agricultural counties, which had a low general rate for indictable offenses, had the highest rate of any section of the country for offenses against morals. At an earlier period, according to Pike, the counties in England in which crime was most prevalent were those adjoining Scotland, because of the lack of organized government in those counties, and these high rates continued until the final amalgamation of the counties.[3]

Joly found similar variations among the eighty-six departments (counties) in France, and he made an analysis of internal migration in relation to crime rates. He found, for instance, that the Corsicans were prosecuted more often when living in their native department than when living elsewhere in France. When the crime rate of Corsica was considered as the number of prosecutions in Corsica of persons born in Corsica, the department had next to the highest rate of the eighty-six departments; it dropped to sixty-fifth position when the crime rate was considered as the number of prosecutions of persons born in Corsica regardless of whether the prosecutions were in Corsica or in other departments. Similarly, the department which was next to the lowest in its rate at home rose to the thirty-sixth rank when prosecutions away from home were included. Some departments retained the same rank in the two methods of computing the rates, but others showed these very significant changes.[4]

The *Uniform Crime Reports* data presented in table XIV show the variation in the frequency of specific types of crime in different regions of the United States.[5] Subject to the qualifications mentioned earlier, the statistics indicate that New England had the lowest rates for homicide, rape, and aggravated assault. The

[1] Enrico Ferri, *L'omicido nell' antropologia criminale* (Torino, Italy: Bocca, 1895), pp. 241-325.

[2] Gustav Aschaffenburg, *Crime and Its Repression* (Boston: Little, Brown, 1913).

[3] Luke O. Pike, *A History of Crime in England* (London: Smith, Elder, 1873-76).

[4] Henri Joly, *La France Criminelle* (Paris: Cerf, 1889), pp. 45-46.

[5] Federal Bureau of Investigation, U.S. Department of Justice, *Uniform Crime Reports for the United States, 1971* (Washington: Government Printing Office, 1972), pp. 62-67.

TABLE XIV

Crime rates, 1971, by geographical division
(offenses per 100,000 inhabitants)

Division	Homi-cide	Forc-ible rape	Rob-bery	Aggra-vated assault	Bur-glary	Lar-ceny over $50	Auto theft
United States	**8.5**	**20.3**	**187.1**	**176.8**	**1148.3**	**909.2**	**456.5**
New England	3.2	11.0	97.8	97.3	1128.0	813.8	716.9
Middle Atlantic	7.9	15.4	344.9	165.3	1169.4	870.9	562.9
East North Central	7.9	19.8	206.6	143.3	1035.3	845.0	448.3
West North Central	4.5	15.9	88.1	104.5	836.2	735.0	314.2
South Atlantic	12.6	21.3	170.5	246.8	1109.0	907.4	332.4
East South Central	13.1	16.8	67.8	189.1	743.9	537.4	253.7
West South Central	11.0	22.2	108.9	208.8	1035.5	749.3	337.8
Mountain	6.5	25.9	95.7	173.5	1208.6	1204.8	420.2
Pacific	7.2	32.2	201.1	213.6	1794.2	1413.4	613.8

East South Central region (Alabama, Kentucky, Mississippi, and Tennessee) had the lowest burglary, larceny, robbery, and automobile theft rates. The highest rates for forcible rape, burglary, and larceny were found in the Pacific states (Alaska, California, Hawaii, Oregon, and Washington); the highest aggravated assault rate appeared in the South Atlantic region (all East Coast states south of Pennsylvania); the highest robbery rate was in the Middle Atlantic states (New Jersey, New York, Pennsylvania); the highest automobile theft rate was in New England; and the highest homicide rate in the East South Central region. By individual states, North Dakota had the lowest forcible rape, robbery, aggravated assault, and burglary rates, Vermont the lowest homicide rate, Mississippi the lowest rate for larceny, and South Dakota the lowest automobile theft rate. South Carolina had the highest homicide rate, California the highest larceny and burglary rates, New York the highest robbery rate, Florida the highest aggravated assault rate, Alaska the highest forcible rape rate, and Massachusetts the highest automobile theft rate.

Thirty-five years ago, Lottier analyzed sectional crime rates in the United States and reported a center of concentration for murder in the southeastern states, with somewhat regular gradients to the north and west; robbery was concentrated in the middle central states, with an axis running from Tennessee and Kentucky to Colorado, and with decreasing rates on either side of this axis. Shannon repeated this study fifteen years later and found essentially the same pattern. The rate for crimes against the person showed definite regional concentration, but crimes against property did not show such marked concentration, probably because they were not based on the total property values in the states in question.[6]

---

[6] Stuart Lottier, "Distribution of Criminal Offenses in Sectional Regions," *Journal of Criminal Law and Criminology*, 29:329-344, September-October, 1938. Lyle W. Shannon, "The Spatial Distribution of Criminal Offenses by States," *Journal of Criminal Law, Criminology, and Police Science*, 45:264-273, September-October, 1954.

Certain types of towns, also, have high crime rates. Lombroso reported that in every province in Italy certain villages had acquired reputations for special crimes; one was noted for murder, another for robbery, and another for swindling. Artena, for instance, had thirty times as many highway robberies as the average community in Italy, and had been noted as a home of robbers since the twelfth century.[7] Similarly, certain types of towns in America have been noted for high crime rates for short periods. Frontier towns, river towns, and resort towns are somewhat outstanding in this respect. Mining towns generally have higher rates than agricultural towns of the same size.

Such broad comparisons of crime rates have been made in many countries over a long period of time. In general, the various geographical divisions hold nearly the same ranks year after year. For regions, the ranks remain nearly the same whether the crime rates are computed for the larger cities or for the smaller cities in the regions. Various attempts have been made to explain the differences. Aschaffenburg believed that the differences in rates of crimes against the person in different provinces in Germany were related to the consumption of alcohol, while larceny was related to poverty, and crimes against public officials to the heterogeneity of population. Niceforo concluded that the differences in the crime rates in Sardinia were due to differences in racial origin of the population. In the United States, the high crime rates in the southern states are generally interpreted as due to the large number of Negroes, but it is evident that homicides, at least, cannot be explained so simply, for the death rate by homicide for white persons in the South is approximately five times as high as in New England, and the Negro homicide rate in New England is slightly lower than the white homicide rate in the same area.[8]

Gastil, like Pettigrew and Spier, has attributed these variations to differences in community organization and traditions of orderliness.[9] Such explanation is consistent with the differential association theory, which predicts that if the ratio of criminal behavior patterns to anticriminal behavior patterns in a region remains approximately the same, the crime rate will remain approximately the same. Once started, a tradition of violence or theft is passed on to generation after generation. For example, in Upper Egypt, as in Sicily, a tradition which requires that revenge be taken for insults and other harms has given this region extraordinarily high homicide rates for centuries. On the other hand, the same region has extraordinarily low rates of conviction for drunkenness, owing to a strong antialcohol tradition stemming from the Islam religion. An illustration of such traditions in exag-

---

[7] Cesare Lombroso, *Crime, Its Cause and Remedies* (Boston: Little, Brown, 1911).

[8] H. C. Brearley, *Homicide in the United States* (Chapel Hill, N.C.: University of North Carolina Press, 1932).

[9] Raymond D. Gastil, "Homicide and a Regional Culture of Violence," *American Sociological Review*, 36:412-427, June, 1971; T. F. Pettigrew and R. Spier, "The Ecological Structure of Negro Homicide," *American Journal of Sociology*, 47: 621-629, May, 1962.

gerated form was found in the thievery patterns of the criminal tribes of India:

> The Bhamptas are a tribe who give an infinity of trouble. . . . The Bhampta is a marvellously skillful pickpocket and railway thief. He frequents fairs, landing-places, bazaars, temples—any place, in fact, where there is a crowd. He is always on the lookout for his prey. . . . The Bhamptas are trained to crime from their earliest childhood, so it is not wonderful that they should become very expert. The children are initiated into the profession of their life by lessons in the pilfering of shoes, cocoanuts, and any odds and ends that they may come across. If they are slow or stupid they are encouraged to improve by the application of a stick. The boys soon become adept. . . . Adults generally work in small gangs of three or four. One of them stealthily removes an ornament from someone in the crowd, or adroitly picks a pocket, or, jostling the victim, boldly snatches his bag or satchel, and instantly passes his booty to one of his accomplices, who in turn passes it on to another; and in an incredibly short space of time the stolen property is far away. . . . Again a Bhampta sees a well-to-do person in the street. He makes a great show of brutally beating a small boy. The boy screams and yells and rushes for protection to the prosperous-looking stranger, who shields the child and expostulates with the Bhampta. The latter in apparent anger snatches away the boy from his protector, while the young rascal, who has been well trained, kicks and struggles for all that he is worth. The sympathizer has had enough of it, and is glad to let the youngster go. Later on he realizes that his purse has disappeared.[10] ●

Rural-urban distributions

Statistics from many countries, and in many periods of time, indicate that urban areas have higher crime rates than rural areas. Two general types of relationship between crime and size of community can be observed, just as two types of relationship were observed between crime and age, sex, race, and nativity.

A. Official statistics indicate that the number of serious crimes per 100,000 population tends to increase with the size of the community. In 1971, the rate of robberies known to the American police varied from 30.5 in towns of less than 10,000 population to 633.4 in cities of over 250,000. This trend is roughly the same for other types of crime and in other years, except that the rates in cities over 250,000 are sometimes less than in cities of 100,000-250,000.

Similar tendencies have been reported for European countries and for Canada. Of all the males born in Norway in 1933, 5.08 percent had become registered offenders by January 1, 1958. Among the boys living in Oslo, however, 9 percent had become offenders, as compared to 8 percent of the residents of other cities and 4 percent of the country residents.[11] Among a sample of 3,032

---

[10] Edmund C. Fox, *Police and Crime in India* (London: S. Paul, 1911), pp. 234-237. See also Paul F. Cressey, "The Criminal Tribes of India," *Sociology and Social Research,* 20:503-511; 21:18-25, July-September, 1936; and Clarence H. Patrick, "The Criminal Tribes of India, with Special Emphasis on the Mang Garudi: A Preliminary Report," *Man in India,* 48:244-257, July-September, 1968.

[11] Nils Christie, *Unge Norske Lovovertredere* [Young Norwegian Lawbreakers] (Oslo: Universitetsforlaget, 1960), pp. 76, 304.

Danish men who in 1953-1954 were twenty-one years of age or more, 9.6 percent were violators of the criminal code. Thirteen percent of the men living in Copenhagen were violators, as compared to 8.8 percent of those living in towns with populations of 2,000-19,000, and to 6.2 percent of those living in rural districts and small towns with less than 2,000 inhabitants.[12] Offenses committed by rural criminals might not be reported or recorded as readily as offenses committed in urban areas, but the urban rate generally so far exceeds the rural rate that it is reasonable to conclude that there is in fact a great excess of crime in urban places. Moreover, a large proportion of urban crime also is overlooked, and it is not at all certain that this proportion is any less than the proportion of rural crime that is overlooked.

B. The extent to which the crime rate in urban areas exceeds the crime rate in rural areas is not the same under all conditions. In some rural areas the crime rate, especially for some types of offenses, is higher than the rate in urban areas:

1. The amount of the excess of crime in urban areas varies by offenses. In American cities of over 250,000, murder and rape rates are about five times as high as the rates in towns of 10,000; burglary, larceny, and aggravated assault are about three times as high; automobile theft is over six times as high, and robbery about twenty-five times as high. In certain respects, the number of crimes decreases as the distance from the large city increases. Burglaries or robberies were committed against 59.6 percent of the stores belonging to a chain in the city of Chicago in a two-year period, while only 29.8 percent, or exactly one-half the proportion, were burglarized or robbed in the suburban area within twenty-five miles from the center of Chicago in the same period. Moreover, the proportion of stores burglarized or robbed decreased by twenty-five-mile zones steadily until it reached 6.2 percent in the zone 100-125 miles away from the city.

Lottier, in a more extensive analysis of the distribution of crimes, found that murders, assaults, rapes, and robberies known to the police decreased consistently in the commutation area of Detroit to a distance of twenty miles from the city hall, but that burglaries, auto thefts, and larcenies did not show a consistent decrease. He also found the same crimes against the person decreasing in the entire metropolitan area of Detroit within a radius of two hundred miles, but again the crimes against property showed no such consistent decrease. He suggested that the difference in the two types of crimes may be due to the fact that crimes against the person were calculated in proportion to the number of persons, but crimes against property were not calculated in proportion to the amount of property.[13] Boggs, similarly, recently proposed that even crimes against the person are not

---

[12] Preben Wolf, "Crime and Social Class in Denmark," *British Journal of Criminology*, 13:5-17, July, 1962.

[13] Stuart Lottier, "Distribution of Criminal Offenses in Metropolitan Regions," *Journal of Criminal Law and Criminology*, 29:37-50, May-June, 1938.

accurate because they are not calculated in proportion to the number of "exposures" of offenders and victims to each other.[14]

For the United States as a whole, the rural rates are slightly higher than the urban rates for homicide, about equal for rape, about one-half as high for assault, and from about one-fourth to about one-third as high for robbery, burglary, larceny, and auto theft.

2. The amount of the excess of crime in urban areas varies by area. In an earlier period, frontier towns, river towns, and resort towns were noted for high crime rates, despite the fact that they were not large in size. Further, Radzinowicz demonstrated that in the southern districts of Poland the crime rates decreased as communities increased in size, that even in other sections of Poland many small communities had higher crime rates than many large communities, and that communities of the same size varied immensely in crime rates.[15] Also, in some other European countries the rates for larger cities have been shown to be lower than the rural rates. Christie's study of all males born in Norway in 1933 showed a clear overrepresentation of offenders in the most densely populated areas, which also had the highest number of policemen per 1,000 inhabitants. However, the most sparsely populated area—Finnmark, the northernmost county in Norway—had an offender rate which was approximately the same as that of the densely populated industrial areas. Finnmark, which is populated by Lapps as well as by Norwegians, also has one policeman for each 500 inhabitants, as compared to a ratio of 1 to 12,000 in other sparsely populated counties and to a ratio of 1 to 400 in Bergen and Oslo.[16]

Studies in Iowa and Kansas found regular increases in delinquency rates from the most rural to the most urban counties. However, a study of the distribution of delinquency in Wisconsin indicated that the counties containing cities have high delinquency rates, but that certain isolated rural logging counties also have high rates. Wiers found in Michigan that the most urban county had the highest delinquency rate, but that the sparsely settled logging counties had higher rates than the southern agricultural counties.[17] It must be concluded that certain contemporary rural

[14] Sarah L. Boggs, "Urban Crime Patterns," *American Sociological Review,* 30: 899-908, December, 1965.

[15] Leon Radzinowicz, "Criminality by Size-Groups of Communities," manuscript, 1946.

[16] Christie, *Unge Norske Lovovertredere,* pp. 78-80, 305.

[17] Charles N. Burrows, "Criminal Statistics in Iowa," *University of Iowa Studies in the Social Sciences,* vol. 9, no. 2, 1930; Mapheus Smith, "Tier Counties and Delinquency in Kansas," *Rural Sociology,* 2:310-322, September, 1937; Morris G. Caldwell, "The Extent of Juvenile Delinquency in Wisconsin," *Journal of Criminal Law and Criminology,* 32:148-157, July-August, 1941; and Paul Wiers, "Juvenile Delinquency in Rural Michigan," *Journal of Criminal Law and Criminology,* 30:211-222, July-August, 1939; see also idem, *Economic Factors in Michigan Delinquency* (New York: Columbia University Press, 1944).

sections have special criminalistic traditions, just as in an earlier period certain frontier areas had such traditions.

3. The amount of excess of crime in urban areas varies in time. There is evidence that as improved communication and transportation have reduced the differences between urban and rural districts, the differences in the crime rates of the two areas have decreased. The *Uniform Crime Reports* data indicate that, since about 1945, the rural rate in the United States has increased more rapidly than the urban rate. This general trend is found in some but not all areas of the United States and in some but not all nations of the world. In Sweden, the conviction rate in rural districts has in the past seventy-five years steadily approached the conviction rate in city districts. The same trend is found in France, but the opposite trend is found in Finland. An analysis of conviction rates in Iowa for the period 1865-1925 showed that the rural rate had been consistently lower than the urban rate and did not show any significant tendency to approach the urban rate.[18]

It has been suggested that the excessive criminality of the city is due to the selective migration from the country of those who are most likely to commit crimes. Kinberg gave statistics indicating that about half the vagrants in Sweden were born in the country and half in the towns, but that the persons who became vagrants migrated from the country to towns four times as frequently as the general population did and migrated from towns to country less than half as frequently as the general population did.[19] Also, the excessive criminality of the city has been explained as due to the impersonality and greater criminal opportunities of city life in comparison with rural life.[20] Criminals tend to migrate to areas in which other criminals operate, and these areas may be either cities or rural districts.

Further, patterns of criminal behavior have become established in some rural districts, and persons migrating to those districts tend to become criminals, just as do persons migrating to urban areas in which criminal behavior patterns are prevalent. A recent study of the delinquents living in Daka found that the delinquents born in rural areas began their delinquent careers rather late, and their delinquency rate increased with age; the urban-born delinquents started their delinquent careers earlier than did those from rural areas, but their delinquency rate decreased with age.[21] Thus,

---

[18] Thomas P. Monahan, "The Trend in Rural and Urban Crime," manuscript, 1937, based principally on the data in Burrows, "Criminal Statistics in Iowa."

[19] O. Kinberg, "On So-Called Vagrancy," *Journal of Criminal Law and Criminology*, 24:552-583, September-October, 1933.

[20] See Marshall B. Clinard, "The Process of Urbanization and Criminal Behavior: A Study of Culture Conflicts," *American Journal of Sociology*, 48: 202-213, September, 1942.

[21] Study cited in G. Houchon, "Les Mécanismes Criminogènes dans une Société Urbanien Africaine," *Revue Internationale de Criminologie et de Police Technique*, 21 (1967): 271-292. See also T. C. N. Gibbens and R. H. Ahrenfeldt, *Cultural Factors in Delinquency* (London: Tavistock, 1966), pp. 40-41.

the significant conditions are the area's ratio of anticriminal behavior patterns to procriminal behavior patterns, and the nature and extent of participation in these behavior patterns. It should be noted, however, that relatively little organized research work has been done on rural criminality. Clinard has made one of the best studies, concluding that rural criminality is explained by the person's identification with delinquents and his conception of himself as reckless and mobile, an explanation which is consistent with differential association.[22] ●

Intracity distributions

It has been evident for many decades that criminals and delinquents are much more numerous in some city areas than in others. Shaw, McKay, and their collaborators have amplified this information and organized it in relation to the general pattern of the large American city. By an analysis of the rates of delinquency in various areas of Chicago and other cities, they reached the following six conclusions: *First,* the rates of delinquency vary widely in different neighborhoods. None of the boys residing in some areas are arrested, while in other neighborhoods more than one-fifth of the boys are arrested in one year. This variation has been found in each of fifteen cities, and the neighborhoods with the highest rates have been designated "delinquency areas."

Second, the rates are generally highest in the low-rent areas near the center of the city and decrease with the distance from the center of the city. Also, the rates are high near large industrial or commercial subcenters of the city and decrease with distance from those subcenters.

Third, the areas which have high rates of truancy also have high rates for all juvenile court cases, for all boys' court cases, and for all adult commitments to the county jail. The areas which have high rates for boy delinquencies also have high rates for girl delinquencies.

Fourth, the areas which had high rates in 1900 also had high rates in 1930, although in the meantime the national composition of the population of the area had changed almost completely. When Germans and Swedes occupied an area near the center of the city, their children had high rates of delinquency; when they were replaced by Polish, Italian, or other national groups, the juvenile delinquency rates in the area were essentially the same.

Fifth, the delinquency rate of a particular national group such as German or Polish shows the same general tendency as the delinquency rate for the entire population, namely, to be high in

---

[22] Clinard, "Process of Urbanization." See also Marshall B. Clinard, "Rural Criminal Offenders," *American Journal of Sociology,* 50:38-45, July, 1944; William P. Lentz, "Rural Urban Differentials and Juvenile Delinquency," *Journal of Criminal Law, Criminology, and Police Science,* 47:331-339, September-October, 1956; and Marshall B. Clinard, "A Cross-cultural Replication of the Relation of Urbanism to Criminal Behavior," *American Sociological Review,* 25:253-257, April, 1960.

the areas near the center of the city and low toward the outskirts of the city.

Sixth, delinquents living in areas of high delinquency rates are the most likely to become recidivists, and among all recidivists they are likely to appear in court several times more often than those from areas with low delinquency rates.[23]

The above conclusions have been criticized on the ground that the statistics from which they were drawn were not valid measures, but the conclusions have been substantiated by studies in other localities by other authors. The question which has been raised most persistently, perhaps, is whether the statistics of arrests or of juvenile court appearances do not give a biased measure of delinquencies because of the poverty of the families in the areas which are reported as having the highest delinquency rates.[24] Wealth and social position provide a certain degree of immunity against arrest and incarceration.[25] Also, certain national or religious groups maintain welfare agencies which take problem cases that would otherwise be referred to the police or to the juvenile court, while other national and religious groups have no agencies of this nature. Even when allowance is made for these probable statistical biases, some concentration of ordinary crime and delinquency seems to remain. In the District of Columbia the juvenile court statistics showed *less* concentration of cases in the high-delinquency areas than did the unofficial statistics of other agencies.[26] Of course, white-collar crime is not concentrated in the areas which have the highest official delinquency rates.

The "concentration," it should be noted, is a concentration of the residences of criminals and delinquents, rather than of the crimes and delinquencies themselves. Generally, the places at which crimes are committed are close to the residences of the criminals. This is especially characteristic of crimes against the person, for the offender and the victim are usually of the same race, the same economic class, and also of the same neighbor-

---

[23] Clifford R. Shaw and Henry D. McKay, *Juvenile Delinquency and Urban Areas,* rev. ed. (Chicago: University of Chicago Press, 1969). See also V. V. Stanciu, *Criminalité a Paris* (Paris: Presses Universitaires de France, 1967). For excellent summaries of research on delinquency areas, see Terrence Morris, *The Criminal Area* (London: Kegan Paul, 1958); and Judith A. Wilks, "Ecological Correlates of Crime and Delinquency," appendix A in President's Commission on Law Enforcement and Administration of Justice, *Task Force Report: Crime and Its Impact—An Assessment* (Washington: Government Printing Office, 1967), pp. 138-156.

[24] Christen T. Jonassen, "A Re-evaluation and Critique of the Logic and Some Methods of Shaw and McKay," *American Sociological Review,* 14:608-617, October, 1949; and Jackson Toby, "The Differential Impact of Family Disorganization," *American Sociological Review,* 22:505-512, October, 1957.

[25] James F. Short, Jr., and F. Ivan Nye, "Reported Behavior as a Criterion of Deviant Behavior," *Social Problems,* 5:205-213, Winter, 1957.

[26] Edward E. Schwartz, "A Community Experiment in the Measurement of Juvenile Delinquency," *National Probation Association Yearbook,* 1945, pp. 157-181.

hood.[27] A study of Seattle indicated that serious property crimes, such as larceny and robbery, tend to occur in the central segment of the city, and are perpetrated by persons residing in that segment of the city. For example, 63 percent of the robberies and 40 percent of the burglaries were committed in the central segment, and 41 percent of those arrested for robbery and 34 percent of those arrested for burglary resided in the central segment.[28]

Although the concentration of the residences of delinquents and ordinary criminals near the industrial and commercial centers is demonstrated in an adequate sample of large American cities, the centers of concentration are not the same in European, Asiatic, or Latin American cities. In fact, a study of residences of criminals in Peiping indicated a concentration in the slum areas at the gates of the city rather than in the center of the city, and much the same distribution is reported in the older European cities, although special studies of residences of delinquents have not been made. DeFleur found that in Cordoba, Argentina, the residences of delinquents are in pockets of poverty scattered throughout the city, with some concentration in the central zone and in the peripheral zones.[29] In some smaller cities in the United States, the residences of delinquents are in the low-rent areas adjacent to the railway tracks or to the "dumps" on the outskirts of town. Because of the rapid expansion of American cities, especially those east of the Rocky Mountains, the areas of poverty in these cities tend to be located near the center. Thus, the high delinquency areas tend to be concentrated in the areas of greatest poverty, whether those areas are near the center of the city or on the outskirts.[30] In a study of offenses known to the police of Seattle, Schmid found that the census tracts with high crime rates tended to be characterized by low family status, low occupational status, low economic status, and a high rate of population mobility.[31] It is not correct, however, to conclude from this that poverty is the cause of crime.

Two principal interpretations of the concentration of delinquents have been presented. The first is in terms of social organization in the neighborhood. The areas of concentration in large American cities, and especially Chicago, where the problem has been studied

[27] Henry Allen Bullock, "Urban Homicide in Theory and Fact," *Journal of Criminal Law, Criminology, and Police Science*, 45:565-575, January-February, 1955.

[28] Calvin F. Schmid, "Urban Crime Areas: Part II," *American Sociological Review*, 25:655-678, October, 1960.

[29] Lois B. DeFleur, "Ecological Variables in the Cross-Cultural Study of Delinquency," *Social Forces*, 45:556-570, June, 1967. See also N. S. Hayner, "Criminogenic Zones in Mexico City," *American Sociological Review*, 11:428-438, August, 1946; and Theodore Caplow, "The Social Ecology of Guatemala City," *Social Forces*, 28:113-133, December, 1949.

[30] See John Mack, "Full-time Miscreants, Delinquent Neighbourhoods, and Criminal Networks," *British Journal of Sociology*, 15:38-53, March, 1964.

[31] Calvin F. Schmid, "Urban Crime Areas: Part I," *American Sociological Review*, 25:527-542, August, 1960.

most intensively, are areas of physical deterioration, congested population, decreasing population, economic dependency, rented homes, foreign and Negro population, and few institutions supported by the local residents. Lawlessness has become traditional; adult criminals are frequently seen and have much prestige. Gangs have continued to exist, with changing personnel, for fifty years in some of these areas. At a particular time a gang may have senior, junior, and midget branches. The techniques, codes, and standards are transmitted from older to younger offenders. Delinquencies begin here at an early age, and maturity in crime is reached at an early age. Boys fourteen or fifteen years of age steal automobiles and commit robberies, while in other areas delinquents of the same age are committing petty thefts. They not only acquire skill in the execution of crimes, but also prepare for avoidance or mitigation of penalties. They know the techniques of "fixing," of intimidating witnesses, of telling plausible stories in court, of appeals to sympathy. Consequently the influences toward delinquency are strong and constant.

At the same time, the antidelinquent influences are few, and organized opposition to delinquency is weak. Parent-teacher associations do not exist, nor do other community organizations which are supported principally by the people of the neighborhood. Because the population is mobile and heterogeneous, it is unable to act with concert in dealing with its own problems. Schools, social work agencies, and even churches are supported by people who reside elsewhere, and these agencies are for the most part formal and external to the life of the neighborhood.

The residents of these neighborhoods probably know much better than do the members of the middle classes the details of any graft and dishonesty in their city's politics. The American culture which they see is a culture of competition, corruption, deceit, graft, crime, delinquency, and immorality. They see practically nothing of the culture of cooperation, decency, and law-abidingness in which some Americans are immersed from infancy. Thus they come in contact with a rather lawless neighborhood, and the rather dishonest public culture of America, but are isolated from the predominantly law-abiding culture of the primary groups in the middle-class American population. That they would behave differently if they came into contact with a different culture pattern has been shown in a comparison of a delinquency area of Boston with a delinquency area of Cairo. In the Boulac area of Cairo, a high-delinquency area, 35 percent of the delinquents arrested in 1952 had committed crimes against the person, while in the Roxbury section of Boston the comparable percentage was eight. Similarly, 65 percent of the Roxbury delinquents, but only 25 percent of the Boulac delinquents, committed crimes against property. These variations are the result of cultural differences in what American and Egyptian slum-dwellers learn about an individualistic orientation to life—that is, in what they know is true about the role of "fate" in their personal affairs, as compared to the role of other persons. Boulac residents have learned that *people* have caused one's misfortunes. They behave accordingly:

> In Boulac society, the individualism of Roxbury society is lacking. . . . Persons, in themselves, are more important to an individual than his belongings. When an individual's success, or his status, or his recognition is hindered or threatened, he usually thinks in terms of some person or persons hindering his success, or threatening his status, or discouraging his recognition. Thus he may try to revenge himself by removing the cause—in this case, the person concerned.[32]

The second interpretation is that competitive processes select out constitutionally inferior, or psychologically inferior, persons who would have high delinquency and crime rates wherever they lived. As a matter of fact, those who reside in the areas of high delinquency rates at a particular time are of three types: recent immigrants, remnants of the earlier residential groups, and failures in the better residential districts who have moved into the cheaper rent areas. A study of Danville, Illinois, supported the selective migration interpretation by finding that while the residences of adult criminals were concentrated near the center of the city, very few criminals had been reared in that area.[33] However, most of them had been reared in families in which other members were delinquent, which might mean merely that they were reared in other areas of high delinquency. In studies of delinquency in nonmetropolitan areas, Polk and Halferty found that small towns contain a "trouble making subculture," and that school failures drift into it after having been "locked out" of the system supporting accomplishments by legitimate means. Participants in the subculture become delinquent, and they also become socially handicapped. Even when they migrate to urban areas, they are not able to participate fully in legitimate opportunity structures because they are economically, educationally, socially, and culturally disadvantaged.[34]

The most important evidence on this point is Shaw and McKay's finding that the delinquency rate remained practically constant over a thirty-year period despite an almost complete change in the national composition of the population. This indicates that the delinquency rate is more likely to be a function of social conditions in an area than of the biological or psychological traits of people who reside there. When a national group, such as Greeks or Mexicans, first settled in an area of deterioration in an American city, the children did not play

---

[32] Saied Euwies, "A Comparative Study of Two Delinquency Areas," *National Review of Criminal Science* (U.A.R.), 2:1-15, November, 1959.

[33] D. R. Taft, "Testing the Selective Influence of Areas of Delinquency," *American Journal of Sociology,* 38:699-712, March, 1933.

[34] Kenneth Polk and David S. Halferty, "Adolescence, Commitment, and Delinquency," *Journal of Research in Crime and Delinquency,* 3:82-96, July, 1966; Kenneth Polk, "Delinquency and Community Action in Nonmetropolitan Areas," appendix R in President's Commission on Law Enforcement and Administration of Justice, *Task Force Report: Juvenile Delinquency* (Washington: Government Printing Office, 1967), pp. 343-347.

with the children of the residents and did not become delinquent. But, as contacts developed, the delinquency rates increased. Consistently, a detailed study showed that when an immigrant group first settled in Los Angeles, only 5 percent of the children of juvenile court age appeared in juvenile courts; five years later this percentage had increased to 46, and after another decade 83 percent of their children appeared in the juvenile court.[35] The ethnic characteristics in this case remained constant, but the opportunities for assimilation of the culture of the American city increased, and in their neighborhood this meant assimilation of delinquency and crime.

The location of delinquency areas near the commercial or industrial centers is related to the rents in those centers. But low rents do not cause delinquency. Rents are low because accommodations are poor, and the accommodations are not improved because of the expectation that the commercial and industrial activities will expand, causing the nearby areas to be annexed to the business sections. When poor migrants arrive, they settle in these areas of deterioration where the rents are low, but some of them move out to better residential districts as soon as they accumulate sufficient capital. In this case, their delinquency rates go down. Negroes, Italians, Puerto Ricans, and Mexicans have dispersed less than other national or racial groups, and for that reason are likely to continue to have problems of delinquency.

Although areas of high delinquency contain an abundance of prodelinquent behavior patterns, many persons residing in them are not delinquent, and these persons live under the same conditions of poverty as do the delinquents. For example, within any given area, the female delinquency rate is customarily much lower than the male delinquency rate, although the wealth of parents, housing conditions, and many other external conditions are the same for girls and boys. Furthermore, in areas with relatively high delinquency rates, less than half of the boys can be identified as past or present delinquents, and about half are engaged in regular school work or occupations and show no sympathy whatever for the delinquent boys. Mack found that, in a Scottish city, the precinct with the highest crime rate produced an annual average of eleven offenders per 100 households during the years 1948-1960; the highest density street in this precinct produced twenty offenders per 100 houses per year. For this street, 32 percent of the households produced two or more offenders over a period of ten years, and another 7 percent of the households had a record of only one offense in the period. Thus, three out of five households in the most criminal area of the city had no criminal record at all, and only one out of three was "criminally

---

[35] Pauline V. Young, "Urbanization as a Factor in Juvenile Delinquency," *Publications of the American Sociological Society*, 24 (1930): 162-166; idem, *The Pilgrims of Russia-Town* (Chicago: University of Chicago Press, 1932).

active" in the sense that two or more offenders were produced in ten years.[36]

One explanation of the presence of nondelinquents in areas of high delinquency is the limitation on contact with delinquency patterns, even in the most delinquent areas. A delinquency area is seldom solidly delinquent; rather, there are certain streets or parts of streets on which at a particular time most delinquents reside, and on other streets the children may associate with each other in relative isolation from the behavior patterns of delinquents. Sometimes one or more national groups within a general residential area are isolated from the rest of the population, or a few members of one such group may be isolated within a larger area of another nationality. For example, in the 1930s the delinquency rate in Seattle's Japanese colony, which was in a very deteriorated, high-delinquency area, was lower than in the best residential areas.[37] Further, some children are kept from frequent or intimate contact with delinquency patterns because of their retiring, quiet, and unaggressive dispositions, and others, especially girls, are kept from such associations by careful and capable parents or siblings. Some children may refrain from delinquency because they have formed attachments at school with teachers, or at other agencies with other leaders; and their interests have been developed and their lives organized around lawful activities.[38]

A second, but consistent, explanation is that punishment of delinquents makes the career of a delinquent unattractive to some of the children in the areas of high delinquency. Of the young adults in the so-called Forty-Two Gang in Chicago in the 1930s, about one-third were killed by the police or by private parties, and another third were committed to prisons or reformatories. Killing young criminals or committing them to prison is a dramatic, but generally ineffective, way of presenting anticriminal behavior patterns to those who remain behind. Nevertheless, some of the boys in the vicinity must have avoided delinquency because of the outcomes of the older boys in the gang.

Yet punishment sometimes inadvertently operates as a prodelinquent influence, despite the attempt to use it as a device for presenting anticriminal behavior patterns. All children are somewhat delinquent, but only some are caught, punished, and, thus, publicly defined and labeled as delinquents. This first public appearance as a delinquent or criminal is highly critical, for thereafter the child's associations with law-abiding persons are restricted, and he is thrown into intimate association with the behavior patterns of other delinquents. A boy who is consistently criminal is not defined as law-abiding if he commits a

---

[36] Mack, "Full-time Miscreants," p. 44.

[37] N. S. Hayner, "Delinquency Areas in the Puget Sound Region," *American Journal of Sociology,* 39:314-328, November, 1933.

[38] See William F. Whyte, *Street Corner Society* (Chicago: University of Chicago Press, 1943), pp. 104-108.

single lawful act, but a boy who is consistently law-abiding is likely to be publicly defined as a criminal if he is caught committing a single criminal act.

It is clear that even in the areas of highest delinquency many nondelinquent and antidelinquent behavior patterns are available.[39] Whether a particular child becomes delinquent or not depends upon the ratio of his participation in this kind of behavior pattern, as compared with prodelinquency behavior patterns, just as is the case with a child that lives in a more affluent area. The difference is in the availability of the two kinds of behavior pattern, not in the process by which they are learned.[40] ●

The gang

Among the influences in a neighborhood, the mutual stimulation of children in association is one of the most important. Many studies have shown that delinquencies are generally committed by two or more children acting together. Of 500 delinquents studied by Glueck, 492, or 98.4 percent, chummed largely with other delinquents, while despite the fact that the 500 nondelinquents used as a control group lived in similar neighborhoods, only 37, or 7.4 percent, of them had intimates among delinquents.[41] Lentz found that 22 percent of a group of rural training-school boys were known to be members of delinquent gangs, while 87 percent of the urban boys were members of such gangs.[42] In a study of the first delinquencies of boys admitted to the Ohio Boys Industrial School, it was found that the median age of the first contact with the police or courts for delinquency was 13.1 years; of boys whose first official delinquency occurred before this age, 77 percent were with companions when the act occurred; of those whose first delinquency occurred after the age of 13.1, 73 percent were with companions. Companions were present in 100 percent of the boys' involvement in gang fights, but in only 56 percent of the cases of first running away from home.[43] Reiss and Rhodes found that the probability of an individual boy committing a specific kind of delinquent act depends upon the commission of that act by his two best friends. However, the relationship varies considerably with the type of delinquency. Vandalism and petty larceny were commonly committed by two or three members of the "best friends" triad. But in most of the triads in which at least one member committed

---

[39] Cf. Solomon Kobrin, "The Conflict of Values in Delinquency Areas," *American Sociological Review*, 16:653-661, October, 1951.

[40] See Jon E. Simpson, Simon Dinitz, Barbara Kay, and Walter C. Reckless, "Delinquency Potential of Pre-Adolescents in High-Delinquency Areas, *British Journal of Delinquency*, 10:211-215, January, 1960.

[41] Sheldon and Eleanor Glueck, *Unraveling Juvenile Delinquency* (New York: Commonwealth Fund, 1950), p. 164.

[42] Lentz, "Rural Urban Differentials," p. 335.

[43] Thomas G. Eynon and Walter C. Reckless, "Companionship at Delinquency Onset," *British Journal of Criminology*, 12:162-170, October, 1961.

automobile theft or assault, in fact only one member committed the offense.[44]

In most areas of high delinquency, some boys are organized for crime in definite working groups, which they call "cliques" or "gangs," in which the labor is precisely divided. In robbery, for example, one boy drives the car, a second acts as lookout, while a third carries the gun and has the principal responsibility of entering the store. The assignment of tasks, of course, varies with the type of offense. This kind of organization is comparable to the division of labor among professional pickpockets. The term *gang* or *delinquent gang* is generally used for a somewhat larger and less definite group. The definition of *gang* is not clear. Inquiries among university students indicate that more than two-thirds of the men had, during childhood, been members of groups which were called gangs, and that approximately a third of the women had such memberships. Most of these groups were described as harmless in their activities, though inclined to mild rowdyism, and the name *gang* was applied largely in a spirit of bravado. Bloch and Niederhoffer attribute gang behavior of this kind to the problems arising in the transition from the status of child to adult; they find gang behavior in many cultures.[45]

These childhood gangs are different from neighborhood delinquent gangs. In some areas of high delinquency, all the boys who live on one street, or the boys of one ethnic group, belong together for the purposes of fights and are known by a common name. Frequently a portion of the neighborhood boys of about the same age and with somewhat similar attitudes toward delinquency or toward "play" (which might involve delinquency) have a common meeting place on a corner and engage in many common activities without any other formal organization. A stranger would not be permitted to associate with these groups, and certain boys in the neighborhood might be ostracized, but otherwise the group is inclusive. Other gangs are much more formally organized, with names, leaders, passwords, and slogans, and they may persist, with changing personnel, for several decades. A "delinquent gang in this sense is a means of disseminating techniques of delinquency, or training in delinquency, of protecting members engaged in delinquency, and of maintaining continuity in delinquency."[46] It is not necessary that there be bad boys inducing good boys to commit offenses. It is generally a mutual stimulation, as a result of which each boy commits delinquencies which he would not commit alone.

---

[44] Albert J. Reiss, Jr., and Lewis Rhodes, "An Empirical Test of Differential Association Theory," *Journal of Research in Crime and Delinquency*, 1:5-18, January, 1964.

[45] Herbert A. Bloch and Arthur Niederhoffer, *The Gang: A Study in Adolescent Behavior* (New York: Philosophical Library, 1958).

[46] Cf. John B. Mays, "A Study of a Delinquent Community," *British Journal of Delinquency*, 3:5-19, July, 1952.

So far as structure is concerned, then, neighborhood delinquent gangs may consist of loosely federated small cliques, or street clubs with rather informal and rapidly changing leadership, or of organizations with an age hierarchy and specific leadership.[47] Among 225 gangs studied in Warsaw in 1953-1955, only 24 percent had an age hierarchy and specific leadership; another 24 percent was said to have "rudimentary organization," and the remaining 53 percent were "non-organized."[48]

One analysis has characterized both the loose federations of cliques and the street clubs as "near groups," rather than as groups.[49] The argument underlying this characterization is that these gangs are merely loose federations of individual boys who are trying to work out their own emotional problems in gang activities. There is little consensus, little identification with the group, and rapidly changing leadership. Thrasher observed the unstable quality of Chicago delinquent gangs in the 1920s.[50] It is not at all certain, however, that emotionally disturbed boys are attracted to delinquent gangs in a disproportionate degree. One study of street clubs in Chicago found only about 10 percent of the members emotionally disturbed enough to be referred to a casework agency.[51] It appears, however, that even the gangs that are highly organized for some purpose such as protection of their "turf" from invading gangs, and which have senior, junior, and midget sections, are so poorly integrated that the gang may disintegrate if a leader is arrested or moves out of the neighborhood.

Delinquent gangs may be classified according to activities as well as according to the type of organization involved. One such classification developed from observations of the kinds of delinquent gangs arising in the slum areas of large American cities: gangs oriented to criminal activities, gangs oriented to conflict and violence, and gangs oriented to the use of drugs.[52] This classification refers to gangs in different locations and in different

---

[47] Ruth Shonle Cavan, *Juvenile Delinquency* (Philadelphia: J. B. Lippincott, 1969), pp. 259-260.

[48] A. Pawelczynska, "Grupy nieletnich przestepców," *Archives Kryminologi*, 1 (1960): 113-163.

[49] Lewis Yablonsky, "The Delinquent Gang as a Near-Group," *Social Problems*, 7:108-117, Fall, 1959.

[50] Frederic M. Thrasher, *The Gang* (Chicago: University of Chicago Press, 1927), pp. 35-37.

[51] Charles H. Shireman, *The Hyde Park Youth Project, May 1955—May 1958* (Chicago: Welfare Council of Metropolitan Chicago, n.d.), p. 147.

[52] Richard A. Cloward and Lloyd E. Ohlin, *Delinquency and Opportunity: A Theory of Delinquent Gangs* (Glencoe, Ill.: Free Press, 1960). See also Yablonsky's classification: delinquent gangs, violent gangs, and social gangs. The latter are not delinquent. Lewis Yablonsky, *The Violent Gang* (New York: Macmillan, 1962), pp. 149-150. Cohen and Short stimulated classifications of these kinds by identifying three kinds of male delinquent subcultures: the "parent" subculture, the conflict-oriented subculture, and the drug addict subculture. Albert K. Cohen and James F. Short, Jr., "Research in Delinquent Subcultures," *Journal of Social Issues*, vol. 14 (1958), no. 3, pp. 20-37.

periods of history. In 1963, Short and his co-workers could find no criminally oriented gangs in Chicago, and it took more than a year of extensive inquiries to locate a drug-oriented group.[53] It should be emphasized, moreover, that no classificatory system is airtight—the gangs that fight also steal occasionally, and gangs involved in the pursuit of "kicks" also engage in various forms of theft, as well as in violence.[54]

In all three types of gangs described by Cloward and Ohlin, members of the gangs are committed to a set of norms in opposition to those held by law-abiding groups of the larger society. They have "withdrawn their attribution of legitimacy to certain of the norms maintained by law-abiding groups of the larger society and have given it, instead, to new patterns of conduct which are defined as illegitimate by representatives of official agencies."[55] The activities of gangs follow rules which are specifically provided and supported by the delinquent subcultures described in chapter 5, but the activities of the members, and of the gangs themselves, should not be confused with the delinquent subcultures. Because of inconsistencies in the general social structure, certain forms of delinquent activity become essential requirements for the performance of some social roles. This kind of delinquent activity is subcultural delinquency, and the "rules for delinquency" which underlie it constitute a delinquent subculture. However, explanation of the process by which the "rules for delinquency" come into existence, develop, and change, is different from explanation of the behavior of delinquents, whether these delinquents perform their delinquencies alone or in gangs.

The delinquent gang is, above all, an important agency for diffusion of the values that make up delinquent subcultures. Acts of delinquency which have the support of a gang are likely to recur with great frequency, for delinquent behavior is a prerequisite for acceptance and status in the gang.[56] In gangs

---

[53] James F. Short, Jr., Ray A. Tennyson, and Kenneth I. Howard, "Behavior Dimensions of Gang Delinquency," American Sociological Review, 28:411-428, June, 1963.

[54] James F. Short, Jr., "Street Corner Groups and Patterns of Delinquency: A Progress Report," American Catholic Sociological Review, 24:13-32, Spring, 1963.

[55] Cloward and Ohlin, Delinquency and Opportunity, p. 19.

[56] The following material is based on Cloward and Ohlin, Delinquency and Opportunity, pp. 10-11, but it stresses the difference between gang activities and the delinquent subcultures on which gang activities are based. Cloward and Ohlin are vague about whether theirs is a theory about the behavior of delinquents, a theory about delinquent gangs, or a theory about the origin of delinquent subcultures. Their use of the terms gang and subculture synonymously contributes to this vagueness. We consider as primary the problem of explaining how delinquent values come into existence, and we view the problem of how these values are diffused as secondary. Cloward and Ohlin state that they are concerned with the first problem: "Why do delinquent norms, or rules of conduct, develop?" (P. ix.) However, their book is devoted principally to discussion of how delinquent rules of conduct, once they are in existence, get distributed to individuals.

oriented to criminal activities, this means that a boy's social position in the gang can be maintained only if he can "score" now and then, and if he can exhibit the behavior patterns of a "real man" or a "thief."[57] In street gangs devoted primarily to fighting and violence, a member's social position depends upon frequent exhibitions of "heart," and skill in the use of violence. Fighting gangs are almost constantly engaged in negotiations with each other, and, as demonstrations of strength, many agreements, alliances, and contracts are made. "These are generally pseudo-bargains, which serve as means for gang members to flex muscles they are unsure they have.[58] In one city, the bulk of the assaultive incidents among members of street gangs involved contests in which the preservation and defense of gang honor was the central issue and where "little of the deliberately-inflicted property damage represented a diffuse outpouring of accumulated hostility against arbitrary objects."[59] In short, it was found that even "non-utilitarian" violence in the form of assaults on innocent victims is very rare. In gangs oriented to the use of drugs, the individual member can lay claim to "rep" only if he frequently displays his ability to obtain drugs and to increase the experience of the "kick."

Gang activities furnish continuity between criminal activities as a juvenile and criminal activites as an adult. Not all gang members become adult criminals, by any means, but gang activities sometimes afford the young an opportunity to acquire the values and skills that are necessary to becoming a competent adult criminal. A study of 711 active Negro male gang members in Philadelphia indicated that the rate for each type of delinquency rose gradually each year from the average age of first contact with the police (13.4 years) to a peak at 15-16 years, and then decreased in the last year of juvenile status.[60] The average time between the first and second contacts with the police was fourteen months, while the average interval between the ninth and tenth contacts was 3.6 months. Of 580 gang members who moved out of juvenile status between January 1 and October 15, 1962, 41 percent acquired criminal records in this period. These data indicate that once gang delinquencies begin, there is a chain reaction in which each delinquent act becomes a stimulus for commission of another act within a briefer period, indicating gang members' increasing acceptance of the norms and values of the gang.

Further, participation in gang activities makes a delinquent difficult to change, for his behavior belongs to an explicit net-

---

[57] See John Irwin and Donald R. Cressey, "Thieves, Convicts and the Inmate Culture," *Social Problems,* 10:142-155, Fall, 1962.

[58] Yablonsky, *The Violent Gang,* p. 157.

[59] Walter B. Miller, "Violent Crime in City Gangs," *Annals of the American Academy of Political and Social Science,* 343:97-112, March, 1966.

[60] Gerald D. Robin, "Gang Member Delinquency: Its Extent, Sequence, and Typology," *Journal of Criminal Law, Criminology, and Police Science,* 55:59-69, March, 1964.

work of expectations and obligations. Most delinquent and criminal behavior is the property of groups rather than of individuals, in the way the French language or English language is the property of collectivities rather than of individuals, but in the case of gang behavior, the ownership of the delinquency is more explicit and obvious. Accordingly, efforts to induce a member to feel shame or guilt are blocked by the rationalizations and reassurances which the group provides.

The member of a delinquent gang organized primarily for pursuit of material gain by such illegal means as theft, fraud, and extortion adopts values which regard members of the conventional world as "suckers," which see the world of business as a world of rackets, and the world of politics as a world of graft. However, the solutions to problems of lower-class boys provided by delinquent gangs are primarily *status* rewarding, rather than economically rewarding.[61] In conflict gangs, for example, the role-model is the "bopper" who displays the courage and bravery of the hero, the successful warrior. A youth can obtain "rep" in such a gang if he is tough and destructively violent; he must not be weak. Short and Strodtbeck have shown that leaders of conflict gangs often respond to status threats by instigating aggression against persons outside the gang.[62]

In gangs oriented to drug use, the member learns that to be important he must be a "cat," a "hipster" who is detached from the life-style and everyday activities of "squares."[63] A "cat," moreover, does not "retreat." He "hustles," meaning that he lives by his wits rather than by routine labor. The so-called retreatist gang (the addict subculture) thus provides each of its members with a system for achieving status in a group which the gang views as "elite," a group which assigns prestige to those who work regularly and hard in the nonconventional occupations summarized by the term "hustle."[64]

Cloward and Ohlin's thesis is that gang behavior is motivated by failure, or the anticipation of failure, in achieving success-goals by socially approved means. This thesis is similar to that of Albert K. Cohen, who stresses the function of the gang in resolving the status frustrations of working-class boys.[65] Lower-class male adolescents find themselves at a competitive disadvantage in gaining access to legitimate routes to success. If they attribute their failure to injustice in the social system, rather than to their own inadequacies, they may (a) bend their efforts

[61] Short, "Street Corner Groups and Patterns of Delinquency," p. 22.

[62] James F. Short, Jr., and Fred L. Strodtbeck, *Group Process and Gang Delinquency* (Chicago: University of Chicago Press, 1965), pp. 185-198.

[63] Harold Finestone, "Cats, Kicks, and Color," *Social Problems*, 5:3-13, July, 1957.

[64] Alan G. Sutter, "Worlds of Drug Use on the Street Scene," chap. in Donald R. Cressey and David A. Ward, eds., *Delinquency, Crime, and Social Process* (New York: Harper and Row, 1969), pp. 802-829.

[65] Albert K. Cohen, *Delinquent Boys: The Culture of the Gang* (Glencoe, Ill.: Free Press, 1955).

to reforming the social order, (b) dissociate themselves from it, or (c) rebel against it. "Democratizing the criteria of evaluation without at the same time increasing the opportunities available to lower-class youngsters will accentuate the conditions that produce feelings of unjust deprivation."[66] A sense of injustice, then, springs from a sense of being discriminated against.

It should not be concluded, however, that persons with limited opportunities, or persons who are discriminated against, perceive these restrictions as status deprivation. For example, boys (but not girls) from rural areas and small towns have lower occupational aspirations than those from larger urban places—independent of intelligence and socioeconomic differences. Low-status rural youth, therefore, are less likely than low-status city youth to perceive their status as a consequence of deprivation.[67] Consistently, a study of delinquency in the most affluent nations of the world concluded: "Resentment of poverty is more likely to develop among the relatively deprived of a rich society than among the objectively deprived in a poor society."[68] Using a crude measure of perceived status deprivation, Reiss and Rhodes found that only 28 percent of a sample of delinquents and 16 percent of a sample of nondelinquents perceived that their clothing and housing were not as good as that of their fellow students.[69] Similarly, an Ohio State study found only a slight association between delinquency proneness and perception of limited opportunity, and a Chicago study indicated that many of the values of members of delinquent gangs closely resemble the values of the middle class.[70] DeFleur has pointed out that Latin cultures have been characterized by rigid class structures in which "remaining in one's station" is more heavily emphasized than striving for status. Accordingly, short-run hedonism, rather than status deprivation, is a major motive for delinquency.[71]

---

[66] Cloward and Ohlin, *Delinquency and Opportunity*, p. 121.

[67] William H. Sewell and Alan M. Orenstein, "Community of Residence and Occupational Choice," *American Journal of Sociology*, 60:551-563, March, 1965.

[68] Jackson Toby, "Affluence and Adolescent Crime," appendix H in President's Commission on Law Enforcement and Administration of Justice, *Task Force Report: Juvenile Delinquency and Youth Crime* (Washington: Government Printing Office, 1967), pp. 132-144.

[69] Albert J. Reiss, Jr., and A. Lewis Rhodes, "Status Deprivation and Delinquent Behavior," *Sociological Quarterly*, 4:136-149, Spring, 1963.

[70] Judson R. Landis, Simon Dinitz, and Walter C. Reckless, "Implementing Two Theories of Delinquency: Value Orientation and Awareness of Limited Opportunity," *Sociology and Social Research*, 47:408-416, July, 1963; Robert A. Gordon, James F. Short, Jr., Desmond S. Cartwright, and Fred L. Strodtbeck, "Values and Gang Delinquency: A Study of Street-Corner Groups," *American Journal of Sociology*, 69:109-128, September, 1963. See also Delbert S. Elliott, "Delinquency and Perceived Opportunity," *Sociological Inquiry*, 32:216-226, Spring, 1962.

[71] Lois B. DeFleur, *Delinquency in Argentina: A Study of Cordoba's Youth* (Pullman, Wash.: Washington State University Press, 1970), p. 148.

The gang-formation process is initiated when the individual frustrated delinquent finds encouragement and reassurance for his acts of deviance by "searching out others who have faced similar experiences and who will support one another in common attitudes of alienation from the official system."[72] The gang of peers forms a new social world in which the legitimacy of the individual's delinquent conduct is strongly reinforced. Occasionally the "social world" extends far beyond any gang, becoming a social movement. This was somewhat the character of the "hippie" and "student protest" cults of the 1960s.[73]

Once individuals start seeking support from others who feel alienated from the prevailing social norms, a gang has begun to form. But before gang activities can begin, there must be effective interaction between the actors in a collective problem-solving process.[74] Cohen describes this problem-solving process as a "conversation of gestures," which serves at least four important functions.[75] *First*, it permits the gang members to explore the extent to which each is willing to go in accepting alternative rules for action. *Second*, it enables them to explore the extent to which they can rely on each other for support if they take a daring, rebellious, or delinquent path. *Third*, it gives each member an opportunity to test the degree to which his techniques for neutralizing the influences of law-abiding society are accepted by others.[76] *Fourth*, it enables the gang collectively to try out various courses of delinquent action and to judge the commitment that each member of the gang is willing to make to each type of action.

This process of alienation is abetted by the very processes by which law-abiding society attempts to deal with delinquent activities. As deviance has developed as an area of concern in sociology, an increasing number of sociologists have begun to write about the importance of "labeling" in creating deviance in the first place. Behavior which might be rather routine to the actor becomes a "problem" only because someone else, usually an official agency, labels it "deviant."[77] In the case of delinquency, this labeling process might ignore one actor who has violated

---

[72] Cloward and Ohlin, *Delinquency and Opportunity*, p. 126.

[73] John C. Ball and Frida G. Surawicz, "A Trip to San Francisco's 'Hippieland': Glorification of Delinquency and Irresponsibility," *International Journal of Offender Therapy*, 12 (1968): 63-69.

[74] Cohen, *Delinquent Boys*, p. 59.

[75] Ibid., pp. 60-61. Cf. Cloward and Ohlin, *Delinquency and Opportunity*, pp. 140-142.

[76] Gresham M. Sykes and David Matza, "Techniques of Neutralization: A Theory of Delinquency," *American Sociological Review*, 22:664-670, December, 1957.

[77] See, for example, Edwin M. Lemert, *Social Pathology* (New York: McGraw-Hill, 1951); Howard S. Becker, *Outsiders: Studies in the Sociology of Deviance* (New York: Free Press, 1963); John I. Kitsuse, "Societal Reaction to Deviant Behavior: Problems of Theory and Method," *Social Problems*, 9:247-256, Winter, 1962; and Kai T. Erikson, "Notes on the Sociology of Deviance," *Social Problems*, 9:307-314, Spring, 1962.

the law but stigmatize another as a delinquent. Tannenbaum referred to this process as a "dramatization of evil":

> The first dramatization of "evil" which separates the child out of his group for specialized treatment plays a greater role in making the criminal than perhaps any other experience. It cannot be too often emphasized that for the child the whole situation has become different. He now lives in a different world. He has been tagged. A new and hitherto nonexistent environment has been precipitated out for him.
>
> The process of making the criminal, therefore, is a process of tagging, defining, identifying, segregating, describing, emphasizing, making conscious and self-conscious; it becomes a way of stimulating, suggesting, emphasizing, and evolving the very traits that are complained of.[78]

Consistently, one of the earliest studies of delinquent gangs pointed out that the societal reactions to gang behavior make gang members more acutely aware of the gang's isolation from the values of the law-abiding community:

> It does not become a gang, however, until it begins to excite disapproval and opposition, and thus acquires a more definite group-consciousness. It discovers a rival or an enemy in the gang in the next block; its baseball or football team is pitted against some other team; parents or neighbors look upon it with suspicion or hostility; "the old man around the corner," the storekeepers, or the "cops" begin to give it "shags" (chase it); or some representative of the community steps in and tries to break it up. This is the real beginning of the gang, for now it starts to draw itself more closely together. It becomes a conflict group.[79]

The specific direction taken in a gang's activities depends upon access to various directives for illegal actions, as well as upon the accessibility to directives for legal actions. Thus, a gang, like a person, takes a delinquent course rather than a nondelinquent course because a delinquent subculture in the form of rules, norms, values, and beliefs is more readily available than an antidelinquent subculture with its norms, values, and beliefs. In this connection, Miller maintains that the dominant motivation underlying gang behavior is the attempt by gang members to achieve standards of value as they are defined in lower-class urban areas.[80] By the same token, a gang moves into one kind of delinquency rather than another because of the norms, values, and beliefs available to it.

An individual frustrated by his condition of poverty may relieve his tension by accepting a nondelinquent solution, such as renouncing all worldly things and becoming a hermit, or moving into the political arena to effect economic reforms. Alternatively, he may simply work harder, holding down two jobs at the same time.[81] Or he may solve the problem by adopting any of a

---

[78] Frank Tannenbaum, *Crime and the Community* (New York: Ginn, 1938), pp. 19-20.

[79] Thrasher, *The Gang*, p. 30.

[80] Walter B. Miller, "Lower Class Culture as a Generating Milieu of Gang Delinquency," *Journal of Social Issues*, 14 (1958): 5-19.

[81] Harold L. Wilensky, "The Moonlighter: A Product of Relative Deprivation," *Industrial Relations*, 3:105-124, October, 1963.

number of delinquent solutions, one of which might be a burglary pattern, or a shoplifting pattern, or even an embezzlement pattern. Which of the delinquent solutions is adopted by the individual depends upon their availability to him. Similarly, whether a delinquent gang composed of persons dissatisfied with their lot in life moves in the direction of a particular kind of delinquency depends upon the availability of directives for action, and of training for action. In this connection, Cloward and Ohlin say that "the individual must have access to appropriate environments for the acquisition of values and skills associated with the performance of a particular role, and he must be supported in the performance of the role once he has learned it."[82]

Negatively, this means that gangs oriented to stealing will not develop where values favorable to stealing are not readily available, that gangs oriented to violence will not develop where behavior patterns favorable to violence are scarce, and that gangs oriented to drug use will not develop in areas where drugs and knowledge about their "good" effects are rare. Positively, gangs oriented to property offenses develop in areas in which the criminality of adults makes the values conducive to property offenses, and the opportunities for displaying adoption of these values, both readily available.

Gangs oriented to conflict arise in areas where access to legitimate channels to success-goals are denied, where the opportunity to learn values conducive to renouncing the importance of "success" and values conducive to theft also are denied, and where values supporting violent actions are available. Thus, the conflict gang is composed of young men who are unable to "make it" legitimately, but also are unable either to "make it" by theft or to "explain away" their failure, and who are able to seize upon patterns for manipulation of violence as a route to high status. Some support for this point is found in Short's observation that of sixteen Chicago gangs, containing a total of 598 members, the six gangs most oriented to conflict, and three of the four gangs least oriented to conflict, were Negro.[83] This suggests that the status deprivation of Negroes produces conflict-oriented gangs only when the conflict values available to be learned outweigh the nonconflict values. As Short and others have said: "Given culturally supported requirements for aggressive responses, such characteristics of lower-class life as public drinking, milling behavior, and a high incidence of guns may precondition the occurrence of acts of violence which involve individuals who could not have been differentiated from their peers by any personality assessment, even an hour before the occurrence of violence."[84]

---

[82] Cloward and Ohlin, *Delinquency and Opportunity*, p. 148.

[83] Short, Tennyson, and Howard, "Behavior Dimensions of Gang Delinquency," p. 425.

[84] James F. Short, Jr., Fred L. Strodtbeck, and Desmond S. Cartwright, "A Strategy for Utilizing Research Dilemmas: A Case from the Study of Parenthood in a Street Corner Gang," *Sociological Inquiry*, 32:185-202, Spring, 1962.

Gangs oriented to drug use occur among persons faced with failure in the use of both legitimate and illegitimate means for achieving success goals, and they occur in areas where the opportunities for obtaining drugs and for learning how to use them are available.[85]

In sum, delinquent gangs provide alternative channels for gaining status or symbols of status. Whether the kinds of opportunities provided by gangs are present in an area of a city, and whether specific *forms* of illegitimate channels of opportunity are present, depends upon the traditions of the people in the area—traditions of beliefs, values, and rules of conduct that are integrated closely enough so that they can be called a "subculture." Yablonsky, like Cloward and Ohlin, has argued that gang members are boys who have been satiated with delinquency behavior patterns and, at the same time, alienated from antidelinquency behavior patterns.[86] Nettler, like Sykes and Matza, has argued that the behavior of gang members, like that of other delinquents, is based on values extending from those held by most members of the society, and that delinquency, therefore, is better understood as a form of conformity than as a form of deviation.[87] •

Individuals and institutions in a neighborhood may disseminate delinquent and criminal behavior patterns, intentionally or inadvertently. The "fence," the junkman, and other persons who are willing to purchase stolen goods, stimulate delinquencies both by failing to present antidelinquency patterns to children who offer stolen goods for sale, and by presenting the procriminal behavior patterns implicit in their purchase of the goods. Sometimes the person who influences the standards of the children may be another child. The following account was written by a middle-aged student regarding his own childhood. It shows the effect of one new arrival in the community upon the lives of the juvenile inhabitants.

Neighborhood agencies

I lived near the edge of a town of about fifteen thousand population. My father was a lawyer. My chief companions were boys of about my own age, one being the son of a Methodist preacher, one the son of a Baptist preacher, and one the son of the fireman at the Tuberculosis Sanitarium. The son of the Methodist preacher knew much more

---

[85] Richard A. Cloward, "Illegitimate Means, Anomie, and Deviant Behavior," *American Sociological Review*, 24:164-176, April, 1959. See also Howard S. Becker, "Marihuana Use and Social Control," *Social Problems*, 3:25-44, July, 1955; and "Becoming a Marihuana User," *American Journal of Sociology*, 59:235-242, November, 1953.

[86] Yablonsky, *The Violent Gang*, pp. 170-194. See also Martin R. Haskell, "Toward a Reference Group Theory of Juvenile Delinquency," *Social Problems*, 8:220-230, Winter, 1961.

[87] Gwynn Nettler, "Good Men, Bad Men, and the Perception of Reality," *Sociolmextry*, 24:279-294, September, 1961; David Matza and Gresham M. Sykes, "Juvenile Delinquency and Subterranean Values," *American Sociological Review*, 26:712-719, October, 1961.

about the world than the rest of us did. He told us a great deal about sex matters and about gangsters. Under his guidance we built a cave, secured some detective stories, and had what we regarded as a regular den of iniquity in the cave. Eventually, with the help of a few others, we constituted a small gang which threw rocks at the street cars, broke windows in empty houses, shot pigeons belonging to other boys, stole fruit from orchards and candy from stores. We did not learn all of these things from the son of the Methodist minister; he undoubtedly learned much from the rest of us. We worked out our plans together. But our delinquent tendencies started soon after he arrived in the neighborhood and ceased soon after his father was called to another church.

Illegal agencies ordinarily are located in a neighborhood against the wishes of the members of that neighborhood. To a degree, this is true of bookmaking enterprises and illegal lotteries, but often such operations depend on community residents for patronage. Houses of prostitution are another matter, for their patrons ordinarily do not come from the local area. The neighbors oppose them, but they are unable to produce the legal and political pressures necessary to force them to move. Negroes and other minority groups suffer most from such vice districts. A situation existing in Chicago over a half-century ago continues today in many American cities:

The chief of police [of Chicago] in 1912 warned prostitutes that so long as they confined their residence to districts west of Wabash Avenue and east of Wentworth Avenue, they would not be disturbed. This area contained at that time the largest group of Negroes in the city, with most of their churches, Sunday Schools and societies. . . . That many Negroes live near vice districts is not due to their choice, nor to low moral standards, but to three causes: (1) Negroes are unwelcome in desirable white residence localities; (2) small incomes compel them to live in the least expensive places regardless of surroundings; while premises rented for immoral purposes bring notoriously high rentals, they make the neighborhood undesirable and the rent of other living quarters there abnormally low; and (3) Negroes lack sufficient influence and power to protest effectively against the encroachments of vice.[88]

Such agencies are not likely to produce sexual delinquencies because of the sex standards involved, but organized criminals in a neighborhood contribute to more general crime and delinquency rates in three interrelated ways. *First,* by their opulence the persons engaged in organized crime demonstrate to the people of the neighborhood, and especially to the young, that crime does pay.[89] *Second,* by their very presence they demonstrate the existence of a rich vein of corruption in political and law-enforcement organizations, making it difficult for parents to convince their children that people get ahead in the world by good,

---

[88] Chicago Commission on Race Relations, *A Study of Race Relations and a Race Riot* (Chicago: Author, 1922), pp. 343-344.

[89] See Irving Spergel, *Racketville, Slumtown, Haulburg: An Exploratory Study of Delinquent Subcultures* (Chicago: University of Chicago Press, 1964); and Gerald D. Suttles, *The Social Order of the Slum: Ethnicity and Territory in the Inner City* (Chicago: University of Chicago Press, 1968).

hard, honest labor in the service of family, country, man, and God. *Third,* the presence of organized crime in a neighborhood lowers the status of the people in the district, just as do conditions of squalor, with the result that anticriminal admonitions become less effective—the people have less to lose if convicted of crime.[90] The Reverend Martin Luther King summed up the contemporary situation as follows:

> The most grievous charge against municipal police is not brutality, although it exists. Permissive crime in ghettos is the nightmare of the slum family. Permissive crime is the name for organized crime that flourishes in the ghetto—designed, directed, and cultivated by the white national crime syndicates operating numbers, narcotics, and prostitution rackets freely in the protected sanctuaries of the ghettos. Because no one, including the police, cares particularly about ghetto crime, it pervades every area of life.[91]

Recreational agencies also contribute to the delinquency of the children in the neighborhood. It has become commonplace to state that most of the delinquencies of children occur in the search for recreation. One general notion in this regard is that the only recreations generally available in deteriorated neighborhoods are those furnished by commercial concerns. Since these concerns are interested primarily in securing a profit, they offer whatever recreation produces the largest revenue, regardless of the welfare of the patrons. The result is that many of the neighborhood dance halls, pool rooms, school stores, and other recreational institutions are "injurious" to many juveniles. A more realistic interpretation is that such institutions merely serve as gathering places for neighborhood youth, thus providing opportunities for dissemination of delinquent attitudes and standards. The same process of dissemination occurs when youth gather on street corners or in public playgrounds.

Another notion is that the *absence* of places of organized public recreation, particularly playgrounds, somehow contributes to the delinquency rate of a neighborhood. A great proportion of the studies of the relation between recreation and delinquency have been conducted by persons or agencies who have a stake in the promotion of recreational programs, and the methods used to reach the conclusion that "lack of wholesome recreation" is a cause of delinquency are dubious. It is obvious that delinquency, like baseball or swimming, is a "spare-time" activity, but this does not mean that delinquency results from an absence of baseball fields or swimming pools.

From the point of view of the differential association theory, there are three possible ways in which playground participation may be related to delinquent behavior. *First,* the activities may

---

[90] Jackson Toby, "Social Disorganization and Stake in Conformity: Complimentary Factors in the Predatory Behavior of Hoodlums," *Journal of Criminal Law, Criminology, and Police Science,* 48:12-17, May-June, 1957.

[91] Martin Luther King, Jr., "Beyond the Los Angeles Riots: Next Stop, The North," *Saturday Review,* November 13, 1965, p. 34.

have little effect on the participant's attitudes regarding delinquency but may keep him from committing delinquencies during some of his waking hours; he cannot play baseball and participate in burglaries at the same time. *Second,* the participant may come into contact with delinquent behavior patterns; the playground may become the gathering place of the delinquents in the neighborhood and may, in fact, serve to promote a strong ingroup feeling among them. *Third,* the playground director may be able to present antidelinquent behavior patterns to the participant, or the participant may in other ways come into contact with antidelinquent behavior patterns.

Thus, participation in the playground activities may be neutral, or it may be conducive to either delinquency or nondelinquency, depending upon the nature of the associations experienced. If the neighborhood baseball team is made up of delinquents, then an excellent and enthusiastic baseball player is more likely to become delinquent than is a boy who abhors baseball, other things being equal. On the other hand, if the members of the neighborhood baseball team arc antidelinquent in their attitudes and behavior patterns, then the probability that a good and enthusiastic baseball player will become delinquent is lower than the probability that a boy who abhors baseball will become delinquent, other things being equal.

"Other things" never are equal, however. The boy who hates baseball may be an excellent and enthusiastic pool player in a neighborhood where pool players view stealing as a form of play, thus increasing the probability of his delinquency if he engages in his favorite form of recreation. But if the values of the pool players are antidelinquent, then the probability of his delinquency is diminished. The process of "selecting" delinquent or antidelinquent companions depends in part, then, on the person's recreational interests and abilities. Yet it would be absurd to explain a person's delinquency or nondelinquency by assessing his pool-playing or baseball-playing ability.

Further, selection or rejection of delinquent or antidelinquent companions is itself a function of previous associations with antidelinquent and delinquent behavior patterns. An excellent baseball player with strong antidelinquent identification and intimate association with antidelinquent behavior patterns might give up baseball rather than play with delinquents. A boy without such strong counteracting values may join the team and become delinquent. Moreover, a person with reference groups which are antidelinquent in their behavior patterns may join a baseball team made up of delinquents and not become a delinquent himself. In this sense, an individual's "selection" of a delinquent, nondelinquent, or antidelinquent play group depends on his prior associations with delinquent and antidelinquent behavior patterns, just as does his delinquency itself. As Sherif has said:

As he [man] passes from one group situation to another from time to time, he reacts to the demands, pressures, and appeals of new group situations in terms of the person he has come to consider himself and aspires to be. In other words, he reacts in terms of more or less consistent ties of belongingness in relation to his past and present identifications and his future goals for security of his identity, and also status and prestige concerns. . . . The groups to which an individual relates himself need not always be the groups in which he is actually moving. His identifications need not always be with groups in which he is registered, is seen to be, or announced to be a member. . . . In many cases, of course, the individual's reference groups are at the same time his membership groups. However, in cases where the individual's membership groups are not his reference groups, it does not follow that the groups in which he actually interacts will not have an effect on him.[92]

ARNOLD, DAVID O., ed. *The Sociology of Subcultures.* Berkeley, Calif.: The Glendessary Press, 1970.

BLAKE, JUDITH, & KINGSLEY DAVIS. "Norms, Values, and Sanctions." Chapter 13 in *Handbook of Modern Sociology,* edited by Robert E. L. Faris, pp. 456-484. Chicago: Rand McNally, 1964.

CLINARD, MARSHALL B. "A Cross-cultural Replication of the Relation of Urbanism to Criminal Behavior." *American Sociological Review,* 25:253-257, April, 1960.

CLOWARD, RICHARD A., & LLOYD E. OHLIN. *Delinquency and Opportunity: A Theory of Delinquent Gangs.* Glencoe, Ill.: Free Press, 1960.

COHEN, ALBERT K. *Delinquent Boys: The Culture of the Gang.* Glencoe, Ill.: Free Press, 1955.

COHEN, ALBERT K. *Deviance and Control.* Englewood Cliffs, N.J.: Prentice-Hall, 1966.

COHEN, ALBERT K. "The Sociology of the Deviant Act: Anomie Theory and Beyond." *American Sociological Review,* 30:5-14, February, 1965.

COHEN, ALBERT K., & JAMES F. SHORT, JR. "Research in Delinquent Subcultures." *Journal of Social Issues,* vol. 14 (1958), no. 3, pp. 20-37.

DeFLEUR, LOIS B. "Ecological Variables in the Cross-Cultural Study of Delinquency." *Social Forces,* 45:556-570, June, 1967.

DELANEY, LLOYD T. "Establishing Relations with Anti-Social Groups and an Analysis of Their Structure." *British Journal of Delinquency,* 5:34-45, July, 1954.

Suggested readings

---

[92] M. Sherif and C. W. Sherif, *Groups in Harmony and Tension* (New York: Harper, 1953), pp. 160-161. See also Robert K. Merton and A. S. Kitt, "Contributions to the Theory of Reference Group Behavior," in Robert K. Merton and Paul Lazarsfeld, eds., *Continuities in Social Research: Studies in the Scope and Method of the American Soldier* (Glencoe, Ill.: Free Press, 1950), pp. 40-105.

EMPEY, LAMAR T. "Delinquent Subcultures: Theory and Recent Research." *Journal of Research in Crime and Delinquency,* 4:32-42, January, 1967.

GLASER, DANIEL, ed. *Crime in the City.* New York: Harper and Row, 1970.

GORDON, ROBERT A. "Issues in the Ecological Study of Delinquency." *American Sociological Review,* 32:927-944, December, 1967.

LONGMOOR, E. S., & ERLE F. YOUNG. "Ecological Interrelationships of Juvenile Delinquency, Dependency, and Population Mobility." *American Journal of Sociology,* 41:598-610, March, 1936.

MARTIN, JOHN M., ROBERT E. GOULD, & JOSEPH P. FITZPATRICK. "Delinquency In Its Community Context." *Social Service Review,* 42:325-334, September, 1968.

MORRIS, TERRENCE. *The Criminal Area.* London: Kegan Paul, 1958.

POLK, KENNETH. "Juvenile Delinquency and Social Areas." *Social Problems,* 5:214-217, Winter, 1957-58.

ROBIN, GERALD D. "Gang Member Delinquency: Its Extent, Sequence, and Typology." *Journal of Criminal Law, Criminology, and Police Science,* 55:59-69, March, 1964.

ROBINSON, W. S. "Ecological Correlations and the Behavior of Individuals." *American Sociological Review,* 15:351-357, June, 1950.

SHANNON, LYLE W. "The Distribution of Juvenile Delinquency in a Middle-Sized City." *Sociological Quarterly,* 1967, pp. 365-382.

SHORT, JAMES F., JR., & FRED L. STRODTBECK. *Group Process and Gang Delinquency.* Chicago: University of Chicago Press, 1965.

SUTTLES, GERALD D. *The Social Order of the Slum: Ethnicity and Territory in the Inner City.* Chicago: University of Chicago Press, 1968.

TOBY, JACKSON. "Social Disorganization and Stake in Conformity: Complementary Factors in the Predatory Behavior of Hoodlums." *Journal of Criminal Law, Criminology, and Police Science,* 48:12-17, May-June, 1957.

WHYTE, WILLIAM F. *Street Corner Society.* Chicago: University of Chicago Press, 1943.

10 Home and family

Since the family has almost exclusive contact with the child during the period of greatest dependency and greatest plasticity, and continued intimate contact over a subsequent period of several years, it plays an exceptionally important role in determining the behavior patterns which any individual follows. No child is so constituted at birth that it must inevitably become a delinquent or that it must inevitably be law-abiding, and the family is the first agency to affect the direction which a particular child will take. Probably it is for this reason that a large proportion of the criminological research and thinking during this century has been directly or indirectly concerned with the relationship between crime and delinquency on the one hand and various kinds of home conditions and child-rearing practices on the other hand.

Although each family unit is expected to train its children in some efficient way so that they will not become delinquent, there is no real science of child-rearing, and such knowledge as is developed is not available to or utilized by many families. The task of child-training was comparatively simple in early society but has become extremely difficult in modern life. In preliterate life both parents were reared in a rather simple, harmonious culture, as were also the grandparents, other relatives, and neighbors. The result was a steady and harmonious pressure upon the child which formed his character without difficulty and with a minimum of conflicts. This is impossible in modern society, where the persons in charge of the training of the child cannot be consistent. Parents are in conflict with each other, with grandparents, with schoolteachers, and with movie and television actors. Moreover, parents are in conflict, probably more than previously, for the affection of the child. In this situation the harmonious pressure of consistent authorities is impossible.

It is not even possible for one parent to be consistent with himself, for he does not have the support of a consistent culture to keep his policies stable. These inconsistencies undoubtedly affect the degree of obedience which parents can exact from children and, generally, the degree to which children can be controlled. Further, obedience and control depend largely upon the prestige of the parents, and this is affected by both the consistency of the demands they make upon a child and their status in the community. The poverty, physical features, competitive ability and comparative attainments, language, and social status of the parents in comparison with other persons with whom the child is acquainted may destroy the prestige of the parents so that the behavior patterns presented are relatively ineffective.[1] ●

Types of homes and of family relationships

The homes from which delinquent children come are frequently characterized by one or more of the following conditions: (a) other members of the family criminalistic, immoral, or alcoholic, (b) absence of one or both parents by reason of death, divorce, or desertion, (c) lack of parental control because of ignorance or illness, (d) home uncongeniality, as evidenced by domination by one member, favoritism, oversolicitude, overseverity, neglect, jealousy, crowded housing conditions, interfering relatives, (e) racial or religious differences, differences in conventions and standards, foster home, or institutional home, (f) economic pressures, such as unemployment, poverty, mother working.

Three general methods have been used in the effort to determine the importance of these conditions as "factors" in delinquency. One of the methods is to evaluate the home as a whole, by means of some rating device or scale. The home is customarily appraised by setting a "normal" standard for homes and concluding that the home conditions are the cause of delinquency if most delinquents come from homes below this normal. In an earlier period, the "Whittier Scale for Grading Home Conditions" was utilized; this scale had a maximum grade of five on each of five items: necessities, neatness, size, parental conditions, and parental supervision. The median score of 162 delinquents on this scale was fourteen, while the median score of fifty nondelinquents in a control group was twenty-two.[2] After a short period of use, the Whittier Scale and similar score cards disappeared. The rating of a home as "bad" or "good" was to a large extent determined by the values and the social class position of the investigator. The use of such rating scales showed that, while children who get into the juvenile courts come, in more than fair proportion, from homes ranked as "poor" or "bad," none of the children in some homes of this kind, and only some of the children in other such homes get into the juvenile court, while on the other hand some delinquent children come from homes ranked as "good."

---

[1] See W. H. Sewell, P. H. Mussen, and C. W. Harris, "Relationships Among Child Training Practices," *American Sociological Review*, 20:137-148, April, 1955; David C. Sottong, "The Dilemma of the Parent as a Culture Bearer," *Social Casework*, 36:302-306, July, 1955; Bernard C. Rosen, "Conflicting Group Membership: A Study of Parent-Peer Group Cross-Pressures," *American Sociological Review*, 20:155-161, April, 1955; and Albert J. Reiss, Jr., "Delinquency as the Failure of Personal and Social Controls," *American Sociological Review*, 16:196-208, April, 1951.

[2] J. H. Williams, "The Whittier Scale for Grading Home Conditions," *Journal of Delinquency*, 1:273-286, November, 1916; and Mabel R. Fernald, Mary H. S. Hayes, and Almena Dawley, *A Study of Women Delinquents in New York State* (New York: Century, 1920), p. 216.

A second method is evaluation of the influence of the home by a general study of individual cases. By using this method in two pioneering studies, William Healy first estimated that the home was a "major factor" in delinquency in 19 percent of a series of a thousand cases studied in Chicago and a "minor factor" in 23 percent; 230 of the delinquents came from homes having "extreme lack of parental control." In a second study of a series of a thousand cases in Chicago, Healy estimated that 46 percent came from homes said to have "extreme lack of parental control."[3] This method permits the investigator to evaluate the meaning which a particular set of home conditions has for the specific child, and thereby to make allowances for the fact that "bad" homes do not always produce delinquent children. However, the method is subjective, and the findings are likely to reflect the preconceptions of the investigator. During a period when rather strict discipline is the fad in child-rearing, homes without such discipline are likely to be designated as delinquency-producing; but when permissiveness is the fad in child-rearing, then the homes using strict discipline are likely to be so designated. Furthermore, whether the home is designated as a "factor" in the delinquency of a child may depend on the likelihood that the home can be modified by welfare agencies—a home which can be modified may more readily be designated as a factor than one which apparently cannot be modified.

A third method is statistical. The technique varies from simple calculation of the comparative incidence of certain home conditions among delinquents and nondelinquents to more sophisticated techniques of holding certain variables constant while determining the degree of association between delinquency and one other variable. Thus the method aims at the identification of certain specific home conditions which are associated with delinquency, rather than at measuring the influence of the home as a whole. This is the most popular method currently in use, and it will be illustrated in the sections which follow.[4] ●

One of the most obvious elements in the delinquency of some children is the criminalistic behavior of other members of the child's family. Burt concluded from his study in England that vice and crime were present five times as frequently in the homes

Criminality in the home

---

3 William Healy, *The Individual Delinquent* (Boston: Little, Brown, 1915), pp. 130-131, 134; William Healy and Augusta F. Bronner, "Youthful Offenders," *American Journal of Sociology*, 22:50, July, 1916.

4 An excellent review and critique of the work with this method was prepared for the President's Commission. See Hyman Rodman and Paul Grams, "Juvenile Delinquency and the Family: A Review and Discussion," appendix L of President's Commission on Law Enforcement and Administration of Justice, *Task Force Report: Juvenile Delinquency and Youth Crime* (Washington: Government Printing Office, 1967), pp. 188-221.

from which delinquents came as in the homes of nondelinquents.[5]
The Gluecks reported that 84.8 percent of the offenders released
from the Massachusetts Reformatory had been reared in homes
in which there were other criminal members; also they found
that 86.7 percent of the juvenile delinquents and 80.7 percent of
the women delinquents whom they studied were from such
homes.[6] In their most recent study, the Gluecks found drunkenness, crime, or immorality in the homes of 90.4 percent of
500 delinquent boys and in the homes of 54 percent of the 500
nondelinquents comprising the control group.[7] The National
Council on Alcoholism estimates that 30 to 40 percent of all
delinquent youths come from homes where parental excessive
drinking or alcoholism exists.[8] The McCords found that the sons
of criminals had a higher rate of criminality than did the sons of
noncriminals.[9] Interestingly enough, however, the sons of criminals who had been rejected by their fathers had higher crime
rates than those who did not. Johnson hypothesizes that this
difference comes about because "rejection by the father creates
aggressive tendencies which are channeled into crime because
the father serves as a role model,"[10] an interpretation which is
consistent with the theory of differential association.

Thus the homes in which delinquents are reared are to a significant degree situations in which patterns of delinquency are
present. These patterns do not generally result in exact copies
by the children; rather it is the attitudes toward certain kinds of
delinquency and criminality which are likely to be most significant. It has been shown that farm boys who prefer farming as an
occupation, as compared with farm boys who prefer nonfarm occupations, more frequently have participated in a family value system
functionally related to farming.[11] There is no reason to believe
that boys participating in a value system functionally related to
crime should not, similarly, enter criminality more frequently
than those not participating in such direct, primary-type influences. Two psychiatrists have concluded that parents' unwitting
sanction or indirect encouragement is a major cause of, and the

---

[5] Cyril Burt, The Young Delinquent, 4th ed. (London: University of London
Press, 1944).

[6] Sheldon and Eleanor T. Glueck, Five Hundred Criminal Careers (New York:
Alfred A. Knopf, 1930), pp. 111-112; One Thousand Juvenile Delinquents
(Cambridge, Mass.: Harvard University Press, 1934), p. 79; Five Hundred
Delinquent Women (New York: Alfred A. Knopf, 1934), p. 72.

[7] Sheldon and Eleanor Glueck, Unraveling Juvenile Delinquency (New York:
Commonwealth Fund, 1950), pp. 110-111.

[8] Annual Report, 1967 (New York: National Council on Alcoholism, 1968), p. 6.

[9] Joan McCord and William McCord, "The Effects of Parental Role Model on
Criminality," Journal of Social Issues, 14 (1958): 66-75.

[10] Elmer H. Johnson, Crime, Correction, and Society, rev. ed. (Homewood, Ill.:
Dorsey Press, 1968), p. 88.

[11] Murray A. Straus, "Personal Characteristics and Functional Needs in the
Choice of Farming as an Occupation," Rural Sociology, 21:257-266, December,
1956; see also A. O. Haller and William H. Sewell, "Occupational Choices
of Wisconsin Farm Boys," Rural Sociology, 32:37-55, March, 1967.

specific stimulus for, truancy and various kinds of delinquency."[12] Wolfgang and Ferracuti have shown that a "subculture of violence" exists in the American urban lower class, and this subculture is carried by families as well as by other groups.[13] Severy studied 296 delinquent and nondelinquent high school students—selected so that half were males and half were Mexican-Americans—over a four-year period. Among these youths, if there was low original exposure to deviance of family members (crudely measured by offense rates, "seriousness of offenses," and "depth of involvement in the formal legal structure"), increasing exposure led to deviance, but when family exposure was originally high, increasing exposure led to rejection of delinquency.[14] ●

The modification of home conditions by death, divorce, or desertion has generally been believed to be an important reason for delinquency of the children. This belief is found even in nonliterate tribes, for the Ama-Xosa, a Bantu tribe in southern Africa, have a proverb, "If the old bird dies, the eggs are addled." Research reports indicate that from 30 to 60 percent of delinquents come from broken homes, and the percentages tend to cluster around 40 percent. The proportion of delinquent girls coming from broken homes is greater than the proportion of delinquent boys coming from such homes, and the proportion of delinquent Negroes is greater than the proportion of whites.[15]

The broken home

Polk has shown that the judicial process tends to select children from broken homes; among the cases of male juveniles which the Los Angeles Probation Department closed at intake in one year, 43 percent were from broken homes, while 50 percent of those placed on probation and 58 percent of those institutionalized came from broken homes.[16] Similarly, Nye found that 24 percent of the most delinquent boys in a high school came from broken homes, as did 48 percent of the boys in a training school, indicating that a selective principle was operating.[17]

Seventy-one percent of all felony cases admitted to Florida prisons in 1969-1970 came from broken homes—64 percent of the white prisoners and 80 percent of the black prisoners. Half the

---

[12] Adelaide M. Johnson and S. A. Szurek, "Etiology of Antisocial Behavior in Delinquents and Psychopaths," *Journal of the American Medical Association,* 154:814-817, March 6, 1954.

[13] Marvin E. Wolfgang and Franco Ferracuti, *The Subculture of Violence: Towards an Integrated Theory in Criminology* (London: Social Science Paperbacks, 1967), pp. 153-163.

[14] Lawrence J. Severy, "Exposure to Deviance Committed by Valued Peer Group and Family Members," *Journal of Research in Crime and Delinquency,* 10:35-46, January, 1973.

[15] Thomas P. Monahan, "Family Status and the Delinquent Child: A Reappaisal and Some New Findings," *Social Forces,* 35:250-258, March, 1957.

[16] Kenneth Polk, "A Note on the Relationship Between Broken Homes, Disposition, and Juvenile Delinquency," manuscript, 1958.

[17] F. Ivan Nye, *Family Relationships and Delinquent Behavior* (New York: John Wiley, 1958), pp. 43-44, 47-48; see also Philip M. Smith, "Broken Homes and Juvenile Delinquency," *Sociology and Social Research,* 39:307-311, June, 1955.

prisoners' homes had been broken before they were thirteen years old.[18] Similarly, an English study showed that the homes of over a third of a group of Borstal boys were broken before the boys reached age 15. Of 300 boys in British detention centers in 1961, 44 percent were from broken homes.[19]

So far as delinquency itself is concerned, statistics on broken homes are meaningless except in comparison with similar percentages for nondelinquent children or for the total population. Burt found about twice as many broken homes in a delinquent group as he did in a control group in England, and the Gluecks found about the same ratio among a group of delinquent boys and a control group in the United States.[20] In the Cambridge-Somerville study, significantly more delinquents than matched nondelinquents came from broken homes. Slocum and Stone, using the self-reporting technique, found a significant correlation between broken homes and delinquency.[21] Barker found that the coefficient of correlation between the juvenile delinquency rate of an area and the percentage of parents divorced was +.79, which could mean that both the delinquency rate and the divorce rate are determined largely by other conditions, such as the local community culture.[22]

Christie studied all males born in Norway in 1933; by January 1, 1958, 5 percent of these males were registered offenders. The homes of 17.4 percent of the offenders and 12.7 percent of the nonoffenders were broken by death, divorce, or separation, a ratio of 1.36 to 1. Among the persons whose parents were still alive, 6 percent of the homes of offenders and 3 percent of the homes of nonoffenders were broken by divorce or separation.[23] This indicates that the broken home is not closely linked with the delinquency of adolescent males. A study by similar methods of delinquent girls in Chicago yielded the conclusion that 66.8 percent of the delinquent girls and 44.8 percent of the schoolgirls came from broken homes, or a ratio of 1.49 to 1. This indicates that a break in the home has a greater influence on girls than on boys.[24]

---

[18] *Seventh Biennial Report* (Tallahassee: Florida Division of Corrections, 1971), pp. 100-101.

[19] T. C. N. Gibbens, *Psychiatric Studies of Borstal Lads* (Oxford: Oxford University Press, 1963); Charlotte Banks, "Violence," *The Howard Journal*, 9:1-13, 1965.

[20] Glueck and Glueck, *Unraveling Juvenile Delinquency*, p. 122.

[21] William McCord and Joan McCord, *Origins of Crime* (New York: Columbia University Press, 1959); Walter Slocum and Carol L. Stone, "Family Culture Patterns and Delinquent-Type Behavior," *Marriage and Family Living*, 25:202-208, 1963.

[22] Gordon H. Barker, "Family Factors in the Ecology of Juvenile Delinquency," *Journal of Criminal Law and Criminology*, 30:881-891, January-February, 1940.

[23] Nils Christie, *Unge Norske Lovovertredere* [Young Norwegian Lawbreakers] (Oslo: Universitetsforlaget, 1960), pp. 105, 111.

[24] See Margaret Hodgkiss, "The Influence of Broken Homes and Working Mothers," *Smith College Studies in Social Work*, 3:259-274, March, 1933. See also Monahan, "Family Status and the Delinquent Child."

Various explanations of the difference between boys and girls in respect to the incidence of broken homes have been suggested. Weeks found that the type of delinquency must be held constant when comparing the incidence of broken homes among boy and girl delinquents.[25] The boy and girl delinquents in his study came from broken homes in approximately the same proportion when the delinquency was ungovernability, running away, or immorality. Girls are more frequently referred for this type of offense, and cases of this type were referred to the juvenile court largely from sources other than the police, indicating that the broken home probably has more to do with referral of cases to the court than with actual causation of delinquency. The broken home had essentially the same significance for boys and for girls when comparison was restricted to similar delinquencies.

Toby has suggested that such weak control is exercised over adolescent males in American families that there is little difference between supervision in a well-integrated family and a disorganized one. Hence, there is no appreciable relationship between broken homes and delinquency among adolescent males. But for girls and preadolescents the well-integrated family gives firm supervision, whereas the disorganized family is unable to do so. Therefore, girls and preadolescents from disorganized households are more likely to be exposed to criminogenic influences than girls and preadolescents from well-integrated households. Differential exposure, then, as well as differential reporting and recording practices, may account for the apparent positive relationship between broken homes and delinquency observed in these populations.[26] The same interpretation could be given to Polk's finding that 69 percent of a group of Negro delinquents placed on probation came from broken homes, as compared with 46 percent of the white cases.[27] ●

Discipline and training

Almost everyone agrees that the most important difference between the situations of delinquent and nondelinquent children is in "home discipline." As Peterson and Becker note, "If one endorses the common assumption that capacities for internal control are complexly but closely related to previously imposed external restraints, then parental discipline assumes focal significance

---

[25] H. Ashley Weeks, "Male and Female Broken Home Rates by Types of Delinquency," *American Sociological Review*, 5:601-609, August, 1940. See also Nye, *Family Relationships and Delinquent Behavior*; and Theodore N. Ferdinand, "The Offense Patterns and Family Structures of Urban, Village and Rural Delinquents," *Journal of Criminal Law, Criminology, and Police Science*, 55:86-93, March, 1964.

[26] Jackson Toby, "The Differential Impact of Family Disorganization," *American Sociological Review*, 22:505-512, October, 1957; cf. Christie, *Unge Norske Lovovertredere*, pp. 111-112, 305.

[27] Polk, "Note on the Relationship Between Broken Homes, Disposition, and Juvenile Delinquency."

as a factor in delinquency."[28] The Gluecks found "unsuitable" supervision by the mother in the homes of 64 percent of the delinquent children and in the homes of only 13 percent of the nondelinquents; also, discipline by the mother was "lax" in 57 percent of the delinquents' homes and in 12 percent of the nondelinquents' homes.[29] Bandura and Walters found that parents of aggressive-destructive boys relied to a greater extent than did the parents of a control group on disciplinary methods involving ridicule, physical punishment, and deprivation of privileges.[30] Trasler's theory is that the punishment-oriented type of child-rearing—used primarily in working-class families—results in less successful socialization to law-abiding norms than do the love-oriented and "character building" practices of middle-class families.[31]

Home discipline, which often means "training" or "socialization," fails most frequently because of indifference and neglect. While it cannot be concluded that children of working mothers are necessarily neglected, the fact that a mother works often affects the training of the child.[32] In some homes of working mothers, like some homes of nonworking mothers, the children are thrown on their own resources as soon as they are physically able. As a result, they are thrust into contact with the behavior patterns of persons outside the home. Whether they become delinquent or not depends upon the community patterns encountered. A study of 312 boys in Los Angeles probation camps found that they were characterized by premature autonomy, attitudinal distance from the family, and lack of factual knowledge about family members.[33] This process has a double impact in inner-city areas: neglect of training by parents is more extensive in slum areas than in middle-class residential areas, and at the same time delinquent subcultures thrive in the slums of American cities. Consequently, the probability that a neglected child will come into contact with an excess of delinquent behavior patterns is higher in ghetto areas than in others.

Many of the complaints in juvenile courts originate with parents who charge their own children, especially girls, with ungovernability. No one wants his son or daughter to be a delin-

---

[28] Donald R. Peterson and Wesley C. Becker, "Family Interaction and Delinquency," chap. in Herbert C. Quay, ed., *Juvenile Delinquency: Research and Theory* (New York: Van Nostrand, 1965), pp. 36-99.

[29] Glueck and Glueck, *Unraveling Juvenile Delinquency*, pp. 113, 131.

[30] Albert Bandura and Richard H. Walters, "Dependency Conflicts in Aggressive Delinquents," *Journal of Social Issues*, vol. 14 (1958), no. 3, pp. 52-65.

[31] Gordon B. Trasler, "Criminal Behavior," in H. J. Eysenck, ed., *Handbook of Abnormal Psychology*, 2nd ed. (London: Pittman Medical Publications, 1970); Robert Everett Stanfield, "The Interaction of Family Variables and Gang Variables in the Aetiology of Delinquency," *Social Problems*, 13:411-417, Spring, 1966.

[32] Elizabeth Herzog, *Children of Working Mothers* (Washington: Department of Health, Education, and Welfare, 1960), pp. 18-20; Eleanor E. MacCoby, "Children and Working Mothers," *The Child*, 5:83-89, June, 1958.

[33] Peter S. Venizia, "Delinquency as a Function of Intrafamily Relationships," *Journal of Research in Crime and Delinquency*, 5:148-173, July, 1968.

quent. But public accusation against a child by his own parents weakens the subsequent influence over the child, while at the same time it throws the child into association with delinquent behavior patterns. This behavior of parents is sometimes due to lack of affection and concern for the child, sometimes to exasperation which is eventually expressed inconsistently and sometimes violently. Moreover, this behavior of parents seems to be concentrated largely in the lower socioeconomic classes, where there is a relative lack of nonjudicial resources for dealing with the problem behavior of children. Porterfield reported that 100 percent of 437 college men and women reported delinquencies in their pre-enrollment years of the same types as those for which children are before the juvenile courts. However, while these persons had engaged in much the same delinquent behavior as the children who appeared before the juvenile court, their own parents and others did not make formal complaints against them, and they did not develop into consistent delinquents in the manner in which the children who appeared before the court did.[34] The child who appears in the juvenile court is labeled a criminal, despite legal theory to the contrary, and as a result he is impeded in adjusting to the larger society, and the society is impeded in adjusting to him.

A special problem of training and discipline appears in the migrant family. Parents who were effective in training their children in the communities of Europe or in the rural areas of the southern United States often find themselves incompetent in the slum areas of the large American city. The rules for living are different, and the community control agencies are different. Children usually acquire the new ways of behaving before their parents do, and then look on their parents with contempt. It is therefore difficult for the parents to make the homes attractive to the children, or to control the children, with the result that the children are often thrown upon their own resources, which means the resources of the delinquent subcultures which surround them.[35]

Foster children are often believed to be more inclined toward delinquency than are other children. The truth of this belief cannot be determined, for there are no good comparisons of the two kinds of groups on this point, and it would be extremely difficult to select adequate samples for such comparisons. Probably the belief is based on occasional observations of foster children who become delinquent and on *a priori* beliefs. Certainly only a small minority of foster children become delinquent. ●

---

[34] Austin L. Porterfield, "Delinquency and Its Outcome in Court and College," *American Journal of Sociology,* 49:199-208, November, 1943; idem, "The Complainant in the Juvenile Court," *Sociology and Social Research,* 28:171-181, January, 1944.

[35] See S. N. Eisenstadt, "Delinquency Group-Formation Among Immigrant Youth," *British Journal of Delinquency,* 2:34-45, July, 1951; and Richard A. Cloward and Lloyd E. Ohlin, *Delinquency and Opportunity* (Glencoe, Ill.: Free Press, 1961), pp. 194-211.

General processes

From the preceding analysis of home conditions in relation to delinquency, five principal processes appear. *First,* a child may assimilate within the home by observation of parents or other relatives the attitudes, codes, and behavior patterns of delinquency. He then becomes delinquent because he has learned delinquency at home. A detailed study of a group of seventeen transsexuals (males who acquire some secondary female sex characteristics by the use of female hormones), who all lived and "passed" as women, indicated that every one of the subjects came from a broken home where the father was not present.[36] However, children of the same age and sex probably are more important than parents in presenting patterns of behavior, whether the patterns presented are delinquent or antidelinquent.

Second, parents determine both the geographic and the social class locus of the home in the community, and the locus of the home, in turn, largely determines the kind of behavior patterns the child will encounter. If the home is in a high-delinquency area, the probability that the child will encounter many delinquent patterns is greater than it is if the home is located in a low-delinquency area. Similarly, being a member of a lower socio-economic class may greatly affect the child's denial or acceptance of the dominant values of the society.[37]

Third, the home may determine the prestige values of various persons and also the type of persons with whom intimacy later develops. The child may learn to reject members of certain minority groups, policemen, social workers, or others. He learns to appraise persons by their bearing, clothing, language, or occupation as important or unimportant, and this appraisal later affects his acceptance or rejection of the behavior patterns which are presented. He learns, in other words, to pay little attention to the behavior patterns, whether criminal or anticriminal, presented by some persons, and to pay close attention to those presented by other persons.

Fourth, a child may be driven from the home by unpleasant experiences and situations or withdraw from it because of the absence of pleasant experiences, and thus cease to be a functioning member of an integrated group. Nye found that delinquency is higher in unbroken but unhappy homes than it is in broken homes.[38] The child may become prematurely autonomous, overtly displaying total indifference both to the expectations of parents and to their disapproval.[39] In the best study that has been made of this process, Werthman showed how lower-class juvenile gang

---

[36] James P. Driscoll, "Transsexuals," *Trans-action: Social Science and Modern Society,* 8:28-37, March-April, 1971.

[37] Albert K. Cohen, *Delinquent Boys: The Culture of the Gang* (Glencoe, Ill.: Free Press, 1955); Solomon Kobrin, "The Conflict of Values in Delinquency Areas," *American Sociological Review,* 16:653-661, October, 1951; and Walter B. Miller, "Lower Class Culture as a Generating Milieu of Gang Delinquency," *Journal of Social Issues,* 14 (1958): 5-19.

[38] Nye, *Family Relationships and Delinquent Behavior,* p. 47.

[39] Venizia, "Delinquency as a Function of Intrafamily Relationships."

boys lose membership in groups conducive to nondelinquency, including family groups, and at the same time become members of groups owning values and norms which sanction stealing and fighting. He suggests that by the time the delinquent is ready to assume adult responsibility, his choices have been so limited by his premature autonomy that he is incapable of making the transition to a nondelinquent role.[40] The important point is that isolation from the family is likely to increase the child's associations with delinquency behavior patterns and decrease his associations with antidelinquency behavior patterns. However, it is entirely possible that the reverse sometimes takes place: the child could become isolated from the patterns of the delinquent home and thereby increase his associations with antidelinquent behavior patterns.

Fifth, the home may fail to train the child to deal with community situations in a law-abiding manner. That is, delinquency patterns may not be present in the home, but the home may be neutral with respect to delinquency of the child. This failure to present antidelinquency patterns may be due to neglect of training because of the absence of the parents or because of the unconcern of parents, or it may be due to overprotection in the form of failure to acquaint the child with the kinds of delinquencies he will be expected to resist or with the taboos of the outside world. Moreover, as Trasler has pointed out, some parents may be unable to verbalize the norms their children will later be expected to follow. Again, whether such a "neutral" child becomes delinquent or not will depend upon his associations with delinquent and antidelinquent patterns outside the home.

Most of the conditions which have been found to be associated with delinquency can be interpreted in relation to the fourth and fifth of the processes which have been outlined. The fact that the mother works away from home, that the father is dead, that the family income is low, that the housing facilities are very inadequate, that the parents are incapable of coping with the behavior of the child, are unconcerned, or are extremely harsh in their discipline—all of these may fall within the framework of the fourth and fifth processes. In both of those processes, the active condition is assimilation of delinquent behavior patterns from associates. These two processes are important because they increase the probability that a child will come into intimate contact with delinquents and will be attracted by delinquent behavior. If the family is in a community in which there is no pattern of theft, the children do not steal, no matter how much neglected or how unhappy they may be at home. There are cases in which

---

[40] Carl Werthman, "The Function of Social Definitions in the Development of Delinquent Careers," appendix J of *Task Force Report: Juvenile Delinquency and Youth Crime,* pp. 155-170. See also idem, "Juvenile Delinquency and Moral Character," chap. in Donald R. Cressey and David A. Ward, eds., *Delinquency, Crime, and Social Process* (New York: Harper and Row, 1969), pp. 611-632.

parents neglect and abuse their children, are in dire poverty, are frequently intoxicated, and in many respects are vicious; in spite of such home conditions, the children engage in practically no delinquencies.

A sixth process also has been suggested. This is the persistence in the community of habits of disobedience formed in the home. This notion is frequently discussed in commonsense terms of the failure of the child to develop habits of obedience. It also is discussed in psychiatric terms of resentment of authority. Both views assume that there is a generalized attitude toward authority. That is questionable, for disobedience of one kind or another develops in a large proportion of the children reared in modern homes due to the impossible demands made on them and to the inconsistency in the enforcement of home regulations. Psychoanalysts have emphasized the Oedipus complex as an important source of delinquency. This complex consists of hatred of the father because of rivalry for the affections of the mother; because the father is the authority in the home, the boy transfers hatred of authority when he becomes active in the outside community. It is difficult to determine the extent to which such transference occurs. Children who are very disobedient at home are frequently well behaved in the home of a neighbor or in school. A study of seventy-four adult male prisoners found no correlation between the subjects' attitudes toward public law and morality and their attitudes toward their parents.[41]

A seventh process also is frequently suggested: psychological tensions and emotional disturbances in the home. There is no doubt that tensions accompanying or resulting from favoritism, rejection, insecurity, harshness, rigidity, irritation, and other conditions characterize many homes and affect many children. Observation of such home conditions among delinquent groups has resulted in the proposition: "The problem child is a child with problems." The delinquent is considered as emotionally disturbed, and his emotional disturbance is considered the product of emotional disturbances in his home. Psychiatrists and psychoanalysts have brought this notion into prominence, and it probably is the most popular interpretation of juvenile delinquency at present.[42] However, it is not at all certain that there is an undue incidence of emotional disturbances among delinquents or in the homes of delinquents.

Furthermore, a most significant theoretical question regarding this interpretation of delinquency has not been adequately

---

[41] Norman Watt and Brendan A. Maher, "Prisoners' Attitudes Toward Home and the Judicial System," *Journal of Criminal Law, Criminology, and Police Science,* 49:321-330, November-December, 1958.

[42] For an illustration of this viewpoint see David Abrahamsen, "Family Tension, Basic Cause of Criminal Behavior," *Journal of Criminal Law and Criminology,* 40:330-343, September-October, 1949; and Beatrice R. Simcox and Irving Kaufman, "Treatment of Character Disorder in Parents of Delinquents," *Social Casework,* 37:388-395, October, 1956.

answered. Granted that juvenile delinquents sometimes come from homes characterized by family tensions and emotional disturbances, how do these tensions produce delinquency? Obviously, they may produce delinquency through the fourth and fifth processes described above; that is, through increasing the probability of contacts with delinquency behavior patterns or through failure of the family to acquaint the child with the taboos of the community. Psychological tensions and emotional disturbances at home may drive the child away from home and into contact with delinquents. A girl who finds no affection at home may find affection in illicit relations with boys, or she may find it in nondelinquent activities in the school or community. A child does not necessarily become delinquent because he is unhappy. Children in unhappy homes may take on delinquency patterns if there are any around for them to acquire. Certainly they will not start giving away their personal possessions according to the custom of some Indian tribes, for this pattern is not present in urban America.[43] ●

It might be expected that all children in the homes in which the processes described above apparently are operating would become delinquent. As a matter of fact, many of the children in such homes are not delinquent. One study found that in 372 two-child families in which one child was delinquent, the other child was delinquent in 20 percent of the families, and the character was not known in 2 percent. In 333 six-child families in which one child was delinquent, 12 percent of the siblings were known delinquents, 82 percent nondelinquents, and 6 percent unknown.[44] This shows a relatively small proportion of the siblings delinquent, and indicates that the home conditions as such do not completely determine behavior. It is probable, however, that some of the siblings were too young to be involved in delinquencies and the proportion delinquent might be increased if the figures were restricted to children above the age of ten or twelve years. Moreover, the home changes greatly in some cases by reason of the death of a parent, a change in economic status, formation or discontinuance of habits and attitudes by parents, or other conditions; thus the home of one child is not the same as the home of another child in the same family. Also, parental affection and supervision vary considerably in a home at a particular time for the different children, so that a child might not, on that account, have the same home as his brother. Finally, many of the associations which an individual has with delinquent and antidelinquent behavior patterns outside the home are adventitious. It is not

Delinquent and non-delinquent siblings

---

[43] Cf. Warren Dunham and Mary E. Knauer, "The Juvenile Court in Its Relationship to Adult Criminality," *Social Forces*, 32:290-296, March, 1954.

[44] William Healy and Augusta F. Bronner, *Delinquents and Criminals: Their Making and Unmaking* (New York: Macmillan, 1926), p. 104.

necessary to believe that every turning point in the life of an individual is a choice directed by a deep-seated and fundamental trait of personality. ●

Order of birth

Many studies have been made of the relation between birth order and achievement, intellectual ability, psychopathy, aggressiveness, and other traits of personality and of behavior. The earlier studies generally showed inferiority in the firstborn child, but the later studies have reduced this difference, due principally to an improvement in the statistical procedures. The result is that it is now doubtful whether order of birth has any association with traits of personality or behavior. Two explanations have been offered for the difference which has been found or has been assumed. One of these is biological and is to the effect that the firstborn child is inferior because of the greater difficulty of his birth process. The other explanation is in terms of social relations and includes undeveloped skill of parents in training the child, solicitude of parents because of the newness of the experience, and conflict for the child in passing from a favored position as an only child to a subordinate position when a second child is born.

American studies of birth order and delinquency or crime were made mostly in the 1920s and 1930s, and they were often limited to a small number of cases.[45] The "only child" is generally supposed to be extraordinarily prone to delinquency, but the studies which have been made do not consistently bear this out. The Gluecks found that their group of delinquent boys contained lower proportions of oldest children, youngest children, and only children than did the control group.[46] Nye found that oldest and only children show less delinquency behavior than intermediate and youngest children.[47] Wattenberg reviewed the studies of delinquency and only children and concluded that the *meaning* of being an only child varies among different national, racial, relig-

---

[45] See E. W. Bohannon, "The Only Child in a Family," *Pedagogical Seminar,* 5:475-496, April, 1898; John Slawson, *The Delinquent Boy* (Boston: Badger, 1926), pp. 398-409; Florence Goodenough and Alice Leahy, "The Effect of Certain Family Relationships Upon the Development of Personality," *Pedagogical Seminar,* 34:69, March, 1927; John Levy, "A Quantitative Study of Behavior Problems in Relation to Family Constellation," *American Journal of Psychiatry,* 10:637-654, January, 1931; Curt Rosenow and Anne P. Whyte, "The Ordinal Position of Problem Children," *American Journal of Orthopsychiatry,* 1:430-434, July, 1931; Mannie Parsley, "The Influence of Ordinal Position and Size of Family," *Smith College Studies in Social Work,* 3:274-283, March, 1933; R. F. Sletto, "Sibling Position and Juvenile Delinquency," *American Journal of Sociology,* 39:657-669, March, 1934; and J. A. Shield and A. E. Gregg, "Extreme Ordinal Position and Criminal Behavior," *Journal of Criminal Law and Criminology,* 35:169-173, September-October, 1944.

[46] Glueck and Glueck, *Unraveling Juvenile Delinquency,* p. 120.

[47] Nye, *Family Relationships and Delinquent Behavior,* p. 37; see also Raymond A. Mulligan, "Family Relationships and Juvenile Delinquency," *Pacific Sociological Review,* 1:40, Spring, 1958.

ious, and economic groups, and that, consequently, the status of only child has no consistent relationship to delinquency or other behavior problems.[48]

A study of two groups of juvenile probationers in England showed an overrepresentation of intermediate-aged children, as compared with oldest and youngest in the family.[49] The investigators suggested that this relationship occurs because parents give most of their attention to the oldest and the youngest children, thus "squeezing" the intermediate children out of the family and into gangs. A recent New York study of 246 adult and juvenile probationers found that only 10 percent of the 67 firstborn individuals violated probation, while 32 percent of the later-born probationers violated. The difference was attributed to differential child-rearing practices that had made firstborn individuals more willing clients of probation treatment programs.[50] ●

Marital status

The marital status of adult persons appears to have considerable significance in relation to crime. The rate of commitment to prisons and reformatories per 100,000 population of the same marital status is lowest for the married, next to the lowest for widowed, next for the single, and highest for the divorced. These ranks, however, are affected in part by age. Divorced persons have the highest commitment rate at each age, and this is true for each of the sexes. Divorced males twenty to twenty-four years of age have a rate of commitment about six times as high as either single males of the same age or married males of the same age, while divorced females of that age have a rate about ten times as high as either single females or married females of the same age. Married males have a lower commitment rate than single males in all age groups except fifteen to nineteen; the rate is only slightly lower in the age group twenty to twenty-four, but is significantly lower in later ages. For females, however, the married women have a higher commitment rate at each age except twenty-five to thirty-four, but the difference is not very great except in the age group fifteen to nineteen. These statistics, which are based on commitments to prisons in the United States, are in substantial agreement with the statistics from European countries. It has been found, also, that married persons succeed on parole more frequently than persons of any other marital class, and that those who are compatibly married succeed more often than those incompatibly married. It is not possible, however, to conclude from these statistics that marital status is a direct causative

---

[48] William W. Wattenberg, "Delinquency and Only Children: A Study of a 'Category,' " *Journal of Abnormal and Social Psychology*, 44:356-366, July, 1949.

[49] J. P. Lees and L. J. Newson, "Family or Sibship Position and Some Aspects of Juvenile Delinquency," *British Journal of Delinquency*, 5:46-65, July, 1954.

[50] James B. Mullin, "Birth Order as a Variable of Probation Performance," *Journal of Research in Crime and Delinquency*, 10:29-34, January, 1973.

"factor" in crime. Instead, it can be concluded that marital status is important to criminality and noncriminality because it determines the kinds of behavior patterns with which persons come in contact.

Suggested readings

ABRAHAMSEN, DAVID. "Family Tension, Basic Cause of Criminal Behavior." *Journal of Criminal Law and Criminology*, 40: 330-343, September-October, 1949.

BARKER, GORDON H. "Parental Organizational Affiliation and Juvenile Delinquency." *Journal of Criminal Law, Criminology, and Police Science*, 44:204-207, July-August, 1953.

BRANDIS, WALTER, & DOROTHY HENDERSON. *Social Class, Language and Communication*. London: Routledge, 1970.

COHEN, ALBERT K. *Delinquent Boys: The Culture of the Gang*. Glencoe, Ill.: Free Press, 1955.

HARTNAGEL, TIMOTHY F. "Father Absence and Self Conception Among Lower Class White and Negro Boys." *Social Problems*, 18:152-163, Fall, 1970.

KOBRIN, SOLOMON. "The Conflict of Values in Delinquency Areas." *American Sociological Review*, 16:653-661, October, 1951.

MONAHAN, THOMAS P. "Family Status and the Delinquent Child: A Reappraisal and Some New Findings." *Social Forces*, 35:250-258, March, 1957.

NYE, F. IVAN. *Family Relationships and Delinquent Behavior*. New York: John Wiley, 1958.

SOTTONG, DAVID C. "The Dilemma of the Parent as a Culture Bearer." *Social Casework*, 36:302-306, July, 1955.

STERNE, RICHARD S. *Delinquent Conduct and Broken Homes*. New Haven: College and University Press, 1964.

STRAUS, MURRAY A. "Power and Support Structure of the Family in Relation to Socialization." *Journal of Marriage and the Family*, 26:318-326, August, 1964.

TOBY, JACKSON. "The Differential Impact of Family Disorganization." *American Sociological Review*, 22:505-512, October, 1957.

TOBY, JACKSON. "Violence and the Masculine Ideal: Some Qualitative Data." *Annals of the American Academy of Political and Social Science*, 364:19-27, March, 1966.

TRASLER, GORDON B. *The Explanation of Criminality*. London: Routledge and Kegan Paul, 1962.

VINCENT, CLARK E. "Mental Health and the Family." *Journal of Marriage and the Family*, 29:18-39, February, 1967.

WEINBERG, S. KIRSON. "Juvenile Delinquency in Ghana: A Comparative Analysis of Delinquents and Non-Delinquents." *Journal of Criminal Law, Criminology, and Police Science*, 55:471-481, December, 1964.

11 Social institutions

Many efforts have been made to determine the effects on criminal behavior of the general social institutions. The basic social institutions—familial, economic, governmental, educational, and religious—are organized systems for meeting societal needs. Each organizes some aspects of the individual's behavior, and each is necessary to the continued existence of a society. There are many variations in the specific form and content of the institutions as we move from society to society, and these variations conceivably are linked to variations in crime rates among societies.

As was indicated in chapter 5, however, intersocietal comparisons of institutional structure and functioning, like intersocietal comparisons of crime rates, are very difficult and hazardous. Consequently, most of the research on the subject in the United States has been directed at analysis of the role of the various institutions in determining the variations in crime and criminality in our own society. That is, "family factors," "economic factors," "political factors," etc., in crime have been sought. The family institution, which was discussed in the last chapter, and the economic institution, especially as it affects the distribution of wealth, have received more explicit attention than the other institutions. ●

The economic institution

Many studies have been made of the relation between crime and poverty. These have been directed at two principal questions: Do people of lower economic status commit more crimes than people of higher economic status? Do crime rates increase when poverty increases in periods of economic depression? A survey will be made of the principal findings of these studies, their limitations, and the conclusions that seem warranted.

Studies of the economic status of criminals have indicated that the lower economic class has a much higher official crime rate than the upper economic class. This conclusion has been derived from two types of data: those on the social class membership of criminals and delinquents, and those on delinquency and crime rates of persons living in areas of poverty, as compared to the rates of persons living in other areas of cities.

Variations by social class

The reliability of the official statistics on the socioeconomic class backgrounds of criminals has been questioned even more severely than have statistics on variables like age, race, and area of residence. Many persons maintain that the law-enforcement processes tend to select working-class persons, just as they tend to select

Negroes. Thus it is believed that if a member of the working class and a member of the upper class are equally guilty of some offense, the person on the lower level is more likely to be arrested, convicted, and committed to an institution. Further, most white-collar crimes are not included in sets of official crime statistics. It is not possible at present to compile quantitative data regarding the white-collar crime rate, and therefore it is not possible to make accurate comparisons of the total criminal behavior of the several classes. When white-collar crimes are taken into account, however, they throw doubt on the conclusion that crime is concentrated in the lower economic classes. Reckless is confident that if statistical procedures could be corrected, the distribution of crime by social classes in the United States would show a bimodal curve, with high peaks for members of the upper class and lower class, and a low valley for members of the middle class.[1]

Even for ordinary crimes, the administrative processes are more favorable to persons in economic comfort than to those in poverty. One study found that lower-class boys were significantly overrepresented in the population of training schools; however, when high school students were asked to report on their delinquencies, no significant differences in the delinquency of boys and girls in the different socioeconomic classes were found.[2] However, the statistics on ordinary crime so consistently show an overrepresentation of lower-class persons that it is reasonable to assume that there is a real difference between the behavior of members of this class and of members of other social classes, so far as criminality is concerned. After reviewing the research studies and essays written on the relationship of delinquency and economic conditions, two sociologists concluded that the best evidence indicates that delinquency is basically a working-class phenomenon.[3] If this reasonable conclusion is accepted, the following two observations are warranted.

A. In the United States, official statistics indicate that the largest proportion of delinquent and criminal populations come from the working class, and there is some evidence that the delinquency rate and crime rate of working-class persons exceed the

---

[1] Walter C. Reckless, The Crime Problem, 4th ed. (New York: Appleton-Century-Crofts, 1967), pp. 110-112.

[2] F. Ivan Nye, James F. Short, Jr., and Virgil J. Olson, "Socioeconomic Status and Delinquent Behavior," American Journal of Sociology, 63:381-389, January, 1958. See also Maynard L. Erickson and Lamar T. Empey, "Class Position, Peers and Delinquency," Sociology and Social Research, 49:268-282, April, 1965; Lamar T. Empey and Maynard L. Erickson, "Hidden Delinquency and Social Status," Social Forces, 44:546-554, June, 1966; and William J. Chambliss and Richard H. Nagasawa, "On the Validity of Official Statistics — A Comparative Study of White, Black, and Japanese High-School Boys," Journal of Research in Crime and Delinquency, 6:71-77, January, 1969.

[3] H. L. Wilensky and C. N. Lebeaux, Industrial Society and Social Welfare (New York: Free Press, 1965), p. 189.

rates of other persons. In institutionalized populations, about two-thirds to three-fourths of the men, and about nine-tenths of the women, are members of the working class.

Caldwell, using an occupational rating scale, found that 33.4 percent of the parents of boy delinquents and 52.7 percent of the parents of girl delinquents in Wisconsin correctional institutions were unskilled, in comparison with 11.8 percent of the entire employed population of the state.[4] Similarly, data gathered on 761 delinquents in Passaic, New Jersey, indicated that their fathers' occupational ratings were considerably lower than the rating for the general population of the city.[5] Seventy-three percent of a sample of the children placed on probation in Ceylon in 1944-1956 were classed as "poor" or "very poor."[6] In an analysis of income and delinquency, Chilton found that the forty-two census tracts in Marion County (Indianapolis), Indiana, that had the highest average incomes contained 40 percent of the juvenile-court-age children but produced only 17 percent of the juvenile court cases. The forty-two census tracts with the lowest income contained 37 percent of the juvenile-court-age children but accounted for 65 percent of the juvenile court cases. The law violations by the children in the low-income tracts were heavily weighted with burglary, robbery, assault, and carrying dangerous weapons, while in the high-income-tract children they were over-represented in trespassing, vandalism, automobile theft, receiving stolen goods, and violations of curfew, traffic, and liquor laws.[7]

Comparisons of the occupational status of adult criminals likewise show a disproportionately large representation of unskilled and semiskilled occupations. Warner and Lunt found that while the two lower classes constituted only 57 percent of Yankee City's population, 90 percent of the arrests during a seven-year period were arrests of members of these two classes.[8] Ninety percent of the 932 felons convicted in Washington, D.C., in 1964-1965 had incomes less than $5,000; 56 percent of the adult population of Washington at the time earned less than $5,000.[9] A study in

---

[4] M. G. Caldwell, "The Economic Status of Families of Delinquent Boys in Wisconsin," *American Journal of Sociology,* 37:231-239, September, 1931.

[5] W. C. Kvaraceus, "Juvenile Delinquency and Social Class," *Journal of Educational Sociology,* 18:51-54, September, 1944.

[6] Department of Census and Statistics, *Juvenile Probation in Ceylon* (Ceylon: Government Press, 1957), p. 24.

[7] Ronald J. Chilton, "Middle-Class Delinquency and Specific Offense Analysis," chap. in Edmund W. Vaz, ed., *Middle-Class Juvenile Delinquency* (New York: Harper and Row, 1967), pp. 91-101. See also Ronald J. Chilton, "Continuity in Delinquency Area Research: A Comparison of Studies for Baltimore, Detroit, and Indianapolis," *American Sociological Review,* 29:71-83, February, 1964.

[8] William Lloyd Warner and Paul S. Lunt, *The Social Life of a Modern Community* (New Haven: Yale University Press, 1941), pp. 373-377.

[9] President's Commission on Crime in the District of Columbia, *Report* (Washington: Government Printing Office, 1966), p. 130.

Denmark indicated that 10 percent of a group of offenders came from the upper or middle class, while 27 percent of the general population was in these classes.[10]

Many other studies have shown the same tendency for adult and juvenile delinquents to be concentrated in the lower economic class.[11] One study indicated that prisoners rank themselves lower than they rank their fathers on socioeconomic status, perhaps indicating that the prisoners were unable to maintain the family level of status, let alone improve it through upward mobility.[12]

B. The extent of overrepresentation of working-class persons in the criminal population is not the same under all conditions. In some situations, working-class people have crime rates lower than those of other classes.

1. The ratio of working-class persons to other persons in the criminal population varies by social group. In the Japanese colony in Seattle prior to World War II the children had a very low delinquency rate, despite the fact that the residents were of the working class and were in as great poverty as residents of the area surrounding the colony, who had high rates. Moreover, residents of certain rural areas may be in extreme poverty with little incidence of crime. Shaw found that for the eighty-seven counties of Minnesota the correlation between crime rates and the percentage of the populations on relief combined with the percentage of the populations seeking work was only +.213. By way of contrast, he found a correlation of +.717 between the degree of urbanization of the counties and their crime rates.[13] Sheldon discovered no close relationship between the indexes of economic status and juvenile delinquency when other factors were held constant, but found a significant relationship between indexes of social disorganization and juvenile delinquency when economic factors were held constant.[14] Clark and Wenninger studied the self-reported crimes of public high school students, sixth through twelfth grades, in four communities chosen to represent four class levels—rural farm, lower urban (mostly unskilled occupations),

---

[10] Preben Wolf, "Crime and Social Class in Denmark," British Journal of Criminology, 13 (1962): 5-17.

[11] See, e.g., Hermann Mannheim, John Spencer, and George Lynch, "Magisterial Policy in the London Juvenile Courts," British Journal of Delinquency, 8:13-33, and 8:119-138, June and October, 1957; Terrence Morris, The Criminal Area (London: Kegan Paul, 1958), pp. 164-181; and Ivar Berg, "Economic Factors in Delinquency," appendix O in President's Commission on Law Enforcement and Administration of Justice, Task Force Report: Juvenile Delinquency and Youth Crime (Washington: Government Printing Office, 1967), pp. 305-316.

[12] Harold Bradley and Jack D. Williams, Intensive Treatment Program: Second Annual Report (Sacramento: Department of Corrections, 1958), p. 16.

[13] Van B. Shaw, "The Relationship Between Crime Rates and Certain Population Characteristics in Minnesota Counties," Journal of Criminal Law and Criminology, 40:43-49, May-June, 1949.

[14] Henry D. Sheldon, "Problems in the Statistical Study of Juvenile Delinquency," Metron, 12 (1934): 201-223.

industrial city, and upper urban (mostly executive and professional). They found that the incidence of self-reported crimes
became greater as one moved from rural farm to upper urban to
industrial city to lower urban.[15] This study shows, basically, that
"location" is more important to delinquency than is "social class"
in its pure form. Differences among the socioeconomic classes
within the areas studied were generally insignificant. The study
makes clear that the "working class," so overrepresented in the
crime statistics, consists of the lower-class persons living in the
lower-class areas of large urban communities. The middle-class
children living in the same areas reported delinquencies in about
the same measure as did the lower-class children.[16]

Similarly, girls in the areas of poverty in the typical American
city are in as great poverty as boys, but their delinquency rate is
much lower than the delinquency rate of boys. Moreover, members of groups in extreme poverty have literally starved to death
rather than violate laws. The following is a report on a period of
famine in India in 1943:

> Through all these months the white Brahmin cattle wandered by the
> hundreds through the streets of Calcutta, as they always have, stepping
> placidly over the bodies of the dead and near-dead, scratching their
> plump haunches on taxi fenders, sunning themselves on the steps of the
> great Clive Street banks. No one ever ate a cow; no one ever dreamed
> of it. I never heard of a Bengali Hindu who would not perish with all
> his family rather than taste meat. Nor was there any violence. No gro-
> cery stall, no rice warehouse, none of the wealthy clubs or restaurants
> ever was threatened by a hungry mob. The Bengalis just died with that
> bottomless docility which, to most Americans, is the most shocking thing
> about India.[17]

2. The ratio of working-class persons to other persons varies by
offense. The kind of crime, as contrasted with the fact of crime,
is very significantly related to economic status. One's position in
the economic structure determines opportunities, facilities, and the
requisite skills for specialized crimes. Most studies showing high
ratios of working-class persons have concentrated on crimes
against property, such as larceny and burglary. There is some
evidence, however, that the ratio is somewhat lower for sex
offenses, and in fact the crime rate of the working class may be
lower than rates of other classes for some sex offenses.[18] Similarly, in Detroit a study indicated that working-class persons are
not as overrepresented in the population of automobile thieves as

---

[15] John P. Clark and Eugene P. Wenninger, "Socio-Economic Class and Area
as Correlates of Illegal Behavior Among Juveniles," *American Sociological
Review*, 27:826-834, December, 1962.

[16] Cf. Wilensky and Lebeaux, *Industrial Society and Social Welfare*, p. 186;
and Howard L. Myerhoff and Barbara G. Myerhoff, "Field Observations of
Middle Class 'Gangs,' " *Social Forces*, 42:328-336, March, 1964.

[17] John Fischer, "India's Insoluble Hunger," *Harper's Magazine*, 190:438-445,
April, 1945 (at p. 439).

[18] A. C. Kinsey, W. B. Pomeroy, and C. E. Martin, *Sexual Behavior in the
Human Male* (Philadelphia: Saunders, 1948), pp. 327-393.

they are in other delinquent and criminal populations.[19] And, of course, working-class persons have lower crime rates than other persons for such offenses as embezzlement, misrepresentation in advertising, violation of antitrust laws, and issuing worthless stocks.

Variations by area[20]

Ogburn found a significant association between poverty and crime in a comparison of sixty-two cities.[21] Shaw and McKay compared residential areas within each of twenty-one cities and found a large and consistent relationship between crime and poverty; they also found very high positive correlations by residential areas between boy delinquency and girl delinquency rates, and also between boy delinquency rates and adult crime rates.[22] In an English city, Morris found a correlation of +.74 between delinquency rates and percentage of overcrowded homes, and a correlation of −.76 between delinquency rates and the percentage of middle-class households.[23]

Correlations between crime rates and other indexes of poverty also indicate that crime is associated with areas of poverty. For instance, the economic values of houses in a delinquency area are low; the delinquency rate is higher among renters than among property owners; and the physical condition and equipment of houses in delinquency areas are poor. Reiss and Rhodes studied 9,238 white male Tennessee delinquents of all social classes and found, among other things, that (1) both in areas of high delinquency and in areas of low delinquency, the low-status boy has the greatest chance of becoming delinquent, (2) no matter whether he is of high status, middle status, or low status, the chances that a boy will be a delinquent are greater if he resides in a high-delinquency-rate area than if he resides in a low-delinquency-rate area, (3) the more the lower-class boy is in a minority in the school and residential community, the less likely he is to become a delinquent.[24] All these findings are consistent with the implica-

---

[19] William W. Wattenberg and James Balistrieri, "Automobile Theft: A 'Favored-Group' Delinquency," *American Journal of Sociology*, 57:575-579, May, 1952.

[20] See the discussion of intracity distributions in chapter 9, pp. 180-187, above.

[21] W. F. Ogburn, "Factors in the Variation of Crime Among Cities," *Journal of the American Statistical Association*, 30:12-34, March, 1935. See also James E. McKeown, "Poverty, Race, and Crime," *Journal of Criminal Law and Criminology*, 39:480-483, November-December, 1948; Karl F. Schuessler, "Components of Variations in City Crime Rates," *Social Problems*, 9:314-323, Spring, 1962; Richard Quinney, "Structural Characteristics, Population Areas, and Crime Rates in the United States," *Journal of Criminal Law, Criminology, and Police Science*, 57:45-52, March, 1966; and Karl F. Schuessler and Gerald Slatin, "Sources of Variation in U.S. City Crime, 1950 and 1960," *Journal of Research in Crime and Delinquency*, 1:127-148, July, 1964.

[22] Clifford R. Shaw and Henry D. McKay, *Juvenile Delinquency and Urban Areas* (Chicago: University of Chicago Press, 1942), pp. 141 ff.

[23] Morris, *Criminal Areas*, p. 169.

[24] Albert J. Reiss, Jr., and Albert Lewis Rhodes, "The Distribution of Juvenile Delinquency in the Social Class Structure," *American Sociological Review*, 26:720-732, October, 1961.

tion in the theory of differential association that socioeconomic status is important to delinquency and crime primarily as it affects the probability of association with delinquent and criminal behavior patterns.

The relation between crime rates and economic conditions also has been studied by examination of data on the relationship between fluctuations in business conditions and fluctuations in crime rates. Here, poverty is measured by the poor business conditions constituting an economic depression, rather than by socioeconomic class or by area of residence. Studies of this kind have been under way for more than a century, and the early ones have been summarized and appraised by Sellin.[25] The methods used have seldom been carefully devised, and the indexes of both crime and business conditions have varied widely, with the result that no positive, definite, and valid generalizations can be made. The following are the closest approximations to conclusions from the studies.

Variations in time

1. Serious crimes have a slight and inconsistent tendency to rise in periods of economic depression and fall in periods of prosperity. Thomas found a correlation of $-.25$ between all indictable crimes and economic prosperity in England and Wales for the period 1857-1913, Ogburn a similar coefficient ($-.35$) in New York State for the period 1870-1920, and Phelps a coefficient of $-.33$ in Rhode Island for the period 1898-1926.[26]

2. The general crime rate does not increase significantly in periods of economic depression.[27]

3. Property crimes involving violence show a tendency to increase in periods of depression, but property crimes involving no violence, such as larceny, show only a very slight and inconsistent tendency to increase in depression periods.[28] Radzinowicz found a clear-cut increase in crimes against property in Poland in the depression years of the early thirties.[29] None of the studies

---

[25] Thorsten Sellin, *Research Memorandum on Crime in the Depression* (New York: Social Science Research Council, 1937). See also W. A. Bonger, *Criminality and Economic Conditions,* trans. H. P. Horton (Boston: Little, Brown, 1916).

[26] Dorothy S. Thomas, *Social Aspects of the Business Cycle* (London: Routledge, 1925), pp. 143-144; W. F. Ogburn, "Business Fluctuations as Social Forces," *Social Forces,* 1:73-78, January, 1923; H. A. Phelps, "Cycles of Crime," *Journal of Criminal Law and Criminology,* 20:107-121, May-June, 1929. See also George B. Vold, *Theoretical Criminology* (New York: Oxford University Press, 1958), pp. 177-181.

[27] Albert H. Hobbs, "Relationship Between Criminality and Economic Conditions," *Journal of Criminal Law and Criminology,* 34:5-10, May, 1943; James F. Short, Jr., "A Note on Relief Programs and Crimes During the Depression," *American Sociological Review,* 17:226-229, April, 1952.

[28] See James F. Short, Jr., "A Social Aspect of the Business Cycle Re-examined: Crimes," *Research Studies of the State College of Washington,* 20 (1952): 36-41.

[29] L. Radzinowicz, "The Influence of Economic Conditions on Crime," *Sociological Review,* 33:1-36, 139-153, January-May, 1941.

which cover longer periods of time has shown such significant relationship, perhaps because extraneous factors, such as variations in laws and in administration of the laws, play less part in the longer period.

4. Drunkenness tends to increase in periods of prosperity according to some studies, but shows no significant change according to others. Dorothy Thomas found a correlation of +.34 between prosperity and prosecutions for drunkenness in England in 1857-1913;[30] Winslow found no significant relation in Massachusetts between prosecutions for drunkenness and unemployment.[31]

5. Crimes against the person show no consistent relationship to the business cycle. Some studies have reported increases in crimes against the person in periods of prosperity and find, also, that increase in consumption of alcohol accompanies the increase in crimes against the person.

6. Juvenile delinquency tends to increase in periods of prosperity and to decrease during periods of depression.[32] A recent study suggests that combining statistics on juvenile crime with statistics on adult crime may give the erroneous impression that the general crime rate (all ages) does not change in periods of depression.[33]

Conclusions

Before a general positive conclusion about the relationship between poverty and crime is derived from these three kinds of studies, two negative conclusions should be drawn. *First,* the official criminal statistics, being biased as to class by the exclusion of white-collar crimes and by differences in arresting practices, exaggerate the extent to which crimes are concentrated in the lower class; excessive criminality of the lower class, except in the official crime records, is still questionable. *Second,* even if the official statistics are accepted, they give conflicting evidence. Criminal behavior is related consistently to poverty and low economic status according to studies which compare residential areas of criminals and noncriminals, but is related inconsistently or not at all to poverty and low economic status when chronological periods are compared.

---

[30] Thomas, *Social Aspects of the Business Cycle,* pp. 143-144.

[31] Emma A. Winslow, "Relationships between Employment and Crime Fluctuations as Shown by Massachusetts Statistics," *Report on the Causes of Crime,* National Commission on Law Observance and Enforcement, no. 13, vol. I (Washington: Government Printing Office, 1937), pp. 257-333.

[32] J. O. Reinemann, "Juvenile Delinquency in Philadelphia and Economic Trends," *Temple University Law Quarterly,* 20:576-583, April, 1947; Lowell J. Carr, *Delinquency Control* (New York: Harper, 1950), pp. 83-89; Paul Wiers, "Wartime Increases in Michigan Delinquency," *American Sociological Review,* 10:515-523, August, 1945; idem, *Economic Factors in Michigan Delinquency* (New York: Columbia University Press, 1944); David Bogen, "Juvenile Delinquency and Economic Trend," *American Sociological Review,* 9:178-184, April, 1944.

[33] Daniel Glaser and Kent Rice, "Crime, Age and Employment," *American Sociological Review,* 24:679-686, October, 1959.

The conflicting kinds of evidence suggest that poverty has certain social accompaniments when considered geographically which are lacking when considered chronologically, and that it is these accompaniments of poverty, rather than the economic need, which result in criminal behavior. Poverty in the modern city customarily means segregation in low-rent areas, where people are isolated to a considerable degree from anticriminal patterns and forced into contact with many criminal behavior patterns. It generally means a low social status, with little to lose, little to respect, and little to sustain efforts at self-advancement. It generally means bad housing conditions, poor health, and invidious comparisons in other physical and physiological conditions. It may mean that both parents are away from home during most of the hours the children are awake, and are fatigued and irritable when at home. It generally means that the child is withdrawn from school at the earliest permissible age to enter an unskilled occupation which is not interesting or remunerative and which offers few opportunities for economic advancement. Poverty in a small town may have few of those accompaniments. On the other hand, a depression does not modify significantly the associations of many persons, for rents decrease and families generally occupy the same houses and have the same neighbors as formerly.[34] Poverty, therefore, is significant because of its social accompaniments. The general conclusion is that poverty affects crime and criminality as it determines associations with criminal behavior patterns or isolation from anticriminal behavior patterns. ●

The institution of government

There has been much speculation but relatively little research on the institution of government and the political processes in relation to criminal behavior. Two possibilities for research may be suggested. First, various forms of government might be compared, as the capitalist democracy and the communist "dictatorship of the proletariat." Other comparisons, with less economic involvement, might be made between a democratic system and an absolute monarchy, a dictatorship, or a system of government by tribal council, with the objective of determining the extent to which criminal behavior is related to the general form of the political institution. The reason no organized research work has been done on this problem and the reason such research is infeasible need hardly be mentioned—the lack of comparable data for different nations and systems.

Second, comparison might be made of specific political variables within a nation, such as a Democratic administration with a Republican administration, or the particular policies of one administration with those of another. Discussion of this subject has resulted in many conflicting claims, but the problem seems pecu-

[34] Ruth Shonle Cavan and Katherine H. Ranck, *The Family and the Depression* (Chicago: University of Chicago Press, 1938).

liarly insusceptible to scientific research. In fact, crime statistics inadequately represent the true crime picture in the United States partly because various political administrations juggle the figures so as to "prove" that their policies have reduced crime while the policies of the opposition have increased or would increase crime. Quinney has made an eloquent plea for study of what he calls "the politics of crime."[35] Because of the absence of organized research on the influence of government on crime rates, analogous to that in the area of economic conditions, this problem can be discussed only in general terms.

A prominent theory is that crime is due to the lack of enforcement of laws, and that the solution of the problem of crime is pressure upon the police and courts to enforce the laws strictly. Strict enforcement of laws would certainly reduce crime, but strict enforcement of laws is extremely difficult because the agencies of justice are kept weak and inefficient by the same conditions which produce high crime rates.[36]

A few centuries ago government had prestige because it was based on the divine right of the sovereign. General opposition to strong government developed because of the necessity of breaking away from the regulations which persisted from the feudal period, because of the democratic fear of absolutism, and because of the new problems of the frontiers. In spite of this distrust, the widening area of social interaction and the deadly effects of competition drove many groups to appeal to government for assistance. Many laws have been passed for the purpose of controlling behavior in these impersonal situations, but the legislation has not been supported by a cohesive body of opinion and sentiment. The result has been the anomalous condition of a great amount of legislation and little respect for legislation. Each group rebels against the legislation forced upon it by other groups, and each group attempts to secure legislation to regulate other groups. It is easy to break laws derived from a source that one does not greatly respect, and it is easy to manipulate policies in the interest of one's group when few people have an intense interest in the larger group.

Clinard has indicated that in America the general public attitude toward law obedience is that all laws except those dealing with very serious offenses should be violated if one can get away with it, or that laws should be selectively obeyed according to one's interests.[37] The first can be seen in attitudes toward tax evasion and stock manipulation, in patronage of gambling establishments,

---

[35] Richard Quinney, "Crime in Political Perspective," *American Behavioral Scientist,* 8:19-22, December, 1964.

[36] Cf. Mabel A. Elliott, "Perspective on the American Crime Problem," *Social Problems,* 5:184-193, Winter, 1957.

[37] Marshall B. Clinard, "Secondary Community Influences and Juvenile Delinquency," *Annals of the American Academy of Political and Social Science,* 261:42-54, January, 1949.

in failure to obey traffic regulations, in public intoxication and marijuana smoking, and in political corruption. The second can be seen in the selective obedience of laws governing business, labor, agriculture, and military service.[38]

The general disrespect for law and disrespect for those who make and enforce laws is seen not only in the fact that people break laws but also in the attitudes of those who do not break laws. Legislative bodies, considered as corporate bodies rather than as individuals, are often viewed with contempt, suspicion, and distrust. Novels dealing with legislatures and city councils in the United States over the last four generations have presented these bodies as corrupt, boss-ridden, and inefficient, which they sometimes are. Similarly, the police are regarded as brutal, corrupt, and inefficient. The public attitude toward the courts is perhaps a little more favorable but inclines toward ridicule and contempt for the lower courts for defects of dishonesty, individual inefficiency, and squalid surroundings. In many groups, individuals would generally prefer to be caught breaking almost any nonfelony law rather than be detected eating potatoes with a knife, and in certain groups even felonies are less serious than breaches of etiquette. Prohibition probably made a generous contribution to the development of a code of selective obedience of law.

Officials charged with the enforcement of laws may avoid their responsibility altogether or may enforce the laws only sporadically. The cyclical pattern of "reform" so common to American municipalities is partly a function of sporadic enforcement. But in the United States we have arranged our program for the combat of crime so that we may in fact maintain crime, putting an impossible burden on police and other local officials. They must ignore some crimes—especially organized crime—because they serve on the front line of diplomacy between those citizens who want laws enforced and those who do not. On the one hand, there are community interests in morality, governmental efficiency, and law enforcement. But on the other hand there are also community interests in immorality, soft political jobs, favors, domestic tranquility, and law violation. When both sets of interests are powerful, the police and their superiors must decide what constitutes an "appropriate level" of law enforcement. As the President's Commission concluded, with reference to organized crime, "Politicians will not act unless the public so demands; but much of the urban public wants the services provided by organized crime and does not wish to disrupt the system that pro-

---

[38] For examples of selective obedience see Marshall B. Clinard, *The Black Market* (New York: Rinehart, 1952); Robert E. Lane, "Why Businessmen Violate the Law," *Journal of Criminal Law, Criminology, and Police Science*, 44:151-165, July-August, 1953; and Erwin O. Smigel, "Public Attitudes Toward Stealing as Related to the Size of the Victim Organization," *American Sociological Review*, 21:320-327, June, 1956.

vides these services."[39] Gardiner's 1966 study of "Wincanton," a middle-sized industrial city where municipal officials had long been paid to overlook illegal gambling, suggested that the citizens approved the gambling or were tolerant of it, but were hostile toward corruption.[40] The citizens, in other words, "display both a desire for or toleration of illicit services and a demand for honesty on the part of local officials." Gardiner concluded that the residents of Wincanton fail to see that a community cannot have illegal gambling without corruption. One outcome of conflicting community demands, with consequent assignment of diplomatic rather than law-enforcement functions to the police, is a negotiated social order. A balance is struck; an "understanding" is operationalized; crime is tolerated.

When one is caught, the problem is to "fix" things. This occurs very commonly in the so-called law-abiding groups in relation to traffic violations, gambling, smuggling, liquor, and certain other crimes. In other circles it occurs in relation to shoplifting, picking pockets, robbery, burglary, and murder. There is a prevalent belief among prisoners that their own cases could have been "fixed" if they had had sufficient money. According to that belief, the only reason for being arrested or convicted is poverty. It is probable that no part of the population is better acquainted with the corruption and graft in the legislative, judicial, and police systems, so far as they exist, than are the professional criminals.

Some cities are under the control of political machines, and these are sometimes bipartisan and continue their control regardless of the party in power. The political party is an agency for predatory control. It must serve the general society, but service to the general society is a means to its own welfare. *In the first place,* the ordinary individual does not want to be bothered with political activity and does not have the initiative to get the government to act. He wants someone else to do the work, and the politician steps in to meet this need. *In the second place,* ordinary citizens who do have initiative and force in relation to government often have an individual interest to promote; it may be a financial return to themselves, a crank's utopian scheme, or a fanatic's hostility to established practices. It is necessary that some person or group weigh these many demands against each other and work out compromises that will give some satisfaction to the discontented groups. Politicians, being essentially amoral, calculate these demands in terms of returns to their own welfare. These calculations produce a balancing of extremes, and this is a service to the general society. *In the third place,* the politician is generally a personal friend and benefactor of the people in his

[39] President's Commission on Law Enforcement and Administration of Justice, *Task Force Report: Organized Crime* (Washington: Government Printing Office, 1967), pp. 15-16.

[40] John A. Gardiner, *The Politics of Corruption: Organized Crime in an American City* (New York: Russell Sage Foundation, 1970).

immediate district. He renders many services to them in a warm-hearted manner and without antagonizing them. Even though his benefactions may come from the public treasury, he acts as a personal friend in the midst of a huge impersonal society. One social scientist has made the following general observation:

The political party in our society is an extralegal development but obviously a very indispensable one. This can be explained by the fact that constitutional provisions originally localized and split up power into units and fractions in such a way as to make government unworkable without it. The party supplies the important unity and dynamic which make government move past dead-center equilibrium and function in a positive manner.[41]

Among the services which the political machine renders and from which the politicians are most likely to derive their own direct financial gains, those which are rendered to persons who violate the law or who wish to prevent the enactment of laws injurious to them are very important. It is these services which are generally regarded as corruption. *The first* of these services is protection of law-violators. For every "corrupter" (criminal) there must be a "corruptee" (criminal). Most of the crimes committed by corrupt officials are perpetrated in order to facilitate the crimes perpetrated by the corrupters. The political machine provides immunity for prostitution, gambling, violation of liquor laws, loan-sharking, and other organized crime activities.[42] This, in fact, is so important that organized criminals are sometimes themselves in positions of importance in the local political machine. More often, they contribute heavily to the party treasury in return for their immunity. When these conditions prevail, an individual policeman is completely unable to take action regarding the protected violations of law. His chief of police is equally impotent, for he himself is under the control, either directly or indirectly, of the same machine. The immunity, moreover, is extended to organized criminals even when it becomes evident that this means protection of groups which are engaged in robbery, burglary, murder, and other serious crimes, as was the case in many of the organized bootlegging groups during the period of national prohibition. Equally important is the immunity granted to many huge and "respectable" business concerns which violate the laws regarding fire hazards, safety devices, obstruction of sidewalks, rent control, sanitation, water and air pollution, and other dangers and inconveniences. Certainly a large part of the campaign contributions come from those who expect immunity in the violation of the law, and not all of the persons who expect immunity are organized criminals.

Second, political machines receive support because of the protection they can furnish against injurious legislation. This pro-

---

[41] Edwin M. Lemert, *Social Pathology* (New York: McGraw-Hill, 1951), p. 61.
[42] See Donald R. Cressey, *Theft of the Nation: The Structure and Operations of Organized Crime in America* (New York: Harper and Row, 1969).

tection is sometimes sought by organized criminals, but, generally, it is more useful to business and labor interests. Public utilities, oil companies, agricultural groups, real estate developers, and liquor groups have been particularly active in this sphere. Many industries make huge contributions to political campaigns in order that they may have the goodwill of those who regulate the legislatures, thus preventing enactment of legislation that these industries regard as injurious. This is a form of bribery only slightly concealed.

But corrupt officials are not always merely minor actors in the crimes in which they are involved. A *third* form of corruption is through licenses and contracts for public works and the franchises which are granted to public utilities and other concerns. Here, corrupt officials are the star actors playing a major role in the criminal drama. Some politicians get rich by charging under-the-table fees for building permits and liquor licenses, and for letting contracts for buildings, parks, pavements, and services such as garbage collection and street sweeping. This is a means of enriching the politicians either as individuals or as a machine, usually at the expense of the contractors, who pass the extra costs along to the consumer. The extent to which persons in important political positions become wealthy after securing office is often evidence of the extent of this collusion with private contractors to rob the public treasury.

A *fourth* form of political corruption is inherent in the patronage system. In some political organizations each candidate for an elective office, including the governor, is required to agree in advance that the appointive offices will be filled by the organization. A patronage secretary or a patronage committee may be publicly recognized as in charge of this function. The principal opposition to a state patronage system comes from the township and county politicians, who insist that patronage is the function of the local organization rather than of the state organization. And the principal opposition to federal patronage comes from the state organizations.

It is important to the organization, whether national, state, or local, that it control patronage, for it is through patronage that many of its services are rendered to individuals and groups. First, it may thus reward its members who have rendered services in elections; the result is that a large proportion of offices is filled by inferior persons whose principal loyalty is to the political machine, and whose salaries frequently are an incidental part of their incomes. Second, through control of patronage the organization can control the activities of the officeholders. Third, as a specific form of the second value, the organization can thus grant immunity, in return for campaign contributions, to the agencies which violate the law or are in other ways injuring the community. One of the members of the patronage committee in Illinois some years ago was the president of one of the principal banks of the state. He had membership on the patronage committee because the banks, utility companies, insurance companies, and similar concerns were interested in the selection of bank examiners, public utility commissioners, and other similar officers, who would be friendly and could be controlled. Patronage is the most obvious indication of the fact that the political organization is interested primarily in its own welfare, and only secondarily in the welfare of the society.

In a *fifth* form of corruption, a government official conspires with a businessman or labor leader to cheat the citizens represented by the official. For example, companies with a franchise to tow away illegally parked cars might charge citizens an extra dollar for the service, then pay the dollar to a city official for the privilege of holding the franchise. The persons granting the franchises and the persons holding them are costars in this crime.

A *sixth* form of corruption is fraud in voting. In a recount of votes in Chicago in 1933, fraud was discovered in 29 percent of the ballot boxes and in some wards in every box. In Kansas City 275 election officials and other party workers were indicted for fraud in connection with the election of 1936. A 1948 congressional race in Kansas City culminated in the theft of ballots from the Jackson County courthouse.[43]

The *seventh* form of corruption is similar to the first. But in this form, the relationship is between a corruptee and a corrupter who is also a victim. The small shopkeeper and the automobile driver are sometimes the victim of simple extortion on the part of officials. When a policeman, for a fee, grants a merchant the privilege of violating the law (the first kind of corruption), he supports the more important criminal role of the merchant, who is the principal actor. But when a policeman threatens a citizen with harassment until a bribe is paid, the citizen becomes a supporting actor rather than a star. The citizen's role is that of both criminal (briber) and victim.

As a result of these influences which corrupt politics, honest operation of the police and of the courts is limited. An honest official must make many compromises with the party machine if he is to continue in office, for the system has been operating for many decades, and no single person can change it much. Corrupt politics has a more significant relationship to the vices, organized crime, and white-collar crime than to juvenile delinquency and the felonies for which persons are committed to prison. Nevertheless, juvenile delinquency and adult violations of the criminal code are intimately related to the politics of the local community. The fact that organized crime activities float on a swamp of corruption teaches an insidious lesson to American youth, and especially to the innercity youth, who, in order to survive, must be astute observers of the facts of life: The government is for sale; lawlessness is the road to wealth; honesty is a pitfall; morality is a trap for suckers. How can a boy be expected to "respect

---

[43] Estes Kefauver, *Crime in America* (New York: Doubleday, 1951), p. 261.

authority" when his model authority figure, the policeman, is known to be on the payroll of criminals? How can we reasonably expect boys of the inner city to have standards of honesty, decency, and morality higher than the standards they observe in their own public officials? ●

The institution of religion

Since the church has been instrumental in developing and maintaining a sacred morality among mankind, and since crime often involves violation of this standard of morality, it may rightfully be concluded that a close relationship exists between crime and the religious institution. For example, one Christian criminologist has written, "The Christian believes the underlying cause of criminality is man's alienation from God."[44] From this point of view, criminality represents a failure on the part of the church to train members of society to behave morally, and from this it is easy to conclude that "lack of religious training" is the basic cause of crime. However, this conclusion merely emphasizes the fact that some persons do commit crime, and it does not really explain why they do so.

To the extent that criminality and immorality are synonymous, the problem in criminology is to explain or account for the fact that some persons behave immorally and some do not, and it is not sufficient to state merely that the absence of morality is the cause of immorality. There is no specific evidence regarding the effect of religion, considered as something different from anticriminal values, on crime. Father Fitzpatrick, who analyzed the relationship of religion to delinquency and crime for the President's Commission, drew the following three conclusions:

(1) The relationship of religion to deviant behavior, in this case crime or delinquency, is very obscure. Religion itself is a very varied experience, and its relationship to social behavior is equally varied. It may be irrelevant to deviant behavior; as an instrument of social control it may seek to prevent deviancy; it may positively provoke deviancy. (2) When religion functions as an element in social control, its role may be very ambiguous. It may become the instrument of interest groups in the struggle for power, either protecting vested interests or becoming the motivating force for revolt. (3) In a number of situations in the United States, religiously related programs involving minority groups or the underprivileged may enjoy a bond of identification with the underprivileged which may enable them to be particularly effective.[45]

An older study indicated that delinquents had more favorable attitudes toward religious issues than did nondelinquents, but a

---

[44] Richard D. Knudten, *The Christian Encounters Crime in American Society* (St. Louis: Concordia, 1969), p. 7.

[45] Joseph P. Fitzpatrick, S.J., "The Role of Religion in Programs for the Prevention and Correction of Crime and Delinquency," President's Commission on Law Enforcement and Administration of Justice, *Task Force Report: Juvenile Delinquency and Youth Crime* (Washington: Government Printing Office, 1967), pp. 315-330.

study of 915 girls attending classes in religious instruction revealed that the training "did not contribute to the subjects' ability to apply the principles of moral law to life situations."[46] Similarly, whether or not children attend Sunday school seems to bear only a slight relationship to delinquency. Kvaraceus found that 91 percent of 761 delinquent children were affiliated with some church, and that 54 percent attended church regularly, that 20 percent attended occasionally, and that only 26 percent rarely visited a church.[47] Other studies have reported similar percentages.[48] These studies, of course, do not indicate the percentage of regular church attendants who commit delinquencies, and this percentage is a necessary prerequisite to a detailed analysis of the relationship between church attendance and delinquency.

A questionnaire study of 21,270 Tennessee high school students showed that boys with no religious preference had almost twice as high a delinquency rate as boys with a preference, after the rates had been adjusted for occupational status, subject and parent religious participation, age, and family structure. The rates were highest for youths whose parents did not go to church, lowest for those whose parents attended the same church, and intermediate for those whose parents attended different churches. Jews had the lowest rates. Catholics had the highest rates, but Negro-male Catholics had rates much higher than white-male Catholics, while white-female Catholics had higher rates than Negro-female Catholics. Baptists and fundamentalists had higher rates than nonfundamentalists except in the case of white females, where the rates were about the same.[49]

Among adults in America, Baptists and Catholics have the highest rate of commitment to those prisons which report religious affiliations. However, a survey showed that two-thirds of the membership in the Roman Catholic and Baptist churches comes

---

[46] Warren C. Middleton and Paul J. Fay, "Attitudes of Delinquent and Non-Delinquent Girls Toward Sunday Observance, the Bible, and War," *Journal of Educational Psychology*, 32:555-558, October, 1941; Carmen V. Diaz, "A Study of the Ability of Eleventh Grade Girls to Apply the Principles of Moral Law to Actual and Hypothetical Life Situations" (Ph.D. dissertation, Fordham University, 1952).

[47] William C. Kvaraceus, "Delinquent Behavior and Church Attendance," *Sociology and Social Research*, 28:284-289, March, 1944.

[48] William W. Wattenberg, "Church Attendance and Juvenile Misconduct," *Sociology and Social Research*, 34:195-202, January, 1950; Sheldon and Eleanor Glueck, *Unraveling Juvenile Delinquency* (New York: Commonwealth Fund, 1950), p. 166; M. Dominic, "Religion and the Juvenile Delinquent," *American Catholic Sociological Review*, 15:256-264, October, 1954; John Travers and Russel Davis, "A Study of Religious Motivation and Delinquency," *Journal of Educational Sociology*, 34:205-220, January, 1961.

[49] Albert Lewis Rhodes and Albert J. Reiss, Jr., "The 'Religious Factor' and Delinquent Behavior," *Journal of Research in Crime and Delinquency*, 7:83-98, January, 1970.

from the lower class.[50] A Canadian study showed considerable differences in conviction rates for members of different religious denominations. The highest rate of convictions for indictable offenses per 100,000 population 16 years and older, was 398, for members of Salvation Army. Rates for other denominations were 373 for Roman Catholics, 267 for Anglicans, 244 for Baptists, 237 for Greek Orthodox, 228 for Presbyterians, 212 for United Church, 194 for Lutherans, and 164 for members of the Pentecostal church. The lowest rate, 112, was for Jews.[51] A census taken in the penal institutions of the Netherlands in 1955 showed that Protestants and Catholics were slightly overrepresented, as compared with the general population of the Netherlands, while "other denominations" were slightly underrepresented.[52]

A study of 13,836 Los Angeles delinquents classified 58 percent of them as Protestant, 35 percent as Catholic, 3 percent as Jewish, and 3 percent as "other." The population of Los Angeles at the time was estimated to include 22 percent Catholics and 7 percent Jews.[53] Jews in all other parts of the United States and in Europe also have low crime and delinquency rates, and this condition has been attributed to the close family and community ties among members of this group.[54] A careful analysis of the differences in crime rates of the several denominations in Hungary also resulted in the conclusion that these differences were due not to the variations in the creeds but to variations in the economic, educational, and family status of the members, to the differences in places of residence, and to variations in age and sex.[55] ●

The educational institution

Since the school has been assigned a major role in training children for adult life, crime and delinquency often are attributed to "poor education" or "failure of the schools," just as they have been attributed to "bad homes" and "poor family training." Schools do not have the specific function of preventing delinquency, but they, like the family, are now expected to inculcate juveniles with certain values of a law-abiding society and are expected to provide interesting activities for the child. Probably delinquency and crime are related to the school in much the same way they are related to family conditions, namely, through the

[50] Philip M. Smith, "Organized Religion and Criminal Behavior," *Sociology and Social Research*, 33:262-267, May, 1949.

[51] P. J. Griffen, "Rates of Crime and Delinquency," chap. 4 in W. T. McGrath, ed., *Crime and Its Treatment in Canada* (Toronto: Macmillan, 1965).

[52] W. H. Nagel, "Criminality and Religion," *Tidschrift voor Strafrecht*, 69 (1960): 263-291.

[53] Calvin Goldscheider and Jon E. Simpson, "Religious Affiliation and Juvenile Delinquency," *Sociological Inquiry*, 37:297-310, Spring, 1967.

[54] Robert A. Silverman, "Criminality Among Jews: An Overview," *Issues in Criminology*, 6:1-38, Summer, 1971.

[55] Ervin Hacker, *Der Einfluss der Konfession auf die Kriminalität in Ungarn* (Miskolc: Jun, Ludvig, Janovits, 1930).

effects which school activities have on the students' associations with delinquent and antidelinquent behavior patterns.[56]

On the basis of inadequate statistics, which do not include white-collar crimes, it appears that crime decreases with the amount of formal education. Every ten years the census lists the characteristics of persons in custodial institutions, including the state and federal prisons and local jails and workhouses. These tabulations for 1960 show that the median years of school for the state and federal prison and reformatory populations is 8.6 years, in contrast to the 10.6 years for the general population of the country.[57] In 1966, 83 percent of correctional institution inmates twenty-five to sixty-four years old had not completed high school.[58] State statistics show the same low levels of education. Tests given to 4,662 males received in the California prisons in 1969 placed 40 percent below the eighth grade, 10 percent below the fifth grade; 3 percent were illiterate.[59] It is probable that these levels of educational achievement are lower than the levels among nonoffenders in California, but no comparable information for the general state populations is available. Of the Canadians convicted of indictable crimes in 1961, the rate per 100,000 population 16 years of age and over was 242 for those with no schooling, 369 for those with elementary school only, 252 for those with a high school education, and 66 for those with an educational level above high school.[60]

A large proportion of delinquents do poor school work, and they are retarded in reading, writing, and arithmetic. Kvaraceus reported that all Passaic, New Jersey, delinquents studied had repeated one or more grades, and that most of them did not go beyond junior high school.[61] In Ghana, 25 percent of a group of delinquents had never attended school, and 52 percent had four years or less of schooling; but only 1 percent of a control group made up of nondelinquents had as little as four years of

---

[56] Cf. Albert K. Cohen, "The Schools and Juvenile Delinquency," in Subcommittee to Investigate Juvenile Delinquency, *Education and Juvenile Delinquency, Interim Report, 84th Congress* (Washington: Government Printing Office, 1956), pp. 50-60; Albert J. Reiss, Jr., "Juvenile Delinquency and the Schools," ibid., pp. 63-68; and I. J. Croft and T. G. Grygier, "Social Relationships of Truants and Juvenile Delinquents," *Human Relations*, vol. 9 (1956), no. 4, pp. 436-466.

[57] *1960 Census of Population: Inmates of Institutions* (Washington: Government Printing Office, 1964), p. 24.

[58] President's Commission on Law Enforcement and Administration of Justice, *Task Force Report: Corrections* (Washington: Government Printing Office, 1967), p. 54.

[59] *California Prisoners, 1969* (Sacramento: California Department of Corrections, 1968), p. 31.

[60] Griffen, "Rates of Crime and Delinquency," p. 79.

[61] William C. Kvaraceus, *Juvenile Delinquency and the School* (Yonkers: World Book Company, 1945). See also R. W. Edmiston and E. H. Swaim, "Juvenile Delinquency and Provisions for Education," *School and Society*, 55:195, February, 1942; Bruce Balow, "Delinquency and School Failure," *Federal Probation*, 25:15-17, June, 1961; and George C. Brook, "High School Drop-Outs and Corrective Measures," *Federal Probation*, 23:30-35, September, 1959.

schooling.[62] Among the males who were born in Norway in 1933 and who had become offenders by January 1, 1958, 32 percent had some education beyond elementary school, as compared to 52 percent of the nonoffenders who were born in 1933. Two percent of the offenders and 10 percent of the nonoffenders had four or more years of education beyond elementary school.[63] A similar study of all boys born in Stockholm in 1940 indicated that among those who had acquired a criminal record by age twenty-one, the conviction rate among those who had completed only primary school was ten times as great as the rate among those who had graduated from *gymnasium* (roughly, junior college).[64] The incidence of juvenile delinquency among the 30 to 40 percent of American children who drop out of high school is about ten times that among those who do not drop out.[65] Some years ago, a careful study observed a low level of education among a group of delinquents, which was compared with a control group. Five years after a group of delinquents and a group of controls were first observed by Merrill, 70 percent of the delinquents and 31 percent of the controls were no longer in school. Of the delinquents who had left school, 29 percent left after completing only the eighth grade, and 77 percent left before finishing high school; the comparable percentages for the control group were 6 and 39.[66]

These differences do not prove that formal education, in itself, stops people from committing crimes, for the formal educational level may merely reflect economic status, home conditions, and several other conditions which affect the probabilities for contacts with delinquent and criminal behavior patterns. Like the home, the school may be located in a delinquency area, may affect the prestige values of various types of persons the child later will encounter, may fail to present antidelinquency behavior patterns, or may provide pleasant or unpleasant experiences which affect the child's associations with delinquency behavior patterns.

Perhaps the school's influence on delinquency rates has been largely through the last process. The fact that truancy and delinquency are closely correlated by area, and the fact that truancy so frequently precedes delinquencies involving theft is evidence of this. Among some groups of juveniles appearing before

---

[62] S. Kirson Weinberg, "Juvenile Delinquency in Ghana: A Comparative Analysis of Delinquents and Non-Delinquents," *Journal of Criminal Law, Criminology, and Police Science*, 55:471-481, December, 1964.

[63] Nils Christie, *Unge Norske Lovovertredere* [Young Norwegian lawbreakers] (Oslo: Universitetsforlaget, 1960), pp. 144-147.

[64] Jackson Toby, "Affluence and Adolescent Crime," appendix H in President's Commission, *Task Force Report: Juvenile Delinquency and Youth Crime*, pp. 132-144.

[65] Lucius F. Cervantes, *The Drop Out* (Ann Arbor: University of Michigan Press, 1965), p. 197.

[66] Maud A. Merrill, *Problems of Child Delinquency* (Boston: Houghton Mifflin, 1947), pp. 101-105.

juvenile courts, as many as 60 percent have truanted habitually. Of 2,021 prisoners investigated in one study, 40 percent had first been committed to an institution because of truancy.[67] Frum found that 23 percent of 148 cases of adult recidivism started with juvenile truancy or incorrigibility,[68] and another author estimates that 61 percent of the delinquents aged eight to seventeen are not in school.[69]

The fact that some children dislike school and play truant is undoubtedly related to family conditions and to other conditions outside the school as well as to the school program itself.[70] A study of 21,720 boys and girls in grades seven through twelve in the schools of Nashville indicated that delinquents and truants are more likely to want to quit school and accept the conforming goal of getting a job than they are to want to quit school because they regard the norm of compulsory school attendance as coercive.[71] This suggests that "rebellion" represented by truancy might be ameliorated for some truants and delinquents by an opportunity to undertake a productive role in the labor force. However, the nature of the activities provided by the school probably greatly affects the truancy rate, and truancy, except that it is itself frequently defined as delinquency, probably is important to delinquency largely to the degree that it increases the probabilities of contacts with delinquency behavior patterns.

In a study of the male high school students in a small city in the Pacific Northwest, Polk and Halferty found that blue-collar students who made "A" and "B" grades had the same low rate of delinquency (4 percent) as did the white-collar students earning the same grades. Moreover, one-fifth to one-fourth of the students doing poor or failing work in school became delinquent, whether they were blue collar or white collar.[72] In explaining these and other findings, Polk noted that in small towns school failures are often "locked out" of the system which supports accomplishments by legitimate means, and they drift into "trouble

---

[67] *Justice and the Child in New Jersey,* Report of the New York Juvenile Delinquency Commission, 1939, p. 110, cited in John R. Ellingston, *Protecting Our Children From Criminal Careers* (New York: Prentice-Hall, 1948), p. 277.

[68] Harold S. Frum, "Adult Criminal Offense Trends Following Juvenile Delinquency," *Journal of Criminal Law, Criminology, and Police Science,* 49:29-49, May-June, 1958.

[69] Samuel M. Brownell, "Delinquency, an Important Problem in Education," *School Life,* 36:52-53, January, 1954.

[70] David H. Hargreaves, *Social Relations in a Secondary School* (London: Routledge, 1967).

[71] Albert Lewis Rhodes and Albert J. Reiss, Jr., "Apathy, Truancy and Delinquency as Adaptations to School Failure," *Social Forces,* 48:12-22, 1969.

[72] Kenneth Polk and David S. Halferty, "Adolescence, Commitment, and Delinquency," *Journal of Research in Crime and Delinquency,* 3:82-96, July, 1966.

making subcultures."[73] Even when they later migrate to urban areas, they are not able to participate fully in the legitimate opportunity structures because they are economically, educationally, socially, and culturally disadvantaged. In Polk and Halferty's study, about 80 percent of the students who did poor and failing work in school did not participate in the delinquent culture and did not become delinquent, regardless of social class. Karacki and Toby have made essentially the same observation about the relationship between commitment to school, participation in a delinquent subculture (which they, unfortunately, called "the youth culture"), and delinquency:

> It is our impression that the Dukes failed to develop early in adolescence commitments to adult roles and values which would have mobilized their interests and energies and which would have served to relate them to school and work. In lieu of this, they drew instead upon the youth culture for meaning and purpose, and out of this emerged a delinquent gang. . . . This involvement in the youth culture was incompatible with diligent performance in school.[74]

In reference to adults, the schools have been criticized because the difference in criminality between the educated and uneducated is not greater than it is. This criticism usually is based on the observation that the school fails to present its charges with anticriminal behavior patterns and, instead, remains rather neutral in respect to criminality, concentrating on dissemination of academic and technical skills. Eighty-nine percent of 202 school superintendents stated that primary and elementary teachers should have additional training in recognizing and understanding signs of maladjustment.[75] Ordinarily, the criticism is stated in terms of the school's failure to supply the nation's youth with moral and democratic ideals. But it is only in rather recent years that schools have been expected to take over many of the socializing functions formerly assigned to the family and other primary groups. Moreover, urban areas, which have the best educational facilities, have higher crime rates than rural areas. •

War   Many persons have asserted that crimes increase during war and postwar periods. This assertion has a certain amount of truth, but it oversimplifies the situation. The following propositions are a more adequate statement of the facts.

First, the official statistics on juvenile delinquency show a

---

[73] Kenneth Polk, "Delinquency and Community Action in Nonmetropolitan Areas," appendix R in President's Commission, *Task Force Report: Juvenile Delinquency and Youth Crime,* pp. 343-352.

[74] Larry Karacki and Jackson Toby, "The Uncommitted Adolescent: Candidate for Gang Socialization," *Sociological Inquiry,* Spring, 1962, p. 208.

[75] Commonwealth of Massachusetts, *Special Report of the Division of Youth Service,* House Document No. 3025 (Boston: Legislative Printers, 1957), p. 33.

general trend toward an increase in wartime.[76] This is shown in figure I.[77] The trend, however, is a statistical artifact: rates go down in many communities, while going up in a larger number of communities. Furthermore, the statistics of arrests and convictions of juveniles are not a certain measure of the delinquent behavior of juveniles. Arrests and convictions of juveniles are not only an indication of delinquent behavior of juveniles, but are also an indication of reactions of officials and other adults toward that delinquent behavior. In Liverpool, England, the number of convictions of juveniles increased during the First World War, but the number of unofficial actions in the form of warnings decreased by approximately an equal amount.

Several explanations of the apparent increase in juvenile delinquency in wartime have been suggested. One is that the increase is due to an increase in a "contagion of violence." Children in wartime develop an admiration for the soldier. They are furnished with war toys; they play war games and in other ways take over the patterns of warfare into their own lives. If this theory were correct, it would be expected that assaults and similar crimes of violence would show the greatest increases in time of war, but they do not.

A second explanation, popular between the wars, was that the increase in delinquency is due to an increase in economic hardships due to blockades, rationing systems, and reduced earnings. While this notion may have some relevance for devastated areas, in the United States during World War II, the Korean War, and the Vietnam War, delinquency increased in the midst of unusual prosperity.

A third explanation is that the increase in juvenile delinquency is due to emotional strain in wartime. The inadequacy of this explanation is seen in the fact that some kinds of delinquency increase and some kinds decrease in wartime, and in the fact that the variations in delinquency rates are not uniform. It is difficult to understand why emotional strain should produce an increase in one kind of delinquency and a decrease in another kind.

A fourth explanation, which seems to best fit the facts, is that juvenile delinquency increases in wartime as a result of changes in the family and other local community institutions.[78] Parents

---

[76] See Edward R. Schwartz, "Statistics of Juvenile Delinquency in the United States," *Annals of the American Academy of Political and Social Science*, 261:9-13, January, 1949; Martin H. Neumeyer, "Delinquency Trends in Wartime," *Sociology and Social Research*, 29:262-275, March, 1945; Walter C. Reckless, "The Impact of War on Crime, Delinquency and Prostitution," *American Journal of Sociology*, 48:378-386, November, 1942.

[77] U.S. Department of Health, Education, and Welfare, *Juvenile Court Statistics*, 1966, Statistical Series, no. 90 (Washington: Children's Bureau, 1967), p. 11. Also see table VI, p. 36, above.

[78] See E. Abbott, "Juvenile Delinquency During the First World War: Notes on the British Experience, 1914-1918," *Social Service Review*, 17:192-212, June, 1943.

FIGURE I

TREND IN JUVENILE COURT DELINQUENCY CASES

AND

CHILD POPULATION 10-17 YEARS OF AGE

1940 - 1966 (SEMILOGARITHMIC SCALE)

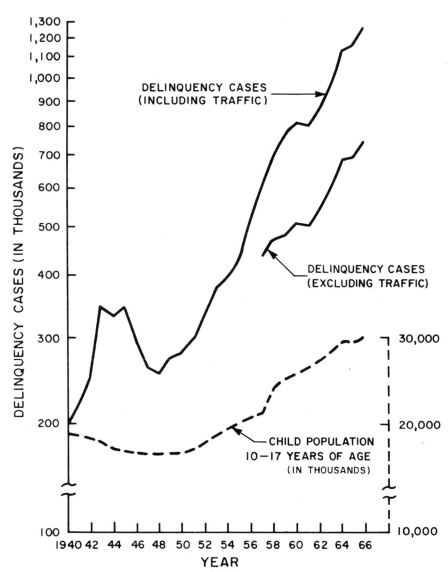

join the army, engage in war industries and other war activities, and neglect the supervision of children. At the same time, many other agencies which ordinarily present antidelinquency values break down as a result of the withdrawal of personnel, lack of interest of adults, and the diversion of money to other uses. With increased mobility, children more frequently come into contact with persons who have delinquent values, and they assimilate delinquent ways of behaving. In invaded and occupied territories, children learn that it is not immoral to steal from, or even to kill, the invader. It has been determined, moreover, that these changes also affect the postwar delinquency rates of children too young to get very involved in delinquency during the war years. In a study of England, Wales, and Scotland, Wilkins found that the highest postwar (1948-1957) delinquency rates occurred among those children who were four or five years old during some part of World War II (1939-1945). Further, youths aged seventeen and twenty-one in 1955 had delinquency rates higher than would be expected on the basis of the delinquency rates of youths whose seventeenth and twenty-first birthdays fell in other years.[79] A study of children reared in Denmark during the nation's critical war years (1943-1944) showed similar results.[80]

Second, the absolute number of adult crimes decreases during wartime because of the mobilization of the young-adult population, but the ratio of crimes committed by adult civilians to the number of adult civilians in the population remains relatively constant.[81] The adult-female crime rate increased greatly in Germany and Austria during both world wars, presumably because females assumed the economic and social roles of the males. To a lesser extent, this occurred in the United States during World War II also.

Third, special wartime regulations are violated with great frequency. There is widespread evidence of extensive violation of price-ceiling and rationing regulations in the United States during World War II.[82] Similarly, the Vietnam War was accompanied by widespread violations of the Selective Service Act. The number of defendants who appeared before U.S. District Courts for draft evasion soared from 516 in 1966 to 2,973 in 1971.

Fourth, postwar crime waves are confined largely to countries which suffer rather complete disintegration of their economic, political, and social systems as a result of the war. Earlier studies

[79] Leslie T. Wilkins, *Delinquent Generations* (London: Home Office Studies in the Causes of Delinquency and the Treatment of Offenders, Report No. 3, 1961), pp. 3, 7-9.

[80] Karl O. Christiansen, "Delinquent Generations in Denmark," *British Journal of Criminology,* 3:259-264, January, 1964.

[81] Edwin H. Sutherland, "Crime," in William F. Ogburn, ed., *American Society in Wartime* (Chicago: University of Chicago Press, 1943), pp. 185-206.

[82] Frank E. Hartung, "White-Collar Offenses in the Wholesale Meat Industry in Detroit," *American Journal of Sociology,* 56:25-35, July, 1950; Clinard, *Black Market,* pp. 28-50, 115-204.

have shown that serious crimes increased significantly in France after the revolution of 1884, in the United States after the Civil War, in Germany and Austria after the war of 1866, in Germany and France after the Franco-Prussian War of 1870-1871, and in Germany and Austria after the First World War.[83] But in nations which did not experience a great disintegration of social institutions, such as England and the United States after both world wars, the crime rates seem to remain rather constant in prewar, war, and postwar periods. This seems to be adequate rebuttal of the argument that young men who have engaged in physical violence during wars will continue similar activities when they return to civilian life. Furthermore, after World War I it was observed that when former servicemen were committed to prison, they were most likely, in comparison with those who had not seen war service, to be committed for fraud, embezzlement, and nonsupport, and least likely to be imprisoned for homicide, burglary, assault, and rape. After World War II this same tendency was found. James V. Bennett, director of the United States Bureau of Prisons, reported that the offenses most commonly committed by veterans committed to federal prisons were embezzlement, fraud, and forgery, while "robbery and homicide, the violent crimes for which one might expect a high proportion of veterans, were well down the list."[84] Bennett indicated further that the imprisonment rate for veterans in all age groups from twenty-five to fifty-four was lower than the rate for nonveterans; the twenty to twenty-four age category, however, had a larger proportion of veterans among the prisoners than were in the general population. He explains these variations in terms of the selective processes of the armed forces. ●

Public agencies of communication

A Gallup poll conducted in 1954 indicated that about 70 percent of a nationwide sample placed some of "the blame" for teenage crime on comic books; an identical percentage placed some of "the blame" on crime and mystery programs on television and radio. Little direct support for this accusation can be found in the statistical data of delinquency and crime rates. People all over the United States read the same comic books and newspapers, see the same movies and television shows, and listen to the same crime broadcasts, but they differ among themselves

---

[83] Edith Abbott, "The Civil War and the Crime Wave of 1860-1870," *Social Service Review*, 1:212-234, June, 1927; Franz Exner, *Krieg und Kriminalität in Oesterreich* (Vienna: Hölder-Pichler-Tempsky, 1927); Moritz Liepman, *Krieg und Kriminalität in Deutschland* (Stuttgart: Deutsche Verlagsanstalt, 1930).

[84] James V. Bennett, "The Ex-GI in Federal Prisons," *Proceedings of the American Correctional Association, 1953*, pp. 131-136; and "The Criminality of Veterans," *Federal Probation*, 28:40-42, June, 1954. See also John C. Spencer, *Crime and the Services* (London: Routledge and Kegan Paul, 1954); and Harry Willbach, "Recent Crimes and the Veterans," *Journal of Criminal Law and Criminology*, 38:501-508, January-February, 1948.

greatly in regard to criminality. Even when the communicator deliberately intends to modify people's attitudes, which is certainly not the case among the personnel of the communication agencies which are said to contribute to crime, there is a great deal of variation in the response. Berelson has said that "effects upon the audience do not follow directly from and in correspondence with the intent of the communicator and the content of the communication. The predispositions of the reader or listener are deeply involved in the situation, and may operate to block or modify the intended effect or even to set up a boomerang effect."[85] This is the same thing as saying that only "some kinds of communication on some kinds of issues, brought to the attention of some kinds of people under some kinds of conditions, have some kinds of effects."[86]

In 1967, 55 percent of the public said they got "most of their news about what was going on in the world" from newspapers, but 64 percent said they got it from television (some respondents named several media).[87] In 1961, newspapers were dominant as a primary source of news by 57 to 52 percent. American newspapers and television news programs have been severely criticized for the part they play in relation to crime. The following charges are made against them. *First,* they promote crime by constantly advertising it and exaggerating its incidence. *Second,* they interfere with justice by "trial by news media," by distortion of news, and by providing advance information to the public, including the criminals, regarding the plans of the police and prosecutors. *Third,* they ordinarily promote indifference to crime, but on occasion create public panic with reference to crime, both of which make consistent and rational preventive law enforcement and judicial correctional procedures very difficult.

News media and crime

The desirability of publishing crime news is not here in question. Rather it is the amount and style of the crime news. English newspapers and television programs publish crime news in the form of brief factual statements. The American crime news is presented vividly and sometimes not distastefully to the reader.[88] Because nothing is said about the millions of persons who lead a consistently law-abiding life, the impression is created that crime is the customary mode of life. Conceivably,

---

[85] B. Berelson, "Communications and Public Opinion," in W. Schramm, ed.. *Communications in Modern Society* (Urbana, Ill.: University of Illinois Press, 1948), pp. 168-185.

[86] Ibid.

[87] Otto N. Larsen, "Violence and the Mass Media," paper delivered at the convention of the American Society of Newspaper Editors, Washington, D.C., April 17, 1969. See also idem, "Controversies About the Mass Communication of Violence," *Annals of the American Academy of Political and Social Science,* 364:37-49, March, 1966.

[88] See Alfred Friendly and Ronald Goldfarb, *Crime and Publicity: The Impact of News on the Administration of Justice* (New York: Twentieth Century Fund, 1967).

this publicity given to crime creates and perpetuates an attitude of indifference to ordinary criminal offenses among persons who are not the direct victims of them. On the other hand, the publicity given to certain sensational crimes does rouse the public to action, and this action could culminate in the creation of strong anticriminal influences in the community. Usually, however, the public action merely consists of requesting the legislatures to increase the severity of punishments for the type of crime in question, after which the whole thing is forgotten.[89] News media could play, and sometimes do play, an important role in mobilizing the public to a more significant kind of anticriminal organization.

The effect of the constant presentation of crime news to the public cannot be demonstrated in specific criminal cases. Occasionally, a criminal states that he got the idea for a crime from a newspaper or television account of the activities of another criminal. But most "crime waves" are fabrications of the press: a sensational crime is committed and given wide publicity in one community; that type of crime becomes "news"; editors begin publicizing hitherto unnoticed crimes of the same type in other parts of the country; and newspaper readers get the impression that the influence of the criminal whose offense was first publicized is spreading throughout the country.

News media on occasion glorify specific criminals and, consequently, increase their prestige among other criminals and among the boys residing in delinquency areas. Newspaper publicity, like commitment to a prison for adults, contributes immensely to one's status in some delinquent groups. Further, news accounts contribute considerably to the self-esteem of professional criminals, who generally are among the most enthusiastic followers of the crime news.

Also, newspapers sometimes interfere with the course of justice by what has been called "trial by newspaper," but which now must also be called "trial by television." Prior to the trial and during the trial, the reporters present such evidence as they have, which is likely to be partisan information, again and again, until the public accepts the implied verdict of the news media and thereafter cannot easily be shaken in its opinion. The newsman's sources of information are almost always the office of the prosecuting attorney or the police; the defendant's version of the case is ignored until the time of the trial itself. A fair trial under such circumstances becomes almost impossible, especially in communities where the judges are elected and where they are afraid of arousing public antagonism. It is quite certain that under such circumstances many innocent persons are convicted, and that many persons who are punished severely would otherwise be given light penalties. However, the number of cases

---

[89] See Edwin H. Sutherland, "The Diffusion of Sexual Psychopath Laws," *American Journal of Sociology*, 56:142-148, September, 1950.

which attract this detailed and continued attention is not large.

The President's Commission pointed out that newspaper, television, and radio reporting are essential to the administration of justice, but the commission also pointed out that a fair trial can be held only if the evidence is presented in the courtroom, not in the press, and jurors do not come to their task prejudiced by publicity. The conflict is not between a hero and a bad guy; it is between two good guys—free press and free trial. The commission cited two recent United States Supreme Court decisions which held that the defendant did not get a fair trial because of prejudicial publicity. In one case, the trial was turned into a "Roman holiday" by the press, and in the other one the presence of television and still cameras in the courtroom during the trial destroyed the "judicial serenity and calm" necessary for a fair trial. Several agencies, including the New York City Police Department and the United States Department of Justice, have restricted the information which law-enforcement officers can disclose to the press prior to a trial.[90] The American Bar Association, similarly, in 1966 drew up rules regarding the release of information to the press by law-enforcement officers and judicial employees.

News media, because they are business concerns, operated for the purpose of profits, are concerned with arousing emotions rather than giving the reader an understanding of the crime situation. Their primary interest is circulation, and public welfare is secondary. Accordingly, presentation of crime news sometimes is designed to throw the public into a panic. Newspapers in England deal with crime news as they do with sickness and financial dangers, that is, quietly and factually. American newspapers, on the other hand, have not realized the dangers of panics of this nature and continue to make the crime stories as colorful as possible.[91] Moreover, the public gets outmoded notions of "inborn criminality," distorted notions about the nature and success of probation and parole, and sensational, "tough" punitive policies rather than a constructive approach to problems of crime causation, law enforcement, and crime control.[92] Taft and England have observed that reporters have a tendency to find trivial motives for crime because the more shockingly trivial the alleged motive, the more newsworthy it becomes, especially when hein-

---

[90] President's Commission on Law Enforcement and Administration of Justice, *Task Force Report: The Courts* (Washington: Government Printing Office, 1967), pp. 48-50.

[91] National Advisory Commission on Civil Disorders, *Report* (Washington: Government Printing Office, 1968), pp. 201-202. See also American Newspaper Publishers Association, *Reporting the Detroit Riot* (New York: Author, 1968).

[92] See F. Perry Olds, "The Place of the Press in Crime Control," *National Probation and Parole Association Yearbook, 1947*, pp. 245-259; Bruce Smith, "Enforcement of the Criminal Law," *Annals of the American Academy of Political and Social Science*, 217:12-18, September, 1941.

ous offenses are involved—"I wanted to see what it was like to kill someone," "I stabbed Pa because he was always criticizing me," "We set fire to the school because the gym teacher bawled us out."[93]

Crime dramatization

Judicial, psychological, sociological, and literary "experts" are in almost complete disagreement regarding the effect of the "comics" on delinquency, just as a few generations ago they were in disagreement as to the effects of "dime novels" and "pulp magazines." The erotic and "blood-and-thunder" literature in these magazines has been severely denounced because of the continued direction of attention to crime, especially violent crime, and the continued presence of sex imagery.[94] Other authors, however, continue to assert that no one has conclusively demonstrated that comic books are detrimental in any way.[95]

Criticism of comic books as contributors to delinquency has waned since the arrival of television, which now is faced with almost the same charges once hurled at comic books and, before that, at movies and radio.

Numerous studies clearly support the contentions of many concerned citizens. These are, as Larsen has summarized them: (1) The menu offered by television is saturated with violent content, including incidents of persons intentionally doing injury to each other. One report to the Federal Communications Commission stated that between the ages of five and fourteen the average American child witnesses the violent destruction of thirteen thousand human beings on television alone. (2) More and more people have ready access to the medium. Children sixteen years of age have spent as much time watching television as they have spent in school. (3) For most persons, but particularly for the poor, television is perceived as the most credible and believable source of information concerning the world as it really is.[96]

Similarly, arguments used to answer the charges made against comic books are now being used to answer the charges against television. Klapper evaluated the results of five studies which contrasted people habitually exposed to media with a violent

---

[93] Donald R. Taft and Ralph W. England, Jr., *Criminology*, 4th ed. (New York: Macmillan, 1964), p. 211. See also Britt-Mari Persson Blegvad, "Newspapers and Rock and Roll Riots in Copenhagen," *Acta Sociologica* (Copenhagen), 7 (1964): 151-178.

[94] See Fredric Wertham, *Seduction of the Innocent* (New York: Rinehart, 1954); and idem, "Mass Media and Sex Deviation," in Ralph Slovenko, ed., *Sexual Behavior and the Law* (Springfield, Ill.: Charles C Thomas, 1965).

[95] See John R. Cavanagh, "The Comics War," *Journal of Criminal Law and Criminology*, 40:28-35, May-June, 1949; Thomas Ford Hoult, "Comic Books and Juvenile Delinquency," *Sociology and Social Research*, 33:279-284, March, 1949; and Edwin H. Pfuhl, Jr., "The Relationship of Crime and Horror Comics to Juvenile Delinquency," *Research Studies of the State College of Washington*, 24:17-177, June, 1956.

[96] Larsen, "Violence and the Mass Media," p. 6.

content and people who were not. He found no significant differences between the two groups, and he therefore concluded that mass media are not a primary factor in deviant behavior and not, per se, a cause of crime and delinquency.[97]

Television programs provide people with temporary philosophies of life, with ideas of their rights and privileges, with fashions in dress, language, etiquette, and child-rearing. They also teach children the words of popular songs, techniques of love-making, and certain criminal techniques. Children impersonate actors in their play, and both children and adults imitate them in their everyday language and conduct. However, what persons perceive when they watch movies or listen to the radio varies with socio-economic, ethnic, religious, and cultural background.[98] Perhaps it is for this reason that many children play as gangsters or robbers after seeing a gangster or crime show, but also play as gangsters or robbers after seeing a love story or musical. And many adolescents make love after seeing gangster or other violent shows as well as after seeing dramatizations of romantic love-making.

Perhaps the major effect of crime dramatization is the creation and perpetuation of an attitude of indifference to ordinary criminal offenses among persons who are not the direct victims of them. Because the impression is created that crime is frequent and usual, the reading and viewing public becomes indifferent to sensational, violent crimes, and even less concerned with ordinary offenses such as burglary and larceny. Thus, dramatization of crime appears to minimize public indignation when crimes are committed and, perhaps, to contribute indirectly to high crime rates. A population for whom crime has become usual cannot present a consistent front against crime. On the other hand, it has not been demonstrated that exposure through news media to the constant dramatization of crime is effective in changing individuals from noncriminals to criminals.

In individual cases, tendencies toward delinquency which have been derived from other sources may be reinforced by the crime stories in comic books, movies, and television presentations, and in some cases specific techniques of delinquency are thus learned. But whether a behavior pattern is followed and whether a specific criminal technique is used will depend upon the child's prior associations with delinquent and antidelinquent behavior patterns in his primary groups. In fact, older studies suggest that children who reside in areas where delinquency rates are high are influenced more significantly by crime and sex movies and radio crime dramas than are those who live in areas of low delinquency

---

[97] Joseph T. Klapper, *The Effects of Mass Communication* (Glencoe, Ill.: Free Press, 1961), p. 37.

[98] Theodore M. Newcomb, *Social Psychology* (New York: Dryden Press: 1950), pp. 90-96. See also Eunice Cooper and Helen Dinerman, "Analysis of the Film 'Don't Be a Sucker': A Study in Communication," *Public Opinion Quarterly*, 15 (1951): 243-264.

rates.[99] This, in general, is what would be expected on the basis of the differential association theory. ●

Conclusion   The general argument of this chapter has been that the causes of crime lie primarily in the area of personal interaction, and that personal interaction is confined almost entirely to local communities and neighborhoods. Negatively, criminal behavior is not affected directly or significantly by variations in the form of the general social institutions—economics, government, religion, and education—or by the media of mass communication. This negative proposition does not deny that the general institutions and mass media have some significance for crime, and certain exceptions and qualifications should be noted. *First,* the crime rate does increase when the general institutions are suddenly disrupted. *Second,* the efficiency of the police system and of the entire system of criminal justice does have an effect on the crime rate. *Third,* the institutions and mass media have a very important indirect effect in that they determine the social organization and interaction patterns of local communities. ●

Suggested readings   BLUMER, HERBERT, & PHILIP M. HAUSER. *Movies, Delinquency, and Crime.* New York: Macmillan, 1933.

BONGER, W. A. *Criminality and Economic Conditions.* Translated by H. P. Horton. Boston: Little, Brown, 1916.

CLARK, JOHN P., & EUGENE P. WENNINGER. "Socio-Economic Class and Area as Correlates of Illegal Behavior Among Juveniles." *American Sociological Review,* 27:826-834, December, 1962.

CRESSEY, DONALD R. *Theft of the Nation: The Structure and Operations of Organized Crime in America.* New York: Harper and Row, 1969.

CRESSEY, PAUL G. "The Motion Picture Experience as Modified by Social Background and Personality." *American Sociological Review,* 3:516-525, August, 1938.

FLEISHER, BELTON M. *The Economics of Delinquency.* Chicago: Quadrangle Books, 1966.

GARDINER, JOHN A. *The Politics of Corruption: Organized Crime in an American City.* New York: Russell Sage Foundation, 1970.

GLASER, DANIEL, & KENT RICE. "Crime, Age and Employment." *American Sociological Review,* 24:679-686, October, 1959.

GOULD, LEROY C. "The Changing Structure of Property Crime in an Affluent Society." *Social Forces,* 48:50-59, 1969.

HARGREAVES, DAVID H. *Social Relations in a Secondary School.* London: Routledge, 1967.

HENRY, ANDREW F., & JAMES F. SHORT, JR. *Suicide and Homicide.* Glencoe, Ill.: Free Press, 1954.

---

[99] Paul G. Cressey, "The Motion Picture Experience as Modified by Social Background and Personality," *American Sociological Review,* 3:516-525, August, 1938; Ethel Shanas and C. E. Dunning, *Recreation and Delinquency* (Chicago: Chicago Recreation Commission, 1942); Howard Rowland, "Radio Crime Dramas," *Educational Research Bulletin,* 23:210-217, November, 1944.

KLAPPER, JOSEPH T. *The Effects of Mass Communication.* Glencoe, Ill.: Free Press, 1961.

LARSEN, OTTO N., ed. *Violence and the Mass Media.* New York: Harper and Row, 1968.

POLK, KENNETH, & DAVID S. HALFERTY. "Adolescence, Commitment, and Delinquency." *Journal of Research in Crime and Delinquency,* 3:82-96, July, 1966.

RADZINOWICZ, LEON. "Economic Pressures." In *Crime and Justice,* edited by Leon Radzinowicz and Marvin E. Wolfgang, vol. 1, pp. 420-442. New York: Basic Books, 1971.

REISS, ALBERT J., JR., & ALBERT LEWIS RHODES. "The Distribution of Juvenile Delinquency in the Social Class Structure." *American Sociological Review,* 26:720-732, October, 1961.

RHODES, ALBERT LEWIS, & ALBERT J. REISS, JR. "Apathy, Truancy and Delinquency as Adaptations to School Failure." *Social Forces,* 48:12-22, 1969.

SELLIN, THORSTEN. *Research Memorandum on Crime in the Depression.* New York: Social Science Research Council, 1937.

SEWELL, WILLIAM H., & VIMAL P. SHAH. "Parent's Education and Children's Education Aspirations and Achievements." *American Sociological Review,* 33:191-209, April, 1968.

SILVERMAN, ROBERT A. "Criminality Among Jews: An Overview." *Issues in Criminology,* 6:1-38, Summer, 1971.

STEFFENS, LINCOLN. *Autobiography.* New York: Harcourt, Brace, 1931.

TOBY, JACKSON. "Affluence and Adolescent Crime." In President's Commission on Law Enforcement and Administration of Justice, *Task Force Report: Juvenile Delinquency and Youth Crime,* Appendix H. Washington: Government Printing Office, 1967.

VAZ, EDMUND W., ed. *Middle-Class Juvenile Delinquency.* New York: Harper and Row, 1967.

12 Processes in criminal behavior

In the life histories of criminals, in the interaction between criminals and others, and in the interaction among criminals, all the processes observed in other areas of social participation may be discovered. Some of these processes have greater significance than others for the understanding of crime. One of the significant processes in the life history of the criminal is maturation. Segregation, conflict, and the competitive development of techniques of crime and of protection against crime appear in the interaction between criminals and the public. Fashion, organization, and professionalization appear in the interaction among criminals. These processes are discussed briefly in this chapter as illustrations rather than as complete analyses. ●

Maturation

A process which may be called *maturation* appears in the life history of persisting criminals. This means merely that criminality in such persons grows in a somewhat consistent course. It does not mean that an individual who starts on this course must follow it to the end, or that he may not begin at some other point than that at which most other criminals begin. Like other terms borrowed by the social sciences from biology, the term *maturation* is misleading but it is used in the absence of a better term.

A person's criminal age is determined by the point he has reached in this process of maturation. The process describes the development of criminality, with reference first to the general attitudes toward criminality, and second, to the techniques used in criminal behavior.[1] A boy who is reared in an area of high delinquency might reach criminal maturity by age twelve or fourteen. He has reached criminal maturity because criminality has become an integrated part of his life style. He plans his offenses, knows how to "fix" things if caught, and thinks of himself as "delinquent" or "bad."[2] When convicted, he takes imprisonment philosophically as a part of his life, just as a newspaper boy who has made what provision he can against the rain takes the rain as a part of his life. The embezzler, on the other hand, may be four times as old as this delinquent, but he has made no provision for immunity in case of detection, and he has no philosophy to support him in his trial and punishment. His character is not integrated; he is immature.

The development of criminal methods in relation to chronological age varies in different crimes. Life histories of persons who in young adult life become robbers and burglars show that criminality proceeds from trivial to serious, from occasional to frequent, from sport to business, and from crimes committed by isolated individuals, or by very loosely organized groups to crimes committed by rather tightly organized groups.[3] This process in

---

[1] See Walter C. Reckless, "The Development of a Criminality Level Index," *Papers of the American Society of Criminology*, 1964, pp. 71-82.

[2] Walter C. Reckless, Simon Dinitz, and Ellen Murray, "Self-Concept as an Insulator Against Delinquency," *American Sociological Review*, 21:744-746, December, 1956. See also Reckless, Dinitz, and Barbara Kay, "The Self Component in Potential Delinquency and Potential Non-Delinquency," *American Sociological Review*, 22:566-570, October, 1957; and Dinitz, F. R. Scarpitti, and Reckless, "Delinquency Vulnerability: A Cross Group and Longitudinal Analysis," *American Sociological Review*, 27:515-517, August, 1962.

[3] See Hutchins Hapgood, *The Autobiography of a Thief* (New York: Fox, Duffield, 1930); Stephen Burroughs, *Memoirs of the Notorious Stephen Burroughs of New Hampshire* (New York: L. MacVeagh, Dial Press, 1924); John Bartlow Martin, *My Life in Crime* (New York: American Library, 1952); Claude Brown, *Manchild in the Promised Land* (New York: Macmillan, 1965); and Bill Chambliss, ed., *Box Man: A Professional Thief's Journey* (New York: Harper and Row, 1972).

crimes of violence reaches its height when the offender is about nineteen years of age and then remains constant for five or ten years, when it either changes into crimes which require less agility and daring, or into the kind of criminal behavior connected with politics, gambling, liquor, and usury, or is abandoned entirely. The Gluecks reported in their study of five hundred graduates of the Massachusetts Reformatory that 31.3 percent of those 21-25 years of age at the beginning of the second five-year period after release committed crimes against property, while of those 36 years or over at this time 10.8 percent committed crimes against property.[4] The nonviolent crimes of a professional nature are continued, however, to an older age.

The process in the life history of embezzlers is decidedly different. Persons who have previous histories of rectitude accept positions of financial trust with no intention of committing a crime, then later become embezzlers by criminally violating their positions of trust. The persons who occupy positions of financial responsibility seldom are psychopathic, feeble-minded, residents of deteriorated slum areas, or in other ways personally or situationally pathological. Consequently, few embezzlers have such characteristics. Usually embezzlements are committed by employees who have held positions of financial responsibility for many years, rather than by recent recruits. Occasionally, embezzlers snatch a large sum of money, or whatever money is on hand, and abscond. The more usual procedure is to abstract relatively small sums over a long period of time.

First, the potential trust violator defines a financial problem which confronts him as "unshareable," that is, as a problem which cannot be shared with persons who, from a more objective point of view, could aid in its solution. In many cases these unshareable financial problems arise from obligations incurred in gambling, extravagant living, or maintaining an extramarital establishment, but they also arise in other ways.

Second, the potential trust violator realizes that he has the ability and opportunity to solve the unshareable problem by violating his position of trust. He realizes that he can solve the unshareable financial problem by using the same technical skills which he had been using in the legitimate aspects of his position.

Third, he defines embezzlement in terms which enable him to look upon it as essentially noncriminal, as justified, or as part of a general irresponsibility for which he is not completely accountable.[5] One popular notion among embezzlers, for example, is that

---

[4] Sheldon and Eleanor T. Glueck, *Later Criminal Careers* (New York: Commonwealth Fund, 1937), p. 109.

[5] Use of such definitions has been described as a "technique of neutralization." See Gresham M. Sykes and David Matza, "Techniques of Neutralization: A Theory of Delinquency," *American Sociological Review*, 22:664-670, December, 1957. For an excellent analysis of criminalistic vocabularies of motive, see Frank E. Hartung, *Crime, Law, and Society* (Detroit: Wayne State University Press, 1965), pp. 62-83, 125-136.

they are merely "borrowing," not "stealing," the entrusted funds. Use of this rationalization enables them to look upon themselves as borrowers and to take relatively small amounts of money over a period of time, always with the intention of repaying it. It is the popularity of this notion, in fact, which accounts for the relatively small proportion of "snatch-and-run" embezzlers. In some cases the embezzler repays the "borrowed" money and his embezzlement goes undetected.

Among apprehended embezzlers, a few are found to have kept a careful record of the amount of the "indebtedness," but most state that after a few abstractions they lost track of the total amount of their "debt." A considerable amount of money may be taken before the embezzler realizes that he cannot possibly repay the amount taken. This realization, which is described by embezzlers as recognition of the fact that they are "in too deep," does not occur in all cases, since some violators are arrested before it takes place; and its absence enables these trust violators to continue rationalizing, even after apprehension, that they were merely borrowing. But when an embezzler discovers that he is "in too deep" he is forced to abandon the notion that he is borrowing and to face the fact that he, an "honest and respectable person," has committed a crime. By using the rationalization that they are borrowing, then, embezzlers are able to remain in full contact with the values and ideals of former and present associates who condemn crime, and when they find that they are "in too deep" and have slipped into a category (criminal) which they know is regarded as undesirable according to that set of values and ideals, they rebel against it. They usually describe themselves as being extremely nervous, tense, emotionally upset, and unhappy. To get rid of these symptoms they may report their behavior to the police, quit taking funds, speculate or gamble wildly in an attempt to regain the stolen funds, or commit suicide. On the other hand, they may identify themselves with criminals and, thus, become reckless in their defalcations, taking larger amounts than formerly and with less attempt to avoid detection and with no notion of repayment.

Thus, in the absence of the rationalization that he is borrowing, an embezzler of this kind cannot reconcile the fact that he is converting money while at the same time he is an "honest and trusted person"; consequently, he either (a) readopts the attitudes of the noncriminal groups with which he identified himself before he violated his trust, or (b) adopts the attitudes of the new category of persons (criminals) with whom he now finds himself identified. After apprehension, those embezzlers who finally come to look upon their behavior as criminal express general disapproval of crime and embezzlement, just as do noncriminals. The crimes are generally committed individually, but occasionally two or more persons are in collusion. Embezzlers are scorned by professional criminals but are regarded by prison officers as model prisoners. A comparatively small proportion of them become recidivists, for the discovery of an embezzlement generally precludes further employment in positions of financial trust.[6]

The processes in the life histories of other types of criminals might also be described. The legal offense category is not the best unit to use in these descriptions. Rather, sociological categories which combine several legal categories should be used as the unit. After a sufficient number of such units have been defined and described, the types which appear can be differentiated from each other with little reference to the legal category.[7]

A few statistical studies have been made from the point of view of the sequential relations between crimes. Some years ago, the Austrian criminologist Grassberger made a study of the arrest records of habitual criminals in New York City which shows that the habitual criminal during his lifetime spreads his crimes over almost the entire field of illegality, and is not confined to a single specialty.[8] More recently, however, a Dutch study of all 21-year-old recidivists (three or more convictions) showed that 75 percent of all their offenses were in the same general category—property crimes, violence, sexual crimes, or traffic violations.[9] Frum found that 63 percent of 148 cases of adult recidivism began with some type of juvenile stealing, 23 percent with truancy or incorrigibility, 13 percent with drunk-vagrancy, and 1 percent with robbery.[10] It is often said that children with problems become "problem children," that these problem children become delinquents, and that these delinquents become criminal adults. But, as our discussion in earlier chapters has indicated, this common belief has not been adequately demonstrated. Studies of the careers of adult criminals show the importance of delinquency as a forerunner of adult crime,[11] but they do not show the immense proportion of delinquents who never reach criminal maturity and, hence, do not move into adult criminality.

The Gluecks treated the process of maturation from a different point of view. They regarded maturation as the underlying influence in reform. According to their conclusions, criminals become

[6] For an extended discussion of embezzlement, see Donald R. Cressey, *Other People's Money: A Study in the Social Psychology of Embezzlement* (Glencoe, Ill.: Free Press, 1953). Paperback edition issued by the Wadsworth Publishing Company, Belmont, Calif., 1971.

[7] See the discussion below, pp. 276-280.

[8] Roland Grassberger, "Gewerbs- und Berufsverbrechertum in den Vereinigten Staaten von Amerika," *Kriminologische Abhandlungen*, Vienna, No. 8, 1933.

[9] W. Buikhuisen and R. W. Jongman, "A Legalistic Classification of Juvenile Delinquents," *British Journal of Criminology*, 10:109-123, April, 1970; see also Julian B. Roebuck, *Criminal Typology* (Springfield, Ill.: Charles C Thomas, 1967).

[10] Harold S. Frum, "Adult Criminal Offense Trends Following Juvenile Delinquency," *Journal of Criminal Law, Criminology, and Police Science*, 49:29-49, May-June, 1958.

[11] President's Commission on Law Enforcement and Administration of Justice, *The Challenge of Crime in a Free Society* (Washington: Government Printing Office, 1967), p. 46.

law-abiding as they mature chronologically; this process of reformation practically stops at the age of thirty-five. They concluded further that those who pass the age of thirty-five and do not reform are much more frequently mental deviates. Thus their proposition was that age has a beneficent effect on those who are not mental deviates, so that they reform before the age of thirty-five; age has no such effect on the mental deviates, and they continue in crime thereafter.[12] The Gluecks reached this conclusion, however, by two very questionable methods: first, a definition of mental deviate so broad that it could be made to include all persons whatsoever; second, a comparison of persons of a given age-span in the first follow-up period with another group of persons of the same age-span in the second follow-up period, and from this drawing conclusions regarding the effect of age. •

Segregation

Segregation may be observed in the interaction between criminals and the public. The extent to which segregation occurs is determined largely by the hatred the group has for the criminal.[13] Sex offenders were completely ostracized in many communities two generations ago, much less completely now. The person with a prison record is still completely ostracized in most small communities and in many occupational groups, but he may become a political leader in larger communities. Thus segregation as a process does not apply universally to all criminals in all groups.

In some earlier societies, criminals lived entirely apart from law-abiding society, in remote regions from which they might issue to make raids upon travelers or householders. Today most criminals live in the midst of society, in certain areas of the cities, where they have developed a symbiotic relation with many kinds of businessmen. While known working-class criminals are segregated in slum areas, the portion of American society that used to be called the "underworld" has blended into the portion considered to be the respectable "upperworld." Nevertheless, admission to the company of thieves is still restricted. It may be secured only by those who have certain abilities, skills, and demeanors that make them acceptable to the criminal establishment. By the same token, persons who do not have other abilities, skills, and demeanors are segregated from the middle-class and upper-class society.

For example, while the leaders of American organized crime operate in collaboration with many so-called respectable businessmen and government officials, they have not been accepted into the social life of the suburban societies where they reside. By an exhibition of humility and understatement in social relationships, especially in relationships of power, they resist segre-

---

[12] Glueck and Glueck, *Later Criminal Careers*, chaps. 10-11.
[13] Pauline Morris, *Prisoners and Their Families* (London: Allen and Unwin, 1965).

gation. Before one Cosa Nostra boss went to prison in 1958, his wealth totalled between $20 million and $30 million. But he lived in a modest house, drove a two-year-old Ford, and owned not more than ten suits, none of which had been purchased for more than about a hundred dollars. He, like other organized crime leaders, followed a pattern set by American businessmen, whose methods and demeanor became smoother, more subtle, and more gentlemanly as they achieved some measure of success.[14] As Daniel Bell has put it:

> As American society became more "organized," as the American businessman became more "civilized" and less "buccaneering," so did the American racketeer. And just as there were important changes in the structure of business enterprise, so the "institutionalized" criminal enterprise was transformed too.[15]

But, taken as a group, American rulers of organized crime are still socially segregated. They once were geographically segregated, and they lived in tenement apartments, each in his own territory. But as their illicit businesses have expanded and become bureaucratized, as they have moved into legitimate businesses, and as the need for personal supervision and control has diminished, they have joined the move of respectable citizens to suburbs like Detroit's Grosse Point, New York's Westchester County, and Chicago's River Forest. Yet they are excluded from offices in civic improvement associations and in the parent-teacher associations, from sailing weekends and from debutante balls in these suburbs. Perhaps they are excluded not because they make their living in crime but because they do not have the social background and social graces which make them eligible to participate. One New York Cosa Nostra boss even went to a psychiatrist to try to overcome his inferiority feelings about his inadequacy in social situations. As such feelings are overcome among the organized crime leaders—as they gain more power, as they extend their influence to wider and wider circles of economic, political, and social activities—they probably will attain the self-confidence and poise necessary for complete assimilation by the "respectables." ●

Progressive conflict

Criminals and law-enforcement agents are engaged in continuous conflict. In this conflict each side tends to drive the other side to greater violence unless the conflict becomes stabilized, on a recognized level, as was the case in Great Britain for some years. In Britain police and criminals both went without guns, and the danger of death was practically eliminated. But now the criminals are

---

[14] See Donald R. Cressey, *Theft of the Nation: The Structure and Operations of Organized Crime in America* (New York: Harper and Row, 1969), pp. 214-220.

[15] Daniel Bell, "Crime as an American Way of Life," *Antioch Review*, 13:131-154, June, 1953. At p. 131.

beginning to arm themselves, and it is quite likely that before long the police will start shooting back, or shooting first.

When the police treat criminals violently, the criminals react violently when they have an opportunity. This spurs the police to greater violence, which again produces more violence by the criminals. It is not evident and perhaps makes no difference which side is responsible for the beginning of this process.

In American cities, for example, there has been progressive armament of both sides and progressive rapidity of shooting. Each side adopted the slogan "Shoot and shoot first." Each side felt that it was dangerous to give the other side a chance. This affected not only the police but also that part of the general public which was repeatedly victimized by criminals. The result was an increasing death rate on both sides.[16] Between about 1960 and 1970 the number of policemen killed by criminals and the number of criminals killed by policemen in the United States almost doubled. However, the *rate* of citizens killed by police probably was higher than the rate of policemen killed by citizens, for the number of policemen in the nation increased tremendously in the decade.

In the absence of settled traditions, this process of progressive conflict begins with arrest, which is interpreted as defining a person as an enemy of society, and which calls forth hostile reactions from representatives of society prior to and regardless of proof of guilt. It is not surprising that the arrested person reacts by further hostility. Thus, in areas where arrests are frequent, especially the ghetto residential areas of Negroes, a tradition of hostility has developed and is assimilated by many persons who have had no personal experiences with the procedures of arrest. During the last generation, as the police have found it necessary to deal with more and more driving offenders and, thus, with a wider and wider cross section of the society, rather widespread hostility toward the police has developed.[17] ●

Competitive development of technology

Both criminals and law-enforcement officers gradually adopt the relevant inventions of modern technology. In early days both proceeded on foot or horseback, then both used bicycles, and now automobiles, with the occasional use of an airplane. In the early days both used clubs as weapons, and now both use guns and chemical mace, with an occasional survival of the knife. Both use bulletproof vests and armored cars. Both, on some occasions, use tear-gas bombs and both may be equipped with gas masks. Kidnapers use adhesive tape, which was practically unknown fifty

---

[16] See Hans W. Mattick, *The Unexamined Death: An Analysis of Capital Punishment*, 2d ed. (Chicago: John Howard Association, 1966), p. 22.

[17] For a history and analysis of motoring offenses, see T. C. Willett, *Criminal on the Road* (London: Tavistock, 1964).

years ago even to physicians, to bind the eyes, mouth, and hands of victims.

When the police develop an invention for the detection or identification of criminals, the criminals utilize a device to protect themselves. When the police began to use the fingerprint technique, criminals began to wear gloves and to wipe surfaces that had been touched by them. The police utilized the radio to notify squad cars of the location of a crime being committed and to direct those cars in the pursuit of criminals. Well-equipped burglars now carry their own shortwave radio sets, tune them in while they are at work, and are informed of an alarm as quickly as are the police. The police are trying to develop selective devices for radio calls which will restrict the calls to police cars. As soon as such a device is "perfected," criminals will devise methods of overcoming it.

The history of the safe furnishes one of the best illustrations of this alternation of progress in the techniques of protection and of crime. Seventy-five years ago, the safe was locked with a key. Full-time safe-burglars learned how to pick these locks, and then the combination lock was invented. The criminals rigged a lever by means of which the whole spindle of the combination could be pulled out of the safe. When correction was made to prevent this, the burglars drilled holes in the safe and inserted gunpowder or dynamite. Then the manufacturers made the safe drill-proof, and the burglars secured harder drills with more powerful leverage. When the manufacturers used harder materials for the safe the clever burglars turned to nitroglycerine, which could be inserted in minute crevices around the door where powder and dynamite would not enter. Then safe-makers developed doors that fitted so perfectly that even nitroglycerine could not be inserted in the cracks. The burglars then adopted the oxyacetylene torch and turned it against the safe, and the manufacturers devised a compound which was proof against the torch.

Somewhere in this process, the burglars began to kidnap bankers and compel them to open the safe, regarding this as easier than mechanical methods of opening safes. To prevent this, the timelock was invented, so that the businessmen could not open their own safes until an appointed hour. Also, when the manufacturers made the safes difficult to open, the burglars hauled the safes away and opened them at their leisure. The manufacturers countered by making the safes too heavy to move, and banks installed night depositories so that businessmen would not have to leave money in their own small safes. The safe-makers experimented with safes which would release gas or great clouds of smoke when disturbed, and burglars then went equipped with gas masks. Some twenty years ago an electronic lock for safes was invented, but the inventor declared that within a short time someone certainly would design tools and devices to pick it. The thermic lance burner, an extraordinarily powerful cutting tool, has recently put the safe-makers on the defensive.

Bank robbery and defense against this crime also show competitive technological trends. For example, small task forces of criminals organized themselves to take advantage of the newly developed automobile before police departments did. In Chicago, especially, criminals jumped in a car, roared into nearby states, robbed a bank and then roared back into Chicago while the local police, still riding bicycles, were pedalling toward the scene of the crime. As soon as the police became technologically and organizationally equal to these bank robbers, the robbers were out of business. Secret pushbuttons to call the police or guards were developed, but bank robbers then took hostages. Also, secret pushbuttons to release tear gas were utilized, but the robbers defended against them. When efforts were made to secure automatic photographs of the scene in order to identify the robbers, the criminals put on masks. When the protective devices against both burglary and robbery became well developed in the larger banks, robbers turned to the smaller banks, which could not afford such expensive equipment. And as the smaller banks improved their protective devices, the criminals directed their attacks against business firms which did not have adequate protection, and the competitive process started all over again. For example, American supermarkets became a prime target for organized robbers, partly because they began providing a payroll-check cashing service. When the robbers returned to the banks, the bankers—who had learned to insure themselves against robbery—more or less gave up. Now many banks simply hand a small sum to any robber that comes in and demands it, and the bank robbery rate has risen enormously as a result. ●

**Fashions
in crime**

Certain types of crimes have disappeared almost entirely. This has generally been due to changes in economic and social conditions, rather than to improved law-enforcement techniques or protective devices. Piracy has practically disappeared, and its disappearance was due to the development of steamships, which were too large and fast for attack by pirates. Train robberies of the type in which a train was stopped and the mail car and the passengers were robbed have been discontinued, but this kind of attack is now sometimes made on bus passengers. Cattle stealing in the form of driving away a herd has ceased, but for it has been substituted the loading of two or three cattle into a truck and delivering them to the city. Robbery of bus drivers has disappeared in cities that require passengers to have exact change, which drops into a strongbox. Prostitution in the form of residential houses has all but disappeared in American cities as job opportunities for women have opened up, as immigration of large numbers of single men has diminished, and as sex standards have changed in such a way that the services of prostitutes are no longer in great demand.

In addition, however, the type and method of crime vary in

ways which closely resemble fashion in other affairs. A criminal makes an attack on a gambling place, and within a short time dozens of other gambling places are attacked. Some criminal selects a hotel for robbery, and quickly dozens of other hotels are robbed. A pickpocket secures a thousand dollars in a certain railway station, and the other pickpockets flock to that station. A wanted criminal hijacks an airplane to Cuba, and the airlines soon have a hijacking problem of serious dimensions. A criminal makes an unusually successful gain by a method which was not customary; other criminals try the method. In recent years, robbery of banks by lone wolf criminals who demand the money in the cash drawer of a teller seems to have become fashionable. •

There is a broad range of informal and formal organization among criminals.[18] One kind of organization is simply a stabilized pattern of interaction based on similarities of interests and attitudes, and on mutual aid. Street-corner groups of delinquents are organizations of this kind. These groups have their own standards, attitudes, and public opinion, an effective system of communication, the shared danger of arrest and incarceration, the common experience of having lived in jail, and common attitudes about outsiders. In other cases, organization means a particular set of roles that has come to be seen as serving express purposes by the persons playing the roles. Such organizations allocate specific tasks to members, limit entrance, and establish rules for their own maintenance and survival. As organizations move from the first form to the second form they become "formal" organizations rather than "informal" organizations.

Organization of criminals

Formal organizations have three characteristics. First, a division of labor is present. This means that there is occupational specialization, with each specialty fitting into the whole. Second, the activities of each person in the system are coordinated with the activities of other participants by means of rules, agreements, and understandings which support the division of labor. Third, the entire enterprise is rationally designed to achieve announced objectives.[19]

These features are matters of degree. Among criminal organizations, the degree to which they are present affects the character of the crimes perpetrated. The criminal tribes of India, the bandits of pre-Communist China, the brigands of southeastern Europe, the smugglers in America and in many European countries in the last

---

[18] Parts of this section are adapted from Donald R. Cressey, *Theft of the Nation*, and from Donald R. Cressey, "The Functions and Structure of Criminal Syndicates," appendix A in President's Commission on Law Enforcement and Administration of Justice, *Task Force Report: Organized Crime* (Washington: Government Printing Office, 1967), pp. 25-60.

[19] See S. J. Udy, Jr., "The Comparative Analysis of Organizations," chap. 6 in James G. March, ed., *Handbook of Organizations* (Chicago: Rand McNally, 1965), p. 687.

century, the Ku Klux Klan, vigilante groups, and feuding families engaged in guerrilla warfare were earlier forms of organized crime. The contemporary Sicilian Mafia also constitutes a formal organization.[20] And the geographically based Cosa Nostra "families"[21] of criminals of Italian-Sicilian descent now operating in the United States fall on the "formal-organization" end of the continuum. Each "family" has formal positions for "boss," "soldiers," and other functionaries, to be described later, and each "family" has a position in the larger cartel and confederation called "the Family," "Cosa Nostra," "the syndicate," "the Mafia," or, simply, "organized crime." Members' organizational activities are tightly coordinated and controlled, not only by the structure itself, but also by a criminal code, the values and rules of which govern many of the interpersonal relationships in which members engage off the job.

Small groups, organized for the execution of a particular type of crime, have existed for centuries. Small criminal groups that operated in England in the Elizabethan period have been described in some detail.[22] Similar groups exist today for the purpose of burglary, robbery, shoplifting, confidence games, picking pockets, and stealing automobiles. Some of these groups have become "professionalized," a process to be described in the next section, and in the next chapter.

These small working groups of criminal and delinquent gangs lie somewhere between the informal organization of street-corner groups and the formal organization of units like Cosa Nostra. They have divisions of labor based on the requirements of specific team operations, but controls over job responsibilities and daily activities are not as extensive or as precise as they are in the Sicilian Mafia or the American Cosa Nostra. For example, the fundamental form of organization among pickpockets is the "troupe," "tribe," or "team" of two, three, or four members. The relationships between the men occupying the positions making up the troupe are "loose, ephemeral, and highly insecure," but there is organization nevertheless.[23] The duties and responsibilities of each position are finely detailed. There is, for example, a position for a criminal whose duty it is to locate the prospective victim and distract his attention. A second position calls for a specialist skilled in actually removing the wallet from the victim's pocket.

---

[20] See Norman Lewis, *The Honored Society* (New York: Putnam, 1964); Luigi Barzini, *The Italians* (New York, Atheneum, 1964); and Robert T. Anderson, "From Mafia to Cosa Nostra," *American Journal of Sociology,* 71:302-310, November, 1965.

[21] Because the "families" are fictive, in the sense that members are not all blood relatives, it is necessary to refer to them in quotation marks.

[22] A. V. Judges, *The Elizabethan Underworld* (London: Routledge, 1930); see also Mary McIntosh, "Changes in the Organization of Thieving," in Stanley Cohen, ed., *Images of Deviance* (Hammondsworth: Penguin, 1971), pp. 98-133.

[23] David W. Maurer, *Whiz Mob: A Correlation of the Technical Argot of Pickpockets with Their Behavior Patterns* (Gainesville, Fla.: American Dialect Society, 1955), p. 84.

A third position requires skills in receiving the wallet or other goods from the man who took it. And a fourth position involves disposal of the stolen goods in legitimate, semilegitimate, or illegitimate channels. The men who fill these positions, even temporarily, are specialists. As in any legitimate organization, a variety of skills is required for effective operations.

"Organization," whether it be that of a working group of criminals, of a legitimate corporation, or of a criminal cartel, means rationality. As the third point (above) suggests, any organization worthy of the name is an apparatus rationally designed to accomplish announced objectives. Among small working groups of criminals, as among syndicated criminals, the objective is to perpetrate offenses which are relatively safe while at the same time profitable. Working groups of criminals, and Cosa Nostra units can be differentiated from juvenile gangs and other less formal criminal groups by the fact that the members of the latter do not participate in a specialized set of positions rationally developed with an eye to efficiency and continuing operations.

The rationality behind the operations of working groups of criminals can be observed in three different contexts.[24] First, the crimes committed by teams of criminals tend to be those whose nature makes it difficult to apprehend and prosecute the perpetrators. Second, the divisions of labor are such that all incumbents must be skilled in the use of techniques which in combination make the whole group's work safe and, therefore, profitable. Third, rational organization for safety and profit is indicated in some, but not all, working groups of criminals by the establishment of at least one position for a "corrupter" and one or more positions for "corruptees." The corruptee position is occupied by public officials who, for a fee, will insure that the group can operate with relative immunity from the penal process. It is as much a part of the criminal organization as any other position.

Syndicated crime is a system based on a further extension of this rational design for safety and profit. Although it is true that the division of labor in the Sicilian Mafia and in Cosa Nostra has been designed for the perpetration of crimes which cannot be perpetrated profitably by small working groups of criminals, let alone by criminals working outside an organization, the critical difference is not merely a difference in size. Small firms selling illicit goods and services must, if they are to capitalize on the great demand for their wares, expand by establishing a division of labor which includes positions for financiers, purchasing agents, supervisors, transportation specialists, lawyers, accountants, and employee-training specialists. The next rational move is consolidation and integration of separate divisions of labor into a cartel designed to minimize competition and maximize profits. Such a monopolistic move is, of course, a rational decision for peaceful

---

[24] See Edwin H. Sutherland, *The Professional Thief* (Chicago: University of Chicago Press, 1937), pp. 217-218.

coexistence. As such, it necessarily involves governmental considerations as well as business considerations. This is the contemporary form of Cosa Nostra.

Investigations of American organized crime

Some criminals, law-enforcement officials, political figures, and plain citizens know from experience that a nationwide cartel and confederation of criminals was established in the United States in 1931 and that it is more powerul today than it ever has been. Some of them have denied the existence of the apparatus because they are members of it. Others have denied its existence because they profit from it. As the Kefauver Committee concluded in 1951, "The money used by hoodlums to buy economic and political control is also used to induce public apathy."[25] But honest officials have for over thirty years been trying to convince the American public that a nationwide alliance does in fact, exist. These men, who are mostly law-enforcement officers, prosecutors, and congressional investigators, know that the activities of organized crime are threatening the foundations of American economic, political, and legal order.

The Cosa Nostra syndicate grew out of the gangs organized to meet the demand for illicit alcohol during the period of national prohibition. Almost from the first, the manufacture, distribution, and sale of prohibited alcohol was in the hands of organized groups, rather than of isolated individuals. There were many such groups, at first organized on a neighborhood or ethnic basis. With increasing competition, violent warfare broke out, some of the smaller units were fused together into larger units, and these larger units then were fused into loosely organized syndicates.[26] The process was exactly the same as in legitimate business, though the methods inclined more to violence and less to fraud than in legitimate business. While the syndicates were using warnings, destruction of property, and murder as means of stifling competition, law-enforcement agents, acting under orders of political leaders, were harassing new manufacturers or dealers who tried to enter the liquor business.

For a considerable part of the period of national prohibition, the leading manufacturer of alcohol was in charge of enforcing the law against illicit manufacture and sale of alcohol. Nevertheless, the syndicated organizations were never secure, and a true nationwide alliance never really developed. Subordinates were ambitious, and some of the gangs were rebellious. Since the entire business was illegal, control depended finally on violence. Near the end of the prohibition period, the basic framework of the current structure of organized crime was established as the final product of a series of "gangland wars" in which an alliance of

---

[25] Special Committee to Investigate Crime in Interstate Commerce (Kefauver Committee), *Third Interim Report* (U.S. Senate Report No. 307, 82d Congress, 1st Session, 1951), p. 174.

[26] See Cressey, *Theft of the Nation*, pp. 29-53.

Italians and Sicilians first conquered other groups, then fought each other. A decision for peaceful coexistence was made in 1931, and that decision, which amounted to a peace treaty, has determined the shape of American organized crime ever since. When the period of national prohibition ended, Cosa Nostra moved into other illicit fields.

Members of Cosa Nostra now control all but a tiny part of the illegal gambling in the United States. They are the principal usurers (loan sharks), and the principal importers and wholesalers of narcotics. They have infiltrated certain labor unions, where they extort money from the employers and, at the same time, cheat the members of the union. The members have a virtual monopoly on some legitimate enterprises, such as cigarette vending machines and jukeboxes, and they own a wide variety of legitimate retail firms, restaurants and bars, hotels, trucking companies, food companies, linen-supply houses, garbage collection routes, and factories. They have corrupted officials in the legislative, executive, and judicial branches of government at the local, state, and federal levels.

One of the earliest warnings that a nationwide crime apparatus exists was made by a defector. In a series of articles appearing in 1939, the former attorney for an illicit New York organization, a man who had occupied a position of "corrupter" for the organization, observed that a nationwide alliance between criminal businesses in the United States was in operation. While in jail he wrote an exposé of political corruption and crime in New York and also made the observation about the nationwide alliance. This was not the first time such an observation was made, but it dramatically foreshadowed statements which have been made in more recent years.

When I speak of the underworld now, I mean something far bigger than the Schultz mob. The Dutchman was one of the last independent barons to hold out against a general centralization of control which had been going on ever since Charlie Lucky became leader of the Unione Siciliana in 1931. . . . The "greasers" in the Unione were killed off, and the organization was no longer a loose, fraternal order of Sicilian black handers and alcohol cookers, but rather the framework for a system of alliances which were to govern the underworld. In Chicago, for instance, the Unione no longer fought the Capone mob, but pooled strength and worked with it. . . . It still numbers among its members many old-time Sicilians who are not gangsters, but anybody who goes into it today is a mobster, and an important one. In New York City the organization is split up territorially into districts, each led by a minor boss, known as the "*compare*," or godfather. . . . I know that throughout the underworld the Unione Siciliana is accepted as a mysterious, all-pervasive reality, and that Lucky used it as the vehicle by which the underworld was drawn into cooperation on a national scale.[27]

More than a decade after this statement appeared in a popular magazine of the time, many members of the public (and some

---

[27] J. Richard Davis, "Things I Couldn't Tell Till Now," *Collier's*, July 22, July 29, August 12, August 19, and August 26, 1939. The quote is from pp. 35-36 of the August 19 issue.

law-enforcement officers) still had no notion that an illicit cartel both performed and controlled some types of crime across the nation. If they heard of "the Mafia," or "the syndicate," or "the outfit," or "the mob," or "the brotherhood," or "the *fratellanza*," they did not believe what they heard, or did not believe it affected them. But the Kefauver Committee in 1951 was able to draw the following four conclusions from the testimony of some eight hundred witnesses who appeared before it:

(1) There is a Nation-wide crime syndicate known as the Mafia, whose tentacles are found in many large cities. It has international ramifications which appear most clearly in connection with the narcotics traffic.

(2) Its leaders are usually found in control of the most lucrative rackets in their cities.

(3) There are indications of a centralized direction and control of these rackets, but leadership appears to be in a group rather than in a single individual.

(4) The Mafia is the cement that helps to bind the Costello-Adonis-Lansky syndicate of New York and the Accardo-Guzik-Fischetti syndicate of Chicago as well as smaller criminal gangs and individual criminals throughout the country. These groups have kept in touch with Luciano since his deportation from this country.[28]

In the next decade, investigating bodies were able to overcome some of the handicaps of the Kefauver Committee, which "found it difficult to obtain reliable data concerning the extent of Mafia operation, the nature of Mafia organization, and the way it presently operates."[29] While *all* such handicaps will not be overcome for some years to come, there no longer is any doubt that several regional organizations, rationally constructed for the control of the sale of illicit goods and services, are in operation. Neither is there any doubt that these regional organizations are linked together by understandings and agreements.

Another series of investigations was set off in 1957, when at least seventy-five of the nation's criminal cartel leaders were discovered at a meeting in Apalachin, New York. They came from many parts of the country, and most of them had criminal records relating to the kind of offense customarily called "organized crime." At least twenty-three came from New York City or New Jersey, nineteen from upstate New York, eight from the Midwest, three from the West, and two from the South. At least two "delegates" were from Cuba, and one was from Italy. No one has been able to prove the nature of the conspiracy involved at Apalachin, but no one believes that the men all just happened to drop in on the host at the same time. Two of the men attending the meeting had met at a somewhat similar meeting of criminals in Cleveland in 1928. The Italian police revealed early in 1968 that some of them also attended a 1957 meeting in a Sicilian motel.

Discovery of the Apalachin meeting stimulated increased investigative action by the United States Attorney General, the Federal

---

[28] Kefauver Committee, *Third Interim Report*, p. 150.
[29] Ibid., p. 150.

Bureau of Narcotics, the Federal Bureau of Investigation, the Internal Revenue Service, and several state and local agencies.

Beginning about 1961, these investigating agencies began to receive intelligence information about the existence of the criminal confederation now commonly labeled "Cosa Nostra," a large-scale criminal organization complete with a commission, a hierarchical structure extending down to the street level of criminal activity. The McClellan Committee in 1963 portrayed this syndicate to a nationwide television audience.[30] Once again, a considerable number of citizens had forgotten, or had never heard, the information on organized crime presented to them over a period of thirty years. They were shocked and surprised when they heard Joseph Valachi, an active member of the confederation, describe the skeletal structure of the organization, its operations, and its membership. The basic points in Mr. Valachi's testimony have now been validated by a wide variety of law-enforcement agencies.[31]

Valachi used the name "Cosa Nostra" when describing the confederation. While it continues to be called the Mafia or the syndicate in some parts of the country, both members and law-enforcement officers now use the "Cosa Nostra" title. Extensive investigations and studies of the structure of Cosa Nostra justify the conclusion that it is indeed an organization, with both formal and informal aspects. When there are specialized but integrated positions for a board of directors, presidents, vice presidents, staff specialists, works managers, foremen, and workers, there is an economic organization. When there are specialized but integrated positions for legislators, judges, and administrators of criminal justice, there is a political organization. Cosa Nostra has both kinds of positions, making it both a business organization and a government. Further, Cosa Nostra exists independently of its current personnel, as does any big business or government. Business, government, and Cosa Nostra go on despite complete turnover in the personnel occupying the various positions making up the organization. If a president, vice president, or some other functionary resigns or dies, another person is recruited to fill the vacant position. No man is indispensable. Organization, or structure, not persons, gives Cosa Nostra its self-perpetuating character.

The highest ruling body in the confederation is the "commission." This body serves as a combination legislature, supreme court, and arbitration board, with some functions of a board of business directors thrown in for good measure, but most of its functions are judicial. Members look to the commission as the ultimate authority on organizational disputes. It is made up of

The structural skeleton

---

[30] Permanent Subcommittee on Investigations of the Senate Committee on Government Operations, *Organized Crime and Illicit Traffic in Narcotics* (U.S. Senate, 88th Congress, 1st Session, 1963, 1964, 1965).

[31] See Peter Maas, *The Valachi Papers* (New York: Putnam, 1968).

the rulers of the most powerful of the twenty-four Cosa Nostra "families," the name given to a geographical unit of the organization. From nine to twelve men usually sit on the commission. The commission is not a representative body, and its members do not regard each other as equals.

Beneath the commission are twenty-four "families," each with its "boss." The "family" is the most significant level of organization and the largest unit of criminal organization in which allegiance is owed to one man, the boss. (Italian words often are used interchangeably with each of the English words designating a position in the division of labor. Rather than "boss," the words *il capo, don,* and *rappresentante* are used.) The boss's primary function is to maintain order while at the same time maximizing profits. Subject to the possibility of being overruled by the commission, his authority is absolute. He is the final arbiter in all matters relating to his branch of the confederation.

Beneath each boss of at least the larger "families," is an "underboss," or *sottocapo*. This position is, essentially, that of vice president and deputy director of the "family" unit. The man occupying the position often collects information for the boss; he relays messages to him; and he passes his orders down to the men occupying positions below him in the hierarchy. He acts as boss in the absence of the boss.

On the same level as the underboss there is a position for a "counselor" or adviser. Such members are referred to as *consiglieri* or *consulieri*. The person occupying this position is a staff officer rather than a line officer. He is likely to be an elder member who is partially retired after a career in which he did not quite succeed in becoming a boss. He gives advice to "family" members, including the boss and underboss, and he therefore enjoys considerable influence and power.

Also at about the same level as the underboss is a "buffer" position. The top members of the "family" hierarchy, particularly the boss, avoid direct communication with the lower-echelon personnel, the workers. They are insulated from the police. To obtain this insulation, all commands, information, money, and complaints generally flow back and forth through the buffer, who is a trusted and clever go-between. However, the buffer does not make decisions or assume any of the authority of his boss, as the underboss does.

To reach the working level, a boss usually goes through channels. For example, a boss's decision on the settlement of a dispute involving the activities of the "runners" (ticket sellers) in a particular numbers lottery game, passes first to his buffer, then to the next level of rank, which is "lieutenant" or *capodecina* or *caporegima*. This position, considered from a business standpoint, is analogous to works manager or sales manager. The person occupying it is the chief of an operating unit. The term *lieutenant* gives the position a military flavor. Although *capodecina* is translated as "head of ten," there apparently is no settled number of men supervised by any given lieutenant. The number of such leaders in an organization varies with the size of the organization and with the specialized activities in that organization. The lieutenant usually has one or two associates who work closely with him, serving as messengers and buffers. They carry orders, information, and money back and forth between the lieutenant and the men belonging to his regime. They do not share the lieutenant's administrative power.

Beneath the lieutenants there might be one or more "section chiefs." Messages and orders received from the boss's buffer by the lieutenant or his buffer are passed on to a section chief, who also may have a buffer. A section chief may be deputy lieutenant. He is in charge of a section of the lieutenant's operations. In smaller "families," the position of lieutenant and the position of section chief are combined. In general, the larger the regime the stronger the power of the section chief. Since it is against the law to consort for criminal purposes, it is advantageous to cut down the number of individuals who are directly responsible to any given line supervisor.

About five "soldiers," "buttons," or just "members" report to each section chief or, if there is no section chief position, to a lieutenant. The number of soldiers in a "family" varies; some "families" have as many as six hundred members, some as few as twenty. A soldier might operate an illicit enterprise for a boss, on a commission basis, or he might "own" the enterprise and pay homage to the boss for "protection," the right to operate. Partnerships between two or more soldiers, and between soldiers and men higher up in the hierarchy, including bosses, are common. An "enterprise" could be a usury operation, a dice game, a lottery, a bookie operation, a smuggling operation, or a vending machine company. Some soldiers and most upper-echelon "family" members have interests in more than one business.

"Family" membership ends at the soldier level, and all members are of Italian or Sicilian descent. About five thousand men are members of "families" and, hence, of the confederation. But beneath the soldiers in the hierarchy of operations are large numbers of employees and commission agents who are not necessarily of Italian-Sicilian descent, although some of them are Italian-Sicilian aspirants. These are the persons carrying on most of the work "on the street." They have no "buffers" or other forms of insulation from the police. They are the relatively unskilled workmen who actually take bets, answer telephones, drive trucks, sell narcotics, etc. In Chicago, for example, the workers in a major lottery business operated in a Negro neighborhood were Negroes; the bankers for the lottery were Japanese-Americans; but the game, including the banking operation, was licensed, for a fee, by a "family" member. The entire operation, including the bankers, was more or less a "customer" of the Chicago "family," in the way any legitimate enterprise operating under a franchise is a "customer" of the parent corporation.

The authority structure sketched out above constitutes the "organizational chart" of Cosa Nostra as it is described by its members. Three things are missing. First, there is no description of the many organizational positions necessary to actual street-level operation of illicit enterprises such as bookmaking establishments and lotteries. As indicated, many of the positions in such enterprises are occupied by persons who are not Cosa Nostra members. Second, and more important, the structure described is primarily only the "official" organization, such as that which might be described by the organizational chart of a legitimate corporation. Cosa Nostra informants have not described, probably because they have not been asked to do so, the many "unofficial" positions any organization must contain. To put the matter in another way, there is no description of the many functional roles performed by the men occupying the formally established positions making up the organization. Third, Third, the structure as described by members is the structure of membership roles, not of the relationships between members and indispensable outsiders like street-level workers, attorneys, accountants, tax experts, and corrupt public officials.[32] These outsiders play roles in organized crime, even if they are not members of a criminal organization.

Corruption of law-enforcement and political systems

Cosa Nostra functions as an illegal and almost-invisible government. However, its political objective is not competition with the established agencies of legitimate government. It is not interested in political and economic reform. Its political objective is a negative one: nullification of government.

Nullification is sought at two different levels. At the lower level are the agencies for law enforcement and the administration of criminal justice. When a Cosa Nostra soldier bribes a policeman, a police chief, a prosecutor, a judge, or a license administrator, he does so in an attempt to nullify the law-enforcement process. At the upper level are legislative agencies, including federal and state legislatures as well as city councils and county boards of supervisors. When a "family" boss supports a candidate for political office, he does so in an attempt to deprive honest citizens of their democratic voice, thus nullifying the democratic process.

The two levels are not discrete. Cosa Nostra members engage in all seven forms of corruption outlined in the previous chapter. If an elected official can be persuaded not to represent the honest citizens of his district on matters pertaining to the interests of organized criminals, he is, at the same time, persuaded that he should help insure that some laws are not enforced, or are enforced selectively. When the political "representative" of a district works to prevent the passing of laws which would damage Cosa Nostra but help honest citizens, the political process

---

[32] For these details, see Cressey, *Theft of the Nation*, pp. 126-185.

has been nullified. But when the same "representative" is paid by criminals to block appropriations for law-enforcement agencies which would fight organized crime, to block the promotion of policemen who create "embarrassing incidents" by enforcing antigambling statutes, and to use his political position to insure that dishonest or stupid administrators of criminal justice are appointed, he is being paid to nullify the law-enforcement process. The American Bar Association's *Report on Organized Crime* concluded, "The largest single factor in the breakdown of law enforcement dealing with organized crime is the corruption and connivance of many public officials."[33] Similarly, the President's Commission concluded, "All available data indicate that organized crime flourishes only where it has corrupted local officials."[34] The operations of organized crime should not be referred to as the operations of the "underworld." The activities of Cosa Nostra members are so interwoven with the activities of respectable businessmen and government officials that doing so directs our attention to the wrong places.

Every Cosa Nostra "family" has in its division of labor at least one position for a corrupter. The person occupying this position bribes, buys, intimidates, threatens, negotiates, and sweet-talks himself into a relationship with police, public officials, and anyone else who might help "family" members maintain immunity from arrest, prosecution, and punishment. The corrupter is not depicted on the organizational charts which informants and others have sketched out as they have described Cosa Nostra's hierarchy, from commissioner to soldier. It is an essential, but "unofficial," functional position, like buffer. It might be occupied by a person who is a soldier, a lieutenant, an underboss, or even a boss. Most frequently, a corrupter position is occupied by the *consigliere*, or counselor.

Although tenure in the role of corrupter is not permanent, it tends to be lengthy. Once a corrupter has established his relationships and connections, it is not easy for a boss to assign another person to the position. Moreover, there is a distinct advantage in centralizing corruption functions in a few positions. A soldier who discovers, perhaps accidentally, that a policeman or public official has a weakness which makes him a likely target of corruption is not allowed to make the bribe or exert the influence himself. In the first place, he might botch the job. In the second place, he might simply have located a man who is already on the payroll. The soldier with ideas merely reports them to a corrupter, who can work the potential dishonesty into the broad scheme of things, including his network of corruptees.

Yet the corrupting functions of a "family" are seldom centralized in a single position. Ordinarily, one corrupter takes care of

---

[33] *Report on Organized Crime* (New York: American Bar Association, 1952), p. 16.

[34] *Task Force Report: Organized Crime,* p. 6.

one subdivision of government, such as the police or city hall, while another is assigned a different subdivision, such as the state alcoholic beverage commission. A third corrupter might handle the court system by fixing a judge, a clerk of court, a prosecutor, an assistant prosecutor, a probation officer. It depends on who you know, and who knows you.

For every corrupter, there must be at least one corruptee. Most corrupt policemen and public officials have been sought out and wooed to a position of corruptee. Men must be recruited and selected for this position just as they must be recruited and selected for a position such as bookmaker or lieutenant. While the officials occupying corruptee positions are not ordinarily members of Cosa Nostra, their positions are part of organized crime's division of labor, just as are low-level positions for street workers. Occasionally, a corrupter does not have to recruit a public official to a corruptee position because the corrupter's "family" has, with the help of the corrupter, recruited him in advance and put him in office.

Demand, supply, and profit

Cosa Nostra, its allies, and its subsidiaries thrive in the United States because a large minority of citizens demands the illicit goods and services they have for sale. As Walter Lippmann observed at the end of the prohibition era, the basic distinction between ordinary criminals and organized criminals in the United States turns on the fact that the ordinary criminal is wholly predatory, while the man participating in crime on a rational, systematic basis offers a return to the respectable members of society.[35] If all burglars were miraculously abolished, they would be missed by only a few persons to whose income or employment they contribute directly—burglary insurance companies, manufacturers of locks and other security devices, police, prison personnel, and a few others. But if the establishment of men employed in illicit businesses were suddenly abolished, it would be sorely missed because it performs services for which there is a great public demand. The organized criminal, by definition, occupies a position in a social system, an "organization," which has been rationally designed to maximize profits by performing illegal services and providing legally-forbidden products demanded by the members of the broader society in which he lives. Just as society has made a place for the confederation by demanding illicit gambling, alcohol and narcotics, usurious loans, and a cheap supply of labor, the confederation has made places, in an integrated set of positions, for the use of the skills of a wide variety of specialists who furnish these goods and services.

It is true, of course, that criminals who do not occupy positions in any large-scale organization also supply the same kinds of

---

[35] Walter Lippmann, "Underworld: Our Secret Servant," and "The Underworld: A Stultified Conscience," *Forum*, 85:1-4 and 65-69, January and February, 1931.

illicit goods and services supplied by the confederation. A gray-haired old lady who accepts a few horse-racing bets from the patrons of her neighborhood grocery store performs an illegal service for those patrons, just as does the factory worker who sells his own brand of whiskey to friends at the plant. Law violators of this kind do not seem very dangerous and, if treated in isolation, such persons cannot be perceived as much of a threat to the social order. Accordingly, they tend to be protected in various ways by their society. The policeman is inclined to overlook the bookmaker's offenses or merely to insist that they not occur in his precinct, the judge is likely to invoke the mildest punishment the legislature has established, and the jailer is likely to differentiate such offenders from "real criminals."

But such providers of illegal services cannot be individual entrepreneurs for long. The nature of the illegal lottery and bookmaking business is such that bookmakers must join hands with others in the same business. Bookmakers and lottery operators are organized to insure that *making* bets is gambling but *taking* bets is not. Other illicit businesses have the same character. Free enterprise does not exist in the field of illicit services and goods—any small illicit business must soon take in, voluntarily or involuntarily, a Cosa Nostra man as a partner.

By joining hands, the suppliers of illicit goods and services (1) cut costs, improve their markets, and pool capital; (2) gain monopolies on certain of the illicit services or on all of the illicit services provided in a specific geographic area, whether it be a neighborhood or a large city; (3) centralize the procedures for stimulating the agencies of law enforcement and administration of justice to overlook the illegal operations; and (4) accumulate vast wealth which can be used to attain even wider monopolies on illicit activities, and on legal businesses as well. In the long run, then, the "small operation" corrupts the traditional economic and political procedures designed to insure that citizens need not pay tribute to a criminal in order to conduct a legitimate business. The demand, and the profits, are too great to be left in the hands of small operators. As the Kefauver Committee reported about the demand for gambling services, "The creeping paralysis of law enforcement which results from a failure to enforce gambling laws contributes to a breakdown in connection with other fields of crime."[36] Organization, not gambling or usury or narcotics distribution or labor racketeering or extortion or murder, is the phenomenon to worry about.

The American demand for illicit goods and services produces huge Cosa Nostra profits, which are then invested in legitimate enterprises in politics. Robert F. Kennedy made the following statement while he was attorney general of the United States: "What is at least disturbing—and for me insidious—is the increasing encroachment of the big businessmen of the rackets into

---

[36] Kefauver Committee, *Third Interim Report*, p. 37.

legitimate business."[37] Cosa Nostra members have been, and are, acquiring and operating legitimate enterprises, ranging from Las Vegas casinos to huge corporations. Moreover, some of them have deposited huge sums in Swiss banks, and they draw on these fruits of crime whenever they want to buy or corrupt another large piece of America.

The business interests of the men attending the 1957 meeting in Apalachin, New York, probably are representative of the kinds of legitimate businesses which have been acquired by organized criminals everywhere. It should be noted, however, that no one has learned the extent of the concealed business interests held even by the Apalachin conferees. Besides their illicit businesses, at least nine of them were in the coin-machine business; sixteen were in the garment industry; ten owned grocery stores; seventeen owned bars or restaurants; eleven were in the olive oil and cheese importing business; nine were in the construction business. Others were involved in automobile agencies, coal companies, entertainment, funeral homes, ownership of horses and race tracks, linen and laundry enterprises, trucking, waterfront activities, and bakeries.

The principal operations of organized criminals are not independent of each other. Bet-taking, usury, narcotics distribution, labor fraud and extortion, corruption of government, and control of legitimate businesses all go together. Legitimate interests serve as an outlet for the vast amounts of money acquired illegitimately and also provide a tax cover. With the aid of lawyers and accountants, some of whom have done a tour of duty as employees of the Internal Revenue Service, members of Cosa Nostra now insure that it is extremely difficult to catch them in income tax evasion. Ownership of legitimate enterprises creates an aura of respectability. Moreover, by investing in legitimate businesses the profits of illicit businesses, the member is able to make his money, which is the fruit of crime and therefore contraband, earn more money. When the contraband money is invested in legitimate businesses, it is almost impossible to trace it to its criminal source. ●

Professionalization

The term *professional* when applied to a criminal refers to the following things: the pursuit of crime as a regular, day-by-day occupation, the development of skilled techniques and careful planning in that occupation, and status among criminals.[38] The professional criminal is differentiated from the occasional criminal, the amateur criminal, the unskilled and careless criminal,

---

[37] Permanent Subcommittee on Investigations, *Organized Crime and Illicit Traffic in Narcotics,* 1963, p. 12.

[38] Reckless has used essentially the same criteria to differentiate "career criminals." Walter C. Reckless, *The Crime Problem,* 4th ed. (New York: Appleton-Century-Crofts, 1967), pp. 287-318. See also Don C. Gibbons, *Society, Crime, and Criminal Careers* (Englewood Cliffs, N.J.: Prentice-Hall, 1968), pp. 245-252.

and the organized criminal. The term *profession* does not carry with it the ideal of public service which is supposed to be characteristic of the legitimate professions, but the professional criminal argues that the ideal of public service is no more developed in the legal profession than in the criminal profession.

Certain types of crimes can be committed without previous experience in crime. Murder by shooting, for instance, may be committed by a person who has no previous experience in murder, and even if he has no experience in shooting. Most crimes, however, require training. Boys in high delinquency areas are taught how to commit thefts of various kinds. The boy who moves into an area at, say, the age of ten years without previous experience in stealing has to learn many criminal techniques and attitudes in order to keep his new-found friends. The other boys show him how to steal articles from department stores, how to steal from a truck, how to steal an automobile. The training extends to knowledge of methods of behavior in case one is caught, knowledge of when to cry and when not to cry, what types of lies to tell the police or the court. Although, from the standpoint of the mature professional criminal, such devices are on a relatively crude and low plane, as is the work of the older amateur burglars and robbers, the criminal maturation of such criminals is much greater than that of episodic offenders such as murderers, embezzlers, and rapists.

Professional theft is a rational extension of this training. Each professional criminal has a highly skilled occupation. At one time the safecracker stood at the head of the criminal professions, for his skill was unusually great, and his plans had to be made with unusual care.[39] Thieves whose occupation requires both manual skill and skill in social manipulation also have high status. These include pickpockets, shoplifters, and confidence men. The crime of picking pockets requires manual skill, but it also requires occupational specialization within a working group and ability to manipulate victims. Most shoplifting is of the casual amateur kind, but some of it involves the use of highly skilled techniques, including social skills which enable the thief to give store clerks the impression that he is a regular customer. The confidence games are based essentially on salesmanship, and they often involve convincing the victim that he should engage in what he thinks is an illegitimate manipulation.[39]

The rationality of a criminal profession extends beyond acquisition of the manual and social skills necessary for executing the crime itself. It includes planning, prior location of spots and victims, and prior preparation for avoiding punishment in case of detection. Arrangements are made in advance for bail, legal services, and fixing the case. It is the rational system for making

---

[39] Bill Chambliss, ed., *Box Man.*

these arrangements, as well as the use of technical skills, which distinguishes professional thieves from ordinary thieves. Yet in professional crime the rationality does not expand to the point where a syndicate is developed, as in organized crime.

Professional thieves, like Cosa Nostra members and other criminals, follow specialized codes of behavior. The codes are not the same for all types of crime or all types of criminals. There are, however, two very general rules. One is a prohibition against informing. "Be a stand-up guy," "Keep your eyes and ears open and your mouth shut," and "Don't sell out" are variations on this theme. The second is a prohibition against dishonesty. "Don't burn your partner," "Be loyal to the mob," and "Be a man of honor," are some of the variations.[40] Unquestionably, these commandments are violated frequently. On the other hand, it is sometimes surprising how much punishment criminals will endure rather than inform on other criminals.

The commandments are enforced by direct and violent punishment in Cosa Nostra, whose table of organization provides for "enforcers" (who make the arrangements for inflicting punishments) and "executioners" (who actually carry out the punishments ordered by enforcers and those above them in the hierarchy). Professional thieves are likely to take punitive action against any member of their group who betrays the group to the police or who holds out more than his share of the spoils. But professional criminals have not been organized in advance to enforce the rules prohibiting organizational disloyalty and organizational dishonesty. They do not, among other things, recruit persons to, or train persons for, well-established enforcer and executioner positions. Unlike Cosa Nostra, working groups of professional criminals are not governments. Perhaps the rules are obeyed most strictly by organized criminals, then by professional criminals, and then by occasional and amateur criminals.

Among professional criminals, a certain lack of concern and sympathy is displayed in dealing with the public, and especially in dealing with victims. This is in part a consequence of, and in part a form of, the segregation of criminals and criminal behavior. Just as a businessman acts on the principle that "business is business," the professional criminal acts on the principle that "crime is crime." There is no place for sentiment in either case.

Amateur criminals, not professionals, stir up the police and public by displays of "toughness" and bravado. A group of young criminals made a successful daylight robbery of a store across the street from a police station, and as they drove away they shot out the window of the station. A young criminal was angered at the way the police had treated his brother, so he set

---

[40] For elaboration of the criminal code and its functions, see Cressey, *Theft of the Nation*, pp. 162-220; and John K. Irwin and Donald R. Cressey, "Thieves, Convicts, and the Inmate Culture," *Social Problems*, 10:142-155, Fall, 1962.

fire to a police car parked in front of the police station. Automobile thieves sometimes make a special effort to steal police cars. Robbers sometimes punish the man who has no money or very little money when he is searched. Similarly, burglars may destroy property in a store if they find no money in the cash register or the safe. A criminal on trial in a courtroom filled with policemen, bailiffs, and spectators secured a gun and tried to shoot his way out of the room. Such acts give the criminal status in his group, but not in the profession of theft. Professionals, who will be discussed in the next chapter, avoid "heat." Professional pickpockets, for example, could easily pick the pockets of policemen, but they refrain from doing so because this would antagonize the police and, in the long run, would lead to restraints on the pocket-picking profession. ●

Suggested readings

ALLSOP, KENNETH. *The Bootleggers and Their Era.* Garden City, N.Y.: Doubleday, 1961.

CAMERON, MARY OWEN. *The Booster and the Snitch: Department Store Shoplifting.* New York: Free Press of Glencoe, 1964.

CATTON, BRUCE. *The War Lords of Washington.* New York: Harcourt, Brace, 1948.

CHAMBLISS, BILL, ed. *Box Man: A Professional Thief's Journey.* New York: Harper and Row, 1972.

CRESSEY, DONALD R. *Criminal Organization.* London: Heinemann, 1972.

CRESSEY, DONALD R. *Other People's Money: A Study in the Social Psychology of Embezzlement.* Glencoe, Ill.: Free Press, 1953.

CRESSEY, DONALD R. *Theft of the Nation: The Structure and Operations of Organized Crime in America.* New York: Harper and Row, 1969.

EDWARDS, LOREN E. *Shoplifting and Shrinkage Protection for Stores.* Springfield, Ill.: Charles C Thomas, 1958.

IANNI, FRANCIS A. J. *A Family Business: Kinship and Social Control in Organized Crime.* New York: Russell Sage Foundation, 1972.

KEFAUVER, ESTES. *Crime in America.* New York: Doubleday, 1951.

KENNEDY, ROBERT F. *The Enemy Within.* New York: Harpers, 1960.

LEVER, HARRY, & JOSEPH YOUNG. *Wartime Racketeers.* New York: Putnam, 1945.

LINDESMITH, A. R. "Organized Crime." *Annals of the American Academy of Political and Social Science,* 217:119-127, September, 1941.

MAAS, PETER. *The Valachi Papers.* New York: Putnam, 1968.

MACK, J. A. "The Able Criminal." *British Journal of Criminology,* 13:44-54, January, 1972.

McCLELLAN, JOHN L. *Crime Without Punishment.* New York: Duell, Sloan and Pearce, 1962.

McINTOSH, MARY. "Changes in the Organization of Thieving." Chapter in *Images of Deviance,* edited by Stanley Cohen, pp. 98-133. London: Penguin, 1971.

MURTAGH, JOHN M. "Gambling and Police Corruption." *Atlantic Monthly,* 206:49-53, November, 1960.

ROBIN, GERALD D. "Patterns of Department Store Shoplifting," *Crime and Delinquency,* April, 1963, pp. 163-172.

ROEBUCK, JULIAN B. "The Negro Numbers Man as a Criminal Type: The Construction and Application of a Typology." *Journal of Criminal Law, Criminology, and Police Science,* 54:48-60, March, 1963.

SALERNO, RALPH F., & JOHN S. TOMPKINS. *The Crime Confederation.* New York: Doubleday, 1969.

STEFFENS, LINCOLN. *Autobiography.* New York: Harcourt, Brace, 1931.

TALESE, GAY. *Honor Thy Father.* New York: World, 1971.

TERESA, VINCENT. *My Life in the Mafia.* New York: Doubleday, 1973.

TYLER, GUS. *Organized Crime in America.* Ann Arbor: University of Michigan Press, 1962.

YEAGER, MATTHEW G. "The Gangster as White Collar Criminal: Organized Crime and Stolen Securities." *Issues in Criminology,* 8:49-73, Spring, 1973.

Behavior systems in crime   13

Most of the work in theoretical criminology has been directed at the explanation of crime in general. Crime in general consists of a great variety of criminal acts. These acts have very little in common except the fact that they are all violations of law. They differ among themselves in the motives and characteristics of the offenders, the characteristics of the victims, the situations in which they occur, the techniques which are used, the damages which result, and the reactions of the victims and the public. Although burglary, robbery, embezzlement, and rape are all crimes, it is almost obvious that they are homogeneous with respect to etiology only in a general way. Even the legal definitions of specific crimes, such as kidnaping, do not always delimit categories of behavior which are homogeneous in regard to their specific causal or genetic characteristics.

Consequently, it is not likely that a general theory of crime can be sufficiently precise or specific to aid greatly in understanding or controlling all types of crime.[1] While a general theory of crime such as the differential association theory organizes criminological knowledge, and is therefore desirable, in order to make progress in the explanation of crime it is also desirable to break crime into more homogeneous units. In this respect, crime is like a disease. The germ theory of disease is a very useful general theory, but even this theory does not apply to all diseases. Progress in the explanation of disease is being made principally by the studies of specific diseases. Similarly, it is desirable to concentrate research work in criminology on specific crimes and on specific "sociological units" within the broad area of crime and within the legal definition of specific types of crime such as kidnaping and burglary.

Several procedures for studying such sociological units within the broad field of crime and within the definitions of specific crimes have been suggested. The typological approach is one such procedure. It has been used by Riemer and by Lottier to define homogeneous units within a specific offense category, embezzlement, and it has been used by Clinard and Wade to define a homogeneous unit, vandalism, as a specific type of delinquency.[2] A second procedure has been to *combine* legal categories of crime in such a way that some of the crimes in each of several legal categories are made into a sociological unit. In the course of an attempt to formulate a sociological theory of embezzlement, for example, it was discovered that the legal term "embezzlement" did not describe a homogeneous class of behavior. Persons whose illegal behavior was not covered by the legal definition were found to have been convicted of embezzlement, and the behavior of some persons who were convicted of offenses such as forgery and confidence game was found to come within the definition of embezzlement. Consequently, a new, sociological definition of the behavior under study was made. This definition enabled the investigator to study certain cases from each of several legal categories, including embezzlement,

---

[1] Cf. Don C. Gibbons, *Changing the Lawbreaker* (Englewood Cliffs, N.J.: Prentice-Hall, 1965).

[2] Svend Riemer, "Embezzlement: Pathological Basis," *Journal of Criminal Law and Criminology,* 32:411-423, November-December, 1941; S. Lottier, "Tension Theory of Criminal Behavior," *American Sociological Review,* 7:840-848, December, 1942; Marshall B. Clinard and Andrew L. Wade, "Toward the Delineation of Vandalism as a Sub-type in Juvenile Delinquency," *Journal of Criminal Law, Criminology, and Police Science,* 48:493-499, January-February, 1958. See also Richard F. Sparks, "Types of Treatment for Types of Offenders," *Collected Studies in Criminological Research* (Council of Europe), Vol. 3, 1968, pp. 129-169; and Sheldon and Eleanor Glueck, *Toward a Typology of Juvenile Offenders* (New York: Grune and Stratton, 1970).

forgery, and confidence game, and to develop a causal theory about this new sociological unit.[3]

A third procedure suggested by sociologists for breaking crime into homogeneous units is the study of "behavior systems." Just as is the case when the typological approach is used, these systems of criminal behavior ordinarily have been defined in such a way that the behavior becomes homogeneous within the definition of a specific legal category. An example of this may be seen in the work of Jerome Hall, who found several behavior systems within the legal category of larceny.[4] Perhaps this procedure holds the greatest promise for criminological research, for by taking the behavior system as the unit of study it is possible to break away from the legal limitations that have often impeded scientific work in criminology; the behavior system can be studied wherever it exists, whether as crime or not crime. ●

The behavior system in crime

The behavior system in crime may be described by its three principal characteristics. *First,* a behavior system is an integrated unit, which includes, in addition to the individual acts, the codes, traditions, *esprit de corps,* social relationships among the direct participants, and indirect participation of many other persons. It is thus essentially a group way of life. It is not merely an aggregation of individual acts. Behavior systems in crime may be illustrated by professional theft, circus grifting, organized crime and racketeering, fraudulent advertising, systematic violation of antitrust laws, and organized manipulation of corporate securities.

Second, the behavior which occurs in a behavior system is not unique to any particular individuals. It is common behavior. It operates in the same manner in a large number of persons, and therefore it should be possible to find causal processes which are not unique to particular individuals.[5]

Third, while common and joint participation in the system is the essential characteristic of a behavior system, it can frequently be defined by the feeling of identification of those who participate in it. If the participants feel that they belong together for this purpose, they do belong together. A professional confidence man and a professional forger would feel that they belonged together, even though they used different techniques, because they have many common interests and standards and can therefore participate in the same system. On the other hand, an

---

[3] Donald R. Cressey, "Criminological Research and the Definition of Crimes," *American Journal of Sociology,* 56:546-551, May, 1951; and Guy Houchon, "Contribution à la Methode Differentielle en Criminologie," *Revue Internationale de Criminologie et de Police Technique,* 18 (1964): 19-32.

[4] Jerome Hall, *Theft, Law, and Society,* 2d ed. (Indianapolis: Bobbs-Merrill, 1952).

[5] See Tamotsu Shibutani, "Reference Groups as Perspectives," *American Journal of Sociology,* 60:562-569, May, 1955.

embezzler would not identify himself with an automobile thief. If these two should meet they would have no common reactions or sentiments growing out of their crimes except such as were common to practically all other persons who violate the laws. Ultimately a behavior system should be defined as a way of life which grows out of a unified causal process. A behavior system in this respect would be similar to a disease, which is differentiated from other diseases by the causal process common to it regardless of the person in whom it occurs.

If a behavior system can be isolated, the problem is to explain that system as a unit. This is similar to an attempt to explain baseball in America. It does not consist primarily of explaining why a particular person becomes a baseball player, and in fact the explanation of why a particular person becomes a ballplayer merely assumes the existence and persistence of baseball as a system. By taking the behavior system as a problem it is possible to avoid some of the methodological difficulties which arise when the act of a specific person is taken as the problem.[6] •

Professional theft as a behavior system

Professional theft is presented as an illustration of a behavior system which can be defined and explained as a unit.[7] The genetic question regarding professional theft is: How does the behavior pattern originate, and how is it perpetuated in our culture? A secondary question is: How does a particular person get into this system?

The principal, but not the only, occupations of professional thieves are confidence games, shoplifting, and pocket-picking. Not all persons who commit these specific crimes are professional thieves. Professional thieves make a regular business of theft. They use techniques which have been developed over a period of centuries and transmitted to them through traditions and personal association. They have codes of behavior, *esprit de corps*, and consensus. They have high status among other thieves and in the political and criminal underworld in general. They associate with each other and do not associate with outsiders on the same basis, and they carefully select their colleagues. They tend to look down upon amateur thieves, referring to them as "neurotic kids," because the crude crimes committed by amateurs arouse the public and make the professional practice of theft more difficult and less profitable.[8] Because of this differential association they develop a common language or argot which is

---

[6] See Robert Dubin, "Deviant Behavior and Social Structure," *American Sociological Review*, 24:147-164, April, 1959; and J. Milton Yinger, "Contraculture and Subculture," *American Sociological Review*, 25:625-626, October, 1960.

[7] See Edwin H. Sutherland, *The Professional Thief* (Chicago: University of Chicago Press, 1937); and Bill Chambliss, ed., *Box Man: A Professional Thief's Journey* (New York: Harper and Row, 1972).

[8] See John K. Irwin and Donald R. Cressey, "Thieves, Convicts, and the Inmate Culture," *Social Problems*, 10:142-155, Fall, 1962.

relatively unknown to persons not in the profession. And they have organization.

A thief is a professional when he has these five characteristics: regular work at theft, technical skill, consensus, status, and organization. The amateur thief is not a professional; neither is the consistently dishonest bond salesman; neither is the Cosa Nostra member who sells illicit goods and services. The case is not quite so clear for the persistent burglar or robber, for there the principal differential is the nature of the technique and the identification. The techniques of the professional thief are much the same as those of the salesman and the actor; they consist of methods of manipulating the interests, attention, and behavior of the victim. The professional thief depends on cleverness and wits, while the robber resorts to force or threat of force, and the burglar relies on both stealth and force. Professional thieves have their group ways of behavior for the principal situations which confront them in their criminal activities. Consequently professional theft is a behavior system and a sociological entity.[9]

The motives of professional thieves are much the same as the motives of other occupational groups: they wish to make money in safety. These desires require no specific explanation. The specific problem is: How do professional thieves remain secure in their violations of the law? Many professional thieves have conducted their illegal activities for a normal lifetime and never been locked up longer than a few days at a time; others have had one or two terms over a period of twenty or thirty years.

Security in professional theft is attained in three ways. *First,* the thieves select rackets that involve a minimum of danger. The confidence game is relatively safe because the victim generally agrees to participate in a dishonest transaction, and when he finds that he is the victim, he cannot make complaint without disgracing himself. For example, the three principal types of big confidence game—the "wire," the "pay-off," and the "rag"—all involve victims who believe that they are defrauding someone. In the "wire" the confidence man convinces the victim that they can delay the telegrams of race results long enough so that the victim can make bets with bookmakers after the race is run, thereby defrauding the bookmakers; in the "pay-off" the victim believes he is defrauding a large racing syndicate; in the "rag" he believes he has inside information regarding the great value of apparently worthless stock.[10]

---

[9] See David W. Maurer, *Whiz Mob: A Correlation of the Technical Argot of Pickpockets with Their Behavior Pattern* (Gainesville, Fla.: American Dialect Society, 1955), pp. 19-28; and Robert L. Gasser, "The Confidence Game," *Federal Probation,* 27:47-54, December, 1963.

[10] David W. Maurer, *The Big Con* (Indianapolis: Bobbs-Merrill, 1940).

Some confidence games do not depend upon the victim's willingness to do something dishonest, but all of them are quite safe.[11] In one recent version of an ancient confidence game, for example, the confidence man telephones the victim and represents himself as a radio announcer who is conducting a quiz program; after the victim answers a simple question, the announcer tells him that he has won an amount of money equal to the amount of money he has in the house and asks him to name that amount; if $100 is mentioned the announcer says he will deliver that amount by messenger; when the messenger arrives he has two checks, one for $100 and the other for $200, and the latter is represented as a "double dividend" which the victim has won instead of the $100; after the victim gives the confidence man the $100 in cash, to prove that he actually had that amount in the house, he receives the bogus $100 check and a receipt for his money, plus the bogus check for the $200 prize; the confidence man then safely disappears. Similarly, shoplifting is relatively safe because the stores do not wish to run the risk of accusing legitimate customers of stealing, and the professional shoplifter makes it a point to look and act like a legitimate customer.[12] Picking pockets is relatively safe because the legal rules of evidence require direct evidence that the thief withdrew the money from the pocket, and that evidence is seldom secured.

Second, professional thieves develop clever and skilled techniques for executing the crimes they select. They do this through tradition, and tutelage. Cleverness and skill may merely mean brashness, as in the case of the thief who, in the sporting-goods section of a large department store, balanced an aluminum kayak on his head and walked out with it. Cleverness and skill also include such things as the utilization of one man to maneuver a victim so that another can pick his pocket, the dexterity required to steal a victim's wristwatch from his wrist, the device whereby one man distracts attention from a shoplifter by kicking or pinching a child so that he will set up a commotion, and the ability to identify, watch, and outtalk store clerks and detectives. Similarly, many ingenious devices for obtaining and carrying shoplifted goods have been invented. These include innocent-looking boxes with false bottoms so that they can be placed over counter merchandise, trousers with hidden pockets and linings, "belly pockets" worn around the waist, false arms, and rubber suction cups attached to strings and elastic bands.[13]

Third, the professional thief makes arrangements to fix those cases in which he may be caught. He expects to fix every such case. He generally does not fix the case himself but employs a professional fixer, for in a larger city one man generally does all

---

[11] See Fletcher Pratt, "The Grift Goes Legit," *Harper's*, June, 1955, pp. 60-65.

[12] See Mary Owen Cameron, *The Booster and the Snitch: Department Store Shoplifting* (New York: Free Press, 1964).

[13] See Lawrence Klingman, "The Booster, the Heel, and the Snitch," *Park East*, January, 1953, pp. 12-17.

of the fixing for all of the professional thieves. The techniques of fixing crimes are as important as the techniques of executing crimes.[14] Whether the fixing is done by the thieves themselves or by their fixer, it is generally accomplished by the direct or indirect payment of money. Usually a promise is made to the victim that his stolen property will be returned, sometimes with a bonus, if he will refuse to push the prosecution or to testify in a way that would damage the thief. The police are sometimes the agents of the criminals in persuading victims to accept restitution. They inform the victim that a criminal trial will cause him great inconvenience and expense, and may be continued for months, after which the victim will have no prospect of recovering his money or stolen property. A large proportion of the cases are fixed in this manner, for the victim is generally more interested in the return of his stolen property than he is in seeing that justice is done to the thieves. If this fails, a policeman may be induced not to make a complaint, or, if a complaint is made, not to testify truthfully, or to give evidence which conflicts with that of the victim or other witnesses. The prosecutor may be induced not to prosecute or, if prosecution is inevitable, to make a very weak effort to bring out evidence which is damaging to the thief. As a last resort, the judge may be bribed to render a decision in favor of the thief, or to impose a minor penalty. It is not necessary that everyone of these officeholders act dishonestly. The only thing necessary is to find one of them who will twist or pervert evidence or decisions. As Maurer has said, "The dominant culture could control the predatory cultures without difficulty, and what is more, it could exterminate them, for no criminal subculture can operate continuously and professionally without the connivance of the law."[15] The President's Commission agrees, saying, "Professional crime would not exist except for two essential relationships with legitimate society: the 'fence' and the 'fix.' "[16]

The profession of theft, then, exists in modern society because victims are more interested in getting their property back than in abstract justice, because police and other officeholders are under the control of political organizations with predatory interests, and because some officials themselves have predatory personal interests. Also, professional theft exists because individuals and business concerns are willing to purchase stolen commodities, and because lawyers are willing to defend professional thieves by every clever argument and device available. In the 1950s, Los Angeles "legitimate businessmen," mostly used car dealers, who purchased stolen automobile radios and other

---

[14] Erving Goffman, "On Cooling the Mark Out: Some Aspects of Adaptation to Failure," *Psychiatry,* 15:451-463, November, 1962.

[15] Maurer, *Whiz Mob,* p. 129.

[16] President's Commission on Law Enforcement and Administration of Justice, *The Challenge of Crime in a Free Society* (Washington: Government Printing Office, 1967), p. 46.

accessories had to be put out of the "fence" business before thefts from automobiles could be reduced. Professional theft exists not only because persons are willing to steal, but also because the rest of society does not present a solid front against theft.

The entrance of a particular person into the professional group is of secondary importance, for the explanation of theft as a profession cannot be found in the life history of one of the members of the profession. Rather it is necessary to understand the profession in order to explain the individual thief. Admission into the profession is not merely an act of will of a person who decides that he would like to be a professional thief. He can no more become a professional thief in that manner than he can become a professional ballplayer. Others must permit him to become a professional thief, just as they must permit a person to become a professional ballplayer. Members of the profession make their entrance by a process of mutual selection.

No one can acquire all of the skills and work safely in cooperation with others without training and tutelage. Lemert has pointed out that check forgery is now a crime committed principally by isolates, rather than a crime committed by professional criminals, as was the case in the nineteenth and early twentieth centuries, largely because the forger no longer needs tutelage by and cooperation with other forgers.[17] Tutelage in professional skills can be given only by those already in the profession. Consequently one gets into the profession by acceptance. If a neophyte satisfactorily performs his "apprentice" or "journeyman" tasks, his responsibilities may be increased until he is finally given the same tasks as regular members of the profession.

Professional thieves do not extend this tutelage to everyone who would like to join them. They extend their assistance, of course, only to those with whom they come in contact in a friendly manner; that is, to fellow lodgers in hotels, rooming houses, or jails, and to waiters, cashiers, and taxicab drivers. The thieves get acquainted with most of these people in a legitimate manner, and confidence develops. They like a certain prospect, and he likes them. They may suggest that he join them, but more frequently he asks to join them because he wants more money than he can make at legitimate work and because their life looks attractive. Doubtless thousands of others with whom they do not come in contact in this manner have the abilities required for professional theft, but they do not happen to meet. Thus entrance into the profession is by selection. The selection is impersonal in the sense that a person must be in a position where he will come in contact with professional thieves in order to develop personal acquaintance. The selection is also personal

---

[17] Edwin M. Lemert, "The Behavior of the Systematic Check Forger," *Social Problems,* 6:141-149, Fall, 1958. See also idem, "An Isolation and Closure Theory of Naïve Check Forgery," *Journal of Criminal Law, Criminology, and Police Science,* 44:296-307, September-October, 1953.

in the sense that the thieves must be attracted to the prospect, and he must be attracted to them. He has a veto on joining the profession, but just as certainly they have a veto on his joining it. ●

Circus grifting

Circus grifting, which has all but disappeared, along with the circus, was a criminal behavior system. It consisted principally of sure-thing gambling, as seen in the shell game, three-card monte, the eight-dice cloth, the cologne joint, and the spindle. In order that circus grifting could be conducted satisfactorily and safely, four elements were necessary: grifters, victims, a dishonest circus management, and dishonest public officials. The behavior system was a combination of these four elements.

Circus grifters came from two principal sources. Some had been grifting previously in state fairs, resort communities, or carnivals, with methods somewhat similar to those used in the circus. Others had been living in a community where the circus was playing, became employed for a day as a shill or assistant in one of the games, proved efficient, and were taken along with the circus and trained in other details of the system. A large proportion of the circus grifters originated in Indiana, where several circuses made their winter headquarters.

Circus grifters formed a relatively cohesive group. They had a saying, "Once a circus grifter, always a circus grifter." The gambling swindles played in the circus were played elsewhere, but seldom with the same abandon. Many people who operated one of these games elsewhere did not succeed in the circus, and many who were successful in the circus were inefficient when they tried to operate the same games elsewhere. The grifters in a particular circus were a somewhat exclusive group while the circus was on the road; the performers did not associate with them. In the early days the grifters rode in the "privilege car" of the circus train. This car was lined with steel to protect the occupants from attacks by angered residents of the community in which the gambling games had been operated. Also the grifters from all circuses associated during the winter season, for many of them spent the winter, or as much of it as their funds permitted, in Hot Springs. The grifter in one circus knew the principal grifters in all the other circuses. This exclusive association was a product of the necessity for training and tutelage in the operation of the gambling games.

Victims were available in practically every community. The general interest in gambling was at the base of the victimization, but to this were added the atmosphere of make-believe and celebration connected with the circus, and the techniques used in appealing to spectators. One of these techniques was the example of the shill, who appeared to be another spectator, but actually was an assistant in the game, and who played and won frequently. Another technique involved an apparent opportunity

for dishonesty; a shill raised one of the shells while the operator's back was turned and enabled the other spectators to see
the pea under the shell, or he bent the corner of the card in the
monte game so that the spectator knew which card to select.
Since this dishonesty seemed to make the gamble absolutely
certain, many spectators tried it, and lost. Finally, the general
method was to induce a spectator to make a start, even without
paying, and he was then ashamed to stop after a win or loss
or two.

Dishonest public officials were found in a large proportion of
the communities in which circuses appeared. Gambling was at
least winked at in most communities, and the officials believed
that some gambling in connection with the celebration at the
time of a circus should be condoned, especially in return for
tickets or money.

Dishonest circus managers were abundant. The circus in the
early part of the century generally depended on the return from
grifting for a substantial part of its income. The circus manager
employed a "privilege man" who had charge of all of the grifting,
and who paid to the circus a percentage of everything taken in
on all of the games. Many of the circus managers started as
grifters and were sympathetic toward the grifters.

Circus grifting was authorized and flourished in practically all
of the circuses in 1880, in all except Ringling's in 1900, and all
except the largest circuses in 1930. Old circus grifters explained
that this decrease was not due to a reduction in the number of
potential grifters, or in the number of potential victims, or in the
number of dishonest public officials. They insisted that the decrease was due entirely to changed attitudes of circus managers.
Moreover, the changed attitudes of circus managers were not due
to an increase in honest motives, but to a change in economic
relationships. In the earlier days a grifting circus could change
its name and thus conceal its identity before returning to a community which had been angered by the crooked gambling games
on the last trip. As the circus increased in size, its name came
to be an asset from the point of view of advertising and could
not be changed without loss of prestige and therefore loss of
income. The loss from the change of name would be greater
than the gain from grifting, and therefore grifting was reluctantly
abandoned. It is for that reason that grifting is now rarely found
and only in the smaller circuses and fly-by-night carnivals.

The principal question is: Why did the circus ever authorize
and participate in grifting? The most immediate answer is that
this was a specific manifestation of a generally dishonest business. Many circuses in early days were fences for stolen horses.
Circus employees were notorious for thefts from clotheslines,
barns, and farmhouses. The circus management frequently dealt
dishonestly with its employees, holding out a part of their wages
and overcharging on expenses. Each circus was unfair in its

competition with the other circuses. The men who put up posters advertising the circus were necessarily sluggers who could fight with the bill plasterers of rival circuses. Many of the attractions were frauds. The "garmagunt" with three heads and eight legs was made of shoe leather. The "Siamese twins" were two separate persons with a flesh-colored belt holding them together during the time they were on exhibition. The "horse with its tail where its head ought to be" was discovered, after payment of ten cents, to be a horse with its tail toward the manger. The exhibit "for men only" proved to be a pair of suspenders. The "emu eggs" sold by the attendant to farmers for $1.50 each proved to be goose eggs. The man who sold balloons hired an assistant to go through the circus grounds and, with his mouth full of tacks, blow a tack through each balloon which had been purchased, thus creating a larger market for balloons. Hundreds of incidents of this nature are recounted in the histories of the circus.

This general dishonesty, in which the circus grifting was embedded, was a product of four conditions. *First,* the circus was a mobile organization. It seldom remained longer than one day in a community, and there were no permanent ties, duties, responsibilities, or relationships. The circus was regarded as queer by the community, and the community was regarded as queer by the circus people. *Second,* the community was hostile toward the circus in several respects. In some places the circus and similar exhibits were prohibited because it was believed that the circus would corrupt the morals of the young. In some communities it was customary for ministers and priests to preach anticircus sermons in all churches on the Sunday preceding the circus. To counteract this influence, Barnum advertised moral lectures as a part of the circus program, but the lectures bulked larger in the advertisements than they did in the program. Opposition also was based on economic grounds. It was believed that the circus took away from the community money which should be spent in the community. *Third,* the people of the community frequently were dishonest in their dealings with the circus. The head of the street department in one city would, on the night before the appearance of the circus, substitute old worn-out manhole covers for the ones then in use, so that many covers would be broken by the heavy wagons in the circus parade. He then presented to the circus a bill for damages each year until the circus became suspicious and discovered the truth. A woman whose home was adjacent to the circus grounds claimed damages of fifty dollars because her laundry on the clothesline was spotted by flies attracted by the circus. A circus promised to give a free ticket to each child in an orphanage and to enough attendants to take care of the children; when the children arrived each one had an adult attendant. *Fourth,* circus personnel were screened through these processes of mobility, opposition, and community impositions. Circus life was a hard, criminalistic, unsociable life, and the personnel became hard, criminalistic, unsociable people. Out of this interaction grew the general dishonesty and grifting. The English circus, which was much less mobile than the American circus, had very little dishonesty.[18] •

Kidnaping is discussed here as an illustration of a legal entity which is not a sociologically homogeneous unit. As kidnaping is studied further, it is possible that behavior systems will be found, that sociologically significant types of kidnaping will be identified, or that certain of the forms of kidnaping will be found to have characteristics in common with certain of the offenses described by another legal term, such as assault or murder. However, the general legal term *kidnaping* will always obscure the multitude of variations in the phenomenon, just as the general legal term *murder* will always obscure the differences between the behavior of a hired killer and the behavior of an unlucky abortionist.

Kidnaping

As a legal entity, kidnaping consists of taking possession of the body of another person, against his will, by force or fraud and in violation of the law. But kidnaping appears in at least twelve forms which are socially distinct and which generally involve different causal processes.

First, kidnaping was the basis of the slave trade, and all those who participated in the slave trade and in slavery were accessory to kidnaping.

Second, impressment was a form of kidnaping in which a sailor was forced to leave a ship in which he had a legal right to be, to board another ship and work there as a sailor.

Third, men were shanghaied by force and compelled to work as sailors in ships. They received wages, but commissions for the crimps who had kidnaped them were deducted from their wages.[19]

Fourth, girls were kidnaped and used for prostitution. This aroused attention in the period just prior to World War I under the name of white slavery, and both federal and state laws were enacted against the practice. Probably few bona fide cases occurred. The laws have been used extensively by girls as means of blackmailing their paramours.

---

[18] See Bert J. Chipman, *"Hey Rube!"* (Hollywood: Hollywood Print Shop, 1933); C. R. Cooper, *Circus Day* (New York: Farrar and Rinehart, 1931); E. C. May, *The Circus from Rome to Ringling* (New York: Duffield and Green, 1932); Gil Robinson, *Old Wagon Show Days* (Cincinnati: Brockwell, 1925); R. E. Sherwood, *Hold Yer Hosses! The Elephants Are Coming!* (New York: Macmillan, 1932); E. H. Smith, "Grift, An Account Based on Statement by Hoke Hammond," *Collier's,* 69:11-12, 20-21, April 8, 1922; M. R. Werner, *Barnum* (New York: Harcourt, Brace, 1923).

[19] See Leon Radzinowicz, "Impressment into the Army and Navy — A Rough and Ready Instrument of Preventive Police and Criminal Justice," chap. 15 in Marvin Wolfgang, ed., *Crime and Culture* (New York: John Wiley, 1968), pp. 287-313.

Fifth, organized criminals were kidnaped by organized criminals and held for ransom, especially during the prohibition period. Since the racketeers were not able to appeal to the police for support and did not wish to advertise their inability to protect themselves, these kidnapings aroused little public attention.

Sixth, kidnaping of wealthy persons for purposes of ransom developed extensively about 1930, so that newspapers announced a new crime in the making. While kidnaping of wealthy and respectable persons for ransom had occurred occasionally in the United States prior to this date, its prevalence increased at that time. But kidnaping for ransom was not new, and kidnaping for other purposes was not new. The only thing that was new was the importance of the victims.

Seventh, a special variety of the sixth form occurs when important political figures, and others, are kidnaped and threatened with death as a means of forcing some political action—such as release of prisoners.

Eighth, offenders took possession of victims in connection with other crimes, such as robbery, as a means of security for themselves. By far the most common form of "kidnaping" at present is forced movement of a robbery victim from one location to another.

Ninth, hijacking of airplanes sometimes involves ransoming the plane itself, the passengers, or both. Sometimes the demanded ransom is money, sometimes a political act. In all cases—as in hijacking simply for transportation or for no rational purpose—kidnaping is involved.

Tenth, illegal arrest is a form of kidnaping. If a policeman takes possession of a person under conditions not authorized by law, he is committing the crime of kidnaping. In this sense, policemen have kidnaped more persons than all other kinds of kidnapers combined. During the economic depression of the 1930s, a special form of this kind of kidnaping appeared in connection with strikes. Special police took pickets, reporters, students, and others to the state lines and pushed them across, with instructions not to return.

Eleventh, children have been kidnaped by lonesome and probably psychopathic women who then reared the children as their own.

Twelfth, parents have kidnaped their own children who have been assigned by the court to the other parent in divorce proceedings, or under other circumstances.

Doubtless other minor forms of kidnaping can be found, but these twelve are a sufficient number to show that kidnaping is not an entity in the causal sense. The twelve forms are, to be sure, somewhat interrelated. Seven of the forms have financial returns as the objective, while the others do not. Moreover, the seven which have financial gain as the objective may be divided into two groups: those in which there is a large demand for victims with a small price per victim, and those in which there is a restricted demand with a high price per victim.

Also, the twelve forms can be divided into kidnapings involving respectable and important offenders and lowly, unimportant victims; and kidnapings in which unimportant offenders abduct important victims. The only form of kidnaping that has aroused great public antagonism is that in which the victims are important and respectable. The much more extensive kidnapings in which the victims were unimportant or not respectable continued for centuries before enough opposition developed to stop the practices. Consequently, explanation of the existence and continuance of one form of kidnaping is likely to be different from explanation of another form. ●

Conclusion

Professional theft and circus grifting have been described in some detail as illustrations of the procedure for studying behavior systems in crime. Neither of these topics has been investigated exhaustively, and the interpretations are therefore tentative and hypothetical. More intensive studies of these two behavior systems and of other behavior systems in crime are needed before general propositions can be developed.

It is not likely that the entire area of crime can be covered in this manner. Certain crimes cluster in systems, are organized, or can logically be combined with other crimes in such manner as to form systems. But other crimes stand somewhat isolated and outside of systems. The behavior systems in crime may be understood more readily than the isolated crimes, and therefore the study of them may yield general propositions that apply to a considerable range of criminal offenses. Then legal categories designating less systematic crimes, and the informal systems used for assigning crimes to these categories, can be combined or redefined in such a way that the behavior designated by them can be studied scientifically and related to the general propositions. ●

Suggested readings

ARNOLD, DAVID O. *The Sociology of Subcultures.* Berkeley, Calif.: Glendessary Press, 1970.

BECKER, HOWARD S. *Outsiders: Studies in the Sociology of Deviance.* Glencoe, Ill.: Free Press, 1963.

CAMERON, MARY OWEN. *The Booster and the Snitch: Department Store Shoplifting.* New York: Free Press, 1964.

CHAMBLISS, BILL, ed. *Box Man: A Professional Thief's Journey.* New York: Harper and Row, 1972.

CLINARD, MARSHALL B., & RICHARD QUINNEY. *Criminal Behavior Systems: A Typology.* 2d ed. New York: Holt, Rinehart and Winston, 1973.

DEBAUN, EVERETT. "The Heist: Theory and Practice of Armed Robbery." *Harper's,* 180:69-77, February, 1950.

DENTLER, ROBERT A., & KAI T. ERIKSON. "The Function of Deviance in Groups." *Social Problems,* 7:98-107, Fall, 1959.

DUBIN, ROBERT. "Deviant Behavior and Social Structure." *American Sociological Review,* 24:147-164, April, 1959.

EINSTADTER, WERNER J. "The Social Organization of Armed Robbery." *Social Problems,* 17:64-82, Summer, 1969.

FERDINAND, THEODORE N. *Typologies of Delinquency: A Critical Analysis.* New York: Random House, 1966.

GIBBONS, DON C., & DONALD L. GARRITY. "Definition and Analysis of Certain Criminal Types." *Journal of Criminal Law, Criminology, and Police Science,* 53:27-35, March, 1962.

HALL, JEROME. *Theft, Law, and Society,* 2d ed. Indianapolis: Bobbs-Merrill, 1952.

JACKMAN, NORMAN R., RICHARD O'TOOLE, & GILBERT GEIS. "The Self-Image of the Prostitute." *Sociological Quarterly,* April, 1963, pp. 150-161.

JACKSON, BRUCE. *A Thief's Primer.* London: Macmillan, 1969.

JENKINS, RICHARD L. *Breaking Patterns of Defeat.* Philadelphia: J. B. Lippincott, 1954.

KITSUSE, JOHN I. "Societal Reaction to Deviant Behavior: Problems of Theory and Method." *Social Problems,* 9:246-256, Winter, 1962.

LEMERT, EDWIN M. "An Isolation and Closure Theory of Naïve Check Forgery." *Journal of Criminal Law, Criminology, and Police Science,* 44:296-307, September-October, 1953.

LEMERT, EDWIN M. "The Behavior of the Systematic Check Forger." *Social Problems,* 6:141-149, Fall, 1958.

MAURER, DAVID W. *The Big Con.* Indianapolis: Bobbs-Merrill, 1940.

MAURER, DAVID W. *Whiz Mob: A Correlation of the Technical Argot of Pickpockets with Their Behavior Pattern.* Gainesville, Fla.: American Dialect Society, 1955.

McKENZIE, DONALD. *Occupation: Thief.* Indianapolis: Bobbs-Merrill, 1955.

SMIGEL, ERWIN O., & H. LAURENCE ROSS. *Crimes Against Bureaucracy.* New York: Van Nostrand, 1970.

SNODGRASS, JON. "The Criminologist and His Criminal: The Case of Edwin H. Sutherland and Broadway Jones." *Issues in Criminology,* 8:1-17, Spring, 1973.

SUTHERLAND, EDWIN H. *The Professional Thief.* Chicago: University of Chicago Press, 1937.

WOOD, ARTHUR LEWIS. "Ideal and Empirical Typologies for Research in Deviance and Control." *Sociology and Social Research,* 53:227-241, January, 1969.

YINGER, J. MILTON. "Contraculture and Subculture." *American Sociological Review,* 25:625-626, October, 1960.

Part 2 THE PROCESSING OF DELINQUENCY AND CRIME

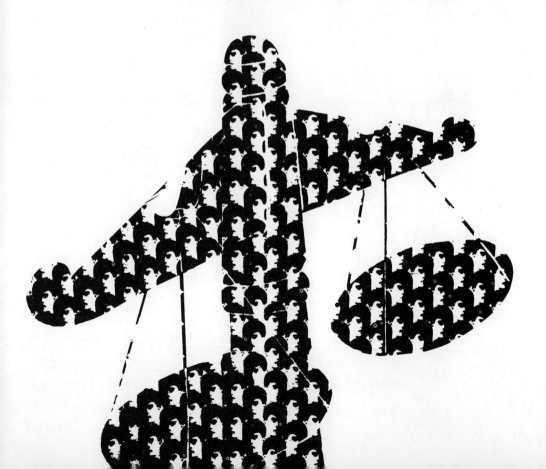

14 Variations in punitive policies

With this chapter we begin the study of various methods of dealing with crime and with apprehended criminals. On a general level, these methods may be described as "societal reactions" to crime and criminality, and, as such, they are subject to analysis and explanation, just as are the criminal reactions themselves. However, social scientists have concentrated on understanding and explaining lawbreaking itself rather than on understanding and explaining the societal reactions to lawbreaking. Consequently, much available information about the societal reactions to lawbreaking has not been organized or integrated, and theoretical problems in the administration of justice are not as sharply delimited as are theoretical problems in criminal etiology. Systematic organization of knowledge in this area is a prerequisite for understanding and explaining present and future policies, and for their efficient direction and administration as well. As a preliminary step toward such integration, four general problems in the control of crime will be specified.

One general problem is closely analogous to the problem of observing variations in the incidence of crime and delinquency. Just as many variations in delinquency and crime rates have been described, careful descriptions of variations in societal reactions to crime should be made. The varieties of methods and policies used in the attempt to control crime are enormous, if they are considered in detail, and an important part of the problem is to classify and generalize these variations in a manner which will make them easier to study and understand. For instance, we can readily observe a great number of variations in reactions to lawbreaking, not only in the United States at present, but in the history of mankind. In some social systems the reaction to lawbreaking is annihilation, in some systems severe corporal punishments, in others imprisonment or probation, and so on.

Similarly, the number of variations in the official policies for implementing the societal reactions to crime—such as policies for police, courts, prisons—is enormous. For example, in some prisons the inmates are tortured, in others they are studiously ignored except when they try to escape, and in others serious efforts are made to "treat" and rehabilitate them. These many variations can be classified tentatively according to their position on a scale ranging from a purely *punitive* reaction or policy to a purely *treatment* reaction or policy, although this classification does not summarize all of the differences. Some societal reactions to crime and, hence, some policies and organizations for control of crime, have been and are directed primarily by punitive considerations, others by treatment considerations, and a final category by a mixture of punitive and treatment considerations.

Second, the general problem of "efficiency" must be analyzed if the materials on control of crime are to be integrated. Is the true crime rate really reduced when police and prosecutors "enforce the law" rather than using discretion and "common sense" in deciding who should be arrested? Is crime control "better" when punitive policies are used than when treatment policies are used? Official policies in recent times have shown a distinct trend toward treatment and away from punishment, but this trend is not based on a demonstration of the superiority of treatment methods. The criteria of efficiency have not been precisely established nor agreed upon, and "better control" cannot be established until such criteria are defined.

One preliminary and general criterion is that the system is most efficient which results in the smallest number of crimes, other things being equal. A small number of crimes may result from either of two things: few people who commit crimes, or few repetitions of crimes by those who commit at least one crime. Hence, according to this criterion, an efficient system would reform those who commit crimes, so that they do not repeat often, and also it would keep others from committing their first crimes, either by "deterrence," which has to do with refraining from crime because of fear of punishment, or by "prevention," which has to do with refraining from crime for other reasons. This statement of the criterion of efficiency leaves many problems unsolved, such as the relation between efficient control of crime and efficiency in other respects, and the relation between reformation and deterrence.

In dealing with problems of efficiency the question also must be raised as to whether the most efficient method or policy for controlling crime in order to reduce crime rates has a chance of being adopted in a given society at a given time. For example, even if it were shown with complete certainty that crime would be greatly reduced by methods which are much closer to "pure" treatment (no punishment) than those now being used in the United States, this policy might not be adopted. In view of what appears to be a punitive societal reaction to lawbreaking, our society probably would reject such a method. Similarly, a policy of extremely severe punishment might be rejected, even if it were shown to be the most efficient method of dealing with criminals, for the society also possesses certain humanitarian attitudes. Further, a policy of strict enforcement or full enforcement of current laws probably would be rejected because it would interfere with those rights summarized by the phrase "due process of law."[1] Or the society

---

[1] See Wayne R. LaFave, Arrest: The Decision to Take a Suspect into Custody (Boston: Little, Brown, 1965), pp. 102-124; Sanford H. Kadish, "Legal Norms and Discretion in the Police and Sentencing Process," Harvard Law Review, 65:904-931, March, 1962; and Herbert L. Packer, The Limits of the Criminal Sanction (Stanford: Stanford University Press, 1968).

might formally adopt the efficient policy of "pure" treatment or severe punishment, only to wink at its enforcement. There is doubt as to whether such a policy would, in the circumstances in which it would be expected to operate, be superior to some other policy which could be carried out in a straightforward manner.

A third general problem is establishment of the relation of the varying reactions to lawbreaking and methods of control to the existing knowledge of the causation of criminal behavior. Every method for control of crime is based, implicitly or explicitly, on a theory of crime causation. However, changes in policies do not immediately follow new discoveries about crime causation, and it may be presumed that some present methods are inefficient because they are based on erroneous theories. Many modifications would be made if police departments, courts, probation departments, and prisons operated strictly in accordance with the criminological theory of emotional disturbances, or with the theory of economic determinism, or with the differential association theory.

The fourth general problem is not unlike the general problem of explaining crime and criminality. The problem may be summarized by the question: *Why* do the policies and methods for dealing with crime vary from time to time and from place to place? If changes in policies are to be controlled, not only the variations, but the causes of the variations must be understood. One basic subsidiary problem in this area is that of accounting for the origins and variations in general societal reactions to lawbreaking, such as the punitive reaction, the treatment reaction, and the "due process of law" reaction.

More specific or detailed subsidiary problems are the following: (a) Explaining the variations in the traditional "modalities" of punishment: severity, uniformity, celerity, and certainty. In some societies punishments may be comparatively severe, uniform, swift, or certain, while in other societies the reaction to lawbreaking may be punitive but not so severe, uniform, etc. The problem is to account for these differences. (b) Explaining variations in specific methods of implementing the punitive reaction, such as the death penalty, corporal punishment, imprisonment, and fines. In some societies the punitive reaction may be implemented almost exclusively by imposing punishment by imprisonment, while in other societies it may be implemented by imposing punishment corporally. (c) Explaining variations in specific methods of implementing the treatment reaction, such as individual casework and community work with criminals, group therapy, and community reorganization. (d) Explaining the differences between the official or formal societal reactions to crime and the unofficial or informal reactions.

The present chapter supplies some of the data on variations in the general punitive reaction to crime, as well as on variations in the use of specific methods of punishment, in different times and places. Chapters 15 and 16 are concerned with variations in other specific aspects of the punitive reaction, with variations in the treatment reaction, with the comparative efficiency of punitive and treatment policies, and with explanation of variations in punishment and treatment. After this "introduction," the treatment and punitive aspects of the various agencies and institutions which deal with the criminal, from the time of his apprehension to the time of his discharge from parole, will be discussed. ●

Definition of punishment

Two essential ideas are contained in the concept of punishment as an instrument of public justice. (a) It is inflicted by the group in its corporate capacity upon one who is regarded as a member of the same group. War is not punishment, for in war the action is directed against foreigners. The loss of status which often follows crime is not punishment, except insofar as it is administered in measure by the group in its corporate capacity. (b) Punishment involves pain or suffering produced by design and justified by some value that the suffering is assumed to have. This is the conventional conception as used in the criminal law. If the pain or suffering is merely accidental, to be avoided if possible, it is not punishment. A surgical operation performed on a prisoner to correct a physical defect is not punishment, for the pain is not regarded as valuable or desirable. The confinement of a psychotic person may involve suffering for him, but it is not punishment. Many of the modern methods of dealing with criminals, especially juvenile court procedures, are not punitive. ●

Variations in the punitive reaction to lawbreaking

Many writers have maintained that punishment is an expression of an instinct of vengeance or the expression of a desire for vengeance which consists of a complex of instincts or processes. Undoubtedly some crimes and other acts which are regarded as wrong upset the equilibrium of society and the interests of individual members, and various punitive reactions which partially restore this equilibrium take place. There is, however, no evidence that these reactions are directed by an instinct of vengeance or by a basic desire for punishment of the offender. Furthermore, the punitive reaction is only one of many reactions to lawbreaking, and it is not at all important in the reactions to offenses occurring among nonliterate peoples.

Three types of wrongs, followed by three types of reactions, no one of which is clearly punitive, were found in nonliterate societies. The first includes tribal and sacral offenses, such as treason, witchcraft, sacrilege, and poisoning. Although such offenses seldom occurred in small, homogeneous groups, when they did occur the societal reaction was annihilation. The group might annihilate the offender by either death or exile; both rendered the offender nonexistent so far as the group was concerned. The reaction of annihilation was closely related to war, social hygiene, and sacrifice. The offender was regarded as an enemy and was processed as an enemy. He also was considered to be polluted, and the tribe attempted to get rid of him and of everything connected with him as a social hygiene measure. Thus, in many societies witchcraft was followed by death, and the body of the offender was thrown into the sea, which was supposed to have cleansing power, or it was buried on foreign soil. His name could not even be mentioned for fear that it might carry pollution with it. An element of sacrifice appears, also, in the reaction to these offenders; the reaction was designed to please the gods.

The second group of wrongs were injuries to private individuals who were not in the same family (gens, clan, tribe). The offenses would now be defined as assault, murder, theft. Generally, they provoked feuds between families. The attitude in these feuds was largely vengeance, and severe suffering was involved. But the reaction to the offense was not a societal reaction; it was private, involving two private individuals and their relatives. By and large, the general community was merely a spectator, although one or the other of the opposing parties was likely to enjoy the approval or tacit support of the "disinterested" remainder of his society.[2] This seems to have been the origin of the system of payment of damages in civil courts, but not of punishment by criminal courts.

The third group of wrongs consisted of injuries to other members of the same family. These wrongs were neither regarded as crimes nor followed by punishment in the sense that the word is used today. In the family, as in the tribe generally, ridicule was the most powerful method of control and was generally sufficient to secure observance of rules. This is illustrated by the Andaman Islanders:

There is no such thing as the punishment of a crime by the society. If one person injured another, it was left to the injured one to seek vengeance if he wished and if he dared. There were probably always some who would side with the criminal, their attachment to him overcoming their disapproval of his actions. The only painful result of antisocial actions was the loss of the esteem of others. This in itself was a punishment that the Andamanese, with their great personal vanity, would feel keenly, and it was in most instances sufficient to prevent such actions. For the rest, good order depended largely on the influence of the more prominent men and women.[3]

Even if a person killed his father, which was in many nonliterate groups regarded as a horrible offense, he was not punished by the other members of the family or by the tribe. The members of the family felt that since the family had already been weakened by the loss of one member, it would be foolish to weaken it still more by injuring the offender. They looked upon such acts, however, with great surprise and disgust.

---

[2] E. Adamson Hoebel, *The Law of Primitive Man: A Study in Comparative Legal Dynamics* (Cambridge, Mass.: Harvard University Press, 1954), pp. 329-330.

[3] A. Radcliffe-Brown, *The Andaman Islanders* (Cambridge: The University Press, 1922), p. 52.

Similarly, among modern nonliterate peoples who are fairly well segregated from civilization, as among primitive peoples, punishment of children seldom occurs.

Travelers everywhere have remarked upon the extreme indulgence toward children. This is very marked among the Eskimos, though perhaps not more so than among the Fuegians of South America. Wherever we have data parents almost never punish or even severely reprove, but such pressure as may be needed is exercised by certain relatives. . . . Chastising the young seems to have been practised in the centres of higher culture, but outside of these limits was practically unknown. . . . In short, the same principles applied to control of the young as to adults, viz., admonition and ridicule. In fact, the whole control of the local group in aboriginal days seems to have been exercised by admonition and mild ridicule instead of by force and punishment.[4]

The Winnebago Indian had the following precepts:

If you have a child and it is naughty do not strike it. In old times if a child was naughty the parents did not strike it but made it fast. When it is quite hungry it will reflect upon its disobedience. If you hit him you will merely put more naughtiness into him. It is said that mothers should not lecture the children, that they merely make the children bad by admonishing them.[5]

In these nonliterate groups, therefore, we find certain motives and attitudes which apparently preceded the punitive reaction to lawbreaking but were not, in themselves, punishment: desire to annihilate an enemy of the group, sacrifice to appease or fend off the wrath of the gods, social hygiene measures to rid the community of pollution, self-redress in cases of private injury, and surprise and disgust at the person who injured his own family. Deliberate and "just" infliction of pain by the group in its corporate capacity was not invented until later.

With the rise of kingship and the king's authority, disposition of wrongdoers became a public matter. The "court" arose and was backed by the central authority. The reaction to wrongs became collective or social rather than private, and wrongs were viewed as crimes—that is, as offenses against the state as well as against the victim.[6] The reaction approached the punitive reaction as we now know it, for severe corporal punishments were inflicted by state officials, but the notion that the pain imposed has some value in itself was not necessarily present. This kind of reaction is illustrated in the following statement about the Anglo-Saxon period in England:

---

[4] C. Wissler, The American Indian (New York: Oxford University Press, 1922), pp. 177-178.

[5] Paul Radin, Crashing Thunder: The Autobiography of a Winnebago Indian (New York: D. Appleton-Century, 1926), p. 463.

[6] Cf. E. Faris, "The Origin of Punishment," International Journal of Ethics, 25:54-67, October, 1914; Max Radin, "Enemies of Society," Journal of Criminal Law and Criminology, 27:328-356, September-October, 1936; Hans von Hentig, Punishment: Its Origin, Purpose, and Psychology (London: William Hodge, 1937).

A detected criminal was either fined, mutilated, or killed, but punishment, as we now understand the term, was seldom inflicted; that is to say, the dominant idea was neither to reform the culprit nor to deter others from following in his footsteps. If a man was killed it was either to satisfy the bloodfeud or to remove him out of the way as a wild beast would be destroyed; if a man was mutilated by having his fore-finger cut off or branded with a red-hot iron on the brow, it was done not so much to give him pain as to make him less expert in his trade of thieving and to put upon him an indelible mark by which all men should know that he was no longer a man to be trusted; if a fine were levied, it was more with a view to the satisfaction of the recipients of the money or cattle or what not, than with the intention of causing discomfort or loss to the offender.[7]

It was not until the modern period that the clearly punitive reaction to crime—the purposive infliction of pain on the offender because of some assumed value of the pain—became popular. Debates regarding the wisdom and efficiency of this societal reaction and of specific policies and methods consistent with it gave rise to three schools of penology: the classical, the neoclassical, and the positive or Italian. The principal arguments of these schools will be used here as illustrations of variations in the punitive reaction to crime, on the assumption that each of the schools arose as a result of or in connection with a variation in general societal reaction to crime, rather than on the assumption that the arguments of the schools caused the variations. The societal reactions reflected in the writings of the members of the neoclassical and the positive schools are conflicting, but both are characteristic of the United States at the present time. They were discussed earlier in the section on schools of criminology.[8]

The classical school, to which Beccaria made one of the first significant contributions, and to which Rousseau, Montesquieu, and Voltaire belonged, maintained the doctrine of psychological hedonism, that the individual calculates pleasures and pains in advance of action and regulates his conduct by the results of his calculations. The implication of the doctrine was that the societal reaction to crime should be the administration of a measured amount of pain. Consistently, the general proposition of the classical school was that it is necessary to make undesirable acts painful by attaching punishment to them and to make the amount of pain thus attached entirely definite, so that the prospective criminal could make his calculations on it, and to make it just sufficient so that the pain would exceed the pleasure. Since the punishment must be one that can be calculated, it must be the same for all individuals, regardless of age, mentality, social status, or other conditions. The question of individual responsibility was not considered, just as it had not been considered in the earlier period

---

[7] W. L. M. Lee, *History of Police in England* (London: Methuen, 1901), p. 10. See also Linton C. Freeman and Robert F. Winch, "Societal Complexity: An Empirical Test of a Typology of Societies," *American Journal of Sociology,* 62:461-466, March, 1957.

[8] See pp. 49-57 above.

when the offender was annihilated.[9] Bentham, the great reformer
of the criminal law in this period, tried to extend hedonistic cal-
culus by working out precise mathematical laws for the infliction
of punishment.

The neoclassical school, which arose at the time of the French
Revolution and the period immediately following, maintained that
while the classical doctrine was correct in general, it should be
modified in certain details: since children and "lunatics" cannot
calculate pleasures and pains, they should not be regarded as criminals or be punished. This principle was to some extent extended
to others, also, by the system of taking into account certain
"mitigating circumstances." The reaction to crime, therefore, was
no longer purely punitive; punishment was imposed on some lawbreakers but not on others.[10] By recognition of the exceptions, individual responsibility was taken into account, and subsequently it
was necessary for administrators of justice to consider the psychology and sociology of crime. The neoclassical argument became
the basic principle of the judicial and legal system of Western
civilization during the last century.

The positive school denied individual responsibility and reflected
an essentially nonpunitive reaction to crime and criminality. Since
the criminal was held to be not responsible for his acts, he was
not to be punished. The adherents of this school maintained that
a crime, as any other act, is a natural phenomenon, just like a
tornado, a flood, a stroke of lightning, or the striking of a snake.[11]
In self-protection, the group might put the criminal to death or
incarcerate him, but these precautions were not punishment. Criminals who could be reformed were to be reformed, and those who
could not be reformed were to be segregated or killed. Denial
of individual responsibility seriously affects the accused crim-

---

[9] In the earlier period, this lack of consideration for responsibility can best
be shown by the penalties imposed upon inanimate objects, insects, and lower
animals. Ives reported a number of instances in which inanimate objects
were punished, and Evans collected a mass of materials regarding the medieval
and modern practice of punishing animals. Much doubt was cast on the
authenticity of Evans's account by Liquori, however, and it is highly probable
that the few cases which may have occurred have little significance from a
theoretical point of view. George Ives, A History of Penal Methods (London:
Stanley Paul, 1914), p. 254: E. P. Evans, The Criminal Prosecution and Capital
Punishment of Animals (London: W. Heinemann, 1906), pp. 143, 175; Sister
Mary Liquori, "The Trial and Punishment of Animals," America, February 1,
1936, pp. 395-396.

[10] In general until the last two centuries, intent was not considered in the treatment of criminals, or was considered only occasionally or incidentally; little
interest in the question of responsibility appeared. Intensive studies of particular communities indicate, however, that generalizations of this nature are
subject to many exceptions.

[11] In Europe, recent attempts to introduce this idea into penal legislation are
properly characterized as pleas for "social defense" against criminals. For
a history of the "new social defense" movement, see Marc Ancel, Social
Defence (London: Routledge and Kegan Paul, 1965).

inal's rights to a jury trial, to counsel, to confront witnesses, and to other safeguards of "due process of law."[12]

In contrast with the societal reactions to crime reflected in these three earlier schools of penology, two present-day reflections of a distinctly "treatment" reaction to lawbreaking are appearing. The first of these is treatment by individual casework, which is based on the premises of the positive school, although differing from it as to procedures. The second cannot be easily named, but it involves a belief that crime is an expression of a situation, generally involving a group, and cannot be "treated" effectively by isolating particular persons for casework but must be handled as a situation or group problem. This might be called group work, but it is different from the group work of most social workers. These two procedures and the societal reaction of which they are a part will be discussed later.[13] ●

Like the general punitive reaction to lawbreaking, the usage of specific techniques for implementing or expressing the punitive reaction has varied from time to time and place to place. During the history of mankind, four principal methods of implementing the punitive policy have been used, but there has been no distinct "evolution" of any one system from the others. Removal from the group by death, by exile, or by imprisonment; physical torture; social degradation; and financial loss all have been used differentially in various historical periods, and they are used differentially today. While it cannot be maintained that any one type of punitive reaction is exclusively characteristic of any one historical period or of any one society, certain emphases upon the different methods can be observed. In the United States at present, for example, all four of the systems are used to some degree, but certainly fines and removal from the group by imprisonment are emphasized.

Variations in use of methods for implementing the punitive reaction

The prevalence of death penalties has varied a great deal in different societies.[14] Such techniques of inflicting death as burning, boiling in oil, breaking at the wheel, the iron coffin, drowning, and impaling have had their greatest frequency not in the earliest or in the more recent societies, but in the society of the medieval period. Impaling and immuring were practiced in Switzerland until about

The death penalty

---

[12] Cf. Jerome Hall, "Science and Reform in Criminal Law," *University of Pennsylvania Law Review*, 100:787-804, April, 1952; and Sidney J. Kaplan, "Barriers to the Establishment of a Deterministic Criminal Law," *Kentucky Law Journal*, 26 (1957):103-111.

[13] See below, pp. 330-336.

[14] As indicated above, it is not always clear that execution of a criminal is punishment in the strict sense of the word. A rather intensive study of the circumstances of the executions must be made to determine whether the executions in certain historical periods were punishments. Such a study has not been made, and it will be necessary, therefore, to accept the uncritical statements now available.

1400, and death by drowning until about 1600. The last case of burning at the stake in Berlin was in 1786. In Frankfurt, Germany, the number of executions was 317 in the fifteenth century, 248 in the sixteenth, and only 140 in the seventeenth.[15] In the cantons of Zürich and Schwyz, 572 executions occurred in the sixteenth century, 336 in the seventeenth, and only 149 in the eighteenth.[16]

In England, however, the situation is somewhat different, for there were only seventeen capital offenses in the early part of the fifteenth century, about 350 in 1780, and then, by 1839, the number was reduced again to about the same as it had been four centuries before.[17] In the earlier part of this period in England, the death penalty was frequently inflicted for religious offenses, but most of the later inflictions were for offenses against property, and many of them for very trivial offenses. In 1814 three boys— aged eight, nine, and eleven—were sentenced to death for stealing a pair of shoes. This was not unusual. During the early part of the modern period, the corpse was gibbeted, that is, remained hanging in chains, and was sometimes soaked in tar so that it would remain for a long time as a warning to evildoers. These objects were seen so frequently that landscape painters considered them an essential part of the scenery and not infrequently introduced them into their landscapes.[18]

Under the leadership of Romilly, Bentham, Peel, McIntosh, Montagu, Cruickshank, and others, and as the power of the common people increased, the use of capital punishment decreased. But as late as 1814, Romilly tried in vain to substitute simple hanging as the societal reaction to treason, in place of the existing penalty of hanging, cutting down alive, disemboweling, cutting off the head, and quartering the body. Although the later penalty was not actually carried out, members of Parliament were afraid that treason would be greatly increased if the law were modified.

During the course of the last century, a very distinct trend away from the death penalty has occurred. About thirty-five countries have abolished it entirely, and in other countries the offenses for which it may be imposed have been generally limited to murder.[19] Of the fifty-two jurisdictions in the United States in 1971, only one (the District of Columbia) had a mandatory death penalty; thirty-six had a permissive death penalty; nine jurisdictions did not permit the death penalty; and six severely restricted its use. The

---

[15] G. L. Kriegk, *Deutsches Bürgerthum im Mittelalter* (Frankfurt, Germany: Rütten und Löning, 1868-1871), 1:200-201.

[16] Karl L. von Bar, *A History of Continental Criminal Law* (Boston: Little, Brown, 1916), p. 299.

[17] See Leon Radzinowicz, *A History of English Criminal Law and Its Administration from 1750* (New York: Macmillan, 1948), 1:42-79, 611-659.

[18] W. Andrews, *Old-Time Punishments* (London: Hull, W. Andrews, 1890), pp. 211-212.

[19] Peter P. Lejins, "The Death Penalty Abroad," *Annals of the American Academy of Political and Social Science,* 284:137-146, November, 1952; and James McCafferty, "Major Trends in the Use of Capital Punishment," *Federal Probation,* 25:15-21, September, 1961.

states which in 1971 did not permit the death penalty or limited it to crimes such as killing a policeman were Alaska, Arizona, Hawaii, Iowa, Maine, Michigan, Minnesota, North Dakota, Oregon, Rhode Island, Vermont, Wisconsin, New Mexico, New York, and West Virginia. Puerto Rico and the Virgin Islands also had abolished capital punishment legislatively. In 1972, the death penalty was declared unconstitutional, and thus abolished, by both the U.S. Supreme Court and the Supreme Court of California.

Several variations may be observed in the use of the death penalty in the United States during the last century. *First,* there was a fluctuating tendency to abolish it. Between 1847, when the first state abolished the death penalty, and 1876, four states prohibited capital punishment. One addition to this list was made in 1907 and another in 1911. From 1913 to 1918, seven other states were added, but five of them restored the penalty after an average experience of two and a half years. Delaware joined the abolition states in 1958, being the first state to do so since 1918. However, in 1961 Delaware restored the death penalty. There are periodic attempts to abolish capital punishment in those states retaining it, and to restore it in those states which have abolished it.

Second, a more pronounced recent variation was substitution of a permissive death penalty for the mandatory death penalty. Courts and juries were given the power of deciding whether one who has committed a capital offense must be executed. In 1918, the death penalty was mandatory on conviction of capital crime in twelve states, in 1938 in five states, and in 1964 and thereafter in none of the states.

Of the states which permitted capital punishment, an average of about one-third each year had no executions. In 1945-1959, Illinois imposed the death penalty on only 1.2 percent of those eligible for it.[20] Maryland in 1936-1961 executed 56 percent of those sentenced to death; in 1936-1940 this percentage was 69; in 1946-1950 it was 56; and in 1956-1960 it was 23.[21] In 1967 there were only two executions by the federal government or by the states which permitted the death penalty,[22] and there have been no executions since that time.[23] Thus, to some extent the introduction of permissive clauses was a technique for abolishing capital punishment in practice while retaining it in law.

Third, public opinion is increasingly opposed to capital punishment. A nationwide Roper poll conducted in the United States in 1958 indicated that 42 percent of the people favored execu-

---

[20] Daniel Glaser, "Survey of the Death Sentence in Illinois" (Chicago: John Howard Association, 1959. Mimeographed).

[21] Legislative Council of Maryland, *Report of the Committee on Capital Punishment* (Baltimore: Author, 1962), p. 54.

[22] Federal Bureau of Prisons, "Executions, 1930-1967," *National Prisoner Statistics,* No. 37, April, 1967.

[23] Willard J. Lassers, "Death Takes a Holiday," *Transaction,* June, 1971, p. 10.

tion rather than life imprisonment of persons convicted of "the worst crimes, like murder." Fifty percent were against the death sentence, and 8 percent had no opinion.[24] In the lowest income groups interviewed, 53 percent were against the death penalty, as compared with 42 percent of the highest income group. Of the Negroes interviewed, 78 percent were opposed to capital punishment. The Gallup poll has been, at intervals, asking a representative sample of the United States population twenty-one and over a standardized question on capital punishment: "Are you in favor of the death penalty for persons convicted of murder?" In 1953, 68 percent of those polled answered "yes." In 1960 this percentage was 52; in 1965 it had declined to 45, and in 1966 to 42. In 1969 the percentage answering "yes" had climbed again to 51; and in December, 1972 the percentage of "yes" opinions was 57.[25]

Fourth, the number of capital crimes has been reduced. There were in the fifty states only twelve capital offenses, and no one state had declared all of these to be capital offenses. Only one crime was punishable by death in fourteen states, two in eight states, and only nine states have as many as six capital crimes.[26] In practice, however, between 1930 and 1967 less than two percent of the 3,857 executions were for crimes other than murder and rape.

Fifth, over the last century the annual number and proportion of executions decreased, largely as a result of the changes mentioned above. The number of executions in the United States decreased rather consistently each year after 1935. Table XV shows that in Ohio the number of death sentences decreased very greatly in proportion to the number of admissions to prison for first-degree murder, while the percent of the death sentences which were actually executed decreased from 1900 to 1915, increased decidedly until 1925, and then remained fairly constant until 1960.

Sixth, executions were closed to the public. While executions were at one time public spectacles, the number of witnesses was increasingly restricted.

Seventh, in place of prolonged torture, the method of execution was made as swift and painless as possible in a large proportion of the states. Electrocution was adopted in New York in 1888, and by 1970 this method was being used by twenty-three states. Ten states now provide for execution by lethal gas, while eight

---

[24] Hans W. Mattick, *The Unexamined Death,* 2d ed. (Chicago: John Howard Association, 1966), p. 36.

[25] *The Gallup Opinion Index,* No. 90, December, 1972.

[26] The exact number of capital offenses is difficult to determine because of the tendency to specify subcategories; for example, Ohio specifies first-degree murder as a capital offense, but it also specifies that killing of a policeman (a form of first-degree murder) is a capital offense. See Leonard D. Savitz, "Capital Crimes as Defined in American Statutory Law," *Journal of Criminal Law, Criminology, and Police Science,* 46:355-363, September-October, 1955.

authorize hanging and one (Utah) offers a choice between hanging and firing squad. In other nations, hanging is the most widely used method of execution. Garrotting survives as the means of execution only in Spain.[27]

In 1930-1970, 3,857 executions by civil authorities occurred in the United States, of which 86 percent were for murder and 12 percent for rape. Of the executed persons, 45 percent were white, 54 percent Negro, and 1 percent other races. Less than one percent were female. About 60 percent of the executions carried out each year since 1930 occurred in seventeen southern and southwestern states, which contain about one-third of the nation's population.[28]

Most societies have to some extent implemented the punitive reaction by corporal punishment. Branding, stocks, pillory, mutilation, confinement in irons and cages, and whipping were used

Physical torture

TABLE XV

Admissions to Ohio Penitentiary for first-degree murder, percent of these with death sentences, and percent of death sentences executed, by five-year periods, 1896-1968[29]

Years	Number of admissions for first-degree murder	Percent of first-degree murder admissions with death sentences	Percent of death sentences which were executed
1896-1900	33	58	58
1901-1905	44	43	74
1906-1910	55	40	59
1911-1915	43	21	45
1916-1920	118	27	59
1921-1925	151	41	82
1926-1930	197	26	69
1931-1935	189	31	78
1936-1940	178	21	84
1941-1945	110	21	87
1946-1950	229	21	77
1951-1955	167	12	60
1956-1960	102	25	54
1961-1965	117	19	21
1966-1968	91	24	0

[27] United Nations, Department of Economic and Social Affairs, *Capital Punishment, 1961-1965* (New York: United Nations, 1967), p. 24.

[28] Federal Bureau of Prisons, "Capital Punishment 1930-1970," *National Prisoner Statistics Bulletin*, No. 46, August, 1971.

[29] Data for 1896-1930 compiled by the Ohio Institute; 1931-1968 data compiled by the Bureau of Research and Statistics, Ohio Department of Mental Hygiene and Correction. Some imprecision in column four is introduced by the fact that the persons executed in any five-year period were not necessarily the same persons admitted during that period.

extensively in the medieval and early modern periods. Such penalties, in general, have increased and decreased in prevalence with the death penalty.

Whipping is the only one of the many varieties of corporal punishment which has been officially retained in Western civilization, and the trend of opinion is very much against it. In Great Britain it was a legal penalty for certain adult crimes and juvenile delinquencies until 1948.

In the United States, whipping is authorized in only one state. Until 1952 it could be used on wife-beaters in Maryland, but it seldom was inflicted. It is authorized in Delaware for several crimes. Of the 7,302 offenders convicted in Delaware in 1900-1942 for crimes which called for whipping, 22 percent were whipped; this percentage was 70 in 1900, 55 in 1910, 30 in 1921, 15 in 1930, 7 in 1940. Few floggings have taken place in this state since 1950.[30]

Social degradation

Shame and humiliation have been used to impose suffering by reduction of the social status of the offender, sometimes temporarily, sometimes permanently. In general, this method of punishment flourished from the beginning of the sixteenth to the end of the seventeenth century, but it is not absent even today. Many techniques for reducing prestige have been used in various societies. Some were used extensively in the societies in which physical torture was the primary method for implementing the punitive reaction. For example, the ducking stool, the stocks, the pillory, the brank, and other devices were not only instruments of corporal punishment, but were used to reduce the status of the offender as well. They were used for minor offenses, such as scolding, giving short weights, forgery, and blasphemy. In the seventeenth century one offender who had stolen cabbages from his neighbor's garden in New York was ordered to stand in the pillory with the cabbages on his head, and in addition was banished from the colony for five years.[31] The brank was a cagelike device placed over the head and provided with a bar which was thrust into the mouth of the offender, thus holding down the tongue; occasionally this bar had spikes on it to prevent any effort to use the tongue. This device was regarded as superior to the ducking stool in dealing with scolds, because the scold could talk between ducks.

The marks of degradation, temporary or permanent, inflicted in an effort to reduce the social status of the offender often did not deter him from further crimes. An English statute of 1698

---

[30] Robert G. Caldwell, *Red Hannah: Delaware's Whipping Post* (Philadelphia: University of Pennsylvania Press, 1947), pp. 69-70; idem, "The Deterrent Influence of Corporal Punishment," *American Sociological Review*, 9:171-177, April, 1944.

[31] Phillip Klein, *Prison Methods in New York State* (New York: Columbia University Press, 1920), p. 23.

which provided for branding on the left cheek was repealed after eight years with the explanation that this penalty

> . . . had not had its desired effect of deterring offenders from the further committing of crimes and offenses but, on the contrary, such offenders, being rendered thereby unfit to be entrusted in any service or employment to get their livelihood in any honest and lawful way, became the more desperate.[32]

Another way of degrading criminals is to deprive them of rights of various kinds following commission of "infamous" and certain other crimes. In the Roman Republic, infamy as the result of the conviction of crime meant loss of the right to vote, to hold office, to represent another in the courts, to be a witness, to manage the affairs of another, and the abridging of the right to marry. During the early modern period, also, certain crimes resulted in infamy. This infamy was produced to some extent merely by the publicity of the trial, but also by the subsequent loss of rights of citizenship. In addition, offenders were branded or mutilated, so that everyone might know that they had been guilty of crimes, and thus they suffered infamy. Loss of rank, mutilation of the body after death, and other methods were used to produce a greater infamy than the public would naturally or ordinarily attribute to the offender. During the feudal period, by bills of attainder, persons convicted of treason or felony might be deprived of their real and personal property, their right to inherit or transmit property, and all rights in the courts. This was known as "civil death."

The following are the principal rights which, at the present, may be lost in various states by the commission of serious crimes. (a) The right to vote is lost by conviction of almost all felonies in all states except Indiana, Massachusetts, New Hampshire, and Vermont. (b) The right to hold public office is lost in most states. Public offices are generally restricted to electors, and therefore the loss of suffrage carries with it the loss of the right to hold office. In addition, certain other restrictions are specified in some states, such as incapacity to serve on a jury or to testify as a witness. (c) The right to practice certain professions or occupations. In addition, in a few states the convicted felon loses the right to make a contract, to marry, or to migrate to a foreign country.[33]

The disabilities produced as the result of conviction are terminated automatically in some states when the sentence is served; in other states they are terminated if the person is not indicted or convicted for another crime within a specified time after the completion of his sentence. In most states the disabilities are removed only by pardon, and in some of them not even by pardon.

---

[32] Luke O. Pike, *A History of Crime in England* (London: Smith, Elder, 1873-1876), 2:280.

[33] Mirjam R. Damaska, "Adverse Legal Consequences of Conviction and Their Removal: A Comparative Study," *Journal of Criminal Law, Criminology, and Police Science*, 59:347-360, September, 1968; and 59:542-568, December, 1968.

Practically all societies have banished some criminals, especially political criminals, but wholesale deportation of offenders is a rather recent invention. Banishment was used in early societies and in ancient Rome, where it was either a prohibition against coming into a specified territory, generally the city of Rome, or a prohibition against going outside a specified territory, such as an island to which the offender had been removed; in either case, banishment might be for life or for a short time. After a long period during which this method for expressing the punitive reaction to crime was seldom used, the method was revived. In England the first modern legalization of transportation was in 1598, and concerned "rogues, vagabonds, and sturdy beggars." However, the law was not used a great deal until the period during which America was colonized. From that time until the American Revolution a considerable proportion of England's criminal population was sent to America. The Transportation Act of 1718 declared that its purpose was both to deter criminals and to supply colonies with labor.[34]

In 1786, after the American colonies had become independent, the policy of transportation to Australia was adopted, and this practice continued until 1867. The total number transported during this period was 134,308, but the average number per year was 474 during the period 1787-1816, and about 3,000 between 1816 and 1838. In England in 1834, the sentence of transportation was imposed on 4,053 persons, death on 480, and imprisonment on 10,716. This shows that at the time, transportation, though at its height, was not being used as frequently as imprisonment. But all except 314 of those sentenced to prison had terms of one year or less, which means that imprisonment was used almost entirely for the relatively trivial offenses.

Transportation was abandoned by England because it was found not to be a good method of reformation or deterrence, because it was expensive, and primarily because it was strenuously opposed by the Australian colonies. John Mitchel, a convict transported for aiding in the Irish rebellion, described the conditions in Australia in 1851 as follows:

There is but one political question now existing—the transportation system. Most of the decent colonists, having families growing up, and feeling the effects of the moral and social atmosphere that surrounds them, and the ignominy of having no country but a penal colony, no servants, no laborers, few neighbors even, who are not men fairly due to the gallows—ardently desire to use this new Constitution, such as it is, to make vigorous protest against the continuance of the penal system.[35]

Many other countries have used transportation in the modern period. Portugal in the sixteenth century sent criminals and women of ill repute to Brazil and later sent criminals to Angola.

---

[34] A. G. L. Shaw, *Convicts and the Colonies* (London: Faber and Faber, 1966), p. 25.
[35] John Mitchel, *Jail Journal* (Dublin: J. Corrigan, 1864), p. 264.

Spain tried transportation in a limited way in the eighteenth century. Russia has used Siberia as a penal colony since 1823. Since 1865 Italy has transported some convicts to the islands along her coast, and France from 1763 to 1766, in 1824, and from 1851 to the present has used transportation to some extent.

Banishment, which is closely related to transportation, is still used as part of the penalty for certain types of crimes. In one of the earliest criminal prosecutions on American soil, the penalty inflicted in 1637 was that the defendant was to be "banished from out of our jurisdiction as being a woman not fit for our society."[36] In 1969-1971, 826 alien criminals were deported; an additional 589 persons were deported as narcotic addicts.[37] A modified form of banishment also is used constantly in the United States at present. It consists of giving a person accused or convicted of an offense a specified number of hours in which to leave the country, town, or state.[38]

(a) In ancient and medieval societies. In nonliterate societies imprisonment was rarely used as a penalty. Similarly, the penalty of imprisonment hardly ever occurred in early Greece; and it was not used at all in the Roman Republic but was used for minor offenses in the Empire. The last code of laws in France previous to the Revolution was made in 1670 and contained no mention of imprisonment as a penalty. Incarceration was sometimes used in France and other countries, however, either as a means of enforcing the payment of fines or as a commutation of death sentences when mitigating circumstances were found.

Imprisonment

In England, imprisonment was used in a few cases in the Anglo-Saxon period, as in a law providing that persons convicted of murder or theft should be imprisoned for 120 or 40 days respectively, before they could be redeemed by their kinsmen. Henry II provided a penalty of imprisonment for one year for perjury, and Henry III provided the same penalty for breaches of the forest law. In 1241 some Jews convicted of circumcising a Christian child were ordered either to pay twenty thousand marks "or else be kept perpetual prisoners." But it was in the reign of Edward I in the latter half of the thirteenth century that incarceration came into extensive use in England, though even in this period it was used primarily as a "squeezer," or means of securing fines.

Thus, in general, until about the last part of the thirteenth century in England, and probably a little later in some of the Continental countries, imprisonment as a penalty was used only for very restricted groups of offenders. It is, therefore, a compara-

---

[36] William O. Douglas, *An Almanac of Liberty* (New York: Doubleday, 1954), p. 135.

[37] Immigration and Naturalization Service, Department of Justice, *Annual Report, 1971* (Washington: Department of Justice, 1972), p. 81.

[38] See Caleb Foote, "Vagrancy-Type Law and Its Administration," *University of Pennsylvania Law Review,* 104:603-650, March, 1956.

tively modern method of dealing with offenders, though its roots run back to the earliest societies.

(b) Imprisonment by the church. The early church authorities did use imprisonment, partly because they were not permitted by law to use the death penalty, and partly because they believed that withdrawal from association with others was rehabilitative. In 1283, a certain Brother John bit his prior's finger "like a dog," and the bishop gave orders to

> . . . keep the said Brother John in prison under iron chains in which he shall be content with bread, indifferent ale, pottage, and a pittance of meat or fish (which on the sixth day he shall do without) until he is penitent.[39]

Though this method was used by the church as early as the fifth century, it was used most extensively during the Inquisition, when it was the most severe penalty that could be inflicted for any offense on those who professed conversion. In 1229, Gregory IX ordered that all who were converted after arrest because of fear of death should be imprisoned for life; this rule was stated by several councils, also. In the Inquisition of Toulouse from 1246 to 1248, of 192 known sentences, all were imprisonment except 43 death penalties imposed on persons who refused to appear; of the 149 prison sentences, 127 were for life, 6 for ten years, and 16 for an indefinite period. Of the 636 sentences imposed by the medieval inquisitor Bernard Giu from 1308 to 1322 (of which 88 were imposed on persons already dead), 300 were imprisonment. Many of these sentences were commuted, however. Such releases were necessary in part because of the lack of prisons, but in general the idea of reformation was taken into account. St. John Chrysostom, the early Christian philosopher, said: "I require not continuance of time, but the correction of your soul; demonstrate your contrition, demonstrate your reformation, and all is done."[40]

This ecclesiastical imprisonment varied from strict confinement in absolute solitude, known as in pace, to congregate life in the corridors of the prisons, with occasional retirement to a cell, which was known as murus largus. As a matter of fact there was much association between prisoners in many institutions, some gambling and feasting, and some grafting by jailers who kept the money of prisoners or food that had been sent to the prison for them, and ordered supplies for prisoners who had long been dead.

(c) Imprisonment in the galleys. The galleys were used considerably as places of confinement for criminals from about 1500 to the early part of the eighteenth century. This practice was a revival of the ancient method of forced labor, although in the earlier period the slaves were not necessarily criminals. It continued until the large sailing vessels were developed to such an extent as to make the galleys unsuitable for competition. In 1602,

---

[39] Quoted in Ives, *History of Penal Methods*, p. 43.
[40] Ibid., p. 38.

Queen Elizabeth appointed a commission to make arrangements for commuting other penalties to galley labor, so that offenders may be "in such sort corrected and punished that even in their punishment they may yeld more profitable service to the Common welth."[41]

In seventeenth-century France, the courts were ordered to refrain from other methods of punishment as much as possible in order to provide crews for galleys. Those who could not work in the galleys, such as women, aged, and infirm, were frequently imprisoned on land during this period, and when the galleys were abandoned, many former slaves were transported or were held in hulks on the shores or in arsenals.[42]

(d) Imprisonment in houses of correction.[43] The house of correction appeared in England about the middle of the sixteenth century, when, on the petition of Bishop Ridley of London for help in dealing with the "sturdy vagabonds" of the city, the king gave his palace at Bridewell to be one of the "hospitals of the city," for the "lewd and idle" and a place for the employment of the unemployed and the training of children. By act of 1576, Parliament provided that a house of correction should be erected in each county, and in 1609 provided penalties for counties failing to erect such institutions. The assumption was that hard work at rather unpleasant tasks would reform criminals, but the possibility of profits was not overlooked. Also, in addition to punitive labor, corporal punishments were used. Justices were ordered to search for "rogues, vagabonds and idle persons" and commit them to institutions, but the institutions also were used for confinement of "lewd women" with illegitimate children who might become a charge on the community and for men who deserted their families. By an act of 1711 the maximum period of confinement in these houses of correction was fixed at three years, and by subsequent legislation the number of offenses for which persons might be committed was greatly enlarged. By the early part of the eighteenth century, the house of correction and the common jail were practically the same in discipline and character of inmates.

---

[41] Ibid., pp. 103-104.

[42] See W. Branch-Thompson, *The English Prison Hulks* (London: Christopher Johnson, 1957).

[43] It is necessary to make a distinction between the house of correction and the workhouse. Technically the workhouse was an institution in which employment was furnished to those able and willing to work, and industrial training was furnished for the young; consequently, it was a part of the poor relief system. The house of correction, on the other hand, was a part of the penal system, designed to protect the poor-relief funds against encroachments by those able but unwilling to work. Thus, the house of correction was designed to compel "sturdy beggars" to work. But as a matter of fact, the two institutions are hardly distinguishable during the larger part of their history in England and America, and no attempt is made in the present discussion to differentiate them precisely; no attention is paid, however, to the workhouse in its pure form.

This system for implementation of the punitive reaction to law-breaking also was used on the Continent during the same period. It began a little later, but was used more extensively than in England. In 1669 one Peter Rentzel established a workhouse in Hamburg at his own expense because he had observed that thieves and prostitutes were made worse instead of better by the pillory, and he hoped that they might be improved by work and religious instruction in the workhouse.[44] A house of correction was established in Waldheim in 1716 with the lower floor for criminals and the upper floor for paupers and orphans, and with complete separation of the sexes on both floors. On entrance the criminals received a "welcome" of ten lashes; work was compulsory and silence was the rule. The staff of the institution included a chaplain, a teacher, and a physician, which was distinctly noteworthy at that time. During the first century of its history this institution received 13,954 persons, of whom 7,921 were criminals, 4,642 paupers, and 1,391 orphans. Almost half of the criminals were convicted of theft, a fourth of begging and vagrancy, and an eighth of sexual offenses; 270 of them were convicted of homicide, which was usually infanticide. Perhaps the most famous house of correction on the Continent was the one established in Ghent in 1775.

(e) Early prison reforms. The early "prison reform" movement, which reached its peak in the last part of the eighteenth century and the first part of the nineteenth century, actually was a movement for the popularization of a relatively new punitive method: imprisonment as a system of punishment. Although imprisonment as punishment was in part the basis of the system of committing offenders to houses of correction, jails, and hulks in the seventeenth and eighteenth centuries, the primary use of imprisonment at that time was for persons awaiting trial. The "reforms" advocated and accomplished were primarily in reference to the prison as a place of detention, and they may be seen best in England and America. Chapter 22 will be devoted to changing societal reactions to crime in America.

In England, from the middle of the sixteenth century there had been considerable publicity regarding prison practices and various suggestions for methods of improvement. Geoffrey Mynshal, committed to prison as an insolvent debtor, while in prison wrote "Certain Characters and Essays of Prison and Prisoners," which was published in 1618. This was the first regular treatise on prison "abuses"; it describes most of the practices and conditions of prison life which John Howard found a century and a half later. In 1699, the Society for the Promotion of Christian Knowledge, with a committee on prisons, was formed. This committee visited many prisons and presented a report in 1702, under the title "Essay towards the Reformation of Newgate and other

[44] F. H. Wines, *Punishment and Reformation* (New York: Crowell, 1895), pp. 115-116.

Prisons in and about London." The following conditions are mentioned: the old criminals corrupt the new; swearing, blasphemy, and gambling; unlimited use of intoxicating liquors; personal lewdness of officers and keepers; and the co-operation of officers with the prisoners in their vices. The committee suggested methods of reducing these conditions as follows: separate confinement in cells, labor while in prison, regular religious services, abolition of fees, prohibition of liquor in prison, retention of hardened offenders until evidence is furnished that they will secure decent employment when released and until they give security for good behavior, and advertisement to the public of the names of those prisoners who have lived decently in prison with the object of securing the help of good people for these prisoners after their release.

During the next century, the investigations, reports, and discussions continued; a few laws were passed; a few individuals in control of prisons undertook to make improvements as suggested by committees. In 1773, Parliament authorized magistrates to appoint chaplains in their jails. This was the first official recognition of the desirability of attempting to reform the prisoners. But in some institutions as late as 1808 the felons were not permitted to attend the religious services.

The great prison reformer of England was John Howard, who in 1777 wrote *The State of Prisons in England* after a personal investigation of practically all the prisons of England. This book contains, after a short summary, a description of each prison, so that it is a mass of concrete details. His general conclusion was:

> If it were the wish and aim of magistrates to effect the destruction present and future of young delinquents, they could not devise a more effectual method, than to confine them so long in our prisons, those seats and seminaries . . . of idleness and every vice.[45]

Howard's work was supplemented by that of other leaders, and several societies for prison reform were formed. Substantial changes were made in prisons, as may be determined by a comparison of Dixon's account of the prisons in 1850[46] with Howard's account of 1777. In fact, Beaumont in 1821 lamented that prisons had changed so much that they were no longer a deterrent. He argued that workmen preferred prison life to the life of freedom, and he urged a return to the earlier methods.[47] Another author berated justices of the peace for indulging "in such costly fads as the separation of male prisoners from females, of adults from children, and of the convicted from the unconvicted, whilst altogether disapproving the extravagant cubic space required either

---

[45] John Howard, *The State of Prisons in England and Wales*, 2d ed. (London: Cadell and Conant, 1780), p. 13.

[46] W. Hepworth Dixon, *The London Prisons* (London: Jackson and Walford, 1850).

[47] B. Beaumont, "Essay on Criminal Jurisprudence," *Pamphleteer* (1821), pp. 1873 ff.

for the cellular confinement or for the useful employment of any prisoners."[48]

This sketch shows that imprisonment as a method of implementing the punitive reaction to lawbreaking rarely occurred in earlier societies. It was adopted by the church and used quite extensively, and then common jails and special prisons for larger and larger proportions of criminals arose, until in the early nineteenth century imprisonment came to be the principal method of punishing serious offenders. In England there has been an unbroken downward trend in the use of imprisonment by superior courts since 1900. For example, such courts gave prison sentences to 89 percent of the felony sexual offenders in 1909-1913, and to 47 percent in 1951-1954.[49]

Financial penalties

Reaction to criminality by general confiscation of property or by imposition of a fine has existed in most literate societies, but there have been great variations in the emphasis placed on this system. The practice developed somewhat as the general punitive reaction developed. When an individual was injured by another, he might claim damages, the amount depending on the injury done and the social position of the injured party. Then the king claimed a part of this payment or an additional payment for the participation of the state in the trial and for the injury done to the state by the disturbance of the peace. About the twelfth century, the victim's share began to decrease and the exactions of the king to increase, until finally the king took the entire payment. These payments were one of the principal sources of revenue, and imprisonment was used largely at this time as a means of compelling the defendant to pay the fine. Fines, therefore, developed out of private damages or civil actions and were in their origin a part of the civil law rather than of the criminal law.[50]

This method became frequent only at the end of the last century, and the current trend toward its greater use is apparent in the following statistics.[51] In Germany in 1882, fines were 22.2 percent of all penalties imposed; in 1934, 54.7 percent; in France in 1900, 35.8 percent; in 1934, 47.8 percent; in Belgium in 1905, 48.0 percent; in 1933, 66.5 percent. In Sweden in 1953, and in Finland in 1959, fines were 95 percent of all sentences imposed.[52]

---

[48] Edward Mullins, *A Treatise on the Magistracy of England* (London, 1836).

[49] Hermann Mannheim, "Comparative Sentencing Practices," *Law and Contemporary Problems*, 23:557-582, Summer, 1958.

[50] L. T. Hobhouse, G. C. Wheeler, and M. Ginsberg, *The Material Culture and Social Institutions of the Simpler Peoples* (London: Chapman and Hall, 1915), pp. 86-119.

[51] George Rusche and Otto Kirchheimer, *Punishment and Social Structure* (New York: Columbia University Press, 1939), pp. 147-150.

[52] Thorsten Sellin, *The Protective Code: A Swedish Proposal* (Stockholm: Department of Justice, 1957), p. 17; and Inkeri Anttila, "Fines for Drunkenness — An Expensive and Ineffective System," *Alkoholpolitik* (Finland, 1960), 3:2-3.

In the United States at present, the imposition of a fine is by far the most frequent method of reacting punitively to crime; probably more than 75 percent of all penalties imposed are fines. This recent trend may be due partly to the increase in trivial offenses growing out of an increased number of technical regulations, but if a particular crime is taken, the same trend is apparent. In Germany, of all penalties for fraud, 11.0 percent were fines in 1882, and 47.5 percent were fines in 1932. In Finland in 1935, 23 percent of the persons convicted of drunkenness were fined; by 1959 the percentage had increased to 58.[53] Fines, then, are being substituted for other penalties.

Courts at present are generally given authority to impose fines within maximum and minimum limits set by legislatures. Sometimes only the maximum level is fixed, sometimes only the minimum. The constitutions of the several states provide that fines "shall not be excessive."

At common law, fines were enforced by executions against property, but now an offender is generally imprisoned in a jail or house of correction in default of payment of the fine. About 60 percent of the persons committed to the Philadelphia County Jail in 1960 were committed for nonpayment of fines. In the Baltimore City Jail on one day in 1970, 410 inmates—about 30 percent of the jail population—were in jail for not paying fines, at the rate of $2.00 per day, and 170 of that number were traffic offenders.[54] When a fine is imposed, the action is tantamount to a declaration that neither the safety of the community nor the welfare of the offender requires the imprisonment of the offender and that the assumed values of punishment can be accomplished without imprisonment. Imprisonment for failure to pay fines is therefore only a means of collecting a debt to the state.[55] Moreover, this type of sentence is inherently discriminatory because severity of punishment is determined solely by the defendant's wealth. In the Scandinavian countries, the amount of a fine is adjusted to the defendant's income and wealth.

The justifications given for this method of implementing the punitive reaction have varied, but at present they consist of the following. *First,* the fine is the most easily and thoroughly remissible of any of the penalties; capital punishment, whipping, or imprisonment once administered cannot be remitted effectively, but a fine that has been paid can be repaid. *Second,* the fine is a most economical penalty; it costs the state practically nothing when used without imprisonment for default. *Third,* the fine is easily divisible and can be adjusted to the enormity of the offense, the character and wealth of the offender, the state of public opinion, and other conditions more easily than any other

---

[53] Anttila, "Fines for Drunkenness."

[54] Robert G. Fisher, "Comment," in Charles H. Whitebread II, ed., *Mass Production Justice and the Constitutional Ideal* (Charlottesville, Va.: Michil, 1970), p. 175.

[55] See Charles H. Miller, "The Fine: Price Tag or Rehabilitative Force?" *National Probation and Parole Association Journal*, 2:377-384, October, 1956.

penalty. *Fourth,* it does not carry with it the public stigma and disgrace that imprisonment does, and therefore does not hamper reformation of the offender. *Fifth,* it affects one of the most general interests of mankind and causes a kind of suffering that is universal; therefore it is efficacious in dealing with the great majority of mankind. *Finally,* it provides an income for the state, county, or city.

Restitution and reparation

In the previous discussion it was observed that the imposition of financial penalties appeared in clear-cut form when the state appropriated all of the payment made by an offender; what had previously been a combination of civil and criminal procedures became thereby distinctly a criminal procedure. The offense came to be regarded as an offense against the state alone; the victim had to initiate a separate civil action to recover damages for the injury done to him.[56] It was found in practice, however, that the injured party had very little success in securing damages under this system, because of the insolvent condition of the typical criminal and the opportunity to hide or transfer his property. Consequently, victims usually made no effort to recover by civil process, or settled out of court by threatening to report the crime to the criminal court if the civil damages were not paid.

For over a century, opinion has been developing in favor of reparation or restitution by order of the criminal court. Several American states at the beginning of the nineteenth century had laws which provided that a person convicted of larceny should return to the owner twice the value of the property stolen. This kind of reaction to crime is essentially nonpunitive, and it probably is a system for implementation of the general nonpunitive reaction which was characteristic of the positive school and which has been gaining popularity in recent times.[57]

It is probable that the system of restitution and reparation is used much more frequently than official records indicate. One of the prevalent methods used by professional thieves when they are arrested is to suggest to the victim that the property will be restored if the victim refuses to prosecute. This results in release in a large proportion of cases, for most victims are more interested in regaining their stolen property than in "seeing justice done." Also, many persons are protected against crime by insurance. The insurance company is interested primarily in restitution, and in many cases the crime probably is not reported, or criminal prosecution is not urged, if restitution is made. Similarly, there are thousands of cases of shoplifting, embezzlement, and automobile theft annually which are not reported to the police by the victim because restitution or reparation is made.

---

[56] Stephen Schafer, *Restitution to Victims of Crime* (London: Stevens and Sons, 1960), pp. 3-7.

[57] See Stephen Schafer, "Restitution to Victims of Crime — An Old Correctional Aim Modernized," *Minnesota Law Review,* 50:243-254, December, 1965.

Restitution and reparation are most frequently used, both officially and unofficially, in connection with minor cases. In the United States, the official method of demanding restitution is used in connection with probation, one condition of the latter often being that the offender make restitution. Probation departments often are primarily collection agencies. The probation department of New York collects about $500,000 a year from probationers for restitution. ●

The general theme of this chapter has been that neither the punitive reaction to lawbreaking nor any specific method of implementing that reaction is rooted in the human organism or in universal traits of human nature. On the contrary, reactions to crime are seen to change with variations in the culture. Some kind of reaction to criminal behavior is universal, but the reaction may be either punitive or nonpunitive. Even when the societal reaction is punitive, there are great variations in the specific methods used to implement the reaction. ●

Conclusion

ANCEL, MARC. *Social Defence.* London: Routledge and Kegan Paul, 1965.

ANDENAES, JOHANNES. "The General Preventive Effects of Punishment." *University of Pennsylvania Law Review,* 114:949-983, May, 1966.

ASCHAFFENBURG, G. *Crime and Its Repression.* Boston: Little, Brown, 1913.

BEDAU, HUGO ADAM, ed. *The Death Penalty in America,* rev. ed. Garden City, N.Y.: Doubleday, 1967.

CALDWELL, ROBERT G. *Red Hannah: Delaware's Whipping Post.* Philadelphia: University of Pennsylvania Press, 1947.

CHAMBLISS, WILLIAM J. "A Sociological Analysis of the Law of Vagrancy," *Social Problems,* 12:67-77, Summer, 1964.

EVANS, E. P. *The Criminal Prosecution and Capital Punishment of Animals.* London: W. Heinemann, 1906.

GARFINKEL, HAROLD. "Conditions of Successful Degradation Ceremonies." *American Journal of Sociology,* 61:420-424, March, 1956.

HENTIG, HANS VON. *Punishment: Its Origin, Purpose, and Psychology.* London: William Hodge, 1937.

HOEBEL, E. ADAMSON. *The Law of Primitive Man: A Study in Comparative Legal Dynamics.* Cambridge, Mass.: Harvard University Press, 1954.

IVES, GEORGE. *A History of Penal Methods.* London: Stanley Paul, 1914.

MAESTRO, M. T. *Voltaire and Beccaria as Reformers of the Criminal Law.* New York: Columbia University Press, 1942.

MARTIN, J. P., & D. WEBSTER. *The Social Consequences of Conviction.* London: Heinemann, 1971.

Suggested readings

MEAD, G. H. "The Psychology of Punitive Justice." *American Journal of Sociology*, 23:577-602, March, 1918.

McCAFFERTY, JAMES A., ed. *Capital Punishment*. Chicago: Aldine-Atherton, 1972.

MOBERLY, WALTER. *The Ethics of Punishment*. London: Faber and Faber, 1968.

OPPENHEIMER, H. *The Rationale of Punishment*. London: University of London Press, 1913.

PACKER, HERBERT L. *The Limits of the Criminal Sanction*. Stanford: Stanford University Press, 1968.

RICO, JOSE M. "L'Indemnisation Des Victimes D'Actes Criminels: Etude Comparative." *Acta Criminologica*, 1:261-305, January, 1968.

RUSCHE, GEORGE, & OTTO KIRCHHEIMER. *Punishment and Social Structure*. New York: Columbia University Press, 1939.

SALEILLES, R. *The Individualization of Punishment*. Translated by R. S. Jastrow. Boston: Little, Brown, 1911.

SAVITZ, LEONARD D. "Capital Crimes as Defined in American Statutory Law." *Journal of Criminal Law, Criminology, and Police Science*, 46:355-363, September-October, 1955.

SCHAFER, STEPHEN. *Restitution to Victims of Crime*. London: Stevens and Sons, 1960.

SELLIN, THORSTEN, ed. *Capital Punishment*. New York: Harper and Row, 1967.

TOBY, JACKSON. "Criminal Motivation: A Sociocultural Analysis." *British Journal of Sociology*, 2:317-336, April, 1962.

WOLFGANG, MARVIN E. "Victim Compensation in Crimes of Personal Violence." *Minnesota Law Review*, 50:223-241, December, 1965.

Punitive policies and social structure

15

In the previous chapter we were primarily concerned with general variations in the punitive reaction to crime and with variations in specific methods of expressing that reaction. Here we will be concerned with the extent to which official reactions are the actual reactions to lawbreaking and with variations in the justifications given for the punitive reaction. In the final pages, several theories which have attempted explanation of the wide range of variations will be reviewed. ●

Variations in execution of official punitive reactions

In the period during which the theories of the classical school were most popular, it was argued that if every crime were followed immediately by extreme suffering on the part of the criminal, crime would almost entirely disappear. The ideal was a punitive societal reaction which would approach as closely as possible an assumed law of nature. The desired attributes of punishment were uniformity, certainty, celerity, and severity, and the basic objective of the classical school was to make these the characteristics of the official, legal system of dealing with lawbreakers. With the rise of the positive school, on the other hand, any method of punishment was regarded with considerable skepticism. The early positivists pointed to intoxication, which often is rather promptly followed by suffering, but which is continued nevertheless. They maintained that a society has the amount of crime it deserves in view of its biological composition and its economic and social conditions, leading to the conclusion that any policy used in dealing with individual criminals is relatively unimportant in determining behavior. Perhaps the same set of social conditions which gave life to the positive school in the first place also effectively blocked the development of a uniform, certain, swift, and severe punitive reaction to lawbreaking.

Uniformity in the classical system referred to the similarity of punishment of all persons who violated a particular law. This uniformity was justified on the ground that it was necessary to have a definite predetermined penalty in order that prospective offenders might take it into their calculations of the pleasures and pains which would result from criminal acts. The pride of the system was its impersonality. In reacting to crime, society was to give no consideration to social status, wealth, religion, previous behavior, age, sex, or any other characteristics or circumstances of the person. The emphasis on uniformity was an expression of the spirit of democracy then strong in European countries.

Certainty of punishment refers to the frequency with which violators are detected, identified, convicted, and punished. Certainty cannot be attained in modern society, especially for such crimes as larceny and burglary, although there probably are great variations in its approximation. Many of these variations were discussed earlier, when it was observed that the value of crime statistics decreases as the distance from the crime in terms of procedure increases.[1] In general, the number of arrests for larceny and burglary probably is not more than 10 percent of the number committed, but this varies from society to society.

Severity and celerity of punishment have, of necessity, varied with uniformity and certainty; and, in fact, it seems impossible to separate any one of these attributes from the others. Many observations of severity have been attempted in support of arguments for and against its effectiveness as a deterrent. But such arguments never have been supported by conclusive evidence, probably because the relationship of severity to the other attributes cannot be controlled. Perhaps severe and swift punishment

---

[1] See chap. 2, pp. 25-31.

would be effective in deterrence and reformation if all offenders were punished in the same way. Also, it is likely that even mild punishments would be effective deterrents for many crimes, especially white-collar crimes, if they were swift and certain.[2] When ten offenders are punished severely and ninety are not even detected in their crimes, then the effects of an official policy of severity cannot be determined. Officially-prescribed punishments, whether severe or not, were not imposed certainly or with any fixed degree of uniformity during earlier historical periods, and surely they are not imposed certainly or uniformly in the United States at the present.[3] This can be observed in the practice of mitigating official penalties and in the practice of imposing punitive policies differentially.

Mitigation of penalties

Penalties officially prescribed as a part of the general punitive reaction to lawbreaking have been mitigated in various ways. One of the early methods used for this purpose was "securing sanctuary." In the thirteenth century, an English criminal could avoid punishment by claiming refuge in a church for a period of forty days, at the end of which time he was compelled to leave the realm by a road or port assigned to him. In the early sixteenth century, instead of being permitted to leave the realm, a criminal who had secured sanctuary might be compelled to spend the rest of his life in an assigned locality in England, the name of which was branded on his thumb for identification. The entire system of securing sanctuary began to decline in the last part of the fifteenth century, and by the middle of the sixteenth century murder, rape, burglary, arson, and a few other offenses no longer carried the right of sanctuary. The whole system was abandoned when the monasteries were broken up.

A second system for mitigation of penalties was "right of clergy." This grew out of the original demand of the church to try its own officers. To be tried by an ecclesiastical court was a distinct advantage, for the church was not permitted to impose the death penalty during a part of the period of its supremacy, and its penalties in general were less severe except for the offenses of heresy and witchcraft. The "clergy" were defined at first in the strict sense, but later the term came to include all who had the clerical tonsure, then all who could read. The test used in determining whether a person could read was generally the first verse of the fifty-first psalm, and a little coaching would enable almost anyone to pass this test. Finally the peers who

---

[2] See William J. Chambliss, "The Deterrent Influence of Punishment," *Crime and Delinquency*, January, 1966, pp. 70-75.

[3] Jack P. Gibbs, "Crime, Punishment, and Deterrence," *Southwestern Social Science Quarterly*, 48:515-530, March, 1968; Charles R. Tittle, "Crime Rates and Legal Sanctions," *Social Problems*, 16:409-423, Spring, 1969; and Theodore G. Chiricos and Gordon P. Waldo, "Punishment and Crime: An Examination of Some Empirical Evidence," *Social Problems*, 18:200-217, Fall, 1970.

could not read received the same benefit of clergy by nature of their position.

"Right of clergy" or "benefit of clergy" was a device by which those who were culturally similar to the lawmakers were made exempt from the more severe penalties. The elites who were responsible for expressing the official punitive reaction did not inflict severe penalties upon their own members but reserved these punishments for the lower classes. While the number of persons who could claim right of clergy increased, the number of times a person could claim the right and the number of offenses for which this right could be claimed were gradually reduced. Thus, as the power of the church elite declined, penalties came to be more nearly the same for those who had the benefit of clergy and those who did not. An act of 1705 provided that even those who claimed the right of clergy might be punished by secular authorities at least to the extent of confinement in a house of correction for not less than six months or more than two years. By the end of the eighteenth century the right of clergy meant nothing.[4]

A third method of mitigation of penalties was the pardon. The prescribed penalties were severe, but the king was permitted to relax the severity in individual cases. Our present system of pardoning probably grew out of this practice. In the modern period, the courts have been authorized to fix penalties within limits set by legislatures, and in this manner to adjust the penalty to the needs of individual offenders.

A fourth method of mitigating penalties was the simple refusal to execute the punishments officially prescribed and imposed. In the seventeenth and eighteenth centuries in England, a period of rapidly shifting standards, property owners demanded severe penalties as a means of protection. But because the common people were increasing in political and social power, these sentences, though imposed, were not executed in a large proportion of the cases, as is shown by the statistics for England in Table XVI.[5]

TABLE XVI

Changes in the proportion of capital penalties executed

Years	Percent
1689-1718*	52.6
1755-1784*	28.3
1785-1814*	25.6
1815-1819	10.5
1820-1826	6.9
1827-1833	4.1

* Counties of Essex, Herts, Kent, Surrey, and Sussex only.

[4] See Jerome Hall, *Theft, Law, and Society*, 2d ed. (Indianapolis: Bobbs-Merrill, 1952), pp. 110-118, 356-363; and George Dalzell, *Benefit of Clergy in America* (Winston-Salem, N.C.: Blair, 1955).

[5] See also Leon Radzinowicz, *A History of English Criminal Law and its Administration from 1750* (New York: Macmillan, 1948), Vol. I, pp. 143-164.

Corporal punishments disappeared from England, just as did the death penalty, because even when courts imposed the sentences, public sentiment prevented their execution. In the last part of the eighteenth century Bentham made the following statement regarding the penalty of branding:

> Burning in the hand, according as the criminal and the executioner can agree, is performed either with a cold or a red-hot iron; and if it be with a red-hot iron, it is only a slice of ham which is burnt; to complete the farce, the criminal screams, whilst it is only the fat which smokes and burns, and the knowing spectators only laugh at this parody of justice.[6]

Similarly, as opposition to the policy of quartering the corpse after execution developed, the method became more and more symbolic, until, in 1820, "quartering" consisted merely of scratching a cross on the neck of the corpse.

Even fines may be remitted by executive or judicial acts. In general at present the governor alone has power to remit fines in state cases, but some variations are found. A practice has developed in some courts of imposing a fine and then, in chambers, allowing a motion in mitigation, by which the fine is reduced. This method was used extensively during the period of national prohibition; publicity was secured by imposing very heavy fines for alcohol violations, and friends were secured by secretly reducing the fines.

Differential imposition of punishments

There is a great deal of evidence that current official punitive policies for dealing with lawbreaking are not imposed in all cases of lawbreaking, and this would indicate that the actual, unofficial, societal reactions to crime are not really reflected in the laws governing the administration of justice. The unofficial reactions to the crimes of persons of one status are different from the reactions to the crimes of persons of another status. Prescribed penalties are mitigated in some cases but not in others. Discriminations have been made and are made because of the age, sex, wealth, education, political prestige, race, nationality, and other characteristics of the offender. For example, in the United States female offenders are less likely than men to be arrested, and female prisoners are held in prison on the average about two-thirds as long for a specified type of offense as male prisoners. It is very difficult to convict females of capital offenses when the death penalty is mandatory, for juries refuse to find them guilty. In fact, for most major crimes, the ratio of convictions to arrests is lower for females than for males.

Powerful groups are usually punished less frequently and severely than less powerful groups, as may be observed in the differential punishments of white-collar criminals compared with

---

[6] Jeremy Bentham, "Principles of Penal Law," in John Bowring, ed., *The Works of Jeremy Bentham* (Edinburgh: W. Tait, 1843), p. 550.

other criminals.[7] Also, numerous studies have shown that the official punitive policy is more frequently applied to lawbreaking by blacks than it is to lawbreaking by whites. The following conclusions have been drawn by one or more investigators: (a) Negroes are more liable to arrest than whites. (b) Negroes have less chance of not being indicted and of having their cases nol-prossed, passed to files, or disposed of in a miscellaneous fashion than do whites. (c) Negroes have a higher conviction rate than whites. (d) Negroes are often punished more severely than whites, but this is not true for all crimes. (e) Negroes are less likely to receive probation and suspended sentences. (f) Negroes receive pardons less often than do whites. (g) Negroes have less chance of having a death sentence commuted than do whites. ●

Variations in the justifications of punitive reactions

Not only have both formal and informal societal reactions to crime varied, but the rationale given for those reactions has varied as well. At various times and places expiation, deterrence, retribution, reformation, income for the state, restoring or promoting the solidarity of the group, and other things have been offered as justifications for the punitive reaction.[8] The justifications are not merely ex post facto rationalizations but, instead, are the reasons or motives men have for punishing in the first place. The particular form the punitive reaction takes depends upon the reasons offered for it or, in other words, upon the kind of value which the punishment is assumed to have. No consistent course of development can be discerned, and certainly at any given time, especially at the present, all the members of a given society do not have the same reason for using the punitive reaction, even if they agree that such a reaction is desirable. Even individuals probably have more than one motive for punishing. Usually investigators infer merely that one or more of the motives is dominant, but not exclusive, in a society. Thomas and Znaniecki, for example, argued that among the Polish peasants they studied, the motive for punishment of crime was the restoration of the situation which existed before the crime and renewal of the solidarity of the group, and that revenge was a secondary consideration.[9]

Exner, the noted German penal law scholar, once remarked, "So far as we can look back, men have always punished and have never ceased to dispute their reasons for so doing."[10] After

---

[7] See Edwin H. Sutherland, *White Collar Crime* (New York: Dryden Press, 1949).

[8] Egon Bittner and Anthony M. Platt, "The Meaning of Punishment," *Issues in Criminology*, 2 (1966): 79-99.

[9] W. I. Thomas and F. Znaniecki, *The Polish Peasant in Europe and America* (Chicago: University of Chicago Press, 1927), 2:1254-1255. See also George H. Mead, "The Psychology of Punitive Justice," *American Journal of Sociology*, 23:577-602, March, 1918.

[10] Franz Exner, *Gerechtigkeit und Richteramt* (Leipzig: F. Meiner, 1922), p. 6.

the early attempts to rationalize punishments by considerations of a transcendental nature, the leading writers in this field insisted that certain social benefits resulted from punishment and constituted the justification of punishment. But little of this literature faced the issue of punishment *versus* other methods of dealing with criminals. It was assumed without argument that punishment was necessary, and the problem was to formulate an acceptable statement of this necessity. Thus, the controversy was largely between adherents of rival concepts of punishment, not between the adherents and opponents of punishment. The political philosophers were concerned, also, principally with the abstract right of the state to punish for crime. Even if one admits that the state has such a right in general, the further problem remains of determining whether punishment is economical in the larger sense. Moreover, the philosophical discussions have been concerned primarily with the purpose or aim of punishment and with the amount and nature of punishment, not with its value in comparison with other methods of dealing with criminals. The following values of punishment have been indicated by those who insist on the desirability of punishment.

Punishment as retribution

At least since the formulation (in about 1875 B.C.) of the Code of Hammurabi ("an eye for an eye and a tooth for a tooth"), it has been urged by leaders and accepted by the general public that the criminal deserves to suffer. The suffering imposed by the state in its corporate capacity is considered the political counterpart of individual revenge. One of England's greatest criminal law scholars, Sir James Stephen, stated: "Criminal procedure is to resentment what marriage is to affection: namely, the legal provision for an inevitable impulse of human beings." This actually is a statement of the aim or purpose of punishment, and not a justification of punishment in terms of the social utilities produced by it. John Dewey argued that we are not relieved of the responsibility for the consequences of our procedure by the fact that the offender is guilty.[11] A justification of punishment must state what future effects punishment will have on criminals. The future is not often considered by those who insist that the criminal deserves to be punished. It sometimes is urged, negatively, that unless the criminal gets the punishment he deserves, the victim will seek individual revenge, which may mean lynch-law if his friends cooperate with him; or the victim will refuse to make complaint or offer testimony, and the state will therefore be handicapped in dealing with criminals.

Punishment as a deterrent

Among those who advocate punishment because of its social utility, some claim that the infliction of pain upon those convicted of crime serves to deter others from crime, and that it has

---

[11] John Dewey, *Human Nature and Conduct* (New York: Henry Holt, 1930), pp. 18-19.

great value for that reason, even if some individuals are not deterred. Generally, the notion that punishment reduces crime is based on the hedonistic assumption that people regulate their behavior by calculation of pleasure and pain. This assumption has been under severe attack for at least fifty years. Dewey emphasized the general fallacy in the assumption: "Deliberation no more resembles the casting-up of accounts of profit and loss, pleasure and pain, than an actor engaged in a drama resembles a clerk recording debit and credit items in his ledger."[12]

Some criminals never consider the penalty. Sometimes this is because they are mentally disturbed, mentally retarded, or acting under the stress of a great emotion. Sometimes the penalty merely makes the prohibited act more alluring. Sometimes the criminal simply does not consider the possibility that he might get caught. At the beginning of this century, Münsterberg accurately summed up the reasons for believing that the pains of punishment are not weighed against the pleasures of crime:

> The hope of escaping justice in the concrete case will easily have a stronger feeling tone than the opposing fear of the abstract general law. The strength of the forbidden desire will narrow the circle of association and eliminate the idea of the probable consequences. The stupid mind will not link the correct expectations, the slow mind will bring the check too late, when the deed is done, the vehement mind will overrule the energies of inhibition, the emotional mind will be more moved by the anticipated immediate pleasure than by the thought of a later suffering. And all this will be reinforced if overstrain has destroyed the nervous balance, or if stimulants have smoothed the path of motor discharge. If the severity of cruel punishment has brutalized the mind, the threat will be as ineffective as if the mildness of punishment had reduced its pain. And, worst of all, this fear will be ruled out if the mind develops in an atmosphere of crime where the child hears of the criminal as a hero, and looks at jail as an ordinary affair, troublesome only as most factors in his slum life are troublesome; or if the anarchy of corruption or class justice, of reckless legislation or public indifference to law defeats the inhibiting counter idea of punishment and deprives it of its emotional strength.[13]

However, a refutation of hedonistic psychology and its conceptions is probably not sufficient to justify the rejection of the broader aspects of the deterrence argument.[14] In a broader perspective, the criminal law and its application by police and courts probably have great effects upon public morality. Although specific severe punishments may have little immediate demonstrable effect in deterring specific criminals, the existence of the criminal code with its penal sanctions probably has a long-run negative effect upon the development of criminalistic ideologies. By means of the criminal law and the procedures

---

[12] Ibid., p. 199.

[13] H. Münsterberg, *On the Witness Stand* (New York: McClure, 1908), pp. 258-260.

[14] See William J. Chambliss, "Types of Deviance and the Effectiveness of Legal Sanctions," *Wisconsin Law Review,* 1967:703-719, Summer, 1967; and Franklin E. Zimring, *Perspectives on Deterrence* (Washington: Government Printing Office, 1971).

for implementing the criminal law, including the imposition of swift and certain punishments, the undesirability and impropriety of certain behavior is emphasized.[15]

> Not the crimes punished, but the crimes prevented should measure the worth of the law. . . . If out of a score of law-abiding persons, only one obeys the law from fear of its penalties, it does not follow that the penal system occupies a correspondingly insignificant place among the supports of social order. For the rules of the social game are respected by the many good men chiefly because they are forced upon the few bad. If the one rascal among twenty men might aggress at will, the higher forms of control would break down, the fair-play instinct would cease to bind, and, between bad example and the impulse of retaliation, man after man would be detached from the honest majority. Thus, the deadly contagion of lawlessness would spread with increasing rapidity till the social order lay in ruins. The law, therefore, however minor its part at a given moment in the actual coercion of citizens, is still the cornerstone of the edifice of order.[16]

When deterrence was regarded as the principal purpose of punishment, penalties were made as public and as brutal as possible—witness the ducking stool, the stocks, the pillory, the public hangings, and the gibbeting of the body so that it might remain as long as possible as an example to the public. Whenever the fiction known as a "crime-wave" is heralded, a demand for an increase in the severity of penalties arises, based on the assumption that the more severe the penalty, the more effectively it will deter others from similar crimes. These demands ordinarily are based on a confusion of penal sanctions as general expressions of hostility to crime on the one hand, and severe punishments as deterrents of specific persons who might be contemplating prohibited acts on the other hand.

Punishment as a means of reformation

It is maintained also that punishment tends to reform criminals and that it accomplishes this by creating a fear of repetition of the punishment, by creating a conviction that crime does not pay, or by breaking habits that criminals have formed, especially if the penalty is a long period of imprisonment which gives the habits no opportunity for expression. Such illustrations as the following are given in support of this argument: If bees swarm out of their hive and sting the boy who molests them, they will not be troubled by him in the future; if they should fly from the hive on the approach of the boy and leave their honey at his disposal, they would be troubled again and again. Moreover, attention is called to the fact that experiments with animals have shown that animals frequently learn an operation more quickly when they are punished for failure than when they are not punished. A city attorney, speaking in defense of punishment, stated:

---

[15] Johannes Andenaes, "The General Preventive Effects of Punishment," *University of Pennsylvania Law Review*, 114:949-983, May, 1966.

[16] E. A. Ross, *Social Control* (New York: Macmillan, 1916), p. 125.

You must inflict pain to get results. It was that way with me when I was a boy: I had been misbehaving and my father gave me an awful whaling and he had to do it only once. I had the same experience in dealing with my son. It is the same way with criminals. You must inflict pain to get results. It is the only language they understand.

Recently, objective tests and measurements have been used in the effort to determine the values of punishment in learning, and these studies are pertinent to the discussion of reformation of criminals since reformation involves a learning process. Experiments are set up in order to measure the relative values of rewards and punishments in relation to animal and human learning and performance. The effects of punishment, even in these experimental situations, cannot be stated as a simple proposition. A mild punishment may promote learning, but a more severe punishment may cause terror and panic which interfere with the whole learning process. Moreover, the social situations in which punishments for crime are inflicted involve variables which are lacking in punishments administered in experimental laboratories.[17]

Changes in schoolchildren's behavior in spite of, or because of, the disappearance of corporal punishment are more relevant to the issue than are laboratory experiments. An eighteenth-century schoolteacher left an itemized list of 1,423,100 corporal punishments which he had inflicted on schoolchildren during his career.[18] A century ago most of the teachers' time in almost all schools was devoted to the maintenance of order and infliction of punishments. The average number of whippings per day in 1845 in a school of about 250 pupils near Boston was 65.6. Nevertheless, nearly four hundred Massachusetts schools were broken up annually because the teacher was unable to maintain discipline. The behavior of schoolchildren in modern schools, in which corporal punishment is seldom inflicted, is much better than in the schools of a century ago, when corporal punishment was extremely frequent. It is evident that the effect of punishment on reformation depends very much on the situation in which the punishment is inflicted.[19]

It is also asserted that respect for law grows largely out of opposition to those who violate the law. The public hates the criminal, and this hatred is expressed in the form of punishment. In standing together against the enemy of their values, they

Punishment and social solidarity

---

[17] For an analysis of the complexities in the effects of punishment see Barry F. Singer, "Psychological Studies of Punishment," *California Law Review*, 58:405-443, March, 1970.

[18] Henry Barnard, *English Pedagogy*, 2d ser. (Hartford: Brown and Gross, 1876), p. 327.

[19] See Johannes Andenaes, "Does Punishment Deter Crime?" *Criminal Law Quarterly* (Toronto), 11:77-93, November, 1968; idem., "Deterrence and Specific Offenses," *University of Chicago Law Review*, 38:537-553, Spring, 1971.

develop group solidarity and respect for these values.[20] As indicated earlier, group solidarity might develop because the penal law process reaffirms law-abiding ideals and attitudes in the general public, not because punishment deters near-criminals. Lundstedt maintained that the significant contribution of punishment is not fear of punishment, but rather the legal sentiments, legal conscience, or moral feeling which have been developed in the general public by the administration of the criminal law during previous generations, and which have become so organized that they regulate behavior spontaneously, almost like an instinct.[21] ●

Testing the effectiveness of punishment

Most of the justifications of punitive reactions and policies have not been made in the abstract but, instead, have been given as rather specific arguments for such methods as corporal punishment, the death penalty, or imprisonment. At present each of these methods is advocated by some on the ground that it has a deterrent effect, an effect on social solidarity, or other desirable effects, just as they were advocated a century or more ago. In the earlier period the arguments were challenged only by counterarguments, while in the recent period the challenges have been based at least in part upon examination and analysis of such empirical data as can be found. Such analyses of evidence amount to attempts to test the arguments, to treat them as hypotheses. This is a scientific procedure, and some of the arguments for the death penalty, together with some of the kinds of data used to refute the arguments, are presented here to illustrate the procedure. Arguments and data regarding the effectiveness of imprisonment will be given later.[22]

The most popular arguments currently made in favor of the death penalty are (a) it is more effective than any other penalty in deterring from murder; (b) it is more economical than imprisonment; (c) it is necessary in order to prevent the public from lynching criminals; and (d) it is the only certain penalty, for murderers who are sentenced to life imprisonment frequently secure paroles or pardons. On the other hand, those who oppose the death penalty argue that the death penalty is not more effective than imprisonment as a deterrent, that the abolition of the death penalty does not promote lynchings, that it reduces the certainty and speed of punishment, that by breaking down respect for human life it tends to promote murder, that errors of justice are irreparable, and that it has undesirable effects on the prisoners

---

[20] See Lewis A. Coser, "Some Functions of Deviant Behavior and Normative Flexibility," *American Journal of Sociology,* 68:172-182, September, 1962.

[21] A. V. Lundstedt, *Superstition or Rationality in Action for Peace?* (London: Longmans, Green, 1925), pp. 47-49, 190-192.

[22] See chap. 23, pp. 496-521.

and the staff in institutions in which it is inflicted.[23] Of these arguments, the one about the deterrent effect of the death penalty is by far the most important.

The most common method of testing the deterrent effect of the death penalty is to compare the homicide rates in states which have abolished the death penalty with the rates in states which retain it. In general, such comparisons show that in abolition states the homicide rate is only about one-third to one-half as high as it is in the other states. However, such comparisons are somewhat biased because the death penalty is authorized in all of the southern states, and the southern states have the highest homicide rate. A more justifiable comparison is between states in a particular section of the United States. Figures II to V show that there is no significant difference in the homicide rates of states which have abolished the death penalty and adjoining states which have retained the death penalty.[24]

The death penalty as a deterrent

The significant difference is not between states which have the death penalty and those which do not, but between the different sections of the country, regardless of whether the states have or do not have the death penalty. The composition of the population and the general culture of the section is much more important than the presence or absence of the death penalty in determining homicide rates. Similar differences are found within states. Vold compared two states which, at the time, had the death penalty. He found the average homicide rate to be 3.9 per 100,000 population in the southernmost Iowa counties and 3.5 in the adjoining Missouri counties. But in the southern tier of Missouri counties the rate was 10.5. The northern tier of Missouri counties is very similar to the southern tier of Iowa counties in culture and composition of the population, but the southern tier of Missouri counties is significantly different.[25]

A second method for testing the deterrent effect of the death penalty is comparison of crime rates just before and just after one or more executions has taken place. If the death penalty has any deterrent value it presumably lies in its actual execution rather than in the legal possibility of execution. Areas in which murderers are actually executed should be compared with areas in which the law prohibits such executions. Moreover, the areas should be sufficiently small (say, counties), so that an execution will produce some influence on the potential murderers in that area. No significant difference was found in this respect

---

[23] Excellent bibliographies on capital punishment appear in James A. McCafferty, ed., *Capital Punishment* (Chicago: Aldine-Atherton, 1972); and in Thorsten Sellin, ed., *Capital Punishment* (New York: Harper and Row, 1967).

[24] Figures II to V are reproduced from Thorsten Sellin, "Homicide in Retentionist and Abolitionist States," in idem., ed., *Capital Punishment,* pp. 135-138.

[25] George B. Vold, "Can the Death Penalty Prevent Crime?" *Prison Journal,* October, 1932, pp. 3-8.

Homicide Death Rates (per 100,000 Population) in Contiguous
Abolitionist and Retentionist States, 1920–1963

FIGURE II

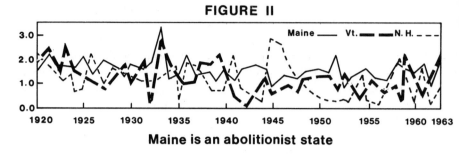

Maine is an abolitionist state

FIGURE III

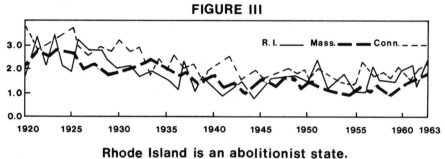

Rhode Island is an abolitionist state.

FIGURE IV

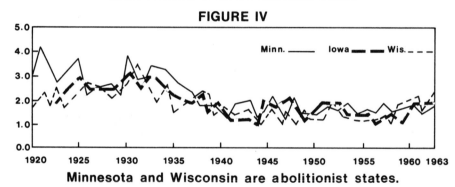

Minnesota and Wisconsin are abolitionist states.

FIGURE V

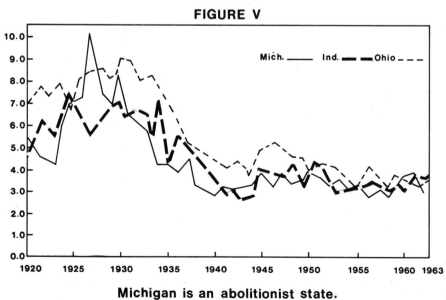

Michigan is an abolitionist state.

in a study of homicide rates sixty days prior and sixty days subsequent to five executions in Philadelphia.[26] In another Philadelphia study, Savitz analyzed the rate of capital crimes for a period
of eight weeks just before and eight weeks after the sentencing
of four men to death. He hypothesized that the greatest deterrence would occur in the locality where the crimes were committed and where the criminal was known. The four cases were
selected because the sentencing was given great publicity in the
newspapers. No significant increase or decrease in the murder
rate occurred; there was no pattern that would indicate deterrence.[27] A more recent Chicago study also indicated that homicide
fluctuates independently of news coverage, executions, and com-
mutations of sentences in capital cases.[28]

The results of the relatively crude comparisons in the United
States are reinforced by comparisons in European countries. On
the average, the European states which have abolished the death
penalty have lower homicide rates (which generally means lower
murder rates in Europe) than states which retain the death penalty. The Scandinavian countries, which have abolished the death
penalty, have homicide rates about one-half as high as England,
which retained the death penalty until recently.

A third method for testing the deterrent value of the death penalty is by comparing, in the states which have abolished the death
penalty, the homicide rates before and after the abolition. The
general conclusion from such comparisons is that the states which
abolished the death penalty have had no unusual increase in homicide rates. Eleven states abolished the death sentence only to
restore it after a few years, on the ground that the murder rate
had increased greatly after the abolition. The statistics show,
however, that the changes in homicide rates were almost exactly
parallel in other states which made no changes in their laws
regarding the death penalty. For instance, Missouri abolished the
death penalty in 1917 and restored it in 1919 on the ground that
murders had increased greatly. But the changes in the homicide
rate in Missouri from 1910 to 1924 were almost exactly the same
in direction and amount as in Ohio, which retained the death
penalty throughout this whole period, and were very much like
the changes in the United States in general. Comparison of the
"before and after" homicide rates of European countries which
have abolished the death penalty also shows that the presence or
absence of the death penalty has no perceptible effect on the
incidence of murder.

---

[26] Robert H. Dann, "The Deterrent Effect of Capital Punishment," *Friends'
Social Service Series*, Bulletin No. 29, 1935.

[27] Leonard D. Savitz, "A Study of Capital Punishment," *Journal of Criminal
Law, Criminology, and Police Science*, 49:338-341, November-December, 1958;
Karl F. Schuessler, "The Deterrent Influence of the Death Penalty," *Annals
of the American Academy of Political and Social Science*, 284:54-62,
November, 1952.

[28] Hans W. Mattick, *The Unexamined Death*, 2d ed. (Chicago: John Howard
Association, 1966), pp. 12-15.

The available statistics do not justify an absolute conclusion regarding the value of the death penalty as a deterrent. The evidence, such as it is, shows a relatively unimportant relation between the murder rate and the death penalty. The argument that the death penalty is an effective deterrent is not, at least, substantiated by the data available.[29] It is based on preconceptions rather than on data, and the preconceptions are taken from the hedonistic psychology which assumes that the psychological processes are much less complex than they are in fact. Even premeditated murders are generally committed under the stress of a great emotion, and the penalty is seldom considered.[30]

The death penalty and certainty of punishment

The advocates of the death penalty argue that it is more certain than imprisonment, because imprisonment is frequently terminated by escape, pardon, or parole. Actually, the death penalty is very uncertain, because it is so seldom imposed even when it is authorized. For example, there have been no executions carried out in the United States since 1967. Also, the argument is made that juries are less willing to convict and witnesses less willing to testify when the penalty is death than when it is a less irreparable penalty. Calvert cites a petition by English bankers in 1830 for abolition of the death penalty for forgery, on the ground that convictions could not be secured because of the severity of the death penalty and for the authorization of a less severe penalty in order that their property might be protected more adequately.[31] Bye found that a slightly larger proportion of convictions was secured in murder cases in states which had abolished the death penalty than in states which retain it.[32] However, in death-penalty states prospective jurors who are opposed to the death penalty have been excused from serving in capital cases, and in some instances this weeding-out process has produced juries which are most likely to convict the accused.[33] Moreover, the percentage of defendants found guilty in murder cases varies widely from county to county even in states which have the death penalty. For example, during the period 1925-1941 Middlesex County, Massachusetts, found 16.8 percent of its cases guilty of murder in the first degree,

---

[29] Jack P. Gibbs, "Crime, Punishment, and Deterrence," *Southwestern Social Science Quarterly,* 1968, pp. 515-530.

[30] See Marvin E. Wolfgang, *Patterns of Criminal Homicide* (Philadelphia: University of Pennsylvania Press, 1958), chap. 10.

[31] E. R. Calvert, *Capital Punishment in the Twentieth Century* (London: Putnam's Sons, 1927), p. 15.

[32] R. T. Bye, *Capital Punishment in the United States* (Philadelphia: Committee on Philanthropic Labor of Philadelphia Yearly Meeting of Friends, 1919), pp. 47 ff.

[33] Hans Zeisel, *Some Data on Juror Attitudes Toward Capital Punishment* (Chicago: University of Chicago Law School—Center for Studies in Criminal Justice, 1968). See also Walter E. Oberer, "Does Disqualification of Jurors for Scruples Against Capital Punishment Constitute Denial of Fair Trial on Issue of Guilt?" *Texas Law Review,* 39 (1961): 545-553.

while in adjacent Suffolk County the corresponding percentage was only 3.9.[34]

The uncertainty of the death penalty also is indicated by the fact that many of the persons sentenced to death are not executed. Of the 124 persons convicted of first-degree murder between 1898 and 1971 in Massachusetts, which had a mandatory death penalty until 1951, 65 were executed, 37 had their sentences commuted, and two died awaiting execution.[35] In Maryland in 1936-1961, 59 percent of those sentenced to death for murder and 51 percent of those sentenced to death for rape were executed.[36] While it is clear that imprisonment is not a completely certain penalty, it also is clear that the death penalty is not a certain penalty until it is actually executed.

Schuessler devised an index of the certainty of the death penalty and showed that the relative occurrence of murder has a slight tendency to decrease as the probability of execution increases. He found that among the death-penalty states, those which executed the largest proportion of the persons convicted of homicide in the period 1937-1949 generally had the lowest homicide rates. However, the correlation coefficient of $-.29$ was not statistically significant. Nor did the homicide rate drop consistently as the risk of execution increased. Also, he found that when a state executes a relatively large proportion of its murderers in one year, the homicide rate does not necessarily drop during the following year.[37]

The death penalty and financial economy

The death penalty often is defended on the ground that it is less expensive than life imprisonment. The per capita cost of imprisonment is about two thousand dollars per year, and the life term may amount to an average of twenty years, making a total of forty thousand dollars. If it is true that an execution costs less than this, the demand for execution would apply equally well to the noncriminal insane, to the mentally retarded, and to criminals who have committed offenses less serious than murder; for execution of such persons also would be cheaper than their maintenance in an institution. But there is some doubt as to whether execution actually is cheaper than imprisonment. First, the trials of death-penalty cases are ordinarily much longer than trials of other cases. As many as a thousand jurors may be examined before twelve are chosen, and a year or more intervenes between arrest

[34] Herbert B. Ehrmann, "The Death Penalty and the Administration of Justice," *Annals of the American Academy of Political and Social Science,* 284:73-84, November, 1952.

[35] Massachusetts Department of Correction, "Some Notes on Death Row and the Death Penalty in Massachusetts," Document No. 5678, June, 1971, p. 1.

[36] Legislative Council of Maryland, *Report of the Committee on Capital Punishment* (Baltimore: Author, 1962), p. 35.

[37] Schuessler, "The Deterrent Influence of the Death Penalty." See also Savitz, "A Study of Capital Punishment."

and sentencing. Second, although the maintenance cost per prisoner may be high, this does not mean that it would increase appreciably if those now executed were committed to prisons. Third, in considering cost of executions, the expenditures for death houses and for the closer custody which must be maintained are usually not computed. It cost over twenty-five thousand dollars a year for the custodial officers in the death house of the New Jersey State Prison.

The irreparability of error with the death penalty

Those who advocate capital punishment consider wrongful conviction as only a remote possibility.[38] But although most mistakes are prevented by the judicial system or by executive clemency, some occur, due to mistaken identification, inadequate circumstantial evidence, framed and simulated evidence, perjury, unreliable expert evidence, overlooking and suppressing of evidence, and excessive zeal on the part of investigators and prosecutors.[39] In a forty-year period, 12.3 percent of the 406 persons sent to Sing Sing Prison for execution were found, upon reconsideration, to have been sentenced in error.[40] Hartung found that in Michigan, which does not have the death penalty, judges and juries erred in 10.9 percent of 759 life-imprisonment convictions for murder in the first degree in 1942-1951.[41] ●

Theories of punishment

Our previous discussion has indicated that there has been no constant desire to make all criminals suffer and that the system used for inflicting suffering on those criminals considered as deserving of suffering has changed from time to time. The punitive reaction to lawbreaking has not been present in all societies; the methods for implementing the punitive reaction which are predominant in some societies are not predominant in others; the extent to which official punitive policies are carried out in practice varies from time to time even within a given society; and the rationale for punishment has taken many forms. A theory which precisely explains or accounts for all of these variations has not been developed. Preliminary attempts to account for at least some of the variations have been made, however, and the major cultural, psychoanalytic, and sociological explanations will be described briefly.

---

[38] See Bernard Lande Cohen, *Law Without Order: Capital Punishment and the Liberals* (New Rochelle, N.Y.: Arlington House, 1970), pp. 24-28.

[39] Charles E. O'Hara and James W. Osterburg, "Some Miscarriages of Justice Analyzed in the Light of Criminalistics," chap. 47 of *An Introduction to Criminalistics* (New York: Macmillan, 1959), pp. 680-685.

[40] Lewis E. Lawes, *Twenty Thousand Years in Sing Sing* (New York: R. Long and R. R. Smith, 1932), pp. 146-147, 156.

[41] Hartung, *op. cit.* See also Otto Pollak, "The Errors of Justice," *Annals of the American Academy of Political and Social Science*, 284:115-123, November, 1952; and Jerome Frank and Barbara Frank, *Not Guilty* (New York: Doubleday, 1957).

One theory which partially accounts for the many variations in the presence and implementation of the punitive reaction to law-breaking may be termed a theory of "cultural consistency." The societal reactions to lawbreaking and the methods used to implement or express those reactions show a general tendency to be consistent with other ways of behaving of the society. This may be observed in a number of ways.

Cultural consistency

First, two centuries ago criminals were disemboweled, quartered, hung in chains, branded, pilloried, ducked, and in other ways tortured, mutilated, and shamed. These practices occurred in a culture in which physical suffering was regarded as the natural lot of mankind, and in which the means of preventing pain were not well developed. Today safeguards against physical suffering have been provided in other fields; a policy of physical torture of criminals cannot be harmonized with the general interest in the reduction of suffering, and the reaction toward crime is away from the strictly punitive.

Second, the price system developed during the modern period, and the methods of punishment have developed somewhat consistently with the price system. Hence, perhaps, came the monetary implications in such phrases as "debt to society" and "pay the price." Just as a price is assumed to bear a constant relation to a commodity, so, it was assumed, the penalty should bear a constant relation to the crime. The aim was "to let the punishment fit the crime." The classical economists insisted that reward should be commensurate with service; the classical criminologists concluded that punishment should be commensurate with disservice or crime.

Third, the ideal of uniformity in the punishment of offenders was stated about the time of the French Revolution, when democracy meant the equality of all persons. Democracy has been reinterpreted since that time, and the policy of uniform penalties has been similarly modified. Moreover, uniformity developed at the time when one cure was used by physicians for all kinds of diseases and all kinds of patients.

Fourth, individualization in medical treatment has developed during the last two centuries and with it individualization in penal treatment. The positive school, which at first was a biological school, insisted that criminals, like patients, differ, and that the offender rather than the offense should be the object of attention. The general trend at present is toward the individualization which the positive school outlined. If this policy of individualization tends to result in a uniform reaction to criminality, it is a uniformity of reaction to all criminals who are similar in type of personality or in situation, rather than uniformity based on the type of crime committed. Ideally, it is a uniformity like that in medicine.

Fifth, only a few generations ago punishment was emphasized in the home, school, and church, and, necessarily, the system for the handling of offenders by the state was consistent. When penal methods were generally abandoned by the home, school, and church, it became difficult for the state to continue exercising penal policies successfully. Now the offender often gets more support and the state less support when the official reaction is severely punitive.

Finally, the penalties tend to be more certain and severe for acts which endanger the values which are highly regarded, and these values change.[42] Perhaps it is for this reason that in several states at present the minimum official penalty for bribing an athlete is greater than the penalty for robbery with a gun.

Somewhat more specifically, two general changes in the method of implementing the punitive reaction have taken place in the last two centuries, and they seem to be correlated: imprisonment has been used more frequently, physical torture and death less frequently. The explanation for this decrease in the use of the methods of torture and killing and for the substitution of imprisonment is not entirely clear, but certain elements of the explanation stand out.

Negatively, imprisonment on an extensive scale was practically impossible in the earlier period. No institutions secure enough for imprisonment of large numbers of persons had been constructed, and the difficulty of building such institutions made their development impractical. More important, with many wars, changes in control, and lack of police or other guardians, such institutions, even if constructed, would have been relatively useless; it was necessary for social life to become more settled before imprisonment could become a popular reaction to lawbreaking.

More positively, a greater appreciation of freedom developed in the modern period, and restriction of freedom came to be regarded as suffering. During the medieval period, which was characterized by an intense interest in theology, suffering could be imposed by excommunication. Similarly, during the modern period, with the interest in democracy and freedom, the loss of freedom means more than it did previously. In the earlier period, prisoners of war and religious prisoners were ordinarily confined in castles, and the life of one imprisoned for crime would not have been significantly different from the life of many persons who had not committed crimes. Many castles of the time were no more pleasant than the prisons; in fact many castles were turned into prisons and then later used as castles again. Because of the increased valuation of freedom, the loss of freedom has come to be regarded as sufficiently punitive even for the worst criminals.

Further, since the time of the industrial revolution, labor power has come to be highly valued. Imprisonment developed at about the time the slave labor system began to wane. Life became valuable. Because of the higher valuation of labor power, it became

---

[42] Cf. Arthur Lewis Wood, "The Alternatives to the Death Penalty," *Annals of the American Academy of Political and Social Science,* 284:63-72, November, 1952.

logical to conserve it instead of destroying it by death or mutilations.

Finally, the more brutal punishments flourished at a time when the social distance between those who imposed the punishment and those who suffered it was very great. The situation changed in this respect in the modern period by the development of democracy and the means of communication. Democracy was important in this way because it meant that the control was secured by persons who had much the same experiences as the defendants; one was tried by his peers who understood his situation and looked upon him as a human being like themselves. The development of the means of communication was important because it brought about an increasing number of contacts between those who committed crimes and others. This enabled a larger proportion of the population to appreciate the situation of those who committed offenses, so that the imposition of pain or suffering was no longer similar to the injury of an animal or of a foreign enemy. Although limitations were imposed by color of skin, socioeconomic status, and other differentiae, contacts that were frequent and intimate increased, with the result of greater understanding and a keener sympathy for criminals.

Psychoanalysts have advanced a theory which correlates the many variations in the punitive reaction with variations in the alternative systems for satisfying aggressive and libidinal instincts. The general notion is that these instincts must be expressed in some fashion and that the criminal serves as a scapegoat for their legitimate expression. Thus, it is maintained that in punishing criminals, society expresses the same urges which are expressed, among criminals, in committing crime. Menninger has recently said, "We need criminals to identify ourselves with, to envy secretly, and to punish stoutly. They do for us the forbidden, illegal things we *wish* to do and, like scapegoats of old, they bear the burdens of our displaced guilt and punishment—'the iniquities of us all.' "[43]

The scapegoat theory

One form of this theory holds that the urge to punish criminals is closely related to sexuality and that the variations in the punitive reaction to lawbreaking tend to follow the variations in social prohibitions against sexual behavior. In societies in which sex taboos are few and lax, punishment is absent or lenient; in periods when sex and sexuality are loudly declaimed, punishment is frequent, open, and severe; in periods when sex becomes more suppressed as a topic of public discussion, punishment is suppressed or hidden. One author accounts for variations in the methods of implementing the punitive reaction in terms of the suppression of a rather fixed amount of libidinal "urge" which is

---

[43] Karl Menninger, "The Crime of Punishment," *Saturday Review*, September 7, 1968, pp. 21-25 ff. See also idem, *The Crime of Punishment* (New York: Viking, 1968).

assumed to be present in the human organism. It is his contention that in the recent period the punitive reaction to lawbreaking is as prevalent as it was in the period when corporal and capital punishments were most popular, but that the method of punishment has merely gone underground. Thus, we no longer openly whip or torture criminals but, instead, torture them secretly, behind prison walls.[44]

A more popular version of this theory deals more directly with aggression. Again, the essential notion is that the human organism, because of unconscious conflicts, contains a fixed amount of aggression, which must be expressed. It may be expressed in criminality; it may be expressed in punishment of criminals; or it may be expressed in other ways.[45] Variations in the punitive reaction to crime, then, would depend upon the availability of alternative outlets for aggressions. The reverse is also thought to be true: limitations on the expression of aggression through punishment of lawbreakers would result in the expression of aggression in other ways, perhaps in criminality itself. It has been intimated that the First World War (aggression) was a substitute for punitive aggression against criminals. That is, the punitive reaction of aggression could not be expressed during the period just prior to the war, but since the aggression had to be expressed, enemies, rather than criminals, became the scapegoats.[46] Hence, it is concluded that societies need criminals for emotional reasons, and they organize the fight against them in such a way that crime is actually maintained.[47]

Punishment of criminals, then, is considered a system for sublimation of aggressive tendencies; persons who are aggressive secure satisfaction in the punishment inflicted, and this satisfaction is socially proper. In this way, many persons can avoid illegal aggressions, just as they avoid them by other kinds of sublimation.[48] The analogy here is with the psychoanalytic theory of the development of the individual. Society is considered to have advanced through the same three stages as are assumed to be present in the psychological development of the human organism. First, there was in social life a stage in which there was free expression of the instincts of sexuality and aggressiveness, and this was the period of no punishment. Next, the expression of the instincts was repressed and, hence, the instincts obtained their outlet in superego activities, directed against their original form; this was the period of severe and open punishments. In the third

[44] Charles Berg, "The Psychology of Punishment," *British Journal of Medical Psychology*, 20:295-313, October, 1945.

[45] David Abrahamsen, *Who Are the Guilty: A Study of Education and Crime* (New York: Rinehart, 1952), p. 287.

[46] Paul Reiwald, *Society and Its Criminals* (New York: International Universities Press, 1950).

[47] Ibid., p. 235.

[48] F. Alexander and H. Staub, *The Criminal, the Judge, and the Public*, rev. ed. (Glencoe, Ill.: Free Press, 1956), pp. 213-223; C. G. Schoenfeld, "Psychoanalysis, Criminal Justice Planning and Reform, and the Law," *Criminal Law Bulletin*, 7:313-327, May, 1971.

stage there has been a further degree of repression, and an open expression of the libidinal and aggressive instincts is no longer tolerated, even in the indirect or symbolic form of punishment. Just as the libidinal and aggressive instincts are said to be repressed and hidden in the unconscious of the individual, the societal expression of such instincts is repressed and hidden behind prison walls. "Inside the prison—the objective equivalent of the unconscious—the same process [instinctual expression] goes on unseen by consciousness and inaccessible to ego-interference."[49]

A few social scientists, largely European, have attempted to relate the many variations in the punitive reaction and its expression and implementation to variations in social structure. The variations have been accounted for by the availability of labor supply, the presence of the lower middle class, the division of labor, and social disorganization.

Social structure theories

(a) Punishment and economic conditions. One theory of punishment is analogous to, or a part of, the economic theory of crime causation. The general notion is that both the punitive reaction itself and the specific methods of implementing that reaction are very much affected, if not determined, by the general economic conditions of the society. Rusche, for example, has advanced the thesis that the primary determinant of the societal reaction to crime is the condition of the labor market.[50] He contends that when the labor market is glutted, and labor therefore is cheap, the reaction to lawbreaking tends to be punitive; but when the labor supply is scarce, and labor therefore is at a premium, the reaction becomes nonpunitive. Also, the methods of implementing the punitive reaction are thought to vary with the condition of the labor market. For instance, it is observed that the galleys were substituted for corporal and capital punishment when it was necessary to secure men for rowing, that the workhouse developed when the state did not have sufficient labor, that transportation began as a means of providing labor for the colonies and stopped because of increased demand for labor at home, that solitary confinement was abandoned because under that system the labor of the prisoners could not be utilized, and that fines developed as revenue measures.[51]

The basic assumption in this theory is that crime is a lower-class phenomenon, and that the societal reaction is a phenomenon of the upper classes, who have political power. When economic conditions are poor and the labor market is glutted, the upper classes impose severe punishments upon the lower classes; but when the economic need of the upper classes for labor cannot be satisfied, they impose few and mild punishments. Actually, the

---

[49] Berg, "Psychology of Punishment."

[50] George Rusche, "Arbeitsmarkt und Strafvollzug," *Zeitschrift für Sozialforschung*, 2:63-78, May, 1933.

[51] George Rusche and Otto Kirchheimer, *Punishment and Social Structure* (New York: Columbia University Press, 1939).

theory breaks down into two arguments, the second of which is as follows: When economic conditions are good, there is no economic need to commit crime, and the crime rate is low; but when there is widespread unemployment, the temptation to commit crime is great. If, the upper classes believe, in times of unemployment criminals can illegally obtain economic necessities in exchange for mild punishments, the crime rate will be high. Therefore, the upper classes impose severe penalties in order to counteract the temptations of the lower classes.

When the two arguments are put together, the formula takes the following form: When poverty increases, crime increases, and, also, the labor market is glutted; and when crime increases and the labor market is glutted, the societal reaction to crime is punitive rather than nonpunitive. Whether it is the crime rate or the condition of the labor market which determines the societal reaction, then, is not clear. However, most economic determinists are not concerned with this lack of clarity, for it is their contention that it is general economic conditions which determine both crime and unemployment rates and, thereby, determine the societal reaction to crime and the means used to implement that reaction. The studies of the crime rate in relation to business cycles, reviewed in chapter 11, throw much doubt upon this assumed relationship between economic conditions, crime, and punishment.

(b) Punishment and the middle class. Another theory of punishment relates variations in the punitive reaction to the presence or absence of the lower middle class. The chief proponent of this theory, however, uses the term *middle class* in a sense uncommon in the United States; also, there is some doubt as to whether he is considering the middle class or something else. The theory is summarized in the following statement: "The disinterested tendency to inflict punishment is a distinctive characteristic of the lower middle class, that is, of a social class living under conditions which force its members to an extraordinary high degree of self-restraint and subject them to much frustration of natural desires."[52]

This statement actually has three component parts: (i) The punitive reaction to lawbreaking ("the disinterested tendency to inflict punishment") grows out of the moral indignation of the public; it does not grow out of the indignation of the person who has been injured by a crime. (ii) Moral indignation is found almost exclusively in the lower middle class and is the product of self-imposed frustration among members of this class. (iii) The punitive reaction increases in frequency and severity when the lower middle class is in control and decreases when the lower middle class decreases in power.

In connection with the second point it is assumed that moral indignation—which is the emotion behind the disinterested tendency to inflict punishment and is a kind of disguised envy—

---

[52] Svend Ranulf, *Moral Indignation and Middle Class Psychology: A Sociological Study* (Copenhagen: Levin and Munksgaard, 1938), p. 198.

is caused by a repression of natural desires. The natural desires of lower-middle-class persons are repressed; the members of the class are morally indignant when crime occurs; and lower-middle-class persons react punitively to lawbreaking. In this view, the theory is not a social structure theory but, instead, a variation of the scapegoat theory.

However, in connection with the third point it is argued that even if the above psychological interpretation is omitted, a correlation between the presence of the lower middle class and the frequency and severity of the punitive reaction to lawbreaking still can be observed. At least the literature suggests that the punitive reaction has always been popular in that social class which may be loosely described as the "petit bourgeoisie," and that it does not prevail in communities where this social class is of little significance. The punitive reaction to crime is said to have been absent among the Teutons, the Chinese, the Hindus, and among primitive groups, which had no class of this kind. Among the Israelites, the punitive reaction did develop strongly, but not until a social class comparable to the lower middle class in modern Europe had grown influential.[53]

One difficulty with this suggestive theory is the lack of precision in the definition of the lower middle class. Ranulf does not define this term precisely, and consequently it is not possible to appraise the theory. Probably what he means by "middle-class psychology" is similar to what is meant by "Puritanism" or "Victorianism." If this be true, then recent variations in the punitive reaction and the methods of implementing it could be related to the rise of the Protestant ethic, in much the same way that Max Weber linked the rise of the spirit of capitalism to the Protestant ethic.[54] The development of an appreciation of the value of labor was shown by Weber to be correlated with the rise of Protestantism, especially Calvinism, and it is not inconceivable that the workhouses and other systems for utilizing the labor of criminals developed along with Calvinism, which emphasized the spiritual value of labor.

(c) Punishment and the division of labor. Durkheim attributed the fluctuations in the punitive reaction to changes in the division of labor of society. His theory may be stated briefly in three propositions. (i) Offenses which attack the collective values of a society elicit more severe punitive reactions than those which attack individual values. Such offenses are treason, heresy, or crimes in which force is used. (ii) Punishments for crime are ordered by tribunals made up of all the people or of only a select number, and they are imposed primarily for the purpose of reinforcing the collective values, not for vengeance, intimidation, or reformation. "We must not say that an action shocks the com-

---

[53] Ibid., pp. 174-186.
[54] For a discussion of Weber's work, see Talcott Parsons, *Structure of Social Action* (New York: McGraw-Hill, 1937), chaps. 14-17.

mon conscience because it is criminal, but rather that it is criminal because it shocks the common conscience."[55] (iii) As the principle of social organization changes from mechanical solidarity to organic solidarity, the punitive reaction to lawbreaking tends to disappear, and in its place is substituted restitution and reparations.

The final proposition is the one used to account for many of the variations in the punitive reaction to crime. The type of societal reaction to crime is determined by the social structure, and the important aspect of the social structure is the complexity of the division of labor. When a society has mechanical solidarity, a solidarity based not upon division of labor but upon similarity of behavior and attitudes, the reaction to legal wrongs is punitive. This punitive reaction is formalized in the criminal law. But in societies in which the solidarity is organic, a solidarity based upon specialization or division of labor, the reaction is nonpunitive, for the desire is to return things to the condition they were in before the offense. However, society in this case is not merely a sort of third-party arbitrator, intervening to compromise disputes between individuals, but applies general and traditional rules of law to particular cases. This nonpunitive restitutive reaction is formalized in the rules of civil law, procedural law, administrative law, and constitutional law. Since organic solidarity is becoming more and more the essential characteristic of the social structure of modern societies, repressive law and the punitive reaction are decreasing in use, and the restitutive law and nonpunitive reaction are increasing in frequency.

(d) Punishment and social disorganization. Another theory which attempts to account for many of the variations in the punitive reaction is stated in terms of the heterogeneity of societies. In general, the notion is that in homogeneous societies the punitive reaction is infrequent and mild, while in heterogeneous societies it is frequent and severe. While heterogeneity does not necessarily imply social disorganization, heterogeneous societies are often considered as being in a condition of social disorganization, and homogeneous societies are considered as organized.

Sorokin has stated a social disorganization theory which is somewhat consistent with Rusche's theory and somewhat inconsistent with Durkheim's theory.[56] He refers to variations in the "ethico-juridical heterogeneity and antagonism" of social groups, and argues that whenever this heterogeneity increases, whatever the reason for the increase, the frequency as well as the severity of the punitive reaction to lawbreaking increases. The greater the increase in the heterogeneity and antagonism, the greater is the increase in the punitive reaction, as formalized in the imposi-

---

[55] Emile Durkheim, *The Division of Labor in Society,* trans. George Simpson (Glencoe, Ill.: Free Press, 1947), p. 81. See also Emile Durkheim, "Deux lois de l'evolution penale," *L'Anne Sociologique,* 14 (1900): 65-95.

[56] Pitirim A. Sorokin, *Social and Cultural Dynamics* (New York: American Book Company, 1937), 2:523-632.

tion of punishments by one part of the group upon the other.[57] The ethico-juridical heterogeneity and antagonism is increased by social crises, including the economic.[58]

In simple statement, this theory holds that the quantity and severity of punishments tend to vary directly with the heterogeneity and antagonism within a society. When a society has homogeneous morality, violations of that morality are infrequent; they do not greatly endanger the group; and the political reaction to them is essentially nonpunitive. But when this network of social relations is broken up, and there is an increase in moral and legal heterogeneity, a condition which may be called disorganization, the official reaction to violations becomes punitive.

The evidence advanced in support of this explanation of variations in the punitive reaction is largely the fluctuations of the reaction in periods of revolution, when heterogeneity increases and the punitive reaction increases. Following the revolution, heterogeneity decreases and the punitive reaction decreases. In periods of revolution the use of death penalties, imprisonments, banishment, transportation, confiscation of property, and all other methods of implementing the punitive reaction increases enormously. For example, in Russia the number of executions averaged about ten to twenty per year in the years 1880-1905; during the revolution of 1905-1907 they were up to about five hundred per year, and even to about thirteen hundred in 1908, thereafter dropping to about one hundred.[59] The same is true in most other revolutions.[60]

These theories are all based on the assumption that certain characteristics of the general culture or social structure determine the general way that criminality is handled in a society. While this assumption is undoubtedly correct, none of the theories specifies the *process* by which certain social conditions produce the societal reactions. For example, the cultural consistency theory does not indicate how culture "works" to change the reactions to crime and criminality, just as the economic determinism theory of crime causation does not indicate how poverty "works" to produce criminality in individuals. On another theoretical level, the process by which persons learn to react differentially to crime could be studied, and the punitive or nonpunitive reaction of an individual could be considered the product of his prior associations with punitive and nonpunitive behavior patterns. One learns to react punitively or in some other way just as he learns to speak English, German, or Japanese. It could be maintained, then, that the "societal" reactions to crime represent the outcome of negotiations between persons

---

[57] Ibid., p. 595.

[58] Cf. Gaston Richard, "Les Crises Sociales et les conditions de la criminalité," *L'Anne Sociologique*, 4 (1900): 17.

[59] Sorokin, *Social and Cultural Dynamics*, p. 601.

[60] See in this connection John N. Hazard, "Trends in the Soviet Treatment of Crime," *American Sociological Review*, 5:566-576, August, 1940.

possessing various learned individual reactions to crime. This application of the differential association principle would place the emphasis upon the study of the process by which societal reactions to criminality change; it would supplement the theories outlined, and it would not necessarily contradict any of them. ●

Suggested readings

ANDENAES, JOHANNES. "The General Preventive Effects of Punishment." *University of Pennsylvania Law Review,* 114:949-983, May, 1966.

ANDENAES, JOHANNES. "The Morality of Deterrence." *University of Chicago Law Review,* 37:649-664, Summer, 1970.

BEDAU, HUGO A. *The Death Penalty in America.* New York: Anchor Books, 1967.

BREHM, JACK W. *Responses to Loss of Freedom: A Theory of Psychological Reactance.* Morristown, N.J.: General Learning Press, 1972.

BROMBERG, WALTER. "Is Punishment Dead?" *American Journal of Psychiatry,* 127:245-248, August, 1970.

CHAMBLISS, WILLIAM J. "Types of Deviance and the Effectiveness of Legal Sanctions." *Wisconsin Law Review,* 1967:703-719, Summer, 1967.

CHAPMAN, DENIS. *Sociology and the Stereotype of the Criminal.* London: Tavistock, 1968.

DALZELL, GEORGE. *Benefit of Clergy in America.* Winston-Salem, N.C.: Blair, 1955.

HONDERICH, TED. *Punishment: The Supposed Justifications.* London: Hutchinson, 1969.

LEVITT, A. "Some Societal Aspects of the Criminal Law." *Journal of Criminal Law and Criminology,* 13:90-104, May-June, 1922.

SALEILLES, R. *The Individualization of Punishment.* Translated by R. S. Jastrow. Boston: Little, Brown, 1911.

SELLIN, THORSTEN, ed. *Capital Punishment.* New York: Harper and Row, 1967.

SINGER, BARRY F. "Psychological Studies of Punishment." *California Law Review,* 58:405-443, March, 1970.

WALDO, GORDON P., & THEODORE G. CHIRICOS. "Perceived Penal Sanction and Self-Reported Criminality: A Neglected Approach to Deterrence Research." *Social Problems,* 19:522-540, Spring, 1972.

WINES, F. H. *Punishment and Reformation.* New York: Crowell, 1895.

WOOD, ARTHUR LEWIS. "The Alternatives to the Death Penalty." *Annals of the American Academy of Political and Social Science,* 284:63-72, November, 1952.

ZIMRING, FRANKLIN E. *Perspectives on Deterrence.* Washington: Government Printing Office, 1971.

16 Treatment of delinquents and criminals

In earlier societies there were few alternatives to the punitive reaction, so that usually either criminals were punished or nothing was done to them. At present, however, when the punitive reaction decreases, a "treatment" reaction is said to increase. While in most areas there still is no positive alternative to the punitive reaction, the trend during the last century has been toward a societal reaction in which the criminal is helped rather than punished. The policy is one of studying the personality of the offender and the social conditions in which he became a criminal, and, by means of knowledge thus secured, attempting to modify the conditions producing the criminality. The reaction is, by analogy with medicine, considered scientific. A positive or constructive program is implied, in contrast with the rather negative or neutral program of punishment. However, if the criminal fails to respond to the constructive program, society protects itself from him by segregating him.

If there is one key to understanding present-day practices in the control of crime, it is the conflict between this treatment reaction and the punitive reaction. Most of the practices of all agencies whose responsibility it is to apprehend and care for criminals are affected by this conflict, whether or not the agencies have an official policy of treatment rather than punishment. One approved reaction to crime is hostility, with insistence that the criminal be made to suffer. Every criminal law specifies a penalty for violation, and almost everyone convicted of violating the law must be at least threatened with punishment. As we have seen, the suffering is justified in various ways: vengeance, retribution, deterrence, reformation. The following statement advocates the punitive reaction:

I warn you to stay unswerving to your task—that of standing by the man on the firing line—the practical, hard-headed, experienced honest policemen who have shown by their efforts that they, and they alone, know the answer to the crime problem. That answer can be summed up in one sentence—adequate detection, swift apprehension, and certain, unrelenting punishment. That is what the criminal fears. That is what he understands, and nothing else, and that fear is the only thing which will force him into the ranks of the law-abiding. There is no royal road to law enforcement. If we wait upon the medical quacks, the parole panderers, and the misguided sympathizers with habitual criminals to protect our lives and property from the criminal horde, then we must also resign ourselves to increasing violence, robbery, and sudden death.[1]

---

[1] J. Edgar Hoover, "Patriotism and the War Against Crime," an address given before the annual convention of the Daughters of the American Revolution, Washington, D.C., April 23, 1936. Quoted by permission of the late Mr. Hoover.

The other approved reaction is one of inquiry designed to secure comprehension of criminal behavior and to work out methods of control based on this comprehension. Suffering may be necessary in the process of control through treatment, but the suffering is incidental, not a direct aim of the process. This second reaction is now most evident in juvenile court procedures, and it is rapidly being extended into criminal courts, prisons, reformatories and the systems of probation and parole. It is reflected, in extreme form, in the following statement:

> . . . imprisonment and punishment do not present themselves as the proper methods of dealing with criminals. We have to treat them psychically as sick people, which in every respect they are. It is no more reasonable to punish these individuals for a behavior over which they have no control than it is to punish an individual for breathing through his mouth because of enlarged adenoids. . . . It is the hope of the more progressive elements in psychopathology and criminology that the guard and the jailer will be replaced by the nurse, and the judge by the psychiatrist, whose sole attempt will be to treat and cure the individual instead of merely to punish him. Then and then only can we hope to lessen, even if not entirely to abolish, crime, the most costly burden that society has today.[2]

It has been argued that these conflicting reactions could and should be combined, the idea being that punishment should be retained but that the pain should be inflicted in a spirit of love rather than hatred. However, it was long ago pointed out by an eminent social psychologist that such a combination is logically impossible.

> . . . the two attitudes, that of control of crime by the hostile procedure of the law, and that of control through comprehension of social and psychological conditions, cannot be combined. To understand is to forgive, and the social procedure seems to deny the very responsibility which the law affirms, and on the other hand the pursuit by criminal justice inevitably awakens the hostile attitude in the offender and renders the attitude of mutual comprehension practically impossible.[3]

This is a popular view at present. It is evident in presentations of the notion that either we must retain punishment and abandon the effort to understand and treat criminology, or abandon the punitive reaction and continue the effort to understand and treat. But one can agree that the two reactions are logically incompatible while at the same time using both of them in practice. In fact, the theory of differential association implies that this seemingly contradictory position is the correct one. The implication is that crime in the generic sense, as well as individual criminal acts, must be understood in order to develop effective policies of control, and that the most important conditions in causing or preventing crime are the reactions of other persons toward crime

---

[2] Benjamin Karpman, "Criminality, Insanity and the Law," *Journal of Criminal Law and Criminology*, 39:584-605, January-February, 1949. The quotation is from page 605.

[3] George H. Mead, "The Psychology of Punitive Justice," *American Journal of Sociology*, 23:577-602, March, 1918. The quotation is from page 592.

and criminality. The reactions which are most effective in pre-venting crime are expressions of antagonism and hostility, and those which are most effective in causing crime are expressions of appreciation. This principle supports either punitive policies or more effective systems for expressing disapprobation, just as it supports programs for expressing appreciation of noncriminal and anticriminal attitudes.[4] Thus, it is possible to combine the attitude of understanding crime in general and the attitude of hostility toward crime in general. Furthermore, acts may remain as pun-ishable by law even if the actual program for changing criminals is one of treatment. Most criminal justice agencies have found it necessary to effect a compromise, on a practical level, between the two reactions. ●

The development of causal explanations of crime probably is more a part of than an explanation for the development of the treatment reaction. Nevertheless, on a formal level it may be observed that attempts to explain criminal behavior have greatly abetted at least the official policy of treatment. In the eighteenth and early nineteenth centuries the will, assumed to be isolated from all other psychological conditions and from social processes and conditions, was practically the only element considered in discussions of behavior, both criminal and noncriminal. The Lombrosian school of criminologists denied the doctrine of free will and attempted to explain crime in terms of causal relation-ships. Their explanation was not at all satisfactory, but it resulted in a demand that crime be regarded as any other natural phenome-non and dealt with as such. Accordingly, the validity or efficiency of the punitive reaction was denied, and what is now called the treatment reaction was supported.

Treatment and the study of crime causation

To the argument of the Lombrosian school has been added the immense weight of authority in the last half-century. By many methods, a valid explanation of crime and criminality is being developed, and the factors associated with crime are being iso-lated. Accompanying this natural science view of crime and criminality is the natural science view that these phenomena can be controlled by comprehension of the processes involved. The emphasis on mental deficiency, psychopathy, differential associa-tion, and status frustration as explanations of crime and delin-quency during the last fifty years has helped establish the view that if criminals are to be reformed, they should be studied, under-stood, and helped. Further, since legal policies have been based on the doctrine of free will, the conclusion that crime and delinquency can be accounted for in terms of social conditions and political

[4] Cf. Johs. Andenaes, "General Prevention — Illusion or Reality?" *Journal of Criminal Law, Criminology, and Police Science,* 43:176-198, July-August, 1952; and Lloyd W. McCorkle and Richard Korn, "Resocialization Within Walls," *Annals of the American Academy of Political and Social Science,* 293:88-98, May, 1954.

practices has created a great deal of controversy. Recent developments in theories of crime, criminality, delinquency, and delinquent behavior have had important implications for changing society rather than criminals' personalities.

It is important to note, however, that the historical development has not been a simple matter of changing practices to fit changes in ideology and theory. Criminological theory has also been greatly affected by changing methods of dealing with crime and criminals. A bit at a time, the methods used for implementing the treatment reaction have encroached on the methods used to implement the punitive reaction, and it has appeared that some of them apparently are no less successful than the punitive policies of earlier days. Then, in the effort to account for the success of the new methods, new criminological theory has been organized. The development has taken on a kind of spiral effect, beginning with modifications in practice, which were not always recognized as in conflict with existing methods and theories. Next, new theory was developed to account for the apparent success of the new practices. Then, with the gradual increase in the popularity of the new theory, deliberate attempts were made and are being made to replace punitive methods with practices consistent with theory. This process can be illustrated by observation of the relationship between development of the juvenile court and changing ideas about delinquency causation. With invention of the juvenile court, nonpunitive methods to accompany the punitive methods of dealing with delinquents under the age of sixteen were introduced. New causal theories of delinquency developed, and they maintained, essentially, that delinquent behavior is a product of emotional maladjustments which can be modified only by the nonpunitive methods used by the juvenile court.[5] It then was said that if sixteen-year-old delinquents could be handled nonpunitively, older persons could be similarly handled. Many persons now argue that control of delinquency and crime would be more effective if a policy of social change replaced both the punitive reaction and treatment methods based on the idea that the offender is somehow sick. ●

The conflict between punitive and treatment reactions

Because the punitive reaction is still very popular, many people assert that the fact that we are now using treatment methods in dealing with juvenile delinquents (and to an increasing extent in dealing with adults) does not cast doubt upon the social utility of the punitive reaction. On the contrary, they argue *for* the social utility of the punitive reaction by maintaining that we have an increasing amount of crime as a result of the shift toward the nonpunitive reaction to crime. Actually, there is no available

---

[5] See Anthony M. Platt, *The Child Savers: The Invention of Delinquency* (Chicago: University of Chicago Press, 1969).

proof that the change toward treatment methods has either increased or decreased crime rates. It is just as logical to assert that crime rates are high because of the survival of the punitive reaction.[6] Although many of the arguments against treatment are mere reiterations of the justifications for punishment which were used when treatment was not an alternative, a more detailed consideration of some of the objections may assist in clarifying the general conflict.

(1) It is asserted by those whose reaction to crime is punitive that the general public cannot be prevented from engaging in a general debauch of crime except by fear of punishment; state officials must continue to terrorize the citizenry. The reply to this objection is that not all of the unpleasantness and suffering would be removed even if the present form of punishment for criminals were completely abandoned. On the basis of the experience when Denmark was without police during a part of the time the Nazis occupied the country, it may be concluded that the penal process, including arrest, does deter.[7] However, even complete substitution of a treatment reaction for the punitive reaction would not necessarily require that the police and other protective agencies be abolished. Whatever the official method of dealing with offenders, there always will be some stigma connected with crime and delinquency.

But the real reason for believing that the substitution of treatment for punishment would not result in a debauch of crime is that social control, after all, lies in the recognition and reward secured by lawful conduct rather than in direct fear of punishment. Not the fear of legal penalties, as such, but the fear of loss of status in the group is the effective deterrent. But this is not really fear; what really occurs is that the person feels that doing a specified thing in violation of a group standard, which also happens to be in violation of the law, would not be in harmony with his personality, would lower him. It does not occur to him to do such a thing. He would feel uncomfortable in violating such a norm and would secure no reward from it. This is the principal method of control, whether or not the conduct is regulated by law. But a man who would not think of breaking into a jewelry store or robbing a liquor store will smuggle jewelry into his country in violation of the law, or will violate the liquor laws or the tax laws, or will engage in other illegalities. His group does not regard such violations as beneath the dignity of one of its members, and he therefore does not have a stake in conformity. Regardless of the official methods of dealing with criminals, we shall retain this method of control by rewarding conformity, rather than control by terror.

---

[6] See Donald R. Cressey, "The Nature and Effectiveness of Correctional Techniques," *Law and Contemporary Problems*, 23:754-771, Autumn, 1958.

[7] Jorgen Trolle, *Syv Maaneder under Politi [seven months without police]*, Copenhagen, 1945.

One weakness of the current criminal justice system is its dependence on the threat of punishment. Although the state can emphasize the necessity for conformity by threatening to punish nonconformists, attitudes of conformity certainly can be developed more effectively than has been done to date.[8] The stress on terror distracts from the need for such development. If attitudes of appreciation for certain values could be developed, laws pertaining to those values would be unnecessary. For example, if everyone in a society had an equal stake in the concept of private property, then trying to terrorize people into respecting property rights would become obsolete.

(2) A second objection is that, if the criminal is not punished, the victim will take the law into his own hands thus engaging either in self-redress or in lynch law. This assertion is based on the belief that there is an unalterable demand for vengeance which will be satisfied by illegal means if it is not satisfied by legal means, and it is consistent with the "scapegoat" theory described in the previous chapter. Most persons demand vengeance under certain circumstances. In offenses involving social relations between blacks and whites in the South, in certain brutal sex offenses, and in offenses involving relations of different social classes, a rather widespread demand for vengeance may arise. In these circumstances, the individual who takes the law into his own hands may receive the support of a group. But most crimes—probably more than 75 percent—arouse the resentment of no particular individual. And even when resentment is aroused, it is generally confined to a very small number of persons, whose resentment is likely to be counteracted by a nonpunitive reaction on the part of other members of the society.

The vengeance reaction is not instinctive. It is the product of social contacts and interactions. The difference between the crimes of immigrants and their native-born offspring, the behavior of lynch mobs, and the fact that the treatment reaction exists all show this.[9] Even if an unconscious desire for vengeance is assumed, it cannot be said that this drive determines its own method of expression. One may secure revenge by a blow with the fist, by spitting, by calling names, by shooting with a gun, by spreading calumny, by voting, by bringing the offender to trial, and, perhaps, by assisting the state to use methods that will reform him.

(3) It is believed that the victim will be unwilling to testify or make complaint if he cannot see his opponent suffer; if there is no alternative to the treatment reaction, he will take the loss

---

[8] See Johannes Andenaes, "The General Preventive Effects of Punishment," *University of Pennsylvania Law Review*, 114:949-983, May, 1966; and idem, "Does Punishment Deter Crime?" *Criminal Law Quarterly*, 11:76-93, November, 1968.

[9] See Alan Valentine, *Vigilante Justice* (New York: Reynal, 1956).

and remain silent rather than go to the trouble of court procedure that will yield him no satisfaction. Against this objection it may be stated that if the treatment reaction were used alone, the victim would still secure the satisfaction of seeing his aggressor put to the trouble of a trial and would secure the satisfaction of a conviction; this would show that the public was on his side, would vindicate him, and would perhaps grant him all the satisfaction he wished. Currently, friends of the criminal are likely to rally to his support in opposition to the hostile procedure of the law. If these friends had any reason to believe that the procedure was designed to improve the offender and would have some efficiency in this respect, they might be more inclined to assist in securing a conviction for his own good. Moreover, no private vengeance is necessary to the prosecution and punishment of about 75 percent of all offenders. For such offenses as drunkenness, prostitution, gambling, abortion, traffic violations, possession of narcotics, and vagrancy the complaint usually is made by a public officer and the testimony is furnished by the same officer and others subpoenaed to appear in court.

(4) Another objection is that group solidarity and respect for the law, now developed by the punitive reaction, would decrease in the absence of this reaction. As we said earlier, these conditions can be developed in a great variety of other ways. They can be developed by collective action toward comprehending the causes of crime and controlling by means of knowledge thus obtained. The only thing needed is that something be presented on which the group can act collectively. Social solidarity might be created by pursuit of the criminal, but it also is created by collective action to cure disease, correct injustices, prevent catastrophes and environmental pollution, save crops from insects, and other actions where comprehension, not punishment, is involved.

Punishment seldom restores the equilibrium of the group at present, because the equilibrium of the group is not much disturbed by crime. Crime is an impersonal event, to be read about in the newspapers, and no direct collective reaction occurs. Many persons carry burglary, robbery, and larceny insurance; for these persons, crime is not a shocking event—the burden of loss is distributed over a period of years in the premiums paid to the insurance company. Even victims not protected by insurance are generally willing to drop the case if restitution can be secured. They usually are interested only secondarily in the offense against the peace and dignity of the society. In general, whole communities are seldom disturbed by crimes or by high crime rates except in spectacular cases, and infliction of punishment therefore has little effect on the community.

As these opposing arguments show, punitive reactions and treatment reactions are both sanctioned ways of behaving in present-day society. For that reason, correctional procedures and programs are not exclusively punitive nor exclusively treatment, even when they are formally set up to deal with delinquents or criminals in one of the alternative ways. •

Limitations of punishment

As the treatment reaction to lawbreaking has become more popular, many arguments (again based on very shaky empirical evidence) have been advanced in support of the general position that punishment is relatively ineffective as a reformative or deterrent device. It has been pointed out in this connection that punishment often has effects which are unanticipated, and that these effects are the opposite of those expected when the punishment was imposed. Thus, the general argument is that the treatment reaction should be substituted for the punitive reaction, since it would not, at least to the same extent, produce these undesirable effects. The following are some of the types of unanticipated consequences produced by punishment.

(1) Punishment often isolates the individual who is punished and makes him a confirmed enemy of society, and his influence may extend to other individuals. When the sole reaction is punitive, criminals are isolated from law-abiding groups and neither understand nor are understood by these groups. Hatred of the criminal by society results in hatred of society by the criminal. In this respect the behavior is much like war, which produces a relatively complete isolation and dissociation of warring nations. When the criminal is effectively ostracized, he has only two alternatives: he may associate with other criminals, among whom he can find recognition, prestige, and means of further criminality; or he may become disorganized, psychopathic, or unstable. Our current practice is to permit almost all criminals to return to society in a physical sense, but to hold them off, make them keep their distance, segregate them, deny them jobs, and otherwise isolate them from law-abiding groups psychologically. If they are to be turned into law-abiding citizens, they must be assimilated, which means that they must be given a stake in the society, like all other citizens.[10]

(2) Punishment develops caution. A painful experience, such as being punished or being stung by bees, will make most persons "think twice" before they repeat the behavior. But, in the case of the bees, "thinking twice" might be a means of securing immunity from the bees while molesting them. The actor has been made cautious by the previous suffering, but he has not been "reformed." Similarly, an unanticipated consequence of current

---

[10] See Donald R. Cressey, "Changing Criminals: The Application of the Theory of Differential Association," *American Journal of Sociology*, 61:116-120, September, 1955; and Rita Volkman and Donald R. Cressey, "Differential Association and the Rehabilitation of Drug Addicts," *American Journal of Sociology*, 69:129-142, September, 1963.

systems for punishing criminals might be cautiousness, not refor-mation. For example, professional and organized criminals have great skill in the execution of their crimes and in addition take many precautions to provide in advance for immunity in case they are caught. The result is that about twenty-five amateur shoplifters are likely to be convicted for each professional shop-lifter (who steals hundreds of times as much as all twenty-five amateurs). After a few convictions, the amateur criminal develops both the professional criminal's caution and the professional crimi-nal's techniques for avoiding arrests.

(3) Punishment creates other unanticipated attitudes. Even if some acts are preventable by terror, this prevention does not prove that punishment promotes the social welfare. Whatever is accomplished by preventing a specific act may be more than offset by general attitudes produced by it. For instance, the state could at least temporarily cut down a neighborhood burglary rate if it dramatically executed ten citizens every time a burglary occurred. Soon the neighborhood would organize against burglary. On a less dramatic level, a boy's practice of lying might be stopped by whipping him, but he might then come to fear the parent who inflicted the punishment, with the result that both his welfare and the welfare of his family are jeopardized. And thus the punitive reaction frequently diminishes the consent of the governed even as particular crimes are successfuly forestalled —lack of respect for law, lack of patriotism, lack of willingness to sacrifice for the state, and lack of initiative. Real efficiency in dealing with delinquents and criminals involves not only the stopping of specific violations of law, but the accomplishment of this result without the loss of other social values.

(4) Punishment often gives offenders high status. In some neighborhoods, going to prison is a sign of manliness. In states whose prisons are scaled from tough maximum-security institu-tions down to relaxed minimum-security institutions, youthful offenders frequently request assignment to the maximum-security institutions, because such assignment will result in high status among their friends when they are released. They try to avoid assignment to reformatories and minimum-security institutions, because incarceration there does not bring the desired prestige. Schrag has shown that, within prisons, positions of leadership go to men convicted of serious offenses, such as robbery, and to men with long punitive sentences.[11]

(5) Punishment generally stops constructive efforts. If a group, in a spirit of hatred, inflicts punishment upon the offender, its members generally sit back, after the penalty is inflicted, with a sigh of relief and with a feeling that the matter is now settled.

---

[11] Clarence Schrag, "Leadership Among Prison Immates," *American Sociological Review,* 19:37-42, February, 1954.

But the situation remains, in general, just about what it was before the punishment was inflicted. Such a punitive reaction may produce fear in the offender, but more than fear is required for an alteration of character, personality, and behavior. Reformation involves more than a determination to change one's behavior because it is painful to do otherwise. It involves a constructive process of reorganizing the conditions that produced the criminal behavior in the first place. The individual must have stimulations, patterns, suggestions, sentiments, and ideals presented to him. He must be given an appreciation of the values which are conserved by the law, and this can occur only if he assimilates the culture of the group which passed the law, or, stated otherwise, only if he himself becomes part of the powerful group that decides which conduct is to be regulated by law. The negative act of prohibiting certain conduct is not sufficient because it does not promote assimilation. ●

Implementation of the treatment reaction: individualization

The official policy of individualized treatment for offenders developed out of the positive school's arguments against the practice of attempting to impose uniform punishments on all persons violating a particular law. It was, and is, argued that policies calling for uniform punishments are as obviously ineffective as would be a policy calling for uniform treatment of all medical patients, no matter what their ailments. This led some persons to advocate that the type of punishment and the severity of punishment be adapted to the individual offender; even today "individualization" is sometimes used to refer to a system for imposing punishments. However, as the treatment reaction has increased in popularity, "individualization" has come to designate a treatment process in which the handling of each case of criminality includes expert diagnosis of individual problems and needs, expert prescription of therapy, and expert therapy—just as clinical medicine includes diagnosis, prescription, and therapy. This is by far the most common meaning of the term in modern correctional parlance. By "individualization," then, is usually meant the general system for implementing the treatment reaction to lawbreaking. Within this general system there are two major methods for administering treatment: casework on an individual or clinical basis, and casework on a group or situational basis. The methods are based upon different conceptions of the process by which criminality develops.

The clinical method

In the early part of the present century the system of individualized treatment for criminals was based almost exclusively on the principle that criminality is a strictly individual disorder which can, therefore, be treated in a clinic, just as syphilis can be treated in a clinic. The principal argument for the clinical method was that the processes of treating offenders should be analogous to the processes of treating medical patients. It was correctly pointed out that two or three centuries ago diseases were not differentiated from each other or explained as natural phenomena; bloodletting was almost the only treatment, varying in amount with the seriousness of the ailment. Since then the germ theory of disease and experimental methods have produced a great variety of treatment methods adapted to particular diseases. By analogy, until recently crime has been handled as sickness was handled two centuries ago—the methods of dealing with criminals consisted of imposing certain degrees of suffering upon them, depending upon their offense. The system of individualized treatment was then introduced.

Ideally, this system included an intensive study of the individual offender for the purpose of learning the basis of his criminality, and application of a program based on the knowledge of the offender and on knowledge previously secured regarding the effective methods of treating such cases. An entirely different program for each criminal was not implied, just as scientific treatment of diseases does not imply the use of an entirely different policy for each patient.[12] Also, when there was no known system for successfully treating an offender's difficulty, he was to be segregated for the protection of society, just as dangerous psychotics are segregated for the protection of society. Furthermore, an attempt would be made to prevent criminality by methods based upon knowledge of crime causation, not by punitive methods alone.

But in the clinical method this medical analogy was then carried to its logical extreme. Because the original arguments for individualization were based on an analogy with clinical medicine, the *methods and theory* used in diagnosing and treating cases of criminality and delinquency were closely analogous to those used in clinical medicine. That is, criminality was assumed to be treatable as an individual disorder independent of the offender's social groups; the diagnoses were very similar to diagnoses of various medical ailments of patients; and the recommendations for treatment were very similar to medical prescriptions for clinical treatment. Even today this interpretation of the individualization system has great popularity among correctional workers, many of whom assume that some cases of criminality, like some diseases such as anemia, are entirely individual disorders, but that most cases of criminality are like the infectious diseases such as syphilis. While group contacts of certain kinds are necessary

[12] See Marguerite Q. Grant, "Interaction Between Kinds of Treatments and Kinds of Delinquents" (California Board of Corrections, Monograph No. 2, July, 1961), pp. 5-14; and Keiichi Mizushima and Richard L. Jenkins, "Treatment Needs Corresponding to Varieties of Delinquents," *International Journal of Social Psychiatry*, 8:91-103, Spring, 1962.

to individual cases of syphilis and to some individual cases of criminality, both ailments can be "cured" in a clinic, without reference to those groups, just as anemia can be cured in a clinic. Individual psychotherapy, as a system for reforming criminals, is perhaps the best example of a current treatment method based on this assumption. Social casework has been greatly influenced by psychiatry, and as a result most of the "diagnoses" made by social workers attached to courts, prisons, and other agencies dealing with criminals are made in clinical terms, just as are most of the diagnoses made by psychologists and psychiatrists. A diagnosis made in clinical terms will be followed, obviously, by clinical treatment of the individual.[13]

The following description of the method once used in the New Jersey Home for Boys illustrates the clinical procedure. The obvious assumption behind the program is that the offender's difficulty can be cleared up by treating it as an almost completely individual disorder. Although the statement was made about fifty years ago, it indicates the official method of "treatment" used by most prisons and by many other agencies today.[14]

First: We make a definite study of each boy when he enters the institution. This study extends over a period of several weeks and is conducted by trained people (psychiatrist, psychologist, director of education, etc.). . . . During the period of these examinations we secure from the Central Parole Bureau, probation officers and other sources, all the information possible about the ward's earlier history, his home and community relations and other vital facts.

Second: Once a week all of the people concerned with the examinations named in the last paragraph meet with the Superintendent for the purpose of comparing reports and consulting as to the best means of promoting the welfare of the ward while in the institution—this is called our Classification Meeting.

Third: We make a definite plan for the development and training of the boy. This plan, or parts of it, at least, are discussed with the boy. We try to secure his co-operation with us for his own development, with a definite purpose in his mind and ours of preparing him for a successful parole. Every boy's case is reconsidered by the Classification Committee within three months, and if the case presents unusual factors, it may be reconsidered several times.

Fourth: As time for his parole approaches, each boy's case is taken up for pre-parole investigation. . . . Home investigations are made, employment and friendly counselors are secured; and the family prepared for the return of the boy. Sometimes the Central Parole Bureau has to prepare the neighborhood or move the family to a new locality, in order to further the interests of the boy.[15]

The group-relations method

The methods for implementing the punitive reaction were generally applied to the offender without regard for his relationships in social groups. He was assumed to have possessed the ability to refrain from delinquency and criminality, regardless of the

---

[13] See Michael Hakeem, "A Critique of the Psychiatric Approach to Crime and Correction," *Law and Contemporary Problems*, 23:650-682, Autumn, 1958.

[14] See the discussion below, pp. 499-507.

[15] State of New Jersey, *Report of State Home for Boys*, 1921, pp. 19-20.

values of the groups in which he had membership. Similarly, the earlier treatment methods were applied to the offender in isolation; criminality was considered an individual disorder, and in the treatment process little consideration was given to the offender's group relations. Gradually, these treatment methods have been supplemented by methods based on an alternative principle, namely that criminality is social in nature and, therefore, can be modified in individual cases only if the criminal's relations with social groups are modified.[16] The proponents of this principle have not extended the medical analogy to include the methods and theory used in diagnosing, prescribing, and "treating." Rather, they contend, as is made explicit in the differential association theory, that persons become criminals principally because they have been relatively isolated from the culture of law-abiding groups, by reason of their residence, employment, codes, native capacities, or something else, or else have been in relatively frequent contact with a rival criminal culture. Consequently they are lacking in the experiences, feelings, ideas, and attitudes out of which to construct a life organization that the law-abiding public will regard as desirable.

Criminality, which is the product of isolation from law-abiding culture and association with procriminal culture, will not be overcome by more isolation. Assimilation of law-abiding culture can come only by contact. As early as 1868 Desprez stated the argument against isolation, with special reference to isolation of prisoners from each other and from the public.

All isolation, even if voluntary, is bad. There is no idea more fallacious than that isolation from the world by prolonged imprisonment will produce moral meditations in the culprit which will be the source of his reformation. It is not sufficient to place a person between four walls in order to improve him. . . . How is it possible to hope or believe for a single moment that gross natures, uncultured and degraded, can find in themselves the force to condemn and sincerely detest their faults, and maintain a firm resolution during the years of detention, in the midst of all the elements of corruption, if the imprisonment is in common, or in apathy and despair, if the imprisonment is in cells?[17]

In the group-relations method, then, diagnosis is directed at analysis of the criminal's attitudes, motives, and rationalizations regarding criminality, with recognition that the character of these behaviors depends upon the kinds of groups in which the individual has memberships, with which he identifies himself, and to which he owes allegiance and loyalty. If the criminality of an individual depends upon such group relations, then the prescription for "treatment" must be a prescription for modification of group relations.[18] As to the "treatment" itself, it is suggested

---

[16] See R. L. Morrison, "Individualization and Involvement In Treatment and Prevention," Ch. 5 in Hugh J. Klare and David Haxby, eds., *Frontiers of Criminology* (London: Pergamon Press, 1967), pp. 85-102.

[17] E. Desprez, *De l'abolition de l'emprisonment* (Paris: E. Dentu, 1868), pp. 18-19.

[18] Cf. Dorwin Cartwright, "Achieving Change in People: Some Applications of Group Dynamics Theory," *Human Relations*, 4 (1951):381-392.

that the group relations which support criminality cannot be directly modified in a clinic in the way that the condition of a person suffering from syphilis can be modified in a clinic; they can be modified only by providing the criminal with new social relations or in some way changing the nature of present group relations.[19]

Numerous policies and programs arising in correctional work during the last hundred years have been explicitly or implicitly based upon recognition of the necessity for modifying criminality by changing the social relationships of delinquents and criminals. Among these are probation, which permits or assists the offender to come in contact with law-abiding groups instead of isolating him behind prison walls; education, self-government, and group therapy in prison, which are attempts to develop social interaction even while the prisoners are physically isolated; parole, which acts in the same way as probation; and various other efforts to assist the offender after release from prison to gain or regain contacts with law-abiding groups.[20]

This method of implementing the treatment reaction by providing contact with the law-abiding culture is important, but it has two shortcomings. *First,* the presence of a cultural pattern does not necessarily result in its adoption. Acculturation comes only as the result of contact, but contact does not necessarily result in acculturation. All persons are in contact with law-abiding culture, and all persons are in contact with criminal culture. Something more than contact is needed. Anthropologists have shown that cultural patterns are diffused among nonliterate groups not radially from a center as the result of spatial proximity, but in selected paths as the result of receptivity to the new patterns. Long-continued contact with a culture produces assimilation, but it accomplishes this by affecting a large variety of elements of the culture.[21] Immediate results in the reformation of an offender also require not only that the cultural pattern be present, but also that the offender be made receptive to it, as can be done with the group-relations method.

Second, offenders frequently find great difficulty in securing intimate contacts with law-abiding groups even if they are receptive to the notion that conformity to the rules of law is desirable. Neighbors may openly display prejudice against criminals. Law-enforcement officers, fearful that offenders will repeat their crimes or will contaminate law-abiding citizens, may hound them until they become convinced that the values embodied in the criminal law support injustice rather than justice. ●

---

[19] See the discussion below, pp. 616-621.

[20] Cressey, "Nature and Effectiveness of Correctional Techniques."

[21] Elihu Katz, Martin L. Levin, and Herbert Hamilton, "Traditions in Research on the Diffusion of Innovation," *American Sociological Review,* 28:237-252, April, 1963.

Because societies and their penal laws have been ambivalent about what should be done with, to, and for criminals, it is not surprising to find that correctional work has been, almost from the beginning, characterized by ambivalent values, conflicting goals and norms, and contradictory ideologies.[22] However, such a state of flux is not necessarily an impediment to correctional innovation. Viewed from one perspective, a state of disorganization or unorganization provides unusual opportunities for innovation. For example, an analysis of the Soviet industrial system concluded that conflicting standards and selective enforcement of an organization's rules permits supervisors to transmit changes in their objectives to subordinates without disrupting the operation of the system; permits subordinates to take initiative, be critical, make innovations, and suggest improvements; and permits workers who are closest to the problem field (usually subordinates) to adapt their decisions to the ever-changing details of circumstances. The following comment about the last point is especially relevant to correctional work:

> The very conflict among standards, which prevents the subordinate from meeting all standards at once, gives him a high degree of discretion in applying received standards to the situation with which he is faced. Maintenance of conflicting standards, in short, is a way of decentralizing decision-making.[23]

As conceptions of "the good society" have changed, conceptions of "good penology" and, more recently, "good corrections" also have changed. This has meant, by and large, that treatment services have been added to correctional work, and treatment roles have been assigned to both correctional workers and their clients. Moreover, these additions have been made without much regard for the services and roles already existing. The process seems different from that accompanying similar growth of manufacturing and sales corporations, for the new treatment roles have been organized around purposes that are only remotely related to the old punitive and custodial ones. This could mean, as in the case of Soviet industry, that anything goes.

But change toward treatment in corrections has been slow and sporadic despite conflicting principles which seem to make anything possible. Ambivalence and conflict in social values and penal theories have produced correctional organizations inadvertently designed to resist change.

In the first place, a shift toward treatment objectives requires changes in organization, not merely in the attitudes or work

Obstacles to innovation

---

[22] Parts of this section are adapted from Donald R. Cressey, "Sources of Resistance to the Use of Offenders and Ex-Offenders in the Correctional Process," chap. in Keith A. Stubblefield and Larry L. Dye, eds., *Offenders as a Correctional Manpower Resource* (Washington: Joint Commission on Correctional Manpower and Training, 1968), pp. 31-49.

[23] Andrew Gunder Frank, "Goal Ambiguity and Conflicting Standards: An Approach to the Study of Organization," *Human Organization*, vol. 17, no. 4, pp. 8-13, Winter, 1958-59. The quotation is from page 12.

habits of employees. In prisons, for example, there is a line organization of custodial ranks, ranging from warden to guard, and salary differentials and descriptive titles (usually of a military nature) indicate that a chain of command exists within this hierarchy. Any prison treatment innovation whose goals cannot be achieved by means of this hierarchy must either modify or somehow evade the organization of custodial ranks.

Secondly, most treatment innovations in correctional work can be introduced and implemented only if the participation, or at least the cooperation, of all employees is secured. In factories, there are separate but integrated hierarchies of management personnel and of workers, and many kinds of orders for innovation can flow freely downward from management offices to factory floors. For example, if the manager of an aircraft factory decides to innovate by manufacturing boats instead of airplanes, a turret lathe operator can readily accept the order to change the setup of his machine in such a way that part of a boat is manufactured. But in correctional work, management is an end, not a means. Accordingly, management hierarchies extend down to the lowest level of employee. The correctional worker, in other words, is both a manager and a worker. He is managed in a system of controls and regulations from above, but he also manages the inmates, probationers, or parolees in his charge. He is a low-status worker in interaction with his warden, chief, or director, but he is a manager in his relationships with inmates or clients. Because he is a manager, he cannot be ordered to accept a proposed innovation, as a turret lathe operator can be ordered. He can only be persuaded to do so.

But even though all correctional employees are managers as well as workers, the agencies and institutions which they manage are not owned by them. Each correctional agency has a number of absentee owners, and these owners have varying conceptions about policy, program, and management procedures. If they were questioned, it is probable that each would have a distinct opinion about treating criminals. Because of differences in theoretical conceptions in the broader society, the contemporary environment of correctional agencies contains overlapping groups with interests in seeing that physical punishments are imposed, groups with interests in reducing physical punishments, and groups with varying ideas for implementing the notion that criminals can be reformed only if they are provided with positive, nonpunitive treatment services. The interests of such groups converge on any particular correctional agency, and the means used by correctional administrators for handling their contradictory directives gives correctional agencies their organizational character.[24]

---

[24] See Philip Selznick, *Leadership and Administration* (Evanston, Ill.: Row, Peterson, 1957); and Mayer N. Zald, "The Correctional Institution for Juvenile Offenders: An Analysis of Organizational 'Character,' " *Social Problems*, 8:57-67, Summer, 1960.

One type of interest group emerges when an existing group sees existing or possible activities of the correctional program as a means for achieving its own objectives. For example, inmate leaders sometimes operate as an interest group and press for control over routine decisions because such control gives them additional power to exact recognition and conformity from other inmates. Political leaders become an interest group when they see a parole agency as a resource for discharging political obligations, and they demand that the agency be so organized that the skills of political appointees, not experts, can be used. Church groups sometimes band together to support or oppose a correctional program on moral grounds. Because there is a strong belief in our society that "doing a good job" is a reward in itself and that laziness and lack of "self-discipline" are sinful, such groups tend to support custody, work programs, and routinization rather than "treatment." Prison guards become an interest group when they perceive that prison discipline for inmates is becoming so relaxed that the guards might be in danger.

Another type of interest group is directly concerned with preventing innovations which threaten the group's existing activities or plans. Police constitute an interest group of this kind. They, even more than correctional workers, are charged with keeping the crime rate low, and they tend to oppose any correctional change which might reduce the degree of custody and surveillance. Similarly, social welfare groups and educational groups oppose any correctional changes which threaten to upset treatment and training routines; industrial groups oppose any organization of employment or employment services which will compete with them; and labor groups oppose any innovation which might reduce the number of jobs for noncriminals.

In this situation, effective action on the part of a correctional administrator depends upon realistic assessment of the power possessed by interest groups. When he makes a commitment to any given group or to any coalition of groups, his freedom of action is henceforth limited. If, at the same time, he decides not to commit himself to other groups or coalitions, his freedom to introduce innovations is limited even more. He is able to make some innovative moves because the mandates given by correctional interest groups ordinarily are stated in broad terms and consequently have broad tolerance limits. For example, the directives coming from interest groups usually specify objectives but ordinarily do not spell out in great detail the means to be used for achieving them. Accordingly, the correctional administrator can "compromise" by adjusting in minor ways the networks of interest groups which differ in significant respects from each other.

The conservatism of corrections is in part a reflection of the necessity for caution in making such compromises. As power and influence are redistributed in the network of interest groups, new forms of correctional activities emerge. These become routinized as a new compromise, a new balance of interests. Correctional personnel at all levels participate in the routinized activities and in that way are allied with correctional interest groups, whether they know it or not. This is the situation in which all employees share policy-making functions with management, making innovation extremely difficult.

If he is skillful, and if his organization is big enough, the correctional administrator can segregate his audiences by giving one part of his organization to one interest group while giving another part to a group with conflicting interests. For example, an interest group made up of social workers might be maneuvered so that it concentrates its concern on the boys' school or on correctional work with children generally, while an interest group composed of law-enforcement personnel might have its interests reflected in a particular prison. Even an entire division of a correctional agency, such as the prison system or the parole agency, may be given to interests supporting a welfare and treatment policy, while another unit is given to interests supporting a punitive and surveillance policy. But the specialization of correctional units should not be overemphasized. Every unit reflects the interests of many different groups, making change difficult.

Perhaps it is ambivalence and conflict in penal theory, together with a complex structure of correctional organizations, that underlies the most striking attitude among correctional workers —an attitude of "standing by." The ambivalence in theory has permitted various interest groups collectively to establish organizational structures which are extraordinarily difficult to change. But interest groups often can be pacified by external appearances and a display of organizational charts, and perhaps it is for this reason that internal pressure for significant innovation rarely occurs.

There certainly is variation from state to state and from agency to agency, but among correctional workers as a whole there is very little concern for the design of innovations which would put real rehabilitative processes into the treatment organizations of prisons and probation-parole agencies. These structures were created some years ago in response to pressures from interest groups. As indicated, however, the mandates given correctional administrators by interest groups tend to be stated in broad terms. Consequently the mere creation of treatment organizations within correctional institutions and agencies pacified some of the groups that supported treatment as a correctional objective. By and large, however, groups pressuring for treatment of criminals have left invention of the processes for administering treatment up to the correctional workers themselves, and correctional workers have not been innovative. Rather than experimenting with techniques based on rehabilitation or treatment principles specifically related to corrections, they have used processes vaguely based on general psychiatric theory. The resistance to innovation here has been more in the form of indifference than in the form of planned conservatism. There are two simple kinds of evidence that this kind of resistance is present in corrections.

First, the establishment of treatment organizations has permitted workers to engage in treatment services without ever defining them. It is extraordinarily difficult to define and identify "rehabilitation techniques" and even more difficult to measure the effectiveness of such techniques.[25] The objective of treatment programs in corrections is to change probationers, prisoners, and parolees so that they will no longer be lawbreakers. Yet it is reasonable to assume that no correctional worker has ever been fired because so few of his clients have changed. Perhaps this indifference to employee efficiency arises because a scientific technique for modification of attitudes has yet to be stated and implemented. Instead of precise descriptions of techniques for changing attitudes, the correctional literature contains statements indicating that rehabilitation is to be induced "through friendly admonition and encouragement," "by relieving emotional tension," "by stimulating the probationer's self-respect and ambition," "by establishing a professional relationship with him," "by encouraging him to have insight into the basis of his maladjustment," etc. We need to know—but we do not know—how these things are accomplished and, more significantly, how, or whether, they work to rehabilitate criminals. Two practicing correctional workers have commented:

Stripped to their essentials, these "instructions" boil down to exhortations to treat, to befriend, and to encourage. In effect, our treatment personnel are often told little more than to *go out there and rehabilitate somehow*—precisely how is not indicated. A military commander who confined his strategic orders to the commands, "Be brave, be careful, and be victorious" would be laughed out of uniform. Often, however, the technical directions given to correctional workers are scarcely more specific.[26]

Because treatment structures have been introduced in defiance of interest groups demanding that corrections be organized for punishment, custody, and surveillance, there has been a tendency on the part of correctional workers to define "treatment" negatively. Rather than identifying what treatment is, they have been content to assert what it is not: Any method of dealing with offenders that involves purposive infliction of pain and suffering, including psychological restrictions, is not treatment. This premise obviously must create strain in a total correctional organization that is expected to be restrictive and punitive. In the processes designed to implement it, there seems to be a mixture of

---

[25] See Cressey, "Nature and Effectiveness of Correctional Techniques."

[26] Richard R. Korn and Lloyd W. McCorkle, *Criminology and Penology* (New York: Holt, 1959), p. 593.

social work and psychiatric theory, humanitarianism, and ethics of the middle class.[27]

Second, because correctional administrators must justify all aspects of their total organization to one interest group or another, the research undertaken by research bureaus located in correctional agencies tends to be somewhat programmatic, rather than the kind that provides the basis for real change in the techniques used to change criminals. For example, research in California indicated that if parole case loads are reduced to fifteen and parolees are accorded "intensive supervision" during the first ninety days after release and then transferred to the normal ninety-man case loads for regular supervision, only slight reductions in parole violation rates occur.[28] But no one knows *why* this experiment, like others, turned out the way it did, principally because no one knows what, specifically, was involved in "intensive supervision" or "intensive treatment" that is not included when the procedure is not "intensive."

Correctional workers should not be blamed or attacked for what appears to be a lack of progress in developing basic principles on which to build sound correctional practice. The condition seems to be rooted in the very nature of the occupation, so that it is not easily changed. At least an attitude of "standing by" seems to be rooted in correctional work in a way that experimental and innovative attitudes are not. Five principal conditions seem to be associated with this conservatism: humanitarianism, poor advertising, bureaucracy, professionalization and inmate resistance.

Humanitarianism as "treatment"

One of the principal handicaps to developing and utilizing treatment techniques in modern corrections arises from the fact that we introduced and continued to justify humane handling of criminals on the ground that such humanitarianism is treatment. In speaking of prisons, for example, we now are likely to contrast the "barbaric" conditions of the eighteenth century with the enlightened "treatment methods" of our time. Yet we do this knowing that an insignificant proportion of all persons employed in American prisons are directly concerned with administration of treatment or training. Perhaps when we say criminals are being "treated," we mean something like, "They are being treated well," i.e., handled humanely.

Correctional workers are increasingly being asked to show the effects of treatment, but they can produce little evidence of

---

[27] See Donald R. Cressey, "Limitations on Organization of Treatment in the Modern Prison," chap. in Richard A. Cloward, Donald R. Cressey, George H. Grosser, Richard McCleery, Lloyd E. Ohlin, Gresham M. Sykes, and Sheldon L. Messinger, *Theoretical Studies in Social Organization of the Prison* (New York: Social Science Research Council, 1960), pp. 78-110.

[28] Ernest Reimer and Martin Warren, "Special Intensive Parole Unit: Relationship between Violation Rate and Initially Small Caseload," *National Probation and Parole Association Journal*, 3:222-229, July, 1957.

efficiency because much of what has been called "treatment" is merely humanitarianism. Budgets for "treatment" have been doubled in some states, but the recidivism rate has remained constant. Over the years, punitive measures, custodial routines, and surveillance measures were relaxed on the ground that such humanitarian relaxation is treatment. Now it is becoming necessary to try to show why this "treatment" has not been at all effective. Occasionally someone argues, usually in connection with a budget request, that no treatment principles have been invented and that, therefore, treatment has never been tried. More often, it is indirectly argued that humanitarianism disguised as treatment has not worked because "inhumane" persons and policies in corrections and in society have opposed it.

Poor advertising

The second condition associated with conservatism in correctional theory and practice, poor advertising, is closely related to the first. Humanitarians have left to correctional agencies themselves both the problem of justifying humanitarianism on the ground that it is treatment, and the problem of implementing that humanitarianism. But correctional workers are by their very nature poor propagandists for the humanitarian view, even if it is called "treatment." Correctional agencies are political units whose budgets and activities are, in the last analysis, controlled by politicians. And most politicians who want to continue being politicians must be opposed to crime as well as to sin and man-eating sharks. It simply is not expedient for governmental workers to advocate being "soft" on criminals, even if they think they can show that being "soft" is more efficient than not being "soft."[29] Police and prosecuting attorneys are excellently organized for promotion of the view that criminals should be dealt with harshly, but correctional workers are not, and probably cannot be, as efficiently organized for promotion of *either* the humanitarian point of view or the treatment point of view.

Bureaucracy and housekeeping

The third condition associated with the conservatism about theory and practice in correctional work is the bureaucratic organization necessary to the continuation of correctional agencies themselves. There is no reason to believe that the bureaucratization of correctional work should involve processes different from the processes of bureaucratization elsewhere. One effect of bureaucratization is conservatism and routinization. On a simple level, any treatment work done by correctional employees must be performed within the framework of an eight-hour day and a forty-hour week, and this means that it must, by and large, be performed at a special work station. On a more complex level, it may be observed that in a bureaucracy there are bureaucrats,

---

[29] See Donald R. Cressey, "Professional Correctional Work and Professional Work in Correction," *National Probation and Parole Association Journal,* 5:1-15, January, 1959.

and a bureaucrat is primarily concerned with housekeeping. It is for this reason that one keen observer of the American scene calls bureaucrats "women in men's clothing." The male principle, he argues, is that of wasteful and reckless experimentation, risk, and creation. The female principle is that of compromise, conservation, monopoly, complacency, and "results."[30] In correctional work, it appears, many employees have become housekeepers rather than reckless experimenters.

In correctional agencies that have grown to the point where professionalism and concordant bureaucracy have appeared, individual innovation, experimentation, and attempted implementation of new treatment ideas must necessarily be controlled. If this is not done, organizational routines might be embarrassingly upset. One control procedure is creation of a "research team," a "research division," or a "planning and development section," which is to contain the experimenters. This custom can block innovation, for the larger the team, the more difficult it is to get concurrence that radically new concepts are worth risking the team's reputation on. After all, if the new treatment plan goes sour, is attacked, ridiculed, and deprecated, the time and energy of all the team members, not just one crackpot, are brought into question.

Profession versus occupation

The fourth condition associated with conservatism among correctional workers is professionalization. Because professional personnel such as social workers, psychologists, and psychiatrists have constituted an interest group pressuring for treatment in corrections, it is somewhat paradoxical to observe that strong resistance to further change is characteristic of this group. There is no doubt that professional personnel have been instrumental in diminishing the punishment-custody-surveillance aspects of corrections, largely in the name of treatment. However, the same personnel tend to be conservative with reference to changes in professional practices themselves. "Professionalization" implies standardization of practice, with the result that the kind of bureaucratization just discussed is perhaps more characteristic of professional personnel than anyone else in corrections.

Among the characteristics of a profession is monopolization of specialized knowledge, including theory and skills.[31] When an occupation is professionalized, access to its specialized knowledge is restricted; definition of the content of the knowledge is uniform; and determination of whether a specific person possesses the knowledge is made by examination. Further, professional personnel ordinarily establish formal associations with definite membership criteria based on possession of the special-

---

[30] David Cort, *Is There an American in the House?* (New York: Macmillan, 1960), pp. 175-176.

[31] See Theodore Caplow, *The Sociology of Work* (Minneapolis: University of Minnesota Press, 1954), pp. 139-140; and Cressey, "Professional Correctional Work and Professional Work in Correction," pp. 2-3.

ized knowledge and specifically aimed at excluding "technically unqualified" personnel. The name selected by the association generally is unusual enough so that not just anyone can use it, again indicating a monopoly on a piece of theory and a set of skills. If the profession has developed a code of ethics, as professions eventually do, the code consists of a number of interrelated propositions which assert the occupation's devotion to public welfare and, more important to conservatism, stipulate standards of practice and standards for admission. Neither practitioners nor trainees can be allowed to "go it alone" in such a way that new or different standards are developed. They must learn the established code and behave according to the standards it implies. They must, in other words, accept the professional culture. In most instances, professions make their conservatism legal by gaining legislation which limits practice to those who have passed a state-administered examination or who are certified by the state upon completion of a specialized course of study, usually in a university. Often it is a crime for uncertified persons to perform the acts reserved to members of the profession. Concurrently, practices such as the privilege of confidentiality about the contents of individual therapy sessions might be reserved for professionals.

Moreover, "professionalization" implies that personnel will not engage in certain practices, just as it implies that certain practices are reserved to an elite group of personnel. Status as a professional person implies a position of high rank involving little or no dirty work. An admiral does not expect to chip paint, and a doctor does not expect to carry bedpans. As nursing has become professionalized in recent years, nurses do not expect to carry bedpans either. And as social work has become professionalized, social workers do not expect to carry baskets of food to the poor. Such activities are "unprofessional." In correctional work, treatment innovations which would require the professionals to perform the equivalent of chipping paint, carrying bedpans, and carrying baskets of food to the poor are bound to be resisted by the professionals. Yet since World War II almost everyone working in the field of treatment has argued that involvement in this kind of work, especially in "group relations therapy," is essential to rehabilitation.

It also should be noted that correctional administrative positions are increasingly being assigned to professional personnel. When this is the case, an administrator's income and status often depend upon his ability to maintain professional practices which over the years have been defined as "standard" and "good." One who is the director of a correctional rehabilitation program or crime prevention program does more than try to treat criminals or prevent crime. He administers an organization that provides employment for its members, and he confers status on these members as well as on himself. In other words, personal and organizational needs supplement the societal needs being met by administration and utilization of various treatment techniques. The personal and organizational needs are met by correctional institutions, agencies, and programs. By utilizing or advocating use of "professional methods" in correctional work, a person may secure employment and income, a good professional reputation, scholarly authority, prestige as an intellectual, the power stemming from being the champion of a popular cause, and many other personal rewards. An agency organized around administration of "professional methods" may fill such needs for dozens, even hundreds, of employees.

Because of personal and organizational investments, personnel dedicated to treating criminals are likely to maintain that criminality is reduced by whatever it is they are doing. Vague statistical measures of efficiency are valuable and useful because they decrease the range of points on which disagreements and direct challenges can occur.[32] Yet any suggestion for radical change is an implicit or explicit criticism, and it therefore is helpful if the efficiency question can be avoided by announcing that the proposed change would introduce procedures that are "substandard" or "unprofessional."

Offenders' resistance to innovation

Probationers, parolees, and prisoners are notoriously resistant to correctional innovations which would change them to significant degrees. First, they usually have good reasons for not trusting the personnel paid to implement any treatment program. Some procedures used in the administration of criminal justice necessarily are based on the theory that society must be hostile toward criminals in order to emphasize the undesirability of nonconformity. Criminals are committed to the care of correctional agencies against their will, and no amount of sugarcoating hides from them the fact that the first duty of correctional personnel is to protect society from criminals, not to treat individual criminals. Criminals often find it difficult to distinguish between correctional procedures designed to punish them and correctional procedures designed to help them.

Similarly, they are not at all confident that correctional personnel ostensibly engaged to help them are not actually engaged to assist in punishing them and keeping them under control. They note, for example, that in most prisons the treatment and rehabilitation specialists are subordinate to officials who emphasize the necessity for maintaining order, even if maintaining order interferes with treatment practices. They know that the prison psychiatrist or social worker might have the task of stopping "rumbles" or of "cooling out" threatening inmates, rather than of rehabilitating criminals. They know that revocation of probation or parole depends as much on the attitudes of the

---

[32] See Donald R. Cressey, "The State of Criminal Statistics," *National Probation and Parole Association Journal*, 3:230-241, July, 1957; and idem, "Nature and Effectiveness of Correctional Techniques."

probation-parole officer as on the behavior of the client. Further, they know that the pressures put on them to reform or become rehabilitated have as much to do with the good of "society" or the good of middle-class property owners as they have to do with the good of the individual criminal himself. Most criminals have very little confidence that the immense amount of data collected on them will be used for their benefit. As a sophisticated ex-convict has written, "The prisoner's need to live and the system's attempt to live for him (and off him) can never be reconciled."[33] In current correctional circumstances, clients have a minimal sense of obligation to the personnel controlling their fate. If, as McCorkle and Korn argued some years ago, criminals are intent on rejecting their rejectors,[34] treatment programs will succeed only if the degree of rejection by society is diminished.

Second, neither criminals nor ex-criminals are convinced that they need either existing treatment programs or any program which might be invented in the future. They cooperate with correctional workers not in order to facilitate their own reformation, but in order to secure release from surveillance as quickly as possible and as unscathed as possible. Prisoners, for example, participate in group therapy, group counseling, and individual treatment programs as much from a belief that doing so will impress the parole board as from a conviction that they, as individuals, need to change.

Once a criminal has gone through the impersonal procedures necessary to processing and labelling him as a law-violator, about all he has left in the world is his "self." No matter what that self may be, he takes elaborate steps to protect it, to guard it, to maintain it. If it should be taken away from him, even in the name of rehabilitation or treatment, he will have lost everything. Old-fashioned punishment-custody-surveillance procedures were designed to exterminate each criminal's self. Modern treatment programs are designed to do the same thing. Although many criminals, especially inmates, have favored "rehabilitation" and "treatment," strong resistance has occurred whenever the rehabilitation technique hints at "brainwashing" or any other procedure which would change the essence of "what I am." A pill or an injection which would change a criminal into a noncriminal without changing the rest of him might be accepted with enthusiasm by most criminals. But attempts to change criminals into noncriminals by significantly changing their personalities or life styles threaten to take away all they have left in the world.

---

[33] W. H. Kuenning, "Letter to a Penologist," in Holley Cantine and Dachine Rainer, eds., *Prison Etiquette* (Bearsville, N.Y.: Retort Press, 1959), p. 132. See also Bengt Börjeson, "Type of Treatment in Relation to Type of Offender," *Collected Studies in Criminological Research* (Council of Europe), Vol. 3, 1968, pp. 174-236.

[34] McCorkle and Korn, "Resocialization Within Walls."

Third, probationers, parolees, and even ex-offenders are not likely to become very excited about any program which expects them to look upon the task of rehabilitating themselves as a full-time job. Criminals, like others, have been taught that efforts at rehabilitation involve "technical," "professional," or even medical work on the part of a high-status employee, not hard work on the part of the person to be reformed. Moreover, for most criminals crime has been at most a moonlighting occupation or a brief, temporary engagement, and it follows that any personal involvement in their own rehabilitation also should be a part-time affair.

Fourth, a special kind of resistance to rehabilitation attempts is encountered in prisons, where inmates are in close interaction and have developed their own norms, rules, and belief systems. Wheeler has shown that inmate attitudes are not as opposed to staff norms as even inmates believe.[35] Nevertheless, for most prisoners, "adjustment" means attachment to, or at least acceptance by, the inmate group. Moreover, an inmate participating in a treatment program, no matter what its character, is likely to be viewed as a nut, as a traitor, or as both. Strong resistance will be encountered when efforts to change individual criminals would, if successful, have the result of making them deviate from the norms of their membership groups and reference groups.[36] Even among probationers and parolees, there is likely to be attachment to the values and beliefs of persons participating in what Irwin and Cressey have described as the "thief subculture," because this subculture stresses norms of "real men" and "right guys."[37]

Fifth, the use of individualized treatment procedures with some criminals is resisted by other criminals because the special handling is viewed as unfair. Criminals, perhaps more than other citizens, are concerned with justice, and one conception of justice views "special treatment" as unjust "special privilege" or "special favor." In prisons, especially, the punitive-custodial-administrative view is that all prisoners are equal and equally deserving of any "special privileges." They are not, of course. But when treatment criteria cannot be understood, handling inmates as special cases is likely to be interpreted to mean that the inmates in question are being given special privileges with reference to restrictive punishment. A prisoner who is released from prison because he has become "adjusted" or "rehabilitated" is not, from a treatment point of view, being granted a special privilege. But

---

[35] Stanton Wheeler, "Role Conflicts in Correctional Communities," chap. 6 in Donald R. Cressey, ed., *The Prison: Studies in Institutional Organization and Change"* (New York: Holt, Rinehart and Winston, 1961), pp. 229-259.

[36] See Harold H. Kelley and Edmund H. Volkart, "The Resistance to Change of Group-Anchored Attitudes," *American Sociological Review,* 17:453-465, August, 1952.

[37] John Irwin and Donald R. Cressey, "Thieves, Convicts and the Inmate Culture," *Social Problems,* 10:142-155, Fall, 1962.

as he is being discharged for treatment reasons, he also is being released from the restrictions deliberately and punitively imposed on him. Accordingly, the discharge is likely to be viewed as a reward for good behavior. More significantly, the prisoners who remain behind are likely to view their continued incarceration as unjust punishment—imposed not because of their crime but because of their prison conduct or the prejudice of the releasing authorities. It is this view that has led, in recent years, to increased criticism of the indeterminate sentence system. ●

Suggested readings

ALLEN, FRANCIS A. "Criminal Justice, Legal Values and the Rehabilitative Ideal," *Journal of Criminal Law, Criminology, and Police Science*, 50:226-232, September-October, 1959.

ANDENAES, JOHANNES. "The General Preventative Effects of Punishment." *University of Pennsylvania Law Review*, 114: 949-983, May, 1966.

CANTOR, NATHANIEL. "Conflicts in Penal Theory and Practice." *Journal of Criminal Law and Criminology*, 26:330-350, September-October, 1935.

CARTWRIGHT, DORWIN. "Achieving Change in People: Some Applications of Group Dynamics Theory." *Human Relations*, (1951) 4:381-392.

CHRISTIE, NILS. "Relativity in Development: An Example from Criminology." Chapter 3 in *Agents of Change: Professionals in Developing Countries*, edited by Guy Benveniste and Warren F. Ilchman. New York: Praeger, 1970.

CRESSEY, DONALD R. "Changing Criminals: The Application of the Theory of Differential Association." *American Journal of Sociology*, 61:116-120, September, 1955.

CRESSEY, DONALD R. "The Nature and Effectiveness of Correctional Techniques." *Law and Contemporary Problems*, 23: 754-771, Autumn, 1958.

EMPEY, LA MAR T. *Alternatives to Incarceration.* Washington: Government Printing Office, 1967.

GRUSKY, OSCAR. "Role Conflict in Organizations: A Study of Prison Camp Officials." *Administrative Science Quarterly*, 3:452-472, March, 1959.

HARLOW, ELEANOR, & J. ROBERT WEBER. *Diversion from the Criminal Justice System.* Washington: Government Printing Office, 1971.

JENKINS, R. L. "The Constructive Use of Punishment." *Mental Hygiene*, 29:561-574, October, 1945.

MECHANIC, DAVID. "Sources of Power of Lower Participants in Complex Organizations." *Administrative Science Quarterly*, 7:349-364, December, 1962.

MEYER, JOEL. "Reflections on Some Theories of Punishment." *Journal of Criminal Law, Criminology, and Police Science*, 59:595-599, December, 1968.

PANAKAL, J. J. "Training for Correctional Work." *Indian Journal of Social Work,* 28:89-94, April, 1967.

ROSE, GORDON. *The Struggle for Penal Reform.* London: Stevens and Sons, 1961.

SALEILLES, R. *The Individualization of Punishment.* Translated by R. S. Jastrow. Boston: Little, Brown, 1911.

SCHWITZGEBEL, RALPH K. *Development and Legal Regulation of Coercive Behavior Modification Techniques with Offenders.* Washington: Government Printing Office, 1971.

SELLIN, THORSTEN. "Correction in Historical Perspective." *Law and Contemporary Problems,* 23:585-593, Autumn, 1958.

STUBBLEFIELD, KEITH A., & LARRY L. DYE, eds. *Offenders as a Correctional Manpower Resource.* Washington: Joint Commission on Correctional Manpower and Training, 1968.

VON HIRSH, ANDREW. "Prediction of Criminal Conduct and Preventive Confinement of Convicted Persons." *Buffalo Law Review,* 21:717-758, 1972.

The police   **17**

After he has been detected, a criminal could become, successively, the concern of many agencies which are organized for the direction and implementation of societal reactions to crime. Hypothetically, he could come into contact with, at least, the police system, the courts, the probation system, the prison system, and the parole system. However, most criminals do not participate in all the programs in the series. Many guilty persons are discharged by the police or courts; others succeed on probation and, consequently, do not come into contact with the prison system; others are sent to prison directly and have no contact with probation or parole agencies.

In almost all instances, however, contact with the police system precedes contact with any subsequent agency or agencies. For this reason, and because in many cases contact with the police system is terminal, the police are in a strategic position with reference to the subsequent behavior of apprehended offenders.

Any punitive reaction by the police has important effects on the success of subsequent attempts at treatment. Even if treatment methods are not used later, either because they are not available or because the guilty person does not encounter them, the methods used by the police in performing their functions affect the probabilities for reformation or recidivism. In some instances, police methods cause offenders to identify themselves with criminals, and in other instances they cause them to abandon such criminal identifications as they may possess at the time of apprehension.

The police are also in a strategic position with reference to crime causation. Among both criminals and noncriminals they frequently are personified as "the law," and respect for law depends upon the behavior of the police more than on any other agents of the state. Most noncriminals have at least casual contact with the police, and in presenting anticriminal behavior patterns to such persons or to apprehended offenders, the prestige of the police is affected by their prior conduct and by their efficiency in performing their duties.

During the course of the last century, the police have also become an increasingly important agency in the total system for control of crime. Punishments have become milder and milder. Imprisonment was substituted for the stock, the whip, and the gallows, and then the conditions of prison life were gradually improved. As Bittner and Platt have observed, "Reform followed reform, and every generation of penologists found the devices of their predecessors barbaric."[1] This development has been matched, step by step, by the growth and increasing influence of organized police departments: "The very same forces that advocated the reduction of severity of punishment also advocated the establishment of a stable police force, while their opponents were as much opposed to mild treatment of offenders as they were opposed to the police."[2]

Currently, the wide distribution of police control has, together with mild forms of punishment, given us an internal pacification of society hitherto unknown in the civilized world. The police, in other words, are managing to protect us from crime more effectively and efficiently than severe punishments ever did.

There are in the advanced nations no longer any hobo jungles, or city slums, or districts of any sort that lie outside the purview of control of the administration of justice. Life and property of everybody, but especially the life and property of the middle and lower classes, are today safer than they were at any time in the past. Indeed, it is fair to say that modern law enforcement has achieved virtually complete control over crime and thus reduced it to a minor social problem.[3] ●

---

[1] Egon Bittner and Anthony M. Platt, "The Meaning of Punishment," *Issues in Criminology*, 2 (1966): 79-99.

[2] Ibid., p. 95.

[3] Ibid., pp. 95-96.

Composition of the police   The term *police* refers primarily to agents of the state whose official function is maintenance of law and order and enforcement of the regular criminal code. Each governmental unit, under the American constitution, may have its own police force. The city has a municipal police force; the small town has a marshal; and the township has a constable. The county may have an organized, uniformed, police force, in the form of a sheriff and his deputies. States now employ approximately ten thousand uniformed police, some of whom are limited to traffic regulation. In the United States there are about forty thousand local law-enforcement agencies, employing approximately 325,000 policemen, sheriffs, constables, marshals, and similar officers, and another 100,000 support personnel. Another 120,000 men serve as government-employed guards. In 1971, there were 2.1 police personnel, excluding civilian employees, for each one thousand inhabitants of the 4,624 cities reporting to the FBI. The police work of the federal government is centralized in the Federal Bureau of Investigation of the Department of Justice, but each federal department may have agents for enforcement of laws pertaining to it, including laws regarding the currency, narcotic drugs, internal revenue, customs, immigration, and post office. The state militia and the army and navy may perform police functions in emergencies.

Two other types of agents are, however, included in the police system. The first of these is the private police. These are privately selected, privately financed, and privately controlled, although they are sometimes commissioned as public agents. Industrial corporations have organized private police forces because they feel that they are not fully protected by public police. About 300,000 private police are employed in the United States. In 1971 Great Britain employed about 110,000 regular public policemen, 15,000 security police such as harbor patrol and the army constabulary, and 90,000 private security industry personnel.[4]

The second type of special police consists of inspectors and examiners who are appointed by public authorities: game wardens, bank examiners, factory and dairy inspectors, and inspectors of weights and measures. The staffs of the Securities and Exchange Commission, the Federal Trade Commission, and analogous state and federal commissions perform police functions in relation to white-collar crimes. By and large, examiners and inspectors officially function to protect consumers from being cheated by businessmen. Because they perform protective services, they are regarded with antagonism by many businessmen,

---

[4] W. E. Randall and Peter Hamilton, "The Security Industry of the United Kingdom," paper presented at the Cropwood Conference, Institute of Criminology, Cambridge, England, June 18-20, 1971.

who consider them "snoopers." At the same time, their work for the consumer is relatively unknown to consumers themselves. If members of the regular police departments enforced laws calling for special inspections and examinations, and publicized this activity as protection of the poor and uninformed, perhaps the ghetto image of the policeman as an adversary would change to an image of him as an ally. Should this occur, however, the policeman's status might decline in the eyes of the businessmen whose taxes contribute heavily to his salary.[5] ●

Conflicts between police responsibility and power

The American policeman is in a difficult position, for in order to do his work efficiently he must adopt more power than the law and the formal organization of his department permit. He is responsible for the enforcement of the criminal law and for the maintenance of order, yet he cannot meet these responsibilities under the power and authority granted him. At the same time, if he exceeds his authority in dealing with certain offenders, he is subject to severe public criticism. He can safely exceed his legal authority only when he deals with people who are not powerful politically and who are, in one sense, helpless.

Also, while the policeman is expected to make crime dangerous for all, he also is expected to use discretion and to exercise certain judicial functions. He must not only know whether a certain act violates the law, but also whether it can be proved that the law has been violated. He must rigorously enforce the law, yet he also must determine whether a particular violation of law should be handled by warning or arrest, for policemen are subject to informal rules which bar the arrest of some persons, and they are not expected to arrest everyone who is known to have violated a law. The courts would find it impossible to do their work if policemen brought all cases into court, and policemen would be in court so much of the time that the force would need to be enlarged enormously. Consequently, policemen must judge and informally settle more cases than they take into court; but the processes by which such settlements are made are not within the scope of their formal authority.[6]

There are numerous similar impediments to the performance of duties which the community ordinarily expects of the police. These include the assignment of administrative duties to the police, the law of arrest, antiquated legal systems, and political control of police activities.

---

[5] This chapter will be concerned with the work of the regular police, and no further attention will be paid to the private police or the specialized public agents who perform police functions for the various divisions of the government.

[6] See Egon Bittner, *The Functions of Police in Modern Society* (Washington: Government Printing Office, 1970), pp. 36-47, 95-106.

Administrative tasks

Many administrative tasks are being imposed upon police. Some of these are concerned primarily with public order, as in the direction of traffic (including installation and maintenance of traffic lights and signals, designation of one-way streets and of zones), granting permits or licenses for taxicabs, taxidrivers, and taxistands, parades, and similar activities, restraining crowds at fires, and aiding in emergencies. Other tasks also are only indirectly concerned with keeping the peace and enforcing the criminal law. They include licensing of amusement parks, dance halls, theaters, concealed weapons, property for advertising purposes, auctioneers, places for handling explosives, and also inspecting theaters and a great variety of other places and activities. The laws which require licensing are increasing rapidly, but the budgets and staffs of police departments are not being increased proportionately, so that inefficiency is almost a necessity. The police must select the laws they will enforce. Suggestions have been made that the regular police should confine their activities to the enforcement of laws against "serious" crimes, and that separate organizations should be developed for dealing with "morals," traffic, and licensing.

The public also has failed to recognize that the control of crime in modern times is extremely difficult and that it can be secured only by continuous, patient effort. Such effort requires a large staff and expensive equipment. The development of modern means of transportation and the resulting mobility of people have immensely increased the difficulties of control. City residents are anonymous. Two generations ago criminals wore masks, but this practice occurs only infrequently today. The criminal is a stranger, and it is difficult to identify a stranger. The crowds on city streets often facilitate escape. To a professional burglar, one block and around the corner in a city is as good as twenty miles in the country.

Also, the very number of crimes impedes the solution of any one of them, yet the police are held responsible for the solution of all. In large American cities at least one murder occurs, on the average, almost every day. A small, specialized homicide squad therefore has little time for study of a particular murder but must rush from one case to another. In England, on the other hand, where murders are less frequent, a specialized force can concentrate on one murder until it is solved. This difference would not be as significant if it were not for the public pressure in the United States to solve spectacular crimes. The pressure is instigated by the news media, and they, more than any other agency, make it impossible for the existing police to develop a policy of consistent work. During a "crusade" inaugurated to solve a spectacular crime, police rules asking for calm, deliberate, and dignified police work are likely to be suspended.

Even if the force has but one set of consistent ends specified for it by the commissioner or superintendent, and even if adherence to those ends is enforced as far as is possible, it is almost inevitable that there will come a time when the commissioner will decide that something must be done "at all costs"—that some civic goal justifies any police means. This might be the case when a commissioner is hard pressed by the newspapers to solve some particularly heinous crime (say, the rape and murder of a little girl). A "crusade" is launched. Policemen who have been trained to act in accord with one set of rules ("Use no violence." "Respect civil liberties." "Avoid becoming involved with criminal informants.") are suddenly told to act ᴉ accord with another rule—"catch the murderer"—no matter what it costs in terms of the normal rules.[7]

The law of arrest

Arrests can be made on warrants, or written orders of the court, by anyone authorized to serve them. Upon application, a warrant may be obtained from a judge when the judge is convinced of the probability that a particular person is guilty of an offense. Under certain conditions, both private citizens and police officers can arrest without a warrant. Private citizens without a warrant, however, have no authority to arrest for misdemeanors, except in some states where they are allowed to arrest for a breach of peace committed in their presence. Officers can arrest for misdemeanors without a warrant if the misdemeanor is committed in their presence.

For felonies, in some states, arrest by a private person without a warrant is not lawful unless the arresting person (a) has reasonable grounds for believing the arrestee is guilty, and (b) the arrestee is guilty. In a greater number of states, a private citizen may arrest for a felony if (a) he has reasonable grounds for believing the arrestee is guilty, and (b) a felony has been committed. In about five other states, a private person has the same powers as police officers generally have in regard to felonies: he can arrest for a felony whenever he has (a) reasonable grounds for believing that a felony has been committed and (b) reasonable grounds for believing that the arrestee committed it.[8] Under common law, neither police officers nor private citizens could arrest for a felony without a warrant unless there were *positive* knowledge that a felony had been committed and there were reasonable grounds for believing that the arrestee was the guilty person.

The law is frequently violated by the police in making arrests. Most police departments, for instance, have rules which authorize officers to make arrests on suspicion quite in opposition to the law.[9] Most of the illegal arrests are designed to protect society. In rural areas where officers are paid by fees—one fee for making an arrest, another for discharging a person from jail, etc.—the

[7] James Q. Wilson, "The Police and Their Problems: A Theory," *Public Policy*, 12 (1963): 189-216. The quotation is from p. 199.

[8] See Rocco Tresolini, Richard W. Taylor, and Elliott B. Barnett, "Arrest Without Warrant: Extent and Social Implications," *Journal of Criminal Law, Criminology, and Police Science*, 46:187-198, July-August, 1955.

[9] See Ed Cray, *The Enemy in the Streets: Police Malpractice in America* (Garden City, N.Y.: Anchor Books, 1972), pp. 36-63.

police are induced to make unjustifiable and illegal arrests in order to get the fees. However, the thousands of unlawful arrests made by urban policemen in "dragnet raids" and in the arrests of drunk persons and vagrants are not necessarily sinister. On the contrary, these arrests reflect, in many cases, "a praiseworthy zeal in the pursuit of the criminal, leading the zealous officer to chafe against, to strain, and occasionally to break the shackles which the law has thrown about his operations."[10] The number of illegal arrests probably would be even greater if more of the suspects made it necessary for a police officer to make an actual arrest before taking them to the police station for questioning or investigation. Often the officer merely says, "You had better talk to the captain about this," or "We had better take a ride down to the station," rather than actually placing the suspected person under arrest, but in many cases the person in question believes that he is being arrested.

The police are severely criticized for making illegal arrests, and they are subject to damage suits by the illegally-detained persons. Yet they also are severely criticized for not arresting persons who apparently have violated the law.[11] Under the law of arrest, if a thief were detained by a private citizen who saw him commit a misdemeanor, and a policeman subsequently arrived on the scene and arrested the offender for the misdemeanor, the arrest probably would be illegal. But a policeman who did not arrest under such circumstances would be subject to severe criticisms, and it is not inconceivable that he would be accused of being in collusion with the offender. Persons charged with concealed weapons are frequently discharged from court on the ground that the officer had no reasonable ground for making an arrest; the fact that concealed weapons were found in the search subsequent to the arrest is of no legal importance, for such evidence is held to have been illegally secured and therefore might not be introduced in the court. However, an officer who did not take such a suspect to court probably would lose his position on the police force. Police have resisted recent United States Supreme Court decisions holding that evidence secured through unreasonable search and seizure, in violation of the Fourth Amendment, shall not be admitted in court against the accused.[12]

---

[10] Lewis Mayers, *The American Legal System*, rev. ed. (New York: Harper and Row, 1964), p. 55.

[11] James Q. Wilson, *Varieties of Police Behavior: The Management of Law and Order in Eight Communities* (New York: Atheneum, 1972), pp. 95-110.

[12] See O. W. Wilson, "Police Arrest Privileges in a Free Society: A Plea for Modernization," chap. in Claude R. Sowle, ed., *Police Power and Individual Freedom: The Quest for Balance* (Chicago: Aldine, 1962), pp. 21-28; Caleb Foote, "The Fourth Amendment: Obstacle or Necessity in the Law of Arrest?" ibid., pp. 29-36; and Albert J. Reiss, Jr., *The Police and the Public* (New Haven: Yale University Press, 1971), pp. 125-134.

Although the police are expected to control crime by enforcing the criminal law, thereby making crime dangerous, they are expected to do so within the legal framework of criminal law and criminal procedure. Among students of the subject there is almost unanimous agreement that the criminal law and criminal procedure are inadequate for the purpose of controlling crime and administering justice. Not only is the law of arrest inadequate, as indicated above, but the police are expected to enforce laws which are unenforceable. Many of the rules of evidence are not adapted to modern conditions, and frustrated police see many criminals escape conviction because of this system. Skolnick has suggested that this frustration stems from a conflict between a set of forces stressing social order, initiative, and efficiency and another set of forces stressing the "rule of law":

Legal restrictions

> The police in democratic society are required to maintain order and to do so under the rule of law. As functionaries charged with maintaining order, they are part of the bureaucracy. The ideology of democratic bureaucracy emphasizes initiative rather than disciplined adherence to rules and regulations. By contrast, the rule of law emphasizes the rights of individual citizens and constraints upon the initiative of legal officials. The tension between the operational consequences of ideas of order, efficiency, and initiative, on the one hand, and legality, on the other, constitutes the principal problem of police as a democratic legal organization.[13]

The "tension" noted by Skolnick has been discussed by Herbert Packer, a professor of criminal law, in terms of a conflict between what he calls a "crime-control model" and a "due process model."[14] On the one hand, there are pressures for the police to control crime, to manage the criminal justice process in such a way that a maximum number of criminals are deterred or discouraged. But a series of United States Supreme Court decisions handed down in the last decade stresses "constitutionalizing" each stage of the criminal process, thus enhancing the capacity of accused persons, rich and poor alike, to challenge the operation of the process on the ground that it invades their rights to privacy, liberty, dignity, and equality (due process model). For example, in the *Mallory* case, a defendant was tried for rape and sentenced to death. Under procedures consistent with the crime-control model, he had been detained from early afternoon until the next morning at police headquarters without being taken before a magistrate, although magistrates were available nearby. He was not told of his right to remain silent, to have counsel, or to be arraigned before a magistrate. By the time he was

---

[13] Jerome H. Skolnick, *Justice Without Trial* (New York: John Wiley, 1966), p. 6. See also Maureen E. Cain, *Society and the Policeman's Role* (London: Routledge and Kegan Paul, 1973), pp. 21-25.

[14] Herbert L. Packer, "Two Models of the Criminal Process," *University of Pennsylvania Law Review*, 118 (1964): 1-68. See also idem, *The Limits of the Criminal Sanction* (Stanford, Calif.: Stanford University Press, 1968).

arraigned, he had made a confession, which was used as evidence to convict him. The Supreme Court reversed the conviction, holding in essence that only the courts can decide to deprive a person of liberty, and that an illegal detention for "investigation" invalidates an otherwise legal confession.[15]

In a second important case, that of *Mapp,* the defendant was convicted of possessing lewd and lascivious pictures and books. She had refused to admit the police to her home, so they entered forcibly, without a search warrant, and seized the illegal material. In reversing the conviction, the Supreme Court held that "all evidence obtained by searches and seizures in violation of the Constitution is, by the same authority, inadmissible in a state court."[16]

The *Gideon* and *Miranda* decisions also stressed the importance of due process of law. Gideon was charged with breaking and entering a Florida poolroom. At his trial, he asked the court to appoint a lawyer for him, but the judge refused. The Supreme Court reversed his conviction, stating, "The right of one charged with crime to counsel may not be fundamental and essential to fair trial in some countries, but it is in ours."[17] In the *Miranda* case, a confession was admitted as evidence against a man charged with rape, but he had not been informed of his constitutional rights to remain silent and to have legal counsel. The Supreme Court reversed the conviction on the ground that he should have been so informed.[18]

Packer summarizes as follows the important differences between the due process model used by the Supreme Court and the crime-control model used by the police and courts in the cases overruled:

> The choice, basically, is between what I have termed the Crime Control and the Due Process models. The Crime Control model sees the efficient, expeditious and reliable screening and disposition of persons suspected of crime as the central value to be served by the criminal process. The Due Process model sees that function as limited by and subordinate to the maintenance of the dignity and autonomy of the individual. The Crime Control model is administrative and managerial; the Due Process model is adversary and judicial. The Crime Control model may be analogized to an assembly line, the Due Process model to an obstacle course.[19]

Besides being necessarily hampered by concern for the rights of accused and suspected persons, the police are unnecessarily hampered by an antiquated system of local boundaries. In the

---

[15] *Mallory v. United States* 354 U.S. 449 (1957). Interpretation of this and the following cases follows closely the analysis by George Edwards (Judge, U.S. Court of Appeals), *The Police on the Urban Frontier* (New York: Institute of Human Relations Press, 1968), pp. 13-17.

[16] *Mapp v. Ohio,* 367 U.S. 643 (1961).

[17] *Gideon v. Wainwright,* 372 U.S. 335 (1963).

[18] *Miranda v. Arizona,* 384 U.S. 436 (1966).

[19] Herbert L. Packer, "The Courts, the Police, and the Rest of Us," *Journal of Criminal Law, Criminology, and Police Science,* 57:238-243, September, 1966.

area within fifty miles of the center of Chicago more than four hundred independent police forces are operating with no central control or organization. In Cook County alone there are over eleven thousand police employed as members of about two hundred separate and uncoordinated agencies. The result is a system of duplicating and conflicting efforts which is necessarily inefficient. Police try to offset the inefficient system by violating the law. When local boundaries seriously hamper their efforts to control crime, police ignore them, or they devise summary methods of extradition, whereby the police in one bailiwick simply shove captured criminals across the boundary line into the arms of the police in the bailiwick in which the crimes were committed.

The police also violate the law in other ways. Since they are charged with the responsibility of controlling crime but are also thwarted in their attempts to do so by the existing legal system, they sometimes take it upon themselves to control by extralegal methods. For instance, violence which is not legally justified is sometimes used at the time of arrest or between the arrest and the court hearing. When such violence, including protracted questioning and various psychological tortures, is used to get confessions from suspected persons, the Fifth, Sixth, and Fourteenth Amendments to the Constitution usually are violated. Those amendments safeguard the rights of suspected persons in courts and make it illegal for a state to deprive any citizen of life, liberty, or property without due process of law. The methods by which these constitutional safeguards are violated in order to obtain confessions from suspects were once referred to as the "third degree." Third-degree practices have declined dramatically in the last thirty years, and especially since 1966, when the United States Supreme Court handed down the *Miranda* decision—which makes it necessary for the police to warn a suspect that he has a right to remain silent, that anything he says may be used against him, that he has a right to have an attorney present during any questioning, and that, if he cannot afford to hire a lawyer, one will be appointed to represent him. Ordinarily, third-degree methods were used against powerless and rather inconspicuous persons.

Although violence designed to coerce confessions has declined, some police departments have in recent years been severely criticized for using excessive force at the times of apprehension, arrest, booking, and detention. The President's Commission reported on national surveys that found "brutality" and "intimidation" at these points to be common in many police departments across the country.[20] In a study made some years ago, 37 percent of the police officers questioned believed that "roughing a man

---

[20] President's Commission on Law Enforcement and Administration of Justice, *Task Force Report: The Police* (Washington: Government Printing Office, 1967), pp. 144-149, 178-190.

up" is justified if he has shown disrespect for the police, and 19 percent believed that such violence is justified when the objective is to obtain information from the subject.[21] A more recent study of police-citizen encounters in Boston, Chicago, and Washington, D.C., suggested that what citizens object to and call "police brutality" is sometimes something less than "roughing a man up." Those complaining of brutality were really making the judgment that they had not been treated with the full rights and dignity owing citizens in a democratic society.[22]

The study found that the most common citizen complaints refer to traditional police practices such as the use of profane and abusive language, commands to move on or get home, stopping and questioning people on the street or searching them and their cars, threats to use force if not obeyed, prodding with a nightstick or approaching with a pistol, and the actual use of physical force or violence itself. Members of minority groups and those seen as nonconformists are the most likely targets of status degradation involving treatment as nonpersons, harassment, and unnecessary searches.

The observers who rode in police cars and who monitored booking and lockup procedures in high-crime precincts of Boston, Chicago, and Washington judged the force used by police to be "improper" or "unnecessary" only if it were used in one or more of the following ways:

If a policeman physically assaulted a citizen and then failed to make an arrest; proper use involves an arrest.

If the citizen being arrested did not, by word or deed, resist the policeman; force should be used only if it is necessary to make the arrest.

If the policeman, even though there was resistance to the arrest, could easily have restrained the citizen in other ways.

If a large number of policemen were present and could have assisted in subduing the citizen in the station, in lockup, and in the interrogation rooms.

If an offender was handcuffed and made no attempt to flee or offer violent resistance.

If the citizen resisted arrest, but the use of force continued even after the citizen was subdued.

In a seven-week period, the observers noted thirty-seven cases, involving forty-four citizens, in which force was used improperly, by these definitions. In three cases, the amount of force was so great that the citizen had to be hospitalized. Encounters with 643 white suspects and 751 Negro suspects were observed. Twenty-seven of the white suspects experienced undue use of force, for a rate of 41.9 per 1000. The comparable rate for the 751 Negro suspects, of whom seventeen experienced undue use of force, was 22.6 per 1000. Thus, the rate of excessive force

[21] William A. Westley, "Violence and the Police," *American Journal of Sociology*, 56:34-41, July, 1953.

[22] Albert J. Reiss, Jr., "Police Brutality — Answers to Key Questions," *Trans-Action*, July-August, 1968, pp. 10-19.

on the white citizens alleged by the police to be offenders was almost twice that of Negro suspects. Sixty-seven percent of the citizens victimized by white policemen were white, and 71 percent of the citizens victimized by Negro policemen were Negro. The study concluded, "The most likely victim of excessive force is a lower-class man of either race."

The most injurious aspect of police violence is that it tends to alienate the public; yet that same public applauds violence when it is used on the more unpopular criminals. Some years ago, a bill to ban third-degree tactics was passed by the lower house of an eastern state, but it was killed when a state senator asked, "Are we to give the criminal an even break? Does the criminal give the law-abiding citizen an even break?" The public, in a sense, also promotes other illegal police methods by severely criticizing the police if they do not control crime, or do not quickly solve spectacular crimes, while at the same time granting them only inadequate legal powers to do so.

Politics

The most serious impediments to efficient crime control by the police are found in the system of political control of police organizations. In some cities, the police force is under the control of politicians who do not wish and will not permit the enforcement of many laws. Appointments of commissioners and superintendents and advancement of policemen from one rank to another are controlled largely by politicians. The politicians therefore control the fundamental policies and practices of the police department.[23] Formally, the police department is organized and operates for the welfare of society; informally, it is organized for the welfare of the politicians. This means both that some crimes must be overlooked and that some criminals must be protected by the police.

Under the control of corrupt politicians, police departments become systematically lawless. This does not mean that every policeman is lawless, but that, as a system, the police operate in a lawless manner. Graft is one form of this lawlessness. Graft, in turn, is usually linked with collusion with professional and organized criminals. The investigations of the United States Senate Special Committee to Investigate Crime in Interstate Commerce revealed extensive collusion between criminals and law-enforcement officers and extensive evidence of graft by law-enforcement officers. For example, it was the committee's judgment that "outright payments for protection were most clearly established" in the case of a sheriff of Orleans, the parish in which the city of New Orleans is located.[24] The sheriff's divorced wife testified that in six years the sheriff had accumulated $150,000, which he kept in a steel box in his home. She also testified that she had seen her husband receive money weekly

[23] See Virgil W. Peterson, "The Chicago Police Scandals," *Atlantic Monthly*, 206:58-64, October, 1960.
[24] Estes Kefauver, *Crime in America* (New York: Doubleday, 1951), pp. 175-176.

from a slot-machine dealer, and that she herself had received money every week from another slot-machine dealer. Another person, who reputedly ran a house of prostitution, came by on Saturdays, bringing "all the food for a week." Similarly, it was revealed that in Tampa a sheriff was the center of a criminal conspiracy to violate gambling laws, and that he received direct payments of protection money. In Philadelphia there were direct payments of approximately $152,000 monthly, "not counting payments to higher-ups." In New York City one bookmaking organization paid over $1 million a year for police protection, and in Los Angeles an entry of $108,000 for "juice," the California term for protection money, was found in the books of a book-making organization.[25]

In many other cities evidence of a politico-criminal-police triumvirate was revealed.[26] In fact, the committee found evidence of corruption and connivance at all levels of government—federal, state, and local. In the federal government the corruption was found to be primarily in connection with the enforcement of income-tax laws, but evidence of illegal activities on the state and local levels took four different forms: (a) direct bribe or protection payments made to the police by criminals; (b) politicians using their influence to protect criminals and further the interests of criminals; (c) police possessing unusual and unexplained wealth; and (d) police participating directly in the business of organized crime.[27]

Illegal activity in police departments is not a recent phenomenon. Federal and state investigating committees have revealed graft and collusion almost every time they have looked for them. The Lexow Committee in New York City in 1894-1895, for example, found that graft was characteristic of the police system rather than of isolated patrolmen.[28] The Seabury Committee a generation later found the same situation persisting.[29] In 1915

---

[25] Special Committee to Investigate Organized Crime in Interstate Commerce, *Third Interim Report,* U.S. Senate Report No. 307, 82d Congress (Washington: Government Printing Office, 1951), pp. 184-185. See also Norton Mockridge and Robert H. Prall, *The Big Fix* (New York: McGraw-Hill, 1957).

[26] For the committee's findings in medium-sized cities, see its *Final Report,* U.S. Senate Report No. 257, 82d Congress (Washington: Government Printing Office, 1951), pp. 37-62.

[27] *Third Interim Report,* pp. 183-184.

[28] New York Legislature, *Report and Proceedings of the Senate Committee Appointed to Investigate the Police Department of the City of New York* [Lexow Committee] (Albany: State Printing Office, 1895), vol. 5, pp. 5311-5388. For a brief description of this investigation, see Lincoln Steffens, *Autobiography* (New York: Harcourt, 1931), pp. 247-284.

[29] New York Legislature, *Report of the Joint Committee on the Government of the City of New York,* 5 vols. (Albany: State Printing Office, 1932). This report has been summarized, interpreted, and amplified in several unofficial books, of which the following are the most important: W. B. Northrop and J. B. Northrop, *The Insolence of Office* (New York: Putnam's Sons, 1932); Raymond Moley, *Tribunes of the People* (New Haven: Yale University Press, 1932); Norman Thomas and Paul Blanshard, *What's the Matter with New York?* (New York: Macmillan, 1932).

the Chicago City Council Commission on Crime found much evidence of collusion between police and professional criminals.[30]

For years, professional thieves have been able to work on the assumption that any case of theft by them in any American city can be "fixed," and that an arrest is merely a temporary discomfort from which no great inconvenience results. This kind of collusion does not involve the whole police system in the sense that graft connected with gambling or prostitution does, but it is a mistake to believe that graft is restricted to situations in which "morals" are regulated. The Lexow Committee found that the same system of bribery used by criminals was also used by commission merchants, contractors, pushcart vendors, bootblacks, and others who wanted to use the public streets for private business. The Seabury Committee reported that the bribery of public officers was the method used in securing special privileges regarding building-zone ordinances, bus franchises, waterfront leases, condemnation cases, weights and measures, taxi regulations, and many other things. Similarly, a recent study of Reading, Pennsylvania, a middle-sized industrial city, revealed that most of the crimes perpetrated by city officials during a period of almost total corruption were committed in order to facilitate the gambling offenses of organized criminals. But the same officials charged under-the-table fees for building permits, for liquor licenses, for employment in city hall, and for contracts to supply the city with goods and services. A 1966 survey of the residents of Reading revealed that the citizens approved of gambling or were tolerant of it, but were hostile toward corruption. The citizens, in other words, "display both a desire for or toleration of illicit services and a demand for honesty on the part of local officials." The residents of the city failed to see that widespread illegal gambling is accompanied by widespread taking of bribes.[31]

Bribery, graft, and corruption are not confined to police departments. And when these conditions are found in police departments, they are not confined to prostitution, gambling, liquor, and other "morals" or "vice" violations. On the contrary, they may develop wherever business concerns or individuals see an opportunity for gain by bribery, and wherever the police see an opportunity to force contributions from such concerns or individuals.

Another consequence of the fact that police departments sometimes are organized for the welfare of corrupt politicians, rather than of society, is inefficient and unqualified personnel. This is unquestionably linked with police dishonesty, since only police

---

[30] Chicago City Council, *Report of the Commission on Crime* (Chicago: Author, 1915).

[31] John A. Gardiner, with the assistance of David J. Olson, "Wincanton: The Politics of Corruption," appendix B in President's Commission on Law Enforcement and Administration of Justice, *Task Force Report: Organized Crime* (Washington: Government Printing Office, 1967), pp. 61-79.

officers who are "right" can be employed by those in political control. Civil service systems which have been set up for the selection and promotion of qualified men are sometimes ignored or circumvented. The public loudly demands that the police control crime, yet it fails to see that policemen are selected carefully, to provide adequate training, to furnish adequate salaries and conditions of employment, and to make possible continuous policies. The average term of office of the chief official of police departments in American cities of a half-million population or more is only about two years, while in London it has been about fifteen years. Even when police are not selected on the basis of political patronage, directly or indirectly, the departments usually are inadequately staffed.

In general, the police are inefficient in performing their duties, as these duties are formally defined, but the inefficiency is due to the fact that the public fails to provide conditions which are essential to efficiency. The police believe, for example, that a universal registration system would facilitate efficient police work. The ordinary American interprets this as an imposition on his personal liberty, although he makes no objection to submitting his fingerprints in other situations. In the same spirit, the public is unwilling to assist the police in other respects. It is extremely difficult for police officers to secure assistance from bystanders in the pursuit of a criminal or the detection of crime. The social conditions which produce high crime rates also produce a police system which cannot deal effectively with crime under existing conditions. It cannot be properly said that the public wants the police to repress and prevent all crime. ●

The punitive reaction and the police

From the time of the formation of the United States there has been a tradition of narrow and restricted authority and power on the part of administrators and executives, including the police. At the same time, the persons occupying such positions are expected to play their roles as administrators skillfully. Like other administrators—in the government, church, educational system, the army, and elsewhere—the police tend to take attitudes of superordination and to assume unofficial powers, often in opposition to the desires of many of their constituents, and in doing so they often adopt punitive measures. The police system is officially an agency which maintains order, serves the public, and captures suspected criminals and takes them to courts for trial.

According to legal and political theory, the rights and duties of the police to inflict punishments are sharply limited.[32] Formally, authority to implement anything approaching a punitive reaction to law violation is restricted to three main areas. *First,*

---

[32] See Jerome Hall, "Police and Law in a Democratic Society," *Indiana Law Journal,* 28:133-177, Winter, 1953.

as noted previously, a limited judicial authority has been conferred upon the police, primarily in connection with minor offenses such as traffic violations, and the exercise of this authority often involves a punitive reaction to the offense. *Second,* police are expected to punish by destroying property which is prohibited by law, such as gambling devices and unregistered equipment for making alcohol. *Third,* police are authorized to confiscate or impound property which is being used in violation of law, with the result that the owner loses the property or is required to pay a fee for its recovery. This may be illustrated by the impounding of arms and by the towing away of illegally parked cars.

However, because they are expected to make crime dangerous, the police, in fact, implement a punitive reaction to crime in many additional ways. The third degree, which entails pain and suffering for the purpose of extorting a confession, is punitive in nature, as is collecting a bribe from a guilty person in lieu of arrest. Brutality in the process of arrest or detention is an expression of hatred and superiority. So far as brutality is defended by the police, it is said to be justified by the fact that many guilty persons escape conviction through technicalities or corruption and thus escape official punishment. The police say, in effect, "We will see that he gets this much punishment anyway."

Even when arrests and detention do not incorporate brutality, they often include intentional imposition of suffering. Police are apt to be discourteous, sarcastic, or rude when arresting persons of lower socioeconomic classes, but courteous and lenient when dealing with persons of high social status. The fact that courtesy was first emphasized in police departments when the police came into frequent contact with automobile drivers, who were not ordinarily of the lower classes, is evidence of this discrimination. In fact, until the police started dealing with automobile drivers, they were mostly workingmen employed by the upper classes and middle classes to control other workingmen. The first police department, established in England in 1829, had something of this form, as did the first regular police forces in New York (1844) and Chicago (1855). The fact that Southern California, with the highest number of automobiles per capita in the world, also has the police with the highest average educational level in the world shows one effect of the encounter between the police and upper- and middle-class automobile drivers. Undoubtedly, the police make distinctions in favor of upper socioeconomic classes because the making of such distinctions is part of our culture.[33] Similarly, the police use punitive methods because the punitive reaction to crime is popular in our culture.

It should not be concluded, however, that any use of force and violence on the part of the police is necessarily "brutality,"

---

[33] See Margery Fry, *Arms of the Law* (London: Gollancz, 1951), pp. 19, 97-98; and T. C. Willett, *Criminal on the Road* (London: Tavistock, 1964), pp. 4, 7, 65-109.

motivated by a desire to inflict punishment. Because some of the persons with whom the policeman deals are dangerous, he must be trained to fight, shoot, and use force. Confronting dangerous men and subduing them is a hazardous business,. and policemen cannot be expected to be gentle at all times. When a policeman's life is at stake, we cannot expect him to follow either the rules of boxing or the rules governing the behavior of television cowboys, both of which stress the propriety of fighting "fairly," like gentlemen. A policeman who fought by these rules would soon use up all his sick leave. The first chapter of a "practical handbook" for American police patrolmen is exclusively devoted to the use of force, and its instructions range from details about how to use an opponent's clothing to restrain him, to how to use a nightstick and how to kill with a gun.[34] On the latter point, the authors give policemen the following lesson:

> You don't have to wait until a suspect is actually assaulting you before you draw your gun. In fiction and on film, the actor portraying a Western Marshal can afford to wait until his assailant has started to draw before he goes for his gun. You cannot. You are in a real-life drama; there are no rehearsals or retakes and mistakes can be fatal.[35] ●

The treatment reaction and the police

Although the fundamental informal policy of police departments is punitive, during the last fifty years there has been a slight trend toward implementation of the treatment reaction to lawbreaking. Changes in police departments in this connection, of course, correspond to changes in other agencies and in the society as a whole. As the treatment reaction has become more popular in the whole society, it also has become popular in police organizations. However, like the implementation of the punitive reaction by the police, the implementation of the treatment reaction is largely unofficial. The activities of the police in this area are usually called "crime prevention"—discouraging or hindering crime by methods which are not designed to produce fear in the recipient.

Most of the activities of crime-prevention divisions of police departments are directed toward what are considered the social conditions leading to delinquency and crime, but the treatment reaction also is implemented in other ways. In exercising their judicial authority, the police certainly screen offenders on the basis of whether or not it is thought that punishment is warranted, but they also sometimes evaluate offenders according to whether or not it is thought that treatment is needed. Especially in dealing with juveniles, the police screen offenders by using discretion as to whether a child should be released or diverted to a guidance clinic for personality help, to a youth agency for

---

[34] David H. Gilston and Lawrence Podell, *The Practical Patrolman* (Springfield, Ill.: Charles C Thomas, 1959), pp. 5-28.

[35] Ibid., p. 23.

club contacts, to some other agency, or to a court.[36] Many police departments now use a quite unofficial process of placing boys on "police probation," sometimes requiring them to do punitive labor such as washing police cars or raking leaves. Guilt usually is assumed, but even if guilt is not assumed, and the policeman makes his decision on the basis of mere probabilities or symptoms of delinquency, expostulation and referral are part of the treatment reaction to crime, just as the infliction of illegal punishments on innocent persons is part of the punitive reaction to crime.[37]

In general, police departments have applied selected principles of social science to their work, and, in so doing, they have put some emphasis on treatment. But for the most part the police deal with persons who have not yet been convicted of crime, and they are expected to treat these persons as if they were innocent. While in a strict sense it is impossible to use such a policy, the possibility for development of correctional programs within police departments is severely limited by it. Some persons have, in fact, criticized the police for developing social-work programs, on the ground that other agencies exist for this purpose and that such programs are extraneous to the official duties of the police. This criticism is similar to the arguments of persons who criticize the police for unofficially inflicting punishments. In the words of a policy statement issued by the International Association of Chiefs of Police, "the police are not in the punishing business any more than they are in the rehabilitating business. The police job is to prevent crime and to detect and apprehend offenders. Treatment of the offender is someone else's job."[38] ●

Trends in police work

Plans for improving the efficiency of the police system have been developed by various persons and agencies, and there has been a slight and inconsistent trend toward following them. This program includes freedom from corrupt politics, larger territorial organization, improvements of personnel, systems of assignments, equipment and scientific techniques, the development of preventive police work, cordial relations between police and public, and the general development of police morale and of police work as a profession.

---

[36] See Irving Piliavin and Scott Briar, "Police Encounters with Juveniles," *American Journal of Sociology*, 70:206-214, September, 1964; Aaron Cicourel, *The Social Organization of Juvenile Justice* (New York: John Wiley, 1968); and Donald J. Black and Albert J. Reiss, Jr., "Police Control of Juveniles," *American Sociological Review*, 35:63-77, February, 1970.

[37] Norman L. Weiner and Charles V. Willie, "Decisions by Juvenile Officers," *American Journal of Sociology*, 77:199-210, September, 1971.

[38] International Association of Chiefs of Police, *The Police and the Civil Rights Act* (New York: Author, 1964), p. 15.

Politics

The fundamental requirement for efficient police work is freedom from corrupt politics. Any other parts of a program for the improvement of the police system are likely to be largely futile unless the impediments caused by corrupt politics are reduced, but development of the other parts of this program may have an indirect influence in producing freedom from politics.

Freedom from corrupt politics does not, of course, mean freedom from outside control. A police department cannot be a self-governing organization. Moreover, freedom from corrupt politics does not mean freedom from pressures of various kinds. It may be expected that powerful people, especially, will always try to pressure the police department for special privileges and for leniency in dealing with their friends.

Corruption in municipal politics seems to be decreasing. The strength of party affiliations and, therefore, the strength of local political control has diminished rather steadily since the Civil War, which left a heritage of party loyalty. Civil service measures have made great inroads on patronage in the last fifty years. Municipal, state, and federal welfare agencies now distribute goods and services to the needy, where forty years ago these things were distributed by political machines, in exchange for votes. Also, businessmen are beginning to revolt against the old system of corruption of government, especially local government, for special privilege.

Further, the police may now secure a measure of freedom even in cities where politics remain corrupt. The executive officer of the police department was traditionally a political appointee, but such officers are increasingly being selected by civil service and given permanent tenure, subject to removal for cause. Furthermore, the police are inactive and uninfluential in politics in comparison with fifty years ago. For example, the Hatch Act forecloses political activity by federal police, and in many states police are forbidden by law or police regulations to participate in such activity. The Illinois State Police are by law 50 percent Democrats and 50 percent Republicans. Also, graft has been increasingly centralized and syndicated, with the result that patrolmen secure little of the proceeds. Accordingly, the police are more inclined to view graft as crime. At the same time, police seem to be gaining a stronger voice in legislative and executive policies, enabling them to get the assistance of others in controlling crime. Similarly, the police are developing programs for educating the public about police problems.

Coordination

There are about 40,000 public law enforcement organizations in the United States, ranging from one-man village units to New York City's twenty-eight-thousand-man department. No national law or coordinating agency sets standards for all these units. One of the fundamental elements of a program for efficient police work is the amalgamation and coordination of these forces. Three tendencies are apparent in this field. One is to develop a regular uniformed county police or else to place all of the constables and marshals of the county under the direction of the sheriff, so that at least within the county the police force will be organized, placed on a civil service basis, and become somewhat professional. A second trend is the development of a single police system for an entire metropolitan area. The large number and great variety of police forces in the area of a great city and its suburbs makes efficiency impossible. Cooperative efforts among the police forces in the metropolitan area of Chicago have been developed, while in Cincinnati a cooperative organization which includes counties in Ohio, Kentucky, and Indiana is now operating. Under a different arrangement, some small police jurisdictions now contract with large jurisdictions for specific police services.[39]

A third trend, development of state police, is already well under way. In 1934, forty-seven state police systems were found in thirty-eight states, of which eleven were regular state police systems, nine highway police systems with general powers over crimes, twenty highway police systems with powers restricted to regulation of traffic, four state sheriffs, and three governors' reserves. By 1971, there were fifty state police, highway patrols, or criminal investigation agencies. In about one third of the states, these agencies had full law enforcement authority.[40] The principal opposition to the extension of state police came from organized labor, which feared that they would be used as strikebreakers. Because of this opposition, many restrictions were placed on state police powers.

Related to this development of regional and state police forces is the tendency toward increased participation of federal police in the administration of justice. Federal police go into operation only when the crimes are of an interstate nature or when federal activities are involved. But in recent years there has been a tremendous increase in the scope of federal criminal jurisdiction, brought about by new federal legislation enacted in response to the needs of a rapidly expanding nation. Federal action against crime is made possible by the commerce clause of the Constitution and also by postal and taxing powers of Congress.[41]

An enormous amount of crime is now of an interstate nature. Because of the mobility of criminals, local agencies are seriously

---

[39] Gordon Misner, "The Police Service Contract in California," *Journal of Criminal Law, Criminology, and Police Science*, 52:445-452, November-December, 1961.

[40] See Clarence Schrag, *Crime and Justice: American Style* (Washington: Government Printing Office, 1971), p. 130.

[41] Albert J. Harno, "Some Significant Developments in Criminal Law and Procedure in the Last Century," *Journal of Criminal Law, Criminology, and Police Science*, 42:427-467, November-December, 1951. See also A. C. Breckenridge, "The Constitutional Basis for Co-operative Crime Control," *Journal of Criminal Law and Criminology*, 39:565-583, January-February, 1949.

handicapped, and a larger organization of police activities is needed. There is no logical reason why all serious crimes should not be defined by federal laws, as is done in Canada, and it is at least an open question whether much of the administrative work might not advantageously be transferred to the federal government.

Personnel

The efficiency of the police system depends upon a careful selection of policemen and adequate training, discipline, and remuneration. In about three-fourths of the cities at present policemen are at least selected by civil service examinations, though some cities still have a large turnover on change of political administration. Of the 3,714 men who applied for positions with the Detroit Police Department in 1964, only 4 percent were placed on the eligible list for appointment. In 1965, the Washington, D.C., police department found 10 percent of its applicants to be eligible for police work; Los Angeles accepted only 2.8 percent of its applicants. A President's Commission survey indicated that, as a result of such selective practices, two-thirds of American police forces were under their authorized strength.[42] The problem of recruiting eligible men is reaching critical proportions in cities that hired a large number of police officers in the years immediately after World War II. These men are now retiring and must be replaced. In 1967, 41 percent of the men in the Los Angeles Police Department were eligible for retirement.

Police training, like selection for police work, has developed extensively during the last fifty years. Most metropolitan police departments now regularly give in-service or continuation training to their police officers. At least fifty colleges or universities offer courses designed for police officers. The Federal Bureau of Investigation organized a National Police Academy in 1935. This training institution ordinarily has a session of twelve weeks, and in each session representatives from thirty-five to forty city, county, or state police departments are accepted for training. In 1969 and 1970 the academy greatly expanded its facilities.

Assignments

This assignment of police to specific tasks and the organization of police work have changed significantly in the years since the automobile, the telephone, and the police radio became popular. August Vollmer developed a program for statistical and ecological studies of crimes as a basis of assignments. If the records of the police department indicate that robberies are concentrated in certain areas, at certain hours, and on certain days of the week, the police force is also concentrated at those places and times. Further, the neighborhood patrolman is tending to disappear, and specialized squads are increasing in number. The word *patrolman* is becoming little more than a designation of rank and no longer describes a type of work. The small number of men now

---

[42] President's Commission, *Task Force Report: Police*, p. 9.

assigned to regular patrol duty is explained in part by the fact
that a citizen in trouble can now telephone police headquarters,
which can dispatch a radio car to his aid. Formerly, the patrolman had to be available on the beat if the citizen were to get help.

Improved communication and transportation have made the
use of specialized squads possible, while changes in the technology of police work have made them necessary.[43] The most
important of these squads is the traffic squad. In some communities, regulation of traffic now occupies the time of as much as
25 percent of the police force. In addition, large cities have pickpocket squads, vice squads, forgery squads, narcotics squads, an
aviation police squad, and other squads and divisions. Because
the members of these squads are mobile experts, the neighborhood patrolman is less important. Some police authorities, however, continue to believe that the neighborhood patrolman is a
necessary unit in police work and should not entirely disappear.

Equipment

The equipment of the police was once quite inadequate in comparison with the equipment of professional criminals. For example, a patrolman on foot was expected to catch a bandit in an
automobile, and, generally, the criminals adopted new inventions
before the police did. Now the police have taken the initiative,
and, by and large, American police departments are the best-
equipped of all police departments in the world. The most striking developments in the equipment of police departments have
been in the means of transportation and communications. Flash
and gong signals were once regarded as important innovations
for communications with the patrolman on the beat. Now the
teletype or telephone-typewriter has been developed for communication between stations, and the police radio for communication between stations and also between stations and cars,
planes, boats, motorcycles, and foot patrolmen equipped with
receiving sets.

Criminalistics

About 25 percent of the arrests for the more serious crimes are
made at the time of the commission of the crime. In the others,
efforts are made to detect and identify the guilty party. This
work is done in part by uniformed men, in part by the specialists
making up the "detective division" of large departments. Detectives are increasingly coming to symbolize the "professional"
policeman who has been trained in methods for utilizing knowledge of the physical, biological, and social sciences in the apprehension of criminals, and in some cities and other centers, scientific methods of crime detection have been developed.

A great variety of techniques for the study of the traces of

---

[43] See Michael Banton, *The Policeman in the Community* (London: Tavistock,
1964), pp. 7, 127; and Elaine Cumming, Ian Cumming, and Laura Edell,
"Policeman as Philosopher, Guide and Friend," *Social Problems*, 12:276-286,
Winter, 1965.

crimes has been invented. Many of these are being used in the larger police departments, though they are generally regarded as useful in a very small proportion of the cases. These include the identification of arms and bullets, identification of clothes, hair, teeth, automobile tires, speech patterns, and many other objects. The techniques of physics and chemistry have been applied to the detection of crime with remarkable success in a small number of cases. The "lie detector" and other devices for determining the truth of testimony are proving to have some value, though they are still definitely in the experimental stage. The Federal Bureau of Investigation has developed these methods further than any other agency in America.

The Bertillon system of physical measurements, invented by a French anthropologist in 1883, was first used in America in 1893 and was regarded at the time as a great invention for purposes of identification. However, it proved to be difficult and expensive in operation and has been replaced by an organized system of fingerprint identification. The FBI has developed a central clearinghouse in Washington which had more than 16 million sets of different criminal fingerprints in 1966, plus about 62 million different civil service and armed forces prints. The total number of fingerprint cards is about 179 million. Each day the FBI receives about thirty thousand fingerprints to be processed, of which about ten thousand are based on arrests.[44] In addition, many states have developed bureaus of identification. Thus a network of local, state, and federal bureaus is developing, by means of which the previous criminal records of persons arrested or convicted may be determined. Many police departments still fail to contribute their records to this system, and this is especially true in misdemeanor cases.

Another method of identification is known as the *modus operandi* system, which was devised by Major Atcherley of the English constabulary. This method is based on the principle that a criminal is likely to use the same technique repeatedly, and that an analysis and record of the technique used in every serious crime will provide means of identification in a particular crime. Some burglars always enter through basement windows, some through doors, some through second-story windows; some always steal silver, some jewelry, some clothing, some money; some come in the afternoon, some in the evening, some early in the morning. An Oslo detective, interviewed in 1965, claimed that when illegal entry to an automobile was made by breaking a window, he could study the window-breaking technique and correctly conclude that the culprit could only be one of four or five men. Most municipal departments make at least informal use of the method.

---

[44] Thomas C. Bartee, "Fingerprint Classification," appendix C in President's Commission on Law Enforcement and Administration of Justice, *Task Force Report: Science and Technology* (Washington: Government Printing Office, 1967), pp. 107-112.

The police departments in some of the European countries are greatly assisted in their work by the system of registration of residents. In many cities this includes a requirement that visitors report to the police within a specified time after they arrive in a city. European detectives would generally be rather helpless if they did not have this information to assist them. In Argentina the citizen is required to carry a registration card, which serves to identify him. American police associations have urged the adoption of some universal system of registration, and some departments have to a slight extent implemented this policy by requiring the registration of all ex-convicts in their bailiwick. As a matter of fact, the fingerprints of a fairly large proportion of all male citizens are on file. Moreover, a very large proportion of the inhabitants of the country are recorded in some manner—in registers for election purposes, gas and electric light companies, the post office, social security, driving licenses, directories of telephone companies and of cities—and when the individual or family changes residence, this is recorded by the same agencies, and also by trucking companies. If this information were organized in a central registration system, it would cause little inconvenience to the average citizen and might be of great assistance in dealing with criminals.

In the last thirty years most large police departments have organized crime prevention divisions, and there has been a growing interest in prevention. With the development of the social sciences, police have come to have a better understanding of crime and delinquency, and this better understanding is undoubtedly related to the growth of prevention programs. However, the concept of preventive police work is not clearly defined. As stated earlier, it often involves on-the-spot adjustment of individual cases. It also seems to include a great variety of activities, including "hounding the hoodlums," attacks on criminal hangouts, frequent patrolling, warning residents and business concerns to keep doors and windows locked, friendly acquaintance with the residents on the beat, friendly relations with boys' gangs, organization of recreational activities in areas where delinquency rates are high, concentrated and cooperative efforts to influence boys who are getting into trouble, and social service work with families or individuals in distress. Thus crime prevention is sometimes thought to include deterrent measures—control through force or fear—as well as other methods. It usually pertains to juveniles.

Preventive police

In some departments, crime-prevention bureaus or divisions are simply another name for women police. At present, policewomen are employed in more than two hundred communities. While some of the preventive work evidently is done to advantage by women, policewomen also carry out many other duties in police departments. They act as matrons in jails and lockups, assist in traffic control and police investigations, detect runaway children, patrol department stores in an effort to apprehend shoplifters, and participate in many other activities. Some policewomen now have the same duties as policemen. However, their primary duties are in connection with prevention of juvenile delinquency, and they use treatment methods much more extensively than do male police.[45]

On the other hand, much so-called preventive work is done by regular policemen, either in special divisions or as a part of the regular police program. This preventive work has been directed largely at establishing recreational and athletic programs. However, efforts also are being made to build up friendly relations with schoolchildren, and to cooperate with youth bureaus and other agencies interested in programs for individuals who seem inclined toward delinquency.

The Police and the public

The police of the United States have been severely criticized, but, on the other side of the coin, the police have found the public to be indifferent to police problems. One of the reactions which criticism and indifference have produced is organized effort to develop friendly understanding with the public. In this effort, police departments have established public relations divisions and "police-community relations" divisions, and have attempted to develop methods which would reduce the amount of irritation provoked by existing procedures. The general aim is to insure that the behavior of police will not arouse public antagonism, either because the public understands the behavior or because the behavior itself is above reproach. But the President's Commission concluded that police training in community relations is still very limited, both in time and in substance. For example, two of the largest police departments devote less than ten hours, out of four hundred hours of training, exclusively to police-minority relations.[46]

Direct efforts toward public understanding of police problems and, hence, of police behavior, have been made in numerous ways. For example, efforts have been made to improve relations with the news media, which often arouse, rather than reflect, public sympathy or antagonism toward the police. Police departments recently have made sincere efforts to cooperate with reporters and to enlist the aid of reporters in publicizing police problems. Similarly, police departments have attempted to create confidence and respect by selecting members of the staff for full-time work in speaking to school assemblies, church groups, service clubs, and other organizations. Also, perhaps much of the recent effort to apply principles of biological, social, and physical science to police work has been aimed more at publicity than at efficiency.

---

[45] For a brief history of police service by women, see Lois Higgins, "Historical Background of Policewomen's Service," *Journal of Criminal Law and Criminology*, 41:822-833, March-April, 1951.

[46] President's Commission, *Task Force Report: Police*, p. 138.

In this effort to establish amicable relations with the public through publicity, there is no doubt that many police departments have become propagandists, which is perhaps necessary in the complex life of the present day.

It is probable, however, that mitigation of public indifference and antagonism will require more than education or propagandization of the public. It is being increasingly recognized by policemen that education of police officers is necessary as well. Methods of dealing with offenders and suspected offenders are changing. Many police departments, for example, now emphasize that their members must be polite and courteous, and attention is being paid to special problems of dealing with minority groups, labor groups, and people in traffic. More fundamentally, however, demonstration of coordinated effort to protect society while at the same time efficiently protecting the civil liberties of individuals probably has more influence than anything else in reducing public antagonism. An earlier observation on the inadequacies of police training in the United States still holds true:

> It can be said of police training schools that the recruit is taught everything except the essential requirement of his calling, which is how to secure and maintain the approval and respect of the public whom he encounters daily in the course of his duties.[47]

One of the advantages which accrues from good relations with the public is high police morale. Present efforts toward professionalization of police service will succeed only if the officer is convinced that the public is supporting him in his work. More and more, high police morale is becoming dependent upon efficient public service rather than upon evidence of physical strength and courage.[48] In no other part of the entire field of criminal justice or of municipal administration is as much enthusiasm shown in regard to the possibility of developing scientific and professional methods as in the police field. ●

Suggested readings

ALEX, NICHOLAS. *Black in Blue: A Study of the Negro Policeman*. New York: Appleton-Century-Crofts, 1969.

BANTON, MICHAEL. *The Policeman in the Community*. London: Tavistock, 1964.

BITTNER, EGON. *The Functions of the Police in Modern Society*. Washington: Government Printing Office, 1970.

CAIN, MAUREEN E. *Society and the Policeman's Role*. London: Routledge & Kegan Paul, 1973.

CICOUREL, AARON. *The Social Organization of Juvenile Justice*. New York: John Wiley, 1968.

---

[47] Charles Reith, *The Blind Eye of History: A Study of the Origins of the Present Police Era* (London: Faber and Faber, 1952), pp. 115-116.

[48] Robert L. Peabody, "Authority Relations in Three Organizations," *Public Administration Review*, 23:87-92, June, 1963; idem, "Perceptions of Organizational Authority: A Comparative Analysis," *Administrative Science Quarterly*, 6:477-482, March, 1962; and Nicholas Alex, *Black in Blue: A Study of the Negro Policeman* (New York: Appleton-Century-Crofts, 1969), pp. 57-84.

COHEN, BERNARD. "The Police Internal System of Justice in New York City." *Journal of Criminal Law, Criminology, and Police Science,* 63:54-67, March, 1972.

CRAY, ED. *The Enemy in the Streets: Police Malpractice in America.* Garden City, N.Y.: Anchor Books, 1972.

CUMMING, ELAINE, IAN CUMMING, & LAURA EDELL. "Policeman as Philosopher, Guide and Friend." *Social Problems,* 12: 276-286, Winter, 1965.

DONNELLY, RICHARD C. "Police Authority and Practices." *Annals of the American Academy of Political and Social Science,* 339: 90-110, January, 1962.

DRIVER, EDWIN D. "Confessions and the Social Psychology of Coercion." *Harvard Law Review,* 82:42-61, November, 1968.

GOLDMAN, NATHAN. *The Differential Selection of Juvenile Offenders of Court Appearance.* New York: National Council on Crime and Delinquency, 1953.

GOLDSTEIN, JOSEPH. "Police Discretion not to Invoke the Criminal Process: Low-Visibility Decisions in the Administration of Criminal Justice." *Yale Law Journal,* 69:543-594, March, 1960.

JAGIELLO, ROBERT J. "College Education for the Patrolman: Necessity or Irrelevance?" *Journal of Criminal Law, Criminology, and Police Science,* 62:114-121, March, 1971.

KADISH, S. H. "Legal Norms and Discretion in the Police and Sentencing Processes." *Harvard Law Review,* 75:904-931, March, 1962.

LaFAVE, WAYNE R. *Arrest: The Decision to Take a Suspect Into Custody.* Boston: Little, Brown, 1965.

LANE, ROGER. *Policing the City: Boston, 1822–1885.* New York: Atheneum, 1971.

MAYERS, LEWIS. *The American Legal System.* Rev. ed. New York: Harper and Row, 1964.

NIEDERHOFFER, ARTHUR. *Behind the Shield: The Police in Urban Society.* New York: Doubleday, 1967.

NIEDERHOFFER, ARTHUR, & ABRAHAM S. BLUMBERG, eds. *The Ambivalent Force: Perspective on the Police.* Waltham, Mass.: Xerox Publishing, 1970.

NIMMER, RAYMOND T. *Two Million Unnecessary Arrests: Removing a Social Service Concern from the Criminal Justice System.* Chicago: American Bar Foundation, 1971.

PACKER, HERBERT L. *The Limits of the Criminal Sanction.* Stanford, Calif.: Stanford University Press, 1968.

REISS, ALBERT J. *The Police and the Public.* New Haven: Yale University Press, 1971.

ROLPH, C. H., ed. *The Police and the Public.* London: Heinemann, 1962.

SCHWARTZ, LOUIS B., & STEPHEN R. GOLDSTEIN. *Law Enforcement Handbook for Police.* St. Paul, Minn.: West, 1970.

SKOLNICK, JEROME H. *Justice Without Trial.* New York: John Wiley, 1966.

SMITH, BRUCE. *Police Systems in the United States.* 2d rev. ed. New York: Harper, 1960.

SOWLE, CLAUDE R., ed. *Police Power and Individual Freedom: The Quest for Balance.* Chicago: Aldine, 1962.

STARK, RODNEY. *Police Riots: Collective Violence and Law Enforcement.* Belmont, Calif.: Wadsworth, 1972.

STEADMAN, ROBERT F., ed. *The Police and the Community.* Baltimore: Johns Hopkins University Press, 1972.

VOLLMER, AUGUST. "Police Progress in the Past Twenty-Five Years." *Journal of Criminal Law and Criminology,* 24:161-175, May-June, 1933.

WILLETT, T. C. *Criminal on the Road.* London: Tavistock, 1964.

WILSON, JAMES Q. *Varieties of Police Behavior: The Management of Law and Order in Eight Communities.* New York: Atheneum, 1972.

18   Detention before trial

After a suspected person has been arrested, it is the duty of the police to take him promptly to a magistrate. This duty often is ignored, and arrested persons are sometimes discharged by the police without a court appearance. If the alleged crime of the person taken before a magistrate is a minor one, the magistrate either discharges or convicts the accused. But if the alleged crime is serious, the magistrate merely considers the conditions under which temporary release on bail or on the suspected person's own recognizance can be granted. Whether the person accused of serious crime is released on bail or not, he is entitled to a "preliminary hearing," also before a magistrate. At this hearing the magistrate determines whether the known evidence against the accused is sufficient to justify further legal proceedings. Defendants who have been denied bail or who cannot meet the requirements for bail must remain in custody while arrangements are made for this preliminary hearing, and the practice of holding accused persons in this way is detention.

The preliminary hearing is wholly for the benefit of the suspect and never results in an official decision that the suspect is guilty. Its purpose is to save obviously innocent persons the expense and trouble of a lengthy trial. The magistrate makes no effort to obtain new evidence and deals only with probability of guilt or innocence. Some states bar newsmen from preliminary hearings, primarily because readers are likely to interpret a "probable cause" action as a finding of guilt. If the known evidence against the accused is not sufficient to justify further court proceedings, he is discharged from custody or from the conditions of bail. However, if there is probability of guilt, the accused person is held for further proceedings by a higher court or is temporarily released on his bail. The practice of holding suspected persons for further legal proceedings after the preliminary hearing also is called detention. •

Release before trial

A person who has been arrested may be held at the police station for a few hours or days and then released without a court appearance; he may secure a release on a writ of habeas corpus; he may secure a temporary release on bail, giving financial security for his return; or he may secure temporary release on his own recognizance or promise to return.

Unofficial release

Persons are frequently released by the police without court appearance. In some instances, such release follows illegal arrest and, hence, illegal detention, but in other cases it is considered the most practical system for dealing with persons rightfully arrested for minor offenses. Illegal arrests include arrests made for failing to bribe an officer, arrests made for the purpose of forcing gambling places to pay graft, and arrests made when there is no evidence of crime. They are followed by illegal detention and, usually, release without trial. This system of release is also used in cases of intoxication, disorderliness, vagrancy, and other misdemeanors, and when so used, it is known as the golden-rule disposition.

Intoxicated persons are often held in the police lockup only until they are sober; vagrants are held until they agree to leave the community; and disorderly persons are held until it is believed that their behavior will be orderly. Of 11,048 adults arrested for drunkenness in Detroit in 1958, 59 percent were charged with the offense; 40 percent were released under the golden rule; and 1 percent were released by the police under other conditions. Of a total of 26,830 arrests of adults for all other offenses (not counting city traffic offenses), 3,847, or 14.3 percent, were released without prosecution. In addition, 666 persons were held as police witnesses, and 26,176 persons were detained for investigation. In sum, of a total of 68,567 adult offenders officially handled by the Detroit police, 35,200, or 51.3 percent, were released by the police without court appearance.[1]

Reports from other cities indicate that the percentage in Detroit is not unusual. Formally, these releases are, with a few exceptions, unjustified. Informally, however, the unofficial release procedure often represents the selection of the best method available at the time. For example, the arrest and temporary detention of intoxicated persons protects them as well as the public. If these

---

[1] Detroit Police Department, *Annual Report, 1958* (Detroit: Police Record Bureau, 1959), pp. 48-52.

persons were taken into court, they would either be dismissed or fined, and since most of them would be unable to pay fines, they would be committed to a house of correction for a short period. None of these methods is of great value in solving the problem of intoxication, but the police method of release probably makes as great a contribution as the alternative methods and is much cheaper. It is evident, however, that if the problems of intoxication are to be solved, more constructive methods must be made available. Some of the other unofficial releases are probably much like those which occur in cases of intoxication.

In some cities, attempts are made to refer offenders in need of help or treatment to appropriate community agencies. In a few places, the threat of prosecution is used to guarantee that the offender follows through with a proposed program of treatment, submits to supervision, makes restitution, or performs some other condition of his release. In Baltimore, this kind of informal adjustment is performed by a magistrate, who holds court in a police precinct station. A special unit of the Detroit probation department disposes of nearly five thousand criminal complaints monthly, mainly complaints of nonsupport or other domestic problems. Warrants of arrest are issued for only about 3 percent of the complaints filed.[2] These informal systems for making the decision about whether an offender should be charged with crime are, like the golden-rule disposition by the police, without the benefit of guidelines from legislatures or top-level policy-makers. "Decisions are to a great extent fortuitous because they are made on inadequate information about the offense, the offender, and the alternatives available."[3]

Release by writ of habeas corpus

In recent years, most habeas corpus writs have been filed by convicted prisoners claiming error in trial proceedings. But the traditional use of the writ has been in connection with pretrial detention. So that citizens are protected from false arrest and illegal detention, habeas corpus writs may be obtained from courts to force the detaining officials to bring the arrested person before a magistrate immediately for a preliminary hearing. If no just reason for holding him can be shown, he must be discharged from custody. The "root principle" of habeas corpus, the United States Supreme Court has noted, "is that in civilized society, government must always be accountable to the judiciary for a man's imprisonment; if the imprisonment cannot be shown to conform with the fundamental requirements of law, the individual is entitled to his immediate release."[4]

Although the arrested person usually must apply to the court for a writ, some judges are known to have issued them informally

---

[2] President's Commission on Law Enforcement and Administration of Justice, *Task Force Report: The Courts* (Washington: Government Printing Office, 1967), p. 6.

[3] Ibid., p. 7.

[4] *Fay v. Noia*, 372 U.S. 391, 402 (1963).

from their homes, and writs also have been issued immediately after arrest. Some professional and organized criminals have attorneys constantly prepared to secure a writ, and sometimes the attorney arrives at the police station with the writ even before the police arrive with the prisoner. The police, in order to have an opportunity to question the arrested person, and for other reasons, frequently detain defendants incommunicado. This is done by hiding the suspect in a "cold-storage" cell, or by shifting him frequently from one lockup to another. Some years ago a series of fifteen outlying station houses in Detroit constituted a "loop," and prisoners were shifted from one to another of these stations for a period of a week or ten days and then released. The abuse of the use of the habeas corpus writ by attorneys, then, prompted police to use illegal methods to avoid its use.

Release on bail

The principal official method of securing release before trial is the use of bail. A promise is made to pay the state a specified sum of money if the accused person does not appear for trial. *Bail* is the name for the financial security which is pledged, but the term also is used to refer to the entire system whereby one is released after having given such security. The right to bail is guaranteed in the constitutions of thirty-five of the states in all cases except capital charges. As a general rule, magistrates are required by law to grant release on bail, but the law also gives them wide discretion as to the amount and character of the bail. They can effectively prevent release by setting the bail at a high figure, or by requiring security of a kind which is extremely difficult to obtain.

In early English law, a person charged with a crime could be released if a friend would act as his keeper and thus act as surety for his appearance in court. The person who acted as surety was liable for the punishment if the accused was not delivered. Later the surety pledged his property, which generally consisted of his house or land, but still remained essentially the keeper of the prisoner. The real estate of friends is still used as security in small towns and to some extent in cities, but in the city many defendants have no friends who own property available for bail. Professional bondsmen and corporate surety companies have filled this gap, and such agencies now provide surety. There are about three thousand bondsmen in the United States. Most of them act as semi-independent agents of about a dozen surety companies. One Ohio surety company has 672 agents in forty-seven states, who write five thousand to six thousand bonds a month. In 1965, the company grossed about $2.5 million.[5]

In most places, an accused person can pay a relatively small fee to a company or to a professional bondsman for providing the financial security necessary to his release. The security thus obtained is called a bond or a bail bond, and it has become customary to refer to the status of one who has been released on bail as "out on bond." The usual bail for a person charged with

---

[5] *Wall Street Journal*, June 1, 1966.

burglary is about $5,000. Surety companies generally will provide a $5,000 bond for about $100 or $150, but in some communities the rates are much higher than this. In Illinois, a defendant can obtain release by depositing with the court a downpayment of 10 percent of the total amount. A refund of 90 percent of the downpayment is given if the defendant appears in court at the appointed time.

In some jurisdictions it has become common practice to require traffic offenders to provide what is called "cash bail." This is a sum fixed at an amount approximately equal to the fine customarily imposed for the offense of which the person is accused. If one who has paid such a sum desires a trial, he appears in traffic court at a specified time, but if he does not desire a trial, he simply does not appear, forfeiting the cash. The great majority of persons who post such sums forfeit them, and a large proportion of offenders consider them as fines. In practice, one who forfeits such a cash sum is absolved from further liability for the offense, forfeiture of the cash being tacitly accepted by the police and courts as satisfactory. Although it relieves the police and courts of a great deal of work, there is no real legal basis for this custom. Ordinarily, bail is in no sense a punitive measure, and the forfeiture of bail does not absolve the offender from prosecution. He can be rearrested and tried, and even if he is acquitted, the forfeited bail is not returned to him.

The ordinary system of providing financial security for persons charged with crimes has been criticized on several points. The chief criticism is that police departments and courts have inadequate facilities for determining whether financial security is needed, how much security is needed, and how adequate the security which is offered may be. The amount required is therefore generally determined by the charge against the defendant rather than by his character and responsibility. This bears heavily on the poor and makes bail practically prohibitive for them.

Although the proportion of persons failing to make bail varies widely from place to place, a recent study of large and small counties shows that it often is substantial:[6]

	Percentage of felony defendants unable to make bail
Large counties:	
Cook (Chicago)	75
Hennepin (Minneapolis)	71
Jefferson (Louisville)	30
Philadelphia (Philadelphia)	14
Small counties:	
Brown, Kansas	93
Rutland, Vermont	83
Putnam, Missouri	36
Anchorage, Alaska	28
Catoosa, Georgia	6

---

[6] President's Commission, *Task Force Report: The Courts*, p. 37.

A study of New York City bail practices found that almost half of all defendants could not obtain the funds for bail. Twenty-five percent failed to make bail at $500; 45 percent failed at $1,500; and 63 percent at $2,500. Thirty-eight percent of the persons unable to post bail in New York City were detained for from fifty to ninety-nine days prior to the trial. The investigators believed that bail was often intentionally set so high that the accused would not be able to obtain the necessary funds, so as to give the offender a "taste of jail" or to "protect society." This practice was condemned in the following terms: "It is fundamental that the state has no right to punish a person until his guilt has been established beyond a reasonable doubt. And there is no support in the law for the proposition that a person may be imprisoned because of the speculative possibility that he may commit a crime."[7]

In effect, therefore, a poor person of excellent character and responsibility charged with a crime of which he is completely innocent has no alternative to detention in an institution.[8] This hardship cannot be defended by the argument that poor persons should not commit crimes, for many of them are actually innocent. On the other hand, the financial security has little value if the defendant is not responsible and is not willing to return to court. Since the court has no facilities for investigating the security which is offered, and since professional bondsmen, as a group, are closely allied with the underworld, the security is generally inadequate. Some years ago Moley described a professional bondsman in St. Louis who had been arrested twelve times, but who was security for bonds aggregating $670,295, although his real property was worth not more than $20,000, and the encumbrances against this property were greater than its assessed valuation.[9] This is an exaggerated case so far as amounts are concerned, but it is not exaggerated so far as the principle is concerned. Sometimes bondsmen do not even own the property they schedule. In 1965 an Oklahoma bootlegger-turned-bondsman was found to be using as "security" property owned by a church. If one court refuses to accept the property as security, a bondsman might peddle it to other courts until he finds one that will accept it. He feels secure in doing this because he knows that relatively few bonds are forfeited, and that even when they are forfeited, the court does not force collection.

A second criticism of the bail system is that it involves collu-

---

[7] Caleb Foote, James P. Markle, and Edward A. Wooley, "Compelling Appearance in Court: Administration of Bail in Philadelphia," *University of Pennsylvania Law Review*, 102:1031-1079, June, 1954. See also Charles Ares and Herbert Sturz, "Bail and the Indigent Accused," *Crime and Delinquency*, 8:12-20, January, 1962.

[8] Caleb Foote, "The Bail System and Equal Justice," *Federal Probation*, 23:43-48, September, 1959.

[9] Raymond Moley, *Our Criminal Courts* (New York: Minton, Balch, 1930), pp. 49-50.

sion between the police, the courts, and the professional bondsmen. The occasional offender asks the police how he can secure
bail, and the police suggest a bondsman or inform a runner for a
bondsman that the defendant has no bondsman. Fees are then
divided with officers of the police and courts. The bondsman also
acts as "fixer" for professional criminals.

Several suggestions for improving the bail system have been
made, and there has been a slight tendency to follow them in
practice. *First*, it has been proposed that one bureau should have
complete control of all the work of granting bail, recommending
forfeitures, and collecting forfeited bonds in a city. This organization has been arranged in several cities with varying degrees of
success. It results in better inspection of securities, so that bonds
can always be kept within the value of the securities listed, and
it prevents bondsmen from peddling bonds from one court to
another. It appears to have no effect on other aspects of the bail
problem.

Second, it is argued that this bureau, or a section of this bureau,
should be responsible for investigating the character of the defendant for the purpose of determining whether release should be
granted without financial security, or under no conditions at all.
Under present constitutional provisions an outright refusal of bail
is not permissible in the United States in most cases, but such
refusal is permissible in England. Probably a great proportion of
offenders could be released on their own recognizance, a system
which eliminates the necessity for bail and for detention. Under
the sponsorship of the Manhattan Bail Project, law students interviewed and appraised the responsibility of adult prisoners appearing in magistrates' felony courts and then either recommended or
did not recommend that the man be released on his promise to
return to court at a given time for trial. Of the first 275 defendants released under this system, only three did not fulfill their
promises.[10] Congress introduced a similar program into the federal court system in 1966, and many cities have introduced similar
"bail reform" programs. A 1970 survey showed that cities with
these programs detained only 23 percent of their defendants while
cities with traditional bail practices detained 36 percent.[11]

Third, it has been suggested that bail would not be necessary
if hearings and trials were more prompt.

As an alternative to the existing conditions of detention, bail
has decided advantages. Perhaps the most important of these is
that it permits persons who are merely accused of crime to avoid
the financial hardships, the physical unpleasantness, and the punitive aspects of being detained in a police lockup or jail. ●

---

[10] Herbert Sturz, "An Alternative to the Bail System," *Federal Probation*, 23:
12-17, December, 1962.

[11] Paul Wice and Rita James Simon, "Pretrial Release: A Survey of Alternative
Practices," *Federal Probation*, 34:60-63, December, 1970.

Punitive aspects of detention

When a person is charged with a crime, it is important that he should be available for trial. However, under the American system of government, the method of securing his presence at the trial should involve a minimum of hardship on him, as he might be innocent. The rule of presumption of innocence until guilt is proved, strictly speaking, refers only to the preponderance of evidence in a trial in court. The rule of evidence is that the defendant is assumed to be innocent rather than guilty, and the evidence must then be sufficient to convict. But this rule is, with limitations required by practical considerations, considered sound social policy in other situations. Of course, if the rule were made absolute, there would be no justification even for arrest, let alone for detention before trial. A 1970 statute authorized preventive detention for persons charged with dangerous crimes or crimes of violence in the District of Columbia, but it was used only twenty times in the first ten months.[12] Methods for predicting dangerousness have not been developed, and probably cannot be developed. Nevertheless, it is sometimes necessary that the state detain some persons suspected of crime, thus imposing hardships on persons who might be innocent.

The imposition of these hardships could be nonpunitive, but it is, in fact, punitive. The constitutional view is that even when persons are actually guilty, they are to be treated, so far as practicable, on the presumption of innocence. In this view, detention is something like confiscation of property for public purposes, or drafting men for the army in time of war, or requiring attendance at public schools, or summoning citizens for service on a jury, where the hardships are reduced to a minimum consistent with public purpose. Furthermore, it is observed that, especially for first offenders, the arrested person is in a very impressionistic condition, and sympathetic handling and understanding will have great effect at this point, just as unnecessary and unwarranted hardships will be very damaging. In general, therefore, the official view is that those persons who are detained awaiting trial should be treated at least as well as those drafted into the army, and that the conditions of life in a detention institution should be at least equal to those in an army camp.

Just as police sometimes argue that punitive arrest methods are justified because many guilty persons avoid conviction, it is sometimes suggested that the hardships of detention should be severe and punitive. Generally, the argument is that a large proportion of guilty persons avoid official punishment and that they should at least suffer severe hardships in detention, as a deterrent to others or as a retributive or reformative measure. However, the hardships are imposed upon innocent as well as guilty persons, and no one has argued that people can be kept innocent by punishing the innocent. Even when this unofficial policy is not

---

[12] Nan C. Bases and William F. McDonald, *Preventive Detention in the District of Columbia: The First Ten Months* (New York: Vera Institute of Justice, 1972).

voiced, it is the informal principle on which most detention institutions are operated. This may be observed in the types of institutions which are used as places of detention and in the manner in which these institutions are maintained and operated.

The institutions used for detention are of the following four types: the station lockup, the small-town municipal jail or lockup, the county jail, and the special detention institutions for women and children. *Station lockups* are maintained in connection with the precinct stations in large cities. Few criminals serve sentences in these institutions, and few suspected persons are held for court proceedings for more than a few days. Persons arrested in the precinct are kept in custody until arrangements for a preliminary hearing or a trial can be made, or they are released without trial after a few hours. *Small-town municipal jails* usually are under control of police departments or marshals, and they resemble city police-station lockups. However, in addition to persons awaiting hearings or trials, the populations of these institutions include offenders serving sentences, usually in lieu of payment of fines ordered by the court. Ordinarily the personnel of these institutions make few, if any, distinctions between those persons awaiting court proceedings and those being punished. There are approximately eleven thousand police and village lockups in the United States. About half of the persons detained in such lockups awaiting hearings or trials are not convicted.

County jails usually are under the control of the sheriff, and they generally are used for three different purposes. *First,* they serve as lockups for persons arrested by the sheriff's staff and awaiting trials or hearings. *Second,* they serve as detention institutions for persons who are accused of felonies and who, in preliminary hearings, have been bound over to a grand jury or ordered to await disposition by higher courts. *Third,* county jails are used as penal institutions, ordinarily for misdemeanants whose sentences are under one year. No serious attempt is made to treat these offenders, and they are not ordinarily carefully segregated from those persons merely awaiting court proceedings. Of 31,187 persons detained in Wisconsin county jails overnight or longer in 1956, only 6,811 were sentenced prisoners.[13]

Ordinarily, if the court to which a person is taken after having been detained in a police, village, or county lockup has final jurisdiction, as in misdemeanor cases, it tries the case and either releases the individual or fixes a penalty. But if the court does not have final jurisdiction in a case and serves to provide a preliminary hearing only, it may discharge the suspect from custody, release him on bail, or commit him to the county jail to await further proceedings by a grand jury or a higher court. Persons held for trial in the federal courts usually are detained in

---

[13] Sanger B. Powers, "Day-Parole of Misdemeanants," *Federal Probation*, 22: 42-46, December, 1958.

county jails; in 1960 the average number of days of detention for all such persons aged twenty-two and over was twenty-six, for persons aged eighteen to twenty-one, the average was twenty-seven, and for those aged seventeen and under, the average was eight.[14] No recent data on the period of detention of those awaiting trial in other courts are available. About two-thirds of the prisoners confined in county jails on any given day have been convicted.

Special institutions and procedures for children have been developed in some jurisdictions. Children of juvenile court age are generally permitted to remain at home after a complaint is made against them; a summons is issued for the parents to bring the children to court at the appointed time. But it is frequently necessary to detain children because of the serious nature of the offense, the condition of the home, or the possibility that the child will try to escape from the jurisdiction of the court. Jails and lockups are frequently used as places of detention for juveniles, but in most states recent laws have placed restrictions on this use of such institutions. In general practice, however, these laws are frequently violated, especially in districts that do not have specially organized juvenile courts. Between 50,000 and 75,000 children are still held annually in county jails and police lockups.

Various arguments have been presented regarding the comparative values of public detention homes, private orphanages and shelters, and private foster homes for the detention of children. The general criterion used for evaluation is the extent to which effective physical detention is combined with a nonpunitive program for those detained. Thus some institutions of any one type may be satisfactory, and other institutions of the same type may be unsatisfactory. It is generally agreed that specially designed and constructed institutions are most suitable to implementation of the treatment reaction to juvenile delinquency.[15] The personnel of juvenile detention institutions usually consider mere detention to be insufficient, just as do the personnel of detention institutions for adults. The important difference between them is that in most adult institutions the desire is to supplement detention with punishment, while in most juvenile institutions the desire is to supplement detention with treatment.

The maintenance and operation of detention institutions

In 1965, more than 19,000 persons were employed to staff American lockups, jails, and workhouses. Of these, only 500—about 3 percent—performed rehabilitative duties, and some of the 500 were employed on a part-time basis. The national average is one psy-

---

[14] U.S. Bureau of Prisons, *Federal Prisons, 1960* (Washington: Department of Justice, 1961), p. 60.

[15] A full discussion of specialized institutions for detention of juveniles will be found in Sherwood Norman, *The Design and Construction of Detention Homes for the Juvenile Court* (New York: National Probation Association, 1947); and idem, *Detention Practices* (New York: National Probation and Parole Association, 1960).

chologist for each 4,300 inmates and one teacher for each 1,300 inmates. However, most of the professional personnel work is in the larger institutions, leaving the vast majority of local institutions with custodial personnel only.[16]

In general, the physical conditions in the county and city detention institutions are decidedly worse than the conditions in the state prisons where criminals are confined after conviction of serious offenses. Those who are officially presumed to be innocent, many of whom are actually innocent and almost all of whom are detained because they do not have the money or influence to obtain release on bail, are subjected to conditions much worse than those for persons already convicted of serious crimes. Criticisms of these conditions have been made for nearly a century, by both American and foreign observers. The president of the International Prison Congress in 1907 said that nothing as bad as the American jails had been known in the history of the world except in the prisons of Turkey in the thirteenth century. The conditions most frequently criticized at present are filth, vermin, fire hazard, inadequate food, inadequate plumbing, inadequate lighting and ventilation, lack of segregation of persons with infectious diseases, universal idleness, lack of provision for medical care, special privileges for favored prisoners (sometimes including a key to the prison door), and inadequate security against escape. Fishman, who was inspector of jails for the federal government for some time, defined the jail thus:

Jail: An unbelievably filthy institution in which are confined men and women serving sentences for misdemeanors and crimes, and men and women not under sentence who are simply awaiting trial. With few exceptions, having no segregation of the unconvicted from the convicted, the well from the diseased, the youngest and most impressionable from the most degraded and hardened. Usually swarming with bedbugs, roaches, lice, and other vermin; has an odor of disinfectant and filth which is appalling; supports in complete idleness countless thousands of able-bodied men and women, and generally affords ample time and opportunity to assure inmates a complete course in every kind of viciousness and crime. A melting pot in which the worst elements of the raw material in the criminal world are brought forth blended and turned out in absolute perfection.[17]

From the viewpoint of differential association, the fundamental criticism of the jail is that it permits association of convicted and unconvicted prisoners. Approximately one-third of the inmates in county jails are awaiting trial, and most of the others are serving sentences imposed after conviction. The effect of this association with convicted prisoners not only leads the person accused of crime to identify with criminals, but such contacts often cause moral deterioration. The sheriff directing one of the

---

[16] President's Commission on Law Enforcement and Administration of Justice, *Task Force Report: Corrections* (Washington: Government Printing Office, 1967), p. 75.

[17] Joseph F. Fishman, *Crucibles of Crime* (New York: Cosmopolis Press, 1923), pp. 13-14.

nation's largest county jails, in Cook County, Illinois, criticized his own and other county jails as follows:

County jails, as presently constituted, are for all practical purposes agencies for the creation of a community of interest on the part of those who violate the law. They establish contacts and a continuing association among law violators. They afford a machinery for perpetuating and transmitting the culture and tradition of crime. And they insure the maturation of delinquent and criminal attitudes as well as professional criminal skills among the young by the indiscriminate lodging of all types of persons under one framework of concrete and steel.[18]

It is possible to exaggerate the importance of contacts with convicted criminals, however. It is not clear that detention in a city police lockup in which no convicted prisoners are held is any less injurious than detention in a county jail in company with convicted prisoners. In the lockups, inmates with long prison records seldom are segregated from persons accused of their first crimes. And detention under existing conditions involves association with criminality even when it does not involve association with criminals. •

Explanations of punitive conditions in jails

Punitive and repulsive physical conditions in detention institutions have existed for centuries and have become traditional. In England, John Howard's investigations during the latter part of the eighteenth century and Elizabeth Fry's work during the early part of the nineteenth century were investigations of institutions similar to our police lockups, for the prisons in those periods were used primarily for detention prior to trial. Criticisms of the jails in America—made three-quarters of a century ago, a half-century ago, a quarter of a century ago, and only a few years ago —all sound very familiar. The persistence of physically unpleasant and punitive conditions may be explained partially by the expense of improvements and by inertia among officials. As one authority states: "Jails mean *jobs.* Jails mean *income.* Jails mean *power.* Jails mean *influence.* Jails mean *patronage.* Jails mean *votes.* Against such a formidable defense the offense must devise an attack of atomic power."[19] Thus, sheriffs and other officials responsible for detention institutions resist change because the existing conditions are highly profitable, both in the form of influence and power and in income. Jailers often are paid "turnkey" fees and are granted a certain sum for the daily maintenance of each prisoner in their custody. If the sum is one dollar and the daily costs can be reduced to twenty cents, the jailer is able to pocket eighty cents per prisoner per day. In some communities numerous arrests are made solely for the fees that the police and

---

[18] Joseph D. Lohman, *Mid-Term Report* (Chicago: Cook County Sheriff's Office, 1956), p. 23.

[19] Roberts J. Wright, "The Jail and Misdemeanant Institutions," in Paul W. Tappan, ed., *Contemporary Correction* (New York: McGraw-Hill, 1951), pp. 310-322.

jailer can collect. While the incumbents have merely inherited, not created, such a system, it is understandable that they should resist attempts to improve the physical conditions in prisons by eliminating the system.

However, resistance of officials is not a sufficient explanation; there is some popular sympathy with existing conditions. This sympathy takes two different forms. *First*, accusation is, in fact, taken as equivalent to proof of criminality. The person who is arrested and detained for court proceedings is identified with the persons already convicted of crime. Then, since the societal reaction to the crimes of persons confined in jails usually is punitive, those who are accused but not convicted are punished. But why does the public fail to make the distinction between those awaiting trial and those serving sentences? Perhaps it is because the public has so few contacts with either type of case. The agencies of mass communication ordinarily report in some detail the cases of persons who have been convicted, but only in the most sensational cases are acquittals reported. Also, many persons take the position that even one who is merely accused of crime is at fault and, hence, deserving of punishment. The argument used is that if the accused person had been leading an exemplary life, he would not have been accused or would have been released by the police.

Second, only the poor are held in jail for trial, and it is traditional to discriminate against the poor. A person in wealth or moderate comfort can secure release on bail in most instances. The attitude of the public is, then, one of indifference; it is not in touch with the situation, looks down upon those who get into jail, and does not suffer the hardships in person that would lead to insistence on modification. No matter how jails are operated, the public is complacent. The poor do not have the power or influence to change the situation. Those who have been in jail, whether they were found guilty or not, try to conceal this fact rather than advertise it. Perhaps the situation will be improved in this country as in England, where Bernard Shaw said that the day of improvement was at hand because in a short time every honest man would have spent some time in jail and would know what jails were like. ●

Many persons and agencies have suggested programs for modifying the methods of detention. In general, these suggestions have been made with consideration for the view that the methods of detention should conform to the constitutional notion that accused persons should be handled as if they were innocent. Also, it is thought that certain modifications will reduce the crime rates by eliminating many contacts with criminal behavior patterns and by increasing the prestige of law-enforcement officers. Finally, it is believed that detention facilities for adults should, like the detention facilities for juveniles, adopt methods which will at

Alternatives to present-day detention institutions

least assist accused persons with the problems arising from the fact that they have been detained. The following are some of the important suggestions which have been made:

(a) Bail and release on personal recognizance should be used more extensively, and the number of arrests should be reduced. It has been indicated previously that 60 percent of the arrests in certain cities result in release without prosecution. In addition, between a third and a half of the persons who are prosecuted are dismissed without conviction. It is not possible to determine what proportion of the dismissals results from inefficiency of the courts, but it is probable that both the courts and the police share responsibility. The summons and on-the-spot citation by a police officer may be substituted for arrest in many cases. Citations are now used almost exclusively for violations of traffic regulations, but use of the summons in lieu of an arrest warrant is authorized in the federal system. A Department of Justice study found no substantial default problem in any of the sixty federal districts which use the summons or merely letters to bring to court those accused of misdemeanors or of violations of regulatory statutes.[20] Contra Costa County, California, uses citations extensively for all misdemeanor offenses. Unless an arrest is considered necessary to the protection of the community, court processes, or the defendant, a misdemeanor suspect is released at the scene of the offense if he can identify himself. The officer checks with headquarters through a computer-based intelligence system, and if the defendant is not wanted for another crime, a summons is issued.

(b) The courts should dispose of cases more rapidly. The shorter the period of detention of the average prisoner, the smaller is the number detained at a particular time. A survey of the Cook County, Illinois, jail reported that the jail would contain only 29 people at one time if the average period of detention were one day, 200 if it were one week, 887 if it were one month, and 10,642 if it were one year. Detained defendants should be given priority in setting trial dates, and a statutory limit should be imposed on the length of time an unconvicted person may be detained. Moreover, persons detained prior to trial and thereafter sentenced should be given full credit for all time spent in custody prior to commencement of sentence.

(c) The physical conditions and the programs of jails and lockups should be improved. Perhaps this is the suggestion which is made most frequently. Even if the number of persons committed and the length of the period of detention were greatly reduced, it would still be sound policy to improve the health and sanitary conditions of the places of detention. However, this is not at all an easy suggestion to follow, because the detained persons include many who are intoxicated at the time of arrest, or are diseased, or are ignorant of the conditions of hygiene. But institutions can be made fireproof; sanitary plumbing can be installed; facilities

---

[20] President's Commission, *Task Force Report: The Courts*, p. 41.

for bathing can be made available; diseased persons can be segregated; organized activities can be provided. Some jails provide opportunities for employment, recreational activities, reading, organized educational classes, moving pictures, and counseling. The complete and practically universal idleness of the jail and lockup could be eliminated.

It is suggested, further, that such standards should be maintained by a system of inspection by state officials, who would have authority to close the jails and lockups which do not meet requirements. Indiana, Minnesota, New Jersey, Oklahoma, and Wisconsin now have regular state supervision of jails and lockups, and certain other states inspect jails and lockups "on complaint." Virginia has adopted a plan whereby a state board is given almost complete control over jails and lockups; the board is authorized to prescribe minimum standards for the institutions and to prohibit the confinement of prisoners in institutions not meeting the standards. In Massachusetts, the state Division of Youth Services has these powers in reference to institutions for detention of children.

Also, it is pointed out that if the standards mentioned are to be maintained, it probably will be necessary to enlarge the geographical area served by particular detention institutions. The county apparently is too small a unit to maintain an institution of this nature, especially if the convicted prisoners and the responsible unconvicted prisoners are removed. Counties could combine, or the state could establish jail districts, or the state could own and operate the places of detention in which persons are held awaiting trial for longer than two or three days. Moreover, if larger units were organized, specialized institutions for special classes could be established. This has already started in the detention institutions for women and children but can be developed outside of the large cities only by state management of the places of detention.

(d) Persons awaiting trial should be separated from convicted criminals. Ordinarily, authorities believe that this could best be accomplished by maintaining convicted prisoners in one institution and detained persons in another. Indiana, California, Wisconsin, Virginia, and numerous other states operate camps, farms, and colonies which take many of the convicted misdemeanants out of the county jails. Some cities and counties have provided farm work for convicted prisoners, who are housed separately from those awaiting trial. About 40 percent of the inmates sentenced to the fifty-eight county jails in California are assigned to camps and farms. Los Angeles County operates a 2,800-acre farm for about one thousand men, and the city of Los Angeles maintains a 600-acre farm for alcoholics. Numerous jurisdictions have established "halfway houses" for chronic alcoholics, and it has been claimed that about a third of the men treated in such houses do not continue as problem drinkers.[21]

---

[21] Edward Blacker and David Kantor, "Half-way Houses for Problem Drinkers," *Federal Probation*, 24:18-23, June, 1960.

In Wisconsin, misdemeanants sentenced under the Huber law are permitted to work at regular jobs outside the jail. About one-third of the 10,000 persons sentenced to Wisconsin's county jails in 1960 were sentenced under this law; of the 3,215 prisoners involved, 2,281 actually were employed outside the jails.[22] Work furlough, work release, or community work programs—the terms are synonymous—are now operating in thirty states. A study of a California program found the recidivism rates to be about the same for a work furlough group and a nonfurlough group.[23]

(e) Dependents of those detained in jail awaiting trial should be cared for by the state or other governmental unit in charge of the jail. If the state finds it necessary to detain in an institution a person against whom a charge of crime is made, the duty of providing for those dependent upon the detained person follows logically as a corollary. Whether the person is subsequently found guilty should make no difference in the care during the period of detention before trial.

(f) Those who are acquitted should be indemnified for financial losses suffered as the result of the detention. Such a system has prevailed for a long time in some European countries. By act of 1911, Massachusetts authorized indemnification, in case of acquittal or discharge, for financial losses if the detention awaiting trial exceeded six months. But there is no reason for such a long minimum period. The general arguments in favor of indemnification are as follows: First, when private property is taken for public use, the owner is compensated; likewise, when the state requires an individual to give his time or services to the state, he is compensated. The state does not compensate the person who is deprived of his property because the state was enriched, but because the individual suffered a loss at the hands of the state. The person detained for trial is deprived of his liberty for the sake of public welfare; if the trial shows that this detention was not justified, he should be compensated for the loss which he has suffered for the sake of public welfare. Second, in workmen's compensation laws the state has ruled that an employer, though he is not at fault, must compensate a workman for injuries. The principle involved in indemnification is the same as that of workmen's compensation laws—spread the loss on the public rather than impose it on one individual. Third, indemnification would be desirable because it would tend to prevent needless arrests, would tend to speed up the courts, and would tend to create a public opinion favorable to greater efficiency in police departments, detention institutions, and courts in general. ●

Detention of witnesses   The material witness who is detained in a city or county jail awaiting trial has received little consideration. Some years ago the newspapers reported a case of a person who was knocked

---

[22] Stanley E. Verhulst, "Report on the Progress and Promotion of a County Work Release Program (Wisconsin's Huber Law)," (Madison: State Department of Public Welfare, 1963), p. 4, mimeographed.

[23] Alvin Rudolph, T. C. Esselstyn, and George L. Kirkham, "Evaluating Work Furlough," Federal Probation, 35:34-38, March, 1971.

down and robbed; he could not furnish financial security for his appearance at the trial, and he was therefore detained in jail for three months as a material witness, while the person accused of the crime was released on bail. Although witnesses make up an insignificant percentage of the persons handled by law-enforcement and detention personnel, it is important that their rights be respected. Performance of the task of testifying for purposes of public justice should not impose a hardship on these persons. They, like the persons accused of the crimes, are held at the demand of the state and should likewise not be detained unless the necessity is definite, and if detained should be treated in a decent manner. The American Law Institute has proposed that if a witness is unable within three days to secure financial sureties, he be examined in the presence of the defendant and his deposition be authorized for use in the trial, in case he is not available at the time of the trial. ●

Suggested readings

ARES, CHARLES, & HERBERT STURZ. "Bail and the Indigent Accused." *Crime and Delinquency,* 8:12-20, January, 1962.

FLYNN, EDITH ELIZABETH. "Jails and Criminal Justice." Chap. 2 in *Prisoners in America,* edited by Lloyd E. Ohlin, pp. 49-85. Englewood Cliffs, N.J.: Prentice-Hall, 1973.

FREED, DANIEL J., & PATRICIA WALD. *Bail in the United States.* Washington: National Conference on Bail and Criminal Justice, 1964.

FRIEDLAND, MARTIN L. *Detention Before Trial: A Study of Criminal Cases Tried in the Toronto Magistrates' Courts.* Toronto: University of Toronto Press, 1965.

FRIENDLY, ALFRED, & ROBERT L. GOLDFARB. *Crime and Publicity: The Impact of News on the Administration of Justice.* New York: Twentieth Century Fund, 1967.

GOLDFARB, RONALD. *Ransom: A Critique of the American Bail System.* New York: Harper and Row, 1965.

GRUPP, STANLEY E. "Work Release in the United States." *Journal of Criminal Law, Criminology, and Police Science,* 54: 267-272, September, 1964.

MATTICK, HANS W., & ALEXANDER B. AIKMAN. "The Cloacal Region of American Corrections," *Annals of the American Academy of Political and Social Science,* 381:109-118, 1969.

MATTICK, HANS W., & RONALD P. SWEET. *Illinois Jails: Challenge and Opportunity for the 1970's.* Chicago: Center for Studies in Criminal Justice, University of Chicago Law School, 1970.

McGEE, RICHARD A. "Our Sick Jails." *Federal Probation,* 35:3-8, March, 1971.

O'CONNOR, GERALD G. "The Impact of Initial Detention Upon Male Delinquents." *Social Problems,* 18:194-199, Fall, 1970.

PAPPAS, NICK, ed. *The Jail: Its Operation and Management.* Washington: U.S. Bureau of Prisons, 1970.

QUEEN, S. A. *The Passing of the County Jail.* Menasha, Wis.: Banta, 1920.

RUDOFF, ALVIN, T. C. ESSELSTYN, & GEORGE L. KIRKHAM. "Evaluating Work Furlough." *Federal Probation,* 35:34-38, March, 1971.

STURZ, HERBERT. "An Alternative to the Bail System." *Federal Probation,* 23:12-17, December, 1962.

VON HIRSCH, ANDREW. "Prediction of Criminal Conduct and Preventive Confinement of Convicted Persons." *Buffalo Law Review,* 21:717-758, 1972.

WICE, PAUL, & RITA JAMES SIMON. "Pretrial Release: A Survey of Alternative Practices." *Federal Probation,* 34:60-63, December, 1970.

The criminal court

19

The substantive laws with which criminal courts are concerned contain threats of punishment for infraction of specified rules. Consequently, the courts are formally organized primarily for implementation of the punitive societal reaction to crime. While the informal organization of most courts allows court personnel to use discretion as to which guilty persons actually are to be punished, the threat of punishment for all guilty persons always is present. Also, in recent years a number of formal provisions for the use of nonpunitive and treatment methods by the criminal courts have been made, but the threat of punishment remains, even for the recipients of the treatment and nonpunitive measures. For example, it has become possible for courts to grant probation, which can be nonpunitive, to some offenders; but the probationer is constantly under the threat of punishment, for if he does not maintain the conditions of his probation, he is imprisoned. As the treatment reaction to crime becomes more popular, the criminal courts may have as their sole function the determination of the guilt or innocence of accused persons, leaving the problem of correcting criminals entirely to outsiders. Under such conditions, the organization of the court system, the duties and activities of court personnel, and the nature of the trial all would be decidedly different from their current status. ●

Organization of the American court system

Although there are variations among the states, the organization of the criminal courts includes the following types: (a) Inferior courts, such as justice-of-the-peace courts, police courts, magistrates' courts, municipal courts, and recorders' courts. These inferior courts serve the dual purpose of rendering final decisions, subject to appeal, in minor cases and giving preliminary hearings in felony cases. They also consider release on bail or on the suspected person's own recognizance. (*b*) Trial courts, such as county courts, district courts, circuit courts, superior courts, and quarter sessions courts. The county is usually taken as the unit, even when the circuit includes several counties. These courts render final decision, subject to appeal, in cases which have come up for trial from the preliminary hearings. They also dispose of cases appealed from the inferior courts. (*c*) Specialized branches of the above-mentioned courts, such as traffic courts, morals courts, and domestic relations courts. These courts deal only with specified types of offenses. (*d*) Appellate courts and supreme courts. Such courts take cases on appeal from the trial courts and have original jurisdiction in a restricted field.

Each of these courts is customarily a separate unit. The justices of the peace and the magistrates in a particular city ordinarily act without reference to each other or to other courts, except to consider the possibility of reversal of decisions by higher courts. Proposals for unification and simplification of court structures have long been part of suggestions for court reform. A slight trend toward coordination of the different courts is evident. For example, years ago the legislature of Illinois authorized a municipal court of Chicago to take the place of scattered and uncoordinated justices of the peace and of police courts. The chief justice of this court has wide powers in regard to the assignment of judges and cases and in regard to organization of work. The federal courts were unified in 1922. Many other cities and states have taken similar action. Colorado in 1962 transferred the work of its justice-of-the-peace courts to county courts; Vermont created district courts to replace municipal courts in 1965. The development of state judicial councils is another example of the trend toward organization of court work. Such councils collect statistics and make suggestions for new legislation dealing with changes in court procedures and administration. Also, in some states, associations of judges and of prosecuting attorneys have taken positive action toward coordination of the various units in the court system.

It has been suggested that all the work of criminal justice should be integrated. The police, the courts, the prisons, the probation and parole boards, and perhaps other related agencies would, according to this plan, be brought together under one director. At present they are distinct units, in accordance with the theory that judicial and executive branches should be separate, and consequently they are frequently working at cross-purposes.

Prosecution in misdemeanor cases is customarily initiated by complaint of a victim or witness of the offense; frequently the police officer who makes the arrest is the complaining witness. The complaint and evidence are presented in the inferior court,

Initiation of prosecution and the grand jury

and the whole matter is settled there, subject to an occasional appeal.

In felony cases the procedure is more complicated. The complaint is made by a victim or witness, and the prosecutor hears the evidence. If he decides that the case should be prosecuted, he must present the evidence to the inferior court where the defendant is arraigned. If the inferior court decides that the evidence is sufficient, the prosecutor must, in many states, present the evidence again to the grand jury.[1] If the grand jury regards the evidence as sufficient, the offender is indicted, and the prosecutor must then present the evidence in a trial court. This procedure involves one informal hearing of the evidence by the prosecutor and two formal preliminary hearings before the case goes to trial. The whole procedure is sometimes necessary even if the accused person pleads guilty.

However, the tendency is toward permissive use of initiation by "information," rather than the absolute requirement of an indictment or the absolute prohibition of an indictment. At present only fifteen states require indictments in all felony cases. Twenty-three states permit the use of either the indictment or an accusation in writing, called an "information," by the prosecuting attorney in all felony cases. Ten states require indictments in certain felony cases but permit initiation of prosecution by information in other types of felony cases.[2] For almost a century, the state of Connecticut has permitted the initiation of prosecutions by information in most felony cases, and the tendency elsewhere has been toward elimination of the duplication found in the grand jury system. Those who favor the use of the information claim that the indictment does not protect the accused person, that it encumbers the whole process, that it delays decisions and thus facilitates the acquittal of the accused, that it is generally a perfunctory rubber-stamping of the prosecutor's evidence, and that it is a useless expense. Those favoring the grand jury system argue that the validity of these criticisms has by no means been demonstrated.[3] The possibility of the indictment as a check on the prosecutor's information is desirable, even if it is seldom used.

The grand jury also has authority to initiate general investigations, but, since the evidence in most cases must be collected and presented by the prosecutor, this work has not been very

---

[1] The term *grand* came into use because in England the number of jurors, originally, was twenty-three, almost double the number composing the trial, or *petit,* jury — twelve. In some states, twenty-three is still the rule, but in other states, sixteen or less are required. In Michigan a single judge can perform the functions of a grand jury. See Seymor Gelber, "A Reappraisal of the Grand Jury Concept," *Journal of Criminal Law, Criminology, and Police Science,* 60:24-27, March, 1969.

[2] R. Lee Benson, *The Grand Jury* (Baltimore: Research Division of the Legislative Council of Maryland, 1958), pp. 33-36.

[3] Louis B. Schwartz and Stephen R. Goldstein, *Law Enforcement Handbook for Police* (St. Paul, Minn.: West, 1970), pp. 12-13.

effective. A severe criticism of the grand jury from this point of view was made some years ago by a grand jury foreman, who showed the helplessness of a grand jury which was anxious to make an investigation of banking practices, racketeering, police corruption, and other serious and organized forms of lawlessness. Because of the inactivity of the prosecutor in regard to these forms of lawlessness, the grand jury was confined to minor routine cases.[4]

Since about 1940 the United States Supreme Court has been holding that grand juries and trial juries alike ought to be bodies truly representative of the community, in the sense of being cross sections or representative samples from the community. However, an analysis of grand jury service in the United States Criminal Court, Southern District of California, showed that the principle of a representative jury had not been operative.[5] Instead, the membership of the grand juries showed considerable economic and social bias. During a thirteen-year period the persons nominated for grand jury service included four times a representative number of proprietors, managers, and officials, and one and one-half times a representative number of professional and semiprofessional workers. On the lower economic levels, only twenty-six craftsmen, foremen, and kindred workers were nominated, whereas 167 would have been nominated if the panel had been representative. Similarly, the representative number of operatives was 198, but only two were nominated in the thirteen-year period. ●

The prosecutor

The prosecutor is the most important person in the judicial system under present conditions. The prosecutor determines whether a particular case shall be prosecuted. He determines whether a compromise shall be accepted. (Generally a compromise means that the defendant pleads guilty to a lesser offense and receives the lesser penalty called for by that offense.) He is responsible for the organization and presentation of evidence before the court, and upon his efficiency in doing this the decision of the court depends. He is generally very influential in regard to the disposition of cases, suggesting to the judge or jury the appropriate penalty.

At the same time, the prosecutor is generally elected and, as is true of other elected officials, this means subservience to the wishes of the politicians. It also means distraction of attention from his official business for the sake of political activities. Small-county prosecutors work on a part-time basis for low salaries that are supplemented by income from private practice, often involving a conflict of interest. The urban prosecutor must

---

[4] William Feathers, *Grand Jury Report* (Cuyahoga County, Ohio, December 21, 1933).

[5] W. S. Robinson, "Bias, Probability, and Trial By Jury," *American Sociological Review*, 15:73-78, February, 1950.

be careful not to antagonize any large organized group, and his record must show a large proportion of convictions in cases which go to trial. It is customary in elections for the prosecutor to present statistics on this point. Accordingly, prosecutors are in the business of producing favorable statistics. They avoid trials unless they are confident of conviction, or unless the case is well publicized. Thus, the prosecutor's reaction to crime must be, and is, selectively punitive. If he is to continue in his position or advance to a higher political office, he must seek the severest punishments possible in some cases, but he must intentionally fail to prosecute other cases. Justice William O. Douglas of the Supreme Court has claimed that the quality of prosecutors has "markedly declined," and he observes that prosecutors "sometimes treat the courtroom not as a place of dignity, detached from the community, but as a place to unleash the fury of public passion."[6]

In larger communities the prosecutor has a staff of assistants— as many as 200 in Los Angeles and 150 in Chicago. The assistant prosecutors secure their positions in many cases because they have been active in political organizations, and their reactions to crime must be similar to those of the prosecutor. They are generally inexperienced in the work at the time they are appointed; those in small towns engage in private practice while in office, and they are dismissed when the political administration changes. Almost fifty years ago the Wickersham Commission criticized the prosecutor system on grounds which are still highly relevant:

Taking the country as a whole, the features which chiefly operate to make the present-day criminal justice in the states ineffective are: want of adequate system and organization in the office of the average prosecutor, decentralization of prosecution whereas law and order have come to be much more than local concern, diffusion of responsibility, the intimate relation of prosecution to politics, and in many jurisdictions no provision for a prosecutor commensurate with the task of prosecution under the conditions of today. . . . The system of prosecutors elected for short terms, with assistants chosen on the basis of political patronage, with no assured tenure, yet charged with wide undefined powers, is ideally adapted to misgovernment.[7]

Although each state has a single code of criminal laws, the prosecutorial function, like the police and the courts, is fragmented. Texas has 317 county or local prosecutors. There is need for, at least, statewide coordination of and assistance to the many local prosecutors' offices. In Alaska, Delaware, and Rhode Island, state attorneys general have full responsibility for all prosecutions. The suggestion has been made that the

---

[6] William O. Douglas, "A Challenge to the Bar," Notre Dame Lawyer, 28:497-508, Summer, 1953.

[7] Alfred Bettman, "Report on Prosecution," in National Commission on Law Observance and Enforcement, Report No. 4 (Washington: Government Printing Office, 1931), pp. 11-12, 14.

prosecutor should be removed from direct control of local politics by providing for his appointment by the governor from a list nominated by the judicial council and for his removal only by the governor on recommendation of the judicial council. The prosecutors in this case would be assistants of the attorney general of the state.

The prosecutor is tending to become a criminal investigator, also. Several prosecutors have made great reputations by vigorous campaigns for law enforcement, in which they have made investigations, secured evidence, and initiated prosecutions. In many counties the prosecutor has his own staff of investigators. Also, the police departments in some jurisdictions assign a number of policemen to the prosecutor's office for this work, and the number thus assigned seems to be increasing. Students of the administration of criminal justice have generally opposed this trend toward expansion of the work of the prosecutor, because he already has an enormous task, because it produces friction between police and prosecutor, and because there is no reason to think the prosecutor will be more efficient than the police in making investigations. ●

The lawyer for the defense

Legal defense for a person on trial was generally prohibited in early English law, but has now become a general right. As early as 1701 the Pennsylvania legal code provided for the right of defendants to be represented by counsel.[8] A large proportion of criminal cases is in the hands of a small number of professional criminal lawyers. These lawyers are often recommended to the accused persons by the police and court attendants and in more general ways are dependent on cooperation of government officials. For example, they must deal with officials in arranging for interviews with their clients, in negotiating bail, in bargaining for a charge or a sentence, and in many other ways. Accordingly, they tend to be more active in politics than are other lawyers, tend to find their friends among persons whose social status is lower than that of businessmen, and tend to substitute social skills of dealing with officials for the professional technical skills of dealing with the law.[9] Criminal lawyers have been very influential as members of legislatures in preventing the enactment of bills for the reform of criminal procedure and of court organization:

The prepondering cause of the failure of American justice is the American lawyer. . . . Any system so constructed that improvement and symmetrical growth are inimical to the material welfare of its

---

[8] Richard L. Perry, ed., *Sources of Our Liberties* (New York: Associated College Presses, 1960), pp. 325, 429.

[9] Arthur Lewis Wood, "Informal Relations in the Practice of Criminal Law," *American Journal of Sociology*, 62:48-55, July, 1956. See also idem, "Professional Ethics Among Criminal Lawyers," *Social Problems*, 7:70-83, Summer, 1959.

personnel is fundamentally unsound. Alone among industrial and business enterprises and the "learned" professions, reform inevitably reacts to the material injury of the legal profession. Every proposal of value means loss of income, loss of power, and loss of position to the lawyer. Simply stated, the lawyer cannot reform the system nor permit others to reform it and survive.[10]

If the defendant is unable to hire his own lawyer, the court may assign one. Following recent Supreme Court rulings, all states must make provision for an assigned counsel in felony cases. Additionally, twenty-eight states make the provision for misdemeanor cases.[11] In practice, however, the person charged with a misdemeanor seldom has an assigned counsel. A relatively capable attorney usually was assigned in capital cases, but this is not true in other felony cases.[12] In a few recent cases, state prisoners have won new trials after appeals based on the claim that though they were furnished counsel at the trial, the service rendered by such counsel was so incompetent that the petitioner was in effect without the assistance of counsel.[13] Sixty percent of the offenders defended by private counsel in the Cook County Criminal Court during a two-year period were represented by the same thirty-five attorneys. Eighty percent were represented by forty-two attorneys.[14]

The assigned-counsel system is the only method used to provide legal services to poor defendants in about 2,750 of the 3,100 counties in the United States. There are currently about 185 public defender offices; they are distributed among 13 states, but a third of them are in California and Illinois.[15] The public defender devotes his entire time to the defense of poor persons charged with crimes. The public defender system is found in ancient Rome, in fifteenth-century Spain, and in many European countries in recent decades. In this country it was first adopted in Los Angeles in 1913, and since that time has been authorized in about half the states. In most of these states, the legislation is merely "enabling," which means that a city or county can elect to set up a defender's office, but Connecticut and Rhode Island have established the

---

[10] I. P. Gallison, "A Layman Looks at Justice," *Journal of the American Judicature Society*, 16:176-181, April, 1933.

[11] See Emery A. Brownell, "Recent Developments in Legal Aid and Defender Services," *Federal Probation*, 23:41-44, March, 1959.

[12] Special Committee of the Association of the Bar of the City of New York and the National Legal Aid and Defender Association, *Equal Justice for the Accused* (New York: Doubleday, 1959), pp. 63-68.

[13] Mayers, *American Legal System*, p. 30.

[14] Don T. Blackiston, "The Judge, the Defendant, and Criminal Law Administration" (Ph.D. dissertation, University of Chicago, 1952).

[15] Junius L. Allison, "Legal Aid for the Indigent Accused of Crime," chap. 8 in Simon Dinitz and Walter C. Reckless, eds., *Critical Issues in the Study of Crime* (Boston: Little, Brown, 1968), pp. 245-248.

public defender on a statewide basis.[16] In Los Angeles, the public defender's office defends approximately five thousand persons annually, or about 60 percent of the criminal cases coming before the superior court.

The public-defender system seems superior to the system of assigned counsel. Delays are reduced, frivolous technical motions seldom made, and the expense to the state is reduced. At the same time, it provides more efficient protection to the accused than does the assigned counsel. Because of their specialization, public defenders could help develop public opinion and criminal procedure as assigned counsels cannot.

Bar associations in some states, recognizing the inefficiency of assigned counsels, have advocated voluntary defenders paid by the bar association or some other group as preferable to public defenders paid by the state. Under this method, popularly known as "judicare," a defendant who is unable to retain a lawyer would be permitted to select one from a list maintained by the court or some other public or private agency. This method is currently used only with reference to indigent persons involved in civil cases. It would be superior to the public-defender system, because under that system the defense attorney and the prosecutor are likely to be members of the same political party and therefore under political control. Moreover, men who work together on a day-to-day basis, even in a so-called adversary system, are likely to reach understandings and agreements that are not necessarily in the best interests of defendants. Since most cases are settled in conference between the prosecutor and the defender, these are important considerations.[17] ●

The judge

At present the trial judge has two rather separate duties. First, he must preside at the trial. If the case is tried before a jury, he must supervise selection of jurors, enforce the rules of evidence, and declare law to the jury. In the courts of some states he may even express to the jury his opinions about the innocence or guilt of the accused person, provided he makes it clear that the jury need not follow his opinion. He may order a jury to acquit a defendant, and when a jury returns a verdict of guilty, the judge, if he believes there is no evidence of guilt, may set it aside and order a new trial. However, he may not order a jury to convict, nor can he set aside a verdict which is favorable to the defendant unless the verdict has been induced by fraud. When the defendant pleads not guilty but waives jury trial, the judge not only interprets the law and the rules of evidence, but he determines whether or not the defendant is

---

[16] See David Mars, "Public Defenders," *Journal of Criminal Law, Criminology, and Police Science*, 46:199-210, July-August, 1955.

[17] See David Sudnow, "Normal Crimes: Sociological Features of the Penal Code in a Public Defender Office," *Social Problems*, 12:255-276, Winter, 1965.

guilty. Among other things, supreme court judges also examine evidence, without a jury, in cases appealed to them.

The judge is well qualified, in general, to perform this first duty. When the courts are efficient, judges who are honest and capable are in control of a careful investigation to determine guilt or innocence. An approach to the Continental system, in which the judge actually directs the trial, would appear to be desirable. This method has been well developed in the juvenile courts and is being constantly extended in the courts for adults, particularly in the specialized courts.

The second duty of the judge is to impose just sentences according to the law on those persons found guilty. When the influence of the classical school was at its height, this imposition of sentences was considered as rather routine. Since the law ordained specific punishments for specific offenses, when it had been legally determined that the defendant had perpetrated an offense, the judge simply ordered administration of the appropriate punishment. In theory, he had no choice in the matter, just as the present-day judge in some states theoretically has no choice about the imposition of a mandatory minimum for some offenders. While there were many exceptions in practice, the offense, not the offender, was technically the object of attention. But, with changes in societal reactions to crime, the offender became more important, and the judge was given a wide range of alternative methods for dealing with offenders.

In general, unless he has some assistance, the judge is not able to impose sentences effectively. The evidence in court is designed to show merely the fact of guilt or innocence; such evidence is not relevant to the purpose of determining which of various sentencing alternatives should be used in specific cases of persons who have been proven guilty. If sentences are to be "just" according to modern standards, it is necessary to know the background and character of the offender, and the possible effects of the different methods of dealing with him. In many cases the judge currently must fix penalties or suggest treatment by guessing at the character of the person on the basis of his appearance and of incidental information that has come out during the course of the trial. It was said of some Philadelphia magistrates' courts that convictions of drunks and vagrants were "obtained by sight and smell alone," and that the magistrates were indifferent to the charges listed in the records.[18] On the other hand, a study of 1,437 convictions in the Philadelphia Court of Quarter Sessions concluded that the sentences were consistent with the criteria for sentencing established in the statutes.[19]

---

[18] Caleb Foote, "Vagrancy-Type Law and Its Administration," *University of Pennsylvania Law Review*, 104:603-650, March, 1956.

[19] Edward Green, *Judicial Attitudes in Sentencing* (New York: St. Martin's Press, 1961), pp. 48-49.

Judges vary immensely in their policies. One judge in New York placed 7 percent of those convicted on probation; another judge, dealing with offenders of the same types, placed 40 percent on probation. In New Jersey, six judges, rotating among the courts and dealing with the same types of cases, showed similar variation. One of them sentenced 57.7 percent of the convicted persons to imprisonment, and another sentenced only 33.6 percent to imprisonment; the first judge placed 19.5 percent on probation, the second 30.4 percent.[20] In the federal system in 1962, the average sentence for forgery ranged from a high of sixty-eight months in the Northern District of Mississippi to a low of seven months in the Southern District of the same state; the highest average prison sentence for automobile theft was forty-seven months in the Southern District of Iowa, and the lowest was fourteen months in the Northern District of New York. In 1965 the average prison sentence for narcotics violations was eighty-three months in the Tenth Federal Circuit and forty-four months in the Third Circuit. Green found that the Philadelphia judges favored females, youths, and whites, as compared with males, older offenders, and Negroes, but he concluded that these differences were due to the crime rates among the various groups, rather than to bias among the judges.[21] In all Western countries except the United States, excessive sentences are subject to routine review and correction by appellate courts.

Attempts have been made to assist the judges by field investigations conducted by probation officers, by recommendations of psychiatrists, and in other ways. In California, judges must order an investigation by a probation officer before judgment is passed in felony cases, and pre-sentence investigations are similarly required in about one-quarter of the states for certain classes of offenses, generally those punishable by imprisonment in excess of one year. Pre-sentence reports are made in about 90 percent of federal felony cases. It has been proposed that the data thus gathered be organized into prediction tables, to be used to supplement the judge's experience with various kinds of offenders.[22] But in misdemeanor courts systematic gathering of sentencing information is virtually nonexistent. If judges are to retain the sentencing power, they need assistance. For years it has been repeatedly argued that this function should be transferred to a dispositions board composed of representatives of

---

[20] F. J. Gaudet, G. S. Harris, and C. W. St. John, "Individual Differences in the Sentencing Tendencies of Judges," *Journal of Criminal Law and Criminology*, 23:811-818, January-February, 1933. For a bibliography, see Institute of Judicial Administration, *Disparity in Sentencing of Convicted Defendants* (New York: Author, 1954).

[21] Green, *Judicial Attitudes in Sentencing*, p. 63.

[22] Sheldon Glueck, "The Sentencing Problem," *Federal Probation*, 20:15-25, December, 1960.

disciplines concerned with human behavior, such as a psychologist, a psychiatrist, a sociologist, a social worker, and an educator.[23]

In more than half of the states, judges are selected by popular election, and their terms are relatively short. In nineteen states, candidates for the bench run in partisan elections after having won a primary election or after having received their party's nomination at a political convention. In other states, candidates run without party designation. Over 80 percent of the judicial positions in the United States are elective.[24] Voters cannot always know the qualities essential in a good judge, such as personal integrity, adequate legal training, and judicial temperament. Accordingly, some judges try to win votes by self-advertisement, by attending banquets, weddings, funerals, prize fights, and lodge entertainments, by sensational behavior on the bench, and in other ways. Judges have asked to be transferred from the civil to the criminal branch of the court shortly before elections because of the better opportunity for publicity in the criminal court. With the exception of parts of Switzerland, the United States is the only democracy in the world where the practice of selecting judges by popular vote still survives.

In 1940, Missouri adopted a plan whereby judges are nominated by a commission of outstanding citizens, including lawyers. The names of three nominees are submitted to the governor, who selects one. After a judge selected in this manner has served for one year, his name is placed on the ballot, and the voters decide whether he should be retained in office. This plan does away with the defects and disadvantages of both the appointment system and the election system of selecting judges. Ten other states have adopted it. The nominating-commission procedure is also used on a voluntary basis in other states.

A judge's judicial behavior, like the behavior of other persons, is influenced by his participation in the social relationships that make up his experiences. His social-class membership affects his interpretations of the law and colors his attitudes toward various types of offenses and offenders. His prior associations with punitive and nonpunitive behavior patterns affect the particular way he reacts to a particular offender, and the general societal reactions to crime set the limits within which he must operate. The judge's training as a lawyer does not ordinarily include studies in anthropology, psychology, and sociology, which would tend to promote an appreciation for the compli-

---

[23] Nathaniel Cantor, "A Dispositions Tribunal," *Journal of Criminal Law and Criminology,* 29:51-61, May-June, 1931; Theodore Levin, "Sentencing the Criminal Offender," *Federal Probation,* 13:3-6, March, 1949; Richard A. Doyle, "A Sentencing Council in Operation," *Federal Probation,* 25:27-30, September, 1961; and John S. Palmore, "Sentencing and Correction: The Black Sheep of Criminal Law," *Federal Probation,* 26:6-14, December, 1962.

[24] President's Commission on Law Enforcement and Administration of Justice, *Task Force Report: The Courts* (Washington: Government Printing Office, 1967), p. 66.

cated variations found in the behavior of social groups other than his own. A recent study of the decisions of 313 state and federal judges indicates that decisions for or against the defense in criminal cases are significantly related to membership in various groups.[25] For example, there was a greater tendency to decide for the defense among Democrats as opposed to Republicans, among nonmembers of the American Bar Association as opposed to members, among judges who had served as prosecutors as opposed to those who had not, and among Catholics as opposed to Protestants. On their responses to a mailed questionnaire, 119 of the judges were scored on "general liberalism" and on "criminal liberalism." The first score was determined by responses to questions measuring the degree of sympathy for less-privileged groups and the degree of acceptance of social change, while the second score was determined by the degree of agreement with this statement: "Our treatment of criminals is too harsh; we should try to cure, not punish them." Judges with a high "general liberalism" score had a significantly greater tendency to decide for the defense than did judges with low scores on this measure, and this was true also for judges with a high "criminal liberalism" score. •

The importance of clerks and attendants in the judicial process ordinarily is rarely acknowledged. Crime surveys show that these agents, like prosecutors and judges, are subservient to politicians and are sometimes the agents of corrupt bondsmen and fixers. Clerks can manipulate complaint forms so that discharges result. Dates for which trials are set may be changed by clerks without the knowledge of the complaining witnesses so that the defendants will be discharged for lack of prosecution. Contents of indictments and of other secret papers may be revealed to the lawyers for the defense. In some cases the clerks actually advise the court. Some clerks and bailiffs steer cases to professional bondsmen and to lawyers who will split fees with them. Moreover, clerks and agents are in charge of court administration, and, even when no dishonesty is involved, the management of most courts is archaic and inefficient. As the President's Commission stated, "Operation of today's courts requires the professional and continuous gathering and assessment of up-to-date information and statistics for scheduling, calendaring, and budgeting. Business affairs of the courts not directly related to the disposition of cases must also be taken care of."[26] •

Clerks and attendants

---

[25] Stuart S. Nagel, "Judicial Backgrounds and Criminal Cases," *Journal of Criminal Law, Criminology, and Police Science,* 53:333-339, September, 1962; see also idem, "Testing Relations Between Judicial Characteristics and Judicial Decision-Making," *Western Political Science Quarterly,* 15:425-437, September, 1962.

[26] President's Commission, *Task Force Report: The Courts,* p. 81.

The trial   Except in very serious cases, such as capital offenses, a plea of guilty makes a trial unnecessary. If the defendant pleads not guilty, he is entitled to a jury trial, but in many instances he can waive this right and stand trial before a judge. Recent statistics show that the trial plays a very small part in the system of criminal justice, and that the jury plays a small part in the trial. In 1970, 85 percent of those persons convicted in the United States district courts were convicted on pleas of guilty, 10 percent on finding of a jury, and 5 percent on finding of the court.[27] The President's Commission presented similar statistics on the number and percentage of guilty-plea convictions in trial courts of general jurisdiction in those states in which reliable statistical information was available.[28] These are shown in table XVII.

TABLE XVII   Number and percentage of guilty-plea convictions

State (1964 statistics unless otherwise indicated)	Total convictions	Guilty pleas Number	Guilty pleas Percent
California (1965)	30,840	22,817	74.0
Connecticut	1,596	1,494	93.9
District of Columbia (year ending June 30, 1964)	1,115	817	73.3
Hawaii	393	360	91.5
Illinois	5,591	4,768	85.2
Kansas	3,025	2,727	90.2
Massachusetts (1963)	7,790	6,642	85.2
Minnesota (1965)	1,567	1,437	91.7
New York	17,249	16,464	95.5
Pennsylvania (1960)	25,632	17,108	66.8
U.S. District Courts	29,170	26,273	90.2

The jury   The jury originated as a protection against the despotism of the king and frequently has been acclaimed as the "palladium of our liberties." According to legal theory, the business of the jury is to determine, on the basis of evidence, a question of fact: Did the accused person commit the crime? It is supposed to be a problem in logic similar to the problem which confronts a scientist in a laboratory. In practice, however, the prosecutor tries to select jurymen who will be antagonistic to the accused, and the attorney for the defense tries to select jurymen who will be sympathetic. One tries to exclude all persons not of the same race, religion, politics, or occupation as the accused, and the other tries to exclude all persons who are of the same race, religion, politics, or occupation. A famous criminal lawyer, Clarence Darrow, described the process of selecting a jury in the following terms:

[27] *Federal Offenders in the United States District Courts, 1970* (Washington: Administrative Office of the U.S. Courts), p. 2.
[28] President's Commission, *Task Force Report: The Courts*, p. 9.

Jurymen seldom convict a person they like, or acquit one that they dislike. The main work of a trial lawyer is to make a jury like his client, or, at least, to feel sympathy for him; facts regarding the crime are relatively unimportant.

I try to get a jury with little education but with much human emotion. The Irish are always the best jurymen for the defense. I don't want a Scotchman, for he has too little human feeling; I don't want a Scandinavian, for he has too strong a respect for law as law. In general I don't want a religious person, for he believes in sin and punishment. The defendant should avoid rich men who have a high regard for the law, as they make and use it. The smug and ultrarespectable think they are the guardians of society, and they believe the law is for them.

The man who is down on his luck, who has trouble, who is more or less a failure, is much kinder to the poor and unfortunate than are the rich and selfish.[29]

In some cases, several thousand prospective jurors have been examined before twelve were secured. In one Chicago trial, 9,425 persons were summoned for jury duty, and 4,821 were examined before twelve were finally selected. Ninety-one days were required to select a jury in one San Francisco case. However, this procedure is not due to the jury system as such, for there is evidence that in some courts, especially the federal courts, the jury is generally selected expeditiously.

Jury trial is necessarily slower and more cumbersome than trial before a judge, and about half the states have made legislative provision for waiver of the jury trial and substitution of trial by the judge. Few cases go on trial by jury in some states where this legislation has been in existence for some time. Over 48 percent of the persons who pleaded not guilty in Massachusetts superior courts in 1970 waived the jury trial.[30] The weight of opinion is distinctly in favor of retaining the right to a jury trial but of facilitating the waiver of the jury.

A series of studies indicates both that juries tend to follow the technical instructions given them by the judges and that in jury-room deliberations the leaders are those who are most articulate and assertive, which means that the leaders tend to come from the upper socioeconomic levels.[31] It also has been found that male jurors tend to try to complete the jury's task, while female jurors tend more to react to the other jurors and to display social solidarity.[32]

---

[29] From a statement made at an anniversary dinner of the Quadrangle Club, Chicago, in 1933. See also James A. Dooley, "The Trial Court," *The Law School Record* (University of Chicago), vol. 3 (1954), no. 2, pp. 1 ff.

[30] Commissioner of Correction, *Statistical Reports 1970* (Boston: Massachusetts Public Document No. 115), p. 70.

[31] Rita M. James, "Jurors' Assessment of Criminal Responsibility," *Social Problems,* 7:58-69, Summer, 1959; and Fred L. Strodtbeck, Rita M. James, and Charles Hawkins, "Social Status in Jury Deliberations," *American Sociological Review,* 22:713-719, December, 1957; Rita M. James, "Status and Competence of Juries," *American Journal of Sociology,* 64:563-570, May, 1959.

[32] Fred L. Strodtbeck and Richard D. Mann, "Sex Role Differentiation in Jury Deliberations," *Sociometry,* 19:3-11, March, 1956.

Evidence and testimony

The great proportion of the evidence in a trial is furnished by the witnesses for the two sides. Several problems arise in regard to such evidence. The first is that it is very difficult to induce witnesses to appear in court and give testimony. In cases involving organized crime, terrorism may be involved. In other types of cases, witnesses are reluctant to go to court because of the great inconvenience involved. They may be required to go to court again and again, at great financial loss to themselves. Defense attorneys often attempt to obtain as many continuances as possible, on the theory that witnesses for the prosecution, including victims, eventually will grow tired of the inconvenience of coming to court. In the United States district courts, witnesses are paid $4 a day. A $40-a-day truckdriver in 1965 appeared 16 times as a witness in a murder case being tried in a District Court, for a loss of $576. Other witnesses complain that they are insulted, manipulated, and otherwise treated as pawns in a game. Consequently, many witnesses do not disclose to anyone the fact that they have important evidence, and many crimes are not reported to the police. Much of the evidence provided by witnesses could be supplied by means of telephone, two-way radio, or two-way television.

A second problem is the honest mistakes which witnesses frequently make. One sometimes remembers what he wants to remember. Also, his memory is a combination of what was witnessed and of other things that were heard or imagined subsequent to the occurrence. Delusions of perception occur also. Psychologists have been working for some time on the comparative accuracy of replies to leading questions, and of narrative accounts on the part of various groups.[33] The only check on mistakes in testimony in court is the testimony of other witnesses, but this adversary system places undue stress on the witness and makes it difficult for him to contribute in a meaningful way to the proceedings. Under the heading "How to Humiliate and Subdue a Recalcitrant Witness," a book written for prosecutors and defense attorneys contains the following advice:

When you have forced the witness into giving you a direct answer to your question you really have him under control; he is off-balance,

---

[33] See, for example, Donald Slesinger and E. M. Pilpel, "Legal Psychology: A Bibliography and a Suggestion," *Psychological Bulletin,* 26:679-692, December, 1929; Alfred Kuraner, "The Consistency of Testimonial Accuracy," *Journal of Criminal Law and Criminology,* 22:406-413, September-October, 1931; H. E. Burtt, *Legal Psychology* (New York: Prentice-Hall, 1931); D. S. Gardner, "The Perception and Memory of Witnesses," *Cornell Law Quarterly,* 8:391-409, April, 1933; Manfred S. Guttmacher and Henry Weihofen, *Psychiatry and the Law* (New York: W. W. Norton, 1952), pp. 360-397; Maximilian Koessler, "Fallibility of Testimony and Judicial Accident Risk," *Case and Comment,* 62:12-16, November, 1957; Jack B. Weinstein, "The Law's Attempt to Obtain Useful Testimony," *Journal of Social Issues,* vol. 13 (1957), no. 2, pp. 6-11; Henry A. Davidson, "Appraisal of Witnesses," *American Journal of Psychiatry,* 110:481-486, January, 1954; Israel Gerver, "The Social Psychology of Witness Behavior with Special Reference to the Criminal Courts," *Journal of Social Issues,* 13 (1957):23-29.

and usually rather scared. This advantage should be followed up with a few simple questions such as, "You did not want to answer that question, did you?" If the witness says that he wanted to answer it, ask him in a resounding voice, "Well, why did you not answer it when I first asked you?" Whatever his answer is you then ask him, "Did you think that you were smart enough to evade answering the question?" Again, whatever the answer is you ask him, "Well, I would like for the jurors to know what you have behind all this dodging and ducking you have done!" . . . This battering and legal-style "kicking the witness around" not only humiliates but subdues him.[34]

A third problem is dishonesty in testimony. The only official check on dishonesty is the oath and the possibility of prosecution for perjury. In a few famous cases, witnesses have not been permitted to testify because they were atheists, to whom the oath would have no meaning. In general, the oath probably has little significance to a large proportion of the witnesses in courts. Judges and others believe that there is an immense amount of perjury in testimony, but few persons are convicted of perjury.[35] From 1956 to 1965 only 376 persons were convicted of perjury by the federal courts; the same figure for 1971 was 46.[36]

For some time, efforts have been made to invent devices which will detect guilty knowledge. The "lie detector" currently has the best standing of any of these devices. This instrument registers the emotional changes which occur as the result of questions presented, but, unfortunately, the emotional changes are not necessarily due to lies. Probably the "lie detector" is of less value in the direct detection of lies than in the detection of emotional conditions which may be utilized by the examiner to induce a confession.[37] Various drugs are being used to some extent for the same purpose. It is reported that these drugs induce a state of semiconsciousness in which one will truthfully answer questions. This method, also, is still in the experimental stage, and its results certainly should not be used as evidence in the courtroom.

Fixing the case

The courts and other agencies of justice find constant pressure placed upon them by friends of the defendant. Members of the family, church, lodge, trade union, club, business firm, neighborhood, and other groups swear to the good character of the defendant and ask for leniency. This may be due to close personal friendship or may represent a desire to protect the reputation of the group. In any case it represents a personal and sympathetic appeal based on a nonpunitive reaction to the offense. Alder-

---

[34] Lewis W. Lake, *How to Win Lawsuits Before Juries* (Englewood Cliffs, N.J.: Prentice-Hall, 1954), pp. 164-165.

[35] David Dressler, "Trial by Combat in American Courts," *Harper's*, 222:31-36, April, 1961.

[36] Attorney General of the United States, *Annual Report, 1971* (Washington: Department of Justice, 1972), p. 17.

[37] See Fred E. Inbau and John E. Reid, *Lie Detection and Criminal Interrogation* (Baltimore: Williams and Wilkins, 1953).

men take care of thousands of tickets for traffic violations, as a part of their preparations for the next election. Other political leaders, from the precinct up, perform similar services either directly or indirectly, and they extend their services to persons charged with serious crimes. In some cities almost any case can be fixed at some point in the judicial process, which means either that the case is dropped entirely, or that the penalty is mitigated. Pressure is most frequently placed upon victims of crimes to induce them to refuse to prosecute, and upon the police to induce them to present uncertain and confusing testimony. The inferior court or the magistrate's court is the place where most of these provisions for fixing operate. One of the Tammany leaders stated, "Give me ten magistrates and you can have the whole supreme court."

The "sporting theory" of justice

Formally, the essential business of a trial is to determine a question of fact: Did the accused commit the crime? In the performance of that duty, tricks and surprises are no more justifiable than in determining a fact in a laboratory. In practice, however, the criminal trial is regarded as a game between two lawyers, who pose as adversaries. Large audiences were attracted in the past, and in some sections of the country criminal trials still are an important source of amusement. Each side tries to win the case and takes advantage of every possible trick, surprise, and technical device. It is not at all unusual for as many as fifteen formal motions to be introduced in a case, each of which involves debate, possible continuances, and decisions by the court. When a case is continued, witnesses disappear and public sentiments weaken, and the chance for conviction decreases. One legal writer used an analogy with warfare, stating that the trial involves scouting the enemy's position and strength, stratagems, tactics, skirmishes, and battles. "Opposing counsel are charged with the responsibility of so conducting their campaign that ultimate victory will result."[38] Under the adversary system it is unusual for either attorney to have adequate information; it is even more unusual for them voluntarily to share any information they possess. The defense counsel is obligated to act only in ways favorable to his client, but often the client would benefit if there were a frank exchange of information with the prosecutor. It has been suggested that each side should be required to submit a list of witnesses who are to be called, with an abstract of the evidence to be presented. This would make it possible to reach a decision without the surprises which are not a part of real justice. Since this suggestion and most other suggestions for the reform of criminal procedure would strengthen the state in the trial, they are opposed by criminal lawyers and have made little progress in the legislatures.

---

[38] Leonard Moore, "Modern Practice and Strategy," *Practicing Law Institute,* 1946, p. 1; quoted in Jerome Frank, *Courts on Trial* (Princeton: Princeton University Press, 1949), p. 8.

Many of the legal conflicts which would have been conducted in the courtroom in earlier days in accordance with the sporting theory of justice are now settled in the office of the prosecutor by a process of bargaining. This, also, involves conflict between the opposed attorneys, but it is not sport, for there is no audience. Each side tries to make the best possible bargain. The attorney for the defense will go to trial, with certain exceptions, if he feels certain of acquittal. The attorney for the state will go to trial, also with certain exceptions, if he feels certain of a conviction. In the intermediate cases each is willing to negotiate, and this generally takes one of two forms.

In the first form of bargaining, a plea of guilty to a lesser offense than the one charged may be entered. Among prisoners, this practice is known as "copping a plea." A charge of grand larceny may be reduced to petty larceny; theft of an automobile may be reduced to tampering with an automobile or theft of a tire; murder may be reduced to manslaughter; and so on. In most instances, such reductions represent informal attempts to mitigate severe penalties, but in many cases they also indicate a desire for expediency on the part of court personnel. Sometimes the reduction is given as a reward to criminals who have testified against their partners in crime. A study of 1,336 New York City cases in which lesser pleas were accepted reveals the prosecuting attorney's officially-stated reasons for accepting lesser pleas.[39] In about 54 percent of the cases, mitigation of a severe penalty was the stated reason for accepting the lesser plea, while in 36 percent the prosecutor reported that he had a weak case. In 4 percent of the cases both a weak case and a desire for mitigation apparently were involved, and in 6 percent no reason for the plea could be found.

A plea of guilty to a lesser offense satisfies the prosecutor, for he has an immense burden of work and cannot go to trial on all cases, and the plea enables him to settle the case expeditiously. He is able to record, for purposes of coming elections, that he has obtained a conviction. However, it should be recognized that the acceptance of lesser pleas is not necessarily inimical to justice. It would be physically impossible to try all cases if guilty pleas were not obtained, and often the bargaining enables court personnel to modify the law informally so that it best suits the individual case. The attorney for the defense is satisfied, for his client has escaped a severe penalty which might have been inflicted. As Judge Charles Breitel has noted:

If every policeman, every prosecutor, every court, and every post-sentence agency performed his or its responsibility in strict accordance

The "bargain theory" of justice

39 R. G. Weintraub and R. Tough, "Lesser Pleas Considered," *Journal of Criminal Law and Criminology*, 32:506–530, January–February, 1942. See also Abraham S. Blumberg, *Criminal Justice* (Chicago: Quadrangle Books, 1967).

with rules of law, precisely and narrowly laid down, the criminal law would be ordered but intolerable.[40]

Moreover, there are practical advantages in disposing of most cases without trial. The results are more prompt and certain, and pleas of guilty conserve scarce resources for the most important cases.

In the second general form of bargaining, a plea of guilty to the offense charged is entered in exchange for the prosecutor's promise of probation or a light sentence. Even if he is guilty, the defendant has a legal and moral right to plead not guilty if he believes that the state cannot prove its case against him. The prosecutor must not only know that the defendant committed the offense, but he must prove that fact. He usually is anxious to bargain for a guilty plea in cases in which proof would be difficult. It is the prosecutor's privilege to recommend a light or a heavy sentence to the judge, but the judge, of course, need not follow the recommendation. In practice, however, judges usually go along with the arrangements made between the defendant and the prosecutor, since considerable saving to the state is effected by a guilty plea, which makes a lengthy trial unnecessary. Many prisoners insist that prosecuting attorneys do not always keep their promises to recommend a light sentence, but, instead, merely use the bargaining system to trick the defendant into pleading guilty. Also, defendants who have bargained for a light sentence often are shocked when the judge imposes a heavier sentence than the one recommended by the prosecutor. While it would be difficult to prove, it is probable that a grave injustice is done to many defendants who insist on their right to a jury trial and refuse to bargain. An extreme penalty is sometimes ordered not solely because a crime has been committed but in part as punishment for refusing to plead guilty, thus causing the court personnel the inconvenience of holding a trial. For example, two men who had refused to accept an offer of two-year sentences in exchange for pleas of guilty to robbery were sentenced to twenty years by a trial judge.

It is not possible to determine what proportion of the reductions of charges and the promises of light sentences involve corruption. Not all of these bargains, however, are equally honest. In one study of ninety-seven felony convictions, bargaining was admitted in 56.7 percent of the cases, but there was no evidence of bribery.[41] Neither is it possible to determine how much corruption is involved in the cases which are dismissed by motion of the prosecutor. Certainly corruption is involved in some of them,

---

[40] Charles Breitel, "Controls in Criminal Law Enforcement," *University of Chicago Law Review*, 42 (1960):427-435.

[41] Donald J. Newman, "Pleading Guilty for Considerations: A Study of Bargain Justice," *Journal of Criminal Law, Criminology, and Police Science*, 46:780-790, March-April, 1956. See also idem, *Conviction: The Determination of Guilt or Innocence Without Trial* (Boston: Little, Brown, 1966).

but it is equally certain that the prosecutor performs an important public service in sifting out the cases which should not go to trial, either because of the innocence of the accused, the triviality of the offense, the undue severity of the potential punishment, or the inadequacy of the evidence.

The principal danger of plea-bargaining, the President's Commission concluded, "lies in the fact that it is so informal and invisible that it gives rise to fears that it does not operate fairly or that it does not accurately identify those who should be prosecuted and what disposition should be made in their cases."[42] Viewed in its best light, plea-bargaining is a system for adjusting the general criminal-law rules to the circumstances of specific offenses and the characteristics of individual offenders.

"Cash register" justice

Some cases are rushed through the courts with scant attention of any court official. This type of justice is well known in the traffic courts, where the whole procedure is mechanical. Perhaps the assembly-line procedure is inevitable, in view of the large number of traffic cases, but many citizens are irritated by it. The poor and uninfluential persons accused of other minor offenses are rushed through the courts in exactly the same manner.

The volume of misdemeanor cases is overwhelming. In one year three Atlanta judges of the municipal court disposed of more than 70,000 cases; in Detroit over 20,000 misdemeanor and nontraffic petty offenses are handled by a single judge each year; until 1966, when more judges were provided, the District of Columbia Court of General Sessions had four judges to process the preliminary stages of more than 1,500 felony cases, and to hear and determine 7,500 serious misdemeanor cases, 38,000 petty offenses, and an equal number of traffic offenses per year.[43] A Philadelphia court disposed of fifty-five cases of vagrancy, drunkenness, and disorderly conduct in fifteen minutes; four men were tried, found guilty, and sentenced in seventeen seconds.[44] It is difficult for a person to retain much respect for the system of justice after he sits in an inferior court for a few sessions and sees the inadequate information on which decisions are based. From the standpoint of the number of cases settled and the number of persons affected, these are the "supreme courts"; they are inferior courts only with reference to the character and training of the judges, the efficiency of the machinery, and the type of justice dispensed. At no point, in a very large proportion of cases, is there an opportunity for an adequate consideration of the facts in the case either by the prosecutor or by the court. "Clearing the docket," not dispensing justice, is a primary objective. Cases are dismissed, guilty pleas are entered, and bargains are struck, all with a view to "moving the cases."

---

[42] President's Commission, *Task Force Report: The Courts*, p. 4.
[43] President's Commission, *Task Force Report: The Courts*, p. 31.
[44] Foote, "Vagrancy-Type Laws," p. 605.

The audience and publicity

One of the rights for which the common people fought two centuries ago was the right to a public trial. This right is no longer highly prized by accused persons. On the contrary, a few defendants currently secure the highly prized privilege of being tried in the judge's chambers or of having the judge come to the courtroom at an unusual hour so that they are protected against a public trial. The right to a private trial has been granted in the juvenile court, and it has been argued that restrictions similar to those in the juvenile court should be authorized for all trials, so that the audience could be confined to those who have a particular and justified interest in the case. Many trials are unquestionably an invasion of the accused person's right to privacy. Probably the most notorious offenders in this respect are reporters and photographers.[45] In some jurisdictions where the judges have little self-respect and are anxious for publicity, the constant flashing of the photographers' lights interferes seriously with the trial and certainly results in a lowering of the public's respect for the court. Aside from this, the tendency is toward greater privacy, for the courtroom is generally arranged so that the audience hears almost none of the evidence except in jury trials. ●

The court as a welfare agency

The conventional court system is an expression of a principle of conflict. The theory is that the state has been injured by a crime and in return should injure the offender by punishment, and also that the truth regarding guilt can best be determined by a conflict between opposed lawyers. The juvenile court, on the other hand, has been built on a different principle. Its work proceeds on the hypothesis that the delinquent child and the state have much in common, and that the interests of both will be promoted by efforts to help or treat the child rather than injure him. Some branches of the criminal court, also, have adopted the principle that future crime can best be prevented by helping and treating the accused. Provisions for probation and psychiatric service are the best illustrations of this, and both have been adopted in many criminal courts in more or less restricted form. They are to be discussed in chapter 21. "Family courts" and divorce courts are organized on somewhat the same principle as the juvenile court. The prosecutor frequently brings together persons who have been quarreling and, by conciliation, induces them to drop the prosecution. In many so-called plea bargaining cases the prosecutor actually dismisses charges or reduces them, with no hint of adversary bargaining, so that nonpunitive and treatment methods can be used. It is certainly possible that this procedure will become more prominent in the future. However, criminal

---

[45] Gilbert Geis and Robert E. Talley, "Cameras in the Courtroom," *Journal of Criminal Law, Criminology, and Police Science*, 47:546-560, January-February, 1957.

courts obviously cannot become generally nonpunitive in their methods of dealing with criminals, for punitive sanctions are an intrinsic part of the criminal law. ●

Suggested readings

BLUMBERG, ABRAHAM S. *Criminal Justice.* Chicago: Quadrangle Books, 1967.

BOK, CURTIS. "The Jury System in America." *Annals of the American Academy of Political and Social Science,* 287:92-96, May, 1953.

CHAMBLISS, WILLIAM J. "A Sociological Analysis of the Law of Vagrancy." *Social Problems,* 12:67-77, Summer, 1964.

DAWSON, ROBERT O. *Sentencing: The Decision as to Type, Length and Conditions of Sentence.* Boston: Little, Brown, 1969.

D'ESPOSITO, JULIAN C., JR. "Sentencing Disparity: Causes and Cures." *Journal of Criminal Law, Criminology, and Police Science,* 60:182-194, June, 1969.

ENKER, ARNOLD. "Perspectives On Plea Bargaining." In President's Commission on Law Enforcement and Administration of Justice, *Task Force Report: The Courts,* appendix A, pp. 108-119. Washington: Government Printing Office, 1967.

GREEN, EDWARD. *Judicial Attitudes in Sentencing.* New York: St. Martin's Press, 1961.

GROSMAN, BRIAN A. *The Prosecutor: An Inquiry into the Exercise of Discretion.* Toronto: University of Toronto Press, 1969.

HOOD, ROGER. *Sentencing the Motoring Offender.* London: Heinemann, 1972.

JAMES, RITA M. "Status and Competence of Jurors." *American Journal of Sociology,* 64:563-570, May, 1959.

KALVEN, HARRY, JR., & HANS ZEISEL. *The American Jury.* Boston: Little, Brown, 1966.

KERPER, HAZEL B. *Introduction to the Criminal Justice System.* St. Paul, Minn.: West, 1972.

LADINSKY, JACK. "Career of Lawyers, Law Practice, and Legal Institutions." *American Sociological Review,* 28:47-54, February, 1963.

MAYER, MARTIN. *The Lawyers.* New York: Harper and Row, 1967.

MAYERS, LEWIS. *The American Legal System.* Rev. ed. New York: Harper and Row, 1964.

MILLER, FRANK W. *Prosecution: The Decision to Charge a Suspect with Crime.* Boston: Little, Brown, 1969.

NEWMAN, DONALD J. *Conviction: The Determination of Guilt or Innocence Without Trial.* Boston: Little, Brown, 1966.

OHLIN, LLOYD E., & FRANK J. REMINGTON. "Sentencing Structure: Its Effect Upon Systems for the Administration of Criminal Justice." *Law and Contemporary Problems,* 23-497-507, Summer, 1958.

RUBIN, SOL. *The Law of Criminal Correction*. St. Paul, Minn.: West Publishing Co., 1963.

SMITH, ALEXANDER B., & HARRIET POLLOCK. *Crime and Justice in Mass Society*. Lexington, Mass.: Xerox, 1972.

SUDNOW, DAVID. "Normal Crimes: Sociological Features of the Penal Code in a Public Defender Office." *Social Problems*, 12: 255-276, Winter, 1965.

WALKER, NIGEL. *Crime and Punishment in Britain*. Edinburgh: University Press, 1965.

WALKER, NIGEL. *Sentencing in a Rational Society*. London: Penguin, 1972.

The juvenile court 20

At common law, a century and a half ago, children were tried and punished for violations of law in the same ways as adults, with the exception that a child under seven years of age was regarded as not responsible and therefore as incapable of committing a crime, while a child between the ages of seven and fourteen was regarded as having the possibility of such discernment as would make him responsible, and this was to be decided in each case by an examination. A child under seven years of age, therefore, could not be punished by order of the court, while a child between the ages of seven and fourteen could be subjected to all forms of punishment that were suitable for adults. In the course of time the maximum age was raised in some American states from seven to ten or some other age, but it still happens that children under fourteen years of age are arrested, held in jail, tried in court, and punished in the same ways as adult criminals. ●

Origins and development of the juvenile court

Differential reactions to the offenses perpetrated by children and those committed by adults have been developing for more than a century. While the official reaction to the offenses of both groups has been slowly changing from a punitive to a nonpunitive reaction, this change has been much more pronounced in the case of juveniles. At least the official policies for dealing with juvenile offenders have incorporated more treatment methods than have the official policies for dealing with adult offenders. As early as 1824 a juvenile reformatory was established in New York State so that children, after conviction, would not be confined with adult criminals. The laws of Illinois in 1831 provided that for certain offenses the penalties for minors might differ from those for adults. In 1861 the legislature of Illinois authorized the mayor of Chicago to appoint a commissioner before whom boys between the ages of six and seventeen could be taken on charges of petty offenses; this commissioner had authority to place the boys on probation, to send them to reform schools, and, generally, to use treatment methods. In 1867, this work was transferred to the regular judges of the courts. Separate hearings for juvenile offenders were required in Boston in 1870 and in all parts of the state of Massachusetts in 1872. In 1877, both Massachusetts and New York State authorized separate sessions with separate dockets and records for juvenile cases. During the last quarter of the nineteenth century, cases of truancy and incorrigibility of children were heard in some places by probate courts, without juries or the ordinary legal technicalities and formalities.[1]

These policies were combined and were supported by a consistent theory, which had been lacking in the earlier developments, and thus the juvenile court came into existence in 1899 in Chicago. The two significant points about this new court were: *First,* the age below which a child could not be a criminal was advanced from seven to sixteen years, which was in line with changes that had been made elsewhere. But whereas the previous law had made no definite provision for dealing with culprits below the age of responsibility, the new law did make provision for dealing with them under the softer name *delinquents.* *Second,* the work of the court was placed under chancery, or equity, jurisdiction. For several centuries dependent children had been under chancery jurisdiction; in principle all children were wards of the state if their parents were not willing or able to care for them; in practice the protection of dependent children was confined almost entirely to those who had property. The juvenile court law of Chicago was merely a logical extension of this principle of guardianship by the court of chancery to all children who were in need of the protection and guardianship of the state, and thus was made to include delinquent children.

The juvenile court movement developed rapidly after the Chicago court was authorized. Twenty-two states had somewhat

---

[1] For an excellent discussion of the history, trends, and problems of the juvenile court, see Anthony M. Platt, *The Child Savers: The Invention of Delinquency* (Chicago: University of Chicago Press, 1969).

similar laws within ten years. By 1925 all except two states—Maine and Wyoming—had such laws, and by 1945, when Wyoming passed its law, all states had juvenile court laws. In 1932, a federal law authorized the federal courts to divert juvenile cases to the juvenile courts of the several states. The Federal Bureau of Prisons and the Federal Children's Bureau attempted to develop the policy cooperatively, with the hope that most of the federal juvenile cases could be turned over to the states. But in the first two years very few of the federal juvenile cases were thus diverted, due principally to the fact that the maximum age jurisdiction of the juvenile courts in most of the states excluded a large proportion of the federal cases, and partly to the fact that many of the states did not have adequate facilities for handling federal delinquents. Consequently, in 1938 the federal government adopted a juvenile court act. The juvenile court movement has spread to other continents, and most of the civilized countries now have specialized juvenile courts.

The juvenile court movement has developed administratively as well as geographically. The age of the children coming under the court's jurisdiction has been raised from sixteen to seventeen or eighteen and in some places even to twenty-one. Adults who commit crimes against children or contribute to the delinquency or dependency of children are included in the jurisdiction of many juvenile courts. Many administrative tasks have been assumed by the juvenile court, including adoption proceedings, mothers' pensions, recreational work, and educational work. These tasks are ordinarily administered as part of the preventive program of the court. ●

Comparison of the juvenile court and criminal court

A comparison of the juvenile court with the criminal court is difficult because of the large number of variations in the procedure and organization of each court. At present, the actual practices of some juvenile courts do not differ a great deal from the practices of some criminal courts. Perhaps there is as much variation among juvenile courts as there is between juvenile and criminal courts. The following comparison refers to the conventional criminal court, without its unofficial modifications, and to the juvenile court in its ideal form.

The expected reaction of the criminal court personnel to crime is punitive—they seek, with some exceptions, to implement a punitive reaction to an offense. In contrast, the expected reaction of the juvenile court personnel is that of treatment—they seek, with some exceptions, to implement a treatment reaction to the offender. The *ideal* of the juvenile courts is that the personnel "are not looking outwardly at the act but, scrutinizing it as a symptom, are looking forward to what the child is to become."[2] ●

---

[2] White House Conference on Child Health and Protection, *The Delinquent Child* (New York: Appleton-Century-Crofts, 1932), p. 257.

Criminal Court	Juvenile Court
1. Trial characterized by contentiousness; two partisan groups in conflict.	1. Hearing charactertized by scientific methods of investigation.
2. Purpose of trial to determine whether the youth is delinquent and the general condition and character of the youth.	2. Purpose of hearing to determine whether the youth is delinquent and the general condition and character of the youth.
3. Elaborate machinery for securing information regarding the character of the juvenile.	3. Elaborate machinery for securing information regarding the character of the juvenile.
4. Such information, if secured, may not be introduced as a part of the evidence.	4. Such information is the basis on which a decision is made.
5. Punishment if convicted.	5. Protection, guardianship, and treatment by the state if the existing conditions show the need.
6. Correctional methods in a specific case determined not by the needs of the particular individual but by the legislature, in advance, for all who violate the law in question, with reference primarily to other actual or potential criminals.	6. Correctional methods in a specific case determined by the needs of the particular individual without reference to other actual or potential delinquents.

The characteristics of the juvenile court, stated in more detail, are as follows.

Character-istics of the juvenile court

A "blanket" definition of "juvenile delinquency" or of a "delinquent child" is provided. The state of Illinois, for example, once used the following definition of a delinquent child:

Broad definition of delinquency

A delinquent child is any male who while under the age of 17 years, or any female child who while under the age of 18 years, violates any law of this state; or is incorrigible, or knowingly associates with thieves, vicious or immoral persons; or without just cause and without the consent of its parents, guardian or custodian absents itself from its home or place of abode, or is growing up in idleness or crime; or knowingly frequents a house of ill repute; or knowingly frequents any policy shop or place where any gambling device is operated; or frequents any saloon or dram-shop where intoxicating liquors are sold; or patronizes or visits any public pool room or bucket shop; or wanders about the streets in the night time without being on any lawful business or lawful occupation; or habitually wanders about any railroad yards or tracks or jumps or attempts to jump onto any moving train; or enters any car or engine without lawful authority; or uses vile, obscene, vulgar, or indecent language in any public place or about any school house; or is guilty of indecent or lascivious conduct.[3]

In the standard juvenile court law formulated by the National Probation Association, in California, and in the District of Columbia, the concept of delinquency is similarly avoided. These laws are even more general than the Illinois law, and they simply establish the fact that juvenile courts have jurisdiction over children who behave in certain general ways. For example, in the standard act, jurisdiction is established over "predelinquents . . . whose occupation, behavior, environment, or associations are injurious to his welfare," and over delinquents "who violate any state law or municipal ordinance."[4] Definitions of the dependent child also are stated in general terms.

The behavior of "predelinquent" and dependent children is quite different from behavior which, except for the age of the offender, would be crime. However, a careful distinction between the three kinds of cases often is not made. As Tappan pointed out, "Whether a child be held delinquent, neglected, or dependent may depend chiefly on the petitioner and his motive rather than either the child's conduct or his more basic problem of adjustment."[5]

It was not through oversight that the juvenile court was given jurisdiction over delinquent, "predelinquent," and dependent children and officially has used essentially the same procedures for all. The purpose is supposed to be the same in all three cases: to determine whether the child needs special guardianship by the state. The elements of guilt, responsibility, criminal intent, and punishment are, theoretically, not considered. The omnibus definitions of delinquency are a logical extension of this theory. The assumption is that the results of contact with the juvenile court are beneficial, not harmful or punitive, and, consequently, precise descriptions of proscribed acts are not necessary.

In practice, some criteria for distinguishing between lawbreakers and nondelinquents must be used by the courts, and, although the result is called "adjudication" or "finding" rather than "conviction" or "acquittal," the criteria used are very similar to those used in the criminal courts. For example, a juvenile court using the Illinois statute reprinted above would have to

---

[3] *Illinois Revised Statutes* (Chicago: Burdette Smith, 1949), pp. 1315-1316.
[4] National Probation Association, *A Standard Juvenile Court Act* (New York: Author, 1943), p. 10. For an enumeration of items mentioned in juvenile court laws as constituting delinquency, see Sol Rubin, "Legal Definitions of Offenses by Children and Youth," *Illinois Law Forum*, 16:512-523, Winter, 1960.
[5] Paul W. Tappan, *Juvenile Delinquency* (New York: McGraw-Hill, 1949), p. 20.

consider the question of guilt or intent in order to determine whether a child has *knowingly* associated with thieves or *knowingly* frequented a gambling house. Thus, *delinquency* becomes a mere softening of the word *crime*, for in distinguishing between delinquency and predelinquency, the juvenile court in fact considers delinquents as "young criminals." Of the 150,067 children detained in California juvenile halls in 1970, 44 percent were detained for specific offenses, such as assault, burglary, and automobile theft; 43 percent were detained for "delinquent tendencies" indicated by behavior such as truancy, incorrigibility, and hitchhiking; 2 percent were detained after their delinquency had been adjudicated by a court; and 7 percent were cases of dependency or neglect.[6] In the United States, about 75 percent of the children referred to juvenile courts are predelinquency or lawbreaking cases; about 20 percent are dependency and neglect cases; and about 5 percent are involved in special proceedings, such as adoption.

Equity, or chancery, jurisdiction

Equity courts stand for flexibility, guardianship, and protection, rather than rigidity and punishment. Consequently, friends of the juvenile court insist that children's cases should fall within the equity jurisdiction rather than the criminal jurisdiction. Supreme courts have approved of this in several decisions. But the methods used in juvenile courts actually are not chancery procedures, and it appears that the analogy has been used merely to rationalize the abandonment of the basic elements of due process of law. In many jurisdictions almost all the procedural safeguards of the criminal law were removed in children's cases, so that the court became a child-saving agency whose decisions were supported by the coercive power of the state.

Informal procedures

Whether the jurisdiction is that of equity or not, procedure in the juvenile court is generally required, by law, to be "summary" or informal. The proceedings begin with a *complaint* against a child or youth. He may be arrested and detained in a jail or a juvenile hall, but he usually is merely summoned to appear in court with his parents. Next, the juvenile is *arraigned*. If he has been locked up in detention, he usually is entitled to an arraignment within forty-eight hours. This procedure, called "initial hearing" or "intake interview," is quite informal. A court official—often a probation officer—tells the juvenile of the charge against him.

---

[6] *Crime and Delinquency in California, 1970* (Sacramento: Department of Justice), p. 102.

Then he either dismisses the juvenile entirely, disposes of the case with an action called "counselled, warned and released," or files an official petition for a court hearing. In California, the intake officer also can officially place the juvenile on probation—called "informal probation" because there has been no adjudication of delinquency. The juvenile and his parents must consent to this action. Most delinquency cases are settled by intake officers, just as most criminal cases are settled by prosecuting attorneys. Thus, the hearing and adjudication process is avoided by dealing with the juvenile unofficially, especially when there is no real evidence of delinquency. In recent years, about half the delinquency cases reported to the United States Children's Bureau by juvenile courts around the nation have been unofficial.

For those cases not disposed of at the arraignment, a *hearing* may be held immediately. More commonly, the intake officer files an official *"petition in behalf"* of the juvenile at this stage. This actually is a petition for a future hearing before a judge. Next, there is a *social investigation* by a probation officer. In some states this investigation is not held until after the court has indicated that a child is delinquent, but the trend is toward prehearing investigations. The investigations involve not merely the questions of fact regarding a specified offense, but the whole social situation of the child—especially his home and neighborhood conditions. Physical and psychiatric examinations sometimes are made also. The information secured in this way is supposed to be the basis of decisions and policies. A Minnesota study suggested that probation officers believe that analysis of the juvenile's attitude toward his offense, family data, and previous delinquent problems are the most important parts of investigation reports; but the same officers believed that juvenile court judges were most interested in present offense data, previous delinquency problems, and the juvenile's attitude toward the offense.[7] Whether the investigation comes after an immediate hearing or before a hearing, the child is either placed in detention or released on his own recognizance, called "parole" in some juvenile courts. He usually is entitled to bail, but this procedure is seldom used.

Following the social investigation, a *hearing*, corresponding to the trial in adult courts, is held. The juvenile court judge may hear the case either in his chambers or in the courtroom, but the courtroom is generally arranged so that spectators are so far removed from the bench or table at which the judge is sitting that they cannot hear the conversation. The records are customarily

---

[7] Seymour Z. Gross, "The Prehearing Juvenile Report: Probation Officers' Conceptions," *Journal of Research in Crime and Delinquency*, 4:212-217, July, 1967.

regarded as confidential, and some states prohibit the publication of information on juvenile court cases or printing a photograph of a child in the juvenile court.

The general practice in the hearings is to exercise care in weighing evidence, but without the same observance of forms as in the criminal courts. In some courts the specific charge is not considered as important as is the fact that a child needs help with his alleged problems. Thus, the juvenile court acts as a social agency as well as a court.

Even in the juvenile courts said to operate under equity jurisdiction, many elements of criminal procedure may be found. *First,* the rights to counsel and trial by jury are retained, largely due to the fear that the Supreme Court might otherwise find the law unconstitutional.[8] However, the necessity of exercising such rights is minimized, and few children or parents demand an attorney or a jury trial. It has long been the rule that jury trials are inconsistent with both the law and the theory upon which juvenile courts were founded.

Second, juvenile court decisions may be appealed to the criminal courts. In forty states and the District of Columbia special provisions are made in the law for such appeals. The number of appeals has always been very small, however. The proportion of juvenile court cases appealed steadily declined during the first sixty years of juvenile court history, but it is now increasing.

Third, delinquency, while given a blanket definition by some phrases, is defined also by some specific phrases, in imitation of the criminal law.

Fourth, the juvenile courts in their reports frequently classify offenses in terms of the criminal law, such as grand larceny, burglary, etc. Similarly, in an early New York case it was stated by a criminal court that an adult defendant charged with receiving stolen property could not offer the defense that since the property had been purchased from a "juvenile delinquent," not from a "thief" or a "criminal," it was not "stolen."[9]

Fifth, most judges impose sentences that are distinctly those of the criminal court, including fines and imprisonment. From the point of view of juvenile court theory, commitment to an institution is a substitute for home training, not an infliction of punishment. But almost everyone—especially juvenile delinquents—

Criminal procedures

---

[8] National Council of Juvenile Court Judges, *Counsel for the Child* (Chicago: American Bar Center, 1966).

[9] *Pollack* v. *People,* Supreme Court of New York, Appellate Division, 1913. 154 App. Div. 716.

views institutionalization as punishment. For example, juveniles placed on probation are threatened with the pain of incarceration if they again get into trouble. Despite welfare ideology, the juvenile justice system is generally regarded as a system for punishing bad children. In the minds of the juvenile, the parents, the neighbors, the police, and others, juvenile court action is a criminal process. That this belief is not unrealistic is seen in the fact that most complaints against or petitions in behalf of juveniles are filed by police officers. In California, about 90 percent of the boy delinquency cases and 80 percent of the girl delinquency cases are referred by police.

Because juvenile courts in fact deprive persons of their liberty, as do criminal courts, they now must show concern for due process of law. In 1967 the United States Supreme Court rendered a highly significant decision in the area of juvenile court procedure. It ruled in the *Gault* case, that juvenile courts must grant to children many of the procedural protections required in criminal trials by the Bill of Rights.[10] The Court was impressed with the kind of observations made above, and with the kind of observation made by the President's Commission:

> In theory the juvenile court was to be helpful and rehabilitative rather than punitive. In fact the distinction often disappears, not only because of the absence of facilities and personnel but also because of the limits of knowledge and technique. In theory the court's action was to affix no stigmatizing label. In fact a delinquent is generally viewed by employers, schools, the armed services—by society generally—as a criminal. In theory the court was to treat children guilty of criminal acts in noncriminal ways. In fact it labels truants and runaways as junior criminals. In theory the court's operations could justifiably be informal, its findings and decisions made without observing ordinary procedural safeguards, because it would act only in the best interests of the child. In fact it frequently does nothing more nor less than deprive a child of liberty without due process of law—knowing not what else to do and needing, whether admittedly or not, to act in the community's interest even more imperatively than the child's.[11]

The *Gault* decision specified that the child and his parent must be given specific notice in writing of the specific charges that must be met at the hearing; that the child and his parent must be notified of the child's right to be represented by counsel; that

---

[10] *In Re Gault,* 387 U.S. 1 (1967).

[11] President's Commission on Law Enforcement and Administration of Justice, *Task Force Report: Juvenile Delinquency and Youth Crime* (Washington: Government Printing Office, 1967), p. 9. See also Edwin M. Schur, *Radical Non-Intervention: Rethinking the Delinquency Problem* (Englewood Cliffs, N. J.: Prentice-Hall, 1973), pp. 29-78.

a lawyer must be appointed if the parents are unable to afford one; that children and their parents must be advised of the child's privilege against self-incrimination, such as the right to remain silent rather than be a witness against himself; that admission or confessions obtained from a child without the presence of counsel must be given the greatest scrutiny in order to insure reliability; and that, in the absence of a valid confession, confrontation and sworn testimony by witnesses available for cross-examination are essential for a finding of "delinquency."

The extension of these rights, long available to adults, would seem to require an overnight transformation of juvenile court procedures. As indicated, juvenile courts were founded on the notion that strict application of the ordinary rules of criminal procedure would interfere with the desired relationship between the child and the court officials. The *Gault* decision demands that these rules be applied. But a 1968 study of hearings in three urban juvenile courts indicated that the Supreme Court directives were being avoided.[12] In keeping with the Court's decision, the study covered only those hearings in which individuals were charged with delinquency, who were subject to commitment to an institution, and who were not represented by an attorney. The general finding was that the courts were not systematically applying the principles of the *Gault* decision. For example, in two of the courts, parents were fully informed of the child's right to retained or appointed counsel in only two of 131 cases. Informing the juvenile of his right to silence occurred in only twenty of 121 relevant cases, and in seventeen of these cases— all in one court—the advice given by the judge was prejudicial. Of the 122 cases deemed relevant for purposes of the right to confrontation, full opportunity for cross-examination of witnesses was found in thirty-seven, or 30 percent. The investigators concluded, "Despite the Supreme Court's concern for protecting youths in jeopardy of losing their liberty, juveniles were at the time of this study and presumably still are remanded to penocustodial institutions without being afforded their constitutional rights."[13] It should be noted, further, that most juvenile court cases are disposed of informally, with no hearing before a judge and, hence, with few procedural safeguards. ●

Jurisdiction over children's cases varies widely from state to state and even from county to county within a state. Independent juvenile courts have been created in about half the states, but in

The court having jurisdiction

---

[12] Norman Lefstein, Vaughan Stapleton, and Lee Teitelbaum, "In Search of Juvenile Justice: Gault and Its Implementation," *Law and Society Review*, 3:491-562, May, 1969.

[13] Ibid., p. 535.

many of these states the juvenile court is independent only in certain counties. The juvenile court usually is a specialized branch of some other court, generally a county court or a probate court. Because county court judges preside over many of the independent courts, the independent courts are scarcely distinguishable from the others.

In thirty-seven states, the District of Columbia, and in parts of another state, the juvenile court has exclusive jurisdiction in children's cases, with certain exceptions. In the other states, the child may be taken either to the juvenile court or to a branch of the criminal court. Also, provision is frequently made in states in which the juvenile court has exclusive original jurisdiction that the judge may transfer cases involving serious offenses to the criminal court. In some states the juvenile court does not have any jurisdiction over juveniles charged with offenses which, if committed by adults, would be punishable by death or by life imprisonment.

Good reasons exist for the opinion that the juvenile court should have original, exclusive, and complete jurisdiction over all cases of delinquency of juveniles. The fact that in some states the jurisdiction of the juvenile courts and the criminal courts is concurrent, as well as the fact that serious offenses are excepted from the jurisdiction of the juvenile court, reveals that the authors of juvenile statutes obviously were confused. It is asserted that the child is not responsible for crime and should not, therefore, be punished; yet violations which in the criminal law call for the most severe punishments are excepted. ●

Age jurisdiction

Age jurisdiction also varies widely from state to state. The maximum age for boys in juvenile courts is sixteen years in six states, seventeen in nine states, eighteen in thirty-five states, and twenty-one in one state. The maximum age for girls is sixteen in five states, seventeen in seven states, eighteen in thirty-eight states, and twenty-one in one state.[14] In some states a youth taken into the juvenile court before he reaches the maximum age of juvenile court jurisdiction remains within the jurisdiction of the juvenile court until a later age, generally until he is twenty-one.

Many juvenile courts also have jurisdiction over certain adults. Forty-three states have laws which make it possible to deal

---

[14] National Council on Crime and Delinquency, "Correction in the United States," in President's Commission on Law Enforcement and Administration of Justice, *Task Force Report: Corrections* (Washington: Government Printing Office, 1967), appendix A, p. 136.

through the courts with parents or others who contribute to the delinquency or dependency of children, and in thirty-one states and parts of six others it is the juvenile courts which have this jurisdiction, with limitations in some states. The juvenile court in a few states is given jurisdiction over the following specified groups: adults deserting or failing to support juveniles, adults accused of crimes against children, adults violating child-labor laws, parents failing to comply with the compulsory school law or concealing the birth of a child, adults aiding a child to escape from an institution, adults furnishing children in institutions with contraband items.

The justifications offered for extending the jurisdiction of the juvenile court to these adults are that it keeps the child, even as a witness, out of the criminal court; that it is easier to deal with all the significant personnel together; and that judges in other courts hesitate to use the ordinary criminal sanctions in dealing with such offenders, and consequently discharge them with a futile warning. However, the informal procedures of the juvenile court do not safeguard civil rights, and many persons have therefore argued that the juvenile court hearing should not be used in dealing with adults. One judge wrote, for example:

> The hearing, instead of remaining an investigation, would frequently become an inquisition; instead of impartial inquiry into the condition of a juvenile it might become a contested court trial with the judge as the accuser; instead of frankly admitting misconduct the child, probably cautioned or coached, would admit nothing and involve no one; instead of getting confidence and cooperation from parents, relatives and friends, one would be likely to find them on guard against being incriminated or incriminating anyone.[15] ●

The judge

The judge of the juvenile court is elected in certain cities or counties in six states, appointed by the governor in certain cities or counties in five states, and by the president of the United States in the District of Columbia. In by far the largest proportion of counties, the judge is elected as judge of the ordinary local court, then later assumes the duties of a juvenile court judge. In most rural counties there is only one judge for all types of cases; the judge of the county circuit, or district court, of which the juvenile court is a part, acts ex officio as judge of the juvenile court. In the larger cities where the juvenile court is more completely separated from the court of which it is a branch, and one judge gives full time to juvenile court work, the judge of the juvenile court is appointed by his associates in most

---

[15] G. Loevinger, "The Court and the Child," *Focus*, 28:65-69 ff., May, 1949.

cases. When the appointment is not made in this way, the judges frequently rotate, each one taking one month, or two months, or perhaps a year in the juvenile court. This method of rotation does not necessarily select judges who are best able to deal with juveniles, but one study indicated that Iowa juvenile court judges conceive of their role as one approximating the role defined in juvenile court philosophy, rather than as one approximating that of the criminal court judge.[16] A recent study of juvenile court judges revealed that half had not received undergraduate degrees; one-fifth had received no college education at all; one-fifth were not members of the bar. Almost three-quarters of the judges devoted less than a quarter of their time to juvenile and family matters, and their judicial hearings often were little more than fifteen-minute interviews.[17]

Because the definitions of delinquency and the rules of law regarding juvenile court procedures are not precisely stated in most instances, the judge plays an exceedingly important role in the official proceedings. It is his duty to order that the best available procedures be applied to delinquents. At the same time, it is his duty to protect the rights of all juveniles coming before the court, and to declare children and youths "delinquent" and, hence, subject to supervision, only when there are legal grounds for doing so. Familiarity with behavioral science is necessary to the efficient performance of the first duty. For this reason, some persons have recommended that judges should be persons trained in principles of child welfare rather than in law. The second duty, however, requires decisions on issues of law. In view of the *Gault* decision, it is not possible to dispense with the legal character of the juvenile court or with the requirement that judges be trained in law.

It is possible, however, for very much of the work to be done under the supervision of the judge by persons who have not had legal training. Most cases are now settled by intake officers who have no legal training. In about one-third of the states, the law gives juvenile court judges authority to appoint referees, who make tentative disposals of the cases petitioned for a hearing, subject to the judge's subsequent approval. This power to appoint referees makes it possible to extend the court to rural districts that are far from the place where the sessions of the court are held. If no such arrangement is made, offenses are passed over, or a justice of the peace is appealed to for the exercise of his

---

[16] F. James Davis, "The Iowa Juvenile Court Judge," *Journal of Criminal Law, Criminology, and Police Science*, 42:338-350, September-October, 1951.

[17] President's Commission, *Task Force Report: Juvenile Delinquency and Youth Crime*, p. 7.

coercive power, or some other unsatisfactory method is adopted because of the inconvenience of attending the sessions of the juvenile court. ●

The procedure called sentencing in the criminal courts generally is named "disposition" in the juvenile courts. The disposition of a case and the treatment of the juvenile theoretically are determined by the whole investigation, of which the court procedure is only a part. In a very large proportion of courtroom cases, the referee or judge gives advice to the parents, lectures the juvenile, and dismisses the case. But most cases do not get to the courtroom at all; they are settled unofficially by the intake officers. No petition is filed; no court record or formal charge is made; and no hearing is held.

> **The disposition**

The major methods used in disposing of official cases are continuance, probation, commitment, and referral to an agency or to an individual. The continuance is designed as a test of the offender and his parents without special assistance or supervision by the court. It differs from dismissal of the petition (often called "adjustment" or "discharge") largely in that the judge feels that further action of the court *might* be necessary. It also differs from probation, which includes, theoretically at least, supervision and guidance by a probation officer. Probation is used in a large proportion of the cases in places where juvenile court methods have developed. But in places where the judge has had no special training in the problems of juvenile delinquency, where there are no social workers, psychologists, or psychiatrists, the child is either dismissed or committed to an institution. In ten states the juvenile court judge is authorized to commit juveniles directly to institutions for adult offenders. In another third of the states a child committed by the juvenile court to an institution for delinquent children may be administratively transferred to an institution for adults convicted of crime.[18] Referral to a social work agency, to a foster home, or to a qualified individual often is a condition of probation. ●

If it could be demonstrated that the juvenile offense rate in areas possessing juvenile courts is lower than the rate in areas without such courts, then, all other things being equal, there would be little question about the success of the juvenile court. This fact has not been demonstrated, however, for two reasons. *First,* in

> **The success of the juvenile court**

---

[18] President's Commission, *Task Force Report: Juvenile Delinquency and Youth Crime*, p. 6.

order to make such a study it would be necessary to locate two areas comparable in every significant respect, so that only the presence of a juvenile court was the differentiating factor. *Second,* it would be necessary to measure the amount of juvenile delinquency in each case. While the first difficulty could be partially surmounted by comparing an area before and after it established a juvenile court, experience in the past has indicated that judicial statistics do not precisely measure the amount of crime or delinquency. In most towns and cities, 95 percent of the children who commit delinquencies serious enough to result in arrests are kept at the police station and then unofficially released by the police. Also, broad definitions contribute to the difficulty of comparing the juvenile offense rates at various places and times. Consequently, the effects of juvenile court work must be measured in some other way.

Two alternative methods, both severely limited by the fact that many youths under the care of the juvenile court commit delinquencies which do not come to the attention of the juvenile court, have been used. First, studies have been made of the subsequent "success" or "failure" of cases handled by juvenile courts. Numerous surveys indicate that about one-third of all juvenile court cases involve repeaters. In the District of Columbia the figure has reached 60 percent, and in one recent year over a quarter of the cases involved juveniles who had been referred to the court three or more times before.[19] Sheldon and Eleanor T. Glueck found that of 1,000 juvenile delinquents in the Boston juvenile court and the Judge Baker Foundation, 88.2 percent had additional delinquencies during the subsequent five years, and that 70 percent of them had an average of 3.6 arrests each.[20] Dunham and Knauer found that 30.6 percent of 500 boys, a random sample of 6,976 cases, coming before the Detroit juvenile court in a ten-year period were registered with the Detroit police department within five years of the time they left the jurisdiction of the juvenile court.[21] Of 1,275 children found guilty by the Glasgow, Scotland, juvenile court in one year, 49 percent reappeared in court at least once during the next seven years.[22]

---

[19] President's Commission, *Task Force Report: Juvenile Delinquency and Youth Crime,* p. 23.

[20] Sheldon and Eleanor T. Glueck, *One Thousand Juvenile Delinquents* (Cambridge: Harvard University Press, 1934), p. 167. See also their *Juvenile Delinquents Grow Up* (New York: Commonwealth Fund, 1940), pp. 16, 26, 43, 59.

[21] H. Warren Dunham and Mary E. Knauer, "The Juvenile Court in Its Relationship to Adult Criminality," *Social Forces,* 32:290-296, March, 1954. See also LaMay Adamson and H. Warren Dunham, "Clinical Treatment of Male Delinquents: A Case Study in Effort and Result," *American Sociological Review,* 21:312-320, June, 1956.

[22] John A. Mack, *Delinquency and Changing Social Patterns* (Glasgow: Charles Russell Memorial Lecture, 1956), pp. 3-4.

A *second* method of appraising the success of the juvenile court is by enumerating the offenders in criminal courts who have previously been in juvenile court. A 1964 study of Ohio prisoners disclosed that 25 percent of the males and 28 percent of the females had been arrested at least once as juveniles.[23] Similarly, the Massachusetts prison reports show that approximately 25 percent of the offenders sentenced to the state prison and the state reformatories have previously been committed to institutions for delinquent children. Consequently, it is evident that a large proportion of the persons appearing in official records for the first time have passed the age of juvenile court jurisdiction.

Such statistical enumerations, of course, do not precisely test the effects of the juvenile court, since it is not clear what proportion of the subjects involved would have been recidivists if they had been dealt with in some other way. Also, insofar as the wards of the juvenile court refrain from subsequent delinquency, it is not clear why they do so. The assumption has been that the treatment methods used in connection with the juvenile court are the explanation. But serious questions have been raised regarding the validity of the belief that individualized treatment methods are valuable in a large proportion of cases, even if they are used. For example, some years ago it was proposed that an intensive study be made of the Cincinnati court, which had a reputation for unusual success in turning delinquents from their careers, but a preliminary investigation showed that the court was far inferior to the Boston juvenile court in its standards of casework and facilities for casework, although it secured at least equally successful results. Consequently, it was concluded that whatever degree of success the Cincinnati court might have could not be explained by its casework methods.

On the basis of such information as has been presented, some authorities have stated that the juvenile court is a dismal failure, while others have become convinced that it is highly successful. Those considering it a success point out that it is unfair to the court to test it in terms of absolute cessation of delinquency. Taft used an analogy with illness, stating that "a hospital is not a complete failure if its patients leave in better health, even though they again contract the same disease for which they were treated."[24] Those who speak most frequently of the failure of the juvenile court probably would not prefer the old criminal procedures. They are seeking the development of a still better substitute for the criminal court. When considered as a substitute for the criminal court, the juvenile court is regarded as a decided success, even if

---

[23] Barbara Ann Kay, "Attitudes Toward Law and Moral Values: Men versus Women Prisoners of Ohio," paper presented at the meetings of the American Society of Criminology, Montreal, 1964.

[24] Donald R. Taft, *Criminology* (New York: Macmillan, 1950), p. 577.

its greatest achievement is the mere recognition of the dignity and potentialities of children and adolescents. ●

Proposed modifications

Among the plans suggested for changes, the two most important are (a) a merger of the juvenile court with a general family court and (b) a transfer of most of the work of the juvenile court to social welfare agencies or to the schools.

The suggestion that the juvenile court be merged with the general family court is made because of the conviction that the various problems of the family are related and should all be handled by one agency. Family courts, or domestic relations courts, would handle all cases of domestic difficulty, including nonsupport, desertion, paternity, divorce, alimony, custody of children, guardianship of children, adoption of children, juvenile delinquency, dependency, and contributing to the delinquency or dependency of children. A successful court of this kind has been operating in Cincinnati since 1914, and such courts are found in parts of at least eighteen states, chiefly in the larger urban areas, and throughout New Jersey and Virginia.

The second suggestion is that the work of the juvenile court be confined to the performance of judicial functions, and that all casework functions be transferred to social work agencies. The suggestion is contrary to the "social agency" view that as a public agency the court cannot refuse to accept any case which might come to it for aid, and it is an endorsement of the legal view that the courts should limit their intake to cases in which there is a specific issue of delinquency.[25] As early as 1903, Aschaffenburg urged that the discipline of school-age children should be transferred to the schools, and that they should not be tried at all in the courts. In recent years, the tendency has been to suggest that the cases of children in trouble be diverted to social welfare agencies, rather than to the school.

The argument for these transfers is based on the observation that court labelling of a juvenile as a delinquent often does more harm than good. The idea is to find alternative means of dealing with juveniles in trouble. As has been indicated, of the selected cases which go to the juvenile court, the large proportion are settled unofficially, without an appearance before the judge. It is proposed, therefore, that this unofficial work be diverted to public or private agencies.[26] The proposal does not assume, of course,

---

[25] For discussion of these two views, see H. Warren Dunham, "The Juvenile Court: Contradictory Orientations in Processing Offenders," *Law and Contemporary Problems,* 23:508-527, Summer, 1958. See also Edwin M. Lemert, *Social Action and Legal Change: Revolution within the Juvenile Court* (Chicago: Aldine, 1970).

[26] See Robert M. Carter, "The Diversion of Offenders," *Federal Probation,* 36:31-36, December, 1972.

that no cases need go to the juvenile court for adjudication. It is an expression of a belief that it is undesirable for a child to appear in a court of any kind, juvenile or criminal, and that such appearances should be obviated as far as possible by the development of extracourt methods of dealing with problem behavior. •

Extension of the juvenile court

The statements made above regarding the characteristics of the juvenile court give an incorrect impression of the present methods of dealing with juvenile delinquents because attention is fixed on the well-organized courts in a few large cities. But 90 percent of the courts that hear children's cases are in counties that have no city of more than 25,000 population, and in such areas few courts can afford even the bare essentials of a juvenile court: separate hearings for children, probation service, and records of social information. Thousands of children are deprived every year of rights which are guaranteed to them by law—the right not to be detained in jails with adult offenders, the right to a separate hearing, the right to be regarded as the ward of the court in need of protection and help rather than of punishment. The loss of these rights causes little protest, because few people speak for such children; if the rights of a professional or other influential class were so denied or abridged, a howl of protest would compel the authorities to obey the law. It is this situation which has prompted proposals for organization of the juvenile court on a statewide rather than on a countrywide basis.

The problem of extending the juvenile court may be approached from another standpoint. Why should not the methods now used in juvenile courts be extended to adults? If we do this, does the separate existence of the juvenile court have an adequate justification?

Two principles have been used to justify the trial and treatment of juvenile offenders separately from adults.

First, the child has been regarded as not capable of committing crime because he does not have sufficient intelligence and experience to formulate an essential element in every crime—criminal intent. But the juvenile court has retained the element of intent, to some extent, in the distinction between delinquency and "predelinquency"; both terms are defined very broadly, and whether a particular juvenile is treated as one or the other is determined largely by his intent. Moreover, if the child under sixteen or even under eighteen or twenty-one is, by law, incapable of having criminal intent, it would appear that many persons over the juvenile court age are similarly incapable. No logical method exists for setting an age level which will separate those who are responsible from those who are not. Juvenile court methods based on the principle of lack of responsibility are, therefore, either not justified or else their very existence logically indicates that they should be extended to adults.

Second, juvenile courts developed because it was believed that criminal courts were based on the assumption that criminals were vicious and depraved, and on the assumption that severe penalties efficiently deter others from crime. It was insisted that the best policy in dealing with children would be to guard and protect them rather than punish them. But, in theory at least, the criminal law and criminal courts are making efforts to reform, protect, and treat adult criminals. Recent changes have made it impossible to state the function of the criminal justice system solely in terms of punishment. It may be observed that this is largely a formal change only, and that in actual practice the object of the law is punishment. But it may also be observed that in actual practice the object of most institutions and programs for juvenile delinquents also is punishment. Certainly the differences between the criminal courts and the juvenile courts are not so great as they were when the juvenile court was invented.

Evidences of the change in attitudes and of the extension of juvenile court methods and procedures to courts for adults are numerous. In 1910 Judge Lindsey, one of the founders of the juvenile justice system, argued that juvenile court methods should be used in half the cases in criminal courts,[27] and similar authoritative statements have been made regularly by students of the subject down to the present. Certain laws also indicate a tendency to extend juvenile court procedures to adults. For example, presentence investigations are required by law in the adult courts of some states, and in many states certain offenders, especially sex offenders, are accorded psychiatric treatment rather than punishment. Also, in many of the specialized courts, such as morals courts and domestic relations courts, the methods are very similar to those of the juvenile court.

But perhaps the best evidence of a changing attitude was the recent attempt to extend the juvenile court methods and ideology to young adults by means of youth-correction-authority acts. The principle involved in this movement was that the juvenile court procedures might well be extended to the group seventeen to twenty-one years of age, because such young adults are not held to be adults in the civil courts or at the polls. This movement was initiated by a report of a committee on delinquency appointed by two social welfare societies in New York City. The committee reported that the methods used in arresting, detaining, trying, and committing young adults were tending in many cases to perpetuate criminal behavior, and it suggested revisions in those procedures.[28] An advisory committee of the American Law Insti-

---

[27] B. B. Lindsey and H. J. O'Higgins, *The Beast* (New York: Doubleday, 1910), p. 149.

[28] Leonard V. Harrison and Pryor M. Grant, *Youth in the Toils* (New York: Macmillan, 1938).

tute, consisting of outstanding lawyers, judges, psychiatrists, sociologists, and correctional workers, worked for two years on the careful formulation of a model act for dealing with young adults, and this model act was recommended to the states for legislative action in 1940. The stated purpose of this act was to substitute "for retributive punishment methods of training and treatment directed toward the correction and rehabilitation of young persons found guilty of violation of law." To this end, a committee called the "youth correction authority" is established, and the judges of all courts except juvenile courts are instructed to commit almost all offenders up to the age of twenty-one to it.

The youth correction authority was given the power to determine what treatment, including probation, shall be given to each offender, to establish facilities for such treatment, and to retain offenders until there is a reasonable probability that discharge will result in no danger to the public. However, the offender may be held beyond age twenty-one only if his case is reviewed by the court. It is clear that the intent was to divide correctional procedure into two distinct parts—trial and treatment—and, hence, to limit the judiciary to the mere determination of whether or not the accused is guilty. Youthful offenders continue to be considered criminally responsible. Considerable controversy has developed as to the desirability of thus depriving the judge of the sentencing power.

While such a proposal reveals a changing attitude toward young adult offenders and a tendency to extend juvenile court procedures to them, the many modifications made as this act was put into practice (in California, Illinois, Wisconsin, Minnesota, Massachusetts, Texas, and the federal government) indicate that the punitive reaction to young adult offenders still prevails.[29] For example, while the model act is designed to benefit young criminals, not juvenile delinquents, in all six states the enacted statutes are mainly instruments for handling juvenile delinquents only. The agency having authority powers in each of two states— Texas and Wisconsin—deals exclusively with juvenile delinquents, and about 90 percent of the case load in Massachusetts and about two-thirds of the case load in California and Minnesota is made up of juvenile delinquents. For the most part, the young adults continue to be handled in the traditional way. Similarly, the intent

---

[29] For descriptions and the evaluations of established programs based on the model act, see Sol Rubin, "Changing Youth Authority Concepts," *Focus*, 29:77-82, May, 1950; Bertram M. Beck, *Five States: A Study of the Youth Authority Program as Promulgated by the American Law Institute* (Philadelphia: American Law Institute, 1951); James V. Bennett, "Blueprinting the New Youth Corrections Program," *Federal Probation*, 15:3-7, September, 1951; Jerome Hall, "Science and Reform in Criminal Law," *University of Pennsylvania Law Review*, 100:787-804, April, 1952; and Paul W. Tappan, "Young Adults Under the Youth Authority," *Journal of Criminal Law, Criminology, and Police Science*, 47:629-646, March-April, 1957.

of the model act in regard to the powers of the court has not been carried out; under the enacted legislation the judge does not lose the sentencing power. He commits a youth or a juvenile to the authority only if he wants him incarcerated. Consequently, the authority is largely restricted to handling persons committed to institutions. To counteract this trend, Massachusetts and California are now in the process of closing down their institutions for juveniles and, thus, dismantling their youth authority agencies.[30]

Despite this failure, some of the elements of the juvenile court seem to be applicable to the criminal court and probably would improve very greatly the work of that organization. Social investigations, use of summons, reformation as the ideal of treatment, informal procedures, and private sessions—all could be used advantageously by the criminal court. It is clear, however, that a blanket definition of "crime," corresponding to the broad definitions of delinquency, could not be used even if the juvenile court procedure were extended to adults. Aside from the fact that there are prohibitions in existing laws and in the constitutional safeguards ensuring due process of law, a blanket definition of crime would be dangerous because of the wide variety of political beliefs in modern society. ●

Suggested readings

BEEMSTERBOER, MATTHEW J. "The Juvenile Court—Benevolence in the Star Chamber." *Journal of Criminal Law, Criminology, and Police Science,* 50:464-475, January-February, 1960.

CALDWELL, ROBERT G. "The Juvenile Court: Its Development and Some Major Problems." *Journal of Criminal Law, Criminology, and Police Science,* 51:493-511, January-February, 1961.

DUXBURY, ELAINE B. *Youth Service Bureaus in California: A Progress Report.* Sacramento: Department of the Youth Authority, 1971.

EMERSON, ROBERT M. *Judging Delinquents: Context and Process in the Juvenile Court.* Chicago: Aldine, 1969.

EMPEY, LAMAR T. "Juvenile Justice Reform: Diversion, Due Process, and Deinstitutionalization." Chapter 4 in *Prisoners in America,* Edited by Lloyd E. Ohlin. Englewood Cliffs, N. J.: Prentice-Hall, 1973.

FOX, SANFORD J. "Juvenile Justice Reform: An Historial Perspective." *Stanford Law Review,* 22:1187-1239, June, 1970.

GLEN, JEFFREY E., & J. ROBERT WEBER. *The Juvenile Court: A Status Report.* Washington: Government Printing Office, 1971.

LEMERT, EDWIN M. *Instead of Court: Diversion in Juvenile Justice.* Washington: Government Printing Office, 1971.

LEMERT, EDWIN M. *Social Action and Legal Change: Revolution within the Juvenile Court.* Chicago: Aldine, 1970.

LERMAN, PAUL, ed. *Delinquency and Social Policy.* New York: Praeger, 1970.

---

[30] See Yitzhak Bakal, "The Massachusetts Experience: Rationale for Closing Institutions," *Delinquency Prevention Reporter,* April, 1973, pp. 1-7.

PLATT, ANTHONY M. *The Child Savers: The Invention of Delin-quency.* Chicago: University of Chicago Press, 1969.

REINEMANN, JOHN. "Fifty Years of the Juvenile Court Movement in the United States." *Mental Hygiene,* 34:391-399, July, 1950.

SHULMAN, HARRY M. *Juvenile Delinquency in American Society.* New York: Harpers, 1961.

WAITE, E. F. "How Far Can Court Procedure be Socialized without Impairing Individual Rights?" *Journal of Criminal Law and Criminology,* 12:339-348, November-December, 1921.

WHEELER, STANTON, & LEONARD S. COTTRELL, JR., with the assistance of ANNE ROMASCO. *Juvenile Delinquency: Its Prevention and Control.* New York: Russell Sage Foundation, 1966.

21   Probation

Although probation is to a large extent a nonpunitive method of handling offenders, it has developed within the framework of a legal system which is basically punitive. Probation methods represent a distinct break with the classical theory on which the criminal law is based, for an attempt is made to deal with offenders as individuals rather than as classes or concepts, to select certain offenders who can be expected, with assistance, to change their attitudes and habits while residing in the free community, and to use a great variety of nonpunitive methods in rendering assistance to those offenders selected. Probation thus is a system for implementing the treatment reaction to lawbreaking. It does not attempt to make the offender suffer; it attempts to prevent him from suffering. Some suffering results from having been placed in the "probationer" status, but, in theory at least, this suffering is not intentional and is avoided as far as possible. Consequently there is no reason for insisting that probation is punishment, as some authors have done in an effort to win approval for the system. •

The nature of probation

From the constitutional point of view, probation is the suspension of a sentence during a period of liberty in the community conditional upon good behavior of the convicted offender. The courts have, without exception, found the constitutional justification of probation in the right of the court to suspend sentence.

But mere suspension of sentence is an act of mercy or judicial leniency which allows "hopeful cases" or first offenders "another chance." Probation is clearly different from the suspended sentence alone, since it includes a positive method of dealing with offenders. While a conditional suspension of sentence by the court is necessary, probation includes supervision, guidance, and assistance of the offender. This assistance has come to be the important part of the probation system.

The suspension of sentence, and hence the threat of punishment, is always present in probation, and it is a reflection of a punitive societal reaction to crime. However, in some states a suspended sentence now can be granted only if the offender is placed on probation; this notion that the offender should be guided and assisted is a reflection of a treatment reaction to crime. Probation, then, represents a kind of compromise between the punitive reaction and the treatment reaction. A definition of probation which reveals this compromise may be stated as follows: Probation is the status of a convicted offender during a period of suspension of his sentence, in which he is given liberty conditioned on his good behavior, and in which the state, by personal supervision, attempts to assist him to maintain good behavior. Court decisions based upon information obtained in presentence investigations of the offender's personality and background are implied. The United States Supreme Court has stated that probation is to be used "to provide an individualized program offering a young or unhardened offender an opportunity to rehabilitate himself without institutional confinement under the tutelage of a probation officer and under the continuing power of the court to impose institutional punishment for his original offense in the event he abuses the opportunity."[1]

The suspension of sentence which permits positive action to be taken may be either a suspension of the imposition of the sentence or the suspension of the execution of the sentence. Most states suspend the execution, but others suspend the imposition, and still others use both methods. In California in 1967, 83 percent of the probation grants to adults by superior courts were suspensions of the imposition of sentence; 12 percent were suspensions of the execution of a jail sentence; and 5 percent were suspensions of a sentence to prison.[2] If the judge imposes a sentence and then suspends the execution of the sentence, and if the offender violates the probation, the judge merely orders the execution of the original sentence. If the judge suspends the imposition of the sentence, he will, in case of violation of probation, have additional information on which to base a decision regarding the sentence which should be imposed.

Whichever method of suspending the sentence is used, it is a

---

[1] *Roberts v. United States,* 320 U.S. 264, 272 (1943).

[2] *Crime and Delinquency in California, 1967* (Sacramento: Department of Justice, 1968), p. 159.

method of suspending punishment, and thus it is to be regarded as an alternative for either of two other major methods currently used in dealing with convicted offenders—imprisonment or release without supervision. It is important to judge probation in relation to these two alternatives; it is frequently judged as though it were an alternative to imprisonment alone.

Some questions of law have arisen regarding probation. A federal court sentenced an offender to serve two years in a penitentiary and then provided that he be released on probation at the end of six months and kept on probation during the remainder of the two years. The higher court held that this was illegal, because the court was really ordering the offender paroled, and the court had no jurisdiction in regard to parole. Again, the court may convict an offender on two counts, then commit him to an institution on the first count and place him on probation on the second count. This, apparently, is not illegal, but it is contradictory to the principle that probation is to be used as a system for keeping offenders out of prison while at the same time giving them assistance. In some jurisdictions, offenders frequently are granted probation with the stipulation that they spend part of the probationary period in the county jail. Forty percent of the persons granted probation by California superior courts in 1970 were given jail sentences as part of the conditions of probation. Four counties gave jail sentences to over 80 percent of their probationers, but one county used this sentence with 14 percent.[3] ●

The origin, development, and scope of probation

As was observed in chapter 15, the punitive reaction was at one time mitigated by methods such as securing sanctuary, right of clergy, judicial reprieve, and technical circumvention of statutes. Probation can be traced to such practices.[4] The common-law practice of suspending sentences temporarily was extended, and courts began to suspend sentences indefinitely, permitting convicted offenders to remain at large on good behavior. Sometimes the offender was compelled to furnish a financial guarantee that he would maintain good behavior, and in some instances restrictions were placed on his freedom. Then volunteers began to assist such offenders during the period of the suspension of the sentence. Among the early volunteers was John Augustus, a shoemaker of Boston, who in 1841 secured the release of a confirmed drunkard from the police court of Boston by acting as surety for him. This offender turned out to be a "sober, industrious citizen" under his care. During the next seventeen years Augustus acted as surety for 1,152 males and 794 females and gave less

[3] *Crime and Delinquency in California, 1970.* (Sacramento: Department of Justice, 1972), p. 17.

[4] Frank W. Grinnell, "The Common Law History of Probation," *Journal of Criminal Law and Criminology*, 32:15-34, May-June, 1941.

formal aid to many others.[5] Such volunteers became more numerous and were, in effect, probation officers before probation had been authorized by statute.[6]

In 1869, a Massachusetts state social agency was authorized by the legislature to accept the custody of juvenile offenders, with the right of placing them in private families. This amounted to probation, and 23 percent of the juvenile offenders convicted in the courts of Boston in the year 1869-1870 were dealt with in this manner. But the first statutory provision for probation with publicly paid officers was the Massachusetts law of 1878, which authorized the mayor of Boston to appoint and pay a probation officer and authorized the municipal court to place offenders on probation. No restrictions were made, as in many subsequent probation laws, regarding the term of probation, the age, previous record, or other characteristics of the offender. The legislature extended this power to all other mayors of the state in 1880, and in 1891 it made mandatory the appointment of probation officers by lower-court judges.

By 1917, twenty-one states had provided for adult probation, and all states had authorized, at least, the suspension of sentences. The states which had the highest percentage of urban population developed probation first, and it gradually spread to the more rural states. Probation was authorized in the federal courts 'in 1925, but those courts had used it without statutory authority for some years prior to that. Most European nations have provision for suspension of sentence, and many have volunteer or philanthropic assistance for persons during the period of suspension of sentence, but few have provided for publicly paid probation officers.

In 1925 probation for juveniles was available in every state, and in 1956 all states made probation available to adult felons as well. However, use of probation in many of these states is limited by statute. Some states do not authorize paid probation officers, and in only fifteen states may probation be granted regardless of type of crime. Crimes of violence, crimes involving the use of a deadly weapon, and crimes carrying a certain penalty often are excepted. Furthermore, in some states, probation may be used only by courts in cities or counties of a specified size, or by courts with specified types of jurisdiction. These statutory restrictions ordinarily are indicative of a conflict between the punitive and treatment reactions to crime, since they are based on the assumption that probation is mere judicial leniency, which should not be available to certain offenders.

---

[5] *John Augustus, First Probation Officer* [reprint of a report by Augustus, with an introduction by Sheldon Glueck] (New York: National Probation Association, 1939), p. vi. See also N. S. Timasheff, *One Hundred Years of Probation* (New York: Fordham University Press, 1941).

[6] See Donald W. Moreland, "John Augustus and His Successors," *National Probation Association Yearbook, 1941*, pp. 1-22.

Evidence of the conflict also may be found in the failure of courts to appoint and pay authorized probation officers and in the failure to use probation when it is authorized by law and when probation officers are provided. About 25 percent of the counties in the United States have no probation service, and probation is seriously handicapped in many other counties by the limitations of part-time, unofficial, and poorly paid probation officers. The rural districts are far behind the urban communities in this respect. In 165 counties in four states, no juvenile probation services were available in 1966.[7] Twenty years ago, a survey of California indicated that in some counties probation was used in less than 12 percent of the felony cases, while in other counties probation was used in over 80 percent of the cases.[8] A Pennsylvania survey revealed that only in a few counties did the courts consider any presentence investigation necessary, that half a dozen counties had no probation service for adults, and that case loads of probation workers were many times higher than those generally considered to be appropriate.[9]

No general statistics covering the entire United States are available. In the federal court system in recent years, about 40 per-

TABLE XVIII

Rates per 100,000 general population for convicted offenders granted probation, parole, or sentenced to prison in census years, Michigan, 1930-1960

Census years as of January 1	Total	Rates per 100,000 general population for offenders		
		On probation	On parole	In prison
1930	270	72	38	159
1940	286	84	56	147
1950	299	105	59	135
1960	363	173	67	123

cent of those convicted in district courts have been placed on probation. The district courts of Massachusetts grant probation to approximately two-thirds of the cases coming before them, and the superior courts use probation in about 45 percent of their cases. Probation probably is used more generally in this state than in many others. In England's superior courts there has been an increase in the proportion of offenders given probation in the years since World War II, but in magistrates' courts (which

---

[7] National Council on Crime and Delinquency, "Correction in the United States," appendix A in President's Commission on Law Enforcement and Administration of Justice, *Task Force Report: Corrections* (Washington: Government Printing Office, 1967), p. 134.

[8] Special Committee on Governmental Administration, *Study of Building Needs of State Correctional Institutions* (Sacramento: State Senate, September 28, 1954).

[9] National Probation and Parole Association, *Probation Services in Pennsylvania* (Harrisburg: Governor's Commission on Penal and Corrective Affairs, 1957).

include juvenile courts), there has been a steady decrease. For example, in the years 1950-1954 about 40 percent of male juvenile delinquents were placed on probation; by 1961 the percentage had declined to 32. But the proportion of adult males put on probation by trial courts increased from 17 percent in 1950 to 22 percent in 1961.[10] Table XVIII shows that in Michigan the number of prisoners per 100,000 population decreased regularly in a 30-year period, while the number of probationers per 100,000 population steadily increased.[11] ●

Organization of probation departments

Two agencies have been suggested as the proper bodies to control probation work—the court and an independent administrative body. Since probation originated in the suspended sentence and hence is regarded as an extension of the judicial function, the control of probation work usually is in the hands of the court. This has carried with it the decision in some states that probation officers can be appointed by no agency except the court. The stated objections to the method are: *First,* the work of supervision is essentially administrative, not judicial. There is no more reason for having probation administered by the courts than for having prisons or reformatories so administered. *Second,* the judge is not able to handle this administrative work efficiently. He has other duties which interfere with his supervision of probation, and the probation department really becomes an independent administrative body. Consequently there has been a trend toward the other method of appointment and supervision of probation officers. The Los Angeles county probation department, for example, is completely separate from the courts and is under the control of a county board of supervisors. It serves the juvenile courts as well as the adult courts. In the juvenile field, sixteen states have centralized state administration for probation services, while in the adult field, thirty-seven states are so organized.[12]

Probation, like the maintenance of detention institutions and the administration of juvenile courts, is primarily a municipal or county responsibility. Most probation workers argue that administration of probation should be a function of the state, and in states which have a strongly centralized system the probation system has operated most effectively. Many counties cannot support the services of full-time probation officers, and in other counties there are so few criminal cases that employment of a full-time, paid worker is not justified. Since parole is almost always administered on a statewide basis, thirty of the fifty states

---

[10] Hugh Barr and Erica O'Leary, *Trends and Regional Comparisons in Probation,* Home Office Studies in the Causes of Delinquency and the Treatment of Offenders, no. 8 (London: Her Majesty's Stationery Office, 1966), pp. 3-9.

[11] Robert J. Glass, *Review of Trends in Adult Corrections over Thirty Years* (Lansing: Michigan Department of Corrections, 1961), table A-3.

[12] President's Commission, *Task Force Report: Corrections,* p. 36.

combine felony probation and parole services for adults, and thirteen do so wholly or in part for juveniles.

Cooperation between the probation departments in various states also produces uniformity and efficiency. Such cooperation is now secured to some extent on an informal level by the National Council on Crime and Delinquency. In addition, some specific interstate agreements have been made. In 1937, for example, twenty-five states entered into interstate compacts for supervision of probationers and parolees from other states, and by 1952 all states had reciprocal agreements of this kind.[13] Also, there is an agreement, made in 1917, that the probation departments in the principal cities will supervise probationers moving into their cities from other districts. ●

Selection of probationers

In almost all jurisdictions adult probation is granted only after the offender has been found guilty. There must be a conviction of a specific offense. However, a few jurisdictions use a procedure comparable to that of the juvenile courts, since persons merely *charged* with crime are placed on probation. For example, in magistrates' courts of Maryland, the defendant may receive the disposition of "probation before conviction." A similar disposition in lower courts in Massachusetts is termed "case continued without finding." In both instances, if an individual stays out of difficulty for a given period of time and follows a recommended course of action, such as outpatient psychotherapy or attendance at Alcoholics Anonymous, the case is closed.[14] Newman gives examples of similar procedures in the lower courts of Kansas, Michigan, and Wisconsin.[15] This "deferred prosecution" procedure is used extensively with juveniles; it has been used by the federal courts in Brooklyn since 1936 and is sometimes called the "Brooklyn plan."[16] The possession of such powers by the court enables the accused person to maintain certain rights which might be forfeited by a conviction, and it eliminates expensive trials, but these advantages might be completely offset by the denial of the traditional rights to due process of law.

The statutes or rules of court make a presentence report mandatory for certain classes of offenses in about one-quarter of the states. In most states and in the federal system a request for a presentence report is discretionary with the judge, although in some of these states probation may not be granted unless a pre-

---

[13] B. E. Crihfield, "The Interstate Parole and Probation Compact," *Federal Probation*, 17:3-7, June, 1953.

[14] President's Commission on Law Enforcement and Administration of Justice, *Task Force Report: The Courts* (Washington: Government Printing Office, 1967), p. 6.

[15] Donald J. Newman, *Conviction: The Determination of Guilt or Innocence Without Trial* (Boston: Little, Brown, 1966), pp. 160-165.

[16] Conrad P. Printzlien, "Deferred Prosecution for Juvenile Offenders," *Federal Probation*, 12:17-22, March, 1948.

sentence report has been prepared. This investigation is for the purpose of determining the characteristics of the prospective probationer and of the conditions surrounding his crime, so that the judge will have factual information on which to base his decision. Even in states where the report is mandatory, many judges do not wait for an investigation; instead, they base their decisions on the offender's statement about himself, his personal appearance, the social status of his family, the nature of the offense, or the recommendations of persons outside the probation department. These are likely to be decidedly inadequate as a basis for policies, and it is largely because of this inadequacy that probation has been brought into ill repute. Pre-probation investigations are mandatory in Illinois, yet in a two-year period 13 percent of the probations granted to felons in Cook County were granted without proper continuance of court proceedings so that the investigation could be made.[17] One judge granted 43.9 percent of his probations within one day of the time of application, and the proportion granted by other judges without time for a pre-probation investigation ranged from 3.1 to 38.7 percent. Probation was granted to nineteen defendants who were not, by law, eligible for probation.

When investigations are made, they are generally made by regular probation officers. Using an analogy with medicine, these investigations are sometimes referred to as "diagnosis," since they provide the factual basis for later individual or group treatment. As Reckless has said, "An adequate pre-sentence investigation not only indicates whether the defendant is probationable; it also gives clues as to the causes of the criminal behavior, the possible extent to which he may be reformed or rehabilitated, and his need for a constructive probation program."[18] The ideal investigation covers such things as the person's attitude toward the offense, his previous criminal record, his family situation, his neighborhood and other group associations, his educational and work history, his personal habits (particularly in reference to the use of alcohol and drugs), his physical and mental health, and his perspective on life. Such ideal investigations are characteristic of large probation departments in which specialized officers can be assigned to the work, but in smaller departments the investigations are likely to be mere routine interviews with the prospective probationer and his family. Sellin has suggested that specially trained personnel, not probation officers, be employed to conduct the presentence investigations, leaving probation workers time to interact with probationers.[19]

---

[17] Don T. Blackiston, "The Judge, the Defendant, and Criminal Law Administration" (Ph.D. dissertation, University of Chicago, 1952).

[18] Walter C. Reckless, The Crime Problem, 5th ed. (New York: Appleton-Century-Crofts, 1973), p. 469.

[19] Thorsten Sellin, "Adult Probation and the Conditional Sentence," Journal of Criminal Law, Criminology, and Police Science, 49:533-556, March-April, 1959.

Probation departments characteristically have insufficient funds for the employment of adequate manpower. In this situation adequate investigation of each case is, of course, impossible. Probation investigation often is handicapped, also, by the fact that the investigator frequently is regarded as a detective by the offender and the other persons interviewed. This attitude is not without some justification, for in some cases, especially when the prospective probationer has insisted that he is innocent of the crime for which he has been found guilty, the investigation takes on some of the characteristics of a retrial. After such an investigation, supervisory work will be extremely difficult, particularly in small departments where investigation and supervision are performed by the same officer.

The absence of organized and central records is a further detriment to probation investigation. In some communities official records are not available to probation investigators. Juvenile court files frequently cannot be cited in preparation of reports of adult probation investigations. Educational and social service records usually are scattered throughout the community, although in large cities social service records are now centralized. The Los Angeles County Probation Department maintains a confidential central registry of all juveniles handled by the law-enforcement agencies in the county, but the registry cards are destroyed when the child reaches his eighteenth birthday. Where probation is administered on a statewide basis, records ordinarily are maintained in a central state file. The maintenance of centralized records not only aids in the investigation of individual cases, but it makes statistical comparison of certain types of classes of offenders possible as well. Analysis of the data in such files might indicate needs for special supervisory and treatment techniques among some groups.

Probation is used, as explained previously, primarily as a substitute for discharge without supervision and for imprisonment. The principle that should be used in determining whether probation should be substituted for discharge without supervision is: Does this offender need supervision and assistance in adjusting to community conditions, and will he profit by this assistance and supervision? The principle that should be used in determining whether probation should be substituted for imprisonment is essentially the same, but includes also the danger to the community during the period of readjustment. For both groups these questions can be answered best by intensive study of individual cases supplemented by analysis of the rates of probation violation by offenders in the past. In 1970, California superior court judges reversed the recommendations of probation officers in about 4 percent of the cases in which probation was recommended and in about 43 percent of the cases in which it was not recommended.[20] ●

---

[20] *Crime and Delinquency in California, 1970*, p. 14.

The terms of probation

The terms of probation are generally fixed jointly by the legislature, the court, and the probation department or staff. The following are generally included: observance of all laws, good habits, keeping good company, regular reports as required, regular work or school attendance, payment of fines or reparation, abstinence from the use of alcohol and drugs, avoidance of unnecessary debts.[21] Often the probationer may not marry, may not become divorced, or may not change his residence without permission of the probation department. Sometimes the probationer is required to live in a specified place. It may be necessary to require him to live at home, not to live at home, or to live in some philanthropic institution. He may be required to undergo specific medical or psychiatric treatment. In some states these terms must be communicated to the probationer in writing in order that there may be no misunderstanding.

Payment of restitution, fines, or costs is frequently imposed not as a sentence, but as a condition for being placed on probation. Of the persons granted probation by California superior courts in 1967, about 58 percent received a fine, an order to pay restitution, or both. Though restitution or reparation is a valuable requirement in many cases, two objections have been made regarding the method by which this is enforced. *First,* probationers may be required to pay so much that their dependents suffer seriously. In Los Angeles County, the probation department investigates all pertinent claims against the offender and regulates payments according to his ability to pay. *Second,* this frequently interferes with other work of the probation department and makes it primarily a collecting agency. Probation officers object to acting as collecting agents, principally on the ground that the assumption of such duties destroys the confidential relationship necessary to constructive casework. Men who have been imprisoned after failing to make restitution payments, thus violating the conditions of their probation, often believe they are being punished not for crime but for failure to pay their debts.

The maximum probationary period is generally fixed by law and is the same as the maximum prison sentence for the offense. Within that limit the court may fix the period of probation and, after fixing it once, may subsequently alter it. In many states the average period of probation for all offenders is less than one year. If treatment or rehabilitation is the actual objective of probation, it is logical to have absolutely indeterminate probation, with no fixed maximum. Some individuals can get along satisfactorily in the community as long as they have the supervision and guidance of a probation officer, but return to crime if that assistance is withdrawn too soon.

About 30,000 probation revocation hearings are held in the United States each year. The probation officer has the duty of in-

---

[21] See Judah Best and Paul Birzon, "Conditions of Probation," *Georgetown Law Journal,* 51:809-836, Summer, 1963.

forming the court if the probationer does not maintain the conditions imposed upon him. At a hearing, the court then either warns the probationer or orders execution of the sentence for the original offense, in which case the time served on probation ordinarily is not counted as part of the prison term. In 1967 the United States Supreme Court ruled that persons on probation have a right to counsel in proceedings to revoke their probation or to reimpose a suspended sentence.[22] Some probationers arrested for a new crime merely have their probation revoked, but others are tried for the new offense. If the probationer is convicted, he may again apply for probation. If a prison term is ordered, the sentence which was suspended for purposes of probation may be ignored, or it may be made to run either concurrently or consecutively with the new sentence. If the probationer maintains the conditions imposed upon him, discharge from probation may, depending on the jurisdiction, come automatically at the end of the probationary period, be ordered by the court before or at the end of the period, or be ordered by the probation officer without court action. •

After he has been granted probationary status by the court, the probationer is assigned to a specified probation officer who administers the probation program. In many instances this is the same officer that made the original probation investigation for the court.

Supervision and guidance of probationers

Assignment

Three systems of probation assignments are used: by districts; by sex, race, or religion; and by problems. The first method, which is used most frequently, gives to one officer all probationers living in a particular district. The second method makes assignments of male probationers to male officers, female probationers to female officers, and similarly for race and religion.[23] The specialization of probation work by problems is possible only in the larger urban probation departments.

Fifty probationers are now generally given as the recommended number to be assigned to one officer, provided he has a densely populated territory and can give his entire time to supervision and guidance. In practice, most probation officers have several times that number of probationers under supervision; in some departments the average case load is as high as four hundred. When the case load is more than about fifty, intensive work with each probationer is impossible. This is in contradiction to the principle of probation, since release without supervision and guidance is mere suspension of sentence. According to probation principles, if offenders do not need supervision and guidance, they should not be placed on probation; if they do need super-

---

[22] *Mempa v. Rhay*, 389 U.S. 128 (1967).

[23] See Don J. Hager, "Race, Nationality, and Religion — Their Relationship to Appointment Policies and Casework," *National Probation and Parole Association Journal*, 3:129-141, April, 1957.

vision and guidance, the number assigned to one officer should be restricted so that his work will be effective.

Effectiveness of supervision and guidance is also limited by the training of the officers to whom the probationer is assigned. As indicated, in some areas officers are unpaid and untrained volunteers, and considerable experience with such officers has resulted in the almost unanimous conclusion that paid workers are essential. But even many of the paid probation officers are untrained, inefficient, and ineffective. This is due largely to the fact that few persons have been trained for the work; the importance of skill is not realized; salaries are small, and the positions are sometimes used as rewards for political service. Few trained probation officers are found outside of large cities, and even in these cities many of the officers have had no training. Among 720 California probation officers studied in 1956 (out of a total of 976 working in the state), 9 percent of those employed in counties with populations over 100,000 and 65 percent of those working in smaller counties had less than three years of college.[24] A survey of 2000 probation officers in 405 courts in the United States indicated that 86 percent had bachelor's degrees; in cities of 500,000 or over, 92 percent had college degrees, but in cities with less than 50,000 population only 55 percent were college-trained.[25] A 1966 survey of juvenile probation officers indicated that in 22 percent of 235 counties studied no college training was required; in 24 counties the probation officer needed no education at all. Adult probation officers in 91 out of 250 counties surveyed (37 percent) needed no college training, and those in 39 counties needed no education.[26] In the Netherlands, and in other European countries, probationers are supervised by a combination of voluntary workers and well-trained full-time probation officers, apparently with great success.[27]

Diagnosis   Ideally, as we indicated previously, experts would always make the diagnosis before the offender is admitted to probation. This procedure is necessary, first, in order to determine whether he should be placed on probation, and, second, in order to determine the policies that should be used by the supervising officer. Though the method of making such diagnoses has not been standardized, and the importance of diagnoses has not been generally realized, it is clear that probation work would be greatly improved if it could be based on precise diagnosis.[28] Until probation has such a basis, it can only be surveillance and kindhearted assistance.

---

[24] Special Study Commission, *Probation in California*, p. 123.

[25] Gladys M. Krueger, *Survey of Probation Officers, 1959*, Children's Bureau Report No. 15 (Washington: Government Printing Office, 1960).

[26] National Council on Crime and Delinquency, "Correction in the United States," pp. 137, 174.

[27] N. Muller, *Work of Rehabilitation in the Netherlands* (The Hague: National Bureau voor Reclassering, 1954).

[28] See Gilbert Geis and Fred W. Woodson, "Matching Probation Officer and Delinquent," *National Probation and Parole Association Journal*, 2:58-62, January, 1956.

Contacts between the probation officer and the probationer are
generally made either in the office of the probation officer or the
home of the probationer. Home visits are more effective because
they enable the probation officer to come into contact with this
most important part of the offender's environment, thus making
possible a better understanding of the offender. Also, since the
attitudes of the probationer's family and other intimate associates
are important in determining his criminality or noncriminality,
contacts with these associates are important in any effort to
modify the offender's criminal attitudes. Yet the number of home
visits per month and the number of hours per visit often are so
small as to be insignificant.

**Routine
reports**

Most probationers are required by court order to report at
regular intervals to the probation officer in his office or some
other place selected by him. Sometimes these reports are made
once a week, sometimes once a month; at one time in Detroit
the probationers who were not working were required to report
daily. The procedure in making these reports varies widely.
In some places the officer merely checks a card which the probationer hands through a window to him. In slightly less perfunctory systems the officer questions the probationer about his work,
companions, recreations, habits, and other things; he gives advice
on many topics—economic, family, legal, habits, reading, self-
improvement, etc. The probationers are frequently required to
bring written reports, such as school reports, reports from
employers, receipts for payment toward support of the family
or for restitution or reparation. Since "supervision" in such
systems is practically nonexistent, it has been suggested that the
system not be called "probation" and that, instead, it be called
what it is, the suspended sentence:

It would be easy to say that we need more and highly trained probation officers, but so long as probation is so conceived that it can be
used as a cover for the kind of clerical and fiscal tasks that probation
officers for adults do in Pennsylvania, there is need for more clerks
rather than for more professional staff. Instead of urging the extension
of probation, we should urge that it be more restrictively used, thereby
reserving it for carefully selected offenders, giving it the status it
should have in accordance with the official definitions, and thus creating the absolute necessity of employing professionally trained people
to administer it. . . . Legislation clearly defining the use of the suspended sentence by the courts could remove from the roster of probationers a considerable percentage of those now there, especially in
states where a suspended sentence now can be granted only when a
probation order is issued, thus forcing the courts in such states to foist
on the probation officers individuals whom they merely wanted to give
a scare—or a kindly favor.[29]

The word *treatment* here refers to the efforts of the probation
officer to guide and assist the probationer. The word is unsatisfactory, for most of the efforts are educational, and we do not
ordinarily think of education as "treatment." But the guidance
and casework efforts of the probation officer do constitute a part

Treatment

---

[29] Sellin, "Adult Probation and the Conditional Sentence," p. 555.

of the general treatment reaction to crime, although they are ordinarily made within the authoritarian frame of reference required by the court. The probationer is both "supervised" (i.e., required to live up to the terms of the probation contract) and guided, assisted, or led toward noncriminality.[30] It is to the latter activities that the word *treatment* is applied. Among probation workers there is a good deal of controversy about whether effective treatment can be executed in the authoritarian setting of probation. One group contends that treatment cannot be forced upon a person, and that, consequently, attempts to treat probationers in the authoritarian setting will usually be unsuccessful. Another group holds that the authoritarian setting is valuable in treatment, or, at least, that the authoritarian frame of reference and the treatment frame of reference can be dovetailed. The conflict between the punitive and treatment reactions to crime and criminality has not been resolved, even in probation work.

The objective in probation work is to change the attitudes of the probationers. A scientific technique for the modification of attitudes has yet to be stated. Instead of descriptions of techniques we find such statements as "by gaining the confidence and friendship of the young man," "through friendly admonition and encouragement," "by stimulating the probationer's self-respect, ambition, and thrift," and "by relieving emotional tensions." It is necessary to know how confidence is secured, or how ambition is stimulated, or how tensions are reduced, and also to know how those processes produce reformation.

In the absence of specific techniques for the modification of attitudes, the general principle which is involved may be recalled. The attitudes of the individual are a product of social interactions. The interactions that are of the greatest importance in determining attitudes are those that are frequent and intimate, as in the family, the play group, and the neighborhood. The procedure for modifying attitudes consists essentially in changing the person's group relations. For this purpose it is necessary either to remove the probationer from the web of his former relations or to insert new elements into that web of relations. While it is easier to remove the probationer from his situation, the modification of the situation is more profitable in the long run.

If it be true that behavior is determined largely in local, personal groups, and that a probation officer can accomplish little by his own direct efforts, the policy of probation must be implemented principally by organization of the local community for helping the delinquent. Efforts of this type have been made in the Chicago Area Projects, where for almost forty years local communities have been organized for probation work as well as

---

[30] See Dale G. Hardman, "The Function of the Probation Officer," *Federal Probation*, 24:3-10, September, 1960; and Lewis Diana, "What is Probation?" *Journal of Criminal Law, Criminology, and Police Science*, 51:189-208, July-August, 1960.

for other programs for the reduction of delinquency.[31] Probation officers are selected, so far as practicable, from the local community. This selection is based on the belief that such officers will be culturally homogeneous with the community and therefore more effective than officers imported from other groups both in influencing the delinquent who is on probation and in inducing other residents of the community to participate in programs for the rehabilitation of the probationer. These other residents give information to the probation officer regarding the behavior of the probationer, which they would not give under any circumstances to an "alien" probation officer. This illustrates the tendency of the community to identify itself with the probation program. While little objective evidence of the success of the area projects in this respect is available, the principle seems to be correct.[32]

Probation officers make many efforts to render material assistance to probationers, in the form of jobs, relief, vocational guidance. Some probation departments maintain regular employment agencies. In many states the probation officers, especially in earlier years, administered mothers' pensions and welfare payments. Such duplication of the work of other community agencies does not appear to be advantageous, and probation departments now generally refer their probationers to these other agencies.

As indicated previously, some judges and some probation officers contend that the achievements of probation departments rest basically on fear of punishment. Fear of imprisonment, and fear of the probation officer because he has the power to recommend imprisonment, is considered the essential factor in rehabilitation. Of course, some fear of the probation officer and of imprisonment is inevitable in the current legal system. But the logic of this argument leads to universal imprisonment of offenders; the logic of probation is that contacts and assimilation in normal groups are most important in modifying behavior; fear places social distance between probationer and probation officer and retards contact and assimilation. However, terror unquestionably has some value in deterring persons from violations of law and the question is whether it cannot be replaced generally by methods which are more effective than terror, and, specifically, whether it is not inconsistent with the principles of probation work and does not interfere with the efficiency of probation work.

The psychiatric school of criminology has a conception that the primary value to be attained in "treatment" is insight by the probationer into the reasons for his delinquent behavior. This school argues that a probationer who attains this insight will be unlikely to violate the law in the future. The probation officer can understand the delinquent only by intensive interviews which probe

---

[31] See Fred A. Romano, "Organizing a Community for Delinquency Prevention," *National Probation Association Yearbook, 1940*, pp. 1-12.

[32] See Donald R. Cressey, "Social Psychological Foundations for Using Criminals in the Rehabilitation of Criminals," *Journal of Research in Crime and Delinquency*, 2:49-59, July, 1965.

the basic motivations of the delinquent, and these interviews at the same time reveal the delinquent to himself. A further value of these interviews, according to this school of thought, is that the probationer in the interviews will develop an identification with the probation officer, and through this identification will tend to behave as the probation officer behaves. Later, the probation worker breaks up this feeling of identification so the probationer can make independent decisions. Although this conception of treatment is currently very popular in the United States, the value of the techniques has not been demonstrated, and the validity of the theories is open to question. The principal reason for skepticism is that the procedure is based on the mistaken assumption that delinquency and criminality can be treated in an office or a clinic just as an infectious disease can be. •

Success and failure on probation

Probation departments generally report that about 75 percent of their probationers succeed on probation. However, the percentage varies a great deal from department to department.

The 11,638 defendants granted probation by the California superior courts in 1956-1958 were followed until December 31, 1963. At that cutoff date, 62 percent had no violations; 7 percent had one violation; 2 percent had two or more violations; and for 29 percent probation had been revoked and not reinstated. The probationers with no violations were considered successes; those whose probation was revoked were considered failures; and those with one or more violations were viewed as neither successes nor failures. One county revoked the probation of about 40 percent of its probationers, and the county at the other extreme revoked in 19 percent of its cases. The highest revocation rates were for persons convicted of forgery and bad checks (46 percent) and automobile theft (41 percent); the lowest revocation rates were for manslaughter (4 percent) and bookmaking (8 percent).[33]

The 75 percent general figure is a rough average of the reports of many departments in many different years.[34] Even in this

---

[33] *Delinquency and Probation in California, 1963* (Sacramento: Department of Justice, 1964), pp. 209-223. See also George F. Davis, "A Study of Adult Probation Violation Rates by Means of the Cohort Approach," *Journal of Criminal Law, Criminology, and Police Science*, 55:70-84, March, 1964; and Friedrich Schaffstein, "Research into the Effectiveness of Probation Results," chap. in Günther Kaiser and Thomas Würtenberger, eds., *Criminological Research Trends in Western Germany* (Berlin: Springer-Verlag, 1972), pp. 74-88.

[34] Ralph W. England, Jr., "What is Responsible for Satisfactory Probation and Post-Probation Outcome?" *Journal of Criminal Law, Criminology, and Police Science*, 47:667-676, March-April, 1957.

sense it is inadequate in at least three respects. *First*, the number reported to be failures is incomplete because the probation officer is not in sufficiently close contact with his probationers to know how many of them commit crimes and also because the identification records of police departments are so restricted that they do not adequately supplement the knowledge of the probation officer. These inadequacies in the official records are being corrected in some jurisdictions.[35] The departments which have the reputation of doing the best probation work show the smallest proportion of successes, probably because they have more complete information regarding the behavior of their probationers than do the departments which are doing their work in a less satisfactory manner.

Second, the statistics of probation departments are confined to behavior during the period of probation and do not include the behavior subsequent to release from probation. Several studies have been made for the purpose of supplying this information. Studies of federal probationers in Alabama have indicated that during a period of from 5.5 to 11.5 years after successful completion of probation 83.6 percent had not been convicted of any crime: 14.3 percent had been convicted of misdemeanors; and 2.0 percent had been convicted of felonies.[36] In another federal district, 82.3 percent of 500 probationers were convicted of no crimes in periods from six to twelve years after completing probation.[37] These studies seem to indicate that the number of failures is not greatly increased after the end of the probation period. However, probationers and former probationers do not avoid arrest as readily as they avoid conviction. In 1970 the FBI studied the fingerprint records of 16,332 offenders who had been released in 1965. Thirty-seven percent of those released on probation with a fine and 56 percent of those released on suspended sentence or probation had been arrested for some offense by December 31, 1969. Eighty percent of the automobile thieves, 76 percent of the burglars, and 69 percent of the narcotics offenders released on probation in 1965 had been arrested.[38]

Third, the "success" of probation in individual cases logically should be determined by comparing it with the success of alternative methods of dealing with offenders. Since probation is generally a substitute either for release without supervision or

[35] Robert H. Vasoli, "Some Reflections on Measuring Probation Outcome," *Federal Probation*, 31:24-32, September, 1967.
[36] Morris G. Caldwell, "Review of a New Type of Probation Study Made in Alabama," *Federal Probation*, 15:3-11, June, 1951.
[37] Ralph W. England, Jr., "A Study of Postprobation Recidivism Among 500 Federal Offenders," *Federal Probation*, 19:10-16, September, 1955.
[38] Federal Bureau of Investigation, *Uniform Crime Reports, 1970* (Washington: Government Printing Office, 1971), pp. 37-42.

for imprisonment, efforts should be made to compare the subsequent behavior of probationers with the subsequent behavior of those released without supervision and those committed to institutions. Such comparison is extremely difficult, however, since probationers generally are selected from the criminal population as those least likely to become recidivists. It is probably for this reason that few comparisons have been made.[41] The FBI study indicated that 83 percent of the automobile thieves, 80 percent of the burglars, and 59 percent of the narcotics offenders released at the expiration of their sentences in penal institutions in 1963 had been arrested by the end of 1967. Conclusions regarding the value of probation are sometimes erroneously based on the number of prison or reformatory inmates who are ex-probationers. Such statistics are inadequate, for they show nothing regarding the number of probationers who do not appear subsequently in institutions.

Almost everyone agrees that probation should be used to some extent. The important question, therefore, is not whether probation in general is a success or failure, but what type of offenders succeed on probation and under what conditions probationers succeed. A few intensive studies contain organized information on this point.[42] These studies agree in the conclusion that the highest rates of violation of probation are found among the probationers who had previous criminal records, previous records of irregular work, low economic status, low occupational level, previous institutional placement, residence in deteriorated or commercial areas, families with records of crime or vice, immoral associates, great mobility in residences, and few or irregular contacts with schools or churches.

Reiss, for example, found that among the probationers from the Chicago juvenile courts, 44.8 percent of those who resided in areas with the highest delinquency rates violated probation, as compared with 30.7 percent of those who resided in the areas of lowest delinquency rates. Similarly, Glaser and Hangren found that probation was violated by 80 percent of thirty cases whose

---

[39] For an excellent example of this kind of comparison, see Dean V. Babst and John W. Mannering, "Probation Versus Imprisonment," *Journal of Research in Crime and Delinquency,* 2:61-69, July, 1965.

[40] Massachusetts Commission on Probation, *Report on an Inquiry into the Permanent Results of Probation,* Massachusetts Senate Document 431 (Boston: State Printing Office, 1924); E. D. Monachesi, *Prediction Factors in Probation* (Hanover: Sociological Press, 1932); J. L. Gillin, "Predicting Outcomes of Adult Probation in Wisconsin," *American Sociological Review,* 15:550-553, August, 1950; Albert J. Reiss, Jr., "Delinquency as the Failure of Personal and Social Controls," *American Sociological Review,* 16:196-207, April, 1951; idem, "The Accuracy, Efficiency, and Validity of a Prediction Instrument," *American Journal of Sociology,* 56:552-561, May, 1951; Daniel Glaser and Richard F. Hangren, "Predicting the Adjustment of Federal Probationers," *National Probation and Parole Association Journal,* 4:258-267, July, 1958; and Judson R. Landis, James D. Mercer, and Carole E. Wolff, "Success and Failure of Adult Probationers in California," *Journal of Research in Crime and Delinquency,* 6:34-40, January, 1969.

leisure time was spent predominantly in association with persons describable as "criminogenic," or in opposition to "respectable" moral standards, while it was violated by only 7 percent of sixty-nine offenders whose recreational activities were describable as taking place in groups predominantly oriented toward socially approved patterns of behavior. These studies make specific the general proposition that excessive intimate association with criminal behavior patterns characterizes second offenders as well as first offenders.

When data on offenders and nonoffenders are organized in statistical form, courts have a basis for intelligent selection of offenders to be placed on probation, and probation officers have a fund of information on which to base treatment policies.[41] Prediction studies utilizing such statistical data have been carried somewhat further in regard to parole than in regard to probation, and prediction instruments are used by several parole boards. The statistical information on probation is not adequate at present from the point of view of reliability, classifications, or significance, but these defects can be corrected. ●

The advocates of probation do not insist that all offenders should be placed on probation, but rather that certain types of offenders will get along better and do less injury to society if they are placed on probation than if they are imprisoned or are dismissed without supervision. The probation policy enables these offenders to remain in the general society, which ordinarily is better than prison as a character-developing institution, and at the same time to receive assistance in modifying the conditions of life which produced their delinquency or criminality.

Appraisal of probation

Probation, furthermore, has the advantage that the probationer, being at liberty, has a better opportunity to make payments toward the support of his family or toward reparation or restitution. In 1956, 84,100 probationers in California paid, through the probation officers, $2,747,000 toward the support of their families, and $902,000 in reparation and restitution.[42] Also, probation, as now operated, is very much cheaper than imprisonment. In New York, the current cost of imprisonment is eighteen times as high as probation per offender dealt with under each system, and in Massachusetts ten times as much. The President's Crime Commission found that the average state spends about $3,400 a year to keep a youth in a state training school. This figure does not include capital costs. The average cost of probation for each youth is about one-tenth of that amount. The national average per capita cost for institutionalization of adult felons is about $1,900; for probation services to adults it is about $140.[43] Proba-

---

[41] Robert H. Fosen and Jay Campbell, Jr., "Common Sense and Correctional Science," *Journal of Research in Crime and Delinquency*, 3:73-81, July, 1966.

[42] Special Study Commission, *Probation in California*, p. 117.

[43] President's Commission, *Task Force Report: Corrections*, p. 28.

tion would cost more if it were properly administered. However, a study in Saginaw County, Michigan, indicated that reducing case loads and improving the quality of probation services actually reduces the total cost of correctional programs.[44]

Certain objections have been raised against probation, of which the most important are the following: (a) probation decreases the average penalty for crime and therefore tends to increase crime; (b) probation replaces the offender in the environment which produced him and is not likely to modify his behavior; (c) probation does not satisfy the desire for revenge and therefore tends to eliminate the incentive for prosecution.

The first objection, as has been shown previously, has little basis in fact. Extensive use of probation does not in itself result in an immense increase of serious crimes. The argument that probation does not alter the environment of the offender is a sound argument and is presented primarily by those who insist that casework must be expanded to include the family, other intimate groups, and larger community if it is to be effective. It is not an argument against probation, but against the specific methods of probationary work. However, a study of California counties indicated that there is no correlation between the percentage of convicted superior-court defendants placed on probation and the rate of failure among these probationers.[45] The recent California "probation subsidy" program also suggests that probation can safely be used for more cases in most counties, even if the probationers are placed in the environment which produced them. Under that program, the state pays counties a fixed sum for retaining in the community on probation felons who otherwise would be committed to state prison.[46]

The last of the objections requires additional comment. The basic idea is that as probation increases, the number of injured persons who will be willing to go to the trouble of prosecuting offenders will decrease, because they will secure so little satisfaction from it. But the amount of injury that must be inflicted in order to satisfy any desire for revenge is variable; a few centuries ago nothing short of the death of the offender would satisfy; at present the desired injury is much less, and it seems to be decreasing. Further, it is quite fallacious to assume that at present the desire for revenge is the only or most important reason for

[44] Alfred C. Ball, The Saginaw Probation Demonstration Project (East Lansing, Mich.: Michigan Crime and Delinquency Council, 1963), pp. 2-3.

[45] Special Study Commission, Probation in California, pp. 93-94.

[46] Robert L. Smith, A Quiet Revolution: Probation Subsidy (Washington: U.S. Department of Health, Education and Welfare, 1971). See also Community Based Correctional Programs: Models and Practices (Rockville, Maryland: National Institute of Mental Health, 1971).

prosecution. Despite the fact that a large proportion of criminal cases involves no particular injured party, if court procedures were speeded up and organized more efficiently and the technicalities reduced, the number of persons, whether motivated by revenge or something else, who would be willing to appear in criminal trials probably would be greatly increased. The desire for restitution also is a general motive, alternative to revenge, for prosecution. Resort to civil courts will not generally serve the purpose of the victim. For, though the judgment of the court may be more certain if the process is civil, most of the offenders are impecunious, and the judgment is worthless to the victim. The criminal court, with its combination of probation and restitution, could be a more effective means of securing financial compensation for injury than the civil court in a large proportion of cases. ●

Suggested readings

ANCEL, MARC. *Suspended Sentence.* London: Heinemann, 1971.

BATES, SANFORD. "The Establishment and Early Years of the Federal Probation System." *Federal Probation,* 14:16-21, June, 1950.

COHN, YONA. "Criteria for the Probation Officer's Recommendations to the Juvenile Court Judge." *Crime and Delinquency,* 9:262-275, July, 1963.

CRESSEY, DONALD R. "Professional Correctional Work and Professional Work in Correction." *National Probation and Parole Association Journal,* 5:1-15, January, 1959.

DAVIS, GEORGE F. "A Study of Adult Probation Violation Rates by Means of the Cohort Approach." *Journal of Criminal Law, Criminology, and Police Science,* 55:70-84, March, 1964.

DICERBO, EUGENE C. "When Should Probation Be Revoked?" *Federal Probation,* 30:11-17, June, 1966.

EMPEY, LAMAR T. *Alternatives to Incarceration.* Washington: Government Printing Office, 1967.

GRINNELL, FRANK W. "The Common Law History of Probation." *Journal of Criminal Law and Criminology,* 32:15-34, May-June, 1941.

HOLTZOFF, ALEXANDER. "The Power of Probation and Parole Officers to Search and Seize." *Federal Probation,* 31:3-7, December, 1967.

LANDIS, JUDSON R., JAMES D. MERCER, & CAROLE E. WOLFF. "Success and Failure of Adult Probationers in California." *Journal of Research in Crime and Delinquency,* 6:34-40, January, 1969.

MEYER, CHARLES H. Z. "A Half Century of Probation and Parole." *Journal of Criminal Law, Criminology, and Police Science,* 42:707-728, March-April, 1952.

OHLIN, LLOYD E., HERMAN PIVEN, & DONNELL M. PAPPENFORT. "Major Dilemmas of the Social Worker in Probation and Parole." *National Probation and Parole Association Journal,* 2:211-225, July, 1956.

SCARPITTI, FRANK R., & RICHARD M. STEPHENSON. "A Study of Probation Effectiveness." *Journal of Criminal Law, Criminology, and Police Science,* 59:361-369, June, 1968.

SCHAFER, STEPHEN. *Restitution to Victims of Crime.* London: Stevens and Sons, 1960.

TIMASHEFF, N. S. *One Hundred Years of Probation.* New York: Fordham University Press, 1941.

YOUNG, PAULINE V. *Social Treatment in Probation and Delinquency.* 2d ed. New York: McGraw-Hill, 1952.

Development of treatment in American prisons

22

We have considered previously the development of imprisonment until it became an established and generally used policy in England about the beginning of the nineteenth century. The present chapter continues this discussion with reference to the development of prisons in the United States, especially after the beginning of the nineteenth century. ●

Early American prisons

Jails and houses of correction were established in the American colonies soon after settlement. The jail was designed originally for the detention of persons awaiting trial. It soon came to be used as a place of punishment after conviction. As was the case in England, this change accompanied increasing opposition to the use of corporal and capital punishments, and it was thus a modification of the prevailing system for implementing the punitive societal reaction to lawbreaking. Convicted drunkards and vagrants, especially, were confined in these institutions. The house of correction began as an institution for vagrants, but before long was not different except in name from many of the jails. The modification in the punitive reaction was made only gradually. For example, the number of persons confined either in jails or workhouses after conviction was small throughout the eighteenth century, and in New York State it was not until 1788 that a general law was passed for the use of jails or workhouses as places of punishment. Previously, commitments to those institutions were made only by a special law in each case.[1]

By present-day standards, the conditions in these jails and houses of correction were horrible. The prisoners spent their time in association, without labor, depending upon charity for their maintenance. There was no attempt to treat the inmates; even religious services were absent. Drunkenness and vice generally prevailed, as had been customary in England. The following description of the Walnut Street (county) Jail in Philadelphia at the end of the Revolutionary War could be duplicated with regard to many other institutions of the time:

> It is represented as a scene of promiscuous and unrestricted intercourse, and universal riot and debauchery. There was no labor, no separation of those accused, but yet untried, nor even of those confined for debt only, from convicts sentenced for the foulest crimes; no separation of color, age or sex, by day or by night; the prisoners lying promiscuously on the floor, most of them without anything like bed or bedding. As soon as the sexes were placed in different wings, which was the first reform made in the prison, of thirty or forty women then confined there, all but four or five immediately left it; it having been a common practice, it is said, for women to cause themselves to be arrested for fictitious debts, that they might share in the orgies of the place. Intoxicating liquors abounded, and indeed were freely sold at a bar kept by one of the officers of the prison. Intercourse between the convicts and persons without was hardly restricted. Prisoners tried and acquitted were still detained till they should pay jail fees to the keeper; and the custom of garnish was established and unquestioned; that is, the custom of stripping every newcomer of his outer clothing, to be sold for liquor, unless redeemed by the payment of a sum of money to be applied to the same object. It need hardly be added, that there was no attempt to give any kind of instruction, and no religious service whatsoever.[2]

The Quakers of Philadelphia made decided efforts to change these conditions. In 1776 Richard Wistar at his own expense provided soup for some of the prisoners in the county jail, when it became known that some of them had died of starvation. Others

---

[1] P. Klein, *Prison Methods in New York State* (New York: Columbia University Press, 1920), pp. 25-26. See also E. W. Capen, *The Historical Development of the Poor Law of Connecticut* (New York: Columbia University Press, 1905).

[2] F. C. Gray, *Prison Discipline in America* (London: J. Murray, 1848); re-issued, with an Introduction by Donald R. Cressey (Montclair, N.J.: Patterson Smith, 1973); pp. 15-16. It has been reported that when the first attempt was made to preach to the prisoners in this Walnut Street Jail, the prison authorities opposed it for fear of an outbreak by the prisoners, but finally agreed on condition that the preacher leave all his valuables outside and that a loaded cannon be placed facing the prisoners, with a man standing ready with a lighted fuse to touch it off. It seems probable that this was more a device of the warden to frighten the preacher rather than the prisoners. J. Thomas Scharf and Thompson Westcott, *History of Philadelphia, 1609-1884* (Philadelphia: L. H. Everts, 1884), 1:444-445, note.

became interested in his efforts, and in that year the Philadelphia Society for Alleviating Distressed Prisoners was formed. Its activities were stopped by the war. It was revived in 1787 with the name Philadelphia Society for Alleviating the Miseries of Public Prisons. About half of its members were Quakers. It had the primary purpose of relieving the physical suffering of prisoners, but soon attempted, in addition, to modify the punitive reaction, largely by advocating reduction of the number of capital penalties and substitution of imprisonment in solitary confinement for the death penalty. ●

Development of the state prison

During the colonial period no institutions similar to the present state prison were established until, in 1773, Connecticut purchased an old mine near Simsbury and turned it into a prison. This was used by the state as a prison until 1827. The prisoners were fastened during the night by heavy chains attached to their necks at one end and the heavy beams above them at the other; in addition heavy iron bars were fixed to their feet. In 1785 Massachusetts provided that persons sentenced to solitary confinement and hard labor should serve the sentence in Castle Island, a military post in Boston harbor, instead of in the county jails and houses of correction, most of which were insecure. Massachusetts authorized a new state prison in 1803. The movement spread rapidly during the last part of the eighteenth and the first part of the nineteenth century. New York erected a state prison in 1796, New Jersey in 1798, Virginia in 1800, Vermont in 1808, Maryland in 1812, New Hampshire in 1812, and Ohio in 1816. The following inscription, placed over the door of the New Jersey state prison, indicates the punitive philosophy which prevailed in such institutions: "Labor, silence, penitence. 1797. That those who are feared for their crimes may learn to fear the laws and be useful. *Hic labor, hoc opus.*"

The immediate motive for the erection of state prisons was not humanitarian concern for prisoners' welfare. Instead, the motive was to obtain greater security for persons sentenced to long terms of imprisonment. The number of prisoners with long sentences was increasing because of the development of opposition to the death penalty. Zephaniah Swift stated that Connecticut authorized a state prison because of opposition to the death penalty and because long-term imprisonment was the only available substitute for the death penalty.[3] This motive stands out more clearly in Pennsylvania than in any other state. The constitution of that state in 1776 directed that imprisonment at hard, punitive labor be substituted for capital punishment. Immediately after the war, under the direction of Benjamin Rush, Benjamin

---

[3] *A System of the Laws of the State of Connecticut* (Windham: Byrne, for the author, 1796), 2:295; L. N. Robinson, *Penology in the United States* (Philadelphia: Winston, 1921), p. 69.

Franklin, William Bradford, Caleb Lownes, and others, a plan
was prepared, which was made law in 1786 and amended several
times during the next decade. By these laws, capital punishment
was abolished for all crimes except murder; corporal punishment
was abolished, and fines and imprisonments were the only penalties left. It was directed that imprisonment should be "with
hard labor, public and disgracefully imposed." At first this
resulted in gang labor on the streets with the prisoners restrained
by ball and chain, dressed in a distinctive garb, and with heads
shaved. They were soon returned to the prison because street
labor was unsatisfactory. At this time, the state had no prison
of its own and therefore made an arrangement that the state
prisoners be kept in the county jails; a part of the expenses of
these institutions was paid from state funds. An unsuccessful
attempt was made in 1803 to secure an institution exclusively
for state prisoners, but it was not until 1818 that the effort
succeeded.

In addition to this desire to obtain more secure places of confinement for long-term prisoners, the hope that these prisoners,
because they were confined for long periods, might be able to
pay the expenses of the institution by their labor was instrumental in the development of the state prison. Doubtless, also,
labor was introduced because imprisonment was not believed
to be sufficient punishment in itself. ●

About the time the state became interested in the maintenance
of prisons of its own, there appeared a new conception of prison
discipline, which resulted in the designation of these institutions
as penitentiaries. The word *penitentiary* had a significance at that
time which it has generally lost at the present, viz., an institution
not for retribution but for producing penitence or penitentiary
reformation. As indicated earlier, the medieval prisons under
the control of the church had this ideal, and the same purpose
was reflected in the law of England passed in 1778 authorizing
a penitentiary. The purpose of this institution was stated by the
law to be: "By sobriety, cleanliness, and medical assistance, by
a regular series of labour, by solitary confinement during the
intervals of work, and by due religious instruction to preserve
and amend the health of the unhappy offenders, to inure them
to habits of industry, to guard them from pernicious company,
to accustom them to serious reflection and to teach them both
the principles and practice of every Christian and moral duty."

This law was framed by Blackstone, Eden, and Howard. Howard
stated: "The term penitentiary clearly shows that Parliament had
chiefly in view the reformation and amendment of those to be
committed to such places of confinement."

This institution was not erected, but the law incorporated the
idea that prisoners should be "amended" and "inured" by constructive action, and it undoubtedly influenced the Quakers of

**The
penitentiary**

Pennsylvania. They developed not only a state prison, but also a new conception of prison discipline which made their institution, and others modeled on it, penitentiaries. These innovators looked upon imprisonment as in itself a sufficiently severe penalty, and they insisted that the prisoner should be assisted in his effort to become rehabilitated. This notion, which is indicative of the rise in popularity of a treatment reaction to crime, was in opposition to the opinion of many persons of the time. Judge Walworth, in declaring whipping in prison a proper punishment, stated in 1826:

> That confinement with labor merely had no terrors for the guilty; that the labor which the human body was capable of performing without endangering its health was but little more than many of the virtuous laboring class of the community daily and voluntarily perform, for the support and maintenance of their families; that to produce reformation in the guilty or to restrain the vicious from the perpetration of crime by the terrors of punishment, it was absolutely necessary that the convict should feel his degraded situation . . .; that the system of discipline adopted by the inspectors under the sanction of the laws was well calculated to have the desired effect of reforming the less vicious offenders and of deterring others from the commission of crime . . .; that it was, however, through terror of bodily suffering alone that the proper effect upon the mind of the convict was produced.[4] ●

The Pennsylvania system

The prison leaders in Pennsylvania contended that association of all types of criminals in prisons is disastrous. They suggested, as had been suggested frequently for several centuries, that prisoners should be kept in solitary confinement. Arrangements for this were made in the Walnut Street Jail, in which the state prisoners were confined. Solitary confinement, it was contended, not only prevented the disastrous association of criminals, but also had the positive virtue of forcing the prisoners to reflect on their crimes, and therefore of producing reformation. During a part of the history of the system of solitary confinement, the prisoners were not permitted to work at anything, and when they were permitted to work, the work was made subordinate to reflection. It was realized that solitude would be injurious if too long continued, and provision was therefore made for association with the following official visitors: the governor of the state, the members of the state legislature, the judges of all courts, the mayors of Philadelphia, Pittsburgh, and Lancaster, the county commissioners and sheriffs, and a committee of the Philadelphia Society for Alleviating the Miseries of Public Prisons. The relation between the prisoner and these official visitors could not have been very intimate. The committee of the society did very well to average four and a half hours a year per prisoner, and their conversation was confined largely to theological

---

[4] Quoted in Klein, *Prison Methods in New York State*, p. 206.

exhortations. The solitude was not frequently broken, therefore. But it was argued that the effect of this solitude was to cause an appreciation of these good men when they did come.

The Western State Penitentiary at Pittsburgh, Pennsylvania, which opened in 1826, adopted this "separate and silent" system. As in the Walnut Street Jail, the prisoners were at first kept in idleness. After a few years, however, they were permitted to work in their cells. But it was in the Eastern State Penitentiary, which was opened in Philadelphia in 1829, that the "Pennsylvania system" really developed. As in the other institutions, the prisoners were to work alone at such occupations as spinning, weaving, and shoemaking, and were to do maintenance work outside their cells only when blindfolded. The system was not practical, and it was formally abolished in 1913. However, strict solitude probably never was enforced. ●

On the demand of Governor John Jay for the improvement of the criminal law of New York State, a commission was sent to Pennsylvania in 1794 to study the new system. After the report of this commission in 1796 a law was passed in New York, reducing the capital offenses to two, and substituting imprisonment for the death penalty and for corporal punishment. Also, the construction of two prisons was authorized. However, Newgate Prison, which opened in 1797, was the only one erected. The institution was small, and there were no provisions for solitary confinement. Newgate proved to be inadequate, and in 1816 another prison, at Auburn, was authorized. A part of this institution was to be used for solitary confinement. By act of 1821, the prisoners in Auburn were divided into three classes: the first class, composed of the "oldest and most heinous offenders," were to be kept in solitary confinement continuously; those in the second class were to be kept in their cells three days a week; and the others one day a week. The cells were small and dark, and no provision was made for work in the cells. This experiment with strict solitary confinement proved to be a great failure; of eighty prisoners who had been in solitary confinement continuously, all except two were out of the prison within two years, as the result of death, insanity, or pardon. A legislative commission which investigated the policy in 1824 recommended that it be abandoned at once, and this recommendation was adopted. Being now thoroughly opposed to the method of solitary confinement, which had not, however, been tried under as favorable conditions as in Pennsylvania, the Auburn authorities provided for work by the prisoners in association but in silence during the day and solitary confinement during the night. This has been known as the Auburn system, in contrast with the Pennsylvania system, which was solitary confinement by day and night. ●

The Auburn system

**The contro-
versy between
the Auburn
and
Pennsylvania
systems**

The literature of criminology during the forty years subsequent to the establishment of the Auburn system is devoted almost entirely to a hot controversy between these two systems. It was carried on largely by two prison reform associations: the Philadelphia Society, mentioned above, which supported the Pennsylvania system, and the Boston Society for the Improvement of Prison Discipline and for the Reformation of Juvenile Offenders, which supported the Auburn system.[5] Both societies were intensely interested in the reformation of offenders; each was convinced of the merits of its method and the demerits of the other method; and both were entirely unscrupulous in their use of statistics to prove their arguments. When Dickens, after a visit to America, wrote his *American Notes,* he included a severe arraignment of the Pennsylvania system, which still further increased the antagonism between the two parties in America.

The Pennsylvania system was tried in a number of the states, but was generally abandoned in favor of the Auburn system after a short trial. The principal advantages claimed for the Auburn system were economic; that is, it cost less to construct the congregate-type prison, and the congregate system made possible more efficient utilization of the labor of prisoners for production of wealth. At the same time, the system of silence was thought to be sufficient for reformation through reflection. European visitors, however, generally secured and carried away an impression that the Pennsylvania system was superior. In 1835, commissioners were sent from England, France, Prussia, and Belgium to examine the American prison systems; they made their visits together and presented practically identical reports to their home governments in favor of the Pennsylvania system. These reports produced a great effect in Europe, and most of the European countries adopted the Pennsylvania system in a modified form.

The controversy between these two systems, after raging for more than half a century, was diverted by the importation of a new system from Europe and Australia. This system was started in an organized manner in the Australian convict camps by Captain Maconochie.[6] His methods were imported into Ireland and England and, under the name of the Irish system, became known to and were discussed by American leaders shortly before the Civil War.

The Irish system consisted of the indeterminate sentence, the "mark system," whereby prisoners could gain their freedom by earning a certain number of "marks," and a form of parole. The first institution using these methods was the Elmira Reformatory in New York, created by law in 1869, but not opened until 1876.

---

[5] See Stewart H. Holbrook, *Dreamers of the American Dream* (New York: Doubleday, 1957), pp. 240-244.

[6] See John V. Barry, "Pioneers in Criminology: XII, Alexander Maconochie (1787-1860)," *Journal of Criminal Law, Criminology, and Police Science,* 47: 145-161, July-August, 1956; and idem, *Alexander Maconochie of Norfolk Island* (Melbourne: Oxford University Press, 1958).

Emphasis was placed on education, productive labor, the mark system, the indeterminate sentence, and parole, all of which were designed to produce reformation. It is not correct to think of this as the first reformatory, for the penitentiaries three-quarters of a century earlier were designed to produce reformation. But with the establishment of the Elmira system, the treatment reaction to crime was more explicitly incorporated into institutional policy. Also, the conflict between the treatment and punitive reactions became institutionalized. It is significant in this connection that the Elmira Reformatory was constructed as a maximum-security penal institution, and that efforts at "treatment" were made in this setting. Similarly, corporal punishment was a part of the Elmira routine.

Almost all reformatories constructed in the United States since 1875 have been based on the Elmira system, including the conflict between treatment and punishment. This system of organized conflict between the treatment and punitive reactions also spread rather quickly to state prisons, so that it is now difficult to draw a line between state prisons and state reformatories so far as methods are concerned. Some state prisons use more definitely reformatory methods than do some reformatories. Fifty years after Elmira was opened, New York prisoners were begging the sentencing judges to send them to Auburn Prison, rather than to Elmira Reformatory, because the disciplinary system at Elmira was so severe. A high official at Elmira boasted of this fact, believing that such a state of affairs was a credit to his institution. •

The first American institution specifically for juvenile delinquents was opened in New York City in 1825 after more than a generation of discussion. It was under the control of a private society called the New York Association for the Prevention of Pauperism, but the state made annual grants for its maintenance. A similar institution under private control was started in Philadelphia in 1826. The first institution of this type under state control was started in Massachusetts in 1847. Even this institution received assistance from private funds. Seven institutions had been opened by 1850, thirty-two more by 1875, and sixty-six more by 1900. At present there are about three hundred state and local training schools. Though these institutions started and made their best progress in the early period under private control, the private institutions at present show no clear superiority to the public institutions. Several institutions have changed from private to public management, though none has changed from public to private management.

From the first, it was contended that these institutions were not penal institutions or prisons, but schools. The children were to be educated or "treated," not punished. This contention was supported by the courts, especially by the Supreme Court in a decision regarding the institution in Philadelphia in 1828. In cer-

Juvenile reformatories and industrial schools

tain respects the institutions incorporated nonpunitive policies, and many efforts were made to reform the delinquents by methods other than solitary confinement: they had self-government, religious teaching, academic teaching, indeterminate sentences, and release on good behavior, which was similar to parole. In the second year of the New York House of Refuge, the president of the board made the following statement, which was quite opposed to the prevailing punitive reaction to lawbreaking: "A child may be made quiet and industrious by beating, but it seldom happens, I believe, that kindheartedness, morality, and intelligence are induced by whipping."[7] Some of these nonpunitive policies were only temporary, and in some respects from the time of their origin the rationale of these institutions was punitive.

The earliest institutions for juvenile delinquents were organized under the dominance of the prison idea. . . . In all regards this was true; the establishments were distinctly prison enclosures, the dormitories were blocks of cells, the dining-rooms were chambers of silence, with only the meagerest provision of the crudest table furniture; the earning capacity of those confined was exploited to the highest possible figure, and education in letters was only provided for during such hours as could not be profitably employed in work; and the greatest ambition and strongest claim for popular approval was a low per capita cost of maintenance.[8]

It seems probable, therefore, that, with temporary exceptions in regard to certain punitive policies, these institutions were, during the first half-century of their history, primarily prisons, and their principal contribution was the removal of juvenile prisoners from association with adult prisoners. Though it may properly be argued that these institutions have changed very much since that time and therefore are not prisons now, at least it is clear that the ideal of the prison for adults has changed, also, and that in practice there is more that is penal in some institutions for juvenile delinquents than in some institutions for adult criminals. The punitive reaction to crime was modified first in connection with juvenile offenses; the modifications spread to offenses of youths, and then to adult offenses. But in no case was the punitive reaction completely replaced. Even today some institutions for juveniles can best be described as congregate prisons.

One of the important developments in juvenile reformatories was the cottage system of architecture, in place of the old cellblock structure. In America the first examples of the cottage system, which was copied from European systems, were a Massachusetts institution for girls and the Ohio School for Boys at Lancaster, established in 1858. This system won general approval,

---

[7] B. K. Peirce, *A Half Century with Juvenile Delinquents, or the New York House of Refuge and Its Times* (New York: Appleton-Century-Crofts, 1869), p. 120.

[8] F. H. Nibecker, "Education of Juvenile Delinquents," *Annals of the American Academy of Political and Social Science*, 23:483, May, 1904.

and most of the state institutions have adopted a similar plan because of the more homelike surroundings and the greater ease of classification. Such surroundings, however, do not necessarily mean that the conflict between treatment and punitive policies is absent. ●

Specialization of prisons

As the previous discussion implies, one of the evident trends accompanying the development of treatment methods in American prisons has been toward specialization of institutions. The jail once was the only penal institution. In the past two hundred years various groups of prisoners have been withdrawn from the jail for incarceration in specialized institutions. Vagrants were first withdrawn and placed in houses of correction. This proved to be abortive, and the houses of correction have now either been abandoned or become identical with the jail except in name. Then state prisons, with differing names, were established for juvenile delinquents, for insane criminals, for young adults, for women, for Negroes, for defective delinquents, for misdemeanants, for the sick, and for other groups of criminals. Thus, in the development of these specialized institutions, the principles which have been used in the selection of offenders have included the governing unit, the seriousness of the crime, the age, color, sex, and mental or physical condition of the offenders. The motives for specialization have included the prevention of contamination of one type of offenders by another and the adaptation of methods of work and of facilities to the characteristics of the special groups of offenders.

Until recent years the principles used in specialization had little, if anything, to do with treatment. Even now the most prevalent principle of specialization is the seriousness of the particular offense of which the prisoner was convicted; the state institutions generally care for felons, the county and municipal institutions for misdemeanants. This kind of differentiation is unsound from both the punitive and treatment points of view, for the particular offense is not a suitable index of character, dangerousness, or needs of the offender. The misdemeanant generally violates a law of the state as well as of the municipality, and the state would therefore be justified in taking charge of the prisoner rather than transferring this work to the local community. Moreover, the number of offenders in the typical county jail is so small that adequate facilities and personnel for segregation of various types of offenders is impractical.

The local prisons of England were taken over by the national government and have been thus operated for more than half a century with improvement in efficiency and great decrease in expense. Several states in America have established state farms for misdemeanants, which, to some extent, take the place of county jails. Indiana, for example, established a state farm for misdemeanants in 1915. The law provides that male misdemeanants are to be sent to this state farm unless their sentences are thirty days or less, in which case they may be retained in the county jail or sent to the state farm at the discretion of the judge. The expenses of transportation are paid by the county, the expenses of maintenance by the state. But state farms, like county jails, are seldom specialized except in respect to the age and sex of inmates. Many misdemeanants are chronic alcoholics or drug addicts who make almost continuous rounds of jails, the street, police stations, and jails again.[9] Special institutions are being established for these men, for they have problems which require special methods of treatment. The remainder of the jail and state-farm population resembles the prison population more than the chronic-alcoholic population.

Specialization of institutions by sex of inmates is now characteristic of all types of prisons—jails, houses of correction, reformatories, and state prisons. When both sexes are confined in one institution, the two departments are separated almost as completely as though they were different institutions.

Another principle of specialization is by age. The desirability of special institutions for juveniles, if they are to be kept in institutions at all, is beyond question. However, the state reformatory for young adults is not clearly justified. It was established on the theory that it would serve younger, less criminal, and more easily reformable men. But 62 percent of the men committed to the Massachusetts State Reformatory at Concord in 1970 were recidivists, as compared to 72 percent of the men sentenced to the Massachusetts State Prison at Walpole. Also, there is considerable overlapping in age. In 1970, 80 percent of the persons sentenced to the Concord reformatory were under twenty-five, and 40 percent of those sentenced to the state prison were under twenty-five.[10] Thus the distinction between the state prison and the state reformatory is not at all clear. It has never been drawn as clearly for women as for men offenders, and at present practically every institution for women offenders might be called a reformatory.

Still another principle of specialization is by the personal characteristics of offenders. The federal government and states with large populations, like California, have been able to establish a series of prisons, graded from "maximum security" to "minimum security" and with quite different programs. Some special institutions have been established for vagrants, some for insane criminals, some for defective delinquents, some for alcoholics, and some for drug addicts. Such arrangements could be considered as specialization on the basis of the kind of punishment considered necessary in each case, but it also is considered special-

[9] See David J. Pittman and C. Wayne Gordon, Revolving Door: A Study of the Chronic Police Inebriate (Glencoe, Ill.: Free Press, 1958).

[10] Commissioner of Correction, Statistical Report, 1970, (Commonwealth of Massachusetts, Public Document No. 115), pp. 33-34, 43.

ization according to the kind of treatment method deemed advisable for the various categories of offenders.[11] In relatively recent years, "classification" of prisoners has come to include recommendation as to the kind of specialized institution in which an offender should be incarcerated, as well as recommendation for a particular kind of program within the institution. Classification will be discussed in the next chapter. ●

Social contacts for prisoners

The solitary confinement of the early Pennsylvania system has been generally abandoned in the United States except as punishment for infraction of prison regulations. Even the rule of silence, which was substituted for this, has been abandoned. Unquestionably, the horrors of prison life have been reduced. Improvements have been made in diet, cleanliness, ventilation, lighting, and methods of discipline. In most institutions the clearest marks of degradation, such as shaving of the head, the lockstep, striped clothing, and the ball and chain, have been eliminated. Also, the monotony of prison life has been reduced. Entertainments have been provided, athletics and other recreations developed, libraries and educational classes provided. Also, visiting and correspondence privileges have been introduced, and college students, potential employers, peer counselors, and others are permitted to enter many prisons for discussions with inmates. These are efforts both to promote contacts among the inmates and between the inmates and the outside world. They are based in part on the conviction that open contacts between prisoners are better than secret contacts which prevail in spite of a formal policy of isolation, in part on the conviction that reformation is a process of assimilation of culture of the outside world and that assimilation of culture is promoted by contact with that culture rather than isolation from it. While the prison in its general plan is a means of isolating offenders from social life, these logically contradictory methods are introduced in the effort to facilitate the reformation of the inmates by breaking down the isolation to some extent. ●

Imprisonment as punishment

Almost all changes occurring in prisons prior to the present generation were directed, explicitly or implicitly, by the doctrine that restriction of a criminal's liberty is, by itself, punishment, and that this punishment is adequate for meeting the societal needs for retribution, deterrence, and reformation.[12] In the early days of their existence, democratic societies were not sure of themselves—they deprived criminals of their freedom and *also* inflicted physical suffering on them. American prisons have abandoned corporal punishments as a regime for supplementing

---

[11] See Richard O. Nahrendorf, "A Correctional Dilemma: The Narcotics Addict," *Sociology and Social Research*, 53:21-33, October, 1968.

[12] See the discussion below, pp. 496-499.

the suffering which "mere imprisonment" is expected to produce. Most prison officials now maintain that men are committed to prisons *as* punishment rather than *for* punishment.

Yet "mere imprisonment" continues to be ordered because it is painful to offenders. It is no coincidence that imprisonment as a system for dealing with criminals arose with the democratic revolutions of the eighteenth century. Neither is it a coincidence that imprisonment has remained as the principal method for dealing with serious offenders in democratic societies. As democracy developed, so did an appreciation of liberty, and restriction of freedom by imprisonment came to be regarded as a proper system for imposing pain on criminals. It was in this period that our current system of criminal laws, each law calling for a measured amount of loss of freedom and, thus, a measured amount of pain, was initiated.

Of course, "mere imprisonment" has never been consistently defined and has meant many things to many people, as has been true of the concept "liberty." In the Walnut Street Jail it meant only perimeter control, with freedom to commit crime and engage in debauchery within prison walls. At the other extreme, it meant confinement of all prisoners in solitary, as in the Pennsylvania system. Now we adopt, or try to adopt, a middle-of-the-road position, allowing inmates physical mobility within the walls but directing their actions and choices. Nevertheless, incarceration *is* intended as punishment in contemporary American society. It is this fact which helps pose the dilemma for contemporary prison workers, who are admonished to treat criminals, as well as to punish them. Only a generation ago it was common to assume that a system or technique for implementing society's punitive reaction to crime was also a method for "correcting" or "reforming" criminals. Now it is ordinarily assumed (perhaps erroneously) that any *real* correctional method is nonpunitive in nature.

While there is wide variation in opinion as to what a positive "treatment" or "rehabilitative" program *is*, there is wide consensus on what it *is not:* A program which involves purposive infliction of suffering is not a treatment program. Psychotherapy, vocational education, counseling, and library privileges are viewed as "treatment" principally because they are nonpunitive, not because they have been demonstrated to be effective methods of changing criminals into noncriminals. Prison workers, then, are to be nonpunitive in an institution which, by definition, is punitive.

The notion that treatment must be nonpunitive if it is to succeed has led to a popular conception of the prison as something other than a prison. The mental hospital is often used as a model of what the prison should become.[13] This is logical only if it is assumed that criminals are not responsible for their actions and are in need of nonpunitive treatment for the sources of that irre-

---

[13] See the statement by Karpman on page 348 above.

sponsibility. Prisons cannot become nonpunitive organizations like mental hospitals, however, because they are used by society for the purpose of inflicting suffering. No hospital for treating *criminality* exists in fact, because in our legal system proof of criminality ("badness") is followed by commitment to a prison, while proof of insanity ("sickness") is followed by commitment to a mental hospital.[14] And the prison remains as a place of punishment because the act of taking away a criminal's liberty is an act performed by the state in a deliberate attempt to produce suffering.

The principal difference between committing a criminal to a prison and a psychotic to a mental hospital lies in the fact that we want the prisoner, but not the psychotic, to suffer from the incarceration. Patients in mental hospitals may suffer from confinement behind bars, but the suffering is not deliberately imposed by the state. Patients are not committed to an institution on the assumption that the suffering resulting from the incarceration will have some positive value in their rehabilitation or in deterring others from becoming patients. This, as we have seen, is precisely the assumption behind committing men to prison, and it is this assumption that makes the prison a place of punishment.

Since the prison is a place of punishment, incarceration cannot officially be ordered or viewed solely as an inconvenient but necessary means to the application of nonpunitive treatment methods. The notion that effective treatment for prisoners must be nonpunitive is in fundamental conflict with one of the tasks society assigns to the prison—purposive infliction of pain. ●

BARNES, H. E. *The Evolution of Penology in Pennsylvania.* Indianapolis: Bobbs-Merrill, 1927.

BARNES, H. E. "The Historical Origin of the Prison System in the United States." *Journal of Criminal Law and Criminology,* 12:42-47, June, 1921.

BROCKWAY, Z. R. *Fifty Years of Prison Service.* New York: Charities Publication Committee, 1912.

CRESSEY, DONALD R. "Adult Felons in Prison." Chapter in *Prisoners in America,* edited by Lloyd E. Ohlin, pp. 117-150, Englewood Cliffs, N.J.: Prentice-Hall, 1973.

DE BEAUMONT, GUSTAVE, & ALEXIS DE TOCQUEVILLE. *On the Penitentiary System in the United States and Its Application to France.* Translated by Francis Lieber. Philadelphia: Carey, Lea and Blanchard, 1833. (Reissued by Southern Illinois University Press, Carbondale, 1964.)

GRAY, F. C. *Prison Discipline in America.* London: J. Murray, 1848. (Reissued by Patterson Smith, Montclair, N.J., 1973.)

Suggested readings

---

[14] See the discussion on pp. 156-157, 347-354, above. See also Donald R. Cressey, "The Differential Association Theory and Compulsive Crimes," *Journal of Criminal Law, Criminology, and Police Science,* 45:25-40, May-June, 1954.

HEATH, JAMES, ed. *Eighteenth Century Penal Theory*. London: Oxford University Press, 1963.

IVES, GEORGE. *A History of Penal Methods*. London: Stanley Paul, 1914.

JOBES, PATRICK C. "Historical Development of Causal Theories of Rational Man." *California Youth Authority Quarterly*, 26:18-27, Spring, 1973.

JOHNSTON, NORMAN. *The Human Cage: A Brief History of Prison Architecture*. Philadelphia: The American Foundation, 1973.

KLEIN, P. *Prison Methods in New York State*. New York: Columbia University Press, 1920.

LEWIS, O. F. *The Development of American Prisons and Prison Customs, 1776-1845*. Albany: Prison Association of New York, 1922.

McKELWAY, BLAKE. *American Prisons*. Chicago: University of Chicago Press, 1936.

MILNER, ALAN, ed. *African Penal Systems*. London: Routledge and Kegan Paul, 1969.

ROBINSON, L. N. *Penology in the United States*. Philadelphia: Winston, 1921.

ROSE, GORDON. *The Struggle for Penal Reform*. London: Stevens and Sons, 1961.

ROTHMAN, DAVID J. *The Discovery of the Asylum: Social Order and Disorder in the New Republic*. Boston: Little, Brown, 1971.

SELLIN, THORSTEN. "Philadelphia Prisons of the Eighteenth Century." *Transactions of the American Philosophical Society*, 43:326-330, pt. 1, 1953.

TEETERS, NEGLEY K. *The Cradle of the Penitentiary: The Walnut Street Jail at Philadelphia, 1773-1835*. Philadelphia: Pennsylvania Prison Society, 1955.

WINES, E. C. *Punishment and Reformation*. New York: Crowell, 1895.

Objectives and conditions of imprisonment

23

The history of imprisonment in the United States reveals a trend toward emphasis on treatment and away from punishment. The view which is now formally expressed by most prison leaders is that the prison should make every possible effort to treat prisoners, within the framework of a system of security. It is observed that practically all prisoners return to free society sooner or later and that the use of punitive methods alone does not produce the desired reformation. Consequently it is emphasized that nonpunitive methods should be used. At the same time, the prison system is organized in such a way that it impedes the efforts at treatment. As a result, treatment programs often are described in official statements of prison policy although they do not exist in fact. It is now becoming popular for prison workers and inmates alike to argue that imprisonment does not rehabilitate and that the paper efforts at rehabilitation ought to be abandoned. The prevailing conflict between punitive and treatment policies in prisons is a reflection of the more general conflicting societal reactions to crime. The analysis presented in the next two chapters is intended as an interpretation of prison conditions in terms of these general societal conditions. ●

Contemporary political and social leaders seem to have a variety of objectives in regard to control of crime, and they consider imprisonment the means for attaining each of them. *First,* as is implied by the relatively recent emphasis on treatment of criminals, conforming citizens want criminals changed, so they will commit no more crimes. The prison is expected to "reform" or "rehabilitate" criminals. *Second,* citizens want protection from criminals. The prison isolates criminals from general society so they cannot commit crimes during certain periods of time. *Third,* many leaders want retribution. The prison is expected to make life unpleasant for people who, by their crimes, have made others' lives unpleasant. *Fourth,* most citizens want to reduce crime rates. The prison is expected to reduce crime rates by reforming criminals, and also by deterring the public from behavior which is punishable by imprisonment.

Objectives of imprisonment

Since the prison has been assigned the task of working toward each of these four goals, attainment of the goals may be considered the objective of imprisonment.

Within the prison, the attempt to perform the duties necessary for the accomplishment of the various tasks assigned—*reformation, incapacitation, retribution,* and *deterrence*—results in conflict. Especially, the conditions necessary for the performance of the first task, reformation, may be in conflict with the conditions necessary for exacting retribution and for maximum incapacitation and deterrence. When reformation is assumed to be induced by treatment, rather than by purposive infliction of pain, the personal conditions which led to inmates' crimes are supposedly determined, and the inmates are then introduced to the personal skills considered important to their reformation. Efficient performance of this task depends on prison conditions which are conducive to free inquiry and to intimate, helpful, constructive action based on the inmates' needs. The conditions viewed as conducive to reformation through treatment, thus, almost never include the purposive infliction of suffering. Such punitive action is considered to detract from the intimate, confidential, amoral relationship necessary to obtaining valid information from inmates, and it also is thought to alienate inmates from personnel when the latter attempt to take positive action for inmate reformation.

On the other hand, retribution and deterrence by purposive infliction of suffering always, obviously, necessitates prison conditions which are punitive, even if the suffering merely results from the severe limitations on personal freedom imposed by incarceration. Moreover, restrictions on freedom-within-walls are deliberately imposed. Some prisons whose administrators stress only perimeter control are often referred to by outsiders and by old-time prison administrators as country clubs, and others— those in which inmtaes engage in petty rackets and debauchery —are viewed as too lax or even corrupt. As a result, rigid systems of punitive control and discipline supplement the punitive conditions brought about by the mere fact of incarceration.

Incapacitation of criminals need not include purposively inflicted suffering, any more than the incapacitation of psychotics by confinement in a hospital need include such suffering. But incapacitation of criminals usually does involve the intentional infliction of suffering, particularly when a system of rigid discipline and control is considered essential to incapacitation. However, it is difficult to determine precisely whether punitive discipline and control are considered part of the routine necessary for gaining the incapacitation objective or, instead, conditions necessary for obtaining the deterrence and retributive objectives. Probably they are regarded as necessary for the attainment of all these objectives.

The administrative problems brought about by the fact that prisons are expected both to treat criminals and punish criminals have been attacked in many ways. In some prisons the problems have been resolved by open abandonment of any serious attempt to treat inmates, on the ground that persons who expect criminals to be reformed by treatment are foolish and misguided. The opposite kind of resolution would be open abandonment of all punitive aspects of incarceration. This solution is frequently advocated by persons who consider punishment unnecessary and inhumane, but it is unrealistic.[1] Another system for resolving the conflict is compromise. Here, the punitive conditions are mitigated in favor of treatment conditions, and treatment conditions are modified in favor of the punitive aspects of imprisonment. This really does not resolve the conflict; it merely makes it less intense. Finally, the problems have been resolved by formally

---

[1] See Don C. Gibbons, *Changing the Lawbreaker: The Treatment of Delinquents and Criminals* (Englewood Cliffs, N.J.: Prentice-Hall, 1965), pp. 130-135.

maintaining that the prison both treats and punishes, while informally abandoning almost all conditions conducive to effective treatment. Perhaps this is the most common contemporary system for resolving the conflict. As two experienced prison administrators have said:

> There does seem to be one problem that all institutions face; the conflicted orientation of the public. . . . Confronted with these contradictory pressures, correctional personnel frequently must decide which to translate into practice and which to honor in public statements. They are like repertory actors, who must vary their performance according to the expectations of a moody and unpredictable public. By and large, they have attempted to resolve this problem by satisfying the more fundamental demands of security by means of concrete action and the demands for increased liberality by means of public statements.[2]

These alternative kinds of solution for the administrative problems may be observed in the varied use of "classification" in prisons. •

Classification

The primary condition against which early American prison reformers argued was the association of all types of criminals in a conglomerate group. At first, "classification" consisted of mere segregation, for purposes of discipline and administrative control, of prisoners according to such criteria as age, sex, race, and dangerousness. Formally, this kind of definition and practice has been abandoned. As the treatment reaction became popular, differentiation was to be made on the basis of individual needs and probable reformability of inmates, and specific treatment programs were to be directed toward individuals who, as the basis for differentiation implied, could most benefit from them.[3] In the last forty or fifty years "classification" has come to refer to this whole system of differentiation according to inmates' needs and individualized execution of treatment programs consistent with the needs. The term is now used to designate the entire process by which prisons attempt to attain the objective of reformation through individualized treatment. This process is said to consist of four separate but coordinated procedures.

First, the prisoner's case history is taken, and his personality studied. This is sometimes performed by a staff of professionally trained workers, such as psychologists, social workers, sociol-

---

[2] Richard R. Korn and Lloyd W. McCorkle, *Criminology and Penology* (New York: Holt, 1959), p. 470. See also Lloyd E. Ohlin, *Sociology and the Field of Corrections* (New York: Russell Sage Foundation, 1956), pp. 15-16.

[3] Paradoxically, rehabilitation programs were introduced before diagnosis. Such programs were at first administered on a "shotgun" basis to all criminals or to all criminals of a certain class, such as an age group. Then, as it became obvious, in the 1920s, that effective treatment was not possible without knowledge of the persons being treated, diagnostic facilities were set up.
up. See Frank Loveland, "Classification in the Prison System," in Paul W. Tappan, ed., *Contemporary Correction* (New York: McGraw-Hill, 1951), pp. 91-106.

ogists, and psychiatrists. The diagnostic procedure ideally involves "the use of every available technique, such as social investigations; medical, psychiatric, and psychological examinations; and educational, vocational, religious, and recreational studies."[4]

Second, the information regarding the prisoner is presented to a classification committee. This committee decides upon a program of individualized treatment and training based upon the diagnosis. Sometimes the classification committee is made up of only the professionally trained staff, but ordinarily it also includes the warden or superintendent, the deputy warden or wardens, the superintendent of industry, the educational director, and the chaplain. Generally, the warden is chairman of a committee consisting of representatives of all administrative departments. The committee assigns the inmate to a designated type of custody—usually minimum, medium, or maximum—to a certain kind of cell or living quarters, to a job, to health services, to educational classes, to recreations, and to other activities and services. The inmate usually appears before the committee within sixty days after his arrival from court.

The third step is application of the treatment policies. The classification committee has the responsibility of seeing that its recommendations are carried out. The diagnostic analysis of the inmate and his background is utilized not only as a basis for a decision as to how he *should* be treated, but also as a basis for his actual treatment.

Finally, the treatment program is kept current with the inmate's changing needs and with new analyses, based on any information not available at the time of the initial classification committee meeting, of the inmate's case. This procedure is known as "reclassification," and it is carried out by the classification committee. Presumably, it guarantees that there will be no dead-end placements nor forgotten men in the prison. The reclassification procedure continues from the time of the first classification until the inmate is released. Consequently the diagnostic report, generally called an "admission summary," the initial classification report, and the reclassification reports presumably comprise a complete preinstitutional and institutional history of the individual.

The classification system and, consequently, the treatment program can, and does, break down at any point in the process. Obviously the entire process depends to a large extent upon the original diagnosis. Yet it is axiomatic that most prisons have insufficient diagnostic personnel. Of the 46,680 persons employed in state institutions for adults in 1966, only 1,124 (2.4 percent) were psychologists, psychiatrists, social workers, or counselors. Thus, for the United States, 1,124 professional personnel carried diagnostic and treatment responsibilities for over 201,000 mis-

---

[4] Robert G. Caldwell, "Classification: Key to Effective Institutional Correction," *American Journal of Correction*, 20:10 ff., March-April, 1958.

demeanants and felons, a ratio of 1 to 179. In southern states the ratio was 1 to 930; in eleven states it was higher than 1 to 500, and in two states it was 1 to 2,000.[5] Some years ago Schnur calculated that inmates who in one month took more than an hour and twenty minutes of service from the whole classification, training, and treatment staff (including institutional parole officers, chaplains, sociologists, social workers, psychologists, psychiatrists, and teachers) were taking more than their fair share.[6]

Even when diagnostic personnel are present, diagnoses accurate enough for treatment planning are rarely made. Inmates often are available for diagnostic interviews only for about two hours in the morning and two hours in the afternoon, the remainder of the time being given over to routine prison activities such as "count," "yard," "bath," "barber," and meals. Accordingly, much of the case history information is hurriedly collected in the allotted periods, often with the aid of inmate clerks. The diagnostic interviews themselves sometimes are only five to fifteen minutes in duration, and on the basis of them an appraisal is made of the inmate's home life, his community life, the etiology of his criminality, and his story of the offense. Also on the basis of these brief contacts the interviewer makes a prognosis as to the probabilities for reformation of the offender, classifies him as to personality type, decides whether the inmate is improvable, unimprovable, or somewhere in between, makes a recommendation for a program of treatment and training, and does many other things.

Even if the diagnoses are accurate, the treatment planning for the inmates might not be based on them. In some institutions the classification committee never meets, or meets only rarely, and the decisions regarding program-planning are made by one person. In other institutions the classification committee meets regularly but bases its decisions on custodial and punitive considerations rather than on treatment. That is, rather than reading diagnostic reports for evidence of inmates' individual needs for specific kinds of treatment, these committees read them for evidence of the kinds of precautions which must be taken to insure incapacitation and just punishment.[7]

Probably most classification committees base their decisions on considerations of custody, convenience, discipline, and treatment, in that order. Thus, it may be decided that a particular inmate must be handled as a maximum security risk, and if, for example, psychiatric services are not available to maximum-risk prisoners,

---

[5] National Council on Crime and Delinquency, "Correction in the United States," in President's Commission on Law Enforcement and Administration of Justice, *Task Force Report: Corrections* (Washington: Government Printing Office, 1967), appendix A, p. 180.

[6] Alfred C. Schnur, "The New Penology: Fact or Fiction?" *Journal of Criminal Law, Criminology, and Police Science,* 49:331-334, November-December, 1958.

[7] See H. G. Moeller, "Changing Trends in Classification," *Proceedings of the American Correctional Association, 1960,* pp. 212-219.

then that decision will mean that psychiatric help will not be available to the inmate in question, no matter what his treatment needs. Stated in another way, it may be observed that for maximum effect on his rehabilitation, a prisoner should work on the prison farm; but if he is not considered a minimum security risk, he cannot be assigned to the farm. When a warden, who knows that he will lose his job if escapes occur, is the chairman of the classification committee, security against escapes takes precedence over everything else. The warden or the deputy warden in charge of custody can, in effect, veto the recommendation of the professional staff or the deputy warden in charge of care and treatment. In this way many institutions which appear to both treat and punish prisoners have solved the conflict by informally abandoning the treatment program.

Also, classification committees may operate merely as assignment boards, in which case the requirements of the institution, rather than the needs of the prisoners, determine the program which is recommended. An inmate who needs vocational training may be assigned to kitchen duties because "someone has to do the maintenance work." In some systems, the official who is responsible for custody brings to the classification committee meetings a list of the institutional jobs which are "open," and inmates are only rarely given an assignment not on that list. Many institutions have established industries which require a certain quota of men for operation, and it sometimes appears that the task of the classification committee is that of keeping the industries going, regardless of whether assignment of an inmate to the industry will aid in his rehabilitation. In the autumn, incoming inmates will be assigned to the cannery, because "if we don't get someone in the cannery, the tomatoes will spoil." Ordinarily, when convenience is the criterion used for assignment, a compromise is made in regard to the treatment objective. The inmate may be required to devote mornings to labor which everyone recognizes as having no rehabilitative value, but he is given the option of participating in a rehabilitative program during the afternoons. Or he may be assigned to the cannery in the autumn, to the nursery in the summer, and to a rehabilitative program in the winter. Again, he may be given a full-time assignment as a janitor, with the recommendation that he enroll in educational classes in the evenings.

It is at the third step in the process that classification work has most frequently broken down in the past and still, perhaps to a lesser extent, breaks down today. When the classification committee does not include custodial personnel, such as the warden or his deputy, the recommendations of that committee are likely to be ignored. In such instances the classification committee is merely diagnostic and advisory; it is an addition to the institutional program but not an integral part of it. Sometimes detailed reports on inmates' needs for particular kinds of treatment are never read by the personnel who are expected to administer the appropriate programs. Sometimes the recommendations are impractical because the institution does not have the facilities for carrying out the recommendations; sometimes the recommendations are considered to be impractical by custodial personnel because they conflict with custodial and punitive programs.[8] In such a system the assignment to workshops, to cellblocks, or to educational grades and treatment programs is made by a correctional officer whose chief criteria for assignment are, again, custody, convenience, and discipline.

Even when both professional and custodial personnel are involved in program-planning, there is no guarantee that the committee's recommendations will be carried out. Treatment recommendations which are not vetoed in the committee might be in conflict with recommendations based on custody and convenience, in which case the latter recommendations are most likely to be acted upon. Also, prisoners may be removed from treatment programs as a form of punishment, or they may be permitted to enroll in educational or vocational programs as a reward for "good behavior" with reference to the punitive aspects of imprisonment. Similarly, participation in treatment programs may be interpreted by individual guards as a form of malingering.

Professional staff members themselves may be extremely negligent in carrying out their own recommendations for treatment. It is apparent, for example, that staff members who are so occupied with report-writing and meetings that they are unable to perform their diagnostic duties also will be too busy to perform their duties as administrators of the recommended programs. The treatment programs then become meaningless and superficial. Twenty years ago, Powelson and Bendix reported, as an illustration of a similar point, the case of a prison psychiatrist who boasted that he could hold fifty "therapy" interviews during a working day. Similarly, in one institution where inmates were selected for group therapy, the custodial officer in charge gave the order that all violators of a certain section of the penal code who were between the ages of twenty and forty, and who were nonveterans, were to appear for group therapy at a given hour.[9] The psychiatrists in only about a dozen states can find time to engage in individual therapy, usually on a very limited basis. Even prison educational and medical programs are often inefficiently administered. The existence of such conditions again illustrates one system for informally abandoning prison programs which are conducive to effective treatment, while maintaining in the formal organization of the institution the ideology that the prison should both punish and treat.

The final step in the classification process, reclassification, also

---

[8] See Stephan G. Seliger, "Toward a Realistic Reorganization of the Penitentiaries," *Journal of Criminal Law, Criminology, and Police Science*, 60:47-58, March, 1969.

[9] Cf. Harvey Powelson and Reinhard Bendix, "Psychiatry in Prison," *Psychiatry*, 14:73-86, February, 1951.

is a point at which the entire system frequently breaks down. When periodic reclassification is required, the classification committee sometimes merely examines the inmate's record for evidence of infraction of custodial rules, or simply rubber stamps his existing program. When reclassification is not required at periodic intervals, the inmate is likely to see the classification committee only at the time of his initial classification and at the time of his pre-parole consideration. If the inmate has a desire for reclassification, he usually can apply to the committee, but his request can be denied on the ground that his work record is poor, or on the ground that he has violated custodial rules, or on the ground that it would not be convenient for the institution if his assignment were changed, as well as on the ground that the desired program, in the opinion of the committee, would be useless to the inmate. Frequently it is difficult to determine just which grounds are used for reclassification, just as it is difficult to determine the grounds for the original classification. Probably the order of precedence is, again, custody, convenience, discipline, and treatment. Application by an inmate for reclassification so that he can participate in a specific treatment program might be interpreted as an attempt to avoid punishment. An inmate with an escape record only very rarely is assigned to a program which would necessitate reclassifying him as a minimum security risk, no matter what his needs in respect to treatment. One prisoner who was working as a saw-filer applied for an assignment in vocational drafting, but this application for reclassification was denied by the committee, at the simple request of a custodial officer, "because saw-filers are hard to find." When such practices are present, reclassification certainly does not guarantee that there will be no dead-end placements nor forgotten men in the prison.

The reception center is the most recent development in the field of classification. The principal difference between classification systems which use reception centers and those which do not is that in the former the inmates are sent to specialized *institutions* on the recommendation of professional workers. All inmates in the state are committed to the reception center and, after a period of about sixty days, during which the diagnostic studies are made, the reception center staff assigns them to appropriate institutions where classification committees take over. The general notion on which such reception center systems are based is that the two most important objectives of imprisonment are reformation and incapacitation. Those prisoners who are most likely to reform and who are least dangerous or desperate, no matter what their offenses or sentences, are to be housed in minimum-security prisons, where the program is largely one of treatment. The inmates who are less likely to respond to treatment and who are somewhat more dangerous are to be kept in secure institutions, where they are subject to the usual classification procedures. But those inmates who do not respond to treatment and who are most desperate and dangerous are to be confined, for the protection of society, in a bastille-type prison. The latter is likely to be a custodial institution, organized for incapacitation rather than for retribution or deterrence, and it only to a slight extent endeavors to provide facilities and staff for treatment.

In some jurisdictions, offenders are referred to reception and classification centers prior to final sentencing disposition. Under federal sentencing procedures, judges can make a final decision as to disposition after committing an offender to the Bureau of Prisons for study and diagnosis. Kansas also provides this service. Cases committed to prison and then studied in the reception center may be referred back to the court with a recommendation for "recall from commitment." The final decision remains with the judge. California's youth authority and department of corrections have developed guidance centers which assign offenders to any of a range of institutions. They also refer cases back to the courts with recommendations for noninstitutional treatment.[10] A 1965 study of this program indicated, in the case of the department of corrections, that over 55 percent of the cases studied in the guidance centers had been granted probation following their return to the courts—a figure that represented 85 percent of the cases for which the guidance center recommended probation.[11] In almost all the cases in which youth authority guidance centers recommended probation, it was granted. In addition to diagnosis, the California guidance center staffs conduct an admission-orientation program, a counseling program, and a group therapy program. In general, an institutional treatment program is supposed to be initiated at these institutions.

When the reception center system is used for assignment of inmates to various institutions, it is subject to the same conflicts as is the classification system within a single institution. Offenders who are obviously reformable are likely to be sent to minimum-security prison farms not because they need farming in their plan of treatment, but because they are "minimum-risk" inmates. Reporting on conditions probably still prevailing in California, Powelson and Bendix observed that when an inmate moved from the guidance center to San Quentin, after his classification on the basis of his case record and test results, he was classified in accordance with the custodial officers' estimates of him as a security risk:

> Our impression is that Custody has a separate and independent system of classifying prisoners which has little, if anything, to do with the recommendations made by the Guidance Center. Each prisoner, who has been classified in the Center on the basis of his case record and a

---

[10] President's Commission, *Task Force Report: Corrections*, p. 20.

[11] Robert L. Smith, *Probation Study* (Sacramento: California Board of Corrections, 1965), pp. 82-89.

battery of tests, is now reclassified in accordance with Custody's estimate of the prisoner as a security risk. The three degrees of security risk—minimum, medium, and maximum—are only remotely related to these earlier findings. They also have little to do with any objective standard which might enable one to distinguish between prisoners of different degrees of security risk. The custodial classification seems to be based rather on the conventional middle-class evaluation of different crimes. Crimes involving violence, sexual or other, are rated as maximum security risks, despite the fact that murderers and sex offenders have the best parole records. Similarly, former escapees from reform schools never get less than a medium security classification, presumably on the ground that once an escapee, always an escapee. Yet, the individual case might well warrant less severe treatment.

To classify prisoners as Custody does, involves a theory of criminality for which there is no evidence. The theory holds that those who have committed crimes most severely punished in our society are most likely to repeat them and are, therefore, least likely to benefit from the program of the Care and Treatment Division. The facts point to the opposite conclusion. . . . The seriousness of a person's crime or the length of his sentence is not a measure of his chances of rehabilitation. This chance can only be judged on the basis of careful examination of the individual case. The custodial classification, in terms of security risk, is therefore unrelated to the program of correction.[12]

It is clear that under the present system of organization the treatment objective of imprisonment cannot be attained without some degree of conflict with the efforts to achieve the incapacitation, deterrence, and retribution objectives. Classification, which has become synonymous with individualized treatment, requires extensive compromise with "custody," sometimes to a degree which makes classification ineffectual. The nature and extent of the compromise in specific institutions depends upon the attitudes of the personnel involved and, indirectly, on the attitudes toward crime of the social group which employs the personnel, ascribes their duties, and provides them with equipment. Public response limits prison officials' attempts to establish treatment programs and the success of attempted programs. The existence of an effective treatment program is not easily discernible to casual prison visitors and is far more difficult for an administrator to demonstrate than is the readily observable fact of a clean, well-maintained, and well-ordered physical plant, equipment, and prison routine. The administrator, then, emphasizes that which is observable and, consequently, rewarding. Also, from the standpoint of prison administrators, one escape or riot could cancel the opportunity to do *any* treatment work with inmates, since successful treatment is not newsworthy, while an escape or riot dramatically focuses public attention on the prison. Consequently, treatment programs must be cautiously attempted only within the framework of custody. Generally, when a society sends to an institution only persons whose behavior is punishable by law, it is to be expected that those persons will be punished while in the institution, even if such punishment interferes with treatment programs. ●

---

[12] Powelson and Bendix, "Psychiatry in Prison," pp. 76-77.

Prison discipline means, conventionally, the regulation or attempt at regulation of the details of prisoners' lives by means of punishment for infraction of rules. In any prison, some minimum of "organization" is necessary in order to provide a division of labor for the staff and for inmates, a schedule of work and meals, a satisfactory relationship with the outside community, and similar arrangements. Employee and inmate work schedules ordinarily must be closely coordinated; meals for inmates must be served and eaten at scheduled times; baths and haircuts must be taken at an assigned period rather than at will; and almost all activities involving choice must be rationed. Although different physical plants and budgets alter the degree of precision needed, the perceived necessity for dominating inmates makes essential a degree of scheduling and coordinating which is higher than the degree ordinarily experienced in democratic societies.

Nevertheless, probably no topic of conversation is as popular, general, or unsettled among prison workers as discussion of the degree and kind of "organization" which is best for institutional operation and for rehabilitation of inmates. Almost all relations between staff members, between staff and inmates, and even between inmates are colored by the positions which are taken, in conversation and in action, on this subject. These positions are based on a variety of conceptions of the "proper" relationships between security measures and rehabilitation measures.

There are many ramifications, however, for such conceptions, when generalized, are notions about the proper balance between responsibility to the group (organization), on the one hand, and individual freedom, on the other. Among prison workers, variation in this respect appears in reference to many aspects of the total program. For example, there are wide differences in evaluations of various "creative activities," such as art, music, hobbycraft, and even school work. One opinion is that such behavior is psychologically therapeutic—it enables the inmate to express himself (minimal restriction), or it enables him to escape momentarily from the repressive organization of prison life. From another viewpoint, however, such activities are viewed as frivolous "wasting of time," as a means of escaping work tasks that need to be accomplished, or as opportunities for inmates to "blow off steam" so that they will more readily accept the organization in which they live.

More significantly, contradictory notions about the proper degree of organization are illustrated by alternative positions taken in reference to inmate discipline. Everyone connected with prisons, including inmates, agrees that there must be "discipline" among the inmates and among staff members. There are wide variations, however, in the meanings of the term and, thus, in the opinions about the degree to which "organization" is vital to institutional functioning and to rehabilitation.

opinions about the degree to which "organization" is vital to institutional functioning and to rehabilitation.

The American Correctional Association's official statement on discipline is couched in language which identifies, but by no means solves, the problem. "Prison discipline," the committee says, is concerned with "the reasonable regulation of everyday institutional life so that the institution will be an orderly, self-respecting community." The aim of discipline, so far as the individual inmate is concerned, is "self-reliance, self-control, self-respect, self-discipline; not merely the ability to conform to institutional rules and regulations, but the ability and *desire* to conform to accepted standards for individual and community life in free society."[13]

The principal difficulty here is with the word *reasonable*. Three basic questions arise: (1) Shall the regulation be reasonable only in the way that the requirement that guards be to work on time and work an eight-hour day is reasonable? (2) Or shall it reasonably attempt to control almost all the details of the prisoner's life by means of punishment for rule infractions? (3) Can "self-reliance," "self-control," and "the desire to conform to accepted standards," actually be induced by either reasonable regulation of the kinds implied in the first two questions, or can it be induced only by nonpunitive "treatment"? These are questions on which prison personnel are in disagreement, and which most prison workers have not satisfactorily resolved even for themselves.

But prison personnel are not alone in their dilemma about prison "organization" or the desirable degree of restrictive "discipline." In their attempts to arrive at a solution regarding the degree to which inmate actions should be regulated (and, therefore, the degree to which regulation is valuable), prison personnel are participating in an unsettled theoretical controversy about the relationship between personality and the "organization" of social relationships.

As Stanton and Schwartz have pointed out, there are social scientists at one extreme who think of the "organization" of social interaction and "personality" as two facets of the same thing.[14] The person is viewed as a product of the kinds of social relationships and values in which he participates; he obtains his satisfactions and, in fact, his essence from participation in the rituals, schedules, customs, rules, and regulations of various sorts which surround him. Moreover, the person (personality) is not separable from the social relationships in which he lives. He behaves according to the rules (which sometimes are contradictory) of the large organization (society) in which he partici-

---

[13] American Correctional Association, Committee on the Model State Plan, *Model of Suggested Standards for a State Correctional System* (New York: Author, 1946), p. 61.

[14] Alfred H. Stanton and Morris S. Schwartz, *The Mental Hospital* (New York: Basic Books, 1954), pp. 37-38.

pates; he cannot behave any other way. On the other hand, social scientists at the opposite pole think of the individual as essentially autonomous, and they view his relationships with the rules and regulations of society and other organizations as *submission* rather than participation. "Personality" is an outgrowth of the effect that the "restrictions" necessary to organization have on an individual's expression of his own pristine needs. These social scientists emphasize "individual self-determination" and attempt to make a distinction between the "real" or "natural" part of the person and the "spurious," "artificial," or "consensual" part. The former is viewed as primary, free, and spontaneous; the latter (obtained from the social relationships making up society) is formal, secondary, and restrictive. In discussing prison organization, these men are likely to emphasize rigidity, cruelty, unresponsiveness, and sadism, without recognizing the usefulness of the organization to the broader society or to the inmates.

Certainly the two theories of the relationship between personality and culture are more complex than this simple statement implies, and probably no social scientist maintains one or the other of them explicitly and with no qualifications. But these ideas, in form even more garbled and unqualified than they have been stated here, have made their way into the policies of prisons. They have come into the prison precisely because members of our society subscribe to both of them. The prison is assigned punitive functions because of concern for the criminal's disruption of the ongoing organization which is society. But at the same time the prison is asked to reform criminals by means which are consistent with the theory that the prison's rules and regulations are harsh, restrictive, and punitive. While groups external to the prison demand that it perform treatment functions, other groups, or perhaps the same groups at a different time, demand that the institution be restrictive and, hence, punitive.

When a prisoner breaks the rules of some prisons, punishment follows as a matter of course. Reports of infractions ordinarily are given to a senior custodial officer or to a subcommittee of the classification committee. A hearing is held, and the inmate is allowed to state his case and, if the offense is a serious one, to call witnesses. The guard reporting the infraction also makes a statement to the disciplinary officer or committee. If the inmate is found guilty, he is punished. In the earlier days, punishment practically always meant some form of bodily suffering. At present, punishment more frequently consists of loss of privileges, such as moving pictures, athletic contests, radio earphones, visiting and correspondence, and educational classes. Also, the "good time" which has been credited to the inmate for early release frequently is revoked, and solitary confinement is used in serious cases. But such practices as confinement in cramped sweat boxes, exposure to extreme heat or cold, standing on a line or in a circle for hours, spraying with a firehose, and stringing up by the wrists are occasionally used, even today.

This system for administration of discipline corresponds roughly to the general system of policing, arresting, trying, convicting, and punishing criminals. But there are three great differences between the contemporary legal system and current prison disciplinary systems. *First,* in prison the inmate is expected to obey not only all laws, but a host of additional rules. Many of these rules and regulations stem from the mere fact that a large number of people must live together within rather narrow quarters, but others are designed to aid the prison in attaining its punitive objectives. Some rules are very general in nature, such as: "Inmates are expected at all times and in all parts of the institution to conduct themselves in an orderly manner and to respect the rights of others." Much behavior which is routine and customary in free society—such as cutting across a lawn, running if one is late for work, leaving unwanted food on a plate, horseplay, personal untidiness, evading work, and oversleeping—is a violation of prison rules. *Second,* inmates accused of rule violations are not represented by counsel, and in fact the procedures summarized in the expression "due process of law" are generally ignored.[15] *Third,* the reaction to a violation of a prison rule is almost never one of treatment, while in the contemporary legal system there are at least formal provisions for treatment in some cases. An inmate who is found guilty by the disciplinary board or officer is almost always punished, even if the punishment is a mere reprimand.

Four principal attitudes or conditions enter into maintenance of the punitive system of discipline: the ideal of reformation by denial of choice, the attitude of dominance, the attitude of retaliation, and the danger of escapes.

(a) The earlier psychology of reformation was based on the assumption that a habit formed by compulsion would be retained after the compulsion was removed. It was felt that since the prisoner failed to make the proper choices before his entrance into the prison, he should be given no opportunity to make choices while in the institution. Instead, all his acts should be imposed upon him. Brockway, an early prison administrator, stated this ideal as follows:

> In order to train criminals for social life they must have a strict régime and learn quick and accurate self-adjustment to a uniform requirement, habituation to the yoke of established custom. Exactness of observance is of the greatest importance . . . so that the newly formed habit of precision calls up the instinctive impulse to social orderliness quite independent of conscious volition.[16]

It is now generally agreed that this theory is incorrect, and policies based on it have already changed to a great extent. However, contemporary conditions of imprisonment are such that lack

---

[15] See Sheldon Krantz, Robert A. Bell, Jonathan Brant, and Michael Macgruder, *Model Rules and Regulations on Prisoners' Rights and Responsibilities* (St. Paul: West, 1973).

[16] Z. R. Brockway, *Fifty Years of Prison Service* (New York: Charities Publication Committee, 1912), p. 355.

of rather uniform conformity to rules by inmates may have adverse effects on any prospect for rehabilitation. Compulsion, thus, might be more conducive to rehabilitation than poor discipline which gives inmates an opportunity to exploit other inmates and also to "beat" the system which society has designed to punish them. An inmate who, while in prison, learns that he can use brute strength, lying, cheating, and stealing to get what he wants from other inmates certainly would not be on the road to rehabilitation. Similarly, poor disciplinary control which permits inmates to use fraud and other crimes to obtain goods, services, and privileges which the prison and society deny them cannot be conducive to the rehabilitation of men who have been sentenced to prison precisely because they obtained such things in an illegal manner while on the outside. Even if we abandon the idea that habits are formed by compulsion, we need not abandon the notion that criminality should be made unattractive to prisoners.

(b) The crime rate in prison is likely to be high unless inmate activities are carefully policed. Just as saturation of a high-delinquency area in a city with policemen is considered by many persons to be a desirable way to prevent crime, so careful scrutiny and regulation of inmate actions is viewed as a necessary and desirable system for preventing prisoners from attacking each other and stealing from each other. In a general sense, prison officials are hired to dominate convicted criminals. It is not surprising, therefore, that some guards attempt to dominate inmates in a specific sense.

A man who is responsible for keeping inmates inside the walls cannot be expected to have the same attitudes toward inmates as a psychologist who has the duty of providing the nonjudgmental, relaxed atmosphere necessary for psychotherapy and counseling. To be effective, personnel who are hired to guard must view inmates as dangerous, scheming, conniving men who are in need of close surveillance and domination. They cannot only watch and wait, in the way traffic policemen sometimes hide behind parked cars waiting for violations, for this would grant inmates an opportunity to gamble the advantages of nonconformity against the disadvantages of possible detection and punishment. They must minimize *potential* violations, and one way to do this is to maximize the domination of individual inmates. This means that they must show their authority, and the making and enforcing of rules and the infliction of punishment are methods of showing this authority. The officer also may express this attitude in subtle ways, such as by saying, "Keep your hands at your sides," to prisoners who are not doing so as they walk by, and then saying, "That's right, keep your hands at your sides," to inmates who have not even thought of having their hands anywhere else. Inmates are believed to have come into the prison because they could not or would not respect the rights of others in free society, and domination of their activities is considered corrective of these deficiencies in social relationships.

(c) Prison officers often have an attitude of retaliation toward the prisoners. Restriction of freedom within walls, like the general restriction of freedom stemming from "mere incarceration," is imposed merely because it is painful to the recipient. The pain may or may not be viewed as having a reformative effect; it is desired as retribution and as a deterrent. Individual officers reporting an infraction of the rules often are disappointed or angry if the offender is not punished. This attitude tends to perpetuate the system of punitive discipline, even when there is a "court" which hears cases of alleged infractions. Something like the following takes place. First, the persons on the disciplinary board ordinarily are the superior prison officials, and, consequently, some guards are eager to report infractions since they feel that such reports indicate that they are alert and capable. Next, since offenders "should get what's coming to them," nonpunishment of an offender is apt to be interpreted by the reporting guard as a reprimand for overzealousness in reporting offenses, even if that is not the motive of the "court." Finally, the "court" is apt, then, to use punitive rather than nonpunitive methods in handling infractions because it feels that employee morale will suffer if there is no punishment.

However, it is not true that officers are free to report all violations to the disciplinary court. On the contrary, inmates know that they can "fire" a guard from a specific post by forcing him to write numerous conduct reports. Court officials who observe that many reports are written on a group of inmates when one guard is on duty and that few are written on the same group when a second guard is on duty are likely to conclude that the first guard is an agitator who cannot get along with the men. If he falls into the inmates' trap, the guard may be transferred to a wall tower or some other post where contact with inmates is minimal. Even in circumstances in which an officer appears to be overenthusiastic and "ticket happy," however, the court must punish the inmates reported. Failure to do so in a consistent manner would be to turn administration of the prison over to the inmates.[17] This, in a sense, is also what occurs when inmates are permitted to "fire" officers.

(d) The great threat to American prison administrators, which is perhaps the principal source of rigid discipline in American prisons, is escapes. Security against escape takes precedence over everything else, and all policies are limited by considerations of the danger of escape. Emphasis on prevention of escapes results from the attempt to attain the objective of incapacitation, but it also results from the attempt to obtain the retaliatory and deterrence objectives. While some prisoners have become so adapted

---

[17] See Gresham M. Sykes, "The Corruption of Authority and Rehabilitation," *Social Forces*, 34:257-262, March, 1956.

to institutional life that they do not wish to escape, in the appropriate circumstances a large number would even attempt to escape from a prison which is as delightful as some of the newspapers picture the actual prisons. Escape by a prisoner is not regarded as a crime in England, Germany, Mexico, Spain, and other nations. "It is regarded as something to be expected of confined men and is punishable by some such method as isolation on reduced rations for two weeks."[18] Yet extreme measures are taken by some European prison directors to prevent escapes. The fundamental reason for opposition to confinement is the fact of confinement, and the most delightful entertainments, recreations, and food will not make such a place desirable to most inmates. Permitting prisoners to determine their own schedules, rules, and routines is, then, likely to be dangerous, for it allows inmates to join forces.

While it would be absurd to contend that the antagonism between prison officials and inmates cannot possibly be eliminated, it appears to be inherent in the prison system in a way that unsanitary conditions or poor food are not. This does not, however, make it impossible to eliminate brutal disciplinary practices which mitigate the effects of treatment programs. But as long as prisons are considered the means for attaining punitive as well as treatment objectives, some aspects of the system of rigid discipline must remain. ●

Efficient administration of prisons has been generally lacking. When personnel are selected on the basis of political patronage, it is very difficult to secure efficiency, even in routine matters. A warden who is a political appointee appoints guards and administrative personnel who have shown some evidence of loyalty to the political party he represents. Often the county or state committee of the political party in office submits a list of loyal party workers from which the warden must make his appointments. When the party in power changes, the warden changes, or, at least, there is a general shake-up of the prison personnel. Over a period of fifty years, the average tenure of 612 wardens was 5.2 years. Only 13 percent held their jobs for ten years or more, and 22 percent were in office one year or less.[19] In only twenty-three states are the superintendents of institutions for adults covered by a civil service or merit system, and such a system for institutional employees does not exist in thirteen states. Professional workers have civil service appointments in thirty-six states, custodial workers in thirty-seven states.[20] Civil service examinations

Administrative and custodial personnel

---

[18] Norman S. Hayner, "Correctional Systems and National Values," *British Journal of Criminology*, 3:163-175, October, 1962.

[19] Walter A. Lunden, "The Tenure and Turnover of State Prison Wardens," *American Journal of Correction*, 19:14-15 ff., December, 1957.

[20] National Council on Crime and Delinquency, "Correction in the United States," p. 181.

do not necessarily assure appointments on the basis of efficiency, since civil service examinations and requirements may be circumvented by making "temporary" appointments. Also, examinations for a high position, such as warden or deputy warden, may be rigged, so that a particular person will almost certainly make the best score and, thus, become qualified for the position. Even when examinations are fairly administered, they may do little more than eliminate the obviously unfit rather than assure the appointments of the most capable men. One study in a maximum-security prison indicated that the best guards, as judged by rating scales, tended to score only average or below average on the civil service examination. Conversely, many of the guards who were rated as "poor" had received high scores on the examination.[21]

Unqualified men obviously cannot, by reason of sheer indifference or ignorance, perform the duties necessary for prevention of waste and for efficient, businesslike operation of an institution. Moreover, filling institutional positions on the basis of political patronage often means that the personnel will be corrupt as well as inefficient.

Appointment of unqualified personnel often means, also, that the prison cannot attain its reformation objective. It is becoming increasingly apparent that the success of treatment programs depends to a large extent upon the attitudes of the subordinate staff toward prisoner participation in such programs. Guards probably have more opportunities for changing inmates' attitudes than any other class of prison workers, yet they are seldom equipped for this exceedingly difficult task.[22] Many released prisoners report that even under the present system guards and industrial workers have more impact on the inmates than do professional treatment specialists. However, 77 percent of the inmates engaged in a special counseling program chose their counselors as the persons who helped them most; 4 percent chose correctional officers. Twenty-one percent of a control group chose correctional officers, and 45 percent chose vocational instructors or job supervisors.[23]

Generally speaking, the status of custodial officers is undergoing a change. In many states, they are called "correctional officers," rather than "guards," in keeping with their new responsibilities. In some institutions, programs for technical training of guards are being developed. Some authorities believe that such programs are likely to result in a closer integration of the punitive

---

[21] Korn and McCorkle, *Criminology and Penology*, p. 503.

[22] Donald R. Cressey, "Social Psychological Foundations for Using Criminals in the Rehabilitation of Criminals," *Journal of Research in Crime and Delinquency*, 2:49-59, July, 1965. See also Charles W. Slack, "Experimenter-Subject Psychotherapy: A New Method of Introducing Intensive Office Treatment for Unreachable Cases," *Mental Hygiene*, 44:238-256, April, 1960.

[23] Alvin Rudoff, *The PICO Project: A Measure of Casework in Corrections*, Second Technical Report (Sacramento: Department of Corrections, 1959), pp. 16-17.

and treatment activities. It takes some time for treatment workers and custodial workers to come to an understanding of each other and to develop coordinated programs through systems of compromise.[24] Preservice and in-service training for guards could, no doubt, accomplish a great deal in this respect.

It must be emphasized, however, that even if institutions secure well-trained personnel, the overload of work and the social structure of the institution generally restrict attempts to develop adequate treatment programs. Occasionally, as in Massachusetts, New Jersey, New York, California, Wisconsin, and the federal prison system, capable leaders have been able to secure appointments on the basis of efficiency and ability, but institutions in these states have not been shown to be outstanding successes as rehabilitation agencies.

Prisons differ significantly from other organizations because their personnel hierarchies are organized down to the lowest level for the administration of the daily activities of men.[25] In a factory, for example, there are hierarchies of management personnel and of the workers. By way of contrast, the guard, who is the lowest-level worker in a prison, is both a worker and a manager. He is managed in a system of regulations and controls from above, but he also manages, in a corresponding system of regulations, the inmates who are in his charge. He is a low-status worker in interaction with administrators, but a higher-status foreman or officer in interaction with inmates. He has no exact counterpart in the business and industrial world. The closest analogy is the overseer of a crew of slaves who are viewed as being "outside" the organization designed to utilize their labor. Even here, however, the analogy is fallacious except as it refers to the guards who serve as foremen of inmate industrial or maintenance crews.

Most guards do not "use" inmates productively any more than they, in their roles as guards, are used productively by prison wardens. They manage and are managed in an organization where management is an end, not a means. This fact makes the guard's job an extraordinarily difficult one. Unlike popular stereotypes which picture the guard as either a brutal sadist with a club or as a robot standing on a wall with a rifle, guards are managers of men. They are responsible for keeping convicted criminals quiet and secure and for supervising groups of men who have no loyalty to the prison. Yet they do not have the help

---

[24] See George H. Weber, "Conflicts Between Professional and Non-Professional Personnel in Institutional Delinquency Treatment," *Journal of Criminal Law, Criminology, and Police Science*, 48:26-43, May-June, 1957. See also idem, "Emotional and Defensive Reactions of Cottage Parents," in Donald R. Cressey, ed., *The Prison: Studies in Institutional Organization and Change* (New York: Holt, Rinehart and Winston, 1961), pp. 189-228.

[25] See Donald R. Cressey, "Contradictory Directives in Complex Organizations: The Case of the Prison," *Administrative Science Quarterly*, 4:1-19, June, 1959. See also idem, "Prison Organizations," in James G. March, ed., *Handbook of Organizations* (Chicago: Rand McNally, 1965), pp. 1023-1070.

of ordinary "incentives" such as wages, promotions, threat of discharge, or even force.

Further, the emphasis upon humanitarianism and treatment in modern prisons has effectively deprived guards of many means of control. At a minimum, custodial practices must be "humane." Thus, inmates cannot be kept docile by severe punishments or severe deprivations; neither can a large number be kept in solitary confinement. Guards control prisoners who must be handled humanely and permitted to work together and in other ways consort with each other. They are expected to exact compliance to rules and restrictive conditions that have been deliberately designed to make inmates' lives unpleasant, but at the same time they are to minimize friction between inmates and staff. They are to contribute to inmate rehabilitation by relaxing, being nondirective, and showing concern for inmate personality problems, but they also are expected to act as policemen, protecting inmates from each other. On top of all this, they are to keep inmates busy at maintenance, housekeeping, and production tasks, to administer justice, and to insure that escapes do not occur. Generally speaking, it is believed that for effective treatment, guards must relax in custodial and disciplinary matters, take the personality needs of each inmate into account, and individualize the handling of inmates accordingly. These practices are viewed either as constituting treatment itself or as a means of assisting (or at least not hindering) the treatment practices of professional personnel such as social workers and psychologists.

The introduction of humanitarianism and treatment in prisons has, therefore, had as one of its effects the introduction of conflicting directives for guards. These conflicting directives make it almost impossible for the guard to do anything which will be judged to be correct by his superiors. If guards attempt to get strict conformity to institutional rules, they risk being accused of antagonizing inmates. Rules must be enforced, but the enforcement must not be so rigid and arbitrary that the inmates are stimulated to riot or rebel. If they attempt to use common sense and discretion in attempting to get conformity to rules, then they risk being accused of not being alert to potential danger or even of corruption. If they enforce discipline and insist on inmate orderliness, they risk undesirable diagnosis as "rigid," "punitive," or "neurotic," for such enforcement theoretically interferes with individualized treatment. But if they relax to a degree that institutional security and organization seem to be threatened, then they risk undesirable diagnosis as lazy or unmotivated. ●

The success and failure of imprisonment

As a means of incapacitation, imprisonment has not been very successful. Very few crimes against outsiders are committed by prisoners during the period of incarceration, but the crime rate in prisons is high nevertheless. The crimes of prisoners are committed principally against other prisoners, prison guards and other officers, and against prison property. Such crimes within prison communities are very frequent. Prison property is seldom safe from theft. Prisoners frequently commit crimes against each other in the form of theft, assault, and murder. Forced homosexual practices and the use of narcotic drugs flourish in many prisons and exist to some extent in most prisons.

Intramural crimes, as well as extramural crimes, vary in frequency in different prisons and are affected by the prison policies. Probably the strict isolation of the original Pennsylvania system was more effective than any other prison policy in incapacitating prisoners. This does not justify a conclusion that the Pennsylvania system is in general most efficient, for other values must be considered.

The success of the prison in deterring the general public from crime is probably much less than its success in incapacitating criminals. Imprisonment certainly has some deterrent effect, but it is difficult to compare the deterrent effects of different prison policies or to isolate the effect of any prison policy from the effect of the whole process of arrest and conviction. The deterrent effect of imprisonment probably increases slightly with the horrors of prison life, though this is likely to be offset by the difficulty of securing convictions if the public feels that the horrors of imprisonment are greater than the horrors of the crimes. Perhaps the fact of incarceration, regardless of conditions within prisons, is the most important factor in deterrence.

The success of imprisonment as a means of reformation is very slight. The statistics on this point are inadequate, but they indicate that the methods thus far developed have not been attended by very significant changes in recidivism. In 1970, 81 percent of the persons committed to federal prisons and reformatories had previous records of commitments to penal or reformatory institutions, and this record is certainly incomplete.[26] In California during 1971, 65,236 felony defendants were disposed of in the superior courts. Of these, 22 percent had no institutional record. Thirty percent had been convicted of minor charges for which the penalty assessed was less than ninety days; 32 percent had previously been convicted and sentenced for periods of ninety days or more, and 16 percent had served a prior prison term.[27] A four-year follow-up study of offenders granted a mandatory release by a

---

[26] *Federal Offenders in the United States District Courts, 1970* (Washington: Administrative Office of the U.S. Courts), p. 62.

[27] *Crime and Delinquency in California, 1967* (Sacramento: Department of Justice, 1968), p. 127.

penal institution in 1965 indicated that 75 percent had been arrested by December 31, 1969; 61 percent of those released on parole had been arrested.[28] Some studies indicate that the crimes ordinarily considered "serious" are decreased by imprisonment and parole. Of 965 California parolees released in 1963 and 1964, 426 (44 percent) had committed new felonies within a three-year follow-up period. Twenty-one percent of narcotic offenders repeated their original crimes. Narcotic offenders and burglars had the highest general recidivism rates: 55 and 51 percent, respectively.[29] Of 311 men released from a Massachusetts reformatory, 56 percent returned to prison—half for new offenses and half for technical parole violations.[30]

In the most comprehensive study that has been made on recidivism, Glaser in 1960 studied a sample of 1,015 men drawn by taking every tenth case from a list of adult males released from federal prisons in 1956. He found that 35 percent of these men could be classed as "failures," a category which included persons returned to prison for new offenses or as parole violators, and persons given nonprison sentences for felonylike offenses. The "successes" included 52 percent who had no further criminal record whatsoever and 13 percent who had been convicted for misdemeanors or arrested (but not convicted) on felony charges.[31] Table XIX shows the percentage of failures in various offense, age, and confinement categories.[32] The high failure rates should not be regarded as the responsibility of the last institution which dealt with these offenders. No institution, receiving the failures of the rest of society, should be expected to reform a very large proportion of them. Also, the institution cannot properly be given the credit for those who reform after imprisonment.[33] Persistence in crime and desistance from crime are affected by conditions other than the institutional policies.

Gottfredson has shown that when certain noninstitutional factors known to be associated with parole success are held constant, differences in the recidivism rates of men released from different prisons tend to disappear. In other words, the eight California

---

[28] Federal Bureau of Investigation, *Uniform Crime Reports, 1970* (Washington: Government Printing Office, 1971), p. 37.

[29] Gene Kassebaum, David A. Ward, and Daniel M. Wilner, *Prison Treatment and Parole Survival* (New York: John Wiley, 1971), p. 293.

[30] Ralph Metzner and Gunther Weil, "Predicting Recidivism: Base-Rates for Massachusetts Correctional Institution at Concord," *Journal of Criminal Law, Criminology, and Police Science*, 54:307-316, September, 1963.

[31] Daniel Glaser, *The Effectiveness of a Prison and Parole System* (Indianapolis: Bobbs-Merrill, 1964), pp. 19-20.

[32] Ibid., p. 474.

[33] See Donald R. Cressey, "The Nature and Effectiveness of Correctional Techniques," *Law and Contemporary Problems*, 23:754-771, Autumn, 1958.

prisons studied—ranging from maximum- to minimum-security, and with different programs—performed equally well with respect to the success criterion used, considering the kinds of risks assigned to them.[34]

Percent of postrelease failures among 1956 federal releases of various ages, by prior involvements in crime

TABLE XI.

	Age at release from prison				
	18-21	*22-25*	*26-35*	*36 and over*	*All cases*
Number of prior sentences for felonylike offenses:					
None	44% (78)[b]	31% (98)	21% (151)	11% (96)	25% (423)
One	52% (31)	46% (37)	34% (105)	25% (48)	37% (221)
Two	57% (23)	52% (27)	45% (64)	28% (40)	44% (154)
Three or more	45% (11)	63% (16)	48% (86)	42% (104)	46% (217)
Age at first arrest:					
16 and under	53% (94)	43% (68)	43% (106)	40% (36)	46% (304)
17-20	37% (49)	45% (73)	41% (116)	28% (78)	38% (316)
21 and over	— —	24% (37)	24% (184)	24% (174)	24% (395)
Time confined:					
18 months or under	44% (78)	39% (96)	27% (202)	24% (157)	31% (533)
Over 18 months	52% (65)	41% (82)	41% (204)	31% (131)	40% (482)
All cases	48% (143)	40% (178)	34% (406)	27% (288)	35% (1015)

[a] "Failure" means return to prison for new offense or as parole violator, or any nonprison sentence for a felonylike offense.
[b] Number of cases in parentheses.

Fundamental and relatively inherent difficulties accompany imprisonment, as has been shown. The prison must necessarily have a low degree of efficiency in reformation. There is a tendency to believe a prison is a success if it does not make offenders worse.

[34] Don M. Gottfredson, "The Role of Base Expectancies in the Study of Treatments," paper read at the meetings of the Western Psychological Association, April, 1959.

Nowadays it is again becoming popular to argue, as it was argued twenty years ago, that we should "break down the walls." More and more concerned citizens and correctional workers are saying that imprisonment, as a principal method for dealing with criminals, should be regarded as undesirable, and that other methods should be substituted for it as rapidly as possible. We have begun to carry out these recommendations. The general tendency in the last generation has been to substitute probation for imprisonment; in many states probation is used for more offenders than is imprisonment, although fifty years ago the ratio could not have been more than one to ten. Now "community treatment programs" are being developed to replace, or supplement, probation.[35]

Nevertheless, the idea that dangerous criminals should be imprisoned has become deeply rooted in the last two centuries, and imprisonment will be with us for some time to come. What is needed is theory and practice which explicitly face the fact that in our present society prisons must, by definition, be abnormally restrictive and, thus, punitive. ●

Suggested readings

BUFFUM, PETER C. *Homosexuality in Prisons*. Washington: Government Printing Office, 1972.

CARTER, ROBERT M., DANIEL GLASER, & LESLIE T. WILKINS, eds. *Correctional Institutions*. Philadelphia: Lippincott, 1972.

CONRAD, JOHN. *Crime and Its Correction: An International Survey of Attitudes and Practices*. Berkeley and Los Angeles: University of California Press, 1965.

CRESSEY, DONALD R., ed. *The Prison: Studies in Institutional Organization and Change*. New York: Holt, Rinehart and Winston, 1961.

FOX, VERNON. *Introduction to Corrections*. Englewood Cliffs, N. J.: Prentice-Hall, 1972.

GALLINGTON, DANIEL J. "Prison Disciplinary Decisions." *Journal of Criminal Law, Criminology, and Police Science*, 60:152-164, June, 1969.

GIBBONS, DON C. *Changing the Lawbreaker: The Treatment of Delinquents and Criminals*. Englewood Cliffs, N.J.: Prentice-Hall, 1965.

GLASER, DANIEL. *The Effectiveness of a Prison and Parole System*. Indianapolis: Bobbs-Merrill, 1964.

HAZELRIGG, LAWRENCE E., ed. *Prison Within Society: A Reader in Penology*. New York: Doubleday, 1968.

NAGEL, WILLIAM G. *The New Red Barn: A Critical Look at the Modern American Prison*. Philadelphia: The American Foundation, 1973.

OHLIN, LLOYD E., ed. *Prisoners in America*. Englewood Cliffs, N. J.: Prentice-Hall, 1973.

---

[35] See Marguerite Q. Warren, *Correctional Treatment in Community Settings: A Report of Current Research* (Washington: Government Printing Office, 1972).

RABOW, JEROME, & ALBERT ELIAS. "Organizational Boundaries, Inmate Roles, and Rehabilitation." *Journal of Research in Crime and Delinquency*, 6:8-16, January, 1969.

ROBINSON, LOUIS N. "Contradictory Purposes in Prisons." *Journal of Criminal Law and Criminology*, 37:449-457, March-April, 1947.

RUDOVSKY, DAVID. *The Rights of Prisoners: The Basic ACLU Guide to a Prisoner's Rights*. New York: Avon, 1973.

SCHRAG, CLARENCE. "The Correctional System: Problems and Prospects." *Annals of the American Academy of Political and Social Science*, 381:11-20, January, 1969.

SHAH, SALEEM A. "Treatment of Offenders: Some Behavioral Concepts, Principles, and Approaches." *Federal Probation*, 30: 29-38, March, 1966.

SPARKS, RICHARD F. *Local Prisons: The Crisis in the English Penal System*. London: Heinemann, 1971.

SYKES, GRESHAM M. *The Society of Captives: A Study of a Maximum Security Prison*. Princeton: Princeton University Press, 1958.

WARD, DAVID A. "Inmate Rights and Prison Reform in Sweden and Denmark." *Journal of Criminal Law, Criminology, and Police Science*, 63:240-255, June, 1972.

WILKINS, LESLIE T. *Evaluation of Penal Measures*. New York: Random House, 1969.

WRIGHT, ERIK OLIN. *The Politics of Punishment*. New York: Harper and Row, 1973.

ZIMRING, FRANKLIN E. *Perspectives on Deterrence*. Washington: Government Printing Office, 1971.

24 The prison community

The policy of individualized treatment developed as a reaction to the eighteenth-century attempts to impose uniform penalties on criminals. Members of the positive school argued that uniform punishments for all criminals could be no more effective than a policy calling for uniform handling of all medical patients, and the alternative eventually proposed was the system of individualized treatment. In the early period under this system, little or no attention was paid to the offender's relations with groups, presumably on the assumption that personality and behavior disorders have little to do with groups and can, consequently, be treated in a clinic, just as tuberculosis can be treated in a clinic. Gradually, the treatment methods based on this "clinical principle" have been supplemented by methods based on the "group-relations principle" that criminality is social in nature and, therefore, can be modified in individual cases only if the criminal's relations with social groups are modified.[1] This trend may be observed in correctional work generally, and it also may be observed in the work with prisoners. ●

Group-relations work in prisons

When considered as a general system for handling criminals, comparable to probation, imprisonment cannot operate on the group-relations principle. Because prisoners, by definition, must in many respects be isolated from law-abiding persons, the reformative influences of any prison are distinctly limited by the very nature of imprisonment. Even the use of treatment methods based on the clinical principle is severely limited by the punitive conditions of imprisonment, although not to the extent that use of methods based on the group-relations principle is limited; it is probably for this reason that in prisons clinical methods currently enjoy a much greater popularity than do group-relations methods. But for at least a century some persons have recognized that the offender can most effectively be trained for participation in law-abiding society by being provided with membership in that society, and this acknowledgment of the importance of group relations to reformation has led to many modifications of the conditions of imprisonment. Implicitly, at least, the group-relations principle has become the basis of many contemporary prison practices and policies. In relatively recent years there has been a growing awareness among prison workers of the necessity for promoting informal contacts between prisoners and law-abiding groups and for studying and developing interaction among the prisoners themselves.

Reduction of prisoner isolation

Although prisoners for the most part continue to be separated from law-abiding groups and from most kinds of social relations in which they will be expected to participate after release, isolation of inmates has gradually been reduced by "prison reforms" undertaken for humanitarian reasons during the last century. Isolation also has been reduced by systems of individualized treatment which, while not explicitly acknowledging the importance of group associations on criminality and reformation, have promoted social relations with law-abiding groups, just as probation and parole have promoted such relations.

For example, visiting and correspondence privileges are restricted in all prisons, yet the very fact that they exist and are being extended reveals implicit recognition of the importance of reducing the degree of prisoner isolation.[2] Mexico and some American states permit prisoners with records of good behavior

---

[1] See the discussion above, pp. 358-360.

[2] See David Rudovsky, The Rights of Prisoners: The Basic ACLU Guide to a Prisoner's Rights (New York: Avon, 1973), pp. 41-68.

to have private visits with their wives and families. Home visits are permitted prisoners in England, Sweden, Poland, and Argentina. Many American jails, and a few prisons, have introduced work-release programs which permit inmates to work in private industry outside the institution during the weekday.

Furthermore, prison administrators always take precautions to see that visitors and correspondents are law-abiding, again implicitly recognizing the effects of group relations upon criminality and reformation. Also, obviously, the general provision in prisons of newspapers, books, magazines, television, moving pictures, and extramural athletic events reduces the inmates' isolation. Even classification, which frequently is used as the best example of a treatment method based on the clinical principle, involves recognition of group effects on the criminality or noncriminality of the prisoners. The separation, by means of classification, of first offenders and habitual criminals must be based on the notion that the behavior of individual first offenders will be positively affected by placing them in association with persons having relatively few criminal attitudes or, at least, that the behavior of first offenders should not be adversely affected by forcing them into membership in groups composed of experienced criminals. Similarly, educational, vocational, religious, and even individual psychotherapy programs may be interpreted as efforts to reform inmates by providing them with associations representative of the noncriminal world and by modifying their skills in such a way that upon release they will abandon membership in the groups which promoted their criminality. All such privileges and treatment programs are administered, of course, within the framework of prison security, discipline, and punishment.

The group-relations principle for treatment also has been recognized in programs designed to develop a prison social life somewhat comparable to the social life outside prisons. One basis for such programs is the notion that if prisoners are to be reformed, they must be permitted to participate in social situations which are to some extent representative of the kinds of noncriminal social interaction in which they will be expected to participate upon release. Another basis, of course, is the hope that inmate participation programs will simplify administrative problems of discipline and control. One of the earliest specific attempts to promote social interaction among prisoners was the development of self-government systems.

Self-government by prisoners

As early as 1793, a modified system of self-government was used in the Walnut Street Jail in Philadelphia. In the institutions for juvenile delinquents in New York and Boston in the first few years of their history, the delinquents had a self-governing court and voting participation in the election of some of the officers. In the Massachusetts state prison, about 1845, the prisoners were organized into a society for improvement and mutual aid, primarily by discussion of topics of interest to the prisoners; the warden was president of the organization, and it was clearly not spontaneous, but was imposed upon the prisoners.[3] In the 1860s, Brockway organized a system in the Detroit House of Correction which he described as "almost complete self-government."[4] In 1895, William George founded the George Junior Republic at Freeville, New York, with the principle of self-government very prominent. Apparently it was this institution, rather than the earlier precedents, which was important in the development of self-government in the next two generations, for one of the directors of this Republic was Thomas M. Osborne, who became the chief advocate of self-government.[5]

Despite favorable accounts of the custodial accomplishments of a system of self-government in some institutions, and despite the theoretical value of a system which stimulates participation in groups which hold noncriminality as an ideal, many students of prison systems have grave doubts about it. A recent poll of fifty-two state penitentiary wardens brought replies from forty-four, only seven of whom had inmate councils in their institutions.[6] Similarly, in 1962 only eight of the thirty-two federal prisons had inmate councils.[7]

There are two principal objections to inmate councils and other forms of self-government. First, if the council in fact has any power to govern, it tends to be controlled by inmates who manipulate it to their own advantage. Powerful prisoners use the weapons of imprisonment, including solitary confinement and deprivation of privileges, against inmates who do not do their bidding. When this occurs, self-government represents a neglect of duty on the part of officials, for one function of prisons is protection of inmates from outsiders and from each other.[8] The system of inmate government used by Brockway in a Boston house of correction some years ago resulted in frequent escapes; the officers of the league were arrogant toward the prison officials and lorded it over the inmates, locking up more in solitary confinement than had ever been locked up under the control of the prison officials. The prisoners finally pleaded to have it abolished. After a trial of

---

[3] O. F. Lewis, *The Development of American Prisons and Prison Customs, 1776-1845* (New York: Prison Association of New York, 1922), pp. 169-170.

[4] Z. R. Brockway, *Fifty Years of Prison Service* (New York: Charities Publication Committee, 1912), p. 97.

[5] See T. M. Osborne, *Society and Prisons* (New Haven: Yale University Press, 1916); W. D. Lane, "Democracy for Law Breakers," *New Republic,* 18:173, March 8, 1919; and Frank Tannenbaum, *Osborne of Sing Sing* (Chapel Hill, N.C.: University of North Carolina Press, 1933).

[6] J. E. Baker, "Inmate Self-Government," *Journal of Criminal Law, Criminology, and Police Science,* 55:39-47, March, 1964.

[7] Daniel Glaser, *The Effectiveness of a Prison and Parole System* (Indianapolis: Bobbs-Merrill, 1964), p. 219.

[8] Donald R. Cressey, "Achievement of an Unstated Organizational Goal: An Observation on Prisons," *Pacific Sociological Review,* 1:43-49, Fall, 1958; see also Amitai Etzioni, "Two Approaches to Organizational Analysis: A Critique and a Suggestion," *Administrative Science Quarterly,* 5:257-278, September, 1960.

self-government for about a year, the inmates of the New Jersey State Reformatory at Rahway abandoned it by a vote that was practically unanimous. Ward politics had developed; cliques were formed; the shrewd prisoners were elected to offices; and prisoners against whom grudges were held were punished. When, shortly after World War II, Oahu Prison in Hawaii moved away from an authoritarian system of administration to a more democratic system, an inmate council was established with unusually broad responsibilities and direct access to the warden on policy matters.[9] At first, this did not disturb the order of the prison, for the old, custodially-oriented inmates gained election to a majority of the seats. Gradually, however, the council was taken over by younger inmates, who referred to themselves as a "syndicate," and who used the privileges granted as devices for demanding even more privileges; a wave of violence, disorder, and anarchy then occurred.[10] A similar sequence took place in the New Jersey State Prison at Trenton.[11]

Second, in response to incidents such as those indicated above, inmate councils have tended to become mere window dressing. They are made up principally of inmates called "square Johns" or "do-rights," and these types of inmates do not have the respect of the real inmate leaders. They take actions which are of little significance to the government of the prison, and all their actions are subject to veto by the warden. A principal function of contemporary inmate councils, for example, is one of communicating inmate preferences in respect to recreational matters—the movies and television programs to be shown, and the radio programs to be received on the headsets provided in the cells. The councils also organize various safe activities, such as athletic tournaments and campaigns for blood bank donations.[12]

These experiences with self-government do not necessarily show that it will be impossible to establish successful self-government systems in the future. It should be recalled, however, that the current system of imprisonment is so designed that inmates can have no loyalty to the prison which keeps them confined, and no loyalty to any majority of their fellow prisoners.

The honor system is similar to self-government only in that it places responsibility upon prisoners and gives them a chance to make choices. Under the honor system, the prison officials grant, as rewards for good behavior and loyalty, privileges which are conditional upon continued good behavior and loyalty. The loy-

The honor system

---

[9] Richard H. McCleery, "The Governmental Process and Informal Social Control," chap. 4 in Donald R. Cressey, ed., *The Prison: Studies in Institutional Organization and Change* (New York: Holt, Rinehart and Winston, 1961), p. 171.

[10] Ibid., pp. 172-181.

[11] Gresham M. Sykes, *The Society of Captives: A Study of a Maximum Security Prison* (Princeton: Princeton University Press, 1958), pp. 119-120.

[12] Glaser, *Effectiveness of a Prison and Parole System*, pp. 217-219.

alty is partly to the officials and partly to other inmates. The prisoner who is given privileges or other rewards in return for his promise not to escape or violate prison rules does not want other trusted prisoners to suffer in case he breaks his trust. Further, because the other prisoners want the privileges, they help the officials control the potential violator. It is obvious that most criminals cannot be converted into men of honor and transformed into noncriminals simply by saying, "From now on I am going to trust you." Although inmates released from honor camps and minimum-security honor institutions have lower parole violation rates and recidivism rates than do other prisoners, this record might be due merely to the fact that only the men who are considered most likely to reform are permitted to participate in such programs.

Group therapy   Since World War II, group therapy has become relatively popular in prisons, and it often is considered a system, similar in principle to self-government, for reforming prisoners by giving them experience in social groups. Although there are many forms of group therapy, it usually consists of a program in which small groups of inmates meet regularly and discuss their problems; a therapist —either trained or untrained—guides the discussion but does not restrict it.

The current emphasis on group therapy, also called "group psychotherapy," "group counseling" and "group psychoanalysis," grew out of the difficulty of treating mental disease cases individually during World War II. There is an almost unanimous opinion that group therapy is a markedly effective technique for dealing with mental patients. In this area, the chief contribution of group therapy has been elimination or reduction of social isolation and egocentricity, or, stated positively, the assimilation of isolated or egocentric patients into clinical groups.

The group-relations principle applied to intramural treatment of prisoners ideally goes beyond this program of group integration in the narrow sense and attempts, by means of prison groups, to present inmates with anticriminal behavior patterns. The aim is not mere reduction of isolation and belligerence among prisoners as they operate in the prison situation, but the provision of positive contacts with groups which will directly or indirectly implant in the prisoner the anticriminal values of the larger society.[13] In California, for example, Department of Corrections staff members believe that participation in their program lessens endorsement of the inmate code (positive attitude change), reduces prison disciplinary reports, and lowers the likelihood of being returned to prison.[14] It is probable that group-therapy programs in prisons do

---

[13] Cf. Lloyd W. McCorkle, Albert Elias, and F. Lovell Bixby, *The Highfields Story* (New York: Holt, 1958), pp. 68-80; and Don C. Gibbons, *Changing the Lawbreaker: The Treatment of Delinquents and Criminals* (Englewood Cliffs, N.J.: Prentice-Hall, 1965), pp. 146-147.

[14] Gene Kassebaum, David A. Ward, and Daniel M. Wilner, *Prison Treatment and Parole Survival: An Empirical Assessment* (New York: John Wiley, 1971), p. 14.

not ordinarily have this positive objective but, instead, merely attempt to provide permissive situations which enable inmates both to discuss their problems with each other freely and to "ventilate" their "suppressed hostilities" toward the courts, the police, and the prison. According to the proponents of the clinical principle, but not those of the group-relations principle, this "reforms" inmates by enabling them to rid themselves of certain individual emotional disorders which are considered the causes of their criminality. There is little difference between the aims of such programs and the aims of individual, clinical psychotherapy.

Group therapy has been used extensively in the New Jersey prisons and reformatories, where it was called "guided group interaction," and in the California institutions, where it is called "group counseling." Both labels were invented in an attempt to avoid confusion with the use of group therapy as practiced by psychiatrists and to avoid the implication that all inmates are mentally abnormal.[15] The therapists in these programs are primarily prison guards and tradesmen. They have tried to go beyond mere ventilation and reduction of isolation, attempting in a more positive way to utilize the group for reformation of offenders.[16] It has been stated, for example, that in guided group interaction "the major emphasis is on the group and its development, rather than on an attempt at exhaustive psychoanalysis of individuals in the group."[17] Similarly, cognizance of the group-relations principle seems to be indicated by the following definition and statement of the aims of guided group interaction: "The use of free discussion in a friendly supportive atmosphere to re-educate the delinquent to accept the restrictions of society by finding greater personal satisfaction in conforming to social rules than following delinquent patterns."[18]

It is not clear how these aims at reformation are specifically accomplished, but guided group interaction and group counseling programs seem to be based, implicitly or explicitly, on four principal assumptions about the processes by which the group sessions contribute to individual reformation. Three of these assumptions are consistent with the clinical principle, only one with the group-relations principle.

---

[15] Lloyd W. McCorkle, "Group Therapy," in Paul W. Tappan, ed., *Contemporary Correction* (New York: McGraw-Hill, 1951), pp. 211-223; Norman Fenton, *An Introduction to Group Counseling in State Correctional Service* (New York: American Correctional Association, 1958); Norman Fenton et al., *Explorations in the Use of Group Counseling in the County Correctional Program* (Palo Alto, Calif.: Pacific Books, 1962); and Guy Houchon, "Introduction au Group Counseling Pénitentiaire," *Bulletin De L'Administration Pénitentiaire* (Belgium), 17:311-327, December, 1963.

[16] See James Robinson and Marimette Kevorkian, *Intensive Treatment Project, Phase II, Parole Outcome: Interim Report* (Sacramento: California Department of Corrections, 1967).

[17] Lloyd W. McCorkle, "Group Therapy in the Treatment of Offenders," *Federal Probation*, 16:22-27, December, 1952.

[18] Ibid.

First, there seems to be an assumption that free discussion of an inmate's problem and personality characteristics by and with an inmate group and a therapist will both enable him and force him to "face the facts" of his case by "getting beneath the surface."[19] Inmates who have had experiences similar to his will not let him lie, bluff, or provide ex post facto justifications for his criminal behavior. Presumably, the inmate eventually will accept his fellow inmates' friendly denunciations of his behavior and rationalizations more readily than he would accept the rejections and denunciations of the same behavior and rationalizations by an outsider.

Second, it apparently is assumed that stimulation to "face the facts" will give the individual "insight" by enabling him to see that his problems are due to such attitudes as "resentment of authority," or "feelings of guilt," or "frustration." Such insight, combined with the opportunity to ventilate, presumably will reform him. This is obviously in keeping with the notion, based on clinical principle, that if a criminal is able to dissipate the "tensions" and "anxieties" arising from his emotional disturbances, he will be reformed.[20]

Third, it seems to be assumed that guided group interaction will give the inmate experience in accepting the analyses, opinions, and arguments of others in the inmate group, and that this, in turn, will give him needed practice in accepting the general "restrictions of society." This assumption is consistent with the individualistic, clinical notion that there is a war between "the individual" and "society." One variety of this idea in criminology is that the individual, because of something in him, "breaks through" the restrictions of society and follows criminal patterns. For reformation, the something in him must be modified, and this can be done in a clinic.[21] Another variety, possibly the one used in guided group interaction, is that the criminal's character makeup is egocentric rather than altruistic—he thinks in terms of "I" rather than "we" and, consequently, follows delinquent patterns. By guided group interaction this individualistic makeup, which is considered as being in opposition to the spirit of "society" and "group living," purportedly is removed by the therapist and the fellow inmates, who will not let the individual "get away with" the expression of his egocentric character. But according to the group-relations principle, the problem is not one of "individual versus society," but, instead, of one kind of values (criminal) versus another kind of values (anticriminal). What we

[19] See J. Douglas Grant and Marguerite Q. Grant, "A Group Dynamics Approach to the Treatment of Nonconformists in the Navy," *Annals of the American Academy of Political and Social Science,* 322:126-136, March, 1959.

[20] See Norman Fenton, *Group Counseling: A Preface to its Use in Correctional and Welfare Agencies* (Sacramento: Institute for the Study of Crime and Delinquency, 1961), pp. 46-50.

[21] Sees Hans J. Eysenck, "The Effects of Psychotherapy," *International Journal of Psychiatry,* 1:102-116, 1965.

attempt to correct in our prisons is not nonconformity or lack of satisfaction in conformity to "social rules" or "restrictions of society," but, instead, conformity and satisfaction in conformity to the norms and values of which we, the lawmakers, do not approve.

A fourth implicit assumption is consistent with the group-relations principle. It is expected that each participant in the group sessions gains experience in the role of a law-abiding person, and that this experience will carry over to the life outside the session and outside the prison. Here, the reformative effect of the sessions is considered as operating not on the inmate as his criminal behavior and attitudes are analyzed and denounced, but, instead, on the inmate as he does the analyzing and denouncing.[22] As the participant attempts to change the behavior of others, he necessarily recognizes that behavior as undesirable. And he must identify with and "take the side" of anticriminal groups when he condemns law violation and law violators. He becomes a reformer, rather than a reformee, and in denouncing the criminality of others, he denounces his own criminality. Possibly, the entire group will become "anticriminal," thus supporting the new anticriminal views of individual participants. Status in the group may be assigned according to the degree of "pro-reform" behavior which is exhibited. If this occurs, there has been a real modification of the social relations of each participant in the group, and the group itself has become an effective medium of change. The personal satisfaction which a participant now obtains from denouncing criminal behavior and values actually is satisfaction in conforming to *anticriminal* social norms.

It is by no means certain that group counseling and similar group-therapy programs transfer allegiance from criminal to anticriminal values. An extensive and careful study of a California prison in which inmates were randomly selected to participate or not participate in group counseling and "group living" showed that the experimental group did not subsequently have lower parole violation rates.[23] Group therapy rarely deals with "natural groups" in the prison. Perhaps it is for this reason that any anticriminal attitudes acquired in the group sessions receive little support in the general prison community, and rarely carry over to situations outside the prison. Wheeler has shown that the private attitudes of prisoners are quite different from the attitudes they express

---

[22] See Donald R. Cressey, "Changing Criminals: The Application of the Theory of Differential Association," *American Journal of Sociology*, 61:116-120, September, 1955; Rita Volkman and Donald R. Cressey, "Differential Association and the Rehabilitation of Drug Addicts," *American Journal of Sociology*, 69:129-142, September, 1963; and Donald R. Cressey, "Social Psychological Foundations for Using Criminals in the Rehabilitation of Criminals," *Journal of Research in Crime and Delinquency*, 2:49-59, July, 1965.

[23] See Kassebaum, Ward, and Wilner, *Prison Treatment and Parole Survival*, pp. 207-251.

publicly, and that in their private attitudes many inmates are not antagonistic to therapy.[24] Consistently, Garabedian found that recalcitrant, "antisocial" inmates join treatment programs when they are sponsored by inmates, but are reluctant to participate in those initiated by officials.[25] An inmate critic of group counseling in California has noted that the "class line" between inmates and staff effectively blocks group-oriented efforts, and that too often staff attitudes toward inmates are sterile, clinical, and "devoid of human warmth."[26] ●

The prison community

Very little is known, even by prisoners and prison workers, of the kinds of social interaction which take place among prisoners.[27] Prisoners, by definition, are persons who have been forcibly removed from the social relations in which they have been participating and locked in institutions where, we are prone to say, they "serve their time," "pay their debt to society," and, perhaps, "learn their lesson." But they do more than pay, and serve, and learn in the institutions. They *live* in them. For varying periods of time, each prisoner participates in an extraordinarily complex set of social relations, including a wide variety of social contacts, associations, bonds, alliances, compromises, and conflicts between hundreds of prisoners, guards, administrators, teachers, tradesmen, and professional personnel like social workers, psychologists, and physicians.

During the period of participation in this set of social relations, some prisoners apparently become "reformed" or "rehabilitated," while others become "confirmed" or "hardened" criminals. For still others, prison life has no discernible effect on subsequent criminality or noncriminality. In the last twenty years, social scientists have begun to study inmate participation in prison life in some detail, and they are beginning to establish as fact the idea that whether any particular prisoner becomes "reformed," or becomes "hardened," or remains neutral during his prison

---

[24] Stanton Wheeler, "Role Conflict in Correctional Communities," chap. 6 in Cressey, ed., *The Prison*, pp. 234-240.

[25] Peter G. Garabedian, "Legitimate and Illegitimate Alternatives in the Prison Community," *Sociological Inquiry*, 32:172-184, Spring, 1962.

[26] Donald E. Walter, "The Self-Directed Group: An Autonomous Approach to Group Counseling," mimeographed paper prepared in the Prison College Project, California State Prison, San Quentin.

[27] Parts of this section are adapted from Donald R. Cressey and Witold Krassowski, "Inmate Organization and Anomie in American Prisons and Soviet Labor Camps," *Social Problems*, 5:217-230, Winter, 1957-58; Donald R. Cressey, "Foreword" to the reissue of Donald Clemmer, *The Prison Community* (New York: Rinehart, 1958), pp. vii-x; Donald R. Cressey, "Introduction" to Cressey, ed., *The Prison*, pp. 1-12; and John Irwin and Donald R. Cressey, "Thieves, Convicts and the Inmate Culture," *Social Problems*, 10:142-155, Fall, 1962.

experience depends upon the specific nature of his participation in the prison community.[28]

These studies have made two principal points. *First,* the prison community has a distinctive set of values, norms, positions, and roles—the elements that make up a "social system." *Second,* in the course of incarceration, not all inmates come into association with the same sets of norms and values in the same way; they hold different positions and play different roles in a set of relationships which is so confused, entangled, complicated, and subtle that even the participants are unable to see and describe clearly their own involvements.[29]

A chart of a prison's administrative hierarchy, showing the lines of authority, does not begin to describe how the prison is organized, who is responsible to whom, or who influences whom. It is even difficult to draw a picture of the official parts of the organization in this way, although these are the least complex aspects of the system. In addition, there are unofficial components of institutional structure, and it is these that are most complicated and, usually, unstated. In one sense, in fact, whether specific aspects of organization are "official" or "unofficial" depends on whether or not they are clear and observable. If a prison warden can "do something about" some aspects of the institution—such as issuing an order that a certain practice is to be changed—he is dealing with official organization; if there is something going on, the nature of which he cannot clearly state, and which, consequently, he cannot change by order, he is dealing with unofficial organization.

Both the official and the unofficial aspects of social organization are important determinants of behavior, including attitudes, opinions, and beliefs. It is likely, however, that unofficial arrangements are of most significance to inmates, for most of their time is spent in them. The "good" or "bad" feeling between an inmate and a guard, between two inmates, or between the warden and the chef, the vocabulary of the psychologists and the social workers, and the sense of justice among inmates and guards are all part of the inmate's world, and they have a powerful effect on the form of his adjustment in the institution and on his subsequent criminality. Similarly, while prison officers have some

The social system

---

[28] For bibliographies of the extensive literature in this area, see Gresham M. Sykes and Sheldon L. Messinger, "The Inmate Social System," in Richard A. Cloward, Donald R. Cressey, George H. Grosser, Richard McCleery, Lloyd E. Ohlin, Gresham M. Sykes, and Sheldon L. Messinger, *Theoretical Studies in Social Organization of the Prison* (New York: Social Science Research Council, 1960), pp. 5-7; T. P. Morris, "Research on the Prison Community," *Collected Studies in Criminological Research* (Council of Europe), vol. I, 1967, pp. 123-156; and Esther Hefferman, *Making it in Prison: The Square, the Cool, and the Life* (New York: John Wiley, 1972).

[29] Donald R. Cressey, "Adult Felons in Prison," chap. in Lloyd E. Ohlin, ed., *Prisoners in America* (Englewood Cliffs, N.J.: Prentice-Hall, 1973), pp. 117-150.

control over most of the inmate's overt behavior, mostly in the form of authority to punish for deviation, their control is negligible compared to control by prisoners themselves. In a system of friendships, mutual obligations, statuses, reciprocal relations, loyalties, intimidation, deception, and violence, inmates learn that conformity to prisoner expectations is just as important to their welfare as is conformity to the formal controls exerted by "outsiders."[30] Powerful prisoners insist that inmates be orthodox in their statements and actions. And orthodoxy is more important in prison than in outside life, because in outside life a person has freedom of mobility not possible in prisons. Orthodoxy in the ways of behaving of prisoners is promoted by a system of rewards and punishments, the latter emphasizing gossip, laughter, and ridicule, but including, also, corporal punishments and, occasionally, execution.

Informal control may be seen in the persistence of the fundamental principles of prisoner organization, called "the code." An examination of many descriptions of prison life has suggested that the chief tenets of the inmate code can be classified roughly into five major groups.[31] First, there are those maxims that caution: *Don't interfere with inmate interests.* These center on the idea that inmates should serve the least possible time, while enjoying the greatest possible number of pleasures and privileges. Included are directives such as, *Never rat on a con; Don't be nosey; Don't have a loose lip; Keep off a man's back; Don't put a guy on the spot.* Put positively, *Be loyal to your class, the cons.* A second set of behavioral rules asks inmates to refrain from quarrels or arguments with fellow prisoners: *Don't lose your head; Play it cool; Do your own time; Don't bring heat.* Third, prisoners assert that inmates should not take advantage of one another by means of force, fraud, or chicanery: *Don't exploit inmates.* This injunction sums up several directives: *Don't break your word; Don't steal from cons; Don't sell favors; Don't be a racketeer; Don't welsh on debts. Be right.* Fourth, some rules have as their central theme the maintenance of self: *Don't weaken; Don't whine; Don't cop out* (plead guilty). Stated positively: *Be tough; Be a man.* Fifth, prisoners express a variety of maxims that forbid according prestige or respect to the guards or the world for which they stand: *Don't be a sucker; Skim it off the top; Never talk to a screw* (guard); *Have a connection; Be sharp.*

All inmates learn the code by word of mouth, and, to varying degrees, prisoners are guided by the code in their relationships both within the prison and in the free community after release. There is no question that the code is frequently violated, just as the formal legal code is violated. But the fact that a code is violated does not mean that it is not prescribed, nor does it mean

---

[30] See George H. Grosser, "The Role of Informal Inmate Groups in Change of Values," *Children*, 5:25-29, February, 1958.

[31] Sykes and Messinger, "The Inmate Social System," pp. 6-10.

that it has no important effects on the behavior of persons sharing it. The effects of the code may be seen everywhere in the prison community. Men who violate the code by becoming "finks," "rats," or "stool pigeons," for example, do so secretly, not only because secrecy is essential to their "profession," but also because they know they will, at least, lose the support of their fellow inmates if they are discovered. A known informer is ostracized, ridiculed, hissed, scoffed, and generally made to feel miserable. He may be given the "silent treatment," a system in which the ostracism is so complete that other inmates do not even acknowledge the informer's presence, or he may be almost constantly isolated from participation in all but the most rudimentary social life. In extreme cases, informers are attacked, and many prison systems have a special cellblock or a special institution for informers.

The code is not necessarily a "code of honor." The prison community does not have a system of democratic justice. One is guilty if he is not above suspicion or if his associates are not above suspicion. An inmate who has been a witness for the state against another criminal usually is treated as an informer or, at least, as an outsider. However, there are exceptional cases, particularly those in which the witness apparently testified against a disloyal crime partner. To be seen speaking to a guard is a social error, and frequent conversation with guards is in most prisons unthinkable, on the part of both the prisoners and the guards.[32] Professional persons who administer treatment programs are considered hardly different from guards, and inmates are suspicious of men who participate in research projects or group-therapy programs. The code, thus, makes inmates suspicious of all outsiders, and it also makes them suspicious of each other. The inmates as a group must be constantly on guard to prevent individual members from seeking an advantage with the officials by betraying the group.

The code, like other behavior patterns among inmates, arises in part out of the conditions of deprivation in the prison. However, it also consists in part of a more general *criminal* code, brought into the prison and utilized there by career criminals and other sophisticated criminals, and adopted by prisoners.[33] So far as the prison itself is concerned, it is significant that the code helps inmates avoid some of the conditions of deprivation which the prison is expected to impose on them. Yet it should not be concluded that the code is necessarily as "anti-administration" in

[32] See Robert Sommer and Humphrey Osmond, "Symptoms of Institutional Care," *Social Problems*, 8:254-263, Winter, 1960-61; Elmer H. Johnson, "Sociology of Confinement: Assimilation and the Prison 'Rat,'" *Journal of Criminal Law, Criminology, and Police Science*, 51:528-533, January-February, 1961; and Harry A. Wilmer, "The Role of the 'Rat' in the Prison," *Federal Probation*, 29: 44-49, March, 1965.

[33] See Irwin and Cressey, "Thieves, Convicts and the Inmate Culture."

emphasis as it appears to be. On the contrary, the code reflects an important alliance between inmate leaders and prison officials.

We observed earlier that humanitarian and treatment considerations have effectively limited the punitive means available to prison administrators for keeping inmates quietly confined, yet these officials continue to be held responsible for the prisoners' orderly confinement.[34] One solution to this problem is to keep inmates unorganized. This practice permits inmates to work together and to participate in other group activities, but it minimizes the danger of escape or riot. Thus, "incentives" such as parole, good-time allowances, and privileges of various sorts, including the privilege of participating in treatment programs, are administered as rewards to inmates who heed the administrators' admonition to "do your own time."[35]

The very first intensive study of an American prison (done in the 1930's) estimated that in an Illinois prison about 40 percent of the prisoners were not in any way intimately integrated in groups in which strong social relationships existed, and that another 40 percent engaged in some of the superficial practices of group life but were not genuinely affiliated with primary groups.[36] This high percentage of "ungrouped" inmates has continued. It seems attributable to the official system of maintaining control by psychological isolation of inmates. It is much easier to control individual prisoners than to control groups of prisoners.

A second, and more complex, kind of solution to the problem is to enlist, unofficially at least, the aid of some of the inmates. When prisoners far outnumber staff members, it is extremely difficult, if not impossible, to keep each of them psychologically isolated. But control is facilitated if inmate elites develop and enforce norms and values which promote psychological isolation among the other inmates.

Actually, the inmate code which puts emphasis upon being an astute criminal, upon maintaining social distance from the guards, and upon inmate solidarity does precisely this. Thus, inmate leaders operate in such a manner that the important administrative task of maintaining a quiet, secure institution is indirectly supported, rather than subverted. The values and type of organization which inmate elites attempt to maintain are to a large degree systems for exploiting fellow captives, a condition attended by control and repression of inmates by inmates rather than by administrators.[37]

The advice inmates give to each other is the exact counterpart of the officials' admonitions. This includes directives to be rational, not to bring "heat" by antagonizing employees, not to

---

[34] See p. 516, above.

[35] See Richard A. Cloward, "Social Control in the Prison," chap. 2 in Cloward et al., Theoretical Studies in Social Organization of the Prison, pp. 41-48.

[36] Clemmer, The Prison Community, p. 129.

[37] Gresham M. Sykes, "Men, Merchants, and Toughs: A Study of Reactions to Imprisonment," Social Problems, 4:130-138, October, 1956; and idem, The Society of Captives, pp. 76-78.

cause trouble by stealing from fellow inmates, and, generally, to "do your own time."[38] In enforcing the code, of course, the inmate elites necessarily violate it. By insisting that inmates "do their own time," an inmate leader shows that he is not doing his own time.

If inmate control of other inmates is valuable to prison administrators, it can be expected that power of various kinds will unofficially, and perhaps unintentionally, be *assigned* to inmate elites, rather than seized by them. This seems to be the case. Judicious distribution of goods in short supply, including measures of freedom and symbols of power and status, enables administrators to enlist the aid of certain inmates in the task of controlling other inmates. In return for some of the scarce goods, usually called "favors," inmate leaders control the bulk of other inmates. As Cloward has said, "Stability depends upon reciprocal adjustments between formal and inmate systems." McCorkle and Korn studied the prison as a rehabilitative organization and concluded, "Prison officials have generally tended to use the inmate power structure as an aid in prison administration and the maintenance of good order."[39] McCleery has summarized the relationship between administrative organization and inmate organization in the following terms: "The processes by which the formal hierarchy is sustained create the conditions for a parallel hierarchy in the inmate community. Exploitive and authoritarian inmate leaders may be removed to segregation, but others rise to fill their place because their role is necessary in the situation."[40]

Many inmate elites are men who, like the administrators, have a vested interest in maintaining the status quo. A basic tenet in their code is that prisoners must stick together and must not use official channels to gain advantages over other inmates, which is exactly what the leaders do. Officials insist that guards must not fraternize with inmates, and inmate elites insist that prisoners must not fraternize with guards; in this way, both officials and elites control the channels of communication, an important source of power.[41] Like administrators, some convicts insist that all inmates are equal, but by this they mean that "outside" criteria such as occupation, wealth, or criminal notoriety shall not be used to determine the power, prestige, and special privileges within the

---

[38] Glaser, *Effectiveness of a Prison and Parole System*, p. 99.

[39] Lloyd E. McCorkle and Richard Korn, "Resocialization within Walls," *Annals of the American Academy of Political and Social Science*, 293:88-98, May, 1954.

[40] Richard H. McCleery, "Communication Patterns as Bases of Systems of Authority and Power," chap. 3 in Cloward, *Theoretical Studies in Social Organization*, p. 76; see also Gresham M. Sykes, "The Corruption of Authority and Rehabilitation," *Social Forces*, 34:257-262, March, 1956.

[41] McCleery, "Communication Patterns as Bases of Systems of Authority and Power," pp. 52-56. See also McCleery, "The Governmental Process and Informal Social Control," p. 149-188; and Merle R. Schneckloth, "Why Do Honest Employees React Dishonestly?" *American Journal of Correction*, 21:6 ff., March-April, 1959.

institution. Such rules for the behavior of prisoners protect the elite convict's privileged positions and are necessary to maintenance of organizational status quo; when they exist, few inmates can seriously threaten the power positions of the leaders. If special privileges and power were awarded on the basis of extra-institutional criteria, the result would be chaotic dethroning of inmate elites at frequent intervals and, consequently, destruction of co-operative alliances between elites and administrators. At the same time, the inmates' rules operate to keep the bulk of the inmates unorganized.

To take an oversimplified example of administrative-inmate alliances, an inmate might be allowed by a guard to steal a little coffee from the kitchen in return for being cooperative, working hard, discouraging other inmates from violence, and, generally, making the guard's job an easy one. This man then has a vested interest in his coffee-stealing privileges and is likely to take a dim view of other inmates who would steal coffee in such manner and measure that the guard and his superiors would put all coffee under strict control. He then makes the guard's job even easier, for *he* guards the coffee. But he really doesn't guard it—other inmates are prohibited from making inroads on his coffee-stealing privileges by a code which emphasizes the importance of doing one's own time, not bringing heat, sticking together against the administration, and not ratting. Both the prison's coffee supply and the inmate's special coffee ration are thus protected by a man who steals from the supply while enforcing a code which, in these circumstances, prohibits others from doing the same. He exploits other inmates by stealing coffee allotted for their use, and he is permitted to do so by a guard who implicitly recognizes that such exploitation keeps the bulk of the inmates unorganized and, thus, under control. •

Prisonization

One of the amazing things about prisons is that they "work" at all. Any prison is made up of the synchronized actions of hundreds of people, some of whom hate and distrust each other, love each other, fight each other physically and psychologically, think of each other as stupid or mentally disturbed, "manage" and "control" each other, and vie with each other for favors, prestige, power, and money. Often the personnel involved do not know with whom they are competing or cooperating and are not sure whether they are the managers or the managed. But despite these conditions, the social system which is a prison does not degenerate into a chaotic mess of social relations which have no order and make no sense. Somehow the personnel, including the prisoners, are bound together enough so that most conflicts and mis-understandings are not crucial—the personnel remain "organized," and the prison continues to "work." Viewed in this way, the prison is a microcosm of the larger society which has created it and which maintains it, for this larger society also is a unit which continues to "work" despite numerous individual disagreements, misunderstandings, antagonisms, and conflicts.

An offender entering a prison for the first time is introduced to the culture in much the way a child is introduced to the ways of behaving of his elders. The general process by which a child is taught the behavior patterns of his group is called *socialization*, and the somewhat comparable process among inmates has been named *prisonization*.[42] However, like a person moving into a new culture, the new inmate, often called a *fish*, usually not only has to learn new ways of behaving, but also must unlearn some of his former behavior patterns. Also unlike the situation in socialization is the fact that inmates are by no means neutral toward accepting or rejecting the behavior patterns presented to them. Among incoming inmates there is variation in the social class of attainment, social class of origin, age at first conviction, number of contacts with persons outside the prison, post-prison expectations, and in other personal characteristics acquired prior to imprisonment. All of these affect the degree of prisonization.[43] Regardless of these personal characteristics, however, every person entering a penitentiary undergoes prisonization to some extent, if only because he must undergo the process of being assigned a number, a standard set of clothing, and a standard haircut.

All inmates who are new to a particular prison, even if they have been previously incarcerated, must learn the organizational principles of the new community. They learn "the rules" and the many technical details of prison living. In this phase of prisonization, which continues for only a few days or weeks, the inmate is essentially an outsider. He maintains the bulk of the attitudes and behavior patterns he possessed upon admission to the prison but changes his personal habits to comply with the folkways of the prison.

Gradually, the new inmate is subject to other, more pervasive, influences. He accepts his inferior status and grows accustomed to having his name replaced by a number. He wears clothing which is not significantly different from that worn by the other inmates, and he realizes that, from the guard's point of view, he is an anonymous figure. He comes to know the meanings of prison slang or argot, and, no matter how aloof he may hold himself from the other inmates, he finds himself using some of that slang. He refers to the guards as "screws," to the warden by the nickname given him by the inmates, to the psychiatrists and social workers as "bug doctors." He begins to recognize the fact that in many respects the prisoners, not the administrators, control the life in the prison. He becomes aware of his security,

---

[42] Clemmer, *The Prison Community*, p. 298.

[43] Charles W. Thomas, "Prisonization or Resocialization? External Factors Associated with the Impact of Imprisonment," *Journal of Research in Crime and Delinquency*, 10:13-21, January, 1973.

realizing that he owes nothing to anyone for such food, entertainment, recreation, education, and living accommodations as are
furnished him. He begins to look for a comfortable job where, as
he says, "I can do my time without any trouble and get out of
here." He no longer expresses a willingness to "do anything"
the officials might ask him to do. All inmates are subjected to
these "universal factors of prisonization." They are swallowed up
by the prison.

For many men, prisonization does not cease when there is mere
engulfment by the rather routine prison life. The prison community contains other patterns which are learned and accepted
by some inmates. These men learn to gamble, to participate in
homosexual activities, and to hate and distrust prison officials
and, generally, outsiders. They not only accept the prescribed
"prison code," they attempt to enforce it. They not only hear the
prison dogma, they begin to spread it. They not only believe that
the environment should administer to them, they attempt to control the environment through prison politics and conniving. These
and similar changes do not occur in every man, and all of them
usually do not occur in any one man. They are, nevertheless,
characteristic of the prison community. The men who participate
in these aspects of prison life differ from those subjected only to
what Clemmer calls the "universal factors of prisonization,"
largely in attitudes of allegiance to prisoners as a group.

The general effect of prisonization is the introduction, with
varying degrees of efficiency, of all inmates to attitudes, codes,
norms, and values which are in many ways contradictory to anticriminal norms. Because it causes prisoners to identify themselves as persons quite different from noncriminals, even contact
with the "universal factors" will render difficult any effort at
clinical treatment. As Clemmer said:

> Even if no other factor of the prison culture touches the personality of
> an inmate of many years of residence, the influences of these universal
> factors are sufficient to make a man characteristic of the penal com-
> munity and probably so disrupt his personality that a happy adjustment
> in any [outside] community becomes next to impossible. On the other
> hand, if inmates who are incarcerated for only short periods, such as a
> year or so, do not become integrated into the culture except in so far
> as these universal factors of prisonization are concerned, they do not
> seem to be so characteristic of the penal community and are able when
> released to take up a new mode of life without much difficulty.[44]

The men who are most efficiently or completely prisonized
adopt the ideology characteristic of the prison. Most of those who
are integrated to a lesser extent at least outwardly espouse the
same ideology. A series of studies has demonstrated, however,
that inmates show a U-shaped pattern of maximum aloofness to

---

[44] Clemmer, *The Prison Community*, p. 300.

the ideology at the beginning and the end of the prison term.[45] Wheeler concluded from his study that at the beginning and end of their terms, most inmates are primarily influenced by reference groups outside the prison—relatives, friends, and employers whom they have just left or whom they are anxious to rejoin.

Despite the fact that all inmates undergo prisonization, much of the inmate behavior ordinarily considered part of the prison culture is not peculiar to the prison at all. One analysis indicates that a distinction must be made between the *convict subculture* which arises within institutions and the *thief subculture* which is carried into prisons by criminals.[46] The prison code is also part of a *criminal code,* existing outside prisons. Similarly, many inmates come to any given prison with a record of many terms in correctional institutions, and they bring with them a ready-made set of patterns which they apply to the new situation, just as is the case with participants in various outside criminal subcultures. In view of these processes, a clear understanding of inmate conduct cannot be obtained simply by viewing "prison culture" or "inmate culture" as an isolated system springing solely from the conditions of imprisonment.

The thief subculture

The core values of thieves operating in the general community correspond closely to the values which prison observers have ascribed to the type of inmate called the "right guy" or "real man." Things have not changed much since the 1930s, when the sociologist Hans Riemer secured a prison commitment for the purpose of studying the prison community and spent about four months in a state prison without the knowledge of any prisoner or administrative officer that he was not a bona fide offender. He described the two principal types of inmate leaders as follows:

> The prison population is largely in the control of a small group of men which has two divisions. There are the "politicians," "shots," or whatever they may be called in varying institutions, who hold key positions in the administrative offices of the prison. They wield a power to distribute special privileges, to make possible the circulation of special foods or other supplies. They in frequent instances become "racketeers" and use their positions to force money and services from less powerful inmates. These men are seldom trusted by the top level of the prison hierarchy, are frequently hated by the general population because of the exclusive-

---

45 Stanton H. Wheeler, "Socialization in Correctional Communities," *American Sociological Review,* 26:697-712, October, 1961; Peter G. Garabedian, "Social Roles and Processes of Socialization in the Prison Community," *Social Problems,* 11:139-152, Fall, 1963; Charles Wellford, "Factors Associated with Adoption of the Inmate Code," *Journal of Criminal Law, Criminology, and Police Science,* 58:197-203, 1967; and Sheldon L. Messinger, "Issues in the Study of the Social System of Prison Inmates," *Issues in Criminology,* 4:133-141, Fall, 1969.

46 Irwin and Cressey, "Thieves, Convicts and the Inmate Culture."

ness and self-seeking behavior characteristic of them. . . . The other section of this controlling power is held by the so-called "right guys." These men are so known because of the consistency of their behavior in accordance with the criminal or prison code. They are men who can always be trusted, who do not abuse lesser inmates, who are invariably loyal to their class the convicts. They are not wanton trouble makers but they are expected to stand up for their rights as convicts, to get what they can from the prison officials, to never permit an opportunity to pass from which they might secure anything from a better job to freedom. . . . These men, because of their outright and loyal behavior, are the real leaders of the prison and impose stringent control upon the definitions of proper behaviors from the convicts.[47]

Similarly, Clemmer found that the most important characteristic of prison leaders was "being right," although the leaders also were above average in intelligence, experienced in crime, and city-bred.[48]

High status as a "politician," "shot," "merchant," "peddler," or even as a "tough," "hood," or "gorilla" is based principally on conduct within the prison, but status as a "right guy" depends as well upon participation in the "criminal" or "thief" subculture which exists outside prisons. In the thief subculture, as it exists on the street, a man who is known as "right" or "solid" is one who can be trusted and relied upon. High status is also awarded to those who possess skill as thieves, but to be just a successful thief is not enough; there must be solidness as well. A solid guy is respected even if he is unskilled, and no matter how skilled in crime a stool pigeon may be, his status is low.

Despite the fact that adherence to the norms of the thief subculture is an ideal, and the fact that the behavior of the great majority of men arrested or convicted varies sharply from any "criminal code" which might be identified, a proportion of the persons arrested for "real crime," such as burglary, robbery, and larceny, has been in close contact with the values of the subculture. Many criminals, while not following the precepts of the subculture religiously, give lip service to its values and evaluate their own behavior and the behavior of their associates in terms relating to adherence to "rightness" and being "solid." It is probable, further, that use of this kind of values is not even peculiarly "criminal," for policemen, prison guards, college professors, students, and almost all other persons evaluate behavior in terms of in-group loyalties. Whyte noted the mutual obligations binding corner boys together and concluded that status depends upon the extent to which a boy lives up to his obligations, a form of "solidness."[49] More recently, Miller identified "toughness," "smart-

---

[47] Hans Riemer, "Socialization in the Prison Community," Proceedings of the American Prison Association, 1937, pp. 151-155. The quotation is from pp. 152-153.

[48] Donald Clemmer, "Leadership Phenomena in a Prison Community," Journal of Criminal Law and Criminology, 28:861-872, March-April, 1938. See also Clarence Schrag, "Leadership Among Prison Inmates," American Sociological Review, 19:37-42, February, 1954.

[49] William Foote Whyte, "Corner Boys: A Study of Clique Behavior," American Journal of Sociology, 46:647-663, March, 1941.

ness," and "autonomy" among the focal concerns of lower-class adolescent delinquent boys; these also characterize prisoners who are oriented to the thief subculture.[50] Wheeler found that half the custody staff and 60 percent of the treatment staff in one prison approved the conduct of a hypothetical inmate who refused to name an inmate with whom he had been engaged in a knife fight.[51]

Imprisonment is one of the recurring problems with which thieves must cope. It is almost certain that a thief will be arrested from time to time, and the subculture provides members with patterns to be used in order to help solve this problem. Norms which apply to the prison situation, and information on how to undergo the prison experience—how to do time "standing on your head"—with the least suffering and in a minimum amount of time are provided. Of course, the subculture itself is both nurtured and diffused in the different jails and prisons of the country.

As Riemer's discussion of "politicians" and "shots" indicates, there also exists in prisons a subculture which is by definition a set of patterns that flourishes in the environment of incarceration. This is the "convict subculture" which can be found wherever men are confined, whether it be in city jails, state and federal prisons, army stockades, prisoner of war camps, concentration camps, or even mental hospitals. Such organizations are characterized by deprivations and limitations on freedom, and in them available wealth must be competed for by men supposedly on an equal footing. It is in connection with the *maintenance* (but not necessarily with the *origin*) of this subculture that it is appropriate to stress the notion that a minimum of outside status criteria are carried into the situation. Ideally, as we indicated above, all status is to be achieved by means made available in the prison, through the displayed ability to manipulate the environment, win special privileges in a certain manner, and assert influence over others. The central value of the subculture is utilitarianism, and the most manipulative and most utilitarian individuals win the available wealth and such positions of influence as might exist.

It is not correct to conclude, however, that even these behavior patterns are a consequence of the environment of any particular prison. In the first place, such utilitarian and manipulative behavior probably is characteristic of the "hard-core" lower class in the United States, and most prisoners come from this class. After discussing the importance of toughness, smartness, excitement, and fate in this group, Miller makes the following significant observation:

> . . . in lower class culture a close conceptual connection is made between "authority" and "nurturance." To be restrictively or firmly controlled

The convict subculture

---

[50] Walter B. Miller, "Lower Class Culture as a Generating Milieu of Gang Delinquency," *Journal of Social Issues,* vol. 14 (1958), no. 3, pp. 5-19.

[51] Wheeler, "Role Conflict in Correctional Communities," p. 235.

is to be cared for. Thus the overtly negative evaluation of superordinate authority frequently extends as well to nurturance, care, or protection. The desire for personal independence is often expressed in terms such as "I don't need *nobody* to take care of me. I can take care of myself!" Actual patterns of behavior, however, reveal a marked discrepancy between expressed sentiment and what is covertly valued. Many lower class people appear to seek out highly restrictive social environments wherein stringent external controls are maintained over their behavior. Such institutions as the armed forces, the mental hospital, the disciplinary school, the prison or correctional institution, provide environments which incorporate a strict and detailed set of rules defining and limiting behavior, and enforced by an authority system which controls and applies coercive sanctions for deviance from these rules. While under the jurisdiction of such systems, the lower class person generally expresses to his peers continual resentment of the coercive, unjust, and arbitrary exercise of authority. Having been released, or having escaped from these milieux, however, he will often act in such a way as to insure recommitment, or choose recommitment voluntarily after a temporary period of "freedom."[52]

In the second place, the hard-core members of this subculture, as it exists in American prisons for adults, are likely to be inmates who have a long record of confinement in institutions for juveniles. As indicated above, McCleery observed that, in a period of transition, reform-school graduates all but took over inmate society in one prison. These boys called themselves a "syndicate" and engaged in a concentrated campaign of argument and intimidation directed toward capturing the inmate council and the inmate craft shop which had been placed under council management. "The move of the syndicate to take over the craft shop involved elements of simple exploitation, the grasp for a status symbol, and an aspect of economic reform."[53] Persons with long histories of institutionalization, it is important to note, might have had little contact with the thief subculture. The thief subculture does not flourish in institutions for juveniles, and graduates of such institutions have not necessarily had extensive criminal experience on the outside. However, some form of the convict subculture *does* exist in institutions for juveniles, though not to the extent characterizing prisons for felons. Some of the newcomers to a prison for adults are, in short, persons who have been oriented to the convict subculture, who have found the utilitarian nature of this subculture acceptable, and who have had little contact with the thief subculture. This makes a difference in their behavior.

The "straight" subculture

A final category of inmates is oriented to "legitimate" subcultures. Prisoners with this orientation are called "straights," "square Johns," "do-rights," etc. This category includes men who are not members of the thief subculture upon entering prison, and who reject both the thief subculture and the convict subculture while

---

[52] Miller, "Lower Class Culture as a Generating Milieu of Gang Delinquency," pp. 12-13.

[53] McCleery, "The Governmental Process and Informal Social Control," p. 179.

in prison. These men present few problems to prison administrators. They make up a large percentage of the population of any
prison, but they isolate themselves—or are isolated—from the
thief and convict subcultures. Clemmer referred to these men as
"ungrouped," and his statistics, reported above, have often been
interpreted as meaning that the prison contains many men not
oriented to "inmate culture" or "prison culture"—in our terms,
not oriented to either the thief subculture or the convict subculture. This is not necessarily the case. There may be socio-
metric isolates among the thief-oriented prisoners, the convict-
oriented prisoners, and the legitimately oriented prisoners. Whether
or not men in this category participate in cliques, athletic teams,
or religious study and hobby groups, they are oriented to the
problem of achieving goals through means which are legitimate
outside prisons. ●

There are great differences in the prison behavior of men oriented
to one or another of the three types of subculture. The hard-core
member of the convict subculture finds his reference groups
inside the institutions, and, as indicated, he seeks status through
means available in the prison environment. But it is important
for the understanding of inmate conduct to note that the hard-
core member of the thief subculture seeks status in the broader
criminal world of which prison is only a part. His reference
groups include people both inside and outside prison, but he is
committed to criminal life, not prison life. From his point of view,
it is adherence to a widespread criminal code that wins him high
status, not adherence to a narrow convict code. Convicts might
assign him high status because they admire him as a thief, or
because a good thief makes a good convict, but the thief does not
play the convicts' game. Similarly, a man oriented to a legitimate
subculture is, by definition, committed to the values of neither
thieves nor convicts.

Differential participation

On the other hand, within any given prison, the men oriented
to the convict subculture are the inmates that seek positions of
power and influence and sources of information, whether these
men are called "shots," "politicians," "merchants," "hoods,"
"toughs," "gorillas," or something else. A job as secretary to the
captain or warden, for example, gives an aspiring prisoner information and consequent power, and enables him to influence the
assignment or regulation of other inmates. In the same way, a
job which allows the incumbent to participate in a racket, such
as clerk in the kitchen storeroom, where he can steal and sell
food, is highly desirable to a man oriented to the convict subculture. With a steady income of cigarettes, ordinarily the prisoners'
medium of exchange, he may assert a great deal of influence and
purchase those things which are symbols of status among persons
oriented to the convict subculture. Even if there is no well-
developed medium of exchange, he can barter goods acquired in

his position for equally desirable goods possessed by other convicts. These include information and such things as specially starched, pressed, and tailored prison clothing, fancy belts, belt buckles, billfolds, special shoes, or any other type of dress which will set him apart and will indicate that he has both the influence to get the goods and the influence necessary to keeping and displaying them despite prison rules which outlaw doing so.

Since prisoners oriented either to a legitimate subculture or to a thief subculture are not seeking high status within any given prison, they do not look for the kinds of positions considered so desirable by the members of the convict subculture. Those oriented to legitimate subcultures take prison as it comes and seek status through channels provided for that purpose by prison administrators—running for election to the inmate council, to the editorship of the institutional newspapers, etc.—and, generally, by conforming to what they think administrators expect of good prisoners. Long before the thief has come to prison, his subculture has defined proper prison conduct as behavior rationally calculated to "do time" in the easiest possible way. This means that he wants a prison life containing the best possible combination of a maximum amount of leisure time and a maximum number of privileges. Accordingly, the privileges sought by the thief are different from the privileges sought by the man oriented to prison itself. The thief wants things that will make prison life a little easier—extra food, a maximum amount of recreation time, a good radio, a little peace. One thief serving his third sentence for armed robbery was a dishwasher in the officers' dining room. He liked the eating privileges, but he never sold food. Despite his "low-status" job, he was highly respected by other thieves, who described him as "right," and "solid." Members of the convict subculture, like the thieves, seek privileges. There is a difference, however, for the convict seeks privileges which he believes will enhance his position in the inmate hierarchy. He also wants to do easy time, but, as compared with the thief, desirable privileges are more likely to involve freedom to amplify one's store, such as stealing rights in the kitchen and freedom of movement around the prison. Obtaining an easy job is managed because it is easy and therefore desirable, but it also is managed for the purpose of displaying the fact that it can be obtained.

In the routine prison setting, the two deviant subcultures exist in a balanced relationship. It is this total setting which has been observed as "inmate culture." There is some conflict because of the great disparity in some of the values of thieves and convicts, but the two subcultures share other values. The thief is committed to keeping his hands off other people's activities, and the convict, being utilitarian, is likely to know that it is better in the long run to avoid conflict with thieves and confine one's exploitations to the "do-rights" and to the members of his own subculture. Of course, the thief must deal with the convict from time to time, and when he does so he adjusts to the reality of the fact that he is imprisoned. Choosing to follow prison definitions usually means paying for some service in cigarettes or in a returned service; this is the cost of doing easy time. Some thieves adapt in a more general way to the ways of convicts and assimilate the prison-ized person's concern for making out in the institution.[54] On an ideal-type level, however, thieves do not sanction exploitation of other inmates, and they simply ignore the "square Johns," who are oriented to legitimate subcultures. Nevertheless, their subcul-ture, as it operates in prison, has exploitative effects.

Numerous persons have documented the fact that "right guys," many of whom can be identified as leaders of the thieves, not of the convicts, exercise the greatest influence over the total prison population. The influence is the long-run kind stemming from the ability to influence notions of what is right and proper, what McCleery calls the formulation and communication of defini-tions.[55] The thief, after all, has the respect of many inmates who are not themselves thieves. The right guy carries a set of atti-tudes, values, and norms that have a great deal of consistency and clarity. He acts, forms opinions, and evaluates events in the prison according to them, and over a long period of time he in this way determines basic behavior patterns in the institution. In what the thief thinks of as "small matters," however—getting job transfers, enforcing payment of gambling debts, making cell assignments—members of the convict subculture run things.

It is difficult to assess the direct lines of influence the two deviant subcultures have over those inmates who are not mem-bers of either subculture when they enter a prison. It is true that if a new inmate does not have definitions to apply to the new prison situation, one or the other of the deviant subcultures is likely to supply them in the prisonization process. On the one hand, the convict subculture is much more apparent than the thief subculture; its roles are readily visible to any new arrival, and its definitions are readily available to one who wants to "get along" and "make it" in a prison. Moreover, the inmate leaders oriented to the convict subculture are anxious to get new followers who will recognize the existing status hierarchy in the prison. Thieves, on the other hand, tend to be snobs. Their status in prison is determined in part by outside criteria, as well as by prison con-duct, and it is therefore difficult for a prisoner, acting as a prisoner, to achieve these criteria. At a minimum, the newcomer can fall under the influence of the thief subculture only if he has intimate association over a period of time with some of its mem-bers who are able and willing to impart some of its subtle behavior patterns to him.

It seems a worthy hypothesis that thieves, convicts, and "do-rights" all bring certain values and behavior patterns to prison with them, and that total "inmate culture" represents an adjustment or accommodation of these three systems within the

---

[54] John Irwin, *The Felon* (Englewood Cliffs, N.J.: Prentice-Hall, 1970), pp. 61-85.
[55] McCleery, "The Governmental Process and Informal Social Control," p. 154.

official administrative system of deprivation and control. It is significant in this connection that Wheeler has not found in Norwegian prisons the normative order and cohesive bonds among inmates that characterize many American prisons. He observes that his data suggest "that the current functional interpretations of the inmate system in American institutions are not adequate," and that "general features of Norwegian society are imported into the prison and operate largely to offset any tendencies toward the formation of a solidary inmate group. . . ."[56] Similarly, Ward and Kassebaum noted that the thief subculture was not apparent in a prison for women, probably because the behavioral rules contained in it are directed to features of behavior that are not relevant to women; the inmate code in this prison referred principally to participation in homosexuality.[57] ●

Reformation in the prison community

Generally, the organization of prison life is conducive to the retention and development of criminal attitudes, rather than to reformation. As a result of the relationships between prisoners and authorities, some long-term inmates become isolated from intimate contacts with anticriminal behavior patterns and learn that "success" is to be achieved by deception, manipulation, and crime.

The "antireform" emphasis in prison culture

Although inmates learn many criminal techniques from each other and often form alliances for the perpetration of crimes after release, retention of criminal attitudes in prison does not result primarily from mere contamination and individual tutelage of one prisoner by another. Instead, it occurs in response to participation in a community which has *collectively* developed traditions favorable to crime and to the repression of any tendency toward reformation. An inmate of the United States Penitentiary at Atlanta made the following statement:

> I know that prisons are wrong because it is self-manifest that were society to attempt to devise a process for the development of the criminal personality; were society to attempt to perfect curricula for the dissemination of anti-social attitudes; were society to attempt to create institutions for the mass production of criminals; then no finer nor no more effective agency for the attainment of these aims could have been evolved than the prison.
>
> This is no attempt to rejuvenate the corny old chestnut about older prisoners teaching the younger ones techniques toward the more effec-

---

[56] Stanton Wheeler, "Socialization in Correctional Institutions," chap. 25 in David A. Goslin, ed., *Handbook of Socialization Theory and Research* (Chicago: Rand McNally, 1969), pp. 1005-1023. See also Wellford, "Factors Associated with Adoption of the Inmate Code"; Thomas Mathiesen, *The Defences of the Weak: A Sociological Study of a Norwegian Correctional Institution* (London: Tavistock, 1965), pp. 136-142; and Charles W. Thomas, "Toward a More Inclusive Model of the Inmate Culture," *Criminology: An Interdisciplinary Journal,* 8:251-262, 1970.

[57] David A. Ward and Gene G. Kassebaum, *Women's Prison: Sex and Social Structure* (Chicago: Aldine, 1965); see also Charles Tittle, "Sex Differentiation and the Influence of Criminal Subcultures," *American Sociological Review,* 29:492-505, 1969.

tual penetration of strong-boxes and recipes for outwitting the gen-darmerie. Such phenomena serve only for the theses of the more junior penologists and viewers-with-alarm in the ranks of the earnestly public-spirited but sadly misinformed committees for the study and improve-ment of this and that. . . .

It is not the possibility of a non-legitimate vocational training that makes the prison a man-perverting agency of great power and efficiency. It is the doleful fact that some nebulous something happens to a man between the time that he checks into and checks out of a prison; some inculcation of the essence of bitterness and social antagonism, an incul-cation that is not merely a veneering process but a deep inoculation. And this "something" spawns a man who is invariably less desirable as a citizen than he was at the time he stood before the bar of justice.[58]

The "nebulous something" which happens to the inmate is his participation in a group which has developed an *esprit de corps*, with crime and violation of official prison rules as the common interest. The net effect of extensive participation in a group with such an *esprit de corps* is likely to be a definition of one's self as an "elite," as one who has few, if any, obligations to "outsiders" who conform to legal norms. This conception of self is both stimulated and reinforced not only by inmates, but also by the attitudes of prison officials. The social distance between inmates as a class and officials as a class lengthens the social distance between inmates and law-abiding persons generally.[59] Weinberg has described the attitudes of prison officials which are conducive to this increased social distance.[60]

We have already noted, however, that there are variations in the extent to which inmates participate in the antireform and essentially procriminal *esprit de corps* of a prison. Wheeler has shown that inmate attitudes and loyalties most closely resemble those of inmate elites when the inmate in question occupies a position which makes the elite deviant subcultures most visible to him.[61] Similarly, perceiving the prison community in terms of the "thief subculture," the "convict subculture," and the "legit-imate subculture" has implications for predicting the behavior of prisoners when they are released. Most inmates are under the influence of *both* the thief subculture and the convict subculture. Without realizing it, inmates who have served long prison terms are likely to move toward the middle, toward a compromise or balance between the directives coming from the two sources. A member of the convict subculture may come to see that thieves

---

[58] Richard Jordan, "Traumatic Trivia," *The Atlantian*, 3:26-27 ff., July-August, 1941.

[59] Joseph C. Mouledous, "Organizational Goals and Structural Change: A Study of the Organization of a Prison Social System," *Social Forces*, 41:283-290, March, 1963; and Mathiesen, *Defences of the Weak*, pp. 11-16.

[60] S. Kirson Weinberg, "Aspects of the Prison's Social Structure," *American Journal of Sociology*, 47:717-726, March, 1942. See also Bernard B. Berk, "Organizational Goals and Inmate Organization," *American Journal of Sociol-ogy*, 71:522-534, March, 1966.

[61] Wheeler, "Role Conflict in Correctional Communities," pp. 250-256. See also Jon E. Simpson, Thomas G. Eynon, and Walter C. Reckless, "Institutionaliza-tion as Perceived by the Juvenile Offender," *Sociology and Social Research*, 48:13-23, October, 1963.

are the real men with the prestige; a member of the thief subculture or even a "do-right" may lose his ability to sustain his
status needs by outside criteria. The fact that time has a blending
effect on the participants in the two deviant subcultures suggests
that the subcultures themselves tend to blend together in some
prisons. The thief subculture scarcely exists in some institutions
for juveniles. It is probable also that in army stockades and in
concentration camps this subculture is almost nonexistent. In
places of short-term confinement, such as city and county jails,
the convict subculture is dominant, for the thief subculture
involves status distinctions that are not readily observable in a
short period of confinement. At the other extreme, in prisons
where only prisoners with long sentences are confined, the distinctions between the two subcultures are likely to be blurred.
Probably the two subcultures exist in their purest forms in institutions holding inmates in their twenties, with varying sentences
for a variety of criminal offenses. Such institutions, of course,
are the typical prisons of the United States.

Despite these differences, in any prison the men oriented to
legitimate subcultures should have a low recidivism rate, while
the highest recidivism rate should be found among participants
in the convict subculture. The hard-core members of this subculture are being trained in manipulation, duplicity, and exploitation; they are not sure they can make it on the outside; and even
when they are on the outside, they continue to use convicts as
a reference group. This sometimes means that there will be a
wild spree of crime and dissipation which takes the members of
the convict subculture directly back to the prison. Members of
the thief subculture, to whom prison life represents a pitfall in
outside life, also should have a high recidivism rate. However,
the thief sometimes "reforms" and tries to succeed in some life
within the law. Such behavior, contrary to popular notions, is
quite acceptable to other members of the thief subculture, so long
as the new job and position are not "anticriminal" and do not
involve regular, routine, "slave labor." Suckers work, but a man
who, like a thief, "skims it off the top" is not a sucker. At any
rate, the fact that convicts, to a greater extent than thieves, tend
to evaluate things from the perspective of the prison and to look
upon discharge as a short vacation from prison life suggests that
their recidivism rate should be higher than that of thieves.

No study of the recidivism rates of "thieves," "convicts," and
"do-rights" has been made. However, a significant analysis has
been made of the recidivism rates, and of the tendencies for these
rates to increase or decrease with increasing length of prison
terms, for each of four inmate types identified by Schrag.[62] This

---

[62] Donald L. Garrity, "The Effects of Length of Incarceration Upon Parole Adjustment and Estimation of Optimum Sentence: Washington State Correctional Institutions" (Ph.D. dissertation, University of Washington, 1956); and
idem, "The Prison as a Rehabilitation Agency," chap. 9 in Cressey, ed., The
Prison, pp. 358-380.

typology classifies inmates of close-custody prisons as *prosocial,
antisocial, pseudosocial,* and *asocial.*[63] These types correspond
closely to the argot labels used for various types of inmates by
prisoners themselves. Thus, *prosocial* inmates are those who fall
within the "square John," "do-right," or "hoosier" configurations;
antisocial inmates are the "right guys" and "real men"; *pseudosocial* prisoners are the "con politicians," "merchants," and "ped-
dlers"; and *asocial* prisoners are the "outlaws," "hoods," "gorillas," and "ballbusters"; also in the *asocial* category are disturbed
inmates, usually called "dings" or "rapos."[64] Unfortunately, this
typology does not clearly make the distinction between the thief
subculture and the convict subculture, probably because of the
blending process noted above. Schrag's "right guys" (*antisocial*
offenders), thus, might include both men who perceive role
requirements in terms of the norms of the convict subculture,
and men who perceive those requirements in terms of the norms
of the thief subculture. Similarly, neither his "con politician"
(*pseudosocial* offender) nor his "outlaw" (*asocial* offender) seem
to be ideal-type members of the convict subculture. Schrag's
"square Johns" (*prosocial* offenders) closely resemble the "legitimate subcultures" category.

Garrity found that a group of "square Johns" had a low parole
violation rate, and that this rate remained low no matter how
much time was served. "Right guys" had a high violation rate
that decreased markedly as time in prison increased. In Garrity's
words, this was because "continued incarceration [served] to
sever his connections with the criminal subculture and thus
increase the probability of successful parole."[65] The rates for the
"outlaw" were very high and remained high as time in prison
increased. The rates of the "con politician" were low if the
sentences were rather short, but increased systematically with
time served.

Noting that the origins of the thief subculture and the convict
subculture are both external to a prison should change our expectations regarding the possible reformative effect of that prison.

---

[63] Clarence C. Schrag, "Social Types in a Prison Community" (M.A. thesis,
University of Washington, 1944); idem, "Leadership Among Prison Inmates";
idem, "Some Foundations for a Theory of Correction," chap. 8 in Cressey,
ed., *The Prison,* pp. 346-356; and idem, "A Preliminary Criminal Typology,"
Pacific Sociological Review, 4:11-16, Spring, 1961. See also Glaser, *Effectiveness of a Prison and Parole System,* pp. 575-583.

[64] The argot terms for types of prisoners vary from institution to institution.
The terms used above do not include all the inmate types identified by
prisoners. For example, terms such as *wolf, punk,* and *fag* refer to roles in
homosexuality. A notation of types in terms of leisure-time pursuits in the
prison brings forth a still different set of types, as indicated by Morris G.
Caldwell, "Group Dynamics in the Prison Community," *Journal of Criminal
Law, Criminology, and Police Science,* 46:648-657, January-February, 1956.
See also Terence Morris, Pauline Morris, and Barbara Biely, "It's the Prisoners Who Run This Prison," *Prison Service Journal* (England), 1:3-11,
January, 1961.

[65] Garrity, "The Prison as a Rehabilitation Agency," p. 377.

The recidivism rates of neither thieves, convicts, nor "do-rights" are likely to be significantly affected by incarceration in any particular traditional prison. This is not to say, of course, that the *entire system* of imprisonment, in which both the thief subculture and the convict subculture are nurtured, does not contribute significantly to recidivism. In reference to the ordinary custodially oriented prison, the thief says he can do his time "standing on his head," and it appears that he *is* able to do the time "standing on his head"; except for long-termers, imprisonment has little effect on the thief one way or the other. Similarly, the routine of any particular prison is not likely to have significant reformative effects on members of the convict subculture; they return to prison because, in effect, they have found a home there. And the men oriented to legitimate subcultures maintain low recidivism rates even if they never experience imprisonment. ●

Prison riots   Occasionally the relationships between the inmate body, inmate elites, and officials are dramatized in a prison riot. During a riot, the loyalty of inmates to inmates and to criminals, the exploitation of prisoners by their leaders, the antagonistic attitudes of guards and officials toward inmates, and the alliances between elites and officials all become manifest.[66] Perhaps the greatest significance of prison riots is the awakening of the public to the fact that prison life, for both inmates and officers, is full of more misery than most middle-class citizens can imagine.

The contemporary pattern of riots in American prisons was established about twenty years ago. It became common shortly after Chinese prisoners of war held by Americans during the Korean War seized hostages and made demands of their captors. In the spring of 1952, sixty-nine prisoners at the Trenton, New Jersey, State Prison seized four guards as hostages, barricaded themselves in the prison print shop, and stated that they would not surrender until a committee of citizens investigated the conditions of the prison. Within a week, 232 prisoners at the New Jersey Prison Farm in Rahway barricaded themselves in a dormitory with nine hostages and demanded changes in prison conditions; they smashed all the dormitory windows, tore up the plumbing and heating systems, and destroyed their own lockers. A few days later 176 inmates at the Southern Michigan Prison in Jackson seized eleven hostages, barricaded themselves in a cellblock, and wrecked whatever was wreckable; prisoners in other sections of the prison armed themselves with makeshift weapons, wrecked the dining hall, set fire to the laundry, tore up the chapel, library, and gymnasium, and broke thousands of windows.[67] Within a few months similar riots occurred in Idaho,

---

[66] See Donald R. Cressey, "A Confrontation of Violent Dynamics," *International Journal of Psychiatry*, 10:109-124, September, 1972.

[67] For a description of this riot, see John Bartlow Martin, *Break Down the Walls* (New York: Ballantine Books, 1954).

Illinois, Kentucky, Louisiana, Massachusetts, New Mexico, North Carolina, Ohio, and Utah. In addition, potentially serious disturbances were quelled in one prison in California, one in Oregon, and two federal institutions.

The pattern was thus established. None of the riots involved attempts at mass escape. Each seemed to be a semiplanned strike or demonstration designed to call public attention to the conditions of prison life. Hostages were seized; the prisoners barricaded themselves; all destructible property in reach was destroyed; demands were issued, and were followed by bargaining with prison officials or political officials of the state. The formal demands were for better food, better medical care, better recreational facilities, segregation of sex offenders, less rigid disciplinary practices, and more liberal parole practices. This pattern also characterizes contemporary riots, including the one taking place in the prison at Attica, New York, in 1971.[68]

Some prison officials and some prisoners have stated that the demands and bargaining process are only second thoughts of the prisoners. We have seen that "peace" in prison depends upon giving some inmates special privileges and allowing them to exploit other inmates. But should these elites become dissatisfied with the officials' concessions, the idea goes, they can withdraw their pretense of support and define themselves as champions of the "mistreated prisoners." This is the usual role of elites during riots.

A more sociological analysis of the riots of the 1950s and 1960s attributes them to changed social structure of prisons.[69] Much of the power wielded informally by "right guys" and other inmate leaders was removed by "prison reforms" designed to make prisons more humane and more rehabilitative, but the services which the leaders provided for the inmates, and the services which the administrators provided the leaders, were not present in the new organization. The riots, then, were counterrevolutions, rather than revolutions, and they took the form of strikes for return of inmate "rights" which had been lost. Further, when prison administrators appeared to be making little effort to implement the progressive measures to which they gave public allegiance, a basis for widespread inmate dissatisfaction was provided.[70] It has been noted, further, that the "old guard" among officials, like the "old guard" among the inmates, also indirectly participate in the coun-

---

[68] New York State Special Commission on Attica, *Attica* (New York: Bantam, 1972), pp. 114-206; and Vernon Fox, "Why Prisoners Riot," *Federal Probation*, 35:9-14, March, 1971.

[69] Maurice Floch and Frank E. Hartung, "A Social Psychological Analysis of Prison Riots: An Hypothesis," *Journal of Criminal Law, Criminology, and Police Science*, 47:51-57, May-June, 1956.

[70] Lloyd E. Ohlin, *Sociology and the Field of Corrections* (New York: Russell Sage Foundation, 1956), p. 24. See also Clarence Schrag, "The Sociology of Prison Riots," *Proceedings of the American Correctional Association, 1960*, pp. 138-145.

terattacks, in an effort to regain power and privileges lost to the reformers.[71] This pattern is of less relevance today than formerly because more prisoners are now opposed to imprisonment as a general principle, not just because promised programs of rehabilitation have been used to break up old coalitions of power.[72]

Another kind of sociological analysis suggests that a prison becomes a "powder keg" which can be touched off by some precipitating incident only when there is a shift in the semiofficial government exercised by the inmates.[73] In some prisons, gradual transfer of power from the rulers to the ruled has at times reached the point where job assignments, cell assignments, recreational activities, and the granting of special privileges are all in the hands of inmate elites. When the officials then attempt to tighten up their prisons they inadvertently undermine control by "thieves" or "right guys" (who stress inmate solidarity but also are rewarded with special privileges because they emphasize the importance of peaceful coexistence with officials), and transfer leadership to more aggressive and violent "toughs," "gorillas," and "ballbusters," who both individually and collectively seem intent on giving the guards and other officials a hard time, despite the ultimate hopelessness of their position.

The changing character of prisoner organization in recent years has produced a more general shift in inmate power, making prisons more and more like "powder kegs." Race and ethnicity have become increasingly important in the formation of cleavages and identity changes in the convict world. Thus, "many Blacks and Chicanos are supplanting their criminal identity with a racial-ethnic one."[74] Further, a loosening of convict solidarity has driven the "right guy" into the background of prison life. Owing to what is commonly called the "politicalization" of prisoners, especially black ones, the proportion of "gorillas" in most prisons has increased in recent years, while the proportion of "right guys" has decreased. Because the prison now, as always, is a microcosm of the society in which it sits, militancy on the outside is bound to be reflected on the inside. Numerous observers of recent changes in prisons have considered the new militancy a sign of new prisoner power. But prisoner power is nothing new. Inmates have dominated the internal affairs of prisons during most of their two-

[71] Ohlin, *Sociology and the Field of Corrections*, p. 17. See also Lloyd E. Ohlin, "New Trends in Research in the Organization of Correctional Agencies," *Proceedings of the American Correctional Association, 1955*, pp. 256-266; Richard H. McCleery, *Policy Change in Prison Management* (East Lansing: Michigan State University Governmental Research Bureau, 1957), pp. 28-34; David Mechanic, "The Power to Resist Change Among Low-Ranking Personnel," *Personnel Administration*, 26:5-11, July, 1963; and Cressey, "A Confrontation of Violent Dynamics."

[72] John P. Spiegel, "The Dynamics of Violent Confrontation," *International Journal of Psychiatry*, 10:93-108, 125-128, September, 1972.

[73] Sykes, *The Society of Captives*, pp. 109-129.

[74] Irwin, *The Felon*, p. 80.

hundred-year history. What is new is a shift of inmate power from "right guys" to "gorillas." The militant "politicalized" prisoner is likely to take the "gorilla" roles. A black man who, for example, is convinced that he has been victimized by white society and then has been imprisoned only because he tried to undo some of the effects of that victimization is not likely to play it cool in prison, as "right guys" and old guard staff members would have him do. •

If the prison is to be efficient as an institution for reformation, the *esprit de corps* or public opinion among prisoners must be changed. No amount of individual therapy, vocational education, or coercion will do this. In addition, there is little reason to think that the prisoners themselves will develop self-government or other community organizations favorable to changing the prison subcultures. The leaders of the prison population look upon themselves as enemies of society, and on society as an enemy of prisoners. They are not to be induced in ordinary prison circumstances to shift their attitudes. Similarly, so long as the prison is expected to perform its retributive and deterrance functions, it is doubtful that the prison community can be greatly modified to bridge the chasm separating the social worlds of the insiders and the outsiders. The organization of prisoners is in part a reaction to the repressive aspects of the prison's administrative organization, and it therefore seems to be modifiable only slightly or not at all as long as the administrative organization efficiently performs the duties society assigns to it.[75]

In the United States, the most impressive attempts to change prisoner organization by modifying the administrative organization have been made in minimum-security institutions. One of the earliest attempts was made by Howard B. Gill, some years before study of the prison community became popular, at the Norfolk Prison Colony in Massachusetts.[76] The Norfolk program differed from honor systems and self-government systems in that the staff was made a part of the community. Twenty-five inmates were assigned to each "house officer" or caseworker. These officers did not wear uniforms, and their primary duty was to maintain a friendly, cooperative, and sympathetic relationship with the inmates. "Watch officers," whose duties were custodial, were used, but almost all of them remained on, or outside, the wall. They were not considered part of the community. From

Attempts to modify the prison culture

[75] Cf. Eliot Studt, Sheldon L. Messinger, and Thomas P. Wilson, *C-Unit: Search for Community in Prison* (New York: Russell Sage Foundation, 1968).

[76] See Howard B. Gill, "The Norfolk State Prison Colony at Massachusetts," *Journal of Criminal Law and Criminology*, 22:107-112, May-June, 1931; W. H. Commons, T. Yahkub, E. Powers, and C. R. Doering, *A Report on the Development of Penological Treatment at Norfolk Prison Colony in Massachusetts* (New York: Bureau of Social Hygiene, 1940).

the standpoint of conventional prison organization, the case-workers became a part of the informal prison social life, while the watch officers represented a modified type of repressive formal organization. The overall plan, thus, was to give inmates experience in noncriminal social activities and, especially, to modify inmates' attitudes in the direction of noncriminality by placing them in intimate, informal contact with sympathetic men possessing a strong bias against criminality. Today it would be considered a large-scale group-therapy program which handled "natural groups," included all inmates, and operated on principles similar to those used by Alcoholics Anonymous. The Norfolk program was subjected to severe and caustic criticism almost from its beginning, largely because it did not perform the retributive and deterrence functions which the taxpayers demanded. Superintendent Gill was discharged, and a more conventional type of prison organization was established.

Sykes and Messinger, among others, have suggested that the inmate code and status system arise as responses to the deprivations imposed on prisoners.[77] The implication is that the inmate system of organization would decline in importance if the pains of imprisonment were reduced, and that, therefore, the degree of deprivation ought to be reduced if reformation is a goal. Currently, this system for attempting to modify the traditional inmate structure is one of the principal features of prison camps, prison honor farms, institutions for juveniles, and so-called "therapeutic communities" in prison.[78]

The relatively relaxed discipline of such institutions, as well as the effort to understand rather than blame the inmates, weaken the "antireform" organization among the inmates.[79] However, it is possible that such institutions merely select a disproportionate number of inmates oriented to legitimate values and do not select many prisoners who bring with them to the prison an orientation to either the thief subculture or the convict subculture. As we indicated earlier, it is not at all certain that the inmate code and the behavior based on it arise solely because of the deprivations of prison life. To some degree, the values of inmates are carried

[77] Sykes and Messinger, "The Inmate Social System."

[78] See Oscar Grusky, "Some Factors Promoting Cooperative Behavior Among Inmate Leaders," *American Journal of Correction*, 21:8-9 ff., March, 1959; idem, "Organizational Goals and the Behavior of Informal Leaders," *American Journal of Sociology*, 65:59-67, July, 1959; Howard W. Polsky, *Cottage Six* (New York: Russell Sage Foundation, 1962); and Mayer N. Zald, "The Correctional Institution for Juvenile Offenders: An Analysis of Organizational 'Character,'" *Social Problems*, 8:57-67, Summer, 1960; and John M. Wilson and Jon D. Snodgrass, "The Prison Code in a Therapeutic Community," *Journal of Criminal Law, Criminology, and Police Science*, 60:532-542, December, 1971.

[79] David Street, Robert D. Vinter, and Charles Perrow, *Organization for Treatment* (New York: Free Press, 1966), pp. 225-227; Thomas P. Wilson, "Patterns of Management and Adaptations to Organizational Roles," *American Journal of Sociology*, 74:146-157, September, 1968; and Studt, Messinger, and Wilson, *C-Unit*, pp. 192-228.

into the prison from the outside. Accordingly, reducing the pains
of imprisonment will not alone result in modification of the values
of the prisoners. As Wheeler has said:

> While little is known about the relationship between roles played
> inside and outside the prison, there is a strong suggestion that the visible
> inmates are those who have had most experience in exploitative and
> manipulative roles prior to imprisonment—those most schooled in tech-
> niques of aggression and deceit. The combination of greater motivation
> and more well-developed skills among the more criminalistic inmates
> suggests the difficulties facing administrative attempts to decrease their
> visibility and power.[80]

McCleery's reports on changes in Oahu prison indicate that the
orientation of inmates can to some degree be shifted by opening
new channels of communication between staff and inmates.[81] By
means of these channels, Oahu staff members presented their
behavior patterns to inmates, and at the same time the "antireform" and "antiadministration" behavior patterns ordinarily cir-
culating among prisoners were choked off. Because in any prison
it is almost literally true among inmates that "knowledge is
power," a shift in the distribution of knowledge about appropriate
ways of behaving in the prison changed the distribution of power.
This kind of program for changing communication patterns and,
thus, definitions of what behavior is appropriate, is involved when
minimum-security institutions are put into operation. While
merely reducing the pains of imprisonment does not change the
patterns of behavior brought in from the outside, changing the
system of communcation should produce some of the desired
effects. This kind of program has not been fully explored by prison
managers, however. To a degree, it was used at Highfields, a
New Jersey institution housing twenty boys, where the entire
program was oriented toward piercing the boys' strong defenses
against rehabilitation.[82]

Korn and McCorkle have outlined a program which they believe
would minimize the opportunities for deception, manipulation,
exploitation, and dishonesty among inmates in maximum-security
prisons and would, therefore, be rehabilitative.[83] An ideal-type
rehabilitation program for nondisturbed "adaptive" prisoners
would begin and end in a struggle for control. An inmate who,
early in the program, asked, in effect, "Can I dominate you?"
would learn that he cannot deceive the officials involved. If he

[80] Wheeler, "Role Conflict in Correctional Communities," p. 257.

[81] McCleery, "The Governmental Process and Informal Social Control"; idem,
"Communication Patterns as Bases of Systems of Authority and Power"; and
idem, *Policy Change in Prison Management.*

[82] McCorkle, Elias, and Bixby, *The Highfields Story.* See also H. Ashley Weeks,
Youthful Offenders at Highfields (Ann Arbor: University of Michigan Press,
1958).

[83] Richard R. Korn and Lloyd W. McCorkle, *Criminology and Penology* (New
York: Holt, 1959), pp. 540-552.

then proceeded to overt rebellion and asked, "Can anybody stop me?" he would find the answer to be "Yes," and he would be placed in segregation. Any heroic suffering ("You can't break me" and despair ("Doesn't anybody give a damn?") in which he engaged would be countered by extreme caution and rigor in avoiding brutality. He would be given all institutional privileges except contact with other inmates, and clues to proper modes of conduct would not be given by officials. When self-doubt begins to emerge, and the inmate begins to recognize that, "This is getting me nowhere," his accessibility to treatment is considered to be at a high point. He then should be released from segregation suddenly and unexpectedly, so that he will return to the prison population asking himself, "Can I make it?" The emergence of conflict with inmates who have not gone through similar experiences is to be taken as "the one indispensable symptom of change." If the inmate has become alienated from the core values of the inmate social system, then the system has become a great asset to change, rather than its greatest obstacle. The inmate elites would become a source of derogation or threat, rather than a source of security and status. Finally, when the inmate had negotiated the hazards and temptations of the probationary period, he would be transferred to a minimum-custody institution reserved entirely for inmates in this last stage of rehabilitation.

This proposed program is more than a restatement of the old notion that the prisoner's "will" must be broken, although it supports the position of prison authorities whose primary concern is with rigid and secure control of the institution. To a large extent, the program is designed to offset the lack of adequately trained and experienced officers who can exert positive influence on prisoners and still not be corrupted by them.[84] It recognizes that the ordinary prison situation permits inmates to maintain essentially the same kind of deviant attitudes they possessed when they arrived, and it attempts to take individual inmates out of this situation.

Nevertheless, it appears that at the base of the program is the doubtful assumption that mere negative action—the presentation of painful evidence that deviant behavior is undesirable—is sufficient for reformation. For generations, the whole system of imprisonment has been based on this same assumption that criminals who are made to see the error of their ways will somehow become reformed. Consistently, for generations it has been assumed that the whole system of imprisonment need not involve systematic, positive, constructive help for criminals, and the whole system of imprisonment has not been a notable success at reformation. "In a less than perfect society where confinement is used as a means of deterrence and reform, it is possible that the prison is

---

[84] Ohlin, "New Trends in Research in the Organization of Correctional Agencies," p. 261.

a 'success' if only it does not make the offender worse. However, it does not seem overly optimistic to suppose that the prison can do more than simply stand still."[85] ●

AKMAN, DOGAN D., ANDRE NORMANDEAU, & MARVIN E. WOLFGANG. "The Group Treatment Literature in Correctional Institutions: An International Bibliography, 1945-1967." *Journal of Criminal Laws, Criminology, and Police Science*, 59:41-56, March, 1968.

BENNIS, WARREN G. "Theory and Method in Applying Behavioral Science to Planned Organizational Change." *Journal of Applied Behavioral Science*, 1 (1965): 337-360.

BONDESON, ULLA. "Argot Knowledge as an Indicator of Criminal Socialization." *Scandinavian Studies in Criminology*, 2:73-107, 1968.

CHANG, DAE H., & WARREN B. ARMSTRONG, eds. *The Prison: Voices from the Inside*. Cambridge, Mass.: Schenkman, 1972.

CLEMMER, DONALD. *The Prison Community*. Boston: Christopher, 1940. Reissued by Rinehart, 1958.

CLOWARD, RICHARD A., DONALD R. CRESSEY, GEORGE H. GROSSER, RICHARD McCLEERY, LLOYD E. OHLIN, GRESHAM M. SYKES, & SHELDON L. MESSINGER. *Theoretical Studies in Social Organization of the Prison*. New York: Social Science Research Council, 1960.

COHEN, STANLEY, & LAURIE TAYLOR. *Psychological Survival: The Experience of Long-Term Imprisonment*. New York: Pantheon, 1972.

CRESSEY, DONALD R. "Prison Organizations," Chapter 24 in James G. March, ed., *Handbook of Organizations*, pp. 1023-1070. New York: Rand McNally, 1965.

CRESSEY, DONALD R., ed. *The Prison: Studies in Institutional Organization and Change*. New York: Holt, Rinehart and Winston, 1961.

ELLI, FRANK. *The Riot*. New York: Coward-McCann, 1966.

GARABEDIAN, PETER G. "Social Roles and Processes of Socialization in the Prison Community." *Social Problems*, 11:139-152, Fall, 1963.

GIBBONS, DON C. *Changing the Lawbreaker: The Treatment of Delinquents and Criminals*. Englewood Cliffs, N.J.: Prentice-Hall, 1965.

GLASER, DANIEL. *The Effectiveness of a Prison and Parole System*. Indianapolis: Bobbs-Merrill, 1964.

HALL, JAY, MARTHA WILLIAMS, & LOUIS TOMAINO. "The Challenge of Correctional Change: The Interface of Conformity and Commitment." *Journal of Criminal Law, Criminology, and Police Science*, 57:493-503, December, 1966.

Suggested readings

[85] Sykes, "Men, Merchants, and Toughs."

HAZELRIGG, LAWRENCE, ed. *Prison Within Society: A Reader in Penology*. New York: Doubleday, 1968.

HEFFERMAN, ESTHER. *Making it in Prison: The Square, the Cool, and the Life*. New York: John Wiley, 1972.

IRWIN, JOHN. *The Felon*. Englewood Cliffs, N. J.: Prentice-Hall, 1970.

KASSEBAUM, GENE G., DAVID A. WARD, & DANIEL M. WILNER. *Prison Treatment and Parole Survival: An Empirical Assessment*. New York: John Wiley, 1971.

MATHIESEN, THOMAS. *The Defences of the Weak: A Sociological Study of a Norwegian Correctional Institution*. London: Tavistock, 1965.

MINTON, ROBERT J., ed. *Inside: Prison American Style*. New York: Random House, 1971.

MOOS, RUDOLF H. "The Assessment of the Social Climates of Correctional Institutions." *Journal of Research in Crime and Delinquency*, 5:174-188, July, 1968.

MORRIS, TERENCE, & PAULINE MORRIS. *Pentonville: A Sociological Study of an English Prison*. London: Routledge and Kegan Paul, 1963.

PERETTI, PETER O. "A Critique of the Prison and Prisoner Communities as Generating Milieu of Anti-Social and Anti-Legal Attitudes Among Inmates." *Acta Criminologiae et Medicinae Legalis Japonica*, 37:1-14, February, 1971.

PETERSEN, DAVID M., & MARCELLO TRUZZI, eds. *Criminal Life: Views from the Inside*. Englewood Cliffs, N. J.: Prentice-Hall, 1972.

POLSKY, HOWARD W. *Cottage Six*. New York: Russell Sage Foundation, 1962.

SCHRAG, CLARENCE. "A Preliminary Criminal Typology." *Pacific Sociological Review*, 4:11-16, Spring, 1961.

SCHWARTZ, BARRY. "Pre-Institutional vs. Situational Influence in a Correctional Community." *Journal of Criminal Law, Criminology, and Police Science*, 62:532-542, December, 1971.

STREET, DAVID, ROBERT D. VINTER, & CHARLES PERROW. *Organization for Treatment*. New York: Free Press, 1966.

STUBBLEFIELD, KEITH A., & LARRY L. DYE, eds. *Offenders as a Correctional Manpower Resource*. Washington: Joint Commission on Correctional Manpower and Training, 1968.

TITTLE, CHARLES. "Sex Differentiation and the Influence of Criminal Subcultures." *American Sociological Review*, 29:492-505, 1969.

TITTLE, CHARLES R., & DROLLENE P. TITTLE. "Social Organization of Prisoners: An Empirical Test." *Social Forces*, 43:216-221, December, 1964.

WARD, DAVID A., & GENE G. KASSEBAUM. *Women's Prison: Sex and Social Structure*. Chicago: Aldine, 1965.

WILKINS, LESLIE T. *Evaluation of Penal Measures*. New York: Random House, 1969.

25 Prison labor and education

The notion that work should be provided for prisoners is almost as old as the prison system itself. When institutions became places of punishment, rather than places of detention for persons awaiting trial, systems for occupying the time of prisoners also arose. This tendency was to some extent offset by the theory on which the early Pennsylvania prisons were based, namely, that labor interfered with the meditation considered essential for penitence. Idleness as a prison régime is no longer defended on any ground, and, on the contrary, the value of prison labor to inmates and to society is stressesd. Despite this emphasis, idleness in prisons has become increasingly prevalent during the last fifty years. As restrictive legislation and other conditions have reduced the amount of work available for prisoners, increasing stress has been placed on another system for keeping inmates occupied—education.

When labor was introduced into prison, it was regarded primarily as a means of punishment, although the possibilities for profits were not overlooked.[1] In some places, primarily in England, prison labor was almost exclusively punitive, consisting of such methods as the "shot drill"—carrying a cannonball back and forth in a long hall—or treadmills or cranks. Sometimes treadmills and cranks were attached to pumps or other instruments so that the work was productive, but more frequently they were merely attached to a meter which measured the number of units of work performed. A certain number of units had to be performed for each meal, and additional units were assigned to unruly inmates. The laws required that the labor should be "hard and servile" or "publicly and disgracefully imposed."

Although the idea that labor should be provided primarily for punishment was soon superseded by concern for utilization of labor in the production of wealth, the punitive element in labor is still retained in many institutions. Currently, the weight of opinion is that prison labor must be "useful" and must train inmates for postrelease vocations, but the idea that monotonous, hard, unpleasant work is necessary, if the prison is to perform its retributive and deterrence functions, also is popular. Also, systems of monotonous or punitive work, like systems of monotonous discipline and punishment generally, are still justified on the ground that they develop habits of industry, obedience, perseverence, and conformity and, hence, have a reformative or reha-

---

[1] George Rusche and Otto Kirchheimer, *Punishment and Social Structure* (New York: Columbia University Press, 1939), pp. 41-52.

bilitative effect. Similarly, the fact that routine prison labor often is defended on the ground that it "keeps inmates out of mischief" is evidence that it is, to some extent, considered part of the prison's program of incapacitation. Prison labor systems, then, are expected to accomplish the same goals—retribution, deterrence, incapacitation, and reformation—as is imprisonment itself. ●

Trends in labor systems

Concern for profits was important in the development of imprisonment as a replacement for corporal punishment and the death penalty, and this concern has remained. While in recent years restrictive legislation has seriously curtailed the amount of wealth which can be produced with convict labor, prisoners are expected, at least, to "pay their way" by producing goods or performing services which will reduce the number of tax dollars necessary for support of the prison. Even in institutions whose programs are said to be those of treatment, inmates are considered as "owing" the state a proportion of their time.

As a method for production of wealth, prison labor may be either public or private with reference to three items: the maintenance and discipline of the prisoners, the control of the employment, and the control and sale of the products. As may be seen in table XX, the lease system gives a private individual or firm control over all three of these. The contract system gives a private individual control over the employment and the sale of the products, while the public retains control over the maintenance and discipline. The piece-price system gives a private individual control over the sale of the products, but not over the employment or the maintenance and discipline. The public retains control over all three of these in the public account, state use, and public works and ways systems.

TABLE XX

Prison labor systems

System	Maintenance and discipline of prisoners	Control of employment	Control of sale of products	Market area
Lease	Private	Private	Private	Open
Contract	Public	Private	Private	Open
Piece-price	Public	Public	Private	Open
Public account	Public	Public	Public	Open
State Use	Public	Public	Public	State agencies
Public works and ways	Public	Public	Public	State agencies

The three public systems differ from each other in the extent of the market. In the public account system the market is entirely unrestricted. In the state use system the market is restricted to the public institutions in the state in which the goods are produced. In the public works and ways system the market is restricted to the state, and in addition to the "sale" of public buildings or roads. The last system, therefore, is merely a specialized form of the state use system.

The first system of convict labor in America was the public works and ways system. After several temporary experiments with this system during the seventeenth and eighteenth centuries, before the great development of prisons, it was practically abandoned until late in the nineteenth century. It was not until about 1880, when the advent of the bicycle helped create a demand for good roads, that the system flourished. The demand was further increased after the invention of the automobile. The "road gangs" employed by southern states and counties are examples of this system. Some states now make extensive use of the public works and ways system by maintaining forestry camps where prisoners are employed in fire fighting, insect control, and clearance work. Many states also use convict labor almost exclusively in prison construction.

The public account system was used generally in the early state prisons from about 1800 to 1825. Prison officials were responsible for the labor of the prisoners and the sale of the products; sometimes they were given commissions on the sales. The system failed because inadequate equipment, capital, transportation facilities, and demand for prison-made goods made it impossible to keep the prisoners steadily employed. Also, the introduction of machinery in outside industries resulted in production of goods at prices so low that the prisons, which depended on hand labor, could not compete. After the failure of the system in this early period, it was resumed in the decade of the 1880s as a substitute for contract labor and has been utilized to some extent since that time. Perhaps the best current example of this system is supplied by the state prison at Stillwater, Minnesota, where farm machinery and binder twine are produced for sale to Minnesota farmers.

The next system in order of appearance was the contract system, which was authorized as early as 1798 in Massachusetts and was actually used there in 1807. However, the system did not begin to flourish until about 1820. Up to this time it was difficult to use prison labor to advantage, and there was no market for prison products. The merchant-capitalist appeared, and he found that he could use cheap prison labor profitably and could enable the institution to make a profit on it. Thus he supplied the production and marketing organizations which had been lacking in the public account system.[2] The contract system flourished until about 1880, when it was attacked by the rising labor organizations. Auburn prison utilized this system, and the fact that the prison paid for itself was an important stimulus to the diffusion of the "Auburn system" to other states and nations. The number

---

[2] J. R. Commons, *History of Labour in the United States* (New York: Macmillan, 1918), vol. 1, pp. 153-155.

of prisoners employed in contract systems steadily declined after 1880, and since about 1940 no inmates in United States prisons have been employed in them.

A fourth system was the piece-price system, which was similar to the contract system except that the state directed the labor of the convicts, turning over the finished product to a contractor at a specified price per piece. This system was used in the prisons of Pennsylvania in the beginning of the nineteenth century and in New Jersey from 1798 to 1838 in connection with the public account system. Except for a few such temporary trials, it had its greatest development in the decade of the eighties and nineties, when the agitation against the contract system broke out. Although contractors paid for labor on the basis of output, rather than according to the number of hours worked, the piece-price system was merely a subterfuge—really the contract system under a different name and in a somewhat preferable form. This system also steadily declined during the twentieth century; less than 1 percent of the prisoners in the United States are now employed in it, and their work consists primarily of clerical jobs, such as addressing envelopes.

The lease system, which also is similar to the contract system, was authorized in Massachusetts in 1798, and in Kentucky and a few other states in about 1825. The lease system had its greatest development in the South after the Civil War, where convicts were leased to private parties who used their labor in lumber camps, turpentine camps, or other camps, but it is related to the indenture system used in the colonies, generally as a substitute for fines. This system is still authorized by law and used somewhat in the county jails of several southern states. In South Africa, modified forms of the lease system are used extensively. In one form, farmers' associations construct buildings for the accommodation of prisoners and personnel and then turn them over to the Department of Prisons, which puts its own officers in control. Native male recidivists are assigned to these "labor outposts," and the farmers' associations pay fixed daily rates for their labor. In another form, prisoners with short sentences give their permission to be assigned to individual farmers, who pay them a small wage and provide food, clothing, housing, and medical care. Over 40,000 prisoners with terms under four months voluntarily used this program in 1952.[3] In six European countries, prisoners nearing the end of their term are permitted to work for private parties under conditions closely approximating those of complete freedom.[4]

The state use system came into prominence in the decade of the 1880s, when the contract system began to decline. By 1899, the system had been authorized by twenty-four states, and at

---

[3] Herman Venter, *The South African Prison System*, Fact Paper No. 68 (Pretoria: South African Information Service, 1959), pp. 9-10.

[4] Ralph W. England, *Prison Labour* (New York: United Nations Department of Economic and Social Affairs, 1955), pp. 12-13.

present in about half the states it is mandatory that state agencies and institutions purchase prison-made products, such as furniture, inmate clothing, and printed materials, if they are available. In practice, evasions are frequent, and prisons sometimes have difficulty of disposing of goods which compete with commercially produced products, occasionally because the prison products are inferior. The antagonism of trade unions and manufacturers has been aroused by this system, just as it was aroused by the contract and lease systems. If a prison makes furniture for state agencies, privately manufactured furniture cannot be sold to these same agencies. Of the prisoners who are now employed, about 90 percent are in the state use system or the public works system.

However, most prison inmates do not work, and those who are employed work haphazardly. The Hawes-Cooper Law of 1934 authorized the states to regulate the sale within their boundaries of commodities made in the prisons of other states, and shortly thereafter every state enacted laws which prohibited or restricted the sale in the open market of goods made in prisons. These state laws were then supplemented by federal laws barring from interstate commerce most goods made in state prisons. This restriction of the market for prison-made goods has contributed to increased idleness. Glaser reports that less than a fourth of the inmates in state and federal prisons were employed in prison industries, which ordinarily do not include prison housekeeping and feeding tasks, and the work of maintaining prison plants.[5] Moreover, the number engaged in productive labor is padded by overassignment, and probably at least two-thirds of the prisoners are, in fact, idle on an average day. While the assignments of prisoners to educational activities, to treatment programs, and to institutional maintenance have increased, they have not increased sufficiently to compensate for the reduction in productive employment. A recent study of California prison industries found that the employment provided for inmates is little different from idleness.[6] ●

Payment of wages to prisoners is not a new device. As early as 1700, Massachusetts provided that inmates of the houses of correction should receive eight pence out of every shilling they made, under a system in which the masters or relatives furnished tools and materials. For a time, prisoners were held until they paid for their maintenance, but the prisons soon became congested, and the system was modified. After a general failure of the wage system in the colonial period, it disappeared almost entirely for half a century. But in 1853 the Eastern Penitentiary

Wage payments to prisoners

---

[5] Daniel Glaser, *The Effectiveness of a Prison and Parole System* (Indianapolis: Bobbs-Merrill, 1964), p. 226.

[6] California Assembly, Office of Research, *Report on the Economic Status and Rehabilitative Value of California Correctional Industries* (Sacramento: California Legislature, 1969), p. 5.

of Pennsylvania began to pay small wages to prisoners. Other states gradually adopted the same policy. In 1957, thirty-three states paid wages to prisoners, with wages ranging from four cents to $1.30 per day. The Federal Prison Industries, a governmental corporation which operates as the industrial division of the Bureau of Prisons, pays inmates according to the grade of work performed. In 1964, the average wage paid per month for those employed in manufacturing was about forty dollars.[7]

Among the states, wages depend on a variety of things other than the efficiency of the inmate; e.g., good conduct, the number of children in the prisoner's family, and especially the profits of the institution. The institution may fail to make a profit because of conditions over which the prisoner has no control, such as inadequate working capital, poor location of prison, poor choice of industries, poor salesmanship, or poor organization of the work. If prisoners are to be paid at all, they should be paid even when idle, if their idleness is due to no fault of their own. This principle is currently used in twenty states and the District of Columbia, where 90 to 100 percent of the inmates earn money in prison.[8] These include states with above-average per capita revenue, such as Massachusetts and New York, as well as some of the lower-income states, such as Kentucky and South Carolina. Six states permit no inmate earnings in prison, and in five states no more than 10 percent of the inmates earn money.

The former chief of the Section on Social Defense in the United Nations argued that labor is a right of prisoners under the "Universal Declaration of Human Rights" adopted by the United Nations. He stated, further, that prison labor is not treatment, that prisoners should receive the same pay as free men if they do the same work, and that prison labor should be a part of labor in general.[9] ●

Administrative problems

Three general problems confront the administrative officers and professional workers of a prison with reference to the employment of prisoners, even after the system of labor is settled. One of the problems is the assignment of prisoners to their tasks in the prison industry and to institutional maintenance tasks such as cleaning, cooking, and clerical work. With the development of classification committees, a few prisons have developed personnel programs which compare favorably with personnel programs in private industry.[10] The various kinds of jobs are analyzed, and

[7] Bureau of Prisons, Annual Report, 1964, p. 4.

[8] Glaser, Effectiveness of a Prison and Parole System, p. 235.

[9] Manuel Lopez-Rey, "Some Considerations on the Character and Organization of Prison Labor," Journal of Criminal Law, Criminology, and Police Science, 49:10-28, May-June, 1958.

[10] See, for example, George W. Tilden, "Missouri Department of Corrections Occupational Evaluation and Utilization Program," Proceedings of the American Correctional Association, 1964, pp. 200-204.

each prisoner is studied on entrance to determine the kind of work he is equipped to do. The prisoner's preferences and needs are noted, and, in the ideal system, he is given the occupation he wishes if it is possible to do so in view of his capacities and the institutional opportunities. However, in practice, the needs of the institution almost always are given priority over the needs or desires of the inmate. As was pointed out in chapter 23, the criteria used for assignment of inmates to specific tasks probably are custody, convenience, discipline, and treatment, in that order.

A second problem is keeping the prison industries efficient enough to be competitive with outside industries, in face of the low educational levels and poor skills of the inmates who must be employed. So that work can be provided for inmates, prisons use obsolete hand operations.[11] Further, most inmates have little skill, little work experience, poor work habits, and little academic training. They are not able to operate the modern automated equipment that characterizes efficient industrial organizations.[12] In 1952, Correctional Industries at the Michigan state prison picked sweet corn and green beans by hand, using 150 to 180 inmates; today they use complex mechanical pickers and only two inmate operators.[13] Most inmates cannot qualify as operators of the machines. If prison industries are to compete with private industries, inmates must first be trained in the most basic manual work skills, taught to read operators' manuals, trained to write reports, and instructed in such basic mechanical skills as the use of a ruler or a wrench. Thus, in the modern age, the vocational training given in prison schools is almost as essential to employment in the prison as it is to employment outside prison.

Organization of working time poses a third general administrative problem. If prison industry is to be efficient and profitable, interference with work must be reduced to a minimum. At the same time, the reduction in work interference must be consistent with the performance of other necessary activities. It is extremely difficult to organize an efficient prison industry because men are frequently called from work for interviews, visits, band practice, group therapy, school, sick call, discipline, or other routine prison activities. Certain custodial practices also are conducive to inefficiency in inmate work. For example, time must be taken for counts; the inmates must be in their cells at 4:00 P.M. or 4:30 P.M., when the guard is changed; and, for security reasons, inmates usually must bathe, play baseball and basketball, visit the barber, and patronize the commissary during working hours.

---

[11] See Ralph W. England, Jr., "New Departures in Prison Labor," *Prison Journal*, 41:21-26, Spring, 1961.

[12] Ross V. Randolph, "Automation in Industries," *Proceedings of the American Correctional Association*, 1964, pp. 194-200.

[13] Paul Chase, "Correlation of Vocational Education and Correctional Industries," *Proceedings of the American Correctional Association*, 1963, pp. 222-225.

The rate of absenteeism in the San Quentin prison's correctional industries in 1968 was about 12 percent, and on any given day only about two-thirds of the inmates worked a full shift.[14] The rate of sick-leave absenteeism in government and private industry is about 3 percent.

A more fundamental aspect of this problem involves a question of the priority of prison work over more direct treatment programs. Although the increasing idleness in prisons in recent years has been rightfully viewed with alarm, revival of the industrial prison might not, by itself, produce the rehabilitative effects which are demanded of our prisons. Instead, the treatment reaction to crime seems to imply a reduction in the amount of prison labor, so that time can be devoted to more efficient treatment programs. Gill was arguing on this ground for a reduction of prison labor forty years ago:

> The industrial prison has not proven a success penologically. In the early days hard work was the panacea for all ills—especially crime. In these days of social work, scientific medicine and psychiatry, we have come to realize that the cause and cure of crime are by no means merely economic. Practically everyone admits that most men leave prison worse than they enter. This is not the fault of the industries, but it is a strong indication that the present emphasis on industries does not produce the desired results penologically.[15]

In spite of this argument, however, most classification committees and prison administrators still operate as if work were the most important nonpunitive activity in the institution, regardless of whether or not the work is of any value to the inmates. In some institutions, the assumption is that industries which are profitable to the institution must be manned, even if the value of the work to the inmates cannot be rationalized at all. The treatment reaction to crime is not yet so extensive that a prison administrator can choose to assign inmates to specific rehabilitation programs at the cost of closing down an industry such as a cannery. Similarly, the notion that free laborers could be hired to perform the prison maintenance tasks, thereby releasing inmates for treatment, would find few supporters today, even though most persons readily accept such a policy as it pertains to inmates of mental hospitals, who also are being treated. ●

Training and rehabilitation

In recent times, as the treatment reaction to crime has developed, labor has frequently been considered as part of the prison treatment program. Ordinarily, the assumption is that nonpunitive labor of almost any kind will instill in inmates habits of industry, so that in the postrelease period they will work at socially accept-

---

[14] California Assembly, Office of Research, *Report on Economic Status*, p. 9.
[15] Howard B. Gill, "The Future of Prison Employment," *Proceedings of the American Prison Association, 1935*, pp. 179-185.

able occupations and will not commit crimes.[16] Although a part of the treatment reaction, this conception of reformation is very similar to conceptions regarding the reformative effect of punitive labor, or of punishment of any kind. Another popular assumption is that through prison labor inmates learn skills which enable them, in the postrelease period, to support themselves and their families by legitimate means, so that they "do not have to turn to crime." Both assumptions, in turn, are based on the notion that economic need and attitudes toward work, not attitudes toward legal norms, produce crime. The assumption regarding the "habit-forming" values of prison labor was stated as follows by James V. Bennett, former director of the United States Bureau of Prisons:

> The great necessity in prison is work. If I had to manage a prison upon condition that I make my choice of one thing, and only one, as an aid to discipline, as an agency for reform, for its therapeutic value, I would unhesitatingly choose work—just plain, honest-to-goodness work. Of course, I wouldn't like to have to concentrate so on a choice and it would be unwise to be so restricted. Physical examinations, medical treatments, bodily repairs, educational opportunities, spiritual guidance, psychiatry, psychology, are necessary and helpful. But the habit of work is what men most need.

An alternative statement regarding the indirect rehabilitative value of prison labor may be made as follows: Work in prison affects reformation largely to the extent that it is conducive to changes in associations upon discharge from prison, but it also contributes to the morale of the inmates, so that they are psychologically better equipped for making such changes in associations. Many prisoners learn skills which could be used after discharge. But the possession of these skills does not, by itself, produce reformation. Instead, it is at least probable that possession of the skills affects the social mobility of the discharged inmate and that as he moves from the status of an unskilled worker or of an unemployed person to the status of a skilled worker his associations and, consequently, his attitudes toward legal norms also change. Rather than return to the social situation which produced his criminality in the first place, the discharged inmate who has been trained in a useful occupation conceivably will move into a new social situation, perhaps one not conducive to criminality.

Also, the work provided in prisons is indirectly important to reformation under the current prison practices, because absence of work means idleness, not participation in programs aimed more directly at rehabilitation. Since idleness in prisons undoubtedly contributes to the incidence of "prison stupor," because it is conducive to low prisoner morale, and because it affects the incidence of prison riots, it may be concluded that idleness seldom equips inmates for shifts in loyalties from criminal groups to law-abiding groups. Until the treatment reaction and programs based on it become much more extensive than at present, prisons will

---

[16] See Ralph D. Edwards, "Correctional Industries and Inmate Training," *Proceedings of the American Correctional Association, 1963*, pp. 197-200.

necessarily have to provide work programs which contribute to the psychological well-being of inmates who are merely "doing time."[17] Perhaps it is for this reason that prisoners in Scandinavian countries and in Mexico possess the right to work.

Prison labor, then, can contribute to rehabilitation by providing inmates with skills which, in turn, might affect their associations and, consequently, their attitudes toward criminality. It also can contribute to rehabilitation, in a rather negative sense, by keeping inmates occupied so that they leave the prison in good psychological and physical condition.[18]

The importance of continuation after release of the work learned in prison is sometimes minimized. It is asserted that the ex-prisoner does not wish to tell where he learned the trade, that he wishes to throw off everything that reminds him of his prison career, and that, in practice, he seldom learns a trade sufficiently well to pursue it efficiently after his release. Glaser interviewed 140 men four months after they had been released from federal prisons to the supervision of the United States Probation Offices in Chicago, Detroit, Cleveland, and St. Louis.[19] Of these men, twenty-four had not yet found any postrelease employment, and two had had no work assignment in prison, due to hospitalization. Of the 114 men who had worked in prison and who had postrelease jobs, thirty-three reported that some job they had held for a week or longer after having been released from prison was related in some way to a job they had had in prison. The 114 men had held a total of 184 postrelease jobs; forty-seven, or about a quarter of these jobs, were related to prison work experience. Among the forty-seven, twenty-four (51 percent) were considered by the men to be related to relatively unskilled prison work, such as construction labor or unskilled kitchen or dining room work; 31 percent of the forty-seven references (fifteen cases) were to relatively skilled work in the prison, such as machinist, electrician, printer, cook, and baker assignments. The remaining 18 percent (eight cases) of the forty-seven references were to white-collar assignments in the prison, predominantly clerical jobs. However, of the forty-seven men who said their postrelease jobs were related to their prison jobs, twenty-five (52 percent) reported that they had had preprison experience with the job they held in prison. From these data and from responses to a question about the usefulness of the prison work to the forty-seven jobs, Glaser concluded that in about one-tenth of inmate postrelease jobs there are benefits from new learning acquired in prison work; in about 3 or 4 percent of these jobs there are benefits from the preservation of old skills through practice in prison; and in about 5 or 6 percent of the postrelease jobs the prison had provided useful physical or psychological conditioning.

---

[17] Cf. Stanley Cohen and Laurie Taylor, *Psychological Survival: The Experience of Long-Term Imprisonment* (New York: Pantheon, 1972), pp. 100-104.

[18] John R. Stratton and Jude P. West, *The Role of Correctional Industries: A Summary Report* (Washington: Government Printing Office, 1972), p. 26.

[19] Glaser, *Effectiveness of a Prison and Parole System*, pp. 250-251.

While closing down prison industries and freeing inmates from maintenance tasks would be expensive, the expense might be offset in the long run by the development of correctional techniques and programs which would reduce recidivism. Even if prisons became almost exclusively institutions for treatment, however, some kind of work activity probably would be provided, just as work activities are provided as a means of passing the time in mental hospitals. It cannot be argued that prison labor has no rehabilitative effects, but it is doubtful that labor is the most important activity which is, or could be, provided for the reformation of prisoners. ●

Education, as popularly understood, means the process or product of formal training in schools or classrooms. In a broader sense, education includes all of the life experiences which shape a person's attitudes and behavior. Education in prison has been viewed in both ways. On one hand, prison education was once taken to mean little more than the academic school programs which were offered to inmates. This conception of education still persists in many prisons. On the other hand, all intentional efforts to direct inmates away from crime by means of nonacademic, as well as academic, measures are now usually considered as prison education. From this point of view, "education" of prisoners is almost synonymous with "treatment" of prisoners. This broad conception of prison education may be observed in the New York State Correctional Law:

Trends in prison education

> The objective of prison education in its broadest sense should be the socialization of the inmates through varied impressional and expressional activities, with emphasis on individual inmate needs. The objective of this program shall be the return of these inmates to society with a more wholesome attitude toward living, with a desire to conduct themselves as good citizens and with the skill and knowledge which will give them a reasonable chance to maintain themselves and their dependents through honest labor. To this end, each prisoner shall be given a program of education which, on the basis of available data, seems most likely to further the process of socialization and rehabilitation. The time daily devoted to such education shall be such as required for meeting the above objectives.[20]

In this broad sense, the problem of prison education is essentially a problem in reformation. This involves a conversion, a transference of allegiance from one group to another, so that the person is not receptive to criminal behavior patterns, and a redirection of those specific interests and attitudes conducive to contacts with criminal behavior patterns. Little specific knowledge has been acquired regarding the exact techniques for producing the required identification of self with law-abiding groups. But it is essential that prisoners be immersed in the ideals, sentiments, and traditions of law-abiding persons. This means not merely an intellectual comprehension of these traditions, but emotional

---

[20] New York Correctional Law, chapter 864, section 136.

involvement with them. Probably the best way to accomplish this would be by providing inmates with frequent and intimate contacts with people who have the traditions; this is limited by considerations of custody and punishment. An alternative is to provide the contacts, meager and ineffective as they must be in the prison community, by means of educational facilities. Reading and writing can assist in producing the contacts, but contacts also can be provided by means of moving pictures, library facilities, lectures, classroom instruction, discussions with volunteer groups, religious exercises, certain recreations and entertainments, and even individual psychotherapy. Participation in such activities, like participation in prison industries, gives the offender an opportunity, after his release, to change his social position and, conceivably, to associate with persons having strong anticriminal biases.

The church has been interested in the religious instruction of prisoners since the origin of imprisonment. During the medieval and early modern periods preachers and priests visited the prisons more or less regularly and conversed with prisoners in congregate or separate meetings. Some of the early houses of correction had resident chaplains who, in addition to holding regular religious services, attempted to teach the elementary subjects, especially to the children confined in these institutions. The first recorded instance of regular visitation of prisoners in America was by the Quakers of Philadelphia just prior to the Revolutionary War. These laymen, as the preachers after them, distributed Bibles and theological tracts and conversed with the prisoners in the cells. Prior to 1845, few prisons had regular resident chaplains, and these were poorly paid and were, in general, inefficient.

The development of secular educational work in prisons resulted directly from the effort to teach prisoners to read the Bible and the tracts. This effort to introduce secular education met with some resistance. The warden of Auburn prison in 1824 successfully opposed an attempt to teach the younger convicts to read and write. His opposition was based on the "increased danger to society of the educated convict." The same fear was expressed in England about this time.[21]

The first organized educational work in America started in the New York House of Refuge. Provision was made there for two hours a day for each child; one hour of this consisted of learning to read the New Testament, the other of lectures and talks by the superintendent. The following year, the school period was increased to four hours a day, and the work consisted of the three R's, geography, and bookkeeping.[22]

---

[21] O. F. Lewis, *The Development of American Prisons and Prison Customs, 1776-1845* (Albany: Prison Association of New York, 1922), p. 95; Sidney and Beatrice Webb, *English Prisons Under Local Government* (London: Longmans, 1922), p. 157.

[22] P. Klein, *Prison Methods in New York State* (New York: Columbia University Press, 1920), pp. 308, 311.

In practically all institutions for adults up to the middle of the nineteenth century, prisoners were not permitted to meet in groups, and the school work was done at night. As late as 1845, few institutions taught even the three R's, and these few gave a very small amount of time to formal educational work. The first legal recognition of academic education as desirable in penal or reformatory institutions was in 1847, when the legislature of New York State provided for the appointment of two teachers for each of the state prisons to give instruction in English for not less than an hour and a half a day. Within a comparatively short time, many of the prisons in other states made similar provisions. In most places, the educational work continued to be confined to the evening, and no congregate groups were permitted. This continued in some institutions to the present century.

The greatest stimulation to the development of prison schools and other educational activities in prisons came with the increasing popularity of the treatment reaction to crime after the Civil War. The nonpunitive, constructive measures advocated for use in the attempt to reform or treat inmates were largely educational. A growing faith in the importance of academic education to all citizens in a democracy and to the "good life" also permeated prison and reformatory systems. The logic was something like this: If the good citizens are the educated citizens, then the education of bad citizens (prisoners) should make them good. The Elmira Reformatory, which opened in 1876, had a "school of letters" as well as a trade school. Elmira's first warden, Brockway, described the changes in his own attitudes toward reformation during the last half of the nineteenth century, and this description may be taken as an illustration of the changes in public opinion taking place at the time. He stated that he had at first placed his dependence on regular labor, with the expectation that it would form habits that would persist after release; then he was converted in a religious meeting and, for a time, had great faith in the power of religion to modify the behavior of the prisoners; by 1885, he had developed a greatly enhanced estimation of the reformative value of rational education. By rational education, he meant education in its broadest sense, including vocational education, lectures, certain entertainments, group discussions, and the teaching of ethics, as well as the ordinary academic courses. ●

Hindrances to educational work

Among the hindrances to educational work in prisons are the attitudes of the prisoners and the informal organization of the prison. Some of the attitudes are developed outside the institution, but many of them are produced by the prison régime and by the conception that the prisons are primarily places of punishment. The walls and bars needed to prevent escapes keep the punitive and protective functions of the prison continually before the attention of the inmates. Prisoners conventionally react by assuming hostile attitudes toward the institution and all its activities. The school, recreational programs, religious instruction, and other activities struggle against this attitude, but generally with little success. Educational administrators, like wardens and guards, are considered outsiders by inmates. Prisoners who participate in educational activities are looked down upon and, in some prisons, suspected of being stool pigeons.

A second hindrance to educational work is inadequate equipment and organization. Libraries are often housed in the visting room, chaplain's office, or a storage room. Money is not available for expensive vocational educational materials or instructors. In certain places, no room is provided for school except the mess hall. In some institutions, children's school desks are used for adult prisoners. The textbooks are frequently those used in the public schools for children. Some years ago, a class of prisoners was engaged in copying from the blackboard a sentence which read, "How swiftly and pleasantly the hours fly by."

A third hindrance to educational work is the productive industry and maintenance activities of the institution. This involves a difficult problem in the comparative importance of labor and of educational activities. School authorities generally insist that the work should not interfere with the school; the warden, interested in the financial status and the smooth operation of the institution, insists that the school should not interfere with prison labor. The criminal needs a modification of attitudes unless he is to be retained in the institution all his life. Even if labor has some value for this purpose, many other methods also must be used, and these methods are usually included in the educational system. ●

The prison school

In many state prisons any academic training is confined to the first three, five, or eight grades, and the time spent in the classroom is generally no more than five or ten hours per week. The primary objective in such schools is to teach the use of the tool subjects—reading, writing, and arithmetic. In view of the fact that about 10 percent of the admissions to correctional institutions throughout the country are functionally illiterate, these are important subjects. The level of educational achievement in California is higher than in most states. Yet in California prisons in 1969, 2.8 percent of the male felons received from court were illiterate; the median level of educational achievement was the eighth grade, and 28 percent of the men fell below the sixth grade.[23] Similarly, 2.8 percent of the persons admitted to Michigan prisons in 1967 were illiterate; 38 percent had not reached the sixth grade, and 82 percent had not reached the ninth grade.[24]

---

[23] *California Prisoners, 1970* (Sacramento: Department of Corrections, 1972), p. 31.

[24] *Criminal Statistics, 1967* (Lansing: Michigan Department of Corrections, 1969), table B-3.

Other popular subjects include bookkeeping, drawing, stenography, and civics. Comparatively few institutions give courses in any of the social sciences other than civics, although several advisory commissions which have made surveys of education in correctional institutions have recommended that much more emphasis should be placed on the social studies, and especially on those social studies which deal with contemporary life, namely, sociology, economics, and political science. These recommendations have been made on the principle that for purposes of readjustment, inmates should understand the social world in which they live and especially should understand and appreciate the traditions of law-abiding society. Seventy percent of fifty-four inmates questioned in one reformatory stated that an ideal rehabilitation program for them would be based on "the teaching, explanation, and discussion of the fundamental principles for living as a responsible citizen in society."[25]

A few institutions for adults have developed school programs which compare favorably with the school programs of many cities. In California, the prison schools are actually a part of the school system of the city in which the prison is located, and both the administration of the school and the instruction are under the direction of the State Board of Education. The students and equipment are provided by the prison, the teachers and program by the school district. Regular courses from the first grade through high school are given by teachers certified by the board. The content, methods, and procedures employed in the ordinary public schools are followed, and certificates and diplomas are granted by the regular school district, rather than by the prison. In addition to the courses leading to a diploma, a wide variety of the general cultural and technical subjects usually included in adult education programs, such as French literature, social living, and accounting, are offered. New York State and the Federal Bureau of Prisons also have excellent, well-organized, school systems. Institutions for juvenile delinquents have the most adequate schools, while formal education in jails and workhouses is almost entirely lacking.

An innovative educational program was recently conducted for inmates of the National Training School, a federal institution in Morgantown, West Virginia. The project, which was conducted over a period of two years, used "programmed learning" coupled with personal counseling and instruction. Boys had maximum choice in how they occupied themselves, but they were paid in "points" equivalent to money for their accomplishments. They earned no points if they were lazy, and they were fined points for misbehavior. In school, points were awarded to boys who passed a test with a score of 90 percent or higher. Boys also could earn points by working in the cafeteria as janitors before or after

---

25 John F. Sinnott, "The Searchers," mimeographed paper (Green Bay, Wis.: Wisconsin State Reformatory, 1959), p. 2.

school. Bonus points were given for exemplary behavior. By spending the points like money, the inmates could "rent" individual cells, buy special meals, and purchase special items from the commissary and a mail-order catalogue. Jukeboxes and pool tables also were available for rental. With these incentives, inmates averaged a grade advancement of one year's academic level in about five months.[26]

Some prisons now give college-level instruction. The most common form of instruction is correspondence courses, then live instruction by visiting college staff members, television, and a furlough system which allows inmates time out of prison to attend classes.[27] Adams estimates that, in 1967, 850 inmates were enrolled in college-level correspondence courses, and about two thousand were taking regular classes taught by college and university instructors. Highland Junior College, in Kansas, has awarded fifty-five Associate in Arts degrees to inmates of a nearby institution. Several other colleges also award A.A. degrees to inmates.

A common practice in the state prisons is to employ one teacher or superintendent and inmate assistants. Most of the inmate teachers are poorly equipped for the work, although it was once reported that Oklahoma had such success with inmate teachers that it preferred them to civilian teachers. The inmate teachers interviewed by Glaser, however, reported pressure from inmates to give good grades, to allow cheating, and to let class discussions wander for indefinite periods to sports, crime, or other topics irrelevant to the assigned study topic. The inmate teachers who balked at such practices were subject to reprisals, while those that complied were the recipients of reciprocal favors. In general, it is distinctly preferable to have teachers who represent ordinary society, who have had sufficient experience with delinquents and criminals to be able to understand them and to present the school work in ways that appeal to them. Accordingly, in some prisons and in most reformatories and institutions for juvenile delinquents the teaching force is composed entirely of civilians. Some reformatories now use female teachers. Some institutions give standardized educational tests and assign the prisoners to school work according to their abilities as thus measured. By repeating the tests at regular intervals, the students' progress can be measured. When education is considered in its broadest sense, assignments to various activities are made on a clinical basis—in accordance with the clinical principle, inmates' needs and problems are diagnosed, and individual assignments are made on the basis of these diagnoses. ●

---

[26] President's Commission on Law Enforcement and Administration of Justice, *Task Force Report: Corrections* (Washington: Government Printing Office, 1967), p. 53.

[27] Stuart Adams, *College-Level Instruction in U. S. Prisons* (Berkeley: University of California School of Criminology, 1968), pp. 1-14.

The best prison vocational training programs are those in which trade training is correlated with related academic subjects, and in which an attempt actually to teach vocational skills is made. Only a small number of prisons have such vocational programs. In the vast majority of institutions "vocational training" is merely the maintenance, industrial, or agricultural work to which inmates are assigned. It is possible to assign inmates to routine prison work—such as painting, baking, barbering, electrical and mechanical repairing, and tailoring—which will furnish the basis for training. But in most institutions participation in such prison work hardly deserves the name "vocational education." Even in institutions where inmates are assigned to certain work activities on the basis of their needs, the training has not been developed in proportion to the development of techniques for classification and assignment. An inmate is likely to be assigned to painting because he is a painter, not because he needs training in painting.

The vocational training in reformatories for young adults is not much better, on the whole, than in state prisons. The greatest difficulty is that the inmates either stay in the institution for too short a time to acquire a trade, or else shift from one trade to another. The institutions for juvenile delinquents have attempted to give trade training, but they are handicapped by the fact that most of the inmates are young and remain in the institution for only a short time. Even if they develop vocational skill, they cannot acquire positions when they are released. Jails and workhouses characteristically give no vocational training.

Perhaps the most serious current problem regarding vocational education in prisons is that of determining the amount of emphasis which should be placed on this subject in the total correctional program. Until recently vocational training was considered the most essential kind of education, and almost all rehabilitative efforts in the prison were vocational. An emphasis on treatment—sometimes called social education—has superseded the earlier emphasis on vocational training, but it has not made the prison rehabilitative either. Nevertheless, we no longer would be satisfied if the prison produced competent bricklayers; we want it to produce honest bricklayers. After a careful survey of fifteen state reformatories a half-century ago, Nadler concluded that the industrial training in those institutions was not successful, and that it would be preferable to devote the time to changing inmates' attitudes.[28] While vocational education procedures have been greatly improved in recent years, the notion that prisoners' major difficulties can be resolved by vocational training has declined in

**Vocational
education**

---

[28] F. F. Nadler, "The American State Reformatory," *University of California Publications in Education,* vol. 5, no. 3 (1920), p. 420.

popularity. It now appears that vocational education is not important to rehabilitation because of the skills it might provide. Instead, it is important to the extent that it, like both work and academic education, affects the inmate's conception of himself and influences his postrelease associations. ●

Results of prison education

While most existing academic, social, and vocational education programs, like most existing work programs, probably are of slight value in modification of attitudes, many prison administrators and many prisoners have expressed the belief that well-organized prison schools are an excellent reformative influence. Few attempts have been made to measure this influence, and most of these attempts have not been reliable. An elaborate statistical study was made in the Wisconsin state prison, which has an educational system that is decidedly above the average. The general conclusion was that, when other things are held constant, men who do not attend the prison school violate parole in significantly larger numbers than do men who attend the school. However, educational training for less than six months appears to have no effect on recidivism.[29]

An interview study of 120 parolees who had graduated from the trade-training programs of various Michigan institutions indicated that only 14 percent were using their training; 38 percent had not even applied for a job in their area of training.[30] Similarly, Glaser found that of 114 men who had been released from prison four months earlier, and who had found postrelease employment, ninety-five (83 percent) had been involved in some sort of educational activity in prison. These ninety-five men had held 156 postrelease jobs. Of the ninety-five men, twenty-six (27 percent) reported that their prison education had helped them in thirty-one of their 156 jobs. The men said that elementary school education was helpful in nine of the thirty-two jobs, high school education in three, white-collar training such as bookkeeping in another nine, personality improvement courses in five, and mechanical trade courses in the remaining five.[31] Glaser's more general data on the relationship between prison education and recidivism indicate, contrary to the earlier Wisconsin findings, that 39 percent of 361 men enrolled in prison education were "failures" (returned to prison or received a nonprison sentence for a felonylike offense within four years), while 33 percent of 654 men who never enrolled in prison school programs were failures.[32] ●

---

[29] "The Educational Treatment of Prisoners and Recidivism," *American Journal of Sociology,* 54:142-147, September, 1948.

[30] James Gillham and William L. Klime, *The Use of Correctional Trade Training* (Lansing: Michigan Department of Corrections, 1970), p. 19.

[31] Glaser, *Effectiveness of a Prison and Parole System,* pp. 271-272.

[32] Ibid., p. 276.

ADAMS, STUART. *College-Level Instruction in U. S. Prisons: An Exploratory Survey.* Berkeley: University of California, School of Criminology, 1968.

BAIRD, RUSSELL N. *The Penal Press.* Evanston, Ill.: Northwestern University Press, 1967.

BARNES, HARRY E. "Economics of American Penology: State of Pennsylvania." *Journal of Political Economy,* 29:614-642, October, 1921.

EDWARDS, RALPH D. "Correctional Industries and Inmate Training." *Proceedings of the American Correctional Association, 1963,* pp. 197-200.

ENGLAND, RALPH W., JR. "New Departures in Prison Labor." *Prison Journal,* 41:21-26, Spring, 1961.

ENGLAND, RALPH W. *Prison Labour.* New York: United Nations Department of Economic and Social Affairs, 1955.

ENGELBARTS, RUDOLF. *Books in Stir: A Bibliographic Essay About Prison Libraries and About Books Written by Prisoners and Prison Employees.* Metuchen, N. J.: The Scarecrow Press, 1972.

FLYNN, FRANK. "The Federal Government and the Prison-Labor Problem in the States." *Social Service Review,* 24:19-40, 213-236, March and June, 1950.

GILLHAM, JAMES, & WILLIAM L. KLIME. *The Use of Correctional Trade Training.* Lansing: Michigan Department of Corrections, 1970.

GOODSELL, JAMES N. "The Penal Press: Voice of the Prisoner." *Federal Probation,* 23:53-57, June, 1959.

HILLER, E. T. "Development of the Systems of Control of Convict Labor in the United States." *Journal of Criminal Law and Criminology,* 5:241-269, July-August, 1914.

LOPEZ-REY, MANUEL. "Some Considerations on the Character and Organization of Prison Labor." *Journal of Criminal Law, Criminology, and Police Science,* 49:10-28, May-June, 1958.

PROCTOR, CARROLL R. "Prison Industries Apprenticeship Training." *Proceedings of the American Correctional Association, 1963,* pp. 225-235.

RUDOFF, ALVIN, T. C. ESSELSTYN, & GEORGE L. KIRKHAM. "Evaluating Work Furlough." *Federal Probation,* 35:34-38, March, 1971.

RUSCHE, GEORGE, & OTTO KIRCHHEIMER. *Punishment and Social Structure.* New York: Columbia University Press, 1939.

STEINER, JESSE F., & ROY M. BROWN. *The North Carolina Chain Gang.* Chapel Hill, N.C.: University of North Carolina Press, 1927.

WALLACK, WALTER M., GLENN M. KENDALL, & HOWARD L. BRIGGS. *Education Within Prison Walls.* New York: Columbia University Press, 1939.

Suggested readings

The exits from prison are more numerous than the entrances. Entrance into prison on sentence must always be by way of the court, generally in accordance with conditions fixed by the legislature. But one may be released from prison by completion of the full term imposed by the court, or before the end of the full term by an executive who grants a pardon or commutation, or an administrative board that grants a parole or a release on good time. That is, acting by authority of the constitution or statutes, the legislature, the court, an executive, or an administrative board may determine the time of release of a prisoner. Table XXI shows the methods of release for felons in 1970, as reported by the Federal Bureau of Prisons.[1] ●

Pardon and related concepts

Modification of penalties by an executive official may take the form of pardon, commutation, or amnesty. A pardon is an act of mercy or clemency, ordinarily by an executive, by which a criminal is excused from a penalty which has been imposed upon him. It has been held in court decisions that the pardon wipes away guilt and makes the person who committed the crime as innocent as though he had not committed it. Pardon may be either condi-

TABLE XXI

Types of departures from state and federal institutions, 1970

Type of departure	All institutions		Federal institutions		State institutions	
	Number	Per-cent	Number	Per-cent	Number	Per-cent
Conditional releases (includes parole)[a]	61,877	24.4	5,696	21.0	56,181	24.8
Unconditional releases[b]	29,855	11.7	5,993	22.1	23,862	10.5
Deaths, except executions	663	.3	36	.1	627	.3
Executions	—	—	—	—	—	—
Other departures[c]	61,530	24.2	4,988	18.4	56,542	24.9
Transferred	99,912	39.4	10,414	38.4	89,498	39.5
Total departures	**253,837**	**100.0**	**27,127**	**100.0**	**226,710**	**100.0**

[a] Also includes 49 conditional pardons.
[b] Includes 16 full pardons.
[c] Includes escapes, court orders, and authorized temporary absences.

[1] Federal Bureau of Prisons, "Prisoners in State and Federal Institutions, 1968-1970," *National Prisoner Statistics*, No. 47, April, 1972, p. 6.

tional or absolute. The conditional pardon is one in which the guilt is wiped away on condition that the offender perform certain acts or refrain from certain acts specified by the pardoning power, such as leaving the country or abstaining from intoxicating liquors. If a person who has received a conditional pardon fails to perform the required acts, the pardon becomes void, and he may be returned to prison for the remainder of his original term.

Commutation of sentence is a reduction of the penalty by executive order. A sentence is frequently commuted so that it expires at once. Commutation differs from conditional pardon in that it does not wipe away guilt in the eyes of the law, and consequently does not restore civil rights as does a pardon. Massachusetts governors have commuted to life imprisonment 50 percent of the death sentences imposed by juries and courts from 1947 to 1971.[2]

Amnesty is a pardon applied to a group of criminals. In 1945, the president of the United States restored civil rights to all federal ex-prisoners who had served honorably in the armed forces for one year or more. In February, 1953, Britain granted amnesty to 14,260 wartime deserters from the armed forces. Israel declared a general amnesty in July, 1967, to celebrate its victory in a six-day battle with the Arabs. Over five hundred prisoners were released, and the police closed their files on about seventy thousand cases, of which about fifteen thousand were cases of felonies and misdemeanors. Suspended sentences were annulled, fines forgiven, and jail sentences reduced by 25 percent.[3]

A reprieve or respite is a temporary postponement of the execution of a sentence, generally for the purpose of further investigation of the guilt of the prisoner. It is used in connection with the death penalty rather than with sentences of imprisonment.

In the Anglo-American legal system, the power of an executive to grant pardons was derived from the time when the power of the crown was almost absolute.[4] In the American colonies the pardoning power was generally vested in the royal governor, acting either alone or with the governor's council. After the Revolution, because of the fear of executives, the pardoning power was at first retained by the legislative assemblies, but it soon passed to the governors, generally as an expression of the doctrine of separation of powers. Recently the responsibility of the governor has been limited by the development of pardon boards.

In twenty-one states, the governor shares the power to pardon with a board or council, and has no more power than any other member of the board in eight of these states. In twenty-seven states, the governor has the sole and complete power to pardon except in impeachment cases. In seventeen of these states in

---

[2] Massachusetts Department of Correction, "Some Notes on Death Row and the Death Penalty in Massachusetts," Document No. 5678, June, 1971, p. 1.

[3] *Amnesty in Israel* (Jerusalem: Institute of Criminology, The Hebrew University, 1968).

[4] Lewis Mayers, *The American Legal System*, rev. ed. (New York: Harper and Row, 1964), p. 138.

which the governor has final authority, a pardon board or other assistants are appointed for advisory purposes. Some advisory pardon boards, in practice, have complete control of pardons because the governor always adopts the recommendations of the board. On the other hand, some governors rarely accept the recommendations of their advisory boards.

The use of pardons began to decrease steadily about a century ago, and currently pardons are seldom used. In the years 1905-1909, 3.0 percent of those released from federal prisons were released through pardon by the president of the United States. This percentage decreased to 0.009 percent by 1940, when 313 pardons (including 235 restorations of civil rights) were granted, and since then the number of releases by pardon has been insignificant. The same decrease is found in many states. In 1970, only forty-nine conditional pardons and sixteen full pardons were granted to all the adult felons in the United States.

The general rule of pardons is that the more serious the crime and the more severe the sentence, the more probable is release by pardon.[5] The social status of the criminal also affects the decision to pardon. Blacks are pardoned less frequently than whites, especially in southern states, and gentlemen thieves more frequently than thieves of the lower socioeconomic class. Also, in areas where parole is used frequently, pardons are used infrequently. Wolfgang examined recommendations for commutation of sentence, by judges and district attorneys, in the cases of 368 prisoners who had been convicted of murder. The opinion of the judge differed significantly from that of the district attorney in two-thirds of the cases, a situation arising principally because the attorneys supported the pardon board's decision in significantly more cases than did the judges. In only 7 percent of the cases did the board grant commutation when the judge and the attorney both recommended that it not be granted.[6] ●

Good-time laws

Under good-time laws a prison board may release a prisoner before he has served the sentence imposed by the court if he has maintained good conduct in prison. Generally, for every month of satisfactory conduct, a certain number of days is deducted from the inmate's sentence. A usual procedure is to deduct one month from the first year of satisfactory conduct, two months for the second year, and so on, up to six months for the sixth and each succeeding year. A three-year sentence, thus, can be reduced to two years and six months by good behavior; a ten-year sentence can be reduced to six years and three months. A prison board is the administrative authority and can determine whether or not the prisoner has earned the reduction in time, but the legislature makes the schedule of reductions in time. Granting

---

[5] This rule was stated by Henry Cabot Lodge, "Naval Courts-Martial and the Pardoning Power," *Atlantic Monthly*, 50:43-50, July, 1882.

[6] Marvin E. Wolfgang, "Murder, the Pardon Board, and Recommendations by Judges and District Attorneys," *Journal of Criminal Law, Criminology, and Police Science*, 50: 338-346, November-December, 1959.

"time off for good behavior" differs, in this respect, from commutation of sentence by executive order, in which the sentence is shortened because the inmate's behavior has been good, or for other reasons.

As early as 1817, a good-time law was passed in New York State, which provided that first-term prisoners on sentences of five years or less could abridge their sentences by one-fourth for good behavior. Apparently the law was not used. The good-time principle was soon adopted in several other places. Connecticut passed a good-time law in 1821 relating to inmates of workhouses. Tennessee passed its good-time law in 1833, Ohio in 1856. Maconochie put the good-time system into general use in 1842 in the convict colonies in Australia, and Marsangy advocated this method in France in 1846. Despite the earlier precedents in the United States, "time off for good behavior" did not become generally known in American prisons until just after the Civil War, when the news regarding the famous Irish system spread. By 1868, twenty-four states had made provision for reduction of prison terms by good behavior, and at present all states except California have good-time laws.

In addition to "statutory good time," as the general system is called by inmates, prisoners in some states may earn "merit good time" for extraordinary behavior and "industrial good time" for participation in the prison industries. Merit good-time and industrial good-time laws usually operate to reduce the period of time to be served before an inmate is entitled to have his case reviewed by the parole board, rather than to reduce the actual sentence. Industrial good-time laws have been severely criticized by Glaser because of their antitreatment emphasis. Inmates are eager to work at jobs carrying this special good-time allowance, thus forgoing training programs designed to provide them with trades, skills, and attitudes that will be valuable upon release.[7]

Good-time laws represent an attempt to mitigate the severity of sentences, to get good work from the prisoners, to assist in reformation, and, above all, to solve the problem of prison discipine. The two principal objections to good-time laws are that they tend to become mechanical and that they place emphasis on routine conformity to prison rules, rather than on reformation.[8] Prisoners then come to view good time as a right. The usual practice is to credit the new inmate with the maximum amount of good time permitted by law and then to deduct a certain number of days from that time whenever the disciplinary court finds him guilty of serious infraction of the prison rules. Good time may be deducted from the amount of time imposed in a definite sentence, or it may be applied to either the minimum or the maximum period of an indefinite sentence, according to the laws of the state. ●

---

[7] Daniel Glaser, *The Effectiveness of a Prison and Parole System* (Indianapolis: Bobbs-Merrill, 1964), pp. 234-236.

[8] G. I. Giardini, "Good Time — Placebo of Correction," *American Journal of Correction*, 20:3-5 *ff.*, April, 1958.

The indeterminate sentence

The release time of a prisoner may be determined by the legislature, which fixes a definite sentence for the offense, by the court, which receives authority from the legislature to fix definite penalties within the limits set by the legislature, or by an administrative board, which receives from the legislature authority to fix definite penalties within the limits set by the legislature or by the court. When the time of release is determined by an administrative board, and the court merely imposes minimum and maximum limits of the penalty, the sentence is known as an indeterminate sentence. Strictly speaking, the sentence is not indeterminate if the limits are fixed by the court or by the legislature, and it should be called indefinite rather than indeterminate. No state has sentences that are completely indeterminate, and the general practice is to call these indefinite sentences indeterminate.

The administrative board which fixes the penalties is called a parole board, but there is no necessary connection between parole and the indeterminate sentence. *Indeterminate sentence* refers to the fact that the exact period of custody is not fixed before the custody begins, while the term *parole* refers to the fact that a portion of the period of custody may be spent outside the institution. Either may be used independently of the other. The federal government and some states have parole systems but no indeterminate sentences; it would be possible to have indeterminate sentences with complete and final release without supervision. Parole is the status of the prisoner after release from the walls of the institution, while still under the special guardianship of the state. It may be granted either to the prisoner on a definite sentence, though this is usually restricted to the period of freedom granted by the good-time allowance,[9] or to the prisoner on an indeterminate sentence. A person on an indeterminate sentence may be released either conditionally on parole or unconditionally and completely without parole. The two methods, though distinct in principle, are generally combined in practice and must be combined for the greatest efficiency of either system.

Originally, the legislature fixed a definite penalty for each offense. As the treatment reaction to crime has arisen, the trend has been for the legislature to transfer to other agencies the authority to fix definite sentences within limits set by the legislature for each offense or class of offenses. It transferred this authority first to the court and then to the parole board. When the court was given authority to fix limits within the limits set by the legislature, some judges who were opposed to indeterminate sentences made the minimum almost identical with the maximum, giving sentences such as two years and nine months to two years and ten months; thirty to thirty-one years; 150 to 160 years. The legislature tried

---

[9] In the federal system and in Wisconsin an inmate who has served one-third of his time is eligible for release on parole, but if he is denied parole, or if he waives parole, he may be "conditionally released" for a period of time equal to the good-time allowance.

at first to correct these abuses by providing that the minimum set by the court must be not more than one-half, or some other specified fraction, of the maximum. More frequently, the legislatures have deprived the courts of the authority to fix any limits within those set by the legislature and have given authority to the parole boards to fix the sentence within these limits. In that case, the court has authority merely to impose the minimum and maximum sentences provided in the law.

The question arises, Why should either the court or the legislature fix the limits? Why should not the sentences be completely indeterminate and the parole board have complete and unlimited authority to determine the time of release? The sentences of 39 percent of the prisoners committed to state prisons and reformatories in 1960 were definite. Of the indefinite sentences, 17 percent had no minimum limit and 13 percent either had a maximum of twenty years or more or had a maximum of life.[10] The problem of the minimum limit is somewhat different from the problem of the maximum limit.

The principal argument for the minimum limit is that it is needed as a check in case the parole board should become sentimental, inefficient, or corrupt. Generally, this argument is part of the punitive reaction to crime. In some states, a large proportion of the prisoners on indefinite sentences are released as soon as the minimum sentence is served. This is taken as proof that many prisoners would not be punished at all unless the legislature or the court imposed a minimum penalty. As a matter of fact, the few states in which the minimum limit has been removed have witnessed no wholesale prison deliveries.[11] An administrative board given the authority to determine whether a prisoner should be held one year or five years can be trusted to decide whether the prisoner should be held six months or ten months. It is probable that the very existence of the minimum sentence serves as a convenient time of release of all offenders against whom no bad behavior in prison has been recorded. If no minimum were provided, a decision on the merits of each case would be necessary.

The absolute maximum penalty probably results in more injury to society than does the minimum. On the one hand it often is perfectly clear to prison authorities that certain offenders will repeat their offenses as soon as released. Nevertheless, the law requires that authorities release them when the maximum period of imprisonment has been served. On the other hand, the legal maximum is a guarantee that the administrative board will not keep confined for life some prisoners who would be perfectly safe in society. Such mistakes do occur, especially when the inmate in question rebels against the prison routine. Inability to adjust to prison life is erroneously taken as evidence of inability to live a law-abiding life outside prison. But such mistakes seem less likely to be made when a decision is reached by a board that is intimately acquainted with the particular prisoner, than when a legislature prescribes the sentence for an entire class of criminals, or when a court, having only a superficial knowledge of a particular offender, fixes a maximum sentence.

If sentences were absolutely indeterminate, the judge and jury would not know whether a particular offender would be held for one year or for life; they would know only that the administrative board would hold the offender as long as necessary for the protection of society. But the administrative board must be able to do much more efficient work than at present before it can be trusted with authority of this nature. As in many governmental bureaus, the work of the administrative boards tends to become a routinized processing of cases rather than a careful consideration of the needs of each prisoner being sentenced and of the society which has locked him up. ●

Parole

Parole is the act of releasing or the status of being released from a penal institution in which a criminal has served a part of his maximum sentence, on condition of maintaining good behavior and remaining in the custody and under the guidance of the institution or some other agency approved by the state until a final discharge is granted. The term *parole* is used in analogous manner with reference to institutions for mentally disturbed and retarded persons. The conditional pardon, now rarely used, is similar to parole in that both are liberation from an institution on conditions, with restoration of the original penalty if the conditions of liberation are violated. They differ in that conditional pardon carries with it the remission of guilt, and parole does not; parole refers to release from imprisonment only, while conditional pardon may refer to other penalties also.

Parole is related to, but should be distinguished from, probation. Like probation, it represents a break with the classical theory of the criminal law, since an attempt is made to adjust the societal response to the circumstances of the offense and the characteristics of the offender. Also, parole ideally includes treatment in the form of guidance and assistance to the offender, just as probation ideally includes such guidance and assistance. Thus both systems attempt to implement the treatment reaction to crime and criminality.

On the other hand, the influence of the punitive reaction to crime is more clearly present in parole than in probation; parole is less "purely" treatment than is probation. Parole is granted by an administrative board or an executive, and it is always preceded by serving part of a sentence in a prison or in a similar institution, while no formal penalty is imposed in probation, or, if imposed, is not executed. Probationers are considered as undergoing treatment while under the threat of punishment, should they violate the conditions of their probation, but probation is granted by the courts as a substitute for punishment as well as for mere suspension of sentence. Parolees are considered as "in custody" and undergoing both punishment and treatment while under the threat of more severe punishment—return to the institutions from which they have been released. Without the threat of return to prison, release from prison before the maximum term was served would merely represent the workings of the indeterminate sentence, not parole. Since parole is expected both to punish and to treat, the conflicts between punishment and treatment found in prisons are also found in parole.

Parole is a combination and extension of earlier penal practices, although the idea of giving treatment, in the form of guidance and assistance, is relatively new. The first trace of parole was the system of indenturing prisoners. By this means prisoners were removed from institutions and placed under the supervision of masters or employers and could be returned to the institution if they did not behave properly. Later, the supervision was centralized by appointment of state visiting agents with the special function of protecting the juvenile wards of the institutions against cruelty. Several other systems for handling prisoners were combined with the indenture system before a parole system for adults was formed. One of these was after-care of discharged convicts. As early as 1776 American philanthropic societies attempted to help ex-prisoners. Such societies worked most energetically in the 1840s and 1850s.[12] Later the state made efforts in the same direction. In 1845 Massachusetts appointed a state agent for discharged convicts, and this agent used public funds to assist ex-prisoners to secure employment, tools, clothing and transportation to places of employment. Other states appointed similar agents, and they began to ask for continuing the custody over the ex-prisoners. For example, a New York agent for discharged convicts pointed out in his reports that his work could be greatly improved if the state retained custody over prisoners for some time after their release; he suggested that good-time allowances should be used merely to determine the time of release from the institutions, but not from custody.

In the early nineteenth century the English convict colonies in Australia developed a primitive parole system, with little supervision or guidance after release, under the name of ticket-of-leave. This was later made a part of the Irish system and in that form became known to American penologists. When members of the Massachusetts prison board made a plea for a parole system in 1865, they called it "the English ticket-of-leave system." The English Prevention of Crimes Act of 1871 also helped create a

---

[12] For a history of such societies, see H. H. Hart, "Prisoners' Aid Societies," *Proceedings of the National Prison Association, 1889*, pp. 270-287.

demand for a parole system in the United States. That act provided for surveillance by the police for a period of seven years after release from prison of all except those on their first terms. The Massachusetts prison board called attention to this act repeatedly and urged the adoption of a similar law.

Parole in its developed form was first adopted by New York State in the 1869 law which authorized the Elmira Reformatory. It was hailed at the time as a great invention. But it is evident that the system had existed for over fifty years in European countries and, as indicated, in its essential features had a long history in the United States. The parole method was first extended to state prisons by Ohio in 1884, and by 1898 it had been adopted in twenty-five states.

Although parole and the indeterminate sentence are now generally combined in practice, in 1898 only five states had indeterminate sentence laws. By 1922, parole laws had been passed by forty-five states, and since 1922 by all the other states, the last being Mississippi, which enacted a parole law in 1944. Many states make extensive use and others little use of it. In eighteen states, more than 75 percent of the releases from state prisons and reformatories in 1970 were by parole, while in two states less than 10 percent of the releases were by parole; in one state, New Hampshire, 100 percent of the discharges were by parole.[13] Parole is used most extensively in the New England and Middle Atlantic states, and in a few states scattered among the North Central, Pacific, and Mountain regions.

The parole board

The parole board has the duty of determining when a prisoner shall be released on parole. Parole boards are of three principal types, with various combinations of these types: first, a special parole board limited to one institution, which is sometimes composed of institutional staff members, and at other times includes only the warden of the institution as one member of the board; second, a general state parole board which is located in the state department of correction and which has authority to release from any state institution; third, a general state parole board which is located outside of the department of correction and has authority to release from any state institution. In four states the power of the parole board is limited to recommending a disposition to the governor.[14]

The trend during the last forty years has been toward centralization of parole authority and toward removal of the parole board from the department of correction. While this movement was supported by some prison workers on the ground that it relieved

---

[13] U. S. Department of Justice, Bureau of Prisons, "Prisoners in State and Federal Institutions for Adult Felons, 1968-1970," *National Prisoner Statistics,* No. 47, April, 1972, pp. 22-23.

[14] President's Commission on Law Enforcement and Administration of Justice, *Task Force Report: Corrections* (Washington: Government Printing Office, 1967), p. 65.

them of a troublesome responsibility which interfered with their efficiency in the institutional work, it was criticized by others on the ground that the prison staff knows better than any other agency when a prisoner should be released. In forty-one states today the parole board is an independent agency; in seven states it is a unit within a larger department; and in two states it is the same body that regulates the correctional institutions. In no jurisdiction in the adult field is the final power to grant or deny parole given to the staff directly involved in the operation of a correctional institution, but in the juvenile field the great majority of the releasing decisions directly involve the staff of training schools.[15]

Parole boards that are restricted to considering release of only the inmates confined in a single institution usually are dominated by the institution staff. In some states this means that the classification committee which directs and supervises the prisoners also determines when they shall be released. In this way, it is said, the prison rehabilitation programs can be closely coordinated with parole selection and supervision. But in other states domination of the parole board by the institution staff means that the board grants parole as a reward for good conduct in the prison, rather than as a correctional device, that the board seeks to maintain discipline by means of threats in regard to chances for parole, or that the board may be willing to grant paroles indiscriminately when the institution is overcrowded. At the other extreme is the parole board which is entirely independent of the department of correction. In some states, this type of parole board, like governors' advisory boards, is concerned less with the progress of the prisoner than with the possible reactions of the public toward parole. However, California's adult authority has been an excellent example of a competent board of this type. Until recently, the adult authority had independent control over the length of the prison term, program while in prison, length of time on parole, and supervision of parolees.

Parole boards currently include members from all walks of life. For example, the Mississippi board in 1960 included a contractor, a businessman, a farmer, and a clerk; the Florida board included a newspaperman, an attorney, and a man with experience in both business and probation; the Washington board had persons with training and experience in sociology, in government, in law, in the ministry, and in juvenile rehabilitation.[16] When various court, probation, parole, police, and institutional staff members and prison inmates were asked to select the best occupational training for an ideal parole board, there was little consensus.[17] While

---

[15] President's Commission, *Task Force Report: Corrections*, p. 65.

[16] Washington State Legislative Council and the Washington State Board of Prison Terms and Paroles, *Parole Board Structure: A Report on the Structure of Boards in the United States* (Olympia, Wash.: Author, 1960).

[17] Joseph W. Rogers and Norman S. Hayner, "The Ideal Parole Board: Views from the Correctional World and the Society of Captives," *Proceedings of the American Correctional Association, 1963*, pp. 287-300.

all the respondents favored training in law, sociology, and psychiatry, there was a tendency for each respondent to select a representative of his own occupation. ●

Determining the time of release

Most contemporary criminologists agree that if a prisoner is to be released at all, he should be released on parole. All released prisoners, it is held, could benefit from assistance and guidance by parole officers, and society would benefit if all offenders were kept under close surveillance during the period of adjustment immediately following incarceration. Even the prisoners who are released by pardon after proof of innocence could benefit from the assistance which parole officers could provide. Many prisoners are opposed to this policy, and some of them, when the time between eligibility for parole and final discharge is not too great, waive the parole hearing. This opposition is based on a feeling that parole really does not provide assistance or treatment, and it therefore merely extends the period of control by the state. Some criminologists are beginning to adopt a similar view.

Many laymen also are opposed to the policy of paroling prisoners, but this opposition is based on the belief that parole is a form of leniency. In twenty-four states, the opposition is reflected in statutes which exclude certain types of criminals from parole. These are generally the prisoners convicted of the more serious crimes, such as murder, rape, or any offense for which life imprisonment is imposed. Often these offenders are in great need of the guidance and supervision which could be afforded in efficient parole work. If they are dangerous, they need the supervision which parole affords; if they are not dangerous, they at least need the guidance and help which parole officers could give, especially when they have been isolated from free society for long periods of time.

The American Parole Association stated in 1933 that fitness for limited freedom should be the principle used in determining the release time of particular offenders:

Has the institution accomplished all that it can for him; is the offender's state of mind and attitude toward his own difficulties and problems such that further residence will be harmful or beneficial; does a suitable environment await him on the outside; can the beneficial effect already accomplished be retained if he is held longer to allow a more suitable environment to be developed?[18]

While parole boards have generally given lip service to this principle, they usually depart from it. Sometimes the departure is a matter of convenience. For several years about 95 percent of the inmates of New York prisons were released as soon as they had completed the minimum term. Moreover, this procedure was defended, and there is no final proof that it is not as good a method as any. Several studies of successes on parole indicate that the prisoners who remain longer violate parole more

---

[18] *Journal of Criminal Law and Criminology,* 24:791, November-December, 1933.

often than those who remain a shorter time in prison. This may result either from the imposition of longer terms upon prisoners who are least fit for life in society or from the decrease in fitness for life in society with the length of the period of isolation from society.

A second form of departure from the principle arises from interpretation of the phrase, "does a suitable environment await him on the outside?" Two specific prerequisites of parole are frequently made. One is that the prisoner have no "detainer" against him. This requirement is made partly out of courtesy to the jurisdiction in which the prisoner is wanted for a former crime, and partly because success on parole is unlikely if the prisoner goes immediately into another trial or another prison. The second specific requirement is a guarantee of employment. Four objections have been made to this requirement. First, many of the positions which are guaranteed are fictitious. Second, many prisoners who have reached the point where they are best prepared to go out are detained in prison because no jobs are available. Third, the paroled man is exploited because the employer must be notified of the prison record. Fourth, parole officers spend much time in locating positions which the offenders should find for themselves.

Everyone agrees that the prisoner should have employment into which he can go immediately after release. However, a California study has shown that releasing men who have no employment does not necessarily increase recidivism.[19] Several states have modified the employment requirement. New York now uses a plan called "release on reasonable assurance," under which selected parolees are released without a job guarantee if they have a stable home situation, a skill or a trade which reasonably assures employment, or the help of an outside community agency in obtaining employment.[20] It has been found that inmates released under this plan do not have a higher violation rate than those who are assured of a job before they are paroled.[21]

There is variation among the states in the amount of help given prisoners who are seeking employment, so as to become eligible for parole. Similarly, five states give no money to men released on parole, and the others ordinarily pay from five dollars to thirty dollars. Vermont pays one dollar for each month served in prison, up to $100.[22] These funds are in addition to any funds the prisoner might have saved from his paid work in the prison.

---

[19] Ernest Riemer and Martin Warren, *Special Intensive Parole Unit, Phase II, Thirty-Man Caseload Study* (Sacramento: Department of Corrections, 1958), p. i. See also William L. Jacks, "Release on Parole to Plans with and without Employment," *American Journal of Correction*, 24:12 ff., December, 1962.

[20] President's Commission, *Task Force Report: Corrections*, p. 69.

[21] John M. Stanton, "Is It Safe to Parole Inmates Without Jobs?" *Crime and Delinquency*, 12:147-150, April, 1966.

[22] Daniel Glaser, Eugene S. Zemans, and Charles W. Dean, *Money Against Crime: A Survey of Economic Assistance to Released Prisoners* (Chicago: John Howard Association, 1961), pp. 3-4.

A few states have loan funds from which parolees can borrow, and most provide clothing and transportation home. Parolees sometimes cannot afford to buy the expensive tools required for a skilled job such as carpenter or mechanic.

Parole boards also depart from the principle when it would be politically or administratively disadvantageous to release an offender, even if he is rehabilitated. This is especially the case when the board is dealing with men who have committed notorious crimes—release of one man, even if he is rehabilitated, might result in such severe attacks on the board and on the indeterminate-sentence system that the opportunity to use the principle in other cases would be lost. A man must be sacrificed for the system. Similarly, if persons of power react to crime punitively and insist on long terms for certain types of offenders, the parole board may not insist on short terms. The policies and actions of parole boards are usually carefully watched by police, district attorneys, newspapers, prison boards, crime commissions, and other agencies which believe that certain offenders should not be released. These interests must be balanced against the interests of groups which clamor for the idea that the board should release men whenever the board believes they are ready to be released.

No matter what the system for measuring "institutional accomplishment" and "the offender's state of mind" fitness for release can not be determined by looking at the conduct in the institution. Four types of prisoners behave well in prisons: those who attempt to secure an early release by good behavior in order to return more quickly to crime, those who are quite comfortable and conforming while under close control, those who, as square Johns, are quite docile inside prison as well as outside, and those who really profit from the institutional program. The good behavior of the last two groups only indicates fitness for release. On the other hand, some prisoners who behave badly under the surveillance of prison guards get along satisfactorily in the general community.

In a number of institutions, a "progressive merit system" or "graduated release program" has been tried. The prisoner might pass through special "pre-release" classes inside the walls, an honor camp outside the walls, a work furlough program, and a halfway house. Although there is widespread enthusiasm for graduated release programs, a review of the research and experiments undertaken with regard to them found that the more rigorous the evaluation methods the more ambivalent or negative are the findings regarding the efficacy of such programs.[23]

Suffering on the part of prisoners is increased by indeterminate sentences and parole. Most prisoners would prefer sentence of a fixed term in prison plus a fixed term on parole to the agony of

---

[23] Eugene Doleschal and Gilbert Geis, *Graduated Release* (Washington: Government Printing Office, 1971), p. 23.

indeterminacy. Some would even prefer a long term fixed in advance to a short term accompanied by a period of worry and anxiety while they await a decision or "setting" by the parole board. Using a semifree interviewing technique based on some 100 standard questions, Farber found that the following five things are significantly related to the degree of suffering of prisoners: indefiniteness of knowledge as to time of release, feeling of injustice of sentence, feeling of injustice of length of time served, lack of hope of getting a break, and apparent unfriendliness on the outside.[24] The following statement by an ex-prisoner illustrates the effect of the first three of these.

I was sentenced to San Quentin on an indefinite term. The prisoner there has no notion during the entire year regarding the term the parole board will set for him to do. At the end of that year the parole board fixes his maximum, and may later reduce it. That first year is a perfect hell for the prisoner. He keeps asking others who were convicted of a similar offense about the details of their crimes and of their maximum sentences. One man committed the same crime I did and he received a sentence of nine years but he had a long previous record and he was armed. Another man who was a first offender and was not armed got four years. I was a first offender and was armed. Consequently I figured that I will get between four and nine years. But I keep thinking and worrying about it, for every year in prison makes a big difference. My worry interferes with my work, and I get sent to the "hole" for inefficiency in work. That looks bad on my record and I wonder whether it will increase my maximum sentence. This worry drives a person mad. As soon as the sentence is fixed the prisoner can settle down to serve his time, and it is a great relief to have it settled.

The prisoner must be released by some agency unless he is to be held for life. No one can now determine in advance how long the prisoner should be held, and there is little possibility of developing a prediction instrument for doing so. When the sentence is definite, the criminal is given a right to feel that when he has finished that term, he has paid the penalty and balanced the account. This is a dangerous doctrine for criminals or others to hold. There is no such account. Nevertheless, when the sentence is indefinite many criminals are made to suffer unnecessarily and to believe that they are not being treated fairly, with the result that they see the criminal justice system, if not the whole society, as unjust, bigoted, and even corrupt.

Parole is "conditional liberation," that is, liberation on condition that the prisoner live in accordance with specified rules. The con-

Organization of supervision

---

[24] M. F. Farber, "Suffering and Time Perspectives of the Prisoner," *University of Iowa Studies in Child Welfare*, 20:153-227 (1944). See also Stanley Cohen and Laurie Taylor, *Psychological Survival: The Experience of Long-Term Imprisonment* (New York: Pantheon, 1972), pp. 86-111.

ditions are sometimes fixed by law, sometimes by the parole board, and sometimes by other agencies. These conditions may include leading a law-abiding life, abstaining from intoxicating liquors and drugs, keeping away from bad associates, spending evenings at home, refraining from gambling, supporting legal dependents, remaining in a specified territory, not changing residence or employment without permission (sometimes merely without reporting the change), attending church at least once each Sunday, not marrying without permission, not becoming dependent on charity, making reparation or restitution for the crime, and making written or personal reports as required. The attempt to impose on parolees standards of conduct not imposed on law-abiding persons is absurd. Unrealistic rules and conditions usually are mitigated informally by parole officers, who count as "parole violation" only the more serious violations of rules.

The board that has authority to grant paroles generally has supervision over the parolees, but sometimes supervision is under the direction of an independent agency. On the principle that imprisonment and parole should constitute a continuous series of efforts to prepare for a life of complete freedom, there is a theoretical superiority in a parole system in which the board that controls the institution also determines the time of release and supervises the parolees from that institution. This has the disadvantage of duplication of efforts in supervision, for an officer from each of the institutions of the state must work in the same territory. Therefore, in the interest of economy, parole supervision which is more than nominal is generally organized on a territorial rather than an institutional basis.

Parole supervision is little more than nominal in most states, for very few have a sufficient number of officers to make adequate supervision possible. As in probation, caseloads sometimes run as high as two or three hundred per officer. In California, the usual load in recent years has been ninety parolees. An experimental program showed that when the caseloads were reduced to fifteen, and parolees were accorded intensive supervision during the first ninety days after release and then transferred to the regular ninety-man caseloads for regular supervision, only slight reductions in parole violation rates occurred. It also was found that men whose parole release dates were advanced three months violated parole slightly less frequently than did men whose release dates were not advanced.[25] A follow-up study indicated that intensive supervision—defined as a caseload of thirty with frequent controls during the first six months—did not produce rates significantly lower than the rates of men in ninety-man caseloads; about 55 percent of each group

---

[25] Ernest Riemer and Martin Warren, "Special Intensive Parole Unit: Relationship Between Violation Rate and Initially Small Caseload," *National Probation and Parole Association Journal*, 3:1-8, July, 1957.

violated parole in the first year.[26] In Pennsylvania, the case load is about sixty, but a recent study indicated that even with this number, adequate supervision is difficult—only 34 percent of work time was spent in contact with parolees.[27]

At least three different views of supervision, differentially emphasizing punishment and treatment, are found among lay and professional parole workers.[28] One conception, which is rapidly disappearing, is based on the assumption that parole is a system of leniency which permits the early release of many dangerous criminals who should continue to suffer punishment. Consequently, in parole work based on this view, emphasis is placed on supervision rather than assistance, and "supervision" is taken to mean zealous "police work," "parole officer" to mean "police officer." It is assumed that most parolees have not reformed, and that they will commit new crimes if given the opportunity. The parole officers are charged, then, with the duty of keeping parolees under close surveillance and coercing the offender into conformity by means of punishment and threats of punishment.

A second conception is based on the assumption that reformation is a matter of individual self-determination to "make good" in free society. The essential notion is that reformation is practically complete at the time of release, and that the function of the parole officer is to watch the parolee to determine whether he is maintaining the conditions fixed for his parole. A supervisory system based on this view may be characterized as "watchful waiting." Coupled with the idea that society must be protected by a careful watch over the parolee is a belief that the parolee must be protected from society. Parole officers using this system are likely to give direct help and assistance in locating jobs or solving other problems, to lecture, and to use both praise and blame. They believe that frequent contacts will destroy the parolee's initiative or confidence in himself.

Another conception is based on the belief that essential work of promoting adjustment has to be done after release from an institution, and that this requires assistance, not to prevent the parolee from exercising his own initiative, but to assist him in exercising it correctly, so that crimes will not be repeated. While it is not assumed that all parolees are dangerous criminals, it is recognized that "reformation" in the form of self-resolution to "make good" is not always sufficient to prevent recidivism. Parole is viewed as a system for improving the welfare of the parolee (often called a "client") by helping him in his individual

Principles and methods of supervision

---

[26] Riemer and Warren, *Special Intensive Parole Unit, Phase II, Thirty-Man Caseload Study*, pp. 13-16.

[27] William L. Jacks, *A Time Study of Parole Agents* (Harrisburg, Pa. Pennsylvania Board of Parole, 1961), pp. 4-5.

[28] Cf. Lloyd E. Ohlin, Herman Piven, and Donnell M. Pappenfort, "Major Dilemmas of the Social Worker in Probation and Parole," *National Probation and Parole Association Journal*, 2:211-225, July, 1956.

his capacity. Assistance, rather than surveillance, is emphasized, on the ground that we already have police to act as surveillants and detectives. In parole work based on this conception, parole officers are social workers.

In practice, of course, it is difficult to separate supervision and assistance or treatment and even in parole systems emphasizing assistance, the parole officer must do some policing.[29] Also, from the parolee's viewpoint almost any contacts, whether called "assistance" or "supervision," are regarded as snooping. Parole officers, like prison officials, are charged with maintaining a delicate balance between punishment and treatment. That balance seems to be most effectively maintained in supervisory systems where the dominant view is that parolees must be given professional assistance within the framework of the punitive restrictions imposed as conditions of their parole, thus protecting society.

If the parole officer is to be of real assistance to the person on parole, he should have an intimate acquaintance with the personality and background of the offender. This information must be secured before a proper method for dealing with the offender can be determined. In the most efficient systems, the information secured through the original investigation for the institutional classification committee (the "diagnosis"), and the data on the institutional career of the offender are accessible to the parole officer. In addition, an efficient parole officer must have an intimate knowledge of the family and other personal groups into which the individual will go, so that he can attempt to prepare these groups for the parolee's return before parole begins. It is ridiculous to return the parolee to the very circumstances that produced his criminality in the first place.

Even when the parole worker is part of an ideal parole system in which parole agents have time for personal contacts, it is important that he assist the parolee in securing friends and contacts of his own, for the period of parole must end sooner or later. A study of fifty prisoners in the District of Columbia revealed that the men had four main areas of concern about their release on parole; community acceptance, employment, family relationships, and relationships with police and parole officers.[30] The important thing is to make the parolee feel that he is part of society. This is easier said than done, for the criminal justice system up to this point in his life has done much to convince him that he is an outcast and an outlaw. Further, he is likely to be ostracized while on parole. The following statement from a prisoner's letter reveals the feelings of being set apart from law-abiding groups:

---

[29] Cf. Donald R. Cressey, "Professional Correctional Work and Professional Work in Correction," *National Probation and Parole Association Journal,* 5:1-15, January, 1959.

[30] Reuben S. Horlick, "Inmate Perception of Obstacles to Readjustment in the Community," *Proceedings of the American Correctional Association, 1961,* pp. 200-205.

We are the anonymous ones who move amongst you with wary eyes. We are among you but not of you; constantly on guard, lest by an incautious word or gesture we may betray ourselves to you, and thereby lose our anonymity—and your respect. You may find us in your factories, in your garages, on your farms, and, sometimes in your offices and places of business. We live next door, work at the next lathe, sit next to you in the movies. In short—we are your neighbors. Yet we are a group of men set apart, divided by our experiences from those around us. We are the parolees from your prisons; still doing time, still paying our debt to society. Although we walk the streets to all outward appearances free men, we wear invisible numbers. . . .[31]

Supervision in the form of close surveillance is likely to contribute to this attitude, and mere inspection of the parolee's activities will do little to reduce it. In order to reduce the feeling of isolation, and in order that the parolee will not, in fact, be isolated, positive, constructive action must be taken. Contacts with groups which possess a bias against criminality must be developed. The larger the number of intimate associations that can be formed between the parolee and law-abiding groups, the more likely he is to become and remain a law-abiding person. To this end, the federal system and some states have opened "halfway houses" where parolees can live while they attempt to reenter the community.

Violation of parole

The law usually states that any violation of the conditions imposed upon the person on parole constitutes a violation of parole, and that for a violation of parole the person is to be returned to prison. In practice, the supervising parole agent generally uses discretion and permits some violations. Also, many violations are not observed by the parole officer. When a formal declaration of violation of parole is made, a warrant for the arrest of the parolee is issued and served if he can be located.

When a parole violator is arrested, a court trial is not necessary in order to return him to prison, and the decision of the supervising authority usually is final. However, if he has violated his parole by committing a new crime, he may be tried and sentenced for that crime. In many states the violator may be returned to the prison with no hearing at all, although this practice has been held as denial of due process of law. On the ground that persons on parole are still being punished, in violation hearings the usual rights to counsel and to other court procedures designed for protection of accused persons are denied.

If the parole violator is returned to prison, he may be required to serve the remainder of his unexpired term if he was on a definite sentence, or the remainder of the maximum term if he was on an indeterminate sentence. He may lose the good time he had earned prior to his parole, or he may be denied the privilege of earning good time after his return to prison, thus

---

[31] Quoted in James V. Bennett, "Wise Men Have Enough to Do . . . ," *Federal Probation*, 14:25-29, June, 1950.

lengthening his prison term. He may lose his right to another parole, or it may be stipulated that he will not be allowed to apply for a new parole until a certain period of time has lapsed. In some states the length of time to be served in prison after parole violation is determined by statute, in other states by the supervising authority, and in others by the parole board which has control of releases.

In a few states, the prisoner may be returned to the prison without a violation of parole. This may occur in several ways. He may desire to return because he cannot find work outside, or because he wishes to complete a course in trade training. He may be returned by action of the supervisor because the supervisor believes the parolee needs additional training or needs medical care or for other reasons which do not involve a formal violation of the conditions of parole. An appreciable number of returns of this nature is reported in states where the program of training within the institutions is somewhat closely integrated with the parole program.

Discharge from parole

A person may not be kept on parole beyond the end of his maximum sentence to prison. In some states, he cannot be discharged from parole before the end of that maximum period; in others he can be discharged when he has served a shorter period specified by law or by the regulations of the parole board; in others the parole board has complete authority to determine, within the limits of the maximum sentence, how long parole should continue.

Violations of parole are concentrated in the early periods of parole, but the evidence as to the extent of this concentration is not consistent. Of all persons who violated paroles in Washington in 1964, 43 percent had been on parole less than six months, 62 percent for less than a year.[32] Among federal parolees who violated parole in 1961, 49 percent violated during the first six months of parole, and 77 percent during the first year.[33] Of 308 returned parole violators interviewed by Glaser, 17 percent had committed the act for which they were returned to prison within a month of their release, and 6 percent during their first week out of prison.[34] Hakeem found that the violation occurred early in the parole period if the paroled burglar had a previous criminal record, came from a large city, returned to a large city, had an irregular work record, was unemployed at the time of arrest, and had few or no family connections, and that the violation occurred late in the parole period if the circumstances were reversed.[35]

---

[32] "Post-Institutional Behavior of Inmates Released from Washington State Adult Correctional Institutions," *Washington Department of Institutions Research Review*, 19:56, April, 1965.

[33] United States Board of Parole, *Annual Report, 1961*, (Washington: U.S. Department of Justice), p. 19.

[34] Glaser, *Effectiveness of a Prison and Parole System*, p. 81.

[35] Michael Hakeem, "Parole Prediction Variables and the Time Factors in Violations by Burglars," *Journal of Criminal Law and Criminology*, 31:157-165, September-October, 1944.

Civil rights, which are lost in most states on conviction of certain types of crimes, are restored in some states automatically when parole is granted; in others they are restored only when one is discharged from parole; and in others they are restored, if at all, only by a pardon by the governor. In California, the parole board is authorized to restore civil rights to persons on parole at such time and to such a degree as they see fit, except that they cannot restore the right to be an elector, hold public office, or act as trustee.

The deprivation of civil rights was originally devised as a punitive system for placing social distance between the offender and law-abiding citizens. As the treatment reaction to crime has become more popular, however, it has become apparent that if the prisoner is to be released to the community at all, he should be a member of that community and should be made to feel that he is a member of it. To this end, prisoners should be permitted to vote and exercise some of the other rights, even if they cannot hold office. For the maximum degree of reformation and, hence, protection of society, all the prisoner's rights should be automatically restored as soon as he is placed in the outside community, at the beginning of the parole period. Criminals are returned to the community so that law-abiding groups may assimilate them. Assimilation is not promoted by treating them as second class citizens.

Success or failure on parole

The annual reports of parole departments customarily state the parole violation rate as the ratio between paroles granted during a year and paroles violated during the same year. The parole violation rates, calculated by this method, in the several states tend to cluster around 25 percent, with a range of 10 to 40 percent. Even these percentages include only the violations known to parole officers and, in general, are restricted to the relatively serious violations for which paroles are revoked. In many areas the parole staff is not sufficient in numbers or activities to have reliable or complete information regarding the conduct of the parolees. Consequently, considerable skepticism regarding the stated violation rates has developed. In the states in which parole supervision is most efficient, the percentages of success are generally lower than in the states where supervision is superficial.

Also, questions have been raised as to the adequacy of the usual method of measuring parole violations, since most prisoners remain on parole for many years.[36] The proportion of parolees

---

[36] Milton G. Rector, "Factors in Measuring Recidivism as Presented in Annual Reports," *National Probation and Parole Association Journal*, 4:218-232, July, 1958.

released in a specified year who subsequently violate parole some-
time during the parole period generally is higher than the ratio of
paroles violated to paroles granted in a certain year. In a pioneering study, the Gluecks made an analysis of the careers of 500
young adult male offenders paroled from the Massachusetts reformatory and reported that 55.3 percent violated paroles, as recorded
by the parole department of the state, and 5.3 percent more violated paroles by new crimes committed during the parole period
which were not known to the parole department but which were
discovered by the Gluecks in independent investigations. Thus
they concluded that the parole violation rate was 60.6 percent,
while the state department was reporting a parole violation rate
of about 25 percent.[37] Later studies have revealed lower rates.
For example 44 percent of the men paroled from the Illinois State
Penitentiary between 1926 and 1943 were violators.[38] Of 1,015
men released from federal prisons in 1956, 35 percent were classed
as "failures" by 1960.[39] Of 5,553 male offenders paroled in California in 1968, 42 percent had been declared violators by 1969.[40]
Precise comparisons of reports are not possible because the definitions of "violation" and "failure" are not the same in all studies.

The parole violation rate, however it may be computed, refers
only to the period of parole and does not include the career of
the offender after he is released from parole. Numerous excellent
studies have been made of the subsequent careers of ex-prisoners,
beyond the period of parole. One of the first was made in 1888
by Brockway regarding former inmates of Elmira Reformatory.
He concluded that 78.6 percent of those released during the preceding decade were leading law-abiding lives and were self-
supporting at the time of the investigation.[41] The most intensive
studies of this type were made by Sheldon and Eleanor Glueck
and refer to 500 young adult male offenders over a fifteen-year
period, and 1,000 juvenile delinquents over a ten-year period.[42]
They reported that 79 percent of the 500 young male offenders
committed new crimes during the first five-year period after parole,

---

[37] Sheldon and Eleanor T. Glueck, *Five Hundred Criminal Careers* (Cambridge: Harvard University Press, 1930), p. 169.

[38] Hans W. Mattick, "Parole to the Army" mimeographed paper (Chicago: Cook
County Jail, 1958), p. II.

[39] Glaser, *Effectiveness of a Prison and Parole System*, pp. 19-20. See Table
XIX, p. 519, above.

[40] *California Prisoners, 1969* (Sacramento: Department of Corrections, 1970), p. 94.

[41] Z. R. Brockway, *Fifty Years of Prison Service* (New York: Charities Publication Committee, 1912), p. 297.

[42] *Five Hundred Criminal Careers; Later Criminal Careers* (New York: Commonwealth Fund, 1937); *Criminal Careers in Retrospect* (New York: Commonwealth Fund, 1943); *One Thousand Juvenile Delinquents* (Cambridge:
Harvard University Press, 1934); *Juvenile Delinquents Grow Up* (New York:
Commonwealth Fund, 1940).

68 percent during the second five-year period, and 68 percent during the third five-year period. Three and one-half years after release from a Borstal institution in England, 45 percent of a group of 720 boys had no further record of crime.[43]

One study has compared the subsequent careers of a group of prisoners released on parole with the subsequent careers of a group released unconditionally without parole. Five years after discharge from a reformatory, 30 percent of the men released on expiration of sentence and 21.4 percent of those released on parole had been convicted, sentenced, returned to custody, or had paroles revoked for felonies. In addition, 7.3 percent of those released on expiration of sentence and 4.9 percent of those released on parole had been fingerprinted for felonies, but there was no record of conviction.[44] These differences, however, may not be due to the treatment given while on parole; the inmates least likely to commit new crimes probably are selected for parole, while the inmates most likely to commit new crimes remain in prison until the end of the maximum sentence. Perhaps it is for this reason that no recent studies of this kind have been made. Statistics from several states routinely indicate that those released on parole are returned for new crimes less frequently than those released at the termination of their sentences.

During the last generation, over six hundred statistical studies have been made of the factors associated with success or failure on parole.[45] The criterion of failure used in most of these studies is a violation of parole by behavior which is noticed by the parole authorities and which leads to the issuance of a parole violation warrant. Such warrants ordinarily are requested and issued only when the parole agent is reasonably certain that the parolee cannot make an adequate social adjustment, or when a new crime is committed. Consequently, parole violation warrants as a measure of outcome tend to overestimate the actual adjust-

---

[43] Hermann Mannheim and Leslie T. Wilkins, *Prediction Methods in Relation to Borstal Training* (London: Her Majesty's Stationery Office, 1955), pp. 53, 65.
[44] Stanley B. Zuckerman, Alfred J. Barron, and Horace B. Whittier, "A Follow-up Study of Minnesota State Reformatory Inmates," *Journal of Criminal Law, Criminology, and Police Science,* 43:622-636, January-February, 1953.
[45] Bibliographies of such studies are given in Robert M. Allen, "A Review of Parole Prediction Literature," *Journal of Criminal Law and Criminology,* 32:548-554, January-February, 1942; Michael Hakeem, "Prediction of Criminality," *Federal Probation,* 9:31-38, July, 1945; Lloyd E. Ohlin and Otis Dudley Duncan, "The Efficiency of Prediction in Criminology," *American Journal of Sociology,* 54:441-452, March, 1949; Karl F. Schuessler, "Parole Prediction: Its History and Status," *Journal of Criminal Law, Criminology, and Police Science,* 45:425-431, November-December, 1954; Mannheim and Wilkins, *Prediction Methods in Relation to Borstal Training;* and Charles Dean and Thomas J. Duggan, "Problems in Parole Prediction: A Historical Analysis," *Social Problems,* 15:450-458, Spring, 1968.

ment achieved by parolees.[46] Information regarding many of the "factors" or conditions which are said to affect success or failure —such as "home status" and "previous work record"—are customarily taken from unverified statements made by the inmates. Others, such as "social type," "type of offense," and "personality rating," are taken from the official prison documents or from classification committee reports.

These statistical studies are consistent in their conclusions in certain respects and inconsistent in other respects. They show considerable consistency in the conclusions that failures decrease as the age of first delinquency increases, and increase as the number of previous arrests, the irregularity of previous work habits, the frequency of contacts with associates from the institution, and the size of the community in which the offender resided increase. Generally, older offenders succeed on parole more often than do the young offenders, white offenders more often than blacks, sex offenders and murderers more often than those engaged in crimes against property.

The studies either show no consistent relation or a very slight relation between failure on parole and such characteristics as height and weight, intelligence, religious preference, occupation classification, and work habits in the institution. On the other hand, the studies which are pertinent to this point show a close association between success on parole and postrelease behavior such as regular work habits, abstinence from alcohol and drugs, and constructive use of leisure time, as well as between parole success and such conditions as close family ties and residence in low-delinquency areas.

Prediction of success on parole

The information regarding the conditions of success or failure on parole of those who have been paroled in earlier years has been organized into experience tables and used to predict probable success or failure on parole and the probable violation rates for specific groups of parole applicants.[47] For example, in one of the earlier prediction studies, Burgess[48] found that parolees who had more than fifteen "unfavorable" factors (e.g., poor work record, previous criminal career, institutional punishments, and residence in a deteriorated neighborhood) violated parole in 98.5 percent of the cases, while those who had less than five unfavorable factors violated parole in only 24.0 percent of the cases. On the basis of this experience, he predicted that a person who had more than fifteen unfavorable factors was almost certain to violate parole, and that a person who had less than five unfa-

---

[46] Lloyd E. Ohlin, Selection for Parole (New York: Russell Sage Foundation, 1951), pp. 43-45.

[47] For an exceptionally clear description of how experience tables are constructed and used in parole, see Ohlin, Selection for Parole.

[48] A. A. Bruce, E. W. Burgess, and A. J. Harno, The Workings of the Indeterminate-Sentence Law and the Parole System in Illinois (Springfield, Ill. State of Illinois, 1928).

vorable factors had three chances out of four of success on parole. The reliability of the original data, the methods of classification, and the statistical methods of organizing the information are being improved by further studies.[49] Six states have for fifty years been producing most of the parole prediction studies. These are California, Illinois, Massachusetts, Minnesota, Washington, and Wisconsin. The improvement of prediction techniques has been strongly stimulated by the state of Illinois. Since 1933, this state has employed actuarial sociologists to conduct research on parole prediction and to assist the parole board by preparing a prediction of the success or failure of each person who comes before the board. This gives the board organized information, which may or may not be used as the basis of decision by the board.[50]

While the prediction technique has customarily been considered as a device for selecting for parole those prisoners who are most likely to succeed, it is potentially more useful as a device for directing the supervision and guidance of prisoners who are placed on parole. That is, men who are "poor risks" could be given close parole supervision and careful guidance, and men who are "good risks" could be given a minimum of supervision and guidance.[51] In an experimental study, California placed good parole risks under minimal supervision and found that they did as well as they were predicted to do under regular supervision.[52]

Three principal criticisms have been made of this prediction technique as a method of selecting persons for parole. The first is that it does not provide a standard for selecting parolees. Should the parole board grant parole to those who have fifty chances out of a hundred or only to those who have seventy-five or ninety chances out of a hundred? The prediction technique, if adequately developed, may be able to give information regarding the chances of success, but it cannot provide a standard. Moreover, the question recurs: Should prisoners who have little chance of success on parole be held to the end of the maximum sentence and then released without supervision, or should they be released on parole anyhow? It is clear that the prediction technique cannot provide the standards, but prediction studies may assist the parole board in defining the standards. Goodman devised a system whereby an estimate of the "social costs" of paroling and not paroling the various kinds of inmates would be

---

[49] See Leslie T. Wilkins and P. Macnaughton-Smith, "New Prediction and Classification Methods in Criminology," *Journal of Research in Crime and Delinquency*, 1:19-32, January, 1964.

[50] See Daniel Glaser, "Predication Tables as Accounting Devices for Judges and Parole Boards," *Crime and Delinquency*, 8:239-258, July, 1962.

[51] See J. Douglas Grant, "It's Time to Start Counting," *Crime and Delinquency*, 8:259-264, July, 1962.

[52] Joan Havel, *Special Intensive Parole Unit, Phase IV, The High Base Expectancy Study*, Research Report No. 10 (Sacramento: Department of Corrections, 1963), and *The Parole Outcome Study*, Research Report No. 13 (Sacramento: Department of Corrections, 1965).

included in the prediction information submitted to the parole board.[53]

The second criticism is that this technique largely neglects the fact that every prisoner reaches a point where he is a better risk on parole than at any other time.[54] The prediction technique is concerned principally with events and characteristics which preceded the period of imprisonment, only to a slight extent with behavior while in prison, and not at all with the changing attitudes of the prisoner while in prison.[55] In 1936, Laune attempted to take these attitudes into account and to base predictions on them,[56] but a later check on the parolees whose success or failure was predicted by Laune indicates that, in general, prediction by use of objective factors would have been more efficient than the prediction based on inmate attitudes.[57] This does not mean, however, that prediction systems using objective factors are necessarily more valuable than the systems using attitudinal factors when the aim is the efficient *selection* of parolees.

A third criticism is that prediction methods do not predict. The predictive efficiency of an experience table can be measured by comparing (a) the number of errors in prediction occurring when the table is used with (b) the number of errors that would have occurred had the prediction been based on the crudest method available—prediction from total violation rates alone.[58] For example, it might be found, after the parole results are in, that an actuary using an experience table had predicted incorrectly in, say, 30 percent of the cases. On the other hand, it might be observed that 40 percent of the parolees under consideration actually violated their parole, so that the best possible prediction for each individual case, on the basis of this total violation rate alone, would have been "nonviolation." If he had

[53] Leo A. Goodman, "Generalizing the Problem of Prediction," *American Sociological Review,* 17:609-612, October, 1952; idem, "The Use and Validity of a Prediction Instrument: I: A Reformulation of the Use of a Prediction Instrument," *American Journal of Sociology,* 58:503-512, March, 1953. See also Otis Dudley Duncan, Lloyd E. Ohlin, Albert J. Reiss, Jr., and Howard R. Stanton, "Formal Devices for Making Selection Decisions," *American Journal of Sociology,* 58:573-584, May, 1953.

[54] Cf. Norman S. Hayner, "Why Do Parole Boards Lag in the Use of Prediction Scores?" *Pacific Sociological Review,* 1:73-76, Fall, 1958; and Jerome K. Skolnick, "Toward a Developmental Theory of Parole," *American Sociological Review,* 25:542-549, August, 1960.

[55] See Ralph W. England, "Some Dangers in Parole Prediction," *Crime and Delinquency,* 8:265-269, July, 1962.

[56] F. F. Laune, *Predicting Criminality: Forecasting Behavior on Parole,* Northwestern University Studies in the Social Sciences, No. 1 (Evanston, Ill.: Northwestern University Press, 1936); idem, "The Application of Attitude Tests in the Field of Parole Prediction," *American Sociological Review,* 1:781-796, October, 1936.

[57] Lloyd E. Ohlin and Richard A. Lawrence, "A Comparison of Alternative Methods of Parole Prediction," *American Sociological Review,* 17:268-274, June, 1952.

[58] Ohlin and Duncan, "Efficiency of Prediction in Criminology."

predicted "nonviolation" for all the parolees, on the basis of the total violation rate, the actuary would have been incorrect in 40 percent of the cases. By using the experience table, then, he reduces the percentage of error from 40 to 30, an improvment of 25 percent. Ohlin and Duncan reported that all of the twenty-six major experience tables which had been used in research studies produced some reduction in the error of prediction for the original samples; the percentage reduction of error in the various studies ranged from 43 percent down to only 3 percent, with an average of about 12 percent. Hence, it may be concluded that the experience tables do have some predictive efficiency.

However, the predictive ability of the tables generally fails to stand up in follow-up samples to which the tables are applied for the purpose of validation. For example, in the Gluecks' study of 500 young adult male offenders over a fifteen-year period, the factors which were selected as most highly associated with failure in the first five-year period did not apply to the second five-year period, and an almost completely new set of factors was adopted; neither the first nor the second set of factors applied satisfactorily to the third five-year period, and a third set of factors was therefore adopted. When existing experience tables are applied to new samples of parolees, Ohlin and Duncan found, some of them do not significantly decrease the amount of error which would have been present had prediction been based simply on knowledge of the total violation rates alone, and others even *increase* the amount of error.

The general failure of the prediction instruments to predict for new samples may be attributed to four principal kinds of error which occur in practice.[59] *First,* there are many errors which result from lack of association between the "factors" and the actual outcome on parole. At best, the predictive techniques rest on the assumption that some categories of individuals will get involved and other categories of individuals will not get involved in the unknown causal systems which lead to parole violation.[60] Intensive analysis of the cause of parole violation probably would reduce the incidence of this type of error.

Second, errors arise because of sampling fluctuations; that is the characteristics of the new sample may differ from those of the first sample in such a way that the predictive efficiency of the instrument is reduced.

Third, errors occur because of the unreliability of the information used to establish the "factors" and of the "factors" themselves. Although the extent of the unreliability of prison records

---

[59] Cf. Lloyd E. Ohlin, "The Routinization of Correctional Change," *Journal of Criminal Law, Criminology, and Police Science,* 45:400-411, November-December, 1954.

[60] See Robert M. Martinson, Gene G. Kassebaum, and David A. Ward, "A Critique of Research in Parole," *Federal Probation,* 28:34-38, September, 1964.

cannot be precisely determined, research workers agree that these sources of information are notably unreliable. This source of error can be corrected by basing prediction on data collected for the specific purpose of making predictions. Scientific prediction can hardly be based on data collected by prisons for nonscientific purposes. The unreliability of the "factors" is due to lack of rigorous definition and to lack of knowledge of the cause of parole violation.

Fourth, errors correlated with time frequently occur. The prediction tables are based on the assumption that parole conditions remain constant over the years. Actually, many conditions which affect violation rates, but which do not affect the factors used in prediction occur from time to time. Among these are the effectiveness of the treatment measures used in the prison, the policy of the parole board, the employment possibilities for parolees, the efficiency of the parole agent, the efficiency of law-enforcement officers, the policy of the supervising agent in regard to what constitutes "violation," and the attitude of the community toward parole. This type of error constitutes perhaps the most serious obstacle to efficient parole prediction. Lloyd Ohlin developed a technique for routine adjustment of the prediction instrument so that it will take account of such changes in parole conditions.[61]

However, the "condition" which probably has the most effect on violation and nonviolation is the behavior of the persons with whom the parolee interacts, and this social interaction is not precisely taken into account in most prediction systems. Some of the prediction systems in criminology attempt to predict behavior on parole and even throughout life from traits and circumstances in infancy and early childhood. While certain behaviors appear fixed in infancy and remain relatively inflexible throughout life, behavior like crime and serious infraction of parole regulations appears to depend much more completely upon a process of continuing social interaction. If this be correct, the criminal behavior of a person can be accurately predicted only if the behavior of the persons with whom he will come in contact is known. Glaser examined the effects of social interaction by deriving his prediction factors from the differential association theory.[62] He found that such factors derived from this principle are more efficient predictors than are case study personality ratings.[63] A more recent study of parolees from a state training school also concluded that "parolees' social relations rather than their personal character-

---

[61] Ohlin, *Selection for Parole,* pp. 62-64, 119-121.

[62] Daniel Glaser, "A Reconsideration of Some Parole Prediction Factors," *American Sociological Review,* 19:335-341, June, 1954.

[63] Daniel Glaser, "The Efficacy of Alternative Approaches to Parole Prediction," *American Sociological Review,* 20:283-287, June, 1955.

istics are decisive in determining their success and failure on parole."[64]

ANONYMOUS. "A Convict Report on the Major Grievances of the Prison Population with Suggested Solutions." Book 2 of *Inside: Prison American Style*, edited by Robert J. Minton, Jr. New York: Random House, 1971.

ARLUKE, NAT R. "A Summary of Parole Rules." *Crime and Delinquency*, 15:267-274, April, 1969.

ARNOLD, WILLIAM R. *Juveniles on Parole.* New York: Random House, 1970.

BAILEY, WALTER C. "Correctional Outcome: An Evaluation of 100 Reports." *Journal of Criminal Law, Criminology, and Police Science*, 57:153-160, June, 1966.

BARNETT, J. D. "The Grounds of Pardon." *Journal of Criminal Law and Criminology*, 17:490-530, January-February, 1927.

BRIGGS, PETER F., & ROBERT D. WIRT. "Prediction." Chap. 6 in Herbert C. Quay, ed., *Juvenile Delinquency: Research and Theory*, pp. 170-208, New York: Van Nostrand, 1965.

COWDEN, JAMES E. "Predicting Institutional Adjustment and Recidivism in Delinquent Boys." *Journal of Criminal Law, Criminology, and Police Science*, 57:39-44, March, 1966.

COZART, REED. "The Benefits of Executive Clemency." *Federal Probation*, 32:33-35, June, 1968.

DOLESCHAL, EUGENE, & GILBERT GEIS. *Graduated Release.* Washington: Government Printing Office, 1971.

GAYLIN, WILLARD. "No Exit—The Turf of the Federal Parole Board is a Landscape of Illogic." *Harper's Magazine*, 243:86-94, November, 1971.

GLASER, DANIEL. *The Effectiveness of a Prison and Parole System.* Indianapolis: Bobbs-Merrill, 1964.

GOTTFREDSON, DON M., & KELLEY B. BALLARD, JR. "Differences in Parole Decisions Associated with Decision-Makers." *Journal of Research in Crime and Delinquency*, 3:112-119, July, 1966.

HAKEEM, MICHAEL. "Glueck Method of Parole Prediction Applied to 1,861 Cases of Burglars." *Journal of Criminal Law and Criminology*, 36:87-97, July-August, 1945.

HAKEEM, MICHAEL. "The Validity of the Burgess Method of Parole Prediction." *American Journal of Sociology*, 53:376-386, March, 1948.

HAYNER, NORMAN S. "Sentencing by an Administrative Board." *Law and Contemporary Problems*, 23:477-494, Summer, 1958.

Suggested
readings

---

[64] William R. Arnold, "A Functional Explanation of Recidivism," *Journal of Criminal Law, Criminology, and Police Science*, 56:212-220, June, 1965. See also Joseph W. Rogers, "Parole Prediction in Three Dimensions: Theory, Prediction, and Perception," *Sociology and Social Research*, 52:377-391, July, 1968; and Thomas J. Duggan and Charles V. Dean, "Statistical Interaction and Parole Prediction," *Social Forces*, 48:45-49, September, 1969.

KASSEBAUM, GENE, DAVID A. WARD, & DANIEL M. WILNER. *Prison Treatment and Parole Survival: An Empirical Assessment.* New York: John Wiley, 1971.

MANNHEIM, HERMANN, & LESLIE T. WILKINS. *Prediction Methods in Relation to Borstal Training.* London: Her Majesty's Stationery Office, 1955.

MARTIN, JOHN P. *Offenders as Employees.* London: Macmillan, 1962.

MARTIN, JOHN P., & D. WEBSTER. *Social Consequences of Conviction.* London: Heinemann, 1971.

MARTINSON, ROBERT M., GENE G. KASSEBAUM, & DAVID A. WARD. "A Critique of Research in Parole." *Federal Probation,* 28:34-38, September, 1964.

MEYER, CHARLES H. Z. "A Half-Century of Federal Probation and Parole." *Journal of Criminal Law, Criminology, and Police Science,* 42:707-728, March-April, 1952.

MORAN, F. A. "The Origins of Parole." *National Probation Yearbook, 1945,* pp. 71-98.

NEITHERCUTT, M. G. "Parole Violation Patterns and Commitment Offense." *Journal of Research in Crime and Delinquency,* 9:87-98, July, 1972.

OHLIN, LLOYD E. *Selection for Parole.* New York: Russell Sage Foundation, 1951.

OHLIN, LLOYD E., HERMAN PIVEN, & DONNELL M. PAPPENFORT. "Major Dilemmas of the Social Worker in Probation and Parole." *National Probation and Parole Association Journal,* 2:211-225, July, 1956.

ROGERS, JOSEPH W., & NORMAN S. HAYNER. "The Ideal Parole Board: Views from the Correctional World and the Society of Captives." *Proceedings of the American Correctional Association, 1963.*

SCOTT, P. D. "Approved School Success Rates." *British Journal of Criminology,* 4:525-556, October, 1964.

SKLAR, RONALD B. "Law and Practice in Probation and Parole Revocation Hearings." *Journal of Criminal Law, Criminology, and Police Science,* 55:175-198, June, 1964.

SKOLNICK, JEROME K. "Toward a Developmental Theory of Parole." *American Sociological Review,* 25:542-549, August, 1960.

TAKAGI, PAUL, & JAMES ROBISON. "The Parole Violator: An Organizational Reject." *Journal of Research in Crime and Delinquency,* 6:78-86, January, 1969.

WILKINS, LESLIE T., & P. MACNAUGHTON-SMITH. "New Prediction and Classification Methods in Criminology." *Journal of Research in Crime and Delinquency,* 1:19-32, January, 1964.

27 Prevention of crime and delinquency

Two general systems for reducing the frequency of crimes have been tried. One method aims at reducing the amount of repeated crime, the other at forestalling commission of first crimes. The name *crime prevention* has been given to both systems, but it is becoming common practice to consider the effort to prevent recidivism as the method of *reformation,* the effort to forestall first crimes as the method of *prevention.* This terminology is slightly inaccurate, for the policies of execution and of segregation of certain offenders are aimed at reduction of repeated crime, yet they can hardly be considered methods of reformation. Furthermore, a single program or policy, such as imprisonment, may be aimed at both reformation and prevention.

When the punitive reaction to crime was most popular, the usual assumption was that severe punishment both reforms those who are punished and deters or "prevents" others from committing first crimes. Even today, legislative commissions appointed to make suggestions for programs to reduce crime rates generally confine their recommendations to measures designed to increase severity of punishment. However, as we have seen, this policy is being supplemented, and to some extent replaced, by policies based on the treatment reaction to crime. Consistent with this trend, *reformation* and *prevention* are coming to refer exclusively to positive, nonpunitive efforts to rehabilitate criminals and to forestall criminality.

Though punishment is one method of building up anticriminal attitudes in the general public, it is not the most efficient method for preventing crime. The development of habits and attitudes by education, by the spreading of traditions, by the contacts and interactions between those who appreciate the values and those who do not is probably a more efficient method. As we find out more about criminal behavior, we shall have a better basis for the determination of specific policies for this purpose. These policies, if carried out consistently, may be expected to protect society from crime in three ways.

First, they would secure the segregation of persons who have demonstrated their dangerousness by persistent involvement in serious crime. Segregation probably will not reform these offenders, but it will protect society by incapacitating them and by indicating disapproval of serious deviance from legal norms. Apparently in the present state of politics and behavioral science we neither can change some persistent offenders nor significantly modify the social situations promoting persistent crime. We can only defend ourselves from this small category of dangerous persons, and segregation is the most extreme measure of defense. *Second,* these policies would integrate into law-abiding society a larger proportion of citizens, including the vast majority of those who have committed crimes but are not serious threats to the general anticriminal culture. *Third,* these policies would define and identify the social situations from which crimes are most likely to issue, and would make it possible to attack and eliminate those social situations in advance of crime.

Thus crime would be prevented by modifying those who can be and should be modified, segregating those who cannot be modified, and eliminating the social situations which are most conducive to crime and which, thus, produce the necessity for modifying and segregating criminals in the first place.[1] Vigorous implementation of such policies would be as much evidence of social disapproval of crime as would punishment. It is such disapprobation, rather than punishment of individual criminals, which tends to forestall crime among the large majority of the population. ●

Recidivism

As our discussion of probation, prisons, and parole has shown, a large proportion of the offenders under the care of any agency are recidivists. In a special study of 87,600 persons arrested in 1966 and 1967, the FBI found that at least 82 percent had been arrested on a prior charge; 70 percent had been convicted on a prior charge, and 46 percent of those convicted had been imprisoned for ninety days or more. Seventy-five percent of those arrested for murder, rape, felonious assault, and robbery had been convicted of some prior charge.[2] About 85 percent of the offenders admitted to the prisons and reformatories of Massachusetts in 1971, and about 85 percent of the male felons admitted to California prisons in 1969, had been in correctional institutions previously.[3] Similar rates have been compiled for several European countries.[4] Christie found that of all males born in Norway in 1933, 1,035 (5.08 percent) had become registered offenders by January 1, 1958. Twenty-two percent of the 1,035 were recidi-

---

[1] President's Commission on Law Enforcement and Administration of Justice, *The Challenge of Crime in a Free Society* (Washington: Government Printing Office, 1967), p. VI.

[2] *Uniform Crime Reports, 1971* (Washington: Government Printing Office, 1972), p. 36.

[3] Massachusetts Department of Correction, *Criminal Statistics, 1971* (Boston: Author, 1972), table B5; *California Prisoners, 1969* (Sacramento: Department of Corrections, 1970), p. 25.

[4] Marc Blanc and Jean Susini, "Typology of Offenders and Typology of Treatments," *Collected Studies in Criminological Research* (Council of Europe), vol. 3, 1968, pp. 79-126; and Zofia Ostrihanska, "Persistent Recidivists with Early and Late Criminal Records." *Archives of Criminology* (Warsaw), 4:215-222, 1969.

vists, and 4 percent had repeated their offenses three or more times. Of the men who had committed their first offenses at ages 14-17, and who, thus, had from 7½ to 9½ years in which to become recidivists, 36 percent had repeated.[5] During the years since 1955 the number of identified recidivists coming before the criminal courts in England and Wales has increased steadily. In 1955 there were thirty-five thousand offenders found guilty of indictable offenses who had previous indictable offenses on their criminal records; by 1962 this number had increased to sixty-eight thousand; and for 1965 it was estimated to be ninety thousand.[6]

This high rate of recidivism is extremely important, for it means that a large proportion of the crimes committed can be attributed to repeaters. A large part of the work of police, courts, and penal and reformatory institutions must be devoted to recidivists. Moreover, recidivists take more than their share of the time and efforts of agency personnel. Recidivists are overrepresented among the failures on probation and parole, and among prisoner populations. Massive walls, steel cages, and electronic locks are needed principally for recidivists.

The persistence of criminals in their crimes may be explained either in terms of the characteristics and conditions of the offenders or in terms of the inadequacy of agencies of reformation. The first involves a social psychology of the recidivist, the second an analysis of the techniques of reformation. ●

One of the findings of the prediction studies is that, with some exceptions, the personal characteristics and social situations which are associated with criminality in the first place are also associated with persistence in crime. Persons who live in areas having low crime rates, who are reared in nondelinquent homes, and who have a comfortable scale of living are least likely to return to crime after any method of treatment. They, like persons with minor physical ailments, probably "cure" themselves. Repeaters frequently were reared in deteriorated areas, in homes where destitution, vice, and criminality were usual, in isolation from law-abiding groups of the community. Several studies of delinquents indicate that nonrecidivists, as compared to recidivists, are older, have older mothers, are better educated, have fewer known delinquencies, are more intelligent, and are less likely to have a father with a criminal record.[7] Negroes have a higher rate of recidivism

Social psychology of recidivism

---

[5] Nils Christie, *Unge Norske Lovovertredere* (*Young Norwegian Lawbreakers*) (Oslo: Universitetsforlaget, 1960), pp. 51, 55.

[6] F. H. McClintock, N. Howard Avison, and G. N. G. Rose, *Crime in England and Wales* (London: Heinemann, 1968), p. 223.

[7] Dugald S. Arbuckle and Lawrence Litwack, "A Study of Recidivism Among Juvenile Delinquents," *Federal Probation*, 24:45-48, December, 1960; and Jerome Laulicht, "Problems of Statistical Research and Its Correlates," *Journal of Criminal Law, Criminology, and Police Science*, 54:163-174, June, 1963.

than whites, boys have a higher rate of recidivism than girls, and urban-dwellers have a higher rate than rural-dwellers.

One common explanation of recidivism is stated in terms of simple habit formation; persistence in crime is merely persistence of habits. Some of the habits were formed prior to the official reaction, others during the course of the processing. Drug addiction and drunkenness are illustrations of offenses which persist after official treatment as the result of habit formation. It is doubtful, however, whether the term *habit formation* is an adequate explanation of the persistence even of drug addiction or drunkenness. This concept implies physiological mechanisms and leaves the social conditions in obscurity. Both the recidivism of any individual and the high rate of recidivism in some groups are much more complex than is ordinarily conceived when explained in terms of habit formation.

Isolation from law-abiding society has been suggested as another explanation of recidivism. Ordinarily the offender acquires no facility in the manners of law-abiding groups, and he has little opportunity to come in contact with them after or during his period of official treatment. Upon discharge by an agency, the offender is restricted in his group memberships by his occupational skill, his table manners, his methods of conversation, his manners in recreation and in wearing clothes, and other characteristics. If the offender lived previously in law-abiding groups, he is likely to be ostracized, while if he lived previously in criminal groups, he may acquire status by further crime. By his manners, skills, stigma, and other traits he is confined to social groups which reinforce his criminal behavior. If he gets out of these groups, he will do so slowly. This isolation from law-abiding groups occurs more frequently after imprisonment than after other methods of punishment or correction, but it exists to some extent in connection with every method.

Another explanation of the persistence of the criminal is found in the criminality and near-criminality in the general society. Just as a person would secure no satisfaction from smoking in church because a church is not a suitable situation for smoking, an offender can feel comfortable in committing crimes only in situations where that behavior has become customary. The urban areas with high rates of crime and delinquency are also areas with high rates of recidivism in crime and delinquency. Mack found that among the delinquents residing in 1946-1958 on the street with the highest crime rate in a Scottish city, 29 percent had become adult criminals by 1964; the comparable figure for all Scottish delinquents is less than 5 percent.[8] Patterns of dishonesty, however,

---

[8] John Mack, "Full-time Miscreants, Delinquent Neighbourhoods, and Criminal Networks," *British Journal of Sociology*, 15:38-53, March, 1964.

are prevalent outside deteriorated areas as well as within them. Advertisements of toothpaste, medicines, and hundreds of other commodities are notoriously fraudulent in their claims and suggestions. The bribery of purchasing agents by business concerns is almost universal in many trades. In many lines of business, ruthlessness in making money has become an important part of the business code. Trade unions have become involved in racketeering. Political graft and corruption are widespread. Evasion of taxes is commonplace. Thus, lying, cheating, fraud, exploitation, violation of trust, and graft are prevalent in the general society. The offender who becomes reformed must be superior to the society in which he lives.[9] Certainly the reformation of offenders would be very much easier if the general society contained fewer so-called respectable citizens who regularly commit crimes.

Again, the criminal, by reason of his crime and the methods of dealing with his crime, forms associations, loyalties, and attitudes which tend to persist. The offender who manifests a desire to reform is called "yellow," "rat," "square," or "stool pigeon" by his associates. Even violence and threats of violence may be used to keep him a criminal. Opportunities for crime are placed in his way. One offender stated that while on parole he had at least forty opportunities for crime suggested to him in a month but not a single opportunity for legitimate work. Of great significance in this connection is the criminal's feeling of obligation and loyalty to criminals who have assisted him in the past.[10]

Finally, persistence in criminal behavior has been explained as due to personality traits, most frequently as due to pathological traits of personality, such as mental defectiveness, emotional instability, mental conflicts, egocentrism, and psychosis. The Gluecks' explanation of persistence in crime beyond the age of forty is almost entirely in terms of mental deviations which are not corrected by the natural maturation of the individual.[11] Personality characteristics, whether pathological or not, tend to persist in spite of the treatment currently given in any of the correctional processes. Since the situation subsequent to the treatment remains essentially the same as prior to the treatment, and the personality traits remain the same, the old behavior must persist. ●

---

[9] Cf. David Matza and Gresham M. Sykes, "Juvenile Delinquency and Subterranean Values," *American Sociological Review*, 26:712-719, October, 1961. See also David Matza, *Delinquency and Drift* (New York: John Wiley, 1964); and idem, *Becoming Deviant* (Englewood Cliffs, N. J.: Prentice-Hall, 1969).

[10] See John Irwin and Donald R. Cressey, "Thieves, Convicts and the Inmate Culture," *Social Problems*, 10:142-155, Fall, 1962; and Bill Chambliss, ed., *Box Man: A Professional Thief's Journey* (New York: Harper and Row, 1972).

[11] See p. 255 above.

Reformation   The second general type of explanation of recidivism is stated in terms of the inadequacy of the methods of reformation. If the offender were reformed by the first agency with which he came in contact, the crime rate would be greatly reduced. As our previous discussion has indicated, every major policy (e.g., corporal punishment, fines, imprisonment, probation, and parole) has resulted in a large proportion of failures. Such failures may be due to the inefficiency of the theories of reformation which are used, or they may be due to the inability to apply the theories when adequate facilities and personnel are not available.[12] In the following review, we shall be concerned with the theories of reformation and the technical policies based on such theories, rather than with personnel and facilities.

Mechanical methods of reformation   Until the present century, almost all reformative efforts were mass methods designed to modify the criminal in some mechanical manner. In the light of contemporary psychological and sociological knowledge, these methods of reformation are obsolete. However, they maintain a certain popularity among laymen.

The classical theory was that reformation could be accomplished by inflicting a sufficient amount of pain upon the offender. This was a strictly hedonistic theory, and it is still held by considerable numbers in the general public. It has generally been discarded by psychologists and sociologists. Pain undoubtedly has some value in the control of behavior, but the value is more or less completely balanced by the antagonism, isolation, and group loyalties which it produces. Furthermore, the infliction of punishment upon the offender does not change the situation which produced the criminality. In some cases there is not much more justification for punishing a criminal than for punishing a person with tuberculosis or smallpox.

A second method designed to produce reformation was meditation, generally enforced by isolation from all or almost all other persons. The theory was that crime was due to a failure to think, and that meditation would develop remorse and repentance. Early in the nineteenth century Mease made a clear-cut statement of this method of producing reformation. He maintained that repentance was produced by:

> (1) A tiresome state of mind from idle seclusion; (2) self-condemnation arising from deep, long-continued and poignant reflections upon a guilty life. All our endeavors, therefore, ought to be directed to the production of that state of mind, which will cause a convict to concentrate his thoughts upon his forlorn condition, to abstract himself from the world, and to think of nothing except the suffering and the privations he endures, the result of his crimes. Such a state of mind is totally incompatible with the least mechanical operation, but is only to be brought about, if ever, by complete mental and bodily isolation.[13]

---

[12] See Joel Meyer, "Reflections on Some Theories of Punishment," *Journal of Criminal Law, Criminology, and Police Science,* 59:595-599, December, 1968.

[13] James Mease, *Observations on the Penitentiary System and Penal Code of Pennsylvania* (Philadelphia, 1828), p. 73. Quoted in F. C. Gray, *Prison Discipline in America* (London: J. Murray, 1848), p. 30.

Some prisoners have testified that during the period of solitude they thought over their careers, and that this resulted in decisions to desist from crime. In general, however, this procedure has not been effective. Many years ago Hobhouse and Brockway accumulated considerable documentary evidence that isolation results in deterioration and degradation, not reformation.[14] Saleilles maintained that "The constant thought of remorse and, still more, of shame, becomes the greatest hindrance to individual regeneration."[15]

A third method, used in earlier and in later times, was moralizing. By tracts, sermons, and personal exhortations, in the name of God, mother, and country, appeals were made to the offenders. These exhortations generally produce antagonism in prisoners. Exhortation is an extremely important method of social control when it is used by members of a group upon other members of the same group. It is seldom effective when used by one group upon another group.

A fourth method is by inducing the offender to sign a pledge or make resolutions in some other form. This method is based upon the assumption that reformation can be accomplished merely by inducing the offender to "make up his mind" to reform. The fallacy of this assumption is abundantly illustrated every New Year's Day. Reformation involves a complex of social relationships and reinforcements which is not altered by resolutions. Furthermore, when the individual breaks his resolution, as is almost certain to be the case if the attempt at reformation involves nothing more than the resolution, the psychological effect is likely to be injurious.

A fifth method of reformation is mechanical habituation, produced by various compulsory methods, including hard and dreary work in the prison, and rigid prison discipline. The constant surveillance of the offender, which was made possible by Bentham's panopticon type of prisons, was justified by him as resulting in the formation of good habits:

> To render a man totally unable to do mischief, you have only to keep him constantly in sight, after depriving him of such offensive instruments as would render him dangerous to you. Place a man by himself, in an iron cage, for example, and keep him every hour and every minute of his life in sight, and it is evident you can prevent him from doing mischief, whether by making his escape to prey again upon society, or by exerting his powers to any pernicious effect where you have him confined.
>
> To place criminals then under perpetual inspection is the object, the all-powerful object, which it is required to accomplish. If this can be done, without loading society with exorbitant expense, the problem

---

[14] S. Hobhouse and A. F. Brockway, *English Prisons Today, Being the Report of the Prison System Enquiry Committee* (London: Longmans, Green, 1922), pp. 476-589.

[15] R. Saleilles, *The Individualization of Punishment* (Boston: Little, Brown, 1911), p. 195.

respecting a better disposal of criminals than killing them is already resolved.[16]

The panopticon prison was constructed in circular form with a central guard tower, from which one guard could look into all the cells and thus keep all the prisoners under constant surveillance. When this prison architecture was used in the prison at Joliet, Illinois, it was found that the construction which enabled the guard to watch all of the prisoners also enabled any prisoner to watch the guard, and therefore any prisoner could do whatever mischief he pleased while the guard's back was turned. In addition, the condition of constant mutual surveillance produced antagonism in both the guard and the prisoners. The panopticon plan has been abandoned.

These five methods are examples of the efforts to produce reformation in the past. Although they have carried over to the present, they reveal the necessity of understanding the principles of human behavior better than they were understood in the last century.

The clinical method of reformation

Strictly speaking, adherence to the policy of individualized treatment for delinquents and criminals does not imply the use of any specific technique or theory of reformation. Rather, commitment to this policy means only that those conditions considered as causing the individual to behave criminally will be considered in the attempt to reform him. Attention is focused on the criminal rather than on the crime. Generally, an attempt is made to diagnose the cause of criminality and to base the technique of reformation upon the diagnosis. An analogy with the *method* of diagnosis, prescription, and therapy for medical patients is apparent.[17]

The clinical method of reformation has extended this analogy, and it has become similar to clinical medicine in theory and content as well as in procedures. Criminality is considered as a defect or disorder, or as a symptom of a defect or disorder, which can be treated on an individual basis without reference to the offender's groups, just as biological disorders can be treated on an individual basis. An extreme position in this regard is that criminality actually is a biological disorder, treatable by modification of the physiology or anatomy of the individual through lobotomy, castration, interference with glandular functioning, or something else. However, the much more popular view is that criminality is an individual psychological disorder which may or may not have a strictly biological basis. According to this view, the essential difference between clinical medicine and the proper system for treatment of criminals lies in the nature of the disorder being treated—clinical medicine deals with organic disorders, clinical treatment for criminals with psychological disorders, with

---

[16] Jeremy Bentham, "On Houses of Safe-Custody and Industry," *Philanthropist*, 1:229, (1811).

[17] See the discussion above, pp. 356-358.

"mental disease." The clinical method of reformation is, thus, based upon an individualistic, psychiatric theory of criminality.

The essence of the popular individualistic theory is that criminality is an expression of emotional disorders or conflicts in the makeup of the individual. The criminal may be considered as a person who is unable to canalize or sublimate his "primitive," antisocial impulses or tendencies; or he may be considered as expressing symbolically in criminal behavior some unconscious wish or urge created by an early traumatic emotional experience; or he may be considered as possessing some other kind of defective personality component. In any event, the implication for treatment is that the internal emotional maladjustment must be eradicated before the external, behavioral maladjustment (criminality) will be corrected.[18]

The specific techniques for reformation of criminals, then, make no attempt to modify the offender's group relations in any direct way. Rather, the techniques used for treating criminals are the same as the techniques used for treatment of emotionally maladjusted noncriminals. The many clinical techniques for administering therapy to emotionally disturbed persons cannot be reviewed here.[19] Generally, the emotional disorders which are considered as criminality-producing are now usually recognized as the product of social conditions, but the treatment is aimed at modification and correction of the criminal's purported emotional maladjustments rather than at modification of the social conditions. For example, rejection by parents might be considered as the source of the emotional disorder which produced a child's delinquency, yet the therapy might be directed exclusively at the emotional disorder, rather than at the social relationships in the family. The parental rejection is considered as having produced a defect in the individual's personality, a defect which will continue to direct and determine his overt behavior until such time as it is modified by treatment.

One clinical system or technique for modification of criminality through modification of emotional maladjustments or disorders can be broken down into five steps or stages. While this analysis greatly oversimplifies the procedures used in clinical therapy, it illustrates basic operations performed. *First,* in discussions with a therapist the criminal is urged to talk freely about his criminality and the conditions which he thinks are responsible for it. *Second,* the therapist identifies a character defect. This defect may be labeled "feelings of guilt," "resentment of authority," or

---

[18] See Don C. Gibbons, *Changing the Lawbreaker* (Englewood Cliffs, N. J.: Prentice-Hall, 1965), pp. 143-157.

[19] Hakeem has pointed out that over fifty definitions of psychotherapy were necessary to accommodate the variety of viewpoints expressed in one professional conference, and that one textbook lists twenty-six different types and schools of thought of individual therapy. Michael Hakeem, "The Psychiatric Approach to Juvenile Delinquency," in Joseph Roucek, ed., *Juvenile Delinquency* (New York: Philosophical Library, 1958).

any of a host of other terms. *Third*, this interpretation of the interview materials is communicated to the criminal, giving him "insight" into the "basic motivation" for his criminal behavior. *Fourth*, the criminal is urged to recall his life experiences in an attempt to discover the original source of the emotional defect. *Fifth*, the subject's awareness of the source of the emotional disorder may alone "cure" that disorder, and "cure" of the disorder, in turn, "cures" the criminality. However, in some cases, merely "raising unconscious emotional circuits to the surface of consciousness so that they are observed by the individuals in whom they occur"[20] will not be sufficient for eradication of the emotional defects produced by these traumatic experiences, and further guidance and counseling may be necessary.

This system may be seen in the following description, by a psychiatrist, of psychotherapy and "intensive treatment" for prisoners:

> The purpose of this discipline is the uncovering of unconscious material which has been expressed in the form of disordered behavior, of disabling subjective symptoms, or demonstrable derangements of function. This material is uncovered in order to bring it to the awareness of the person suffering from the disability, and for the purpose of helping him to alter favorably his behavior patterns; of effecting as deeply-ranging a change as is possible and is necessary, of the disposition and expression of his impulses. . . . To put it differently, the aim of this therapy would be to assist a person toward the goal of socially-acceptable behavior, through his understanding of the unconscious purposes served by his former unacceptable behavior.[21]

The group-relations method of reformation

Modern sociological and psychological discoveries about the nature of personality have provided an alternative theory upon which to base diagnosis and treatment of criminals. The personality is viewed as "situation determined" rather than "trait determined"; the behavior of an individual is said to be the product of his group relationships, rather than of the presence of specific individual traits or characteristics. The traits which an individual exhibits are the properties of groups, not of the individual alone. John Dewey, in 1922, and Dorwin Cartwright, in 1951, expressed this viewpoint as follows:

> To change the "working character" or will of another, we have to alter objective conditions which enter into his habits. Our own schemes of judgment, of assigning blame and praise, of awarding punishment and honor are part of these conditions. . . . We cannot change habit directly: that notion is magic. But we can change it indirectly by modifying conditions, by an intelligent selecting and weighing of the objects which engage attention and which influence the fulfillment of desires.[22]

---

[20] Justin K. Fuller, "Group Therapy for Parolees," *Prison World,* 14:9-11, July, 1952.

[21] David Sherbon, "Definition of 'Intensive Treatment,'" in Harold B. Bradley and Jack D. Williams, *Intensive Treatment Program: Second Annual Report* (Sacramento: Department of Corrections, 1958), pp. 23-24.

[22] John Dewey, *Human Nature and Conduct* (New York: Henry Holt, 1922), pp. 19-20.

The behavior, attitudes, beliefs and values of the individual are all firmly grounded in the groups to which he belongs. How aggressive or co-operative a person is, how much self-respect or self-confidence he has, how energetic and productive his work is, what he aspires to, what he believes to be true and good, whom he loves or hates, and what beliefs and prejudices he holds—all these characteristics are highly determined by the individual's group membership. In a real sense, they are properties of groups and of the relationships between people. Whether they change or resist change will, therefore, be greatly influenced by the nature of these groups. Attempts to change them must be concerned with the dynamics of groups.[23]

In criminology, the differential association theory is consistent with this conception of the nature of individual behavior. Also, as was pointed out in chapter 16, the general implication of the differential association theory for reformation of criminals is that relations in the culture of law-abiding groups must be promoted, and relations in procriminal culture must be discouraged. Negatively, this means that criminality cannot be modified to any significant extent in a clinic, for clinical methods do not deal with group relations.

Although correctional programs are including more and more provisions for contact with anticriminal culture, a specific set of techniques for promoting reformation by this method has not been worked out. Instead, the contacts provided have been promoted in a rather haphazard fashion, often with no explicit acknowledgment of the group-relations theory of criminality and reformation. Perhaps a general statement of some principles of reformation consistent with the group-relations theory of behavior in general and the differential association theory in particular will provide a basis for explicit attempts to utilize the group-relations principle in correctional programs. Research and experimentation may eventually produce precise, detailed rules of action for correctional workers interested in achieving change in criminals, but current knowledge of the techniques of reformation is very scanty. The following statement, adapted from a more general statement by Dorwin Cartwright,[24] should be regarded as tentative, as directing attention to areas where research and experimentation should prove fruitful:

(*a*) Criminals who are to be reformed and the persons who are to exert influence or change must have a strong sense of belonging to the same group. The two general processes in reformation are the *alienation* of the criminal from groups which support values conducive to criminality and, concurrently, the *assimilation* of the criminal into groups supporting values conducive to law-abiding behavior. The latter process can be accomplished only when the social distance between the criminals and the reformers is small enough to permit a genuine "we" feeling. Consequently, the reformers and the reformees should be similar in social status

---

[23] Dorwin Cartwright, "Achieving Change in People: Some Applications of Group Dynamics Theory," *Human Relations*, 4(1951):381-392.

[24] Ibid.

and ethnic backgrounds; ideally, they would be similar in all respects except attitudes toward law-violation. Neither the view that all criminals are "outsiders" nor the view that correctional workers are "hoosiers" or "cops" is conducive to reformation. However, these two views currently prevail, and it is probably for that reason that nonprofessional persons, such as the family of a girl with whom the criminal is in love, often exert more influence than do the correctional workers themselves.

(b) The more attractive the group to the criminal, the greater is the influence that the group can exert on the criminal. The group must be so constituted that the criminal desires and can achieve status in it. He must be given recognition for anticriminal and non-criminal behavior. In psychiatric terminology, the group must fill his "unmet needs," "provide an opportunity for ego-expansion," etc. Not all persons are attracted to the same groups, and it can be safely asserted that few criminals are attracted to groups in which they are made the object of ridicule, hate, sermons, or tear-jerking sympathy. A judge in New York sent a criminal who had shown remarkable organizing ability in the field of crime to oversee the reclamation of large tracts of abandoned farm land. The criminal acquired status in the community by this method, and his opinion of the behavior that was appropriate to the status no longer included crime. He came to think of himself as a useful member of society. Similarly, the provision of material services by the group may serve to attract criminals to a network of anticriminal personal relations. The correctional worker must appeal to criminals with as much skill as the salesman uses in appealing to customers, and he must produce an effect that will be much more permanent than that produced by salesmen. This appeal must be based on study of the offender's background and past experiences. For example, a delinquent who thinks that Boy Scouts are sissies is not likely to join the Scouts. But if he should join, the group probably will change him only very slowly, for he will resist entering into intimate personal relationships with the other boys.

(c) The more relevant the basis of attraction of the group to the reformation of criminals, the greater will be the influence that the group can exert on the criminal's attitudes and values. This means that groups organized largely for the purpose of occupying the criminal's time—such as hobby and recreational groups —will not have the influence of a group organized for the explicit purpose of changing criminals. If the basis of attraction of the group is some tangential interest which the criminal might have (e.g., an interest in music), the criminal's values regarding criminality are likely to remain unchanged, while his values regarding the tangential interest are changed. He might become a criminal educated in music, rather than a noncriminal. A group in which "Criminal A" and some noncriminals join together to change "Criminal B" probably is most effective in changing "Criminal A." This system is sometimes rather inadvertently used in institutions for delinquents, where one of the older children is appointed as "monitor" or "big brother" for each newcomer. The newcomer takes his troubles to the monitor, and, more significantly, the monitor, even when not consulted, tries to direct and protect the newcomer. The monitor probably benefits more than does his charge. The system also is effective in Alcoholics Anonymous and in Synanon, a self-help organization for drug addicts.[25] It has been tried, in modified form, in several institutions and programs.[26]

(d) The greater the prestige of a group member in the eyes of those who are to be reformed, the greater the influence he can exert. The prestige assigned to a group member may spring from the member's social position outside the group, or it may spring from some attribute or trait which the member seems to possess. In assigning prestige, reformees may use criteria different from those used by other reformers.

(e) Strong resistance will be encountered when the efforts to change individual criminals or the criminal members of a group would, if successful, have the result of making them deviate from the norms of the group.[27] The group must be, first of all, a strongly anticriminal group, so that deviation from group norms will be deviation in the direction of criminality. If the reformers are in such a minority—in numbers, influence, or prestige—that exhibition of essentially "antireform" attitudes is the real basis of group cohesion, any reformation of individuals will be extremely unlikely. The offender who understands the psychological and social mechanisms involved in criminal conduct and who has a stake in the prohibitions against that conduct probably will accept anticriminal values more readily than an offender who does not. Sometimes an understanding of the situation can be secured only if the offender's rationalizations, by which he justifies and defends himself, are broken down. Such an understanding can be promoted only by persons who themselves have some understanding of the psychology and sociology of crime.

(f) The source of pressure on the criminal whose change is sought must lie within the group. The group must not rely upon the criminal to change himself. So far as the processes are concerned, there is no essential difference between abandoning crime

---

[25] Rita Volkman and Donald R. Cressey, "Differential Association and the Rehabilitation of Drug Addicts," *American Journal of Sociology*, 69:129-142, September, 1963; and Michael M. Jasinsky, "Die Anwendungsmöglichkeit der Theorie der differentiellen Assoziation in der Kriminalpädagogik," *Monatsschrift für Kriminologie und Strafrechtsreform*, 53:238-250, September, 1970.

[26] See Keith A. Stubblefield and Larry L. Dye, eds., *Offenders as a Correctional Manpower Resource* (Washington: Joint Commission on Correctional Manpower and Training, 1968). See also Andrew Rutherford, "New Careers for Ex-offenders," *Prison Service Journal*, January, 1971, pp. 2-5.

[27] Cf. Harold H. Kelley and Edmund H. Volkart, "The Resistance to Change of Group-Anchored Attitudes," *American Sociological Review*, 17:453-465, August, 1952.

and backsliding in church. The person who changes has transferred his loyalties from one group to another. The change is
sometimes rapid, sometimes gradual. Often the reformee does not
repent and resolve to do right. Instead, his behavior is modified
by the changes in group relations. Perhaps the most effective
group for reformation of criminals would be one in which status
is achieved by exhibition of "proreform" attitudes. That is, those
persons who show the most marked tendency toward anticriminal
values, attitudes, and behavior would become leaders. Criminality is learned in intimate, personal groups, and noncriminality
and anticriminality are learned in similar groups.

This last principle was demonstrated in an early but highly
significant experiment with hospitalized drug addicts. When the
experiment began, the hospital wards contained an essentially
"antireform" culture, and the ward leaders were the older, more
experienced addicts. The social organization in the wards was
described as follows:

> Pro-social attitudes, such as a desire for psychotherapy or real coop-
> eration with hospital authorities, were frowned upon. Patients who held
> these beliefs were "squares" or "chickens" and were ostracized by the
> dominant antisocial group on the ward. On the regular wards, it was
> found that the bulk of the patients' free time was spent in "breaking up
> jack pots" (group discussion of past addiction or plans for future use
> of the drug), group expressions of hatred and contempt for authority
> (hospital and community), and how to do "easy time" (devices for
> seducing authority so as to get easy or pleasant jobs in the hospital).[28]

In connection with a group-therapy program this antireform
culture was changed. so that prestige was assigned by ward
members to persons exhibiting signs of abandoning the use of
drugs, rather than to persons exhibiting antireform attitudes:

> Continuous observation of the Treatment Ward revealed a significant
> change in the subculture developed on this ward. On the Treatment
> Ward, a premium was placed by the patients "on getting better," as
> evidenced by realistic relations with other patients on the ward and with
> authority figures. Group discussions of drugs for their own sake were
> discouraged. The leaders that evolved were people who could demon-
> strate by their relations to others that they had utilized and benefited
> from "treatment." All the patients on this ward were in a [therapy]
> group. The group was used to explore the personal problems and inter-
> personal experiences on the ward. . . . [The treatment] ward developed
> a pro-social therapeutic climate that fostered psychotherapy. This was
> not true of the other wards of the hospital.[29]

This experiment has great significance for a theory of reformation, since almost all of the participants were reformees. The

---

[28] James J. Thorpe and Barnard Smith, "Phases in Group Development in the
Treatment of Drug Addicts," *International Journal of Group Psychotherapy*,
3:66-78, January, 1953. See also Lamar T. Empey and Jerome Rabow, "The
Provo Experiment in Delinquency Rehabilitation," *American Sociological
Review*, 26:679-695, October, 1961; and Lamar T. Empey and George E. New-
land, "Staff-Inmate Collaboration — A Study of Critical Incidents and Consequences in the Silverlake Experiment," *Journal of Research in Crime and
Delinquency*, 5:1-17, January, 1968.
[29] Ibid.

culture observed among the addicts was not unlike that existing in many prisons, making the task of reformation exceedingly difficult. When the reformees are probationers or released prisoners, the reformer has the advantage of being able to direct the reformee to an anticriminal group or to draw him into group relations which are already anticriminal. Under such circumstances, achievement of reformation should be much easier than it is under conditions in which the subculture itself must be changed.[30]

The courts and correctional agencies are adding professionally trained persons to their staffs to assist in the diagnosis and treatment of offenders. This work is relatively recent in origin, and the proportion of time and energy given to diagnosis is much greater than that given to treatment. Professional training for the specific work of diagnosing and treating criminals and delinquents is nowhere adequate.[31]

Professional services and reformation

The social worker acquires in a training school a theory of interviewing and experience in interviewing. Moreover, he has had some practice in the collection, verification, and application of social data. But the social worker is seldom trained specifically in the field of crime and delinquency, and has no specific knowledge of the processes which lead to delinquency. In recent years, social work has been psychiatrically oriented, and therefore the social worker is usually individualistic in his approach. His clinical theory of reformation makes it difficult for him to work with agencies that are concerned with the immediate welfare of society rather than with the welfare of the criminal.[32]

The psychologist is generally trained to give intelligence, aptitude, interest, and personality tests, and to conduct therapeutic interviews. Almost anyone can be trained in a very short time to give the tests in a routine manner. The contribution of the psychologist, in comparison with those who may acquire the ability to give the tests and interviews routinely, is to be found in the background of knowledge regarding psychology, by reason of which he can make interpretations of test and interview results and of incidents which occur during the interviewing and testing processes. The psychologist, like the social worker, generally has had no acquaintance with the field of criminology prior to employment in correctional work.

The psychiatrist has generally been trained in a medical school; most of his training has focussed on study of the organism, and he has given relatively little attention to behavior problems. Insofar as he gets specialized courses in behavior problems, he becomes

---

[30] See Gibbons, *Changing the Lawbreaker*, pp. 163-174.

[31] Evan Louis Sanchez, *An Analysis of California Correctional Workers' Academic Training and Needs* (Sacramento: California Probation, Parole, and Correctional Association, 1959).

[32] See Donald R. Cressey, "Professional Correctional Work and Professional Work in Correction," *National Probation and Parole Association Journal*, 5:1-15, January, 1959.

acquainted with the major psychoses. He has practically no opportunity to become acquainted with the body of knowledge in psychology or criminology.

The sociologist is the only member of the professional group who ordinarily has an academic training in criminology and penology, for academic work in this field is confined almost entirely to departments of sociology. On the other hand, he has had no training in clinical methods; he has been concerned with research work and general interpretations of crime rather than with the diagnosis and treatment of individual offenders. •

Crime prevention

The methods of reformation, like the methods of punishment, have not been notably successful in reducing crime rates. They have failed most frequently in reforming offenders who have been reared in the situations where crime flourishes most. Thus they have been least effective in dealing with the offenders who come from the most potent crime-breeding situations, from which a considerable proportion of all the criminals who are dealt with by official methods do come. Moreover, a very small proportion of those who commit crimes receive official treatment for the criminal behavior involved. Perhaps as few as 10 percent of crimes result in arrests, and certainly a much smaller percentage result in official action. This is especially true of fraud, bribery, and similar white-collar crimes which flourish in the business world and the political world, and which almost never result in arrest.

The implication of these facts is that the policy of prevention must be emphasized if the crime rate is to be reduced significantly. Punishment and methods of treatment are, at best, methods of defense against criminals or of rescuing criminals. It is futile to take individual after individual out of the situations which produce criminals and permit the situations to remain as they were. A case of delinquency or crime is more than a physiological act of an individual. It involves a whole network of social relations. If we deal with this set of social relations, we shall be working to prevent crime.[33]

The superiority of prevention to correction may be illustrated in the problem of school discipline. Two generations ago corporal punishment was used with great frequency in the schools, and disorder was generally prevalent in spite of the punishment. Orderly behavior then developed, but it did not develop by increasing the severity and frequency of punishment or by "treating" unruly students. Rather the improvement in the behavior of schoolchildren came as the result of improvement in the teachers and the curricula, and in the gradual development of a tradition of orderly behavior, together with liberality in the criteria of good behavior. The school system was adjusted to the needs

---

[33] Cf. Marshall B. Clinard, "Prevention of Crime," *Journal of Correctional Work* (India), 7(1960):1-12.

of the children much better than it had been previously. It is probable that analogous changes must be made in the social organization before great reductions can be made in crime rates. Even the school must again make readjustments if recent increases in disorderliness are to be checked.

Most criminals, in their earlier stages, are probably much like the person who is dishonest in reporting his personal property to the assessor. This man would be willing to make an honest report if others made honest reports. Each individual is driven to dishonesty by the fact that dishonesty is prevalent. In that sense most criminals probably do not need to be reformed, at least in their earlier stages of criminality. Instead, the prevalence of dishonesty needs to be modified so that individual crime is prevented.

Many general programs of crime prevention have been outlined. For example, Bentham, in the last part of the eighteenth century, made a comprehensive outline of the "indirect methods" (that is, methods other than punishment) which might be used to prevent crime. He included such things as taking away the capacity to injure, diverting the course of dangerous desires, decreasing susceptibility to temptations, general education, a code of morals similar to a code of laws, and other things.[34] Ferri, a member of the Italian school, in the last part of the nineteenth century paid considerable attention to the prevention of crime. He had a doctrine of criminal saturation, namely, that a group has the crimes it deserves in view of the type of people and the conditions of the group, and that as long as the type of people and the conditions remain constant, crime will remain constant regardless of methods of punishment. Consequently, he insisted that penal substitutes, or methods of modifying the conditions and traits of people, should be used. He outlined a long list of these, including free trade, reduction in consumption of alcohol, metal (instead of paper) money, street lights, reduction in hours of labor, lower interest on public securities, local political autonomy, and many other things.[35]

Many other elaborate programs for the prevention of crime have been proposed, and these programs have included practically every reform that has been suggested by anyone. The programs tend to be somewhat utopian, principally because the knowledge of crime causation has not been sufficiently precise to isolate the conditions and traits which need attention in programs of prevention. Policies for the prevention of crime are based, implicitly or explicitly, on theories of the causes of crime. Those who believe that crime is due to innate defects advocate a policy of sterilization. Those who believe that it is due to acquired personal defects advocate agencies for education or psychiatric clinics. Those who

General programs of prevention

---

[34] Jeremy Bentham, "Principles of Penal Law," in John Bowring, ed., *The Works of Jeremy Bentham* (Edinburgh: W. Tait, 1843).

[35] E. Ferri, *Criminal Sociology*, trans. J. I. Kelly and John Lisle (Boston: Little, Brown, 1917), pp. 209-287.

believe that it is due to the immediate personal groups advocate reorganization of the family and of the neighborhood. Those who believe that it is due to the more general culture advocate a more general social reorganization.

Almost everything in the universe is found to be associated in some direct or indirect manner with criminality. These multiple factors have not been reduced to a clear-cut system, with immediate and remote relationships established. No universals have been discovered; until they are discovered, programs of prevention as well as programs of punishment and programs of treatment must operate on the trial-and-error principle. No one can show in advance that crime will be significantly reduced if a particular program of prevention is adopted.

The greatest need in crime prevention now is, and always has been, irrefutable facts about crime causation and sound means for transforming that knowledge into a program of action.[36] Until such information is secured, and perhaps even after it is secured, the general public will be opposed to modifications of the status quo, which will in almost all cases increase taxes. Citizens are opposed to crime, to be sure, but they are also opposed to high taxes and individual financial sacrifice. It is easier to make emotional gestures in regard to crime rather than risk capital on studies and changes which might prevent crime. If reliable information on which to base programs of prevention were available, the decision-makers probably could be educated and induced to carry out programs based on such information. However, in view of the fact that persons administering crime prevention programs have vested interests in maintaining only vague procedures for measuring the effectiveness of the programs, such reliable information is not likely to be forthcoming.[37]

Local community organization   The policy implied in the earlier chapters of this book is that control of delinquency lies principally in the personal groups within the local community. It was shown that delinquency is explained principally by an excess of delinquent associations over antidelinquent associations; in such associations, intimacy and the prestige of the source of a pattern are the principal characteristics of associations which result in behavior concordant with that pattern. Moreover, it was shown that the condition in these local and personal groups which has the greatest significance

---

[36] Cf. Eva Rosenfeld, "Social Research and Social Action in Prevention of Juvenile Delinquency," Social Problems, 4:138-148, Fall, 1956; Lyle W. Shannon, "The Problem of Competence to Help," Federal Probation, 25:32-39, March, 1961; and Lamar Empey and Steven G. Lubeck, Delinquency Prevention Strategies (Washington: Government Printing Office, 1970).
1961.

[37] Donald R. Cressey, "The Nature and Effectiveness of Correctional Techniques," Law and Contemporary Problems, 23:754-771, Autumn, 1958. See also James C. Hackler, "Evaluation of Delinquency Prevention Programs: Ideals and Compromises," Federal Probation, 31:22-26, March, 1967.

is the definition of behavior as desirable or undesirable. For example, even in the more extremely deplorable family and neighborhood situations, girls are less delinquent than boys, and this is due to the fact that delinquency is defined as more dangerous and undesirable for girls than for boys.

The closest approximation to a general formula for the prevention of crime and delinquency that can be made at present is that criminal and delinquent behavior must be defined as undesirable by the personal groups in which a person participates. The correlate of this is that lawful behavior must be defined as desirable by such groups. The personal groups in question may be the family, school and neighborhood groups, work or recreational groups, religious groups, or others. Policies for prevention of delinquency and crime, therefore, should be directed primarily at these personal groups. In this sense, control of delinquency and crime lies within the local community. This means, first, that the local community must be the active agency in reducing its own delinquency. The personal groups can be modified through the efforts of local organizations such as the school, the church, the police, welfare agencies, and civic groups. Second, modifications of the general institutional structure are important in reducing crime and delinquency rates to the degree that they affect local community organization.

Experiments in the control of delinquency along the lines suggested in the preceding paragraph were developed in Chicago under the guidance of the sociologists in the Institute for Juvenile Research.[38] The principle involved in these "Chicago Area Projects" is that the persons who reside in an area of high delinquency are induced to form an organization for the purpose of reducing their own delinquency rates. The "natural leaders" in these areas direct the organizations, with some suggestions from outsiders and with financial aid from agencies outside the area. The groups which are most important in the lives of the residents of an area become the agencies through which operations are conducted.

These Area Projects have been in operation for about forty years. The approach has remained the same over the years, although the community committees now attempt both to assist in the rehabilitation of parolees and to prevent delinquency and crime. Undoubtedly, the community units are as important in modifying the attitudes and behavior of the adult participants as they are in directly changing the activities of children and

---

[38] See E. W. Burgess, J. D. Lohman, and Clifford R. Shaw, "The Chicago Area Project," *National Probation Association Yearbook, 1937*, pp. 8-28; Fred A. Romano, "Organizing a Community for Delinquency Prevention," *National Probation Association Yearbook, 1940*, pp. 1-12; Clifford R. Shaw and Jesse A. Jacobs, "The Chicago Area Project," *Proceedings of the American Prison Association, 1939*, pp. 40-53; Clifford R. Shaw and Henry D. McKay, *Juvenile Delinquency and Urban Areas* (Chicago: University of Chicago Press, 1942), pp. 442-446. (Rev. ed., with a new introduction by James F. Short, Jr., 1969.)

youth.[39] Adults who band together to prevent delinquency in their community rather automatically modify their own attitudes. An "antidelinquency" group is formed, and status in the group is achieved by expressions of antidelinquent behavior. This subtle modification of adults' attitudes of indifference to delinquency is itself delinquency prevention, for a new set of social influences for the child is created. The child begins to live in an antidelinquency setting where he, also, gains status by nondelinquent or antidelinquent, in contrast to prodelinquent, activities. Even probationers, parolees, and ex-criminals may work to improve the community and to keep others out of delinquency, thus reforming themselves. In addition, the attempts to deal directly with the behavior of children and youth probably are most effective when the cultural differences between the adults and the children are at a minimum, as is the case in the Area Project communities. The Area Projects, and many similar programs developed in the last decade, have been criticized for using "untrained" workers and "bad" people as leaders, yet the use of such natural leaders is one of the program's greatest assets.

Unfortunately, there is little objective evidence that the projects have reduced the delinquency rates of the subject areas. Some persons connected with the program believe that significant reductions in delinquency rates have resulted, while others connected with the program are skeptical as to the results. Delinquency rates have shown a greater decrease in project areas than in nearby areas, but this difference may be due merely to a difference in delinquency reporting in the two kinds of areas. Perhaps the best that can be said in appraisal of the Area Projects and similar programs is that they are consistent with an important theory of criminal behavior and with the ideals of democracy. Communities which have been indifferent to high delinquency rates must gradually be converted to a set of values which places a premium on nondelinquency.[40]

Establishing such an antidelinquency public opinion obviously is very difficult in areas with highly mobile populations, made up of persons with little stake in conformity to the dominant society. These areas, then, must be brought into the dominant society. The Anti-Crime Crusade of Indianapolis made progress in this direction. The organization was founded by thirty women in 1962, the day after a ninety-year-old woman was beaten and robbed on the street. By 1966, about fifty thousand women were participating. Among the activities of the organization are securing jobs for young people, helping school dropouts return to school, involving adolescents in volunteer work for social agencies and clinics, campaigning for slum cleanups, sponsoring police recruits,

---

[39] See Solomon Kobrin, "The Chicago Area Project—A 25-Year Assessment," *Annals of the American Academy of Political and Social Science*, 322:19-29, March, 1959.

[40] Cf. Walter B. Miller, "The Impact of a 'Total-Community' Delinquency Control Project," *Social Problems*, 10:168-191, 1962.

publicizing the shortcomings of the courts, assisting probation and parole workers, forming block clubs to improve slum neighborhoods, and campaigning for police pay raises. After a few months or years, most such organizations collapse for lack of membership, change goals, regain members, then collapse again.[41]

One feature of most programs for the control of delinquency is emphasis on organized recreation. The emphasis on recreation is essentially negative, in the sense that it implies that juveniles who are engaged in conventional recreation activities will not, at the same time, engage in delinquency. It is a method of occupying the leisure time of children; as such, it does not change attitudes or tendencies regarding behavior. Youth centers, recreational groups, and boys' clubs have been established by social settlements, churches, police departments, and other organizations as a means of occupying the leisure time of the boys. Claims have been made that delinquency rates have been greatly reduced in neighborhoods where recreation centers have been established. Over forty years ago, Healy made the following statement regarding the South End of Boston, and its essence has been repeated in annual reports of community agencies ever since:

Organized recreation

> This is a district in which there has been no marked change of population and in which police attitudes toward delinquency have not altered. In this district three main settlement houses have built up a preventive program, school people have co-operated and churches of several denominations have entered into the spirit of the project by organizing boys' clubs and scout groups. The probation officer of long experience in this district states that the former tendency toward delinquent gang formation is practically overcome. Many of the more difficult cases which we ourselves were accustomed to study came from this part of the city, but we have noted a great decrease of these cases. Ten years ago this probation officer carried in this district a case load regularly of about eighty to ninety offenders, many of them serious. The number has gradually gone down until at the present time he has only twenty-two and asserts that none of them is what he would call a serious offender. Another proof of the value of this preventive program is shown by the fact that while there has been a special effort to draw in the younger potential delinquents, it was possible to hold their interest for years in a constructive program. Many of them now twenty-two or twenty-three years old continue their club activities. The spirit has spread so that there is an overwhelming number of applicants at the various centers.[42]

On the other hand, many recreational centers have become sources of infection for delinquency. At about the time Healy made his statement, a study of the Boys' Club of New York City found that boys who were members of the club had a larger number of delinquencies than boys in the same neighborhood who were not members; that boys who belonged to the club for four years had more delinquencies than those who belonged for one

---

[41] See Ivan Jankovic, "The Natural History of a Social Control Agency," (Cambridge, England: Institute of Criminology, mimeographed, 1971).

[42] William Healy, "Prevention of Delinquency," *Journal of Criminal Law and Criminology*, 24:74-77, May-June, 1933.

year; that they had more delinquencies while members of the club than prior to or subsequent to that membership.[43] It does not seem possible to explain these findings except by the proposition that the club was directly or indirectly promoting delinquency, probably through the association of boys who were inclined to delinquency. It does not necessarily follow that all clubs must have the same effects, but many of them do, probably because they become hangouts for delinquents but not, to the same extent, for boy leaders with antidelinquent orientations. The successful recreation centers are those which somehow manage to provide participants with an excess of definitions unfavorable to delinquency.[44]

Casework with near-delinquents

Certain children have been called *potential delinquents* or *predelinquents*. These terms, from the etymological point of view, are misleading, for every child is a potential delinquent; every child in earlier years is a predelinquent, and every able-bodied person who has passed the earlier years of childhood commits delinquencies more or less frequently. The terms are used, however, to refer to the children who are believed to be extraordinarily likely to become confirmed delinquents. These predelinquents have not been definitely identified, but are believed by certain psychiatrists and social workers to be the children who manifest emotional problems such as enuresis, temper tantrums, sullenness, timidity, and, in later years, difficulties in school and with companions. It is believed that if these problems can be corrected in early childhood by appropriate procedures, the child will develop into a less delinquent adult.

The principal agency which has developed in the attempt to turn these near-delinquents away from their trend toward delinquency is the guidance clinic. Some guidance clinics have been operated by the public schools, some by juvenile courts, some by public welfare departments, some by private welfare agencies, some by state hospitals and mental health organizations, and some by independent agencies organized for this purpose. The clinic staff usually is made up of psychiatrists, psychologists, and social workers. Problem children are referred to the clinic by parents who are anxious about their children, by police, judges, and probation officers, by kindergartens and schools, by welfare societies, and by other agencies and persons. Some of them are referred because they have been delinquent, some because they have deviations in their personal characteristics, and some because of disturbing behavior which is not in violation of the law, such as temper tantrums, bed-wetting, or bashfulness. These children are sometimes divided into behavior problems and personality problems.

---

[43] Frederic M. Thrasher, "The Boy's Club and Juvenile Delinquency," *American Journal of Sociology*, 42:66-80, July, 1936.

[44] See Roscoe C. Brown, Jr., and Dan W. Dodson, "The Effectiveness of a Boys' Club in Reducing Delinquency," *Annals of the American Academy of Political and Social Science*, 322:47-52, March, 1959.

The St. Paul "Community Service" project may be used as an illustration of the work of child guidance clinics. Schools, police, the juvenile court, churches, health agencies, and social welfare agencies were instructed as to the kinds of behavior considered symptomatic of delinquency, and these organizations were encouraged to refer children to the clinic. The following kinds of behavior were considered symptomatic of delinquency:[45]

Bashfulness	Hitching rides	Stealing
Boastfulness	Ill-mannered	Stubbornness
Boisterousness	behavior	Sullenness
Bossiness	Impudence	Tardiness
Bullying	Inattentiveness	Tattling
Cheating	Indolence	Teasing
Cruelty	Masturbation	Temper displays
Crying	Nail-biting	Thumb-sucking
Daydreaming	Negativism	Tics
Deceit	Obscenity	Timidity
Defiance	Overactivity	Truancy from home
Dependence	Overmasculine	Truancy from school
Destructiveness	behavior (of girls)	Uncleanliness
Disobedience	Profanity	Uncouth personality
Disorderliness	Quarreling	Underactivity
Drinking	Roughness	Undesirable
Eating disturbances	Selfishness	companions
Effeminate behavior	Sex perversion	Undesirable
(of boys)	Sex play	recreation
Enuresis	Sexual activity	Unsportsmanship
Fabrications	Shifting activities	Untidiness
Failure to perform	Show-off behavior	Violation of
assigned tasks	Silliness	street-trade
Fighting	Sleep disturbances	regulations
Finicalness	Smoking	Violation of traffic
Gambling	Speech disturbances	regulations
Gate-crashing		

A total of 1,466 children were referred to the clinic during the period of its operation, and of this number 727 were considered as possessing undesirable personality traits or as exhibiting definite behavior problems. These 727 children were given five types of service, including psychiatric treatment, psychological testing and counseling, casework, group work, and tutoring in school projects. Emotional disturbances were considered of major importance in 432 cases, fifty-three of which were treated with "deep therapy." The staff estimated the effect of therapy in the 432 cases, judging that 18 percent had made "major improvement," 65 per cent "partial improvement," and 17 percent "no improvement."[46]

---

[45] Sybil A. Stone, Elsa Castendyck, and Harold B. Hanson, *Children in the Community*, Children's Bureau Publication No. 317 (Washington: Government Printing Office, 1946), pp. 47-48.

[46] Ibid., pp. 70-72.

Studies of child guidance clinics generally indicate that from a fourth to a third of the children treated continue to have problems, and that approximately a third manifest no further difficulties. One study showed no significant difference in the outcome of a group of children receiving psychiatric treatment in a clinic and a group not receiving such treatment.[47] Another study indicated that 47 percent of a group treated in a psychiatric clinic thirty years earlier had been arrested, as compared with 16 percent of a control group; 60 percent of the persons referred to the clinic for delinquency had arrests, as compared to 20 percent of those referred for neuroses or learning problems.[48] Modification of an "undesirable personality trait" undoubtedly is valuable to the individual and to society, but such modification does not necessarily mean that the individual in question will refrain from law violation.

In general, the child guidance clinic seems to be only slightly more successful in dealing with its problems than do the institutions for delinquents and criminals. Doubtless this failure is due to the fact that the problem is not confined to the organism of the child, but involves wider social relationships in the family, the neighborhood, the institutions, and the general culture. However, the child guidance clinic is at a great disadvantage, both in preventing delinquency and in aiding emotionally disturbed children, for it cannot initiate treatment. It must wait for cases to be referred to it. Accordingly, the delinquents seen in clinics are not likely to be drawn from all segments of the population, and, in fact, the clinics might not be serving the delinquents who are most in need of their services.[49]

A ten-year experiment in delinquency and crime prevention by methods which can best be described as casework outside a clinic setting revealed that the professional workers' efforts were not highly successful.[50] In the late 1930s, 650 boys under twelve

---

[47] LaMay Adamson and H. Warren Dunham, "Clinical Treatment of Male Delinquents: A Case Study in Effort and Result," *American Sociological Review,* 21:312-320, June, 1956.

[48] Lee N. Robins and Patricia O'Neal, "Mortality, Mobility, and Crime: Problem Children Thirty Years Later," *American Sociological Review,* 23:162-171, April, 1958.

[49] Helen L. Witmer and Edith Tufts, *The Effectiveness of Delinquency Prevention Programs,* Children's Bureau Publication No. 350 (Washington: Government Printing Office, 1954), p. 40. See also Ralph Schwitzgebel, "A New Approach to Understanding Delinquency," *Federal Probation,* 24:31-35, March, 1960.

[50] Edwin Powers, "An Experiment in Prevention of Delinquency," *Annals of the American Academy of Political and Social Science,* 261:77-88, January, 1949; Edwin Powers and Helen L. Witmer, *An Experiment in the Prevention of Delinquency — The Cambridge-Somerville Youth Study* (New York: Columbia University Press, 1951). See also William McCord and Joan McCord, *Origins of Crime: A New Evaluation of the Cambridge-Somerville Youth Study* (New York: Columbia University Press, 1959); and Jackson Toby, "Early Identification and Intensive Treatment of Predelinquents: A Negative View," *Social Work,* 6:3-13, July, 1961.

years of age were selected for the project from a list of about 1,900 names submitted by teachers, social agencies, police officers, and probation officers. Some of these boys were believed destined to become delinquent, and others were not. The 650 boys were paired on the basis of about one hundred factors, such as age, religion, intelligence, educational performance, personality, neighborhood, and social adjustment. The information regarding these factors had been obtained from social work agencies, schools, interviews with parents, and physical and psychological examinations of the boys. On the basis of these factors, prognostications as to probable delinquency were made. One set of the matched pairs was randomly selected as the "treatment group," while their "diagnostic twins" became the "control group."

The members of the treatment group were given help in educational problems, were given special counseling, guidance, and health services, were taken on camping trips, etc. The control group members were given none of these services. After two or three years, 65 of the boys in the treatment group were dropped because they presented no special problems and were definitely nondelinquent; this left 260 boys in the treatment group. At the end of the experimental period, in 1945, 76, or 23.4 percent, of the 325 treatment-group members had appeared in court for serious offenses, and 90, or 27.7 percent, had committed either serious or minor offenses. Among the 325 control-group members, the proportions were slightly *less* in each instance: 67, or 20.6 percent, had court appearances for serious offenses, and 85, or 26.1 percent, had committed either serious or minor offenses.

At the time of the original diagnosis, delinquent careers were predicted for 70 boys in the treatment group and for 68 in the control group; 23 (32.9 percent) of the members of this treatment subgroup became delinquent, and 27 (39.7 percent) of the control subgroup became delinquent. Similarly, "probable delinquency" was predicted for 163 members of the treatment group and for 165 members of the control group; 14.1 percent of the treatment subgroup became delinquent, as compared to 13.3 percent of the control subgroup. These differences are hardly significant, indicating that the "treatment" had little effect; they also cast doubt upon the feasibility of identifying "predelinquents" accurately. There was evidence, however, that the control-group members who became delinquent were more persistent offenders than the treatment-group members who became delinquent.

One of the significant developments in social work during the last two decades is group work. The development is to some extent based on the desirability of extending casework beyond the person and his family to groups of approximately the same age as the delinquent or near-delinquent who is being treated. Group work with delinquents and near-delinquents may be regarded as falling into two types, both of which are now being used in most large urban communities. First, an individual is induced to become

Group work with near-delinquents

a member of a group, as a means of satisfying his needs as a person. The group may be a ball team, a hiking club, an art-crafts class, or it may be concerned with some other activity. While in this group, the person is given particular attention to aid him in adjusting to the group and to overcome tendencies considered to be conducive to delinquency. At its best, this type of group work does more than merely provide recreational opportunities. It uses an individualistic psychology, and is based on the same general theory as is individual casework. A principal problem is that of inducing children to participate in the groups. One study revealed that group work agencies using this approach are not even "identified closely with the underprivileged and insecure elements in our population, nor with the age groups among which delinquency is most prevalent."[51]

A second type of group work consists in redirecting the activities of a group of persons, all or nearly all of whom are delinquents or near-delinquents. The Chicago Area Projects were the progenitors and the prototypes of a program designed to establish direct and personal contact with "unreached" boys. One of the early applications of this procedure was made by Keltner in St. Louis under the sponsorship of the YMCA. In a deteriorated section of St. Louis, which had been the headquarters of a notorious adult gang, Keltner attempted to redirect the boys' gangs so that they would be assets to the community. After a period of fifteen years, forty of these gangs, now turned into boys' clubs, were carrying on their activities in this section, with an average membership of about twenty-five. Keltner stated that the members were seldom in difficulties with the police, that the older members assisted in developing similar groups for their younger brothers, and that the businessmen of the district wholeheartedly cooperated with the movement.[52]

Most cities now have agencies using this kind of group work, primarily with relationship to delinquent gangs or street-corner groups, rather than with reference to a community or neighborhood. The essential characteristic of this policy, as differentiated from other policies, is that some person attempts to enter into friendly participation with delinquent gang members in order to try to change them into law-abiding citizens, not as separate individuals, but as a group.[53] In a pioneering program conducted in central Harlem years ago, trained workers were assigned to five street gangs, and these workers attempted by informal methods to influence the activities of the gang. At the end of its third year,

[51] Ellery F. Reed, "How Effective are Group Work Agencies in Preventing Delinquency?" *Focus*, 28:170-176, November, 1959.

[52] Harold S. Keltner, "Crime Prevention Program of the YMCA, St. Louis," in Sheldon and Eleanor Glueck, eds., *Preventing Crime* (New York: McGraw-Hill, 1936), chap. 24.

[53] See David M. Austin, "Goals for Gang Workers," *Social Work*, 2:43-50, October, 1957; and David J. Bordua, *Sociological Theories and Their Implications for Juvenile Delinquency* (Washington: U.S. Children's Bureau, 1960).

the program was judged successful.[54] This program set the pattern for many subsequent programs in other areas.[55]

The emphasis on gangs, rather than on neighborhoods, probably has arisen in part because lower-class areas of large cities have become more unstable or less strongly organized—family, ethnic, political, and religious organizations are all weak. Another reason is the pervasive tendency of social agencies to push middle-class patterns of control and conformity:

> The social agency is *society's* instrument for support, rehabilitation and control of deviant population segments. Agencies which serve primarily low income persons derive their major source of funds from middle class people and groups. Policies are determined and programs controlled by a board representing extra-local or non lower-class interests. Staff are recruited for ability to assist a *lower class* population, but within a professional outlook fundamentally determined by *middle class* norms and values. Therefore, the basic structure and dynamic of social agencies has not allowed for determination of policy and program by the local residents of low income areas.[56]

Many persons have advocated widespread modifications of the general institutional structure. Some have done so in connection with preventing crime and delinquency. Many criminologists have suggested that only partial and temporary reduction in crime rates can be expected from the methods currently employed in the attempt to prevent crime and delinquency: repression, clinical treatment, special school classes for "predelinquents," visiting teachers, character education, education of parents, casework and group work with parents and children, domestic relations courts, foster homes, club and camp programs, neighborhood reorganization, etc. According to Taft, for example, none of these cuts the deeper roots of crime. After acknowledging the tremendous difficulties and opposition which institutional modification would entail, he makes the following statement regarding the characteristics of a "crimeless society":

Institutional reorganization

> Since social change implies maladjustment, a crimeless society had best be static. To avoid culture conflict it should be internally homogeneous. On the economic side, a crimeless society must avoid excessive

---

[54] Paul L. Crawford, Daniel I. Malamud, and James R. Dumpson, *Working with Teen-age Gangs* (New York: Welfare Council of New York City, 1950); James R. Dumpson, "An Approach to Anti-Social Street Gangs," *Federal Probation*, 13:22-29, December, 1949.

[55] See Irving Spergel, *Street Gang Work: Theory and Practice* (Reading, Mass.: Addison-Wesley, 1966); Malcolm W. Klein and Barbara G. Meyerhoff, eds., *Juvenile Gangs in Context: Theory, Research, and Action* (Los Angeles: University of Southern California Youth Studies Center, 1964); Malcolm W. Klein, "Juvenile Gangs, Police, and Detached Workers: Controversies in Gang Intervention," *Social Service Review*, 39(1965):183-190; and Solomon Kobrin, "Sociological Aspects of the Development of a Street Corner Group: An Exploratory Study," *American Journal of Orthopsychiatry*, 31(1961): 685-602.

[56] Spergel, *Street Gang Work*, p. xvi.

[57] Donald R. Taft, *Criminology: A Cultural Interpretation* (New York: Macmillan, 1950), pp. 664-666.

competition and greed for material gain and must be planned rather than chaotic. This would be essential to avoid such sources of maladjustment as relative failure, city slums, struggle for speculative gains, monopolistic advantages, and various types of exploitation.

A crimeless society might have to reverse the trend toward impersonal relationships and restore the personalized culture of the past. It might need to restrict human freedom. It might resort to a return to religious superstitions as agencies of social control. Though different in some respects, such a crimeless society would seem more nearly to approximate primitive or peasant society, than does modern society. . . .

A crimeless society should also be largely free from preferential group loyalties which we have found to be at once so cherished and so productive of strife and crime. A society so homogeneous as we have indicated might perhaps accept and enforce a puritanical morality, otherwise it would seem to need a "new morality" permitting considerable freedom of sex and other personal behavior.

Perhaps the most basic change needed in the interest of crime prevention would be the incorporation in our culture of a genuinely scientific point of view which sees criminals as products. Such a society would not hold the individual criminal responsible, though it would continue to hold him in every way accountable for his behavior.

The reader may decide for himself, first which of the changes needed to prevent crime he desires, and second whether the criminogenic conditions he would hate to sacrifice are or are not more desirable than crime prevention. A program of cultural change solely in the interest of crime prevention would be based upon the, perhaps false, assumption that a crimeless society is the one great good. It is not the task of the criminologist to determine what is the major social good.[58]

Saul Alinsky has similarly suggested that crime and delinquency must, in the last analysis, be prevented through institutional reorganization, and he has initiated a program to achieve that reorganization. His program, variously known as the "Back of the Yards Project," the "Industrial Areas Foundation," and the "People's Organization," is not aimed directly at control of delinquency and crime. Instead, it attempts to eradicate "unemployment, undernourished, disease, deterioration, demoralization, and other aspects of social disorganization." The implication is that as these conditions are altered, crime and delinquency rates will decrease. The essence of the following statement, made about twenty-five years ago, has become the rallying cry for those who subscribe to the now-popular idea that delinquency and crime will be prevented only when basic social injustices are eradicated:

It is very clear that if any intelligent attack is to be made upon the problem of youth or the causes of crime the community council will have to concern itself with the basic issues of unemployment, diseases, and housing, as well as all other causes of crime. This the conventional community council cannot do. It is not equipped to attack basic social issues, and its very character is such that it never was meant to do that kind of job. The community council organized to prevent crime will tell you that its function is in the field of crime purely and it has no place in such controversial fields as conflict between labor and capital, private vs. government housing, public health, and other fundamental issues.

---

[58] Ibid., pp. 666-667. See also pp. 756-757 of the third edition of this book (1956).

Intellectually and logically members of such council will admit that one cannot hope to attack the causes of crime unless one gets into all the related fields, yet in actual practice they will vigorously abstain from entering any controversial field. . . . You don't, you dare not, come to a people who are unemployed, who don't know where their next meal is coming from, whose children and themselves are in the gutter of despair —and offer them not food, not jobs, not security, but supervised recreation, handicraft classes and character building! Yet *that is what is done!* Instead of a little bread and butter we come to them with plenty of bats and balls![58] ●

ALINSKY, SAUL D. "Community Analysis and Organization." *American Journal of Sociology*, 46:797-808, May, 1941.   **Suggested readings**

AMOS, WILLIAM E., & CHARLES F. WELLFORD, eds. *Delinquency Prevention: Theory and Practice.* Englewood Cliffs, N.J.: Prentice-Hall, 1967.

BALL, JOHN C., & ALICE SIMPSON. "The Extent of Recidivism Among Juvenile Delinquents in a Metropolitan Area." *Journal of Research in Crime and Delinquency*, 2:72-84, July, 1965.

BELESS, DONALD W., WILLIAM S. PILCHER, & ELLEN JO RYAN. "Use of Indigenous Nonprofessionals in Probation and Parole." *Federal Probation*, 36:10-15, March, 1972.

BORDUA, DAVID J. *Sociological Theories and Their Implications for Juvenile Delinquency.* Washington: U.S. Children's Bureau, 1960.

CONKLIN, JOHN E. "Dimensions of Community Response to the Crime Problems." *Social Problems*, 18:373-385, Winter, 1971.

CRESSEY, DONALD R. "The Nature and Effectiveness of Correctional Techniques." *Law and Contemporary Problems*, 23:754-771, Autumn, 1958.

EMPEY, LAMAR T., & STEVEN G. LUBECK. *Delinquency Prevention Strategies.* Washington: Government Printing Office, 1970.

GIBBONS, DON C. *Changing the Lawbreaker.* Englewood Cliffs, N.J.: Prentice-Hall, 1965.

GLASER, DANIEL. "National Goals and Indicators for the Reduction of Crime and Delinquency." *Annals of the American Academy of Political and Social Science*, 371:104-126, May, 1967.

GROSSER, CHARLES, WILLIAM E. HENRY, & JAMES G. KELLY, eds. *Nonprofessionals in the Human Services.* San Francisco: Jossey-Bass, 1969.

HACKLER, JAMES C. "Evaluation of Delinquency Prevention Programs: Ideals and Compromises." *Federal Probation*, 31:22-26, March, 1967.

HILLS, STUART L. *Crime, Power, and Morality: The Criminal-Law Process in the United States.* San Francisco: Chandler, 1971.

---

[58] Saul D. Alinsky, *Reveille for Radicals* (Chicago: University of Chicago Press, 1946), pp. 81-82.

IRWIN, JOHN. *The Felon.* Englewood Cliffs, N. J.: Prentice-Hall, 1970.

KASSEBAUM, GENE, DAVID A. WARD, & DANIEL M. WILNER. *Prison Treatment and Parole Survival: An Empirical Assessment.* New York: John Wiley, 1971.

KITTRIE, NICHOLAS N. *The Right to be Different: Deviance and Enforced Therapy.* Baltimore: Johns Hopkins Press, 1971.

KLEIN, MALCOLM W., ed. *Juvenile Gangs in Context.* Englewood Cliffs, N.J.: Prentice-Hall, 1967.

MacIVER, ROBERT M. *The Prevention and Control of Delinquency.* New York: Atherton, 1966.

MARTIN, JOHN P., & D. WEBSTER. *Social Consequences of Conviction.* London: Heinemann, 1971.

McKAY, HENRY D. "Differential Association and Crime Prevention: Problems of Utilization." *Social Problems,* 8:25-37, Summer, 1960.

SCHUR, EDWIN M. *Radical Non-Intervention: Rethinking the Delinquency Problem.* Englewood Cliffs, N. J.: Prentice-Hall, 1973.

SHIBUTANI, TAMOTSU. "The Sentimental Basis of Group Solidarity." *Sociological Inquiry,* Spring, 1964, pp. 144-145.

SPERGEL, IRVING. *Street Gang Work: Theory and Practice.* Reading, Mass.: Addison-Wesley, 1966.

STRATTON, JOHN R., & ROBERT M. TERRY, eds. *Prevention of Delinquency: Problems and Programs.* New York: Macmillan, 1968.

TOBY, JACKSON. "Early Identification and Intensive Treatment of Predelinquents: A Negative View." *Social Work,* 6:3-13, July, 1961.

VOLKMAN, RITA, & DONALD R. CRESSEY. "Differential Association and the Rehabilitation of Drug Addicts." *American Journal of Sociology,* 69:129-142, September, 1963.

WARREN, MARGUERITE Q. *Correctional Treatment in Community Settings: A Report of Current Research.* Washington: Government Printing Office, 1972.

YABLONSKY, LEWIS. "The Anticriminal Society: Synanon." *Federal Probation,* 26:50-57, September, 1962.

H